Arthur Hellyer's All Colour
Gardening Book

Arthur Hellyer's All Colour
Gardening Book

This edition produced exclusively for

Acknowledgements

The Publishers are grateful to Bradley-Nicholson Limited for lending the illustration of the Shilton natural gas greenhouse heater used on page 218, and would also like to thank the following for providing the remaining photographs used in this book: Bernard Alfieri, *Amateur Gardening*, Pat Brindley, Kenneth Burras, Robert Corbin, John Cowley, Ernest Crowson, W. F. Davidson, *The Field*, Valerie Finnis, Iris Hardwick, Mrs H. Hodgson, Anthony Huxley, Elsa Megson, Frank Naylor, L. F. Oland, Sheila Orme, Robert Pearson, Ray Procter, Harry Smith and D. Wilridge.

**This edition published exclusively for
W H Smith**

Published by
The Hamlyn Publishing Group Limited
London · New York · Sydney · Toronto
Astronaut House, Feltham, Middlesex, England

Copyright © The Hamlyn Publishing Group Limited 1981
Reprinted 1982
ISBN 0 600 37454 8

The material in this book has been
published previously by The Hamlyn
Publishing Group Limited under the
titles *Arthur Hellyer's All-Colour
Gardening Book* and *Arthur Hellyer's
All-Colour Book of Indoor and
Greenhouse Plants*.

Printed in the Canary Islands (Spain)

Litografía A. Romero, S. A., D. L: TF. 329 – 1981

Contents

Decorative Gardening

Introduction	6
Garden Planning	8
Lawn Making and After-care	14
General Garden Cultivation	22
Simple Ways to Increase Plants	30
Shrubs for Year-round Interest	38
Climbing and Screening Plants	62
Garden Trees	70
Garden Hedges	78
Colourful Perennials	82
Practical Rose Growing	104
Bulbs for Garden Display	114
Making a Rock Garden	126
Annual Flowers	140
A Selection of Biennials	152
Garden Pools	156
Patios and Plants in Containers	160
Bedding Plants	168
Plants for Special Purposes	172
Flowers for Cutting	178

Indoor and Greenhouse Plants

Introduction	190
House Plants	192
Cacti and Succulents	206
Bonsai	214
Greenhouse Management	216
Propagating Plants	228
Growing in Frames	230
Plants for Unheated Greenhouses	232
The Alpine House	236
Plants for Heated Greenhouses	242
Greenhouse Bulbs	274
Greenhouse Climbers	280
Greenhouse Chrysanthemums	288
Orchids	290
Greenhouse Ferns	296
Greenhouse Calendar	300
Index	311
Acknowledgements	319

Decorative Gardening

This is a book about gardening for pleasure. It is concerned with plants grown for decoration in the garden or to provide cut flowers for the home, and since there are many thousands of such plants it has necessarily to be selective. Every effort has been made to choose only the best plants, both in the sense of those which are attractive and able to satisfy a great variety of requirements and also those which are not too difficult to grow and are readily available.

In this last respect, gardeners are deriving increasing assistance from a revolution in marketing methods which began to take effect in the 1960s. A gradual change over from the traditional nursery practice of despatching plants by mail or rail, to a fetch-and-carry trade based on container-grown plants is rapidly introducing gardeners to a great many plants they would not otherwise have known. Most plants that have to travel long distances can only be moved safely from the open ground when in a more or less dormant condition, usually from October to April. Plants must be ordered months ahead or purchased when there is little to indicate their true quality. By contrast, container-grown plants can be bought and established in the garden at almost any time of the year, even when in full bloom or leaf. Customers can see precisely what they are buying and actually pick out for themselves the individual plants they prefer. In this way they are being introduced to hundreds of varieties they would not otherwise have been likely to consider, and their gardens are benefiting.

In the early days of selling plants in containers fears were expressed that it would limit the variety of plants available, since nurseries and garden centres would stock only those plants for which there was a known popular demand. In fact, the opposite has proved to be true. Nurseries are finding it profitable to propagate many beautiful plants which were formerly only known and ordered by a few enthusiasts, but which now are readily purchased when customers see them.

Plants vary greatly in the amount of attention they require and much of the pleasure of gardening depends upon taking due account of this when the garden is planned and planted. Some people enjoy looking after plants and do not in the least grudge the time and labour involved in caring for some of the more exacting kinds, such as the more difficult rock plants accustomed to alpine conditions or plants that have special requirements in soil or feeding or need some protection in cold weather.

Other gardeners – and they are the majority – want to have an attractive garden with the minimum of trouble. To ensure this they must be careful not to cram too many plants into their garden and restrict their choice mainly to those plants that do not require frequent renewal. Above all they should learn to work with, rather than against, their local soil and climate. There are plants to suit every place if one takes the trouble to look for them.

A few well-chosen and well-placed plants can often produce a better effect than a far greater number planted with less fore-thought. Since all plants are likely to need attention at some time, the higher the number of plants in the garden the more work in maintenance there is likely to be. Nor are lawns as labour saving as is often supposed. Mowing, watering, feeding and aerating can all occupy a good deal of time and if labour saving is a prime consideration paving may prove a better proposition than grass. In general, trees and shrubs require the least attention of all plants, particularly if selection is confined to really hardy varieties that are well suited to the often unimproved soil of the garden. Lime-hating plants, such as rhododendrons, azaleas and many heathers, can be grown on chalky soils but only with a great deal of care and attention and this kind of thing is best left to the enthusiasts who enjoy it. For every type of soil there are plants that have adapted themselves to it and a little observation in the locality and enquiries at local nurseries and public parks will soon disclose which these are.

Yet even the toughest and most adaptable of plants will require some care, especially in the early stages. Transplanting itself checks growth, though this can be minimised by careful work and by using well-established container-grown plants.

After planting, while roots are finding their way out into the soil, plants may require firm staking and fairly frequent watering. Feeding at this stage should not be too heavy, for only well-established plants can make full use of the chemicals in the soil and an excess of readily soluble fertiliser or even of animal manure can harm those recently transplanted.

Much of the subsequent care of plants is very largely a matter of common sense directed by observation of what is happening in the garden. Good gardeners acquire a feeling for their plants and quickly observe when something is going wrong. Again, it is much easier to acquire this sensibility if, at the outset, there are not too many plants to be observed.

Many seeds germinate more readily in an artificially maintained atmosphere than they do in the open and similar conditions can also be an advantage when cuttings have to be rooted to increase or maintain the stock of plants. A greenhouse is ideal for these purposes, but a frame is almost as good, especially if it can be

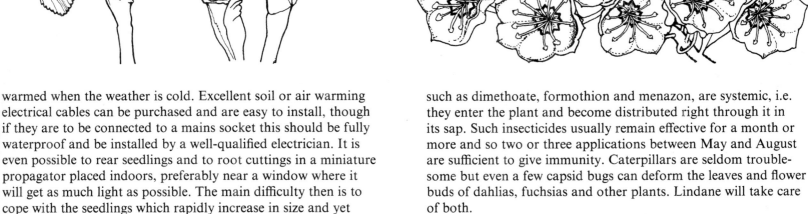

warmed when the weather is cold. Excellent soil or air warming electrical cables can be purchased and are easy to install, though if they are to be connected to a mains socket this should be fully waterproof and be installed by a well-qualified electrician. It is even possible to rear seedlings and to root cuttings in a miniature propagator placed indoors, preferably near a window where it will get as much light as possible. The main difficulty then is to cope with the seedlings which rapidly increase in size and yet cannot be transferred too hastily to the open air lest the sudden change kills them. Here again a garden frame can provide the link, giving protection when required but enabling plants to be fully exposed whenever the weather permits.

Composts ready mixed for seed raising and for growing on seedlings can be purchased from any garden centre or garden shop. The difference between seed composts and growing on composts (usually called potting composts) is principally in the amount of chemical food they contain, the potting composts being richer to cope with the increasing needs of the rapidly growing plants.

These composts are of two basic kinds, soil composts, usually prepared to the John Innes formulae, and no-soil composts usually based on peat, but marketed under trade names without precise disclosure of their contents. Peat composts are much lighter than soil composts and they do not need anything like as much firming (some kinds no firming at all). Both these characteristics save labour, but on the debit side plants do not get such a firm roothold in peat compost and are more likely to topple over or be blown out.

Success with plants in seed trays, pots, boxes or other containers depends largely on proper watering. The aim is to keep the soil nicely moist from top to bottom without being waterlogged. Fortunately most modern seed and potting composts are sufficiently porous to get rid of surplus water readily, so that overwatering is not now as common a cause of failure as it once was. It is dryness that is most troublesome, especially with peat composts which, once they become really dry, turn water aside and are very difficult to moisten again. For this reason they are usually packed at the correct degree of moisture in sealed polythene bags.

Pests and diseases are not as troublesome in the ornamental garden as they are in the vegetable or fruit garden. Greenflies are an almost universal nuisance, appearing suddenly, multiplying rapidly and often disappearing again just as quickly. Nowadays there are plenty of insecticides with which to destroy them. Some,

such as dimethoate, formothion and menazon, are systemic, i.e. they enter the plant and become distributed right through it in its sap. Such insecticides usually remain effective for a month or more and so two or three applications between May and August are sufficient to give immunity. Caterpillars are seldom troublesome but even a few capsid bugs can deform the leaves and flower buds of dahlias, fuchsias and other plants. Lindane will take care of both.

Slugs and snails are perhaps the most damaging flower garden pests since they can devour whole batches of seedlings in a night. Poison baits containing metaldehyde or methiocarb must be placed near plants liable to be attacked, or a solution of metaldehyde can be applied from a watering pot to any place where they may be hiding. Mice, too, can eat seedlings and various bulbs and corms, but they can be trapped, a positive and satisfactory way of destroying them. Birds are much more problematical since they strip winter buds, pull up seedlings and damage flowers yet are themselves so attractive that they cannot be killed. Protection with bird deterrent chemicals seems the most hopeful solution.

Mildew can disfigure the leaves of roses, delphiniums, Michaelmas daisies and some other plants, covering them with a flour-like outgrowth. Dinocap will prevent this happening provided it is applied before the mildew becomes established, but this may mean fairly frequent spraying to protect new growth as it appears. Much the same applies to black spot, one of the most troublesome diseases of roses, but for this it is captan or maneb that will prove most effective.

Virus diseases are common in chrysanthemums, dahlias and lilies and may affect other plants. They cause mottling of the leaves, leaf distortion, stunting, flower deformity and other symptoms not easy to define and sometimes difficult to recognise. Sprays are useless against these diseases except in so far as they control the insects, mainly greenflies, which carry them. As a rule it is best to burn infected plants directly they are recognised since viruses, once introduced, can spread rapidly.

Arthur Hellyer

Garden Planning

Surveying, Paper Plans

To draw a reasonably accurate plan of the plot it is necessary to take a few measurements from the boundaries, usually to the corners of the house. First make a very rough sketch on which to jot down the measurements. Then measure from each corner of the house to the boundary, keeping in line with the house wall. Now draw the house to scale on a sheet of graph paper, mark off the measurements from each corner of the plot to the nearest corner of the house and mark these on the plan.

On this outline plan the features required can now be filled in – paths, beds, borders, and trees. Draw them to scale but do it lightly in pencil at first so that alterations can be made.

If the ground is very irregular or sloping it may be necessary to take some sightings to see what the differences of level are. This can be done with a long plant stake or cane and a spirit-level. Fix the stake upright at a low point in the ground. Keeping the spirit-level perfectly horizontal, sight along it and at the same time move it up and down the stake until it is exactly aligned on the nearest high point of ground. Now measure the distance from the bottom of the stake to the spirit-level. This is the difference in height between the two points of high and low ground.

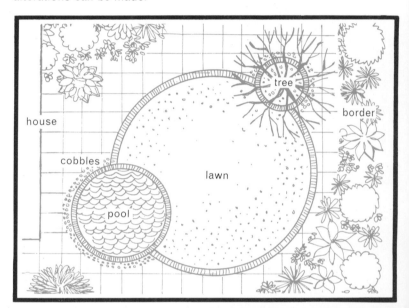

Successful garden planning involves a proper balance between taste and utility. If the garden is to be satisfactory and give lasting pleasure it must be well fitted for the purpose (or purposes, for there may well be several) for which it is required and also be pleasing to the eye. One garden maker may wish to devote most space to flowers, a second to fruit, a third to vegetables. It may be essential to have a place for the baby to crawl with safety, for children to romp or for the washing to be aired. Some gardeners are interested in only a few types of plant, whereas others seek for maximum variety in the available space. It may even be that plants themselves are not a prime consideration, but rather design, which can be largely an architectural matter. Good gardens can be made to suit each of these needs or one garden may be divided into several sections, each with its own purpose or style. The really important point is to be quite clear at the outset what that purpose or style is and to plan accordingly.

In a garden intended for family use a lawn is usually highly desirable, though if space is very limited it may have to be replaced by paving, if only because small areas of grass simply will not withstand the wear of many feet. But where there are small children it may be wise to avoid gravel and cobbles, which can cause nasty cuts, and also bricks, which can be dangerously slippery in wet weather. Non-slip paving slabs laid quite level on a bed of concrete are usually the best substitute for a lawn.

Gardens, or garden features planned exclusively for decoration may be conceived as patterns or as pictures. The former are called formal gardens since they are usually more or less symmetrical and based on regular shapes such as rectangles, circles and ovals. Picture gardens, by contrast, are nearly always informal, based on irregular curves and balanced, but not symmetrical, shapes.

One type of planning may lead to the other, perhaps a formal terrace or patio near to the house looking out on to an informal garden beyond. It is in some ways easier to design a formal rather than an informal garden since its pattern is revealed clearly on a paper plan, whereas the picture garden is very much more a three dimensional affair requiring a perspective drawing for clear depiction. Planting can be used to emphasise the pattern of a formal garden and to create the shapes, vistas and focal points in a picture garden.

Water can be introduced into either style of garden, fountains in a formal garden or cascades in an informal setting, presenting no difficulty if the water is constantly recirculated by an electrically operated pump and proper provision is made for a mains electric supply in the original planning.

Careful planning is essential to the success of any garden. Incorporated in this lovely town garden are many delightful features including a rectangular pool for fish. The grass surround is for ornament only and the walking area is sensibly paved

Quantity Surveying

There are simple ways of estimating quantities of various materials and plants required.

Paving slabs are usually sold by the superficial area they will cover. Measure the length and breadth of each path, preferably in feet, and multiply the figures to get the area in square feet.

Bricks are sold by numbers. 35 laid flat or 53 laid on edge will cover an area of 10 sq. ft.

If paving slabs are sold by weight, approximately 1½ cwt. of ¾- to 1½-in. thick paving will be required for each 10 sq. ft.; or 2½ cwt. of 1½- to 2½-in. thick paving. For 2-in. thick concrete 2½ cwt. of mixed cement and aggregate is required for each 10 sq. ft., and for 3-in. thickness 4 cwt. will be needed.

Gravel for paths and drives is usually sold by the 'yard', which means a cubic yard. If spread 2 in. thick a cubic yard will cover 18 sq. yd.

7 cwt. of 6-in. wide walling stone will make a wall with a face area of 10 sq. ft.

Herbaceous plants are spaced on average 15 to 16 in. apart, so 6 are required for each 10 sq. ft. Shrubs are spaced on average 3 ft. apart so each takes 9 sq. ft.

Turves are normally sold in 3 × 1-ft. strips. 4 turves will cover 12 sq. ft., or 100 turves will cover 33⅓ sq. yd. (300 sq. ft.).

Soil for filling is sold by the cubic yard or ton (about the same). One ton will raise a 10 sq. ft. bed between 2½ and 3 ft.

planting herbaceous plants

planting shrubs

After the garden has been planned the next step is to make an accurate assessment of the materials and plants needed – in this garden the number of plants for the herbaceous border and the weight of crazy paving slabs for the path

Marking Out

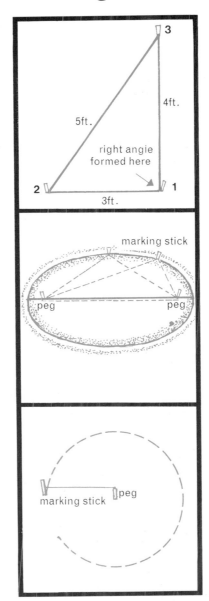

To mark out a right angle, drive in a peg at the corner and from this stretch a garden line to mark one side of the right angle. Drive in a peg against this line exactly 3 ft. from the first peg. Attach a string 4 ft. long to the corner and another exactly 5 ft. long to the second peg. Draw them together to form a triangle and where they touch drive in a third peg. A line stretched between pegs 1 and 3 will be at right angles to the line between pegs 1 and 2.

To mark out a circle drive a peg into the centre. Loop over it a string exactly half the width of the circle required and draw it around at full stretch with a pointed stick inside the loop to scratch along the ground.

To mark an oval use a line to mark out the full length of the oval and midway, another at right angles to mark the width, and drive in a peg at one end of this line. Attach to this peg a piece of string exactly half the length of the oval and draw it tight so that it touches the long line first on one side of the centre and then on the other side. Drive in a peg at each of these points. Measure the length from one of these pegs to the extreme end of the oval on the farther side. Make a loop of string exactly twice this length, throw it over the two pegs on the central line and pulling it taut, use a pointed stick to scratch out the oval on the ground.

Straight edges, circles, ovals and irregular curves should all be carefully marked out on the ground before paths are laid, lawns sown and beds formed and planted. Simple geometrical methods can be used for the regular shapes

Paths and Terraces

All paths and terraces should be laid on a good layer of brickends, clinkers or other hard rubble for drainage. If the surface is to be of paving slabs or bricks, spread on top of this rubble a layer of either sand or mortar on which the paving can be laid absolutely flat. If mortar is used do not spread too much at a time as it soon starts to set. Use a square-edged plank to check the levels from time to time and make sure that each slab or brick is firmly bedded with no tendency to rock.

Paving slabs and bricks can be laid in patterns of many different kinds and some manufacturers supply slabs of different sizes to aid pattern making. For added interest coloured slabs may be used or the materials may be mixed, for example by alternating panels of pebbles or cobblestones with paving slabs or bricks.

Concrete paths should be at least 2 in. thick and individual sections should not be more than 8 ft. long to allow for expansion and contraction. Sides should be formed by setting planks on edge as shuttering between which the concrete is laid.

Excellent brochures giving fuller instructions and showing many examples of path and terrace design are obtainable from the Cement and Concrete Association, 52 Grosvenor Gardens, London S.W.1.

Screens, Arches, Pergolas

Screens can be used to give extra privacy or shelter to some part of the garden or to divide it into sections and are particularly useful as a partial surround for a terrace or patio. They can be made of wood either in the form of open-slat, Canadian-style fencing or solid fencing or they can be made of brick or walling blocks. Particularly attractive are the precast pierced concrete blocks available in a large variety of patterns. Full particulars and illustrated brochures are available from the Cement and Concrete Association.

Arches give elevation to the garden design and in small areas may be preferable to trees since they do not grow. They can be of wood or of metal; timber of 3 × 2-in. section is suitable for their construction. All wood should be treated with a preservative harmless to plants, such as copper naphthenate, and the uprights should be embedded in soil or concrete.

Pergolas are covered walks like a continuous series of arches. Uprights may be of wood, brick or concrete blocks, but the cross members are usually of timber which should be of 4 × 4-in. section and must also be treated with preservative.

The cross members could be of 4 × 2-in. timber on edge for widths up to 8 ft.

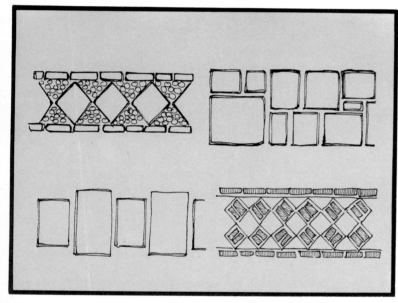

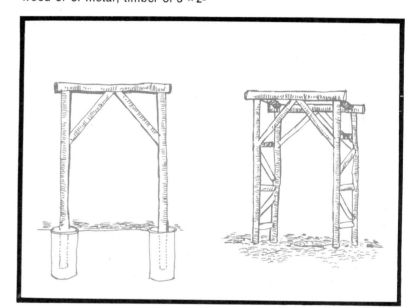

Striking patterns can be made with paving slabs using differing sizes and colours. Further diversity can be given by mixing materials, such as panels of pebbles or cobblestones with paving slabs or bricks

This little terrace has been well screened with pre-cast perforated slabs. These break the wind and provide excellent support for climbing plants. Note the modern plant bowl

Statues and Ornaments

These can be used either as focal points to catch the eye and form the central feature in the garden picture, or be tucked away so that one comes upon them as delightful surprises. Light-coloured statues and ornaments look well against a background of dark evergreen foliage or reflected in water.

Ornaments can be of many kinds. Large vases or jars of stone or terra-cotta make attractive plant containers, and so do old stone troughs. Excellent reproductions of these can be purchased, and some really imaginative garden ornaments are now cast in concrete. Natural rocks are often beautiful, or large rounded boulders gathered from the beach. Japanese gardeners make imaginative use of natural objects of this kind. Large pieces of driftwood can also be attractive.

Ornaments and statues should be used sparingly and placed carefully. Too many give a cluttered appearance, dividing instead of concentrating attention.

Bird tables, bird baths and sundials are all popular ornaments. The first two need to be placed where they can be viewed from the house without disturbing the birds, but a sundial should obviously be put in the open.

It is also possible to purchase sundials for mounting on the side of south-facing walls. Always try to set the dial so that it really does indicate the time.

Garden Buildings

Arbours can be attractive features in themselves, or places from which the garden can be viewed to advantage. They can be built of timber or masonry as little pavilions, or fashioned out of shrubs or trees suitably clipped, or of climbing plants trained over structures such as a deep arch or small pergola. Similar details of material and construction apply.

Sheds and greenhouses are seldom ornamental and it is often a problem to know where to put them in a small garden. A shed may be screened by shrubs or covered with climbing plants, but a greenhouse must stand in an open position with plenty of light. It may have to stand quite close to the house if it is to be heated from the house supply, in which case it may be best to treat it as a conservatory leading from the house to garden or to close in one side of a patio or terrace. It would then be wise to choose a greenhouse glazed to ground level for maximum display.

If a shed or greenhouse is at any distance from the house a path should be made leading as directly as possible to it, so that there is no temptation to take short cuts. It is also convenient to have a paved or gravelled area close to a greenhouse on which pot plants can be stood in summer. If room permits two or three frames may be added for hardening off.

This patio has been given an oriental touch by the careful choice and placing of ornaments combined with the use of dwarf evergreen shrubs. The flat rock bed is an interesting feature

Here an arbour in the form of a short pergola is placed against a wall on a terrace overlooking a sunken garden. The planting masks the formality of the design

Beds and Parterres

Parterre is the name given to any level area of ground occupied by a pattern of beds. In public parks and large gardens the parterres may be wonderfully elaborate but even in small gardens a simple parterre may be an effective feature, particularly near the house where such formal treatment is appropriate. Since it is the geometrical pattern of the beds that gives the parterre much of its charm this should stand out clearly, which means that plants used in the beds must not be so tall that they obscure the pattern. For the same reason it is an advantage if the parterre can be viewed from above, from windows of the house or from a raised terrace or patio. On flat ground it may be possible to obtain this difference of level by lowering the site of the parterre and using the excavated soil to build up a terrace or raised path, but care must be taken to retain the top soil where plants are to be grown and to use the sub-soil for building up paths and terraces.

Beds in parterres are usually designed symmetrically. They may be of any size and shape, arranged round some central focal point such as a pool, fountain, ornament or sundial, or may be diversified with a few taller plants such as topiary specimens to give elevation without obscuring the plan.

Mixed Borders

A mixed border is one in which shrubs and herbaceous plants are used and possibly roses and bedding plants as well. In small gardens this has the obvious advantage that it overcomes the difficulty of finding separate places for different classes of plants, and even in big gardens, mixed borders may prove to be more interesting and to have a longer appeal than single-type borders. However they do need careful planning to ensure that the shrubs do not in time occupy the greater part of the border, leaving little room for anything else.

Usually shrubs are used for the background, or to form bays within which herbaceous plants and roses are grouped in a pleasing way, with bedding plants added in season to fill in any gaps and to extend the flowering period. Bulbs can also be introduced, and with their aid it is possible to have a considerable display from spring to autumn, with something of interest even in the winter months.

Just as herbaceous borders can be replaced by herbaceous beds, so mixed borders can be replaced by mixed beds if these fit in with the site and plan better.

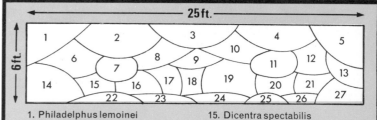

1. Philadelphus lemoinei
2. Buddleia davidii
3. Rosa spinosissima
4. Hibiscus syriacus Blue Bird
5. Choisya ternata
6. Lupin Sweetheart
7. Delphinium Blackmore's Blue
8. Aster Autumn Glory
9. Aquilegia Crimson Star
10. Lupin George Russell
11. Delphinium Swan Lake
12. Sidalcea Monarch
13. Hosta undulata
14. Cytisus nigricans
15. Dicentra spectabilis
16. Anemone elegans Louise Uhink
17. Dianthus Clunie
18. Hosta alba marginata
19. Geranium Johnson's Blue
20. Artemisia frigida
21. Aster Connie Thrower
22. Cotoneaster horizontalis
23. Stachys lanata
24. Nepeta mussinii
25. Daphne collina
26. Dianthus Pink Mrs Sinkins
27. Lavandula Hidcote

The beds in this charming sunken garden have been planted with tulips and wallflowers. Parterres of this type are always best when viewed from above so that the geometrical pattern of the beds can be appreciated

A magnificent display of herbaceous and other plants in an attractive and well-planned border. Roses have been trained up the stone wall to create a colourful background

Vistas and Avenues

Avenues give a great sense of distance, delight the eye by their regularity and invite exploration. They are only possible in gardens of some size, but even in comparatively small gardens a somewhat similar effect can be produced by contriving a vista – a long view enclosed on each side. It may be open-ended so that the eye is carried on to the distance, perhaps to rest on some prominent object such as a fine tree or building, or it may be closed.

A vista may be flanked by trees, shrubs or any plants sufficiently tall to channel the view; it may be paved, grassed or carpeted with low-growing flowers with perhaps a focal point of interest at its end.

When planning an avenue of trees consideration must be given to their ultimate growth. Where space is limited trees of erect, pyramidal or columnar habit are to be preferred, such as Dawyck Beech, Pyramidal Hornbeam and Fastigiate Oak. Erect-growing conifers may also be used, such as the narrow forms of Lawson's Cypress, Leyland Cypress, Irish Yew and Irish Juniper. On a miniature scale the effect of an avenue can be obtained with standard roses or clipped yew or box but for a higher enclosure trees such as limes may be pleached, with branches trained and interwoven along the line of the avenue.

Specimen Plants

Some plants look their best when grown as isolated specimens. The most suitable are plants with a distinctive or symmetrical shape. Japanese maples have this quality and are an ideal size for small gardens. Columnar trees, such as the narrow varieties of Lawson's Cypress, also make good specimens and so do some regularly formed pyramidal trees, such as the Pyramidal Hornbeam, and weeping trees, such as Young's Weeping Birch and the Weeping Pear, *Pyrus salicifolia pendula*. All magnolias look best as single specimens.

Alternatively, evergreen trees or shrubs such as Portugal Laurel may be clipped as specimens.

Good flowering shrubs to plant as specimens include *Berberis stenophylla, Camellia* Donation or any variety of *C. japonica, Cornus alba spaethii, Viburnum tomentosum mariesii* and *Weigela florida variegata*.

Some vigorous roses such as the hybrid musk Penelope make beautiful isolated specimens and some hardy perennials, including pampas grass, rheums, rodgersias and hostas are also good.

In very small gardens it is often more effective to grow one or two well-chosen plants as specimens with a groundwork of low-growing plants or mown grass or paving than to risk overcrowding. Since specimens occupy so conspicuous a place they should be specially well tended.

A vista planned to be seen from the French windows of the house. The path is made more interesting by varying the material and allowing plants to encroach on it

This weeping cedar, named *Cedrus deodara pendula*, makes a highly decorative and symmetrical specimen but will in time grow too wide for a small bed such as this

Lawn Making and After-care

Lawns may serve quite distinct purposes in a garden. They can provide the perfect colour foil to beds of flowers as well as the open spaces. Finely proportioned trees and elegant shrubs can be effectively displayed as isolated specimens surrounded by grass. Lawns are for recreation and for relaxation, for games of skill or for children to play upon. A lawn may also serve a very utilitarian purpose as an airing ground for washing, and in its own right it can be one of the most decorative features in the garden. There are, in fact, many types of lawn and the grasses and methods of cultivation necessary for one may not be the best for another. For ball games requiring a very true playing surface fine grasses and close mowing are essential, but if the lawn is merely to provide a green carpet it may be quite satisfactory to use coarser grasses and to let them retain a great deal more of their growth. Where space is available there is much to be said for combining both types of lawn so that the smooth texture and lighter colour of the close-mown grass contrasts with the rougher texture and darker colour of the grass that is cut an inch or more above soil level. Some bulbs grow well in turf, provided it is not cut until their leaves are about to die down, usually some time in May or June. Daffodils, crocuses and snowdrops are particularly suitable for this kind of planting which combines very satisfactorily with the rough cutting of certain areas of grass.

Mown turf may also be considered as an alternative to paving in some parts of the garden, though it is unwise to use it where there will be heavy wear, since worn grass is unsightly and can be difficult to repair. All the same, the glade type of garden, in which curving beds for trees, shrubs and other permanent plants are separated by grass paths of varying width as well as by wider areas of turf, has become very popular for gardens of medium to large size.

In very small gardens it may be better to dispense with turf altogether or to confine it to a purely decorative role, using it in small panels, only to be walked on when necessary for mowing and other care. There are even some difficult places in shade or in city gardens where grass used in this way may best be treated as an annual, to be reseeded each spring. Well cared for, a quick-growing rye or meadow grass can produce a fine effect in under a month. It is well to remember that the smaller the lawn the more difficult it will be to hide any imperfections.

In special places small lawns can be made of aromatic plants such as chamomile and thyme (*Thymus serpyllum*) but they are more troublesome to look after than grasses and also more costly to establish.

Choosing the Grass

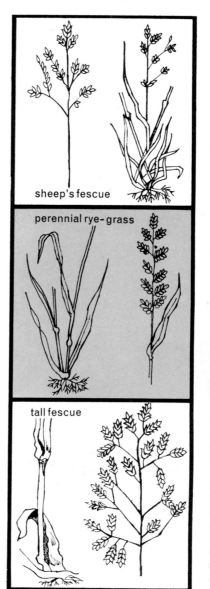

sheep's fescue

perennial rye-grass

tall fescue

There are many different kinds of grass and by no means all are suited to lawn making. Even those that are suitable differ greatly in the kind of turf they produce. One of the advantages of growing a lawn from seed is that grasses can be selected to produce the kind of lawn one wants.

The finest lawns, such as those used for bowls, croquet and putting, are formed from slow-growing grasses with narrow leaves, such as the fescues (*Festuca* sp.) and the bents (*Agrostis* sp.). These lawns need the most care to maintain them in good condition.

Lawns likely to receive a lot of hard wear, such as children's play-grounds or grass paths, are usually made from coarser grasses, such as the perennial rye-grass (*Lolium perenne*), or smooth- or rough-stalked meadow grass (*Poa* sp.). The latter are also good for shady places and so is crested dog's-tail (*Cynosurus cristatus*).

Seedsmen seldom offer individual grasses, but prepare mixtures suitable for particular purposes. Mixtures of fine grasses cost more than coarse mixtures.

When turf is purchased, it is usually very difficult to tell which grasses it contains, but Cumberland or sea-washed turf is always composed of the finest grasses. However, it is expensive and difficult to maintain in good condition and should only be used for high quality, well-maintained lawns.

A well-tended lawn provides a perfect foil for border flowers. In this garden, the lawn is on two levels, joined by a simple flight of steps, which gives added interest

Digging and Levelling

Dig or fork the whole area thoroughly and be particularly careful to remove the roots of all perennial weeds, such as couch grass, bindweed, dandelions, docks, nettles and thistles. If the site is very weed infested, kill these first by watering with a weedkiller, such as paraquat, which will not leave any harmful deposit in the soil.

Occasionally lawns are required to follow the natural contours of the ground however irregular these may be, but usually the aim is either for a level lawn or, at least, for a regular slope. If this involves much movement of soil, care must be taken to keep the topsoil at the surface.

Remove the topsoil to a depth of at least 8 in. and place it conveniently in heaps. Then drive in stakes every 10 ft. or so over the site, and level the tops with a spirit-level and a long, straight-edged plank. Now remove sub-soil from the highest to the lowest places until all are approximately the same distance below the tops of the pegs. Finally, return the topsoil, spreading it evenly all over and giving a final levelling with spirit-level and plank. Slopes can be engineered by sighting across the tops of the pegs, or by using two planks nailed together at the angle of the slope.

Final Preparation

For the final preparation, choose a day when the surface is reasonably dry and the clods of soil break up easily. Before breaking down the surface for seeding or turfing, give it a dressing of a good compound fertiliser, such as Growmore, at the rate recommended by the manufacturers, together with a dressing of granulated peat at 6 to 8 lb. per sq. yd. Then break up the clods with the back of a fork and the smaller pieces with a rake, at the same time removing any large stones, pieces of stick or any remaining weed roots.

Next, tread the whole site carefully, partly to assist in breaking any remaining lumps of soil but even more to ensure that there are no loose places which would settle later and cause hollows in the lawn. Work from side to side moving one way across the plot, and then repeat this at right angles, so that no piece of ground, however small, is missed.

Now rake the whole site again, this time working at right angles to the first raking. At this stage take great care to get the surface quite level with no humps or depressions which would render mowing difficult later on.

It is more necessary to get a very fine crumbly surface if seed is to be sown than it is if turves are to be laid or tufts of creeping grass planted. It is an advantage if seeding, turfing or planting can follow almost immediately after this final preparation is finished.

One of the first steps in producing a lawn is to dig or fork the plot thoroughly. The area above was watered a week earlier with paraquat to kill weeds and native grasses and their roots are being pulled out

During the final raking it is important to ensure that the surface is level. A surprising degree of accuracy can be achieved with the eye alone but more precise levelling can be given with a spirit-level

Sowing

Spring, and late summer to early autumn, are the best periods for seed sowing, though it can also be sown in summer if the seedbed can be kept well watered in dry weather.

Allow from 1 to 2 oz. of seed per sq. yd., the greater quantity when using fine grasses because of their slower germination and growth. Divide the site into yard-wide strips with string, measure out enough seed for each strip and sow each separately. By this means even distribution of seed should be obtained. A still more accurate way is to have two lots of strings, lengthwise and crosswise, so that the plot is marked out in square yards; find a measure that will just hold 2 oz. of seed (or 1 oz. if the lower seeding rate is to be adopted) and scatter one measure of seed over each square. Alternatively, use a wheeled fertiliser distributor to spread the seed, but a little experimenting on a large sheet of paper may be necessary to get the correct adjustment for the required rate of sowing.

Cover the seed by raking it very lightly or by scattering sifted soil over it. Most grass seed is treated by the seedsman with a bird deterrent before it is sold, but if it has not been so treated, black cotton should be stretched between sticks over the site to keep birds away.

When making a lawn from seed, the best results are obtained if the ground is marked out in yard-wide strips each to be sown separately with a measured quantity of seed

Turfing

Turves are usually cut in rectangular strips 3 ft. by 1 ft. and about 1½ in. thick. They are rolled up for ease of delivery, but should be unrolled as soon as possible, for the grass soon turns yellow if deprived of light. Occasionally, turves are cut in one foot squares, and these are preferred by some greenkeepers for very accurate work. Turves can be laid at any time of the year but early autumn is the most favourable season.

If the lawn has straight edges, start laying the turves along one of these, but if the edges are curved, stretch a line a little way in and start the first row of turves against this. Lay the turves lengthwise and see that each is quite level. Remove or add soil where necessary to correct unevenness. Lay the next row of turves so that the joins between them do not coincide with those in the first row and continue in this way so that only the lengthwise joins are continuous, the cross joins all being staggered, like bricks in a wall. Beat the turves gently with the back of a spade to settle them firmly on the soil.

Do not lay small pieces of turf to finish off an edge, but use full turves here and fill in with part turves away from the edge where they are less likely to be dislodged.

A plank is useful to kneel on while laying turves in order to keep the surface of the soil level. A spade is used to beat the laid turves gently to ensure close contact with the soil

Care of New Grass

Seedling grass should appear in anything from eight days to a month from the time of sowing, according to the weather and the type of seed used. If there is much seedling weed with the grass, water it with ioxynil selective weed-killer which can first be used approximately seven to ten days after the grass appears.

When the grass is about 1 in. high, roll it with a light roller. A few days later, when it is between 1½ and 2 in. high, give it its first cutting with the blades of the mower set 1 in. above soil level. The blades must be really sharp or there will be danger of dragging some of the seedlings out of the ground. Small lawns are best cut for the first time with sharp shears

so that this danger is avoided.

Roll lawns from turf occasionally after the first fortnight or three weeks, by which time the grass should be rooting down into the soil. Mowing can commence at about the same time if the turf is laid in spring or summer, but autumn-laid turf will grow very little before the following spring and one autumn cutting will probably be sufficient. Apply a light topdressing of fine peat or a mixture of peat and sand and brush this down into any crevices remaining between the turves.

If new lawns are made in spring or summer, water freely in dry weather, but for seedling grass use a fine sprinkler so that the surface soil is not washed away.

Mowing

Mowing has a marked effect on the character of a lawn since the grasses and weeds that can survive constant close mowing are not the same as those that thrive with less severe cutting. Even the native grass of a site will alter with mowing since it is composed of a mixture of grasses and weeds and the degree of mowing will determine to a considerable extent which become dominant.

For a good quality home lawn mow about twice a week from May to September, and once a week in April and October, with perhaps two or three mowings in winter when conditions are favourable. Set the mower to cut at ¾ in. above soil level. If the lawn is to be used for ball games requiring

a true playing surface, mow more frequently and set the mower to cut at ½ in., or even ¼ in. if the lawn is made up entirely of fine grasses. However, constant close mowing will kill perennial rye grass, meadow grasses and crested dog's-tail.

If the mower is driven by a roller fixed behind the blades it will give the lawn a striped appearance due to the grass being rolled in different directions. With a roller drive it is also possible to cut over the edge of the lawn.

Newly laid turves should be rolled occasionally once they have become established and have rooted into the soil below. This will help to consolidate the lawn and give a really professional finish

Mowing a well-established lawn with a motor mower. Lawn mowers of all types should be sharpened and oiled regularly and cutting height set to suit the purpose for which the lawn is required

Verges

Tidy edges to lawns can greatly improve their appearance. Clip the grass growing horizontally over the edge of the lawn with special long-handled shears or with a mechanical edge trimmer. Do this every time the lawn is mown.

Occasionally, cut the edge of the lawn with a sharp spade or a special edging tool, using a line stretched between pegs or a plank to get an absolutely straight edge. Do not overdo this cutting or the lawn will gradually get smaller and flanking beds or paths wider, but the natural tendency of wear and rolling is to spread the edges and it is right to correct this.

Where paths abut lawns, lay them ½ in. or so below the level of the lawn so that the lawn mower can be used right over the edge, and also leave a channel about 2 in. wide and 3 in. deep between the turf and the path so that the edges of the turf can be clipped easily. It is a good labour-saving idea to lay a line of flagstones between flower borders and lawns, keeping them just below the level of the turf and separated from it by a channel as just described. Plants growing at the edge of the border can then grow out over the flagstones without harming the grass or interfering with the edging.

Feeding

If the mowings are always picked up and removed from a lawn, it will require more feeding than if the lawn mowings are permitted to lie and rot, since by doing this they will return food to the soil. However, decaying grass cuttings will, in time, impart a spongy texture to the surface which is not desirable if the lawn is to be used for games requiring a firm surface. A reasonable compromise is to remove mowings in spring and autumn but leave them in hot summer weather, when they act as a useful mulch.

In either case, lawns must be fed to keep them in good condition. Apply a compound lawn fertiliser in March or April, usually at 4 oz. per sq. yd., but do not exceed the manufacturers' recommended rate. Give a second application at half this rate in June. In September apply a special autumn lawn dressing which will have a low percentage of nitrogen in relation to phosphoric acid and potash. At the same time topdress the lawn with fine peat at 4 oz. per sq. yd. and brush it into the turf.

Be careful to spread fertilisers evenly and at the correct rate. An overdose may scorch or kill the grass. A wheeled fertiliser distributor is particularly useful for even distribution.

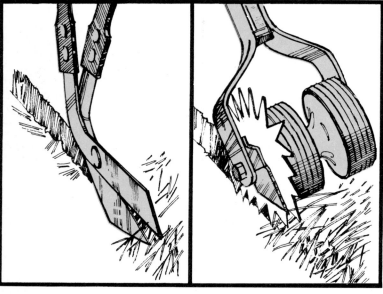

The edges of lawns spread with mowing and ordinary wear and should be cut back occasionally. Here, a special edging tool with a curved blade is being used, but a sharp spade is a good substitute

In September a dressing of finely milled peat will replenish the humus content of the soil, particularly important in a lawn which has been mown closely. This dressing can be brushed in with a besom

Watering

rotary sprinkler

oscillating sprinkler

perforated hose

If lawns are deprived of water, they quickly turn yellow and then brown. The fine grasses may be killed completely and only coarse grasses, clovers and some deep-rooted weeds survive. So watering in dry weather is a very important item in the management of lawns. It is all the more vital if the lawn is closely mown and the mowings are removed, since the soil will be more exposed to the baking effect of the sun.

Water must be supplied in sufficient quantity to soak an inch or so into the soil, but not so fast that it cakes the surface and runs off it. For this reason, fine sprinklers are better than coarse jets. The oscillating type of sprinkler is particularly good since it waters a rectangle and can be moved from point to point in such a way that the whole area is watered to a similar degree.

Contrary to popular belief, it does not matter what time of day water is applied. Give it whenever it is most convenient, whether the sun is shining or not. Be particularly careful to water after fertiliser has been applied if it does not rain thoroughly in a few days, as it is only in solution that the fertiliser is of any use to the grass. If it is left lying on the grass for too long, or in too concentrated a solution, it may damage it.

Brushing and Raking

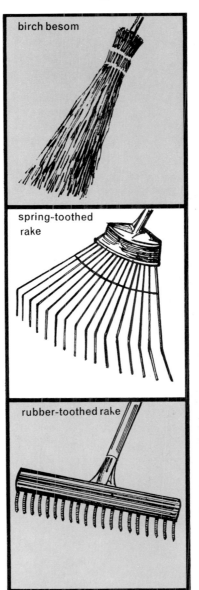

birch besom

spring-toothed rake

rubber-toothed rake

Brushing is necessary to scatter worm casts, which might otherwise be trodden down and smother small patches of grass, to work fertilisers and peat topdressings into the turf, and to get rid of debris, moss etc. particularly after raking. The old-fashioned birch besom is still an excellent lawn brush and is especially useful for collecting leaves and distributing worm casts, though many special lawn brushes are also made.

Raking is necessary to drag out the accumulations of dead but undecayed material which can collect under the surface of the grass, particularly when the soil is acid or the weather dry. It also drags out a lot of moss, though care must be taken to see that it does not actually spread the moss from one part of the lawn to another.

Use a spring-toothed lawn rake for this purpose, not a rigid steel garden rake, which would drag out the lawn grass. Rake about once a fortnight from spring to late summer and then, before applying the autumn fertiliser, give a much more thorough raking or use a slitter or spiker. Rake the lawn first in one direction and then at right angles so that nothing is missed.

Watering is generally necessary in the height of summer if a really green sward is required. Oscillating sprinklers are particularly effective for this job as they cover a rectangle of turf

Brushing the lawn with an old-fashioned birch besom to disperse worm casts and to sweep up debris. This is still a good tool, though there are now many excellent modern lawn brushes on the market

Aerating

Lawns that receive a lot of use, or are frequently rolled, become so hard that air can no longer penetrate to the grass roots and the quality of the turf declines. It is then necessary to loosen it again by slitting or spiking or by a combination of the two.

Slitting is done with a special tool which slices down into the turf and the soil beneath to a depth of an inch or so. Many different models are available, some for hand use, some power driven or for attachment to a power-driven lawn mower.

The simplest form of spiking is with a digging fork. Thrust the tines about 3 in. into the turf, lever backwards on the handle sufficiently to raise the turf slightly and repeat every 6 in. or so all over the lawn. The work can be done more rapidly with special spiking tools, some of which are wheeled backwards and forwards across the lawn.

An alternative to spiking is hollow-tining, in which the solid spike is replaced by a hollow-tine which punches out a core of turf and soil, leaving a little hole. This is most effective, especially if a dressing of sharp grit is given and brushed down into the holes.

Aeration is usually done in early autumn, but may be carried out at any time if the condition of the turf necessitates it.

Weeds

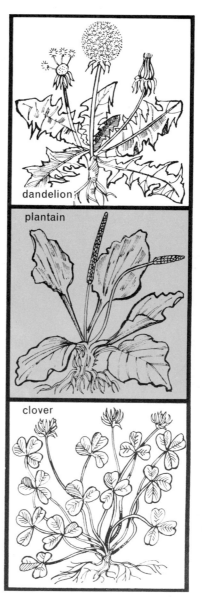
dandelion

plantain

clover

Many lawn weeds can be killed with special weedkillers which may check the grass slightly but do it no permanent damage. They are known as selective lawn weedkillers and the principal kinds are 2,4-D, MCPA and mecoprop, the last being particularly effective against clover. These can be purchased separately or in various mixtures under trade names, ready for dilution with water according to the manufacturers' instructions.

Apply in spring and early summer, a few days after applying fertiliser. Use a watering-can fitted with a sprinkle bar which will deliver the weedkiller at the correct rate if moved across the turf at a steady walking pace. Some persistent weeds can only be eliminated by several applications at intervals of two or three weeks.

Do not use 2,4-D, MCPA or mecoprop on young seedling turf. Ioxynil can be used seven to ten days after germination until the grass is three months old when it will be established.

Lawn sand, a mixture of sulphate of ammonia, sulphate of iron and sand, can also be used to kill lawn weeds. Sprinkle it directly on the weeds or carefully distribute it all over the lawn as recommended by the manufacturer. It is most effective in fine weather in spring or summer. The grass may be slightly scorched but will recover rapidly, provided an overdose has not been given.

A foot-operated spiker is very useful for aerating small areas of grass. A garden fork may also be used for this operation but for larger areas a wheel-mounted aerator will save much time

When making up solutions of weedkiller great care must be taken to follow the manufacturer's instructions. Note the rubber gloves which are being worn to protect the hands from harmful chemicals

Pests

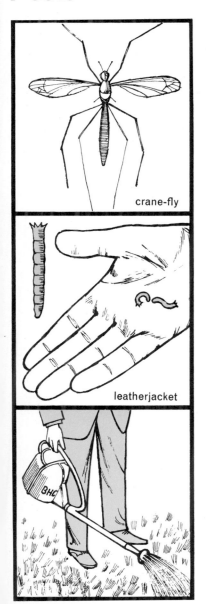

crane-fly

leatherjacket

The principal pest of lawns is the leatherjacket. This is the larva of the crane-fly or daddy-long-legs and is a tough-skinned, greyish grub about an inch in length which lives on the roots of grass and other plants. The grass dies in patches where the leatherjackets are feeding, and if the infested places are heavily soaked with water and a wet sack laid on top, some may come to the surface to breathe and can thus be detected and destroyed. The best remedy, however, for a serious attack is to water the lawn well, especially the brown and yellow patches, with a solution of a suitable insecticide.

Moles and earthworms, though useful in some respects, can be a great nuisance on lawns; the moles by tunnelling beneath the surface and throwing up heaps of excavated soil, the earthworms by covering the lawn with little heaps of soil or worm casts.

Moles can be caught with special spring traps set across their runs, and they can be kept out of a lawn by surrounding it with naphthalene moth balls dropped into holes 4 in. deep and 4 to 6 in. apart.

Worms can be killed by watering the lawn with chlordane at the strength recommended by the manufacturers. The most effective times for application are spring and early autumn.

Diseases

Grass suffers from various diseases just as other plants do. These are likely to be most troublesome between autumn and spring, particularly if a fertiliser containing a high percentage of nitrogen has been applied late in the summer. The grass becomes yellow in patches which later turn brown, symptoms very similar to those produced by leatherjackets, which, however, usually appear in a hot, dry summer. Moreover, a close examination of diseased turf will often reveal white or pinkish thread-like growths of fungus on the dying grass.

Avoid the use of summer fertilisers after July; rake, brush and aerate turf to keep it in good condition. Water the grass with a suspension of 4 per cent. calomel dust stirred into water at 2 oz. per gal., keeping the solution agitated while it is being applied. Proprietary lawn fungicides can also be used as advised by the manufacturers.

Fairy rings are circles of lush, dark green grass surrounding areas of dead or dying grass. They are caused by a fungus in the soil which spreads outwards, first stimulating and then killing the grass. Soak the edge of the ring and just beyond it with sulphate of iron at the rate of 4 oz. per gal. of water, or make use of a lawn fungicide. In bad cases, dig out the whole ring to a depth of 1 ft., replace with fresh soil and re-seed or turf.

Good cultivation is an important factor in promoting a healthy lawn, such as the one shown here. Mixed flower borders provide a gay contrast to the rich green sward

A badly maintained lawn that has become infested with weeds and fungi. The fungi have formed a fairy ring, which, though interesting to look at, is very damaging to the grass

General Garden Cultivation

Plain Digging, Forking

Digging and forking, the simplest method of soil cultivation, consists of turning the soil over to the full depth of a spade blade or the tines of a fork (approximately 10 in.). A spade is better if the ground is covered with grass or weeds since it can be used to chop through their roots, and it is also preferable on sandy soils which tend to slip through the tines of a fork. But for heavy or wet soil or clay a fork is easier to use.

To dig soil properly, open up a trench about 8 in. wide and 10 in. deep across one end of the plot and wheel the soil taken out of the trench to the other end of the plot. Alternatively, divide the plot in half lengthwise, open up the trench across one half only and move the soil across to the other half, then work down one side of the plot and up the other to finish at the end where the work started.

In either case, lift the soil a spadeful (or a forkful) at a time, turning it over and throwing it forward into the trench already made. In this way another trench is formed, to be filled in turn with inverted soil. The last trench is filled with the soil that was displaced from the first trench.

Manure or decayed garden refuse can be spread on the surface and turned in as work proceeds or it can be spread along the bottom of each trench.

All plants with coloured leaves obtain a great deal of their food from the air. From the soil they require water, often in considerable quantities, and various chemicals. They also need good anchorage for their roots, which means that the soil must be reasonably firm but not so hard that roots have difficulty in penetrating it.

The purpose of soil cultivation is to improve the texture of the soil, enable it to store water without becoming waterlogged and to stimulate those natural processes within the soil by which its food reserves are liberated. Feeding may be long term to build up those reserves, or short term to increase the immediately available supply of plant food.

The chemicals most likely to be in short supply are nitrogen, phosphorus and potash and sometimes also magnesium, manganese and iron. All these can be added as chemical fertilisers or in animal manures and animal and vegetable waste in which they are present in varying quantity. The process of decay of these bulky organic materials liberates the chemicals and also produces humus, a brown, structureless, slimy substance which is extremely valuable in improving soil texture. Peat is rich in humus and for that reason is a valuable soil dressing despite the fact that it contributes little chemical food.

Deep cultivation of the soil is only possible when it is vacant. It is never wise to dig near established trees and shrubs, since this will destroy many of their roots which are quite near the surface. Even forking can do damage, though pricking the surface is a useful method of getting rid of weeds, letting in air and stirring in topdressings of fertiliser or manure. Hoeing will produce similar results. Deep rooted perennial weeds cannot be destroyed by such light cultivation.

When plants are moved from one place to another they inevitably suffer some check to growth, though the less the roots are injured or the soil around them disturbed the smaller this check is likely to be. That is the justification for growing young plants in containers from which they can be removed with a complete ball of soil and roots. Such plants can be moved at almost any time of the year, whereas plants dug up from the open ground can as a rule only be moved safely at certain periods of the year.

Most deciduous trees and shrubs (those that lose their leaves in winter) and roses are planted between late October and March. Evergreen shrubs and trees are most safely moved in April, May or October, though with care they can also be moved during mild spells in winter. Most herbaceous plants are best planted in March or April, though some transplant quite well in October.

Using a spade to chop out the turf when first digging a garden plot. Once cultivated a fork will dig just as well and be less laborious to use

Trenching and Ridging

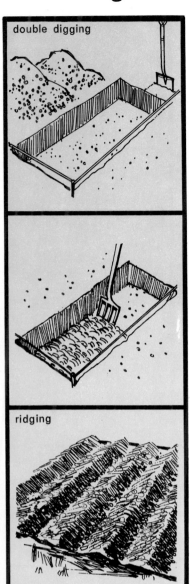

double digging

ridging

Trenching or double digging consists of breaking up soil to twice the depth of the blade of a spade or fork (approximately 20 in.). It is useful for very weedy or poorly drained ground and also in preparation for growing some special crops.

First open up a trench 2 ft. wide across one end of the plot and wheel the soil to the other end or divide lengthwise as for digging and transport the soil to one side. Then get into the open trench and, working from one end to the other, break up the soil in the bottom with a fork, using the full depth of the tines. Manure or garden refuse can be worked in at the same time.

Now mark out a second 2-ft. trench behind the first and dig the soil from it into the first trench, inverting each spadeful (or forkful) so that all grass or weed is buried. When the second trench is completed get into the bottom and break it up as before. Proceed in the same way, trench by trench, filling the last one with the soil taken from the first.

To ridge soil, divide the plot into 3-ft. wide strips and dig or fork each separately from end to end. Throw all the soil towards the centre of each strip so leaving it in steep ridges, with a large surface exposed to wind and frost.

General Conditions

Planting should not be attempted when soil is frozen or is so wet that it sticks badly to tools and boots. When soil is very dry planting should be carried out only if it is possible to keep it well watered until rain falls or plants become established.

The ideal conditions for planting are moist soil and mild, showery weather.

If conditions are not quite ideal it will be helpful to prepare a special planting mixture beforehand and keep this covered with polythene sheeting. A good combination is equal parts of sifted soil, peat and coarse sand, plus a handful of bonemeal to each bucketful of the mixture. A spadeful or so of this is worked around the roots and mixed with the ordinary garden soil as it is returned to the hole.

If soil and/or weather conditions are not right when plants arrive, open up the packages but leave the packing round the roots (or wrap them in damp moss or straw if there is no packing) and put the plants in a shed or garage for a few days, keeping the roots moist. If a longer waiting period seems likely, heel in the plants, that is, plant them temporarily close together in a trench in a sheltered place, making the soil firm around their roots. Lift and replant properly when conditions are right.

heeling in shrubs

Breaking up the subsoil in the bottom of a trench in the process known as double digging. It is a method often used by exhibitors and other gardeners seeking the finest results

Planting under good soil conditions. Note that the spade is relatively clean and firming is possible without puddling the soil which is crumbly without being dry

Special Tools

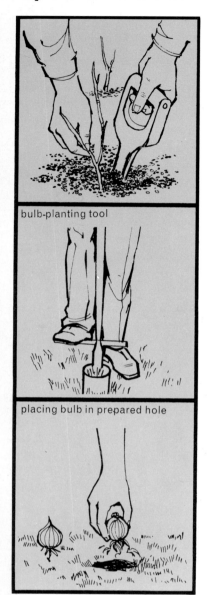

bulb-planting tool

placing bulb in prepared hole

Special planting tools include dibbers, bulb planters and similar but smaller tools for pot plants.

A dibber is a short stick or shaft with a pointed or rounded end with which a hole can be bored in the soil. Large dibbers are often steel shod for easy use and long life. Dibbers are serviceable for planting seedlings and plants with fairly straight, downward-pointing roots, such as hollyhocks, wallflowers, cabbages and cauliflowers. They are not suitable for plants with spreading roots since the hole made is too narrow, nor are they recommended for bulbs since there is a danger that the bulbs will be suspended in holes with a space beneath in which water will collect.

To plant with a dibber, press it well into the soil and withdraw it carefully, inserting the plant roots immediately. Then push the dibber in again an inch or so away and lever it towards the plant to close up the hole.

Bulb planters and similar larger tools cut out a plug of soil, leaving a clean, round hole into which a bulb or pot plant is placed. With bulbs the plug can then be replaced intact leaving practically no trace, even on well-kept lawns. With pot plants the plug is broken up and returned around and over the roots.

Using a Spade

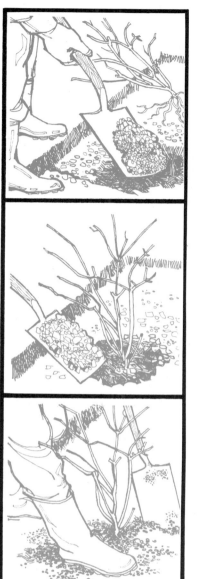

A spade is the most convenient tool with which to plant large plants such as shrubs and trees.

First measure the spread of the roots to be planted. Mark out an area of this size where the plant is to go and dig out a hole a little larger and of approximately the required depth. Place the plant carefully in position and check the depth. This can be done by placing a rod across the hole from side to side next to the stem of the plant. If the old soil mark can be seen – that is, the level on the stem to which the soil came in the place where the plant formerly grew – this should be about 1 in. below the rim of the hole. If the mark cannot be seen the depth of the hole should permit the uppermost roots to be covered with at least 2 in. of soil.

Remove the plant if it is necessary to adjust the depth, and then replace it in position and return the soil, breaking it up in the process and working it between the roots. When all are covered, firm by careful treading all round. Return the rest of the soil and leave the surface level and crumbly.

To support trees and large shrubs, drive a strong stake into the hole before filling in so that there is no danger of injuring roots when inserting the stake. Secure the plant to the stake at once to prevent wind rocking.

Daffodils and other bulbs look delightful when naturalised in irregular drifts in grass. A special tool, shown above, can be obtained for planting which removes a neat core of turf that can be replaced when the bulb has been dropped in

Planting conifers with a spade. The plants are placed close at hand so that the size of the root ball of each can be estimated and a hole of just the right size and depth prepared. Evergreens are a little more difficult to transplant than deciduous shrubs

Using a Trowel

planting bulbs with a trowel

putting in young plant

firming plant with a trowel

Nearly all small plants and bulbs are planted most conveniently with a trowel. A short-handled trowel is less tiring to wrist and arm than a long-handled trowel which saves little in stooping since the plant must in any case be held in position in the prepared hole.

Make the hole sufficiently large to accommodate all the roots spread out in a natural manner and not turned up at the tips. See that each hole is sufficiently deep to allow the collar of the plant (the point where leaves or stems join the roots) to be fractionally below the level of the soil.

Hold the plant in the centre of the hole and return soil around its roots, breaking up any lumps in the process. Make the soil firm around the roots with the knuckles or the handle of the trowel and complete the job with a scattering of loose soil.

If frost occurs after planting make certain that the plants are still firmly in the soil, refirming them if necessary. When planting in spring or summer water freely after planting if the soil is dry.

Container-grown Plants

Many plants are grown and sold in containers so that they can be planted with a minimum check to growth. Such plants may be moved at almost any time of the year provided that the soil around the roots is retained undisturbed and the roots are not broken.

Containers may be conventional clay pots, plastic pots, treated paper pots, polythene bags or tin cans. Whatever their nature, the plants must be removed from them without the soil balls being broken.

With a clay or plastic pot, place one hand over the soil and invert the pot, rapping the edge of it on something firm. Strip off paper pots and polythene bags, first slitting with a knife if necessary. Slit tins vertically on two sides with a can opener so that the plant can be lifted out.

Plant immediately in a hole a little larger than the size of the ball of soil, working fine soil around the edges and making firm.

Water freely for several weeks after planting in spring or summer if the weather is at all hot and dry. Stake large plants securely.

'Balled' plants are lifted from the open ground after which sacking or polythene is wrapped around the roots to prevent soil falling off. Plant as for container-grown plants but do not remove the wrapping until the plant is actually in its hole.

planting container-grown shrub

removing sacking from shrub

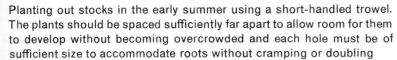

Planting out stocks in the early summer using a short-handled trowel. The plants should be spaced sufficiently far apart to allow room for them to develop without becoming overcrowded and each hole must be of sufficient size to accommodate roots without cramping or doubling

When plants are container grown, they can be planted out at almost any time of the year as there is little root disturbance. This is particularly useful for a new garden when quick results are required. The container must be removed when planting

Aftercare

Cold and drying winds can do much damage to newly planted plants, especially to evergreens. Sacking or polythene screens can be used to protect them or cut branches of evergreens may be thrust firmly into the soil around them as a screen. Never cover plants right over but only give protection round their sides.

Rocking by wind disturbs roots, prevents re-establishment and may cause the death of plants. To prevent this, stake securely all newly planted trees and large shrubs.

Frost may loosen the soil and allow roots to dry out or plants to be blown over. After frost examine new plantings and re-firm the soil where this is necessary.

Even under the most favourable conditions it takes weeks for roots to grow out into the surrounding soil and obtain food and moisture as freely as before being transplanted. In spring and summer keep all new plantings well watered, especially if the weather is hot and dry, until strong new growth indicates that plants are established.

Spread damp peat or grass clippings on the surface around plants to prevent evaporation and conserve moisture in the soil.

Do not feed new plantings with strong fertilisers until they are well established and growing.

protection from wind

spreading peat

Protecting a newly planted shrub with a screen made of sacking and wooden stakes. This is particularly necessary in cold, exposed positions until the plants have become well established

Hoeing

Dutch hoe

draw hoe

The purpose of hoeing is to break up the surface soil – improving thereby the aeration of the soil – and at the same time to kill weeds. Hoeing is also used to thin overcrowded seedlings, a process known as singling. Some gardeners believe that hoeing helps to retain moisture in the soil by creating a loose layer on the surface through which water cannot rise readily. This layer also serves as a blanket to protect the lower soil from the sun's heat.

There are many different kinds of hoe but for the purpose of using them correctly they may be divided into two main groups – Dutch hoes and draw hoes.

A Dutch hoe has a blade set more or less in the same plane as the handle and it is pushed and pulled through the soil, the user usually moving backwards so that the freshly hoed soil is not walked on and flattened.

A draw hoe has the blade set roughly at right angles to the handle and is used with a chopping and pulling action, the user usually moving forwards, though possibly a little to one side of the ground actually hoed.

Dutch hoes are particularly serviceable for cutting off small weeds and keeping the surface tidy, draw hoes for cutting off large or tough weeds and breaking hard ground.

Thinning out seedlings with an onion hoe. This tool, which is like a miniature draw hoe, was originally designed for work on onion crops but is now used for any job needing a small hoe

Mulching

Mulching means spreading some bulky material such as animal manure, decayed vegetable refuse, peat, spent hops, chopped straw or grass mowings on the surface of the soil. It may serve one or all of three purposes: feeding plants, retaining soil moisture and suppressing weeds.

Mulches are most useful if applied in spring and early summer and should be at least 1½ in. thick, preferably more. Feeding mulches may be thinner, according to the richness of the material used.

Mulches are best applied when the soil is reasonably moist. They then act as a blanket on the surface, protecting it from the sun's heat and reducing loss of water by evaporation. If mulches are applied in summer to soil that is already dry, they may have the opposite effect, absorbing light showers and preventing the water reaching the roots of plants. If mulches are applied too early, before the soil has warmed up, they will tend to keep the soil cold.

An alternative to mulches of organic material is a mulch of plastic, usually of thin black polythene, which may be perforated to allow rain to penetrate. Such mulches are very effective in suppressing weeds and in checking surface evaporation, but are not very sightly, and so are generally restricted to the fruit and vegetable gardens.

Lime

Lime can be obtained in various forms. Limestone and chalk are different forms of the same chemical, calcium carbonate, while hydrated lime is chalk that has been heated in a kiln to turn it into quicklime or calcium oxide, and then slaked with water to change it into calcium hydroxide. This is a fine white powder, dusty and choking if inhaled but fairly easily spread, and is best for the garden as it acts quickly on the soil. It is applied at rates varying from 2 to 8 oz. per sq. yd. of ground.

Calcium is an essential plant food but is usually present in sufficient quantity for the needs of plants. The principal reason for applying lime or chalk is to make the soil less acid, since both substances are alkaline (the opposite of acid).

Home kits are available for measuring the acid/alkaline reaction of soil which is expressed as the pH value. $pH7$ is neutral, being neither acid nor alkaline, while figures below 7 show increasing degrees of acidity and above 7 increasing degrees of alkalinity. Plants differ greatly in their preferences, some, such as rhododendrons, preferring acid soils and others, such as brassicas, preferring alkaline soils, but most will grow in soils within a range between $pH6$ and 7. Liming at two- to three-year intervals is most likely to be required on heavily manured and frequently cultivated ground.

mulching

Well-rotted garden refuse is being spread around this bush as a mulch. This will act as a fertiliser, will help to suppress weeds and also to retain moisture in the soil by reducing surface evaporation

Using a soil testing kit to ascertain the pH of soil before applying lime. If the reading is $pH7$ or higher it is unlikely that lime will prove beneficial, but readings below this indicate increasing acidity

Animal Manures

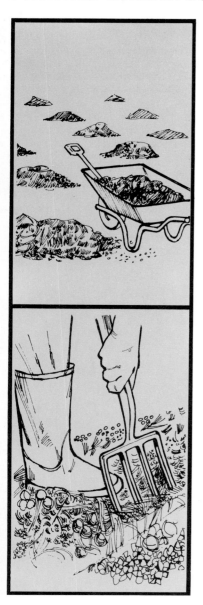

Manures of animal origin vary greatly in character, from the comparatively light texture of horse manure made with straw or peat bedding to the heavy, wet texture of pig manure containing little bedding, or the very rich but rather caustic fresh poultry manure.

The light, bulky manures are best for improving the texture of heavy soils and can be used at rates of 1 cwt. per 6 to 15 sq. yd. Heavy manures are better for light soils and can be used at similar rates. Concentrated manures such as poultry and pig droppings do not greatly improve soil texture and are best used dry, like chemical fertilisers, at rates of 8 to 12 oz. per sq. yd.

All animal manures contain a variety of chemicals which are used by plants as food, not only those most quickly exhausted but also many others, known as trace elements, deficiencies of which can cause some strange symptoms which are often mistaken for disease. The two most important advantages of using animal manures are that the bulky kinds improve the soil texture and all kinds supply some of the essential trace elements – that is, chemicals which are necessary to plants in very minute quantities.

The chemicals in animal manures are not immediately available to plants, but are liberated by decay, a process which starts in the manure heap before it is used.

Garden Compost

Garden compost is the name given to vegetable refuse which has been allowed to rot until it has become dark brown and of even texture throughout. It is a valuable substitute and fulfils the same functions as bulky animal manures, including returning trace elements to the soil. However, if the soil is lacking a particular chemical the plants growing in it will also be deficient and so will any compost made from them.

The best way to prepare compost is to build the garden refuse into heaps about 3 ft. wide, 3 ft. high and of any required length. Pile the heap up in layers 6 to 8 in. thick and spread animal manure over each layer or sprinkle them with Nitrochalk or one of the advertised compost 'accelerators'. If the materials are dry, wet them thoroughly as they are built into the heap. After four to six weeks turn the heap completely inside out. When the whole heap has decayed apply it to the beds in the same way and at the same rates as bulky animal manures.

Do not put badly diseased plants on the compost heap, or weeds that are full of seeds, as disease spores and weed seeds may not be killed in the process of decay. Burn such material, together with branches, twigs and other hard plant matter which will not decay easily.

Animal manure being incorporated into the soil during digging. Such bulky manures will improve the texture of the soil and provide many of the chemical foods required by all plants

Leaves and all soft garden waste can be rotted down into an excellent manure substitute. Air must be able to penetrate the heap. A chemical compost accelerator will hasten decay and so will an adequate supply of water

Compound Fertilisers

Compound fertilisers are composed of several different chemicals to provide a more balanced feed than could be supplied with one chemical only. Most compound fertilisers contain nitrogen, phosphorus and potash in varying proportions and some also supply other chemicals including iron, magnesium and manganese. The percentage of nitrogen, phosphorus (shown as phosphoric acid equivalent) and potash must be shown on the bag or container. It usually appears simply as three figures: for instance, 6:8:4 would mean that the fertiliser contained 6% nitrogen, 8% phosphoric acid and 4% potash. The manufacturer is not obliged to disclose what ingredients are used to obtain these percentages and rarely does so.

Compound fertilisers with roughly equal percentages of nitrogen, phosphoric acid and potash are described as 'well balanced' and are suitable for the general feeding of a wide variety of plants and crops.

Compound fertilisers with a preponderance of one chemical are described as 'high nitrogen', 'high phosphorus' or 'high potash' according to which is in excess and are respectively useful for promoting rapid growth, good root production and ripening.

All compound fertilisers should be used strictly according to manufacturers' instructions and never in larger quantities.

Organic Fertilisers

Organic fertilisers are those containing carbon but, since this is a characteristic of all soil dressings obtained from animal and vegetable waste, the term is often used as if it referred specifically to manure or compost. Plants do not feed directly on organic fertilisers but on the inorganic chemicals that are liberated from them by decay. In consequence, these fertilisers are often slower in action but longer lasting than inorganic fertilisers. Some also provide several different chemicals useful to plants, including trace elements. The following are among the most useful:

Dried blood: supplies mainly nitrogen. Use at 2 to 4 oz. per sq. yd. in spring and summer.

Bonemeal: supplies phosphorus and a little nitrogen. Use at 2 to 6 oz. per sq. yd. at any time.

Castor meal: supplies mainly nitrogen. Use 1 to 2 oz. per sq. yd. in spring or summer.

Fish meal: supplies nitrogen, phosphorus and potash. Use 2 to 4 oz. per sq. yd. in spring or summer.

Hoof and horn meal: supplies mainly nitrogen. Use at 1 to 2 oz. per sq. yd. in spring and summer.

Meat meal: supplies nitrogen and some phosphorus. Use like fish meal.

Spent hops and peat: contains little chemical food (unless added) but improves the soil texture.

Urea formaldehyde: supplies nitrogen. Use at $\frac{1}{2}$ to 1 oz. per sq. yd. in spring or summer.

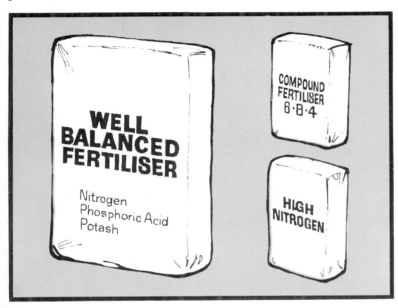

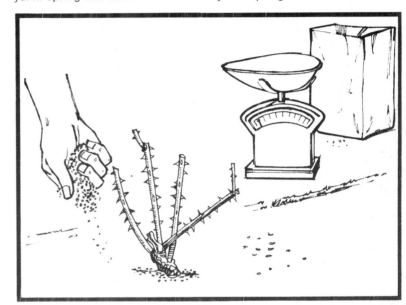

A compound fertiliser being applied to a lawn. Note the scales for accurate weighing of the fertiliser and the way in which the lawn has been marked out into strips to ensure even coverage

Bonemeal will supply the plant with phosphorus and a little nitrogen. It can be applied at any time, at a rate of 2 to 6 oz. per sq. yd., is rather slow acting and will last for many months

Simple Ways to Increase Plants

Sowing in Pots and Boxes

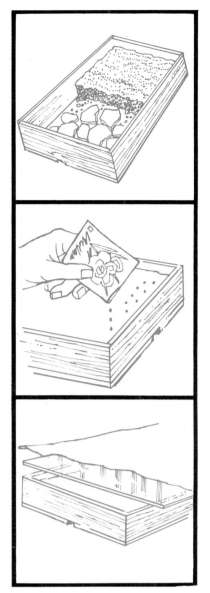

Pots, pans and boxes in which seeds are germinated must be well provided with holes or slits through which surplus water can drain away. Cover these outlets with pieces of broken pot (crocks), small gravel or coarse peat so that they cannot be blocked by fine soil and then fill up with seed compost. Press the compost in gently with the fingers and smooth it off level with a straight-edged piece of wood. Firm composts based on loam, such as John Innes Seed Compost, with a smooth wooden block, but do not firm peat composts. When ready for sowing, the surface of the compost should be about $\frac{1}{2}$ in. below the rim of the receptacle.

Broadcast the seed thinly over the surface of the compost and cover by sifting soil, peat or sand over it. Very small seeds need not be covered at all, but both types should be protected by a pane of glass laid over the container (but not touching the soil) with a sheet of paper on top. The paper must be removed directly the seedlings appear and the glass a day or so later.

Water the seeds thoroughly using a watering-can fitted with a fine rose. For very small seeds, water by holding the pan for a few moments almost to its rim in a tub of water.

One of the most fascinating things about gardening is that it is possible to increase most plants very easily. Some plants actually need to be renewed from time to time; annuals and biennials each year, since they die once they have flowered and set seed; many fast growing herbaceous perennials every two or three years since in that time they can spread too widely for convenience and starve themselves out by exhausting the soil. Some plants are also healthier and produce better quality flowers if renewed annually from cuttings, dahlias and chrysanthemums being notable examples.

There are two basic methods of increasing plants, one from seed; the other, known as vegetative reproduction, by division, cuttings, layers or grafts. Seedlings are genuinely new individuals, starting a fresh life of their own, whereas plants raised by vegetative means are really extensions of their parents, usually retaining every minute characteristic of their parents, sometimes even the pests and diseases which afflicted them. For this reason, it is important to use as parents only plants that are healthy, pest free and of really desirable quality. Seedlings often differ from their parents but vegetatively propagated plants exactly resemble them. All propagation should be done at the most favourable time of the year. Seeds need moisture, air and warmth to germinate and seedlings require light. In a heated greenhouse the first three can be provided at any time, but light is often lacking in winter and so seed sowing is mostly done between February and July.

Out of doors, the soil is usually too cold to permit seeds to germinate before March and it is from then until early September that most seeds are sown, with particular emphasis on the spring, since this gives the seedlings plenty of time to grow into sturdy plants before the winter.

When seeds are sown in pots, pans or trays, special seed compost is generally used. A compost known as John Innes Seed Compost is excellent and can be purchased ready for use. It is prepared with two parts by bulk of sterilised loam, one part granulated peat, and one part coarse sand, plus $1\frac{1}{2}$ oz. of superphosphate of lime and $\frac{1}{4}$ oz. of ground chalk to each bushel of mixture. Alternatively, there are various proprietary seed composts, mostly based on peat.

Out of doors it would not be practical to use relatively expensive composts such as these, but the natural soil of the site can usually be made sufficiently crumbly and congenial by thorough digging followed by a generous topdressing of peat. The final preparation of outdoor seedbeds should be done when the soil is reasonably dry on top and clods break up easily.

A gay border of annuals. The hardy varieties can be sown where they are to flower but most half-hardy kinds are best sown in pots or boxes and germinated in a greenhouse or frame

Pricing Out

Pricking out is the equivalent of transplanting. Under glass it can be done earlier than outdoors, as the tiny seedlings are protected.

The first leaves produced by a seedling are of a different character, and often of simpler outline, than the leaves that follow. They are known as seed leaves or cotyledons. Pricking out is best done when these are fully developed and the next pair have appeared.

As a rule, seedlings are pricked out into the same type of seed compost as that in which the seeds were germinated, but seedlings of vigorous, fast growing plants, such as tomatoes, may go direct into potting compost.

Pricking out is usually into pans or boxes. Prepare the compost and fill the boxes or pots as for seed sowing, ensuring that the compost is moist throughout. Lift the seedlings, a few at a time, with a pointed stick or wooden plant label, carefully separating the plants. Use a small wooden dibber the size of a fountain pen to make a hole in the compost. Holding a seedling by a leaf or leaves (not by its growing tip or stem, neither of which must be bruised) lower the roots into the hole and press soil round them gently with the dibber. Continue until the pan or tray is full, spacing the seedlings at least $1\frac{1}{2}$ in. apart – vigorous kinds 2 in. apart. Water thoroughly from a watering-can fitted with a fine rose to settle the soil further around the roots, and allow to drain. In sunny weather, lightly shade for the first day.

Seedlings Under Glass

watering seedlings

hardening off seeds

Seedlings need a steady temperature, and adequate moisture and light. Too much heat or insufficient light will make them grow tall and thin. With too little heat they will be stunted and may change colour to a bluish-green. Strong sunlight may scorch them, especially if they are short of water. When the seedlings are checked by bad conditions it usually takes some time to get them growing again.

In spring, seedlings can usually take all the light that is going, and may benefit from being placed on shelves near the greenhouse glass. The boxes should be turned regularly. Summer seedlings are likely to need shading from strong, direct sunshine and may be better in an open frame, with glass protection at night only.

Water the seedlings thoroughly from a can fitted with a rose or by standing the containers for a moment or so up to their rims in water.

At least a fortnight before seedlings raised under glass are to be planted out, place them in a frame and give free ventilation whenever the weather is favourable. For the last few days before being planted, remove all protection from the plants unless frost threatens. This hardening off is essential to accustom plants to cooler outdoor conditions. If a frame is not available, stand the seedlings in a sheltered place outdoors, covering with brown paper on cold nights.

Gazanias are readily raised from seed sown under glass, pricked out into boxes and later planted out of doors. They are low-growing plants ideal for rock gardens, banks or the front of sunny borders but not completely winter hardy

Nemesias are highly colourful half-hardy annuals for summer bedding. Seeds are sown under glass in late March to provide plants for setting out in late May or early June

Sowing Broadcast

Broadcasting seed means scattering it as evenly as possible over the surface of the soil. It is the usual method of sowing lawns and also hardy annuals and other plants that are to grow and flower where sown.

To broadcast seed over a large area, such as a lawn, first mark it off in yard-wide strips, then divide the seed into a sufficient number of equal parts so that each strip can be sown separately. Place the measured quantity of seed in a bowl and scatter it from this by hand, taking care to spread it as evenly as possible. Cover the seed either by scattering fine soil over it or by careful raking so that it is stirred into the surface soil.

Smaller areas can be conveniently sown by slitting the seed packet cleanly with a sharp knife, opening it sufficiently to form a little scoop and sprinkling the seed from this. Thin and even sowing is desirable as crowded seedlings are likely to be weak and may suffer from disease. Cover the seed by sprinkling or sifting soil over it. Only lightly cover very small seeds, but large seeds can have a covering of soil equal to their own thickness.

The drawbacks to broadcasted seeds are that it may be difficult to distinguish weed seedlings from plant seedlings, and it is not possible to use a hoe to eliminate weeds.

Sowing in Drills

Drills are little furrows in which seeds are sown. They are then covered by drawing back the displaced soil. It is important that the drills should be of the correct depth to suit the seed to be sown and that they should be of an even depth throughout. If not, some seeds may be buried too deeply and fail to germinate, and some may be covered too thinly and be picked up by birds; in either case, germination will be uneven.

Make drills with the corner of a hoe or with a sharpened stick. Stretch a garden line to mark the exact position of the drill or use a rod for the same purpose. Hold the hoe or stick firmly and draw it through the soil close to the line with sharp but firm movements, so that minor obstructions are overcome. It is much easier to draw good drills in well-prepared seedbeds than in those that contain many large stones, and are uneven and lumpy.

For average seeds, drills should be $\frac{1}{2}$ to $\frac{3}{4}$ in. deep; for very small seeds, $\frac{1}{4}$ in. and for large seeds, such as peas and beans, about 2 in. deep.

Cover the seeds by drawing back displaced soil with a rake, using the flat of the rake to tamp the soil down gently over the seeds.

Mark the position of each drill before removing the line, so that the seedlings can be readily identified and a hoe run through the surface between rows to destroy weeds as they appear.

Limnanthes is a sweetly scented annual that is much sought after by bees. It is readily raised from seed scattered out of doors where the plants are to flower and lightly covered with soil

Sweet peas can either be raised in pots for planting out in spring or, for later flowering, can be sown in drills out of doors where they are to flower. This latter method has been used for these plants

Aids to Germination

vernalising seeds

chipping seed using a penknife

chipping seed using a nail file

Many seeds are conditioned by nature not to germinate until they have passed one winter outdoors. Vernalisation is a means of hastening this natural process or making it more effective. Usually, it is done by exposing the seeds to cold while taking precautions to ensure that they are not damaged by other things.

Berries and fruits of various kinds, including rose hips, are conditioned by being put in sand-filled pots, covered with fine-mesh wire netting to keep out mice, and left for the winter in a sheltered but cold place out of doors, such as against a north-facing wall. In spring the seeds are rubbed out of the rotten flesh and sown in the ordinary way.

Other seeds, such as delphiniums, may be artificially vernalised by being stored for several months in a refrigerator at a temperature of 0 to 1°C. (32 to 33°F.).

Some tough-coated seeds, such as peas, beans and sweet corn, germinate more readily if soaked in water for 24 hours before sowing. A few seeds, including black-coated sweet peas, germinate better if a small chip is removed from the seed coat with a nail file or the point of a penknife. Be careful to make this chip at the opposite side of the seed to the 'eye' – a small wrinkle indicating the position of the growing points – so that this is not damaged.

Thinning, Transplanting

Even when seeds are sown thinly it is probable that in places the seedlings will be overcrowded. They should then be either thinned or transplanted.

Thinning means pulling out surplus seedlings. Do this as soon as the seedlings can be conveniently handled, and take care not to dislodge the seedlings that are to be retained. Press two fingers on the soil on each side of the wanted seedling while others close to it are being pulled out. Thin when the soil is moist but not wet. Do not complete thinning in one operation, but leave about twice the required number of seedlings at first, in case some die or are eaten. About a week later, thin to the final spacing.

Thinnings may sometimes be replanted elsewhere, but generally for transplanting it is better to lift all the seedlings carefully with a handfork so that their roots are damaged as little as possible. Do this when the seedlings are a few inches high (earlier for very small plants) and place the seedlings in a tray or basket. Replant them at once with a dibber or trowel, taking care to drop the roots well into the soil and to make them firm. Water in thoroughly if the soil is at all dry. The most favourable period for transplanting is when the weather is showery and the soil moist.

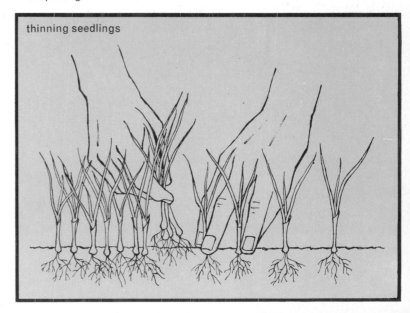

thinning seedlings

The handsome fruits or heps of *Rosa rugosa scabrosa*. The seeds they contain can be sown but will germinate better if not removed from the heps until these have spent a winter out of doors

Calendula Geisha Girl, a very easily grown hardy annual. Seed sown out of doors germinates freely and seedlings must be thinned. If removed carefully the thinnings can be replanted elsewhere

Soft-wood Cuttings

Soft-wood cuttings are made from the young shoots of plants before they have started to harden or ripen. They are used for many herbaceous plants and also for popular greenhouse and display plants, such as perpetual-flowering carnations, chrysanthemums, dahlias, fuchsias, and pelargoniums (including bedding geraniums). Occasionally soft-wood cuttings are used for trees and shrubs, but more usually half-ripe or hard-wood cuttings are used for these.

Select firm, healthy shoots without flowers or flower buds and sever each cleanly below a joint, i.e., the point where a leaf or leaf stalk is attached to the stem. Carefully remove the lower leaves.

Take cuttings of perpetual-flowering carnations by breaking out short sideshoots from mid-way up the plants. Prepare chrysanthemum cuttings from young shoots growing directly from the roots. Take cuttings of pinks by pulling out the top 2 or 3 in. of each shoot at a joint; such pulled cuttings are known as 'pipings'. With all soft-wood cuttings, avoid shoots that are puffy or hollow. Cuttings of delphiniums and lupins are best severed close against the firm crown of the plant.

Half-ripe Cuttings

Half-ripe cuttings differ from soft-wood cuttings in being made from slightly older shoots which have started to become ripe and woody at the base though they are still soft at the tip. Such shoots are usually available in June, July or August, so these cuttings are sometimes referred to as summer cuttings.

Half-ripe cuttings are mainly used as a means of propagating shrubs and shrubby rock plants. Success often depends on taking the cuttings at precisely the right stage of development, and since this can vary from one kind of plant to another, it is impossible to give exact timings. The state of growth is what matters and when in doubt it is wise to take several batches of cuttings at intervals of 7 to 10 days.

The length of the cuttings will also differ greatly according to the growth of the plant from which they are taken. Heather cuttings may be no more than 1 to 1½ in. long, whereas rose or hydrangea cuttings may be 4 to 5 in. long.

Half-ripe cuttings may be taken and prepared exactly as for soft-wood cuttings or, alternatively, they may be taken with a 'heel'. This means that the whole young shoot is pulled away from the older stem with a slip of this attached. This slip or 'heel' must be neatly trimmed with a sharp knife or razor blade before the cutting is inserted.

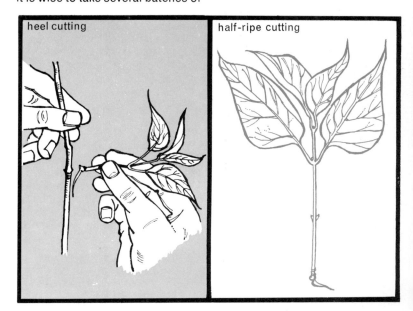

heel cutting / half-ripe cutting

Preparing cuttings of a herbaceous plant. Firm sturdy shoots should be selected, and should be trimmed below a leaf joint with a sharp knife before inserting in compost

Half-ripe wood cuttings of various shrubs rooting in an unheated frame. Note the neat way in which the cuttings have been grouped, and the clear labels which identify them

Success with Rooting

Soft-wood and half-ripe cuttings must be kept in a still, moist atmosphere to prevent flagging while they are forming roots. This can be provided in a small frame with a close-fitting light (i.e. a sheet of glass with a wooden frame) or in a box covered with a piece of glass or polythene film, or within a polythene bag.

Cuttings can be rooted in sand, Vermiculite, peat or special cutting compost. For most purposes a half-and-half mixture of gritty sand and granulated peat will do quite well.

Dip the base of each cutting in hormone rooting powder and then insert it to about one-third its length in the prepared compost, which may be in pots, pans, boxes or a bed, whichever is most convenient. When all the cuttings have been inserted, water them well through a fine rose and cover them with glass or polythene film and shade from strong sunshine. If polythene bags are used, slip one over each pot with an elastic band around to hold it lightly against the sides of the pot.

Water cuttings as frequently as is necessary to keep the compost moist right through. More frequent watering is usually required under glass than under polythene film. When cuttings are well rooted, indicated by renewed growth, carefully separate them and pot singly in 3-in. pots in a soil or peat compost.

Hard-wood Cuttings

Hard-wood cuttings are made from young stems that have completed a season of growth and become hard and ripe. They are used to propagate trees and shrubs, including such fruit bushes as currants and gooseberries. Since they are usually taken in the autumn they are sometimes called autumn cuttings.

As a rule, hard-wood cuttings are considerably longer than softwood or half-ripe cuttings–up to 12 in. for some plants. They may be severed below a joint or taken with a heel like half-ripe cuttings, but their treatment thereafter is quite different. Since they are usually taken at a time of year when growth is virtually at a standstill, they lose moisture very slowly and there is no need to keep them in a still, moist atmosphere. Many can be rooted out of doors, but evergreen shrubs should be protected in a frame. A hormone rooting powder specially for hardwood cuttings may be used.

Insert the cuttings in straightbacked trenches; evergreen cuttings should be covered to onethird of their length, deciduous cuttings to two-thirds their length. Scatter sharp sand in each trench, set the cuttings on this, return the soil and make firm with the foot.

Hard-wood cuttings usually take about 12 months to root.

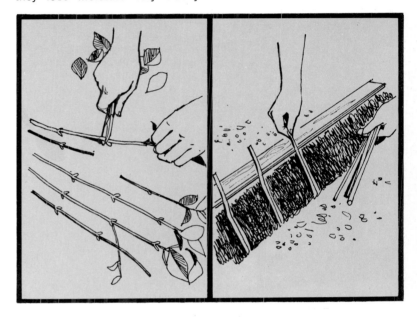

This propagating frame in a small greenhouse is being used for the rooting of dahlia cuttings inserted in pots to keep individual varieties separate. The polythene cover has been removed for watering

Placing hard-wood cuttings in a narrow straight-sided trench. These will remain out of doors over winter so a sheltered position is desirable. They will root within 12 months

Division

Division is the simplest of all methods of propagation, but can only be applied to perennial plants with a more or less spreading habit of growth.

Lift plants carefully with a spade or fork and shake as much of the soil as possible from their roots so as to see where the plant can most readily be split. If it is the type of plant that will divide easily, break it up with the fingers, taking care that each piece has both shoots and roots. If this results in more pieces than are required for re-planting, retain the young outer portions and discard the woody centre portions of the plants.

If the plant is too tough to be broken up with the fingers, thrust two hand forks (or for larger plants, two border forks) back to back through the centre of the clump and lever apart. Repeat if necessary until the pieces are sufficiently small or can be broken by hand.

Some plants with fairly solid crowns, e.g. rhubarb and peonies can be divided if the crown is carefully cut with a knife. It is usually best to wash off all soil before attempting this.

Spring and early autumn are favourable times for dividing plants.

Layering

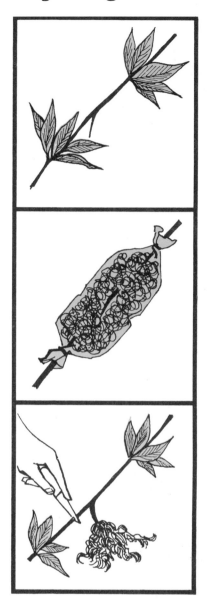

Layering is a method of propagating plants by inducing stems to form roots and then severing them from the parent plant. If the stems can be bent down to soil level they can be layered directly into the soil. Spring and early summer are favourable times for layering, but it can be done at any time.

Choose fairly young, pliable stems and either give each a sharp twist where it can be made to touch the ground most conveniently, or make an incision in it at this point. The incision may pass through a joint or may simply be a ring drawn round the stem with a knife to check the flow of sap. Dust the wound with hormone rooting powder, make a shallow hole in the soil, press the wounded part of the layer into this and secure with a forked stick or a piece of wire bent like a hairpin, and leave until rooted. Sever the layer from the parent plant, but leave for a further week or so and then lift carefully and replant elsewhere. If a shrub has no branches sufficiently pliable or low growing to be bent down to soil level it may still be possible to layer them by bringing the growing medium up to the plant, and air layering it, as illustrated.

Strawberries and violets make runners naturally in summer. These can simply be pegged down to the soil and will form roots.

Shrub layers may take 12 months to form roots, but strawberries, violets and carnations will root in 5 or 6 weeks.

Dividing a well-developed herbaceous plant with the aid of two garden forks which have been thrust into the middle and levered apart. When the clump is a little more manageable, it can be further divided by hand. It is the younger outside portions which make the best plants

Border carnation layering: An incision has been made through a joint in the stem and the wounded portion will be pushed into the soil. With shrubs it may be necessary to wrap damp sphagnum moss enclosed in a sealed polythene sleeve around the wound

What is Grafting?

Grafting is a means of joining two plants together. It is the usual method of propagating apples and pears, is also used for some ornamental trees and shrubs, including garden varieties of rhododendron, and even for a few herbaceous plants such as the double-flowered varieties of *Gypsophila paniculata*.

In all these cases a shoot of the garden variety to be increased is grafted on to the root or stem of an allied species. This shoot is known as the 'scion' and the plant to which it is united as the 'stock' or 'rootstock'. When the two are fully joined together, the stock is prevented from making any top growth and simply provides the roots which anchor the plant and supply it with water and chemicals from the soil. Sap rising from the roots is channelled through the scion from which all further top growth proceeds.

In a grafted plant the nature of the stock determines the character of the roots and to some extent the vigour and growth of the scion, but the scion determines the character of the leaves, flowers and fruits which the plant produces. Grafting, therefore, is not only a means of increasing some plants which are difficult to raise from cuttings or layers, but is also a means of influencing their behaviour to meet particular garden requirements.

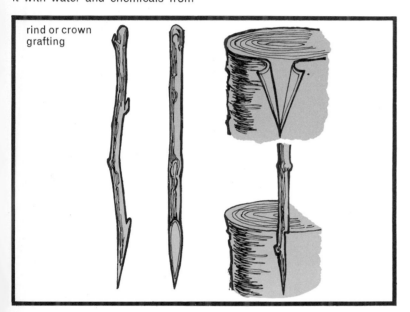

rind or crown grafting

Budding

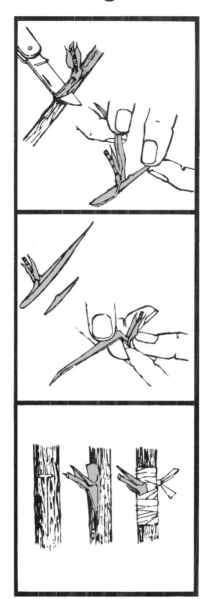

Budding is the name given to the special form of grafting used to propagate most garden roses. It is carried out in summer when roses are in full growth and sap is flowing freely.

To obtain suitable buds, cut strong young shoots from the rose to be propagated. Flowering shoots are suitable immediately the flowers have faded. Cut off the tops and remove all leaves but retain the leaf stalks.

In the angle between each leaf stalk and the stem there will be a little growth bud. Using a sharp knife (a special budding knife is best) cut this out with a shield-shaped portion of bark about 1¼ in. in length. Carefully remove the slip of wood which will be found on the inside of this 'shield'. Cut off the top of the shield ½ in. above the bud. Make a T-shaped incision 1¼ in. long in the bark of the stock, and, using the thin scalpel-handle of the budding knife, raise the flaps of bark so formed.

Slip the shield and its bud beneath these flaps so that the exposed tissues lie snugly against those of the stock. Bind the whole in place with soft raffia or make use of the special ties which can be obtained for this purpose.

Examine about three weeks later, and if the bud has withered, repeat the operation elsewhere on the stock. Remove the top of the stock just above the bud the following March.

Making a whip and tongue graft. The sloping cut on both stock and scion should be as nearly identical in size as possible. The 'tongues' made by the reverse cut serve to hold the two together while they are bound together and waxed

Budding is one of the chief methods of propagating roses and the stone fruits such as almonds and cherries. Specially designed budding knives are available with scalpel-shaped handles to draw back the bark so that the prepared bud can be slipped in easily

Shrubs for Year-round Interest

Shrubs of all kinds make a year-long contribution to the garden scene. Even the deciduous kinds, which lose their leaves in the autumn and do not get any more until the following spring, have interesting branch patterns, sometimes given added attraction by distinctive bark colour. Evergreen shrubs retain their leaves all winter and then stand out in sharp contrast to the deciduous kinds, a factor which needs to be taken into account when siting them. Evergreens with leaves variegated with white, cream or yellow can be particularly valuable in winter.

Some shrubs are grown primarily for the conspicuous beauty of their flowers, some for their berries or other autumn fruits, some for the colour of their foliage, and a few combine two or more of these attractions. There is also great variety in height and habit, from completely prostrate shrubs such as some species of cotoneaster, to almost tree-like specimens, such as the lilacs.

Not all shrubs are equally hardy and this must be considered when selecting and placing them. A few, such as the hardier fuchsias, make a permanent framework of branches in the milder parts of the country, especially near the sea, but elsewhere tend to be killed to ground level each winter, sending up new shoots from the roots the following spring, almost like herbaceous plants.

Some shrubs dislike lime (including limestone) or chalk in the soil and must either be grown in moderately acid soil or be fed with specially prepared iron and manganese fertilisers to make good the deficiencies of these chemicals that commonly occur in alkaline soils. Azaleas and rhododendrons are familiar lime haters and so are many varieties of heather, but not all, since *Erica carnea* together with its numerous varieties, and *E. darleyensis* and *E. terminalis* will all succeed even where there is a fair amount of chalk or limestone.

Shrubs are commonly grouped either with other shrubs or with herbaceous plants and annuals, but some kinds look their best planted as isolated specimens and some can be trained against walls. *Magnolia stellata* is an excellent example of the former type and pyracantha, Japanese quince and ceanothus all do well against walls, where their stiff branches may provide support for genuine climbers, such as the less rampant varieties of clematis.

Most shrubs take several years to attain anything like their full size and this must be taken into account when spacing them. Temporary plants, such as dahlias, annuals and herbaceous perennials, can be used to fill up the ground until such time as the shrubs require it all.

Cultivation

Thoroughly dig all ground intended for shrubs, work in some rotted manure or compost and remove all perennial weeds. Complete preparation several weeks before planting.

Plant deciduous shrubs lifted from the ground in the autumn or winter when the leaves are off the plants. Evergreen shrubs should be planted in early autumn or early spring. Shrubs grown in containers can be planted at any time as long as the roots are not disturbed. Always plant with a spade and make holes sufficiently large to accommodate all the roots spread out naturally. The old soil mark on the stem should lie just below the surface of the soil.

Space small shrubs 2 to 3 ft. apart, medium-sized shrubs 3 to 4 ft. apart and tall shrubs 4 to 6 ft. apart. Many shrubs look attractive when grown as isolated specimens so that they can be viewed from every side.

Feed shrubs each spring with well-rotted manure or compost spread liberally around them, or with a good compound fertiliser such as Growmore at 3 oz. per sq. yd. Never apply lime near lime-hating shrubs.

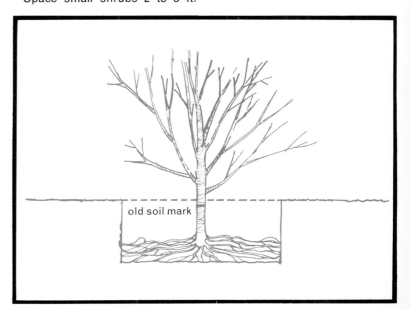

old soil mark

Viburnum opulus nanum, a dwarf variety of the Guelder Rose has white flowers followed by scarlet berries. As an additional attraction the foliage colours brilliantly before it falls in the autumn

Pruning

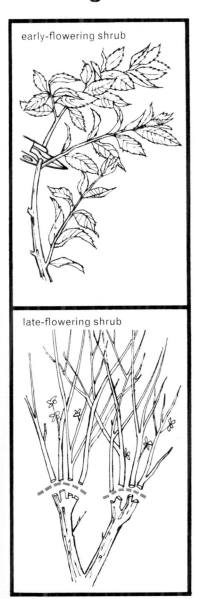

early-flowering shrub

late-flowering shrub

Most shrubs will grow and flower well without any pruning, but pruning is often useful to restrict the size of a shrub and can sometimes be used to improve the quality of the flowers.

Evergreen shrubs are best pruned in spring or early summer, but not while they are flowering. Generally, it is sufficient to cut back branches that are projecting too far and to thin out growth that is overcrowded.

For the purpose of pruning, deciduous shrubs can conveniently be divided into two groups: early-flowering shrubs, or those that flower before mid-summer, and late-flowering shrubs, those that flower after mid-summer.

Prune early-flowering shrubs as soon as they have finished flowering. Cut out most or all of the stems that have just flowered, if possible making each cut immediately above a young, non-flowering stem, a new shoot, or a growth bud from which a new shoot can grow.

Prune late-flowering shrubs in March or April, either by cutting out some of the older branches, or by shortening all branches so that strong, new flowering growth is made.

Bamboos

Most bamboos are perfectly hardy and yet can impart an almost tropical look to a garden. They will grow in any reasonably good soil, can be planted at the waterside or in ordinary well-drained ground and will thrive in sun or shade, though in cold, windy places some of their leaves may become brown in winter. Some kinds spread rapidly by suckers and may have to be chopped back with a spade from time to time. Rooted pieces dug out in the process provide the best means of increase, as if they are replanted they will soon grow into good plants.

Bamboos are excellent for screening. They can be used as a background to other plants, or be planted beside streams and pools.

There are many different varieties and names tend to be rather confused. Some of the best are as follows: *Arundinaria auricoma*, green and gold leaves, 4 ft. high; *A. fastuosa*, deep green, 15 ft.; *A. japonica (Bambusa metake)* light green, 10 ft.; *A. murieliae*, slender, green, 8 ft.; *A. nitida*, small, elegant, green leaves, 8 ft.; *Phyllostachys henonis,* deep green, 10 ft.; *P. ruscifolia,* bright green, 3 ft.

Arundinaria japonica

Arundinaria nitida

Many early-flowering shrubs, such as this forsythia, can be pruned as soon as the floral display has finished. The old flower stems are removed but all young growth is retained

Despite their almost tropical look, most bamboos are completely hardy and very accommodating for they thrive in all but the worst situations. *Arundinaria japonica* is one of many excellent species

Deciduous Azaleas

Deciduous azaleas flower in May and June. They are immensely showy with good-sized flowers in fine clusters and a wonderful colour range, including yellow, orange pink, scarlet, crimson and many intermediate shades. The flowers of some varieties are very fragrant. Bushes grow from 4 to 8 ft. high and as much in diameter. In some varieties, the leaves turn copper and crimson before falling in the autumn. Mollis varieties have larger and earlier flowers than Ghent varieties.

Azaleas are hardy, free flowering and easy to grow in soils that contain no chalk or lime. Where soil is chalky or limy, azaleas can be grown by building up special beds of peat and lime-free loam and by feeding the plants each spring with iron and manganese sequestrols.

They will grow in full sun or partial shade and can be planted in thin woodland. No regular pruning is required, but overgrown bushes can be thinned or reduced immediately after flowering.

Separate colours can be purchased as named varieties, e.g. Anthony Koster, yellow and orange; Dr M. Oosthoek, orange-red; (both mollis azaleas); Fanny, rose, (a Ghent azalea). Good mixtures are also available, usually at a cheaper price, e.g. Knap Hill Hybrids and Exbury Hybrids.

deciduous azalea

Deciduous azaleas are splendid shrubs for lime-free soils, making a spectacular display in May and June. This planting gives some idea of the lovely colours available

Evergreen Azaleas

The evergreen azaleas are low, densely branched spreading shrubs with neat leaves and small to medium-sized flowers, very freely produced in May and June. Their colour range is from white to crimson, but with none of the yellow shades that characterise the taller, more open-branched deciduous azaleas and with greater emphasis on pinks, carmine and scarlet. They are among the most showy of all shrubs when in flower, and being evergreen, give the garden a well-furnished appearance even in winter. Collectively they are often known as Japanese azaleas, one of the most useful sections of which are the Kurume azaleas, so called since they were produced near the town of Kurume in Japan. Because of their origin they are usually included in Japanese-style gardens.

All varieties dislike lime and chalk and prefer peaty or loamy soils in partial shade. They transplant well, even when quite old, need no regular pruning, though they can be thinned immediately after flowering, and are increased by summer cuttings.

Some good varieties are: Addy Wery, vermilion; Benegiri, deep magenta; Christmas Cheer, crimson; Hinomayo, pink; Hinodegiri, carmine; Malvaticum, mauve and Palestrina, white.

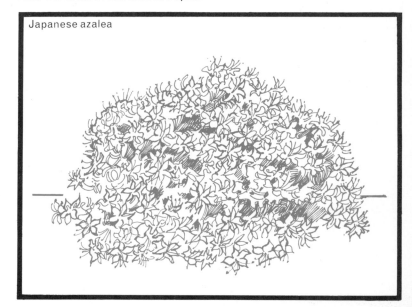

Japanese azalea

This delightful evergreen azalea belongs to the Kurume group and is named Hinomayo. It makes a low, spreading bush with small leaves, and it flowers freely in May or early June

Barberries

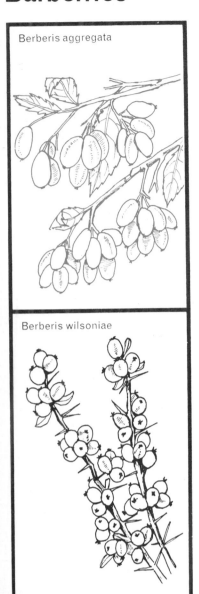

Berberis aggregata

Berberis wilsoniae

Barberry is the popular name for berberis. There are numerous different kinds some of which are evergreen, some deciduous. All have yellow flowers followed by red or purple berries. In general, the deciduous barberries are grown principally for their flowers which make a fine display in spring.

All are hardy and easily grown in almost any soil. They will grow in shade, but flower and berry better in sun. No regular pruning is required, but overgrown bushes can be thinned; the evergreen kinds after flowering, the deciduous kinds in March.

The two most popular evergreen kinds are *Berberis darwinii* with small, holly-like leaves and clusters of orange flowers followed by little purple berries, and *B. stenophylla* with narrow leaves and yellow, sweetly scented flowers. Both make large bushes 8 to 10 ft. high and as much through.

The most popular deciduous barberries are *Berberis wilsoniae*, 3 ft. high with coral-red berries and *B. thunbergii atropurpurea*, 6 ft. high with reddish-purple leaves. *B. aggregata* resembles *B. wilsoniae* but is twice the size.

Buddleias

Buddleia alternifolia

Buddleia globosa

The buddleias are large, branching shrubs which will grow practically anywhere, even on poor chalky or limy soils and in dry, rocky places.

The purple buddleia (*Buddleia davidii*) is the most popular. It produces its long, conical spikes of honey-scented flowers in late summer, and there are several varieties ranging in colour from white through to lavender and intense purple. It will grow 12 ft. in height and width, but can be kept to half these dimensions by pruning each March. Do this either by cutting all stems to about 1 ft. from ground level or allow the plant to retain a framework of stout branches and shorten all other branches to within a few inches of these. Seed is freely produced but self-sown seedlings may vary in colour from their parents.

Buddleia alternifolia makes a big, rounded bush with slender, arching branches wreathed in purple flowers in June. It can be thinned and shaped immediately after flowering, but should not be hard pruned. It can be trained on a main stem or trunk like a small tree.

Buddleia globosa is known as the Orange Ball Tree because its orange flowers are clustered in little balls, in May and June. It grows 10 to 12 ft. high and can be thinned or shortened after flowering.

Berberis darwinii, a splendid evergreen shrub, as valuable for hedge making as for a border or specimen planting. The leaves are small and shaped like those of holly

Royal Red is one of the deepest purple varieties of *Buddleia davidii*. This shrub flowers in late summer and its long, scented flowers attract butterflies. It is for this reason that it is often known by the common name of the Butterfly Bush

Brooms

Spartium junceum

Genista hispanica

Brooms have thin, whippy stems and small, pea-type flowers. They are sun lovers which will grow in any well-drained soil, even those that are rather poor and sandy. Brooms transplant badly so plant from pots or other containers, disturbing the roots as little as possible. Only prune when it is essential to keep the plants in check. Do this by shortening flowering stems as soon as the flowers fade, but never cut into mature wood.

Recommended types are: Common Broom (*Cytisus scoparius*) 6 to 8 ft. with yellow flowers in May and early June, and improved garden varieties such as Cornish Cream, cream; Donard Seedling, rose; Dorothy Walpole, crimson and Lord Lambourne, yellow and red. Also, Early Broom (*Cytisus praecox*) 4 ft., cream, April to May; Portugal Broom (*Cytisus albus*) 6 to 8 ft., white, June; Spanish Broom (*Spartium junceum*) 6 to 8 ft., yellow fragrant flowers, July to August; Spanish Gorse (*Genista hispanica*) 2 ft., yellow, May to June; Mount Etna Broom (*Genista aethnensis*) 12 to 15 ft., yellow, July and Madeira Broom (*Genista virgata*) 6 to 8 ft., yellow, June to July.

There are also dwarf brooms suitable for rock gardens, walls and the front of borders such as *Cytisus beanii, C. kewensis, Genista lydia* and *G. tinctoria plena.*

Camellias

Contrary to popular belief many camellias are quite hardy, but they flower in late winter and spring and in exposed places the flowers may be damaged.

All camellias are evergreen and the shining, dark green foliage is very handsome. All make quite big bushes in time but are rather slow growing and can be thinned immediately after flowering.

Camellias dislike lime and chalk but succeed in most other soils, preferring those of good loamy or peaty nature. They will grow in sun or shade, but do not like very hot, dry places. They can be trained against walls.

There are many different varieties which may be divided into four principal groups: Japonica, Williamsii, Reticulata and Sasanqua.

Camellia japonica varieties are hardy and have showy flowers. Representative are: Adolph Audusson, semi-double, scarlet; *donckelarii,* semi-double, crimson and white; *elegans,* double, rose; Lady Clare, semi-double, pink; *magnoliaeflora,* semi-double, pink; White Swan, single, white.

The *C. williamsii* varieties are a little looser and more open in growth, and are fine garden shrubs. Representative are: J. C. Williams, single, shell pink and Donation, double, pink.

The *C. reticulata* varieties are tall and have very large flowers. *C. sasanqua* varieties have smaller flowers in winter and early spring. Both are more tender.

Camellia reticulata

Cytisus scoparius andreanus, Lord Lambourne, a broom which has for long been a favourite with those gardening on well-drained soils. All brooms are sun lovers and most tend to be rather short lived but some can be easily renewed from seed

The glossy dark green leaves of *Camellia japonica* make it a handsome evergreen shrub and they are a perfect foil for the shapely flowers. Camellias prefer sheltered places and lime-free soils

Caryopteris, Ceratostigma

The chief similarities between caryopteris and ceratostigma are that they are both deciduous, flower in late summer and autumn, and have blue flowers and rather soft stems which are liable to be damaged by frost in winter. Caryopteris is sometimes given the common name of blue spiraea.

Caryopteris clandonensis, the most popular variety, has twiggy branches, small grey-green leaves and little clusters of fluffy looking lavender-blue flowers in August and September. Kew Blue is a variety with deeper blue flowers. If pruned each April almost to soil level, caryopteris will remain reasonably compact, reach a height of about 3 ft. and produce finer flower clusters.

Ceratostigma willmottianum has green leaves, thin, 2-ft. stems and bright blue, phlox-like flowers from July to October. It will also benefit from being cut back each April.

Both caryopteris and ceratostigma like good, well-drained soil and a sunny, fairly sheltered place. Ceratostigma makes an excellent edging plant or it may be used to fill a narrow border at the foot of a sunny wall.

Both shrubs can be increased by summer cuttings.

Cistus

Cistus are called rock roses because they will grow in hot, dry, rocky places and their flowers look like single roses. They are all evergreen and many are quite small shrubs, but most are a little tender and may be damaged or even killed in very exposed places or during unusually severe winters. They are very suitable for sunny banks, terraces and rock gardens.

They will grow in most well-drained soils, including chalky and limy soils. No regular pruning is required but overgrown branches can be shortened moderately in spring. All can be increased readily from seed and also by summer cuttings.

The hardiest kinds are: *Cistus crispus,* also known as Sunset, 2 ft. high, magenta rose; *C. corbariensis,* 3 ft., white; *C. cyprius,* 5 ft., white and maroon; *C. laurifolius,* 5 ft., white and *C.* Silver Pink, 2 to 3 ft., pale pink.

Other fine kinds, needing a little more shelter in winter, are: *Cistus ladaniferus,* known as the Gum Cistus, because its leaves are slightly sticky, 5 ft., white; *C. lusitanicus,* 5 ft., white and maroon; and *C. purpureus,* 4 ft., deep rose and maroon.

Caryopteris clandonensis

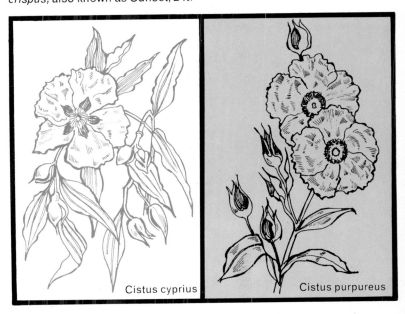
Cistus cyprius

Cistus purpureus

Amongst the shrubs still in flower during October is *Ceratostigma willmottianum.* It should be planted in a sheltered, sunny border and in a well-drained soil. It often dies down to ground level in winter

Cistus purpureus is a charming evergreen shrub of moderate size. It will succeed well in hot, dry rocky places and may be damaged by frost in an exposed place or during a severe winter

Ceanothus

These fine shrubs are mainly of Californian origin. They like good, well-cultivated, well-drained soils and sunny, rather sheltered places. There are two main groups: the evergreen varieties mostly flowering in May and June, and the deciduous ones flowering in summer and early autumn.

The evergreen varieties make densely branched bushes about 6 ft. high with small, neat leaves and little tight clusters of blue flowers. They can be trained against sunny walls where they may reach a height of 10 to 15 ft. In such places forward-growing shoots should be shortened to a few inches annually after flowering.

The deciduous varieties make loosely branched bushes, about 8 ft. high, with sprays of blue or pink flowers. They can be cut hard back each March, which will reduce their height and improve the flower quality.

Good evergreen types are: *burkwoodii,* bright blue, July to October; Delight, rich blue, May; *impressus,* deep blue, May; *lobbianus,* bright blue, June; *thyrsiflorus,* bright blue, June; *veitchianus,* light blue, May.

Good deciduous types are: Gloire de Versailles, soft blue; Perle Rose, rose pink and Topaz, indigo blue.

Ceanothus burkwoodii

Cotoneasters

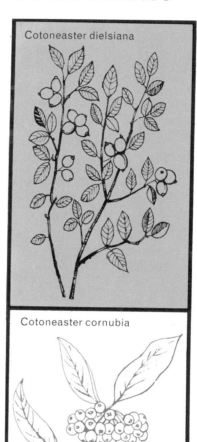

Cotoneaster dielsiana

Cotoneaster cornubia

Cotoneasters are grown primarily for their fine crops of berries in autumn, but many have good evergreen foliage and a decorative habit. They thrive in most soils and in sun or partial shade. They need no regular pruning, but when overgrown can be thinned in spring. All can be readily increased by seed and self-sown seedlings often appear in the garden.

Recommended kinds, all with red berries, are: *Cotoneaster conspicua,* 4 ft., evergreen, dome-shaped bush; *C. cornubia,* 12 ft. or more, deciduous, berries in large clusters; *C. dielsiana,* 8 ft., semi-evergreen; *C. frigida,* deciduous, 15 ft. or more, (can be grown on a main stem or trunk like a small tree); *C. horizontalis,* 3 ft., deciduous, fan-like habit; *C. microphylla,* 3 ft., evergreen, stiffly branched; *C. simonsii,* 6 to 8 ft., deciduous, erect and *C. watereri,* 12 ft. or more, evergreen.

There are also prostrate kinds such as *C. adpressa* and *C. dammeri* which may be used as edging plants or to carpet the ground. *Cotoneaster horizontalis* and *C. microphylla* may be planted against walls, over which they will spread themselves like a fan without any further support.

Trained specimens of ceanothus should be pruned immediately after they have flowered. This is *Ceanothus thyrsiflorus,* one of the hardiest of the evergreen species and a fairly tall shrub

The evergreen *Cotoneaster conspicua decora* makes a compact dome-shaped bush with white flowers followed by deep red berries which usually persist all the winter when this is one of the most cheerful shrubs in the garden

Currants, Elders

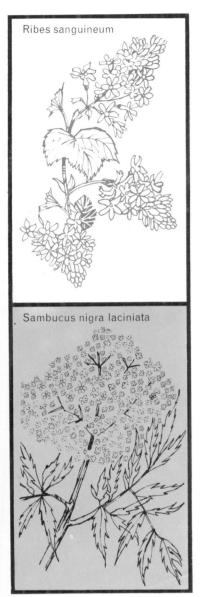
Ribes sanguineum

Sambucus nigra laciniata

It is the American or Flowering Currant, *Ribes sanguineum*, that is grown as an ornamental shrub. It is vigorous, easily grown and makes a fine show with its little clusters of rose-pink or magenta-red flowers in March and April, at about the same time as the yellow forsythia. It will grow in almost any soil, in sun or shade, and can be pruned annually each spring as soon as the flowers fade, by cutting the old flowering stems right out. Pulborough Scarlet is the most brightly coloured variety and China Rose the palest. *R. s. splendens* has extra large clusters of flowers, rosy-crimson in colour.

The ordinary elder, *Sambucus nigra*, is a handsome British shrub, too large and common for most gardens, but it has a golden-leaved variety named *aurea,* which is well worth a place. There is also a variety named *laciniata* with finely-cut green leaves. If pruned back to within about a foot of ground level each March or April, these varieties make bushes of about 5 ft. in height, with even finer leaves than normal. Like the Flowering Currant, they will grow practically anywhere.

Both Flowering Currants and elders can readily be increased by summer or autumn cuttings.

Daphnes

Daphnes are grown for their rich perfume as well as for the beauty of their flowers. Some are evergreen, some deciduous and most are quite small shrubs. All like reasonably good, well-cultivated soils and though a few will grow well in shade, the popular garden kinds enjoy open, sunny places. Most dislike root disturbance and should be purchased, if possible, in containers from which they can be planted with their roots intact. They are better left unpruned. All can be increased by summer cuttings or layers and some by seed.

Daphne mezereum is deciduous, erect, 3 ft. high and flowers on the bare stems in February and March. The flowers, purple or white and very fragrant, are followed by red berries which may produce seedlings. This daphne sometimes dies suddenly and for no obvious reason.

Daphne Somerset, also known as *D. burkwoodii*, is deciduous, 3 ft., freely branched with abundant pink, fragrant flowers in May.

Daphne odora is evergreen, 3 ft.; with clusters of intensely fragrant, purple flowers in February and March. A variety named *aureomarginata* has leaves bordered with yellow and is hardier.

Daphne cneorum is evergreen, 1 ft., with fragrant, rose-pink flowers in May. *D. blagayana* is quite prostrate with creamy-white fragrant flowers in May. Both are suitable for rock gardens.

Daphne mezereum   Daphne burkwoodii

Ribes sanguineum splendens is one of the best of the flowering currants. They overlap in flowering time with the golden forsythias with which they contrast vividly

Daphne cneorum is a choice shrub for the rock garden or the front of a border. During May it is completely covered with fragrant flowers. It requires a lime-free soil

Deutzias

Deutzia scabra

D.s. Pride of Rochester

Deutzias are deciduous shrubs, flowering in spring and early summer. The white, pink or purple flowers are small but numerous. Heights vary from 4 to 10 ft. All kinds are easily grown in most soils that are reasonably well drained. All prefer sunny positions though they will grow in shade. They may be pruned immediately after flowering, when flowering stems can be cut right out, and this practice is recommended as the older stems are inclined to die back in winter.

Deutzia scabra is 8 to 10 ft. high, but rather less through, with a shuttlecock habit of growth and white flowers in June. Pride of Rochester is a good variety with double flowers flushed with purple. There are also several garden varieties similar to *D. scabra* in habit, but shorter and with finer flowers. Recommended are: Mont Rose, rose-pink; Perle Rose, soft rose and Magician, purplish-pink. All can readily be increased by summer or autumn cuttings.

Deutzia elegantissima is 4 to 5 ft. high, with slender, arching stems wreathed in rose-pink flowers in May. Another hybrid of similar habit is *D. rosea*. It has several varieties of which *carminea* is one of the prettiest.

Dogwoods

There are many kinds of dogwood or cornus, and they differ greatly in appearance and requirements. Most are deciduous.

The Westonbirt Dogwood, *Cornus alba sibirica,* and the Yellow-barked Dogwood, *C. stolonifera flaviramea,* are grown for the respectively red and yellow bark of the young stems, particularly attractive in winter and on plants that have been cut hard back the previous April. They will thrive in almost any soil and in sun or shade and have a particular liking for moist soils and the sides of streams. Exactly the same treatment suits *C. alba spaethii,* with golden variegated leaves, and *C. alba sibirica variegata,* with grey-green, silver-edged leaves.

Cornus kousa makes a large shrub or small tree 15 ft. or more, freely branched and spreading, with large white flowers along the stems in June. *C. florida* is similar but rather tender, and *C. florida rubra* has beautiful rose-pink flowers. All need good, well-cultivated, well-drained soils and a sunny, sheltered position.

Cornus mas is also a tall shrub or small tree, with small, but very numerous, yellow flowers on the bare stems in February and March.

Cornus can be increased by summer cuttings or layers and all varieties of *Cornus alba, C. stolonifera* and *C. mas* by rooted suckers dug up in the autumn.

Cornus kousa

Cornus mas

The graceful *Deutzia rosea carminea,* a deciduous shrub some 4 ft. tall and twice as much through with prettily arching branches. It flowers in late May and early June and does best in a sunny position

The attractions of ornamental bark in winter should not be overlooked. The red-barked *Cornus stolonifera* and yellow-barked *C.s. flaviramea* shown in combination above are delightful if hard pruned each spring

Elaeagnus, Garrya

Elaeagnus pungens aureo-variegata is one of the best evergreen shrubs with golden variegated leaves. It makes a big, well-branched bush 10 ft. or more high but can easily be kept much smaller by annual thinning and cutting back in spring. It will grow in practically any soil and in sun or shade though the leaves will be larger and of brighter colour in fairly rich, well-cultivated soil and a sunny place. The flowers are insignificant.

Garrya elliptica is an evergreen shrub of very unusual appearance since in winter it produces long, slender, grey-green catkins, both male and female, borne on different bushes. The male catkins are longer and more decorative, but if a male bush is growing nearby, the female catkins are followed by trails of black fruits. Both types make shapely, well-branched bushes 6 to 8 ft. high or may be trained against walls where they can easily attain a height of 12 ft. They thrive in good, well-cultivated soils and sunny positions, and can be pruned to shape in spring when the catkins have fallen.

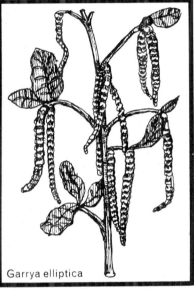

Elaeagnus pungens   Garrya elliptica

Elaeagnus pungens aureo-variegata is grown primarily for its foliage, for the flowers though fragrant are insignificant. On a sunny winter's day there are few brighter plants in the garden

Escallonias

The best varieties of escallonia are evergreen shrubs, freely branched, with numerous small pink or red flowers in summer. Some kinds make excellent hedges or screens and all can be planted in shrub borders or as isolated specimens. They will grow in any reasonably good, well-drained soil and sunny place. They are excellent seaside shrubs and will grow well in inland gardens, though a few are a little tender and not suitable for cold districts. All can be pruned in spring or immediately after flowering as much as is necessary to keep them in bounds, and they can all be increased readily by summer cuttings.

One of the loveliest and hardiest is *Escallonia langleyensis,* 6 to 8 ft., with arching stems wreathed in soft carmine flowers in July. Apple Blossom is similar in habit with pink and white flowers, Donard Seedling has pale pink flowers, and both Donard Brilliance and C. F. Ball are crimson.

Escallonia macrantha has large leaves and deep red flowers and is very popular in seaside areas as a hedge, but is rather tender elsewhere.

Escallonia langleyensis

Escallonias are splendid seaside shrubs and they will also grow well inland, thriving in good, well-drained soils and sunny positions. There are many lovely forms; this one is Apple Blossom

Euonymus

There are both evergreen and deciduous kinds of euonymus which look very different and serve quite different purposes.

The two best evergreen kinds are the Japanese Euonymus (*Euonymus japonicus*) and the Creeping Euonymus (*E. fortunei*). The Japanese Euonymus will grow to 20 ft., but can be pruned hard in spring or summer and is suitable for hedges. It has shining leaves which may be green or variegated with silver or gold. It will withstand sea gales.

The Creeping Euonymus has several varieties, some completely prostrate and useful as ground cover, some with silver or gold variegated leaves which form neat bushes.

The deciduous kinds, known as Spindle Trees, are grown for their clusters of little carmine and orange fruits in autumn. The two best are *Euonymus europaeus* and *E. latifolius*, both 6 to 8 ft. high.

All kinds will grow in almost any soil and in sun or shade. The spindle trees fruit best if more than one bush is planted for cross-fertilisation. All suffer from attacks of blackfly which may be controlled by occasional spraying with menazon or dimethoate in late spring and early summer. Evergreen kinds are readily increased by summer or autumn cuttings, deciduous kinds by seed.

Euonymus japonicus

Forsythias

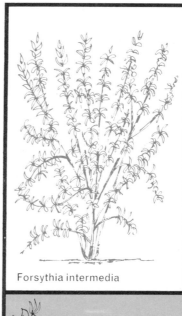

Forsythia intermedia

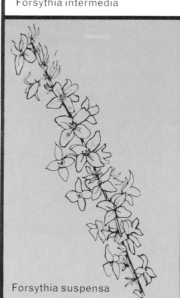

Forsythia suspensa

Forsythia is one of the first shrubs to make a big display in spring. Its yellow flowers open in March and in country gardens the flower buds are sometimes stripped by birds, but this seldom happens in towns. *Forsythia intermedia* Lynwood, with particularly large, deep yellow flowers, is one of the best varieties. It grows 8 ft. high and as much through but can be kept smaller by cutting out all old flowering stems directly the flowers fade. Arnold Giant, a recent introduction from America, is another variety with large, deep yellow flowers.

Forsythia suspensa has paler yellow flowers and longer, more slender stems. It can be trained against walls or fences, even those facing north. All forsythias are deciduous.

Forsythia will grow in almost any soil, though for best results it should be planted in moderately rich, well-cultivated soil and be fed with manure or fertiliser each spring. It will succeed in full sun or in shade. The best flowers are produced on strong, one-year-old stems and pruning, as described above, improves the quality of the flowers. Underplanting with blue-flowered chionodoxa makes a wonderful colour contrast.

Forsythias are readily increased by summer or autumn cuttings.

The highly decorative fruits of the Spindle Tree (*Euonymus europaeus*). It will grow well in almost any soil, in sun or shade, but should be planted in small groups as isolated bushes sometimes fail to fruit for lack of effective pollination

The popularity of the forsythias is a tribute to their qualities as garden shrubs as well as to their ease of cultivation. This variety, Arnold Giant, has especially large flowers of fine quality

Fuchsias

Many fuchsias are rather too tender to be grown out of doors except in very mild districts but some are excellent garden plants, flowering all summer and well into the autumn. They like good, well-cultivated soil and will grow in shady places, but flower more freely where it is sunny.

They should be planted rather deeply as the stems are often killed in winter, but new growth comes up from the roots which are protected by the soil. Stems damaged by frost should be cut out each March, even to ground level if necessary. Pruned in this way most varieties will grow to between 2 and 3 ft.

Fuchsias are easily raised from summer cuttings and it is as well to keep a few rooted cuttings if possible in a frame or greenhouse during the winter in case of losses out of doors.

Among the most reliable varieties are: Alice Hoffman, pink and white; Brilliant, red and purple; Brutus, red and violet; Chillerton Beauty, pink and violet; Lena, flesh pink and violet, double; *magellanica gracilis,* small red and purple flowers; Margaret, scarlet and violet; Mrs W. P. Wood, small pale pink flowers; Tom Thumb, small cerise flowers on a 1-ft. plant; *riccartonii,* small scarlet flowers; Snowcap, red and white; Swingtime, double flowered, red and white and Uncle Charley, pink and lavender.

Hebes

Hebe is the new name for evergreen shrubs formerly known as veronica, and it serves to distinguish them from herbaceous veronicas.

Hebes flower in summer and some varieties go on flowering spasmodically well on into the autumn and even the winter. They make well-branched, rounded bushes with good foliage and small flowers crowded in spikes which may be short or long according to the variety.

All will grow in almost any reasonably well-drained soil. They like warm, sunny places, and some kinds are rather tender and liable to be damaged or even killed in cold districts or severe winters, but all succeed well by the sea.

Regular pruning is unnecessary, but overgrown bushes can be thinned or cut back in spring. All hebes grow readily from summer cuttings.

One of the hardiest kinds is *Hebe brachysiphon* (also known as *H. traversii*), 5 ft., with white flowers in July. Other recommended varieties are: Autumn Glory, violet purple, 18 in., June to August; Great Orme, 3 ft., July to September, pink; Marjorie, light violet, 3 ft., July to September and Midsummer Beauty, lavender, 5 ft., July to November. Alicia Amhurst, deep purple and Simon Delaux, crimson are 3 ft., and flower from July to November. They are more tender, but excellent for seaside gardens.

Fuchsia magellanica gracilis

Fuchsia Mrs W. P. Wood

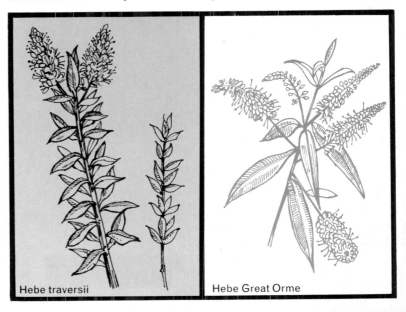

Hebe traversii

Hebe Great Orme

Tom Thumb, a dwarf and hardy fuchsia which will produce its small flowers freely throughout the summer and even later if there are no early autumn frosts

Many forms of hebe, including Midsummer Beauty, provide a striking display of flowers throughout the summer and autumn months. All are evergreen but few are fully hardy

Heathers

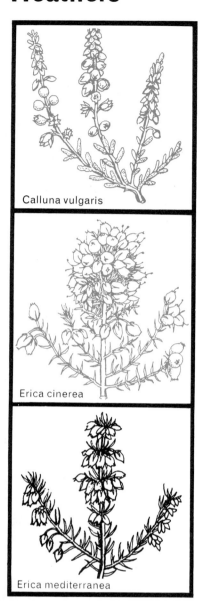

Calluna vulgaris

Erica cinerea

Erica mediterranea

There are a great many kinds of heather, of which the following are representative:

Calluna vulgaris, the Scotch Heather or Ling, flowers from August to October. Good varieties are: Gold Haze, with golden foliage, 18 in.; J. H. Hamilton, double, deep pink, 12 in.; Peter Sparkes, double, pink, 2 ft.; *flore albo pleno,* double white, 18 in.

Erica arborea alpina, the Tree Heath, 6 ft. or more, has white flowers in March and April.

Erica carnea flowers from January to March. Good varieties are: Springwood White, white, 18 in.; Springwood Pink, heather pink, 18 in. and *vivellii,* carmine, 6 in.

Erica ciliaris, the Dorset Heath, rosy red, 1 ft., June to October. There is also a white variety.

Erica cinerea, Bell Heather, June to August. Good varieties are: C. D. Eason, deep pink, 18 in.; *coccinea,* red, 1 ft.

Erica darleyensis, heather purple, 2 ft., November to April.

Erica mediterranea, rosy red, 4 ft., March to May. W. T. Rackliff is white flowered.

Erica terminalis, the Corsican Heath, rosy pink, 4 ft., June to September.

Erica vagans, the Cornish Heath, July to October. Good varieties are: Lyonesse, white, 1 ft., Mrs D. F. Maxwell, cerise, 1 ft.

Daboecia cantabrica, the Irish Heath, 2 ft., has purple and white varieties and flowers from June to October.

Choisya, Hibiscus

The Mexican Orange Blossom, *Choisya ternata,* is an evergreen shrub 4 to 6 ft. high, with shining, light green leaves and clusters of white, scented flowers rather like those of the orange. It flowers most freely in May, but more flowers are usually produced on and off right through the summer and even into autumn. It enjoys good, well-cultivated soil and a sunny, rather sheltered position and is easily increased by summer cuttings.

The Syrian Mallow, *Hibiscus syriacus,* is an erect-growing, deciduous shrub, 6 to 8 ft. high, flowering in August and September. The double or single flowers of various colours resemble those of the hollyhock on a much smaller scale. There are numerous varieties, such as: Bluebird, single, deep blue; Duc de Brabant, double, red; Hamabo, single, blush and crimson; Souvenir de Charles Breton, double, lilac and Woodbridge, single, rose-madder.

All like good, well-cultivated, well-drained soils and sunny places. They transplant rather badly so container-grown plants are to be preferred to those lifted from the open ground. Overgrown plants can be thinned or shortened in April. Propagation is by summer cuttings or layers.

Choisya ternata

Hibiscus syriacus Woodbridge

A group of Scotch Heathers, *Calluna vulgaris,* with the very showy double-flowered variety H.E. Beale in the foreground. This is one of the heathers which must have lime-free soil

Hibiscus syriacus Woodbridge has flowers like small single hollyhocks during August and September. It makes a stiffly branched shrub and likes a good, well-drained soil and a sunny position

Hydrangeas

Hydrangeas give the same kind of massive flower display from midsummer until autumn that rhododendrons give in May and June, though they are not so colourful. All will grow in any reasonably good soil and do not mind chalk or lime, but where this is present, flowers of coloured varieties tend to be pink or red, rather than blue or purple. White varieties are unaffected by the soil. Hydrangeas will succeed in sun or shade.

Hydrangea paniculata is the hardiest kind. Its flowers are creamy-white in conical heads and it will grow 6 ft. tall. By shortening the stems to at least half their length each March the height will be reduced, the size of the flowers increased.

The common garden hydrangeas are varieties of *Hydrangea macrophylla*. They grow 4 to 6 ft. high and more through and should not be pruned hard as this checks flowering. Faded flower heads should be removed in March and overcrowded bushes can be thinned then.

Recommended varieties are: Altona, rose or deep blue; Hamburg, pink, deepening to crimson or purple; Mme E. Mouillière, white; *mariesii*, rosy-pink or blue; Parsival, rosy-red or violet-purple; Vicomtesse de Vibraye, soft pink or light blue; Westfalen, crimson or violet.

Hypericums

All hypericums have yellow flowers freely produced in summer but some are evergreen, and some are deciduous and they can vary greatly in height from creeping plants such as *Hypericum calycinum*, the Rose of Sharon, to erect, freely branched shrubs 5 or 6 ft. high, such as *Hypericum* Hidcote. All are easily grown in any reasonably good soil, and in sun or shade. The Rose of Sharon, which is evergreen, has a particular liking for chalky or limy soils and can be used both to cover hot, sunny banks and as a carpet beneath other shrubs and trees.

Hypericum Hidcote retains many of its leaves in winter. *H. patulum*, which is 3 to 4 ft. high and has slightly smaller, more cup-shaped flowers, is deciduous. *H. moserianum* is only 18 in. high, but is spreading and useful for the front of a border.

Hypericums do not require any pruning, but can be thinned or reduced in size if desired in March or April. The Rose of Sharon can be clipped with shears at the same period to keep it neat and within bounds.

All can be increased by summer cuttings, and the Rose of Sharon can also be very easily increased by separating off rooted pieces at any time between October and March.

Hydrangea paniculata

The handsome *Hydrangea macrophylla mariesii*. Varieties of this type are often called lacecaps because the large outer flowers and beadlike inner ones suggest an old-fashioned lace cap

The Rose of Sharon, *Hypericum calycinum*, is a splendid ground-cover plant for sun or shade, even under trees and other shrubs. An evergreen, it does not grow more than 18 in. tall

Kalmia, Pieris

Both kalmia and pieris are evergreen shrubs which dislike chalk or lime and grow best in loamy or peaty soils in partial shade.

Kalmia latifolia, sometimes known as the Calico Bush, makes a well-branched, rounded bush eventually 6 ft. or more high, but it is very slow growing. It has bright pink flowers, shaped like little Chinese lanterns, which appear in June. It needs no regular pruning, enjoys a topdressing of peat each spring, and does not like being dried out in summer.

There are several different kinds of pieris, all known as the lily of the valley bush, because the little sprays of white, urn-shaped flowers in spring look rather like those of lily of the valley. *Pieris japonica*, 6 to 8 ft. high, is one of the easiest to grow and best in flower, but *P. forrestii* Wakehurst Variety has magnificent rose and scarlet young growth.

Both kalmia and pieris are better unpruned but if overgrown they can be cut back in spring, though this means sacrificing the flowers for one year. They can both be increased by layering in spring.

Lavender, Rosemary

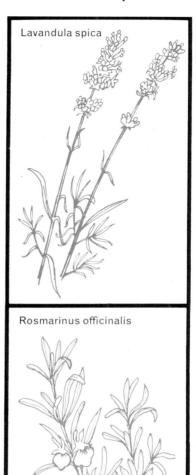

Lavandula spica

Rosmarinus officinalis

Both lavender and rosemary are very popular for their fragrance, as well as for their distinctive evergreen foliage and blue flowers.

Lavender delights in warm, sunny places and chalky or limy soils, though it can be grown in almost any reasonably well-drained soil. The flowers appear in July and can be picked and dried for filling sachets and making pot-pourri if desired. In any case, bushes should be clipped over in August or September to keep them neat. *Lavandula spica*, 3 ft. high with lavender-blue flowers, is the Old English Lavender. Good varieties include Hidcote, 1 ft. high, deep purple and Twickle Purple, 3 ft. high, purple. All have grey leaves.

Rosemary (*Rosmarinus officinalis*) has narrow, shining, dark leaves and makes a bush about 4 ft. tall. The lavender-blue flowers start to open in winter and are at their best in May. *R.o.* Tuscan Blue has deeper blue flowers; *R.o. humilis*, also known as *R.o. prostratus*, is sprawling and will hang down over a wall, but needs a sunny, sheltered place as it is rather easily damaged by frost.

Bushes may be trimmed to shape after flowering. Both lavender and rosemary are readily increased by summer cuttings.

Kalmia latifolia

Pieris forrestii

The individual flowers of *Kalmia latifolia*, the Calico Bush, resemble small Chinese lanterns. This is one of the most beautiful of the early summer-flowering evergreens but it requires lime-free soil

Especially strong colouring is a characteristic of Hidcote, a dwarf lavender which seldom exceeds 1 ft. in height. It makes a splendid edging and can be trimmed after flowering

Leycesteria, Rubus

Leycesteria formosa is popularly known as Himalayan Honeysuckle, though it does not come from the Himalayas or even look like a honeysuckle. It makes a thicket of long, rather soft green stems, hanging out short trails of claret-purple and white flowers in summer, succeeded by dark purple berries. It will grow almost anywhere, in sun or shade, and in rich soil may reach a height of 7 or 8 ft. The older stems should be cut right out each March, leaving only the best young stems for flowering.

Rubus is the general name for the brambles, including the blackberry and loganberry. For decorative purposes there are several fine kinds, such as *Rubus* Tridel, a loose bush with long, canelike stems bearing large white flowers in May and June; *R. odoratus,* making a 7-ft. thicket of tangled stems bearing light magenta flowers from June to August and *R. ulmifolius bellidiflorus,* like a blackberry with fully double pink flowers resembling little pompons in July and August. The Whitewash Bramble, *R. cockburnianus,* is so called because its long stems are white.

All will grow in any reasonably good soil and open or partially shaded position. Flowering stems should be cut out as soon as the last flowers fade.

Lilacs

Everyone loves the Common Lilac, (*Syringa vulgaris*) which blooms in May and fills the air with its pleasant fragrance. It is a deciduous shrub or small tree, eventually growing 12 to 15 ft. high, though it can be kept smaller by thinning out older branches in autumn or winter. It will grow practically anywhere, but enjoys good, well-cultivated soil, which encourages the production of fine flower trusses. So does the regular removal of the faded flowers, though this may be difficult on large bushes.

Syringa persica, the Persian Lilac, is another species with particularly fragrant flowers. It forms a smaller bush than the Common Lilac, reaching 6 ft., and bears small sprays of lavender flowers in May.

There are a number of improved garden varieties with larger flowers, double in some, and in a range of colours from white to deep purple. Recommended varieties are: Charles Joly, double purple; Charles X, single purple; Katherine Havemayer, double mauve; Maud Notcutt, single white; Michael Buchner, double rosy-lilac; Madame Lemoine, double white and Primrose, single primrose yellow.

These garden varieties are often grafted on Common Lilac and then all suckers (shoots growing direct from the roots) should be removed.

Lilacs can also be increased by layering, in which case suckers will be of the same variety as the bush and can be retained or dug up with roots and planted elsewhere.

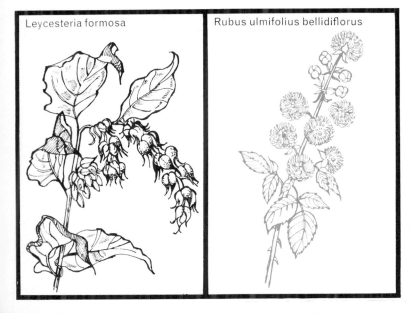

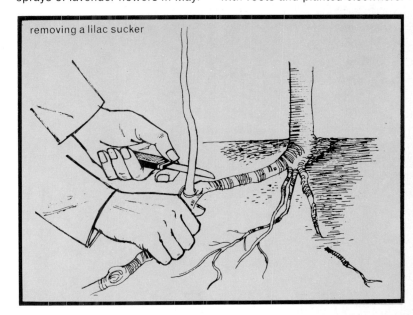

removing a lilac sucker

Leycesteria formosa can be killed to ground level during a hard winter but in the spring it will shoot up again from the base like a herbaceous plant. The flowers are followed by dark purple berries

There are a great many varieties of the fragrant common lilac, *Syringa vulgaris*, some single, some double flowered. This one is Clarke's Giant which has extra large single flowers

Mahonia, Magnolia

Mahonias are evergreen shrubs with shining prickly leaves and clusters or sprays of yellow flowers in late winter and spring. They will grow almost anywhere in sun or shade, but for best results they should be grown in good, well-cultivated soil.

Mahonia aquifolium (the second name means 'holly leaved') is 3 ft. high, flowers from February to April and often carries a good crop of purple berries afterwards. *M. japonica* is 5 ft. or more high and has long trails of lemon-yellow, scented flowers in February and March. *M. repens,* the Creeping Barberry, is 1 ft. high, spreading and excellent for covering and binding a bank. Regular pruning is not necessary but all can be thin-

ned or trimmed after flowering.

The only truly shrubby magnolia is *M. stellata,* an open, well-branched bush 8 to 10 ft. high. The white flowers, produced very freely in March and April, have narrower petals than the flowers of the tree magnolias. It likes a loamy or peaty soil, without chalk or lime, and a sunny sheltered position, for though quite hardy, the flowers may be damaged by frost. No pruning is required. Increase by layering after flowering.

Magnolia stellata

Handsome evergreen leaves and bold flower spikes make the choice *Mahonia lomariifolia* a splendid shrub for a prominent but sheltered position. The flowers appear in winter and early spring

Olearia, Osmanthus

Olearias are evergreens, sometimes known as daisy bushes, because they have small, daisy-like flowers usually very freely produced. The most generally useful is *Olearia haastii,* a shapely bush 6 ft. or more high with neat, rounded leaves and white flowers in July and August. It will grow practically anywhere and is a first-rate town shrub. *Olearia stellulata,* 4 ft. high, with greyish leaves and white flowers in May, is even more decorative but less hardy. It succeeds well near the sea and inland in well-drained soil and sunny, sheltered places. *Olearia macrodonta* has large, holly-like leaves, grows 10 ft. or more high and has large clusters of flowers in June and July, but is

suitable only for the milder parts of the country.

Osmanthus delavayi (also known as *Siphonosmanthus delavayi*) is a densely branched evergreen, 8 ft. or more high, with small, dark green leaves and, in April, little white tubular flowers which are extremely fragrant. It will grow in any reasonably good, well-cultivated soil and sunny or partially shaded position.

Both olearias and osmanthus can be thinned or lightly cut back after flowering. They are increased by summer cuttings.

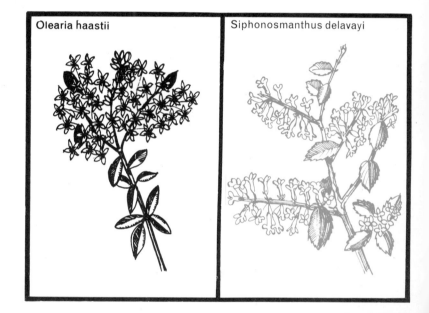

Olearia haastii   Siphonosmanthus delavayi

The small tube-shaped flowers of *Osmanthus delavayi* are produced in clusters in April and are intensely fragrant. It is a very bushy shrub with shining, neat evergreen leaves

Pernettya, Skimmia

Pernettya mucronata is an evergreen shrub making a dense 3-ft. thicket of growth slowly spreading by suckers. It has neat, dark green leaves, little bell-shaped white flowers mostly in May and June, followed by showy berries in a wide range of colours from white to plum purple with some remarkable shades of lilac and rose.

It likes a loamy or peaty soil without chalk or lime, and will grow in sunny or shady places. It needs no pruning and can be increased by digging out rooted suckers in autumn. Davis's Hybrids give all the colours and are self-fertilising, though some other varieties need a male bush as a pollinator since male and female flowers are borne on separate bushes.

Skimmias are also evergreen and berry bearing, but the berries are always scarlet. They also dislike lime and chalk, grow well in loamy or peaty soils in sun or shade. *Skimmia japonica,* 2 to 3 ft. high, with little spikes of white, fragrant flowers in May and June, bears male and female flowers on separate bushes. One male bush is sufficient to pollinate several females, if planted within a few yards. Only the female bushes produce berries, but the males have the best flowers. *Skimmia foremanii* is self-fertile, with flowers of both sexes growing on the same bush. Neither variety needs pruning and both can be increased by summer cuttings.

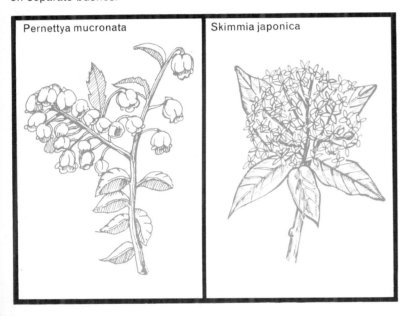

Pernettya mucronata | Skimmia japonica

Philadelphuses

Philadelphus Sybille

Philadelphus Virginal

Philadelphuses are the shrubs which many people wrongly call syringas, a name that really belongs to the lilacs. All kinds of philadelphus are deciduous and have mainly white flowers which are often very sweetly scented. They look and smell like orange blossom, and for this reason are known as mock oranges.

All are deciduous, flowering in June and July. They will grow almost anywhere, but flower more freely in open, sunny places than in shade. Some make very large shrubs but all can be reduced in size by pruning directly the flowers fade, when the old flowering branches can be cut right out and only the best shoots or stems retained to flower the following year.

Two of the most heavily scented mock oranges are *Philadelphus coronarius,* with small, creamy-white flowers and *P. delavayi,* white and purple, tall. *P. microphyllus* is also richly scented, with dainty flowers and small leaves. The most showy are the garden varieties, such as Beauclerk with large, single, white flowers each with a flush of purple in the centre; Belle Etoile, with a more pronounced purple flush; Sybille, similar to Belle Etoile in flower but a smaller bush and Virginal with large, double, white flowers. *P. microphyllus* and Sybille are 3 ft. high – the rest 6 to 8 ft.

All can be readily increased by summer or autumn cuttings.

Pernettya mucronata is a handsome evergreen shrub with small white flowers in May. These are followed by showy berries in a variety of colours including pink, puce, crimson, purple and white

Belle Etoile, one of many varieties of philadelphus or Mock Orange. All have white or cream flowers sometimes, as in this variety, with a purple blotch and many are very fragrant

Phlomis, Senecio

Phlomis fruticosa, called Jerusalem Sage, grows wild in eastern Mediterranean countries and has grey, sage-like leaves. Its whorls of hooded, bright yellow flowers are very decorative in June and July. It grows about 3 ft. high and has rather soft stems which are sometimes damaged by winter frost. Bushes should be trimmed back a little each April to keep them tidy and get rid of damaged growth.

Senecio laxifolius also has rather soft stems and grey, rounded leaves, more leathery than those of the Jerusalem Sage. It grows 3 to 4 ft. high and produces sprays of bright yellow, daisy-type flowers in June and July. Like the Jerusalem Sage it can be damaged by winter frost, but may be pruned in the same way.

Both shrubs like well-drained soils and warm, sunny places and are a good choice for hot, dry borders and banks. Their soft, grey leaves contrast well with the various shades of green that tend to dominate shrub borders, and, being evergreen, they will continue to furnish the garden during the winter.

They can both be increased by summer cuttings.

Potentillas

Potentillas, also known as shrubby cinquefoils, are especially valuable because they are relatively small, compact shrubs which flower all through the summer. They will grow in any reasonably well-drained soil and prefer open, sunny places. All can be pruned each March when either some of the older stems can be removed to thin the bushes, or all stems can be cut to within a few inches of the ground, which will result in a smaller bush and larger flowers. All can be increased by summer cuttings.

There are a number of good varieties all derived from *Potentilla fruticosa,* which is deciduous, has small, deeply divided leaves and strawberry-type flowers. The variety Elizabeth is rather short and spreading with light yellow flowers; Katherine Dykes is deep yellow, 3 to 4 ft. high and similar in diameter; Tangerine has coppery-orange flowers, is 1 ft. high, but may spread over several feet; *vilmoriniana* has silvery leaves and white flowers and *beesii* has silvery leaves and yellow flowers. There are several other varieties, all in the same colour range.

Phlomis fruticosa

Senecio laxifolius

shrubby cinquefoil

Senecio laxifolius is a wide-spreading evergreen shrub and it has abundant daisy-like flowers in midsummer. Care should be taken not to let the soil get waterlogged in winter

Potentilla fruticosa, the Shrubby Cinquefoil. These deciduous shrubs are valuable for their compact habit and long flowering season from early summer to autumn

Pyracanthas

The pyracanthas are known as firethorns, because of their abundant crop of flaming-red berries in autumn and winter. All are strong-growing shrubs with dark green, shiny, evergreen leaves and clusters of white flowers in June. They are often trained against walls, but will grow equally well in the open where they will make fine bushes 6 to 8 ft. high and through, though they can be kept smaller by pruning after flowering. When trained on walls, some pruning is usually required to keep them tidy. Overgrown or badly placed stems are cut out as far as possible without removing the clusters of young berries which will then be just forming.

Firethorns will grow practically anywhere, in sun or shade and in any reasonably good soil. They can be increased by seed or from summer cuttings, but seedlings may take several years to attain flowering and berry-bearing size.

Recommended kinds are: *Pyracantha coccinea lalandii,* with quite large, orange-red berries; *P. atalantioides* (also known as *P. gibbsii*) with smaller, deeper red berries and *P.* Waterer's Orange with orange-yellow berries. Birds may strip the berries in winter, but often leave those of *P. atalantioides.*

Japanese Quince

The Japanese Quince may appear in nurserymen's catalogues either as chaenomeles or cydonia, and is often known by gardeners simply as japonica. Typically it is a freely branched, suckering, deciduous shrub, 3 to 5 ft. high and of almost any width, with scarlet flowers in spring, followed by large fruits (quinces) in late summer. It is commonly trained against walls where it may be in flower by February, but it can equally well be grown as a bush in the open.

In addition to the common scarlet-flowered chaenomeles there are others with white, pink, orange or crimson flowers. Recommended varieties are: Knap Hill Scarlet, scarlet; Nivalis, white; Apple Blossom (also known as *moerloesii*) blush pink and *simonii*, crimson.

All may be grown in any reasonably good soil and in sun or shade. Cut out some of the older stems after flowering each year, to prevent overcrowding, and, when grown against a wall, shorten side growths in June and main stems in August as necessary to fill the available space. Wires or trellis-work should be used to tie shoots to as they do not climb naturally.

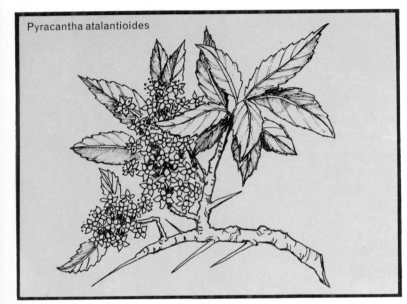

Pyracantha atalantioides

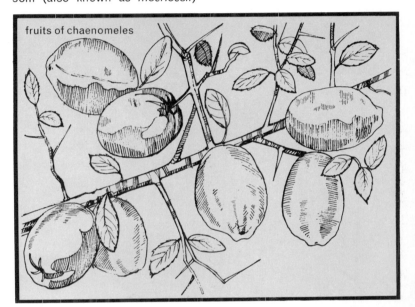

fruits of chaenomeles

Pyracanthas are popularly known as firethorns and they make very attractive wall shrubs. They will also grow equally well as bushes in the open in sun or shade

Chaenomeles superba Knap Hill Scarlet will flower very early in the year when it is trained against a wall. It can also be grown as a bush but it is not evergreen

Rhododendrons

At the height of their flowering season in May and early June, rhododendrons are the most spectacular of all flowering shrubs, and for sheer display none surpass the group of varieties known as Hardy Hybrids. These are also the easiest to grow, for, as their name implies, they are quite hardy, and will thrive in sun or shade and in almost any soil that is not chalky or limy. If chalk or lime is present, they can be grown in specially prepared beds of lime-free loam and peat and will benefit from annual spring feeding with iron and manganese sequestrols.

All hardy hybrid rhododendrons are evergreen and make dome-shaped shrubs eventually 6 to 10 ft. high and as much through. Prun-ing is not necessary, but over-grown bushes can be cut back in spring, one year's flowers being sacrificed.

Rhododendrons transplant easily and even quite large bushes can be moved in autumn. All benefit from an annual spring topdressing of peat or leafmould.

Recommended varieties are: Betty Wormald, deep pink; Britannia, scarlet; Cynthia, rose red; Doncaster, deep red; *fastuosum flore pleno*, mauve, double flowers; Gomer Waterer, blush white and gold; Loder's White; Mother of Pearl, blush turning white; Mrs Furnival, rose and maroon; Pink Pearl, rose pink; Purple Splendour, deep purple and Sappho, white and maroon.

In addition to the hardy hybrid rhododendrons there are a great many other kinds which are excellent garden shrubs, all evergreen and all disliking chalk or lime. They succeed best in loamy or peaty soils and though some will grow in full sun most prefer a partially shaded place. Many are first-class shrubs for planting in thin woodland.

There are a great many varieties, of which the following are representative: *R. augustinii,* light blue, 6 to 8 ft.; Blue Diamond, lavender blue, 3 ft.; *R. cinnabarinum,* orange-red, hanging, tubular flowers, 6 ft.; Dairymaid, cream and red, 6 to 8 ft.; Electra, violet blue, 5 ft.; Elizabeth, bright red, 3 ft.; *R. impeditum,* deep blue, 1 ft., suitable for a rock gar-den; Lady Chamberlain, red and orange, hanging, tubular flowers, 5 ft.; Loderi, white to pale pink, very large, fragrant flowers, 8 ft. or more; May Day, scarlet, 6 ft.; Naomi, various shades of lilac pink and greenish yellow, 8 ft. or more; *R. racemosum,* small rose-pink flowers, 3 ft.; Temple Belle, bell-shaped pink flowers, 4 ft.; *R. williamsianum,* bell-shaped, pale pink flowers, 1½ ft.; Yellow Hammer, yellow, 3 ft.

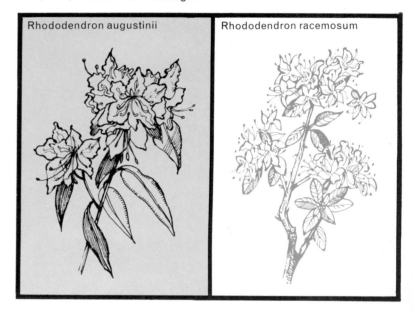

Rhododendron augustinii

Rhododendron racemosum

The hardy hybrid rhododendrons are a natural choice for rather more spacious lime-free gardens. Shown above is *Rhododendron fastuosum flore pleno*, one of the few double-flowered varieties

Rhododendron Blue Diamond is one of many good small varieties. It is a slow-growing, compact shrub and is seen here in front of *Berberis darwinii* and one of the taller red rhododendrons

Rhus, Tamarix

There are several kinds of rhus, all deciduous. *Rhus typhina,* the Stag's-horn Sumach, is a very open-branched shrub or small tree, 10 or 12 ft. high, with long, divided, fern-like leaves and curious erect spikes of crimson flowers in late summer. The leaves colour brilliantly before they fall in autumn. *Cotinus coggygria, (Rhus cotinus)* is a big bush with rounded leaves and tangled masses of silky filaments around the tiny flowers, which gives it the popular names Smoke Tree and Wig Tree. A variety named *atropurpureus* has purple leaves. Rhus enjoy good, well-drained soil and sunny places. They can be increased by digging out rooted suckers in autumn.

There are also several different kinds of tamarix, or tamarisk, which is the popular version of the name, but all are deciduous shrubs with thin, whippy branches set with tiny leaves and with very small but numerous pink or white flowers, the whole effect being very light and feathery. They grow well in light, sandy soils and open places and are first-rate seaside shrubs able to withstand the worst gales. The most beautiful kind is *Tamarix pentandra,* 6 ft. or more high, with rosy-pink flowers in July and August. It can be cut hard back each March if desired, and increased by summer or autumn cuttings.

Cotinus coggygria

Tamarix pentandra

Rhus typhina laciniata, a cut-leaved variety of the Stag's Horn Sumach, is an extremely attractive small tree for the garden. The rich autumn colouring of the leaves makes it especially beautiful

Spiraeas

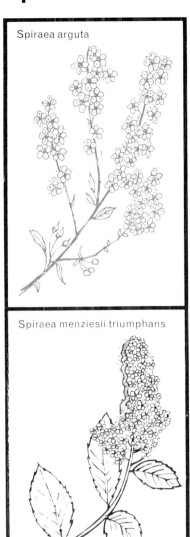

Spiraea arguta

Spiraea menziesii triumphans

Most spiraeas are elegant, deciduous shrubs with slender, often arching branches and numerous small flowers either in clusters or scattered over the stems. All will grow in practically any soil and in sun or shade. Pruning is not essential but overgrown bushes can be thinned in March and the late-flowering kinds, such as Anthony Waterer, can be cut almost to ground level at this time, so reducing their size and improving the quality of the flowers.

Some kinds sucker freely and suckers may have to be dug out if they extend too far. They can be replanted elsewhere if desired. Spiraeas can also be increased by summer or autumn cuttings.

Spiraea thunbergii and *S. arguta* flower in spring and are 4 ft. high. *S. prunifolia plena* flowers in May and has double flowers, *S. vanhouttei* flowers at the same time and has single flowers. Both are about 6 ft. high. So is *S. cantoniensis flore pleno* with double flowers in June. *S. veitchii* is also June flowering and 9 to 12 ft. high. All the foregoing have white flowers.

S. menziesii triumphans has fluffy spikes of rose flowers in July and August and makes a 6-ft. thicket. Far better for small gardens is *S. bumalda* Anthony Waterer only 3 ft. high with cream-splashed leaves and flat heads of deep carmine flowers. This is an outstandingly good shrub.

Anthony Waterer is the best variety of *Spiraea bumalda,* a low-growing but rather spreading shrub with variegated young leaves to complement the carmine flowers

Viburnums

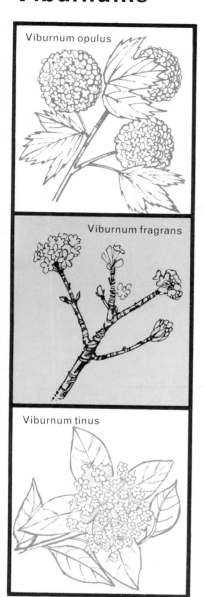

Viburnum opulus

Viburnum fragrans

Viburnum tinus

There are a lot of viburnums and they are nearly all good, easily grown garden shrubs. One, *Viburnum opulus*, grows wild in Britain and is known as the Guelder Rose. It is very beautiful, especially when covered with shining, scarlet berries in the autumn, and there is a shorter variety of it called *compactum* which is a better garden plant. Another variety, *V. o. sterile*, has large round clusters of white flowers in late May and early June and is known as the Snowball Tree.

The Japanese Snowball Tree, *Viburnum tomentosum plicatum*, has smaller but more numerous flower clusters and *V. t. mariesii* has flat clusters of white flowers all along its branches in May. *V. fragrans* has very fragrant clusters of pinkish-white flowers in winter and is 7 or 8 ft. high. *V. carlesii* is even more fragrant, only 4 ft. high and flowers in April and May. All the foregoing are deciduous.

The Laurustinus, *Viburnum tinus,* is evergreen and carries its white and pink flowers from November to April. It makes a big, dense bush 6 to 8 ft. tall. All these viburnums can be grown in any reasonably good soil and in sun or shade. They need no pruning, but if they get too large, can be thinned or cut back in March.

Weigelas

Weigelas were formerly called diervillas. They are all fairly large, deciduous bushes with long arching stems wreathed in little trumpet-shaped pink or crimson flowers in early summer. They will grow practically anywhere, but flower best in open, sunny places. They can be pruned immediately after flowering when all stems that have just carried flowers are cut out, but young, non-flowering stems are kept to flower the following year. This reduces the size of the bushes and improves the quality of the flowers. All can be increased by summer or autumn cuttings.

Weigela florida, 6 to 8 ft. high with rose-pink flowers is the common kind. It has an excellent variety named *variegata*, with paler pink flowers and leaves broadly edged with cream.

There are also a number of good garden varieties. Abel Carrière has large pink flowers; Bristol Ruby is ruby red; Eva Rathke is crimson and more compact than most; Newport Red is deep carmine and Styriaca has small, deep rose flowers, very freely produced. There is also a variety called *looymansii aurea* with rosy-pink flowers and light golden leaves.

Weigela florida

Spectacular layers of flowers, raised tier on tier, are the glory of *Viburnum tomentosum mariesii*. These appear in May and have their perfect foil in the fresh green foliage

Abel Carrière is one of numerous attractive varieties of weigela. All are easily grown shrubs flowering in early summer. They can be pruned immediately after flowering

Winter Sweet, Witch Hazel

The Winter Sweet, *Chimonanthus praecox,* flowers in mid-winter. The pale primrose and purple flowers are not at all showy, but they are very fragrant and scent the air for a considerable distance. The Winter Sweet is a deciduous, open-branched shrub about 8 ft. high. It likes a good, well-cultivated and well-drained soil, and sheltered position as it is not very hardy. It can be trained against a wall, in which case surplus growth can be cut out immediately after flowering.

There are several kinds of witch hazel, or hamamelis, and they too are all deciduous and flower in winter. The most popular is *Hamamelis mollis* with spidery, deep yellow, sweetly scented flowers. It makes a big, loosely branched bush 8 ft. or more in height, but it can be pruned moderately each March to keep it within bounds. A variety named *pallida* has larger primrose-yellow flowers. *Hamamelis japonica* makes an even bigger bush or small tree, with smaller, yellow flowers. It has several varieties, *arborea* with yellow and purple flowers; *rubra* with orange and purple flowers and *zuccariniana* with lemon-yellow flowers. *H. intermedia* is an attractive hybrid of *H. mollis* and *H. japonica.*

Both Winter Sweet and witch hazels are best increased by layering in spring or early summer.

Chimonanthus praecox
Hamamelis mollis

Yuccas

Yucca filamentosa

There are no better shrubs than yuccas to impart a sub-tropical look to a garden, for, though several kinds are reasonably hardy, their large rosettes of stiff, sword-shaped evergreen leaves have a highly exotic appearance.

Yuccas enjoy light, well-drained soils and warm, sunny positions, but may often be seen growing in most unlikely places, even in grimy industrial areas. The creamy-white cup-shaped flowers are borne in summer in long, erect spikes and add to the unusual appearance of the plant. It is widely believed that the flowers are only produced at intervals of many years, but this is untrue as plants in good health will flower annually. No pruning is required, but the faded flower spikes should be cut out.

Yucca filamentosa has rosettes 2 or 3 ft. high with 3- to 4-ft. flower spikes in August. *Y. flaccida* is very similar, but the leaves are less stiff. *Y. gloriosa,* also known as Adam's Needle, is the largest and will, after a few years, make a distinct main trunk several feet high surmounted by large rosettes of leaves and with rather broad 4-ft. flower spikes in August.

Yuccas are increased by offsets and by root cuttings.

Hamamelis intermedia is an attractive hybrid witch hazel. The hazel-like foliage takes on fine autumnal tints and the yellow flowers follow on bare stems. *Gentiana sino-ornata* can be seen below

Stiff, sword-shaped leaves and stout spikes of cupped flowers make *Yucca flaccida* an interesting evergreen shrub. It is especially happy in seaside gardens because of the milder conditions there

Climbing and Screening Plants

Preparing and Planting

Since most climbers will remain undisturbed in the same place for many years the soil should be well cultivated before they are planted. Dig or fork it thoroughly, remove all perennial weeds and work in some well-rotted manure or decayed garden refuse. Complete this preparation with a good dusting of bonemeal, hoof and horn meal or meat or fish meal, or a combination of these before planting.

The general principles of planting climbers are the same as those for any other plants, but there are a few points which apply particularly to climbers, especially when planted against walls or fences. Because the soil near a screen is sheltered from rain it is usually dry and so climbers should be planted a foot or so away from the wall, not hard up against it. If during planting it is inclined slightly towards the wall, it will be easy to tie the plant to the supports provided and this should be done immediately.

Many climbers are supplied in pots or other containers. When planting out remove the container completely, but do not attempt to unravel or otherwise disturb the roots. Work a little moist peat around the ball of soil, make firm and keep well watered for the first few weeks if the weather should be dry.

If lawns and the shorter annuals and bedding plants may be likened to the carpet, rugs and other floor coverings of rooms, climbers may be equated with wallpaper, curtains and pictures. They fulfil an essential part in the furnishing of a well-organised garden and can even play a dominant role in determining its character. It is quite possible, even in the very limited space of a town garden, to create an air of jungle-like profusion by the lavish use of vigorous climbers.

Climbers are of many different kinds. They may be shrubby, with more or less permanent woody stems, as in honeysuckle, roses and wisteria; herbaceous perennial with soft stems dying to ground level each winter, as in Everlasting Pea and Golden-leaved Hop, or annual, completing their growth in one season and then dying, as in nasturtium and sweet pea.

Like other plants, climbers may be evergreen or deciduous and they may be grown primarily for their flowers, for their fruits or for their foliage. Some kinds are tender but it may be possible to grow these against sheltered walls.

Methods of climbing also vary greatly. Some kinds, such as honeysuckle and Russian Vine, twine themselves around anything available, even quite large objects such as trunks of trees. Others, such as clematis and sweet pea, climb by tendrils which cling most readily to string, wire or trellis work. Yet others, such as ivy and ampelopsis, will attach themselves securely to walls and other smooth surfaces by means of aerial roots or adhesive discs.

Roses and various brambles sprawl through other plants and gain some support from their thorns. There are also shrubs, such as pyracantha (firethorn), ceanothus, Japanese quince and Fishbone Cotoneaster (*Cotoneaster horizontalis*), which can readily be trained against walls and, by reason of their stiff stems, are almost self supporting. All the same, trellis or wires can greatly facilitate the training of such plants, since young growths have a natural tendency to grow forwards away from the wall or fence and they can then be drawn back towards it. All such supports should be fixed an inch or so away from the wall so that the growth, tendrils and ties can easily go round them.

When climbers are being selected for planting against houses or other high walls, aspect must be considered since climbers on north-facing walls will get little or no direct sunshine, those on some south-facing walls may get an excess of warmth and those on east-facing walls may be exposed to cold winds. The problem hardly arises with fences since plants quickly rise above them. The soil close to house walls can be very dry, and until climbers become established they may need regular watering.

Humulus lupulus aureus, the Golden-leaved Hop. This is a herbaceous perennial climber which grows very rapidly and is valued for its attractive foliage in summer

Arches and Pergolas

Many climbers grow well on arches and pergolas, which are a continuous linked string of arches covering the path or terrace in a cloister-like manner. Climbing roses, in particular, benefit from the free circulation of air they get when growing in this manner instead of against a wall or fence, but since arches and pergolas afford little or no protection from cold they are not so suitable for the more tender climbers such as solanums and passion flowers (passiflora).

Be sure that all such structures are sufficiently strong and durable to take the very considerable weight of growth they may eventually have to bear. Timber 4 in. square is the minimum size for uprights, and for large structures brick or block piers may be preferred. Cross members should be a minimum of 4 x 2-in. timber, more for structures over 6 ft. wide.

If uprights are bedded in concrete, bring the level of the concrete base above the ground and finish it off with a bevel to run off water. Treat all wood, whether in or out of the ground, with a good preservative, which is harmless to plants. Creosote is not suitable because of the scorching fumes it can give off.

Ampelopsis and Others

Ampelopsis, vines and Virginia Creeper are closely related plants and at different times they have been given different names so that it is sometimes hard to distinguish them in nursery catalogues. What most people call ampelopsis has leaves with three lobes, whereas the Virginia Creeper has leaves which are composed of five separate leaflets. Both cling to walls, fences and trees by little suckers on their tendrils and both turn crimson before their leaves fall in autumn. The correct names of these two fine plants are *Parthenocissus tricuspidata* and *P. quinquefolia* respectively, but they may be listed as *Ampelopsis* (or *Vitis*) *inconstans* and *A.* (or *V.*) *quinquefolia*.

The Grape Vine or *Vitis vinifera* also has several good ornamental varieties, such as *purpurea* with reddish purple leaves and Brandt with leaves which turn crimson in the autumn. Like other vines they climb by tendrils, not by suckers. So does *Vitis coignetiae* with large, rounded leaves that turn scarlet and crimson in the autumn. It is very vigorous.

All these climbers will grow in any reasonably good soil in sun or shade, but will colour best in the sun. If they grow too vigorously they can be thinned or cut back after the leaves fall in the autumn.

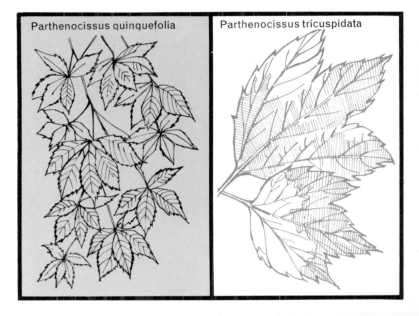

Parthenocissus quinquefolia   Parthenocissus tricuspidata

Climbing roses will succeed well and look very attractive when trained up arches and pergolas. Such structures must be made from strong and durable materials and must be firmly anchored

The self-clinging ampelopsis, *Parthenocissus tricuspidata*, will quickly cover a wall with a dense network of slender growths bearing handsome green leaves. These change to shades of scarlet and crimson before they fall in autumn

Akebia and Others

Akebia, celastrus and polygonum are all very vigorous, hardy climbers that may be used to clothe unsightly objects quickly. Akebia makes many slender stems clothed in leaves composed of three or five separate leaflets, giving it an attractive appearance. The little, deep maroon flowers are curious rather than beautiful, but in sunny, sheltered places they may be followed by cylindrical, violet-coloured fruits.

Celastrus is less attractive in leaf, but it can produce big crops of small yellow and scarlet fruits in autumn. It is important to buy the hermaphrodite form of this plant as other forms may be male or female and will bear no fruits unless two of different sexes are planted. The hermaphrodite has male and female flowers on the same plant.

The climbing polygonum (*P. baldschuanicum*) is often known as Russian Vine. Few climbers grow so fast and it will soon cover a large outhouse or go to the top of a tall tree. From July to October it produces cascades of small, creamy-white or pinkish-white flowers.

All these climbers will grow in any reasonably good soil, the celastrus and polygonum in any aspect, but the akebias in a sunny place. If they grow too far they can be thinned or shortened in February or March.

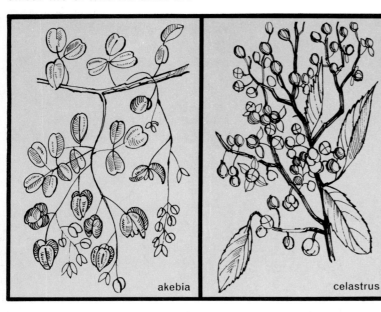

akebia   celastrus

Clematis

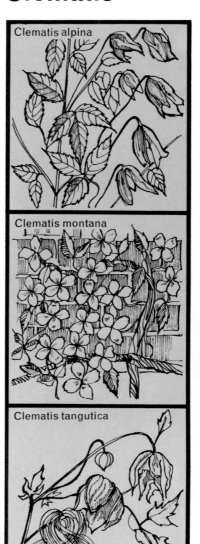

Clematis alpina

Clematis montana

Clematis tangutica

Clematis are among the most valuable of garden climbers because there are a great many varieties, differing in vigour of growth, time of flowering and the size and colour of their blooms. In consequence something can be selected for almost every purpose.

Clematis may be broadly divided into small-flowered kinds, many of which are wild plants introduced to gardens, and large-flowered kinds, most of which are hybrids produced in gardens.

Of the small-flowered species *Clematis armandii* is one of the first to flower, opening its clusters of small white flowers in late March and continuing throughout April. The leaves are evergreen.

Clematis alpina and *C. macropetala* both have little nodding bell-shaped blue or soft mauve-pink flowers in April and May.

Clematis montana has masses of small white or pink flowers in May. It is one of the most vigorous of all clematis, but can be kept in check by shortening side growths in early August.

Clematis viticella has medium size, purple or red flowers in July and August. There are several varieties of it, all very showy.

Clematis tangutica and *C. orientalis* have small yellow flowers from August to October.

Polygonum baldschuanicum, the Russian Vine, grows very quickly and from July to October is covered with cascades of small cream flowers. It will thrive in any reasonably good soil and in sun or shade

There are many varieties of clematis differing in vigour of growth, time of flowering, size and colour. *Clematis montana rubens* has a mass of pale pink blooms in May

The large-flowered clematis are divided into several groups according to their parentage. These groups are *florida*, flowering mainly in May and June; *jackmanii*, flowering mainly in July and August; *lanuginosa*, flowering at different times between June and August; *patens*, flowering mainly in May and June; *taxensis*, flowering mainly from July to September and *viticella*, also flowering mainly from July to September.

There are numerous varieties in each group and the following are representative:

C. florida: Belle of Woking, double-flowered, mauve; Duchess of Edinburgh, double-flowered, white.

C. jackmanii: Comtesse de Bouc-haud, soft pink; Gipsy Queen, violet-purple; *superba,* deep violet-purple; Perle d'Azur, pale blue; Star of India, violet and red.

C. lanuginosa: Beauty of Worcester, violet-blue with some double flowers; *henryi,* white; Lady Northcliffe, lavender; Mrs Cholmondeley, light blue; William Kennett, deep lavender.

C. patens: Barbara Jackman, petunia purple; Lasurstern, purple-blue; Nellie Moser, mauve and carmine.

C. texensis: Gravetye Beauty, red.

C. viticella: Ernest Markham, petunia red; Huldine, pearly white and mauve-pink; Lady Betty Balfour, violet-blue; Ville de Lyon, carmine.

Clematis like good, well-cultivated and well manured soil. They grow best with their roots shaded but their stems in the sun, which can often be done by planting them behind a low-growing shrub or leafy herbaceous plant. The less vigorous can be allowed to scramble up into climbing roses or other plants or they may be trained to wires or trellis. The vigorous kinds may be allowed to grow round trees, climb over sheds or cover walls or fences.

All clematis can be pruned but it is sometimes rather difficult to prune the very vigorous kinds because of the tangle of growth they make. The method of pruning depends upon the group to which the clematis belongs.

Prune *Clematis alpina, C. macropetala* and *C. montana* and their varieties in early August by shortening side growths to 3 or 4 in.

Prune varieties of the *florida* and *patens* groups immediately after flowering by shortening the flowering shoots to strong growth buds.

Prune varieties of the *jackmanii, texensis* and *viticella* groups in February or March, by shortening to 3 or 4 in. each growth made the previous year.

Prune varieties of the *lanuginosa* group like *florida*, if early flowers are required, or like *jackmanii* for late flowering.

Retain all young growth of *C. armandii* but cut out old growth where possible after flowering.

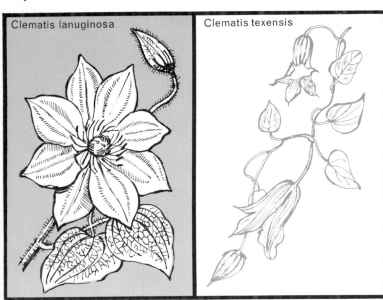

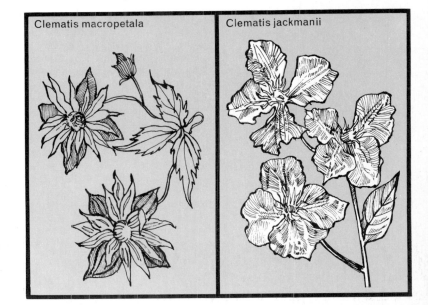

The large-flowered clematis are divided into several groups according to their parentage. One of these is the *viticella* group to which this variety, Ernest Markham, belongs

Clematis prefer to have their roots in the shade and their flowers and stems in the sun and they are often grown behind low-growing shrubs and herbaceous plants. This lovely variety is Countess of Lovelace

Cobaea and Others

Ipomoea purpurea

Thunbergia alata

The three climbers cobaea, ipomoea and thunbergia are often grown from seed and sometimes treated as annuals, being discarded in autumn and replaced by new seedlings in the spring.

Cobaea grows very rapidly, climbs by tendrils and has bell-shaped, light purple or greenish white flowers in summer. Sow seed in February – March in J.I.S. or peat seed compost, prick out seedlings singly into 3-in. pots in J.I.P. No. 1 or peat-based potting compost and later move to large pots or plant in a bed of good loamy soil. Water freely in spring and summer and do not shade. Water very sparingly in autumn and winter and protect from frost. The plants can be grown out of doors in summer from June to October.

Ipomoeas, commonly called morning glory, have blue or purple, wide, funnel-shaped flowers in summer, and climb by twining. Grow in exactly the same way as cobaea. Varieties of *Ipomoea purpurea,* such as Flying Cloud and Heavenly Blue, are annuals but *Ipomoea leari* is a perennial.

Thunbergia alata is a twining plant with white, buff or orange, black-centred flowers, for which reason it is known as Black-eyed Susan. It can be grown in the same way as cobaea, but it is much less rampant and can be used in hanging baskets. It is best treated as an annual and discarded each year after flowering.

Honeysuckles

The botanical name of honeysuckle is lonicera and it is under this that the various kinds of honeysuckle will be found in most nursery catalogues.

Honeysuckles enjoy good, well-cultivated soil, but will grow in most soils either in full sun or in shade. They all climb by twining so if planted against walls they should be provided with wires or trellis for support, but no tying will be needed.

The Common Honeysuckle has two useful varieties, Early Dutch, flowering in May and June, and Late Dutch, flowering from July onwards. Both are very fragrant.

The Japanese Honeysuckle (*Lonicera japonica*), also very fragrant, has smaller creamy flowers in summer. There are several useful varieties such as *aureo-reticulata* with leaves netted with yellow and *halliana* with white flowers changing to dull yellow.

The Scarlet Trumpet Honeysuckle (*Lonicera brownii*) has very showy, scarlet flowers but no scent, and neither have either *L. tellmanniana* with coppery-yellow flowers or *L. tragophylla* with large, bright yellow flowers. The last two are more successful in shade than in sun, and all honeysuckles are liable to be attacked by aphids if planted in very hot, sunny places. The remedy is to spray with a systemic insecticide.

Thunbergia alata is better known to many gardeners as Black-eyed Susan. It succeeds best when treated as an annual and it makes a splendid plant for a hanging basket

There are several beautiful species of the ever popular honeysuckle. This one is *Lonicera periclymenum belgica,* the Early Dutch variety, and it has very fragrant flowers in May and June

Hydrangeas, Solanums

There are several climbing hydrangeas which cling like ivy by means of aerial roots. One, *Hydrangea petiolaris,* has flat circular heads of little creamy-white flowers surrounded by a few large ones like a lace-cap hydrangea. A second, *Schizophragma hydrangeoides,* is similar, but the flower heads are more showy. Both are deciduous, flowering in June – July. A third, *Pileostegia viburnoides,* is evergreen, flowers from August to October and has rather fluffy-looking heads of creamy-white flowers. All like good, rich, rather moist soils and will grow in sun or shade, though pileostegia really prefers a shady place.

The climbing solanums prefer warm, sunny places and like good, well-drained soil. *Solanum jasminoides* has very slender stems that ramble a long way and slaty blue flowers (white in variety *album*) produced from July to October. It is not very hardy and can be killed by hard frost. *Solanum crispum* is tougher and its whippy stems grow to a height of 12 or 15 ft. The heliotrope-blue flowers are produced from June to September in showy clusters.

Ivies

The botanical name of ivy is hedera, and it will usually be found under this name in nursery catalogues. There are a great many varieties, differing in the shape and colour of their leaves, and there are also 'bush' ivies, which do not climb at all but branch out like shrubs. This is the natural habit of ivy when it flowers and bush ivies are produced by taking cuttings from the flowering growths of ordinary ivies.

Ivies climb by roots which cling to any surface. They are hardy evergreens; they will grow in sun or shade -- even quite dense shade -- in practically any soil, and are among the easiest of climbers to grow. They can be cut back or clipped with shears in spring, and any dirt or debris lodged in them can be brushed out.

Good varieties of the common ivy are: Buttercup, with yellow leaves; *caenwoodiana,* with small leaves; Jubilee, dark green leaves with central golden splash; Silver Queen, leaves variegated with creamy-white and pink; *sagittaefolia,* leaves with narrow lobes and *tricolor,* leaves grey-green, white and rose.

Hedera colchica variegata has very large, heart-shaped green and yellow leaves. The leaves of *H. canariensis variegata* are dark green, grey-green and white.

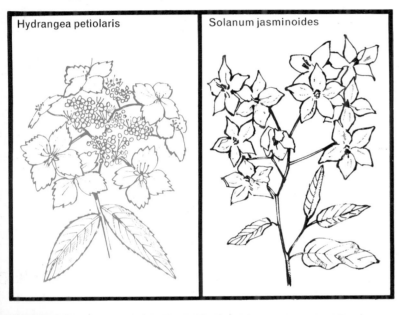

Hydrangea petiolaris

Solanum jasminoides

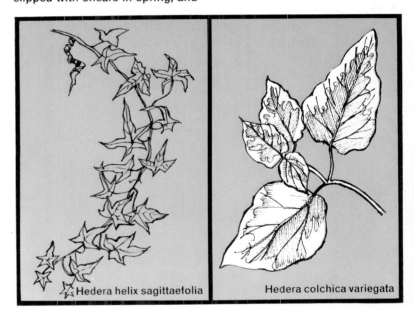

Hedera helix sagittaefolia

Hedera colchica variegata

Solanum crispum basking in the summer sun against a warm, sheltered wall. Solanums prefer a good, well-drained soil and they can be killed by a hard frost

This large-leaved variegated variety of the Persian Ivy, *Hedera colchica dentata variegata,* has excellent decorative qualities. It makes a splendid cover for an old wall or tree stump

Jasmines

Jasminum polyanthum

There are two jasmines that are perfectly hardy and two others that can be grown out of doors in the mildest parts of the country and elsewhere in frost-proof greenhouses. The hardy kinds are the Winter Jasmine (*Jasminum nudiflorum*) with yellow flowers on rather stiff green stems from November to February and the Summer Jasmine (*J. officinale*) with masses of white, sweetly scented flowers on thin twining stems in July and August. The two rather tender jasmines resemble these hardy ones in many respects, the Primrose Jasmine, (*J. primulinum*), looking like a finer, double-flowered Winter Jasmine and *Jasminum polyanthum* being freer flowering and sweeter scented than *J. officinale*, with white flowers flushed with pink outside. The Primrose Jasmine flowers from March to May, *Jasminum polyanthum* from May to July.

All will grow in any reasonably cultivated soil. The Winter Jasmine will grow and flower equally well in sun or shade, but the others prefer sunny places. The Winter Jasmine and Primrose Jasmine must be tied to some kind of support, but the other two will twine themselves around any support, and the Summer Jasmine is especially good for covering fences or walls. Cut back the flowering stems of Winter and Primrose Jasmine when the flowers fade, and thin the others as necessary.

Nasturtium and Others

The Canary Creeper and the nasturtium are closely related, being different kinds of tropaeolum. They are annuals, useful for covering fences, walls and sheds quickly but temporarily since they will die in the autumn after flowering.

Sow seeds of Canary Creeper (*Tropaeolum peregrinum*) in pots or pans in a warm greenhouse or frame in March; pot seedlings singly in 4-in. pots in John Innes No. 1 or peat-based potting compost and plant out in late May or early June in a warm, sunny place. The flowers are small, fringed and canary yellow.

Sow seed of the Climbing Nasturtium, (*Tropaeolum majus*) out of doors in April or May a few inches apart and 1 in. deep in a sunny place where the plants are to grow and thin the seedlings to 1 ft. apart. Spray the plants occasionally with insecticides to kill blackflies and caterpillars.

There is also an annual hop, *Humulus japonicus*, which is very quick growing and has attractive, light green leaves variegated with white in some varieties. This can be grown just like the Climbing Nasturtium, but the perennial hop, *Humulus lupulus*, should be planted where it can grow permanently. It is chiefly valued in gardens in its gold-leaved variety *aureus*.

Tropaeolum peregrinum | Humulus lupulus

The Winter Jasmine is a sprawling plant rather than a true climber and will need an occasional tie to keep its slender stems in position. It will grow and flower in shady places

Tropaeolum speciosum, the Flame Flower, is a slender climber with gracefully divided leaves and vividly coloured flowers. It likes to grow through an evergreen shrub which will shade its roots

Wisteria

Wisterias are beautiful hardy twining plants which bear their pea-type flowers in long trails like laburnum, but usually in some shade of blue, lavender or mauve. There are also white varieties and one, rather rare, pale pink wisteria. All flower in late May and early June.

Wisterias like sunny places and will grow well in most soils, though they like best a good, well-cultivated soil. They can be trained against walls or fences or over pergolas. To keep them tidy and encourage flowering, prune them in late July and shorten all the shoots made that summer to about five leaves. It is also possible to prune these shoots again in autumn to within about 2 in. of the main stems and by this means wisterias may be grown as bushes in the open without any support.

The two most popular kinds are the very fine variety of the Japanese Wisteria (*W. floribunda*) named *macrobotrys* or *multijuga*, with trails of flowers sometimes 3 ft. long, and the Chinese Wisteria (*W. chinensis*) with shorter but very numerous trails of sweetly scented flowers. There are white-flowered varieties of both the Japanese and Chinese Wisteria, and also varieties with double, blue-mauve flowers.

Woody Climbers

There are some shrubs which although not by nature climbing are readily adaptable for training against walls and fences. Of these there are numerous varieties of ceanothus, some evergreen and some deciduous, mostly with blue flowers in late spring or summer, though there are pink-flowered forms. Some are not very hardy and appreciate the protection of a sunny wall. Prune spring-flowering kinds to shape immediately after flowering, and the summer-flowering kinds in April.

The firethorns (pyracantha) are also very popular evergreen shrubs which make excellent wall cover. They produce clusters of small white flowers in early summer followed by heavy crops of scarlet, orange-red or yellow berries in the autumn. All kinds are completely hardy and will thrive on shady as well as on sunny walls. Trim to shape in early summer when the flowering stems can be seen.

Some kinds of cotoneaster also make good wall or fence climbers, particularly the Fish-bone Cotoneaster (*C. horizontalis*) which spreads its fan-like branches against a wall to a height of 5 or 6 ft. without requiring any support or pruning. It has red berries and the leaves turn crimson in autumn.

Japanese Quinces (chaenomeles) with scarlet, crimson, pink or white flowers in early spring also make good wall climbers and will thrive in sun or shade. Shorten misplaced shoots after flowering.

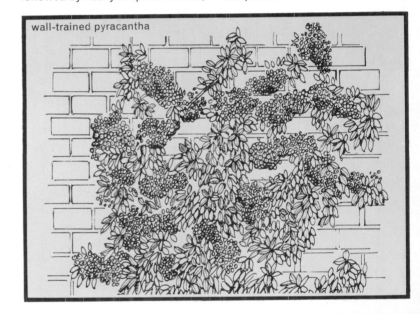

wall-trained pyracantha

In late May and June the magnificent trails of wisteria flowers are a very beautiful sight. Above is *Wisteria chinensis*, a vigorous free-flowering Chinese species

This fresh springtime scene is dominated by a magnificent wall-trained specimen of *Ceanothus impressus*. This species is the hardiest of the evergreen kinds

Garden Trees

Almonds, Peaches

Almonds and peaches are closely related and very similar in appearance and requirements. The Common Almond, *Prunus amygdalus*, is the first to flower, being at its best in March. It makes an open, shuttlecock-shaped head of branches up to 20 ft. high in the common form, and has light pink single flowers, though there are white-flowered and double pink-flowered forms.

The Peach is *Prunus persica*, and it makes a smaller tree, rarely over 15 ft. high, often considerably less. It flowers in April, and the most popular variety, Clara Meyer, has double rose-pink flowers. Iceberg is semi-double and white and Russell's Red, double crimson.

Both almonds and peaches like good, fairly rich, well-cultivated soil and a sunny position. Both are subject to a disease known as leaf curl, which causes the young leaves to turn red, pucker and curl. This is most likely to occur in exposed places and in cold weather. It can be controlled by spraying with Bordeaux mixture or a copper fungicide in late February or early March.

These are first-rate town trees as they do not take up too much room and appreciate the shelter of neighbouring buildings. Any pruning necessary should be done immediately after flowering and then kept to a minimum.

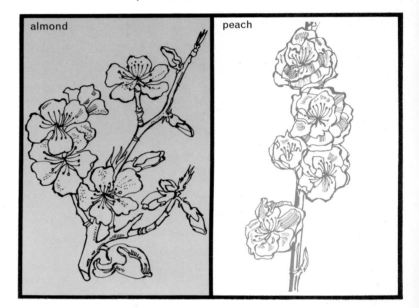

almond   peach

Trees can make or mar a garden. Too many of them, or unsuitable kinds, can rob the garden of light and the soil of food and moisture, making it impossible to grow anything else well. But a few well-placed and well-chosen trees can give a garden distinction and provide welcome summer shade.

Large trees, such as oak, elm, lime, poplar, beech, willow, cedar, pine and fir, are only suitable for large gardens, but there are sometimes narrow, upright-stemmed or fastigiate forms of large trees that can be planted in quite small gardens. Examples are the Dawyck Beech, fastigiate oak and fastigiate Tulip Tree (liriodendron). The Lombardy Poplar is a fastigiate form of the Black Poplar and its branches do not take up much room, but unfortunately its roots penetrate too far to make it a good, small, garden tree.

Conifers, of which cypress, cedar, juniper, fir, larch and pine are familiar examples, differ from other trees in having narrow, sometimes needle-like leaves. Most, but not all, are evergreen. There are not many other evergreen trees, so conifers do play a rather special part in the garden, accentuated by the fact that many are conical in habit in contrast to the more rounded shapes of broad-leaved trees. Though naturally green leaved, some conifers produce varieties with leaves of different colours, usually blue-grey or golden. Most conifers are allowed to branch from ground level but other trees are often grown on a bare trunk and are known as standards.

Once trees are planted they are likely to remain for a great many years, during which time no further deep cultivation can be carried out. Initial soil preparation should therefore be thorough.

Planting holes must be of ample width and it is wise to drive a stout stake into the centre of each hole. Plant so that the soil mark on the main trunk is about 1 in. below soil level. Firm the soil thoroughly around the roots and tie the main stem securely to the stake to prevent wind rocking.

Even if trees are to be grown in grass, a cultivated circle at least 4 ft. in diameter should be maintained around each for the first few years. In addition, young trees should be fed each March with a topdressing of manure or a compound fertiliser used according to manufacturer's instructions. No ornamental tree requires regular pruning, but most will benefit from a little shaping in the early stages to maintain a good balance of growth on all sides while retaining a natural habit. Suckers – growths from the roots and from the main trunk below the head of branches – should also be removed. When removing branches, cut them close to a fork or where they join a larger branch of the main trunk.

This ornamental peach, *Prunus persica* Clara Meyer, is a very popular small tree. During April it is covered in a wealth of beautiful pink double flowers. It grows well in town gardens

Beeches, Birches

The Common Beech, *Fagus sylvatica*, is too large to be grown as a tree in gardens of ordinary size, though it can be hard pruned and used as a hedge. The Dawyck Beech is a fastigiate variety making a very narrow tree, tapering top and bottom, so that it can be accommodated in quite a limited space. The Copper Beech and the Purple Beech are of normal habit with bronze-coloured and deep beetroot-red foliage respectively. They make a splendid contrast to green-leaved trees where there is room for them, but in 20 years may easily be 40 ft. high and 30 ft. in diameter.

The Silver Birch, *Betula pendula*, is one of the few forest trees suitable for planting in fairly small gardens. It is very variable and care should be taken to purchase good forms with really silver-white bark colour and drooping branches. The variety *tristis* is reliable and *youngii* is a smaller tree making a dome of slender branches weeping to ground level.

Both birch and beech will grow in most soils, with birch preferring light, rather sandy or peaty soils, and beech chalk or limestone soils. They can be pruned in autumn or winter, but great care should be taken with birch not to destroy the natural graceful habit of the tree.

Cherries

Together with the crab apples, cherries are the most valuable flowering trees for gardens.

Cherries thrive in a wide variety of soils with a particular liking for those of a limy or chalky nature, and though they prefer open, sunny places they will grow in shade. Their one slight drawback is their susceptibility to bacterial canker disease which may be aggravated by pruning. Nothing much can be done when trees do become infected, indicated by small circular holes in the leaves, dying branches and masses of gum exuding from the bark, and they are best dug up and burned. Any pruning necessary should be done after flowering.

Representative varieties are as follows, but there are many more equally good.

Amanogawa, double soft pink, April – May, narrow columnar habit; Fugenzo, double deep pink, April – May, spreading habit; Kanzan, double deep pink, April, shuttlecock habit; Cheal's Weeping, double deep pink, April, small tree with weeping branches; Shimidsu, double white, May, low, spreading habit; Ukon, double pale greenish yellow, April, well branched; *Prunus sargenti*, single pink, April, shuttlecock habit; *Prunus subhirtella autumnalis*, small, semi-double pale pink flowers, November to February, well branched; *Prunus yedoensis*, single white, March – April, well branched.

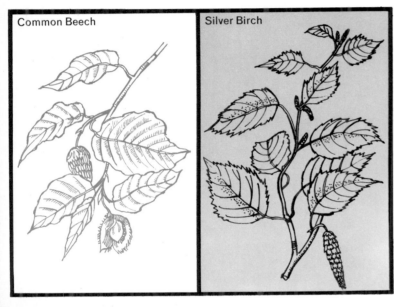

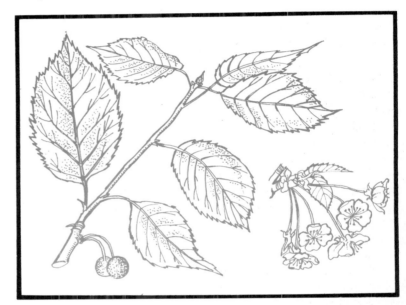

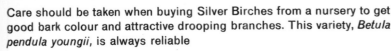

Care should be taken when buying Silver Birches from a nursery to get good bark colour and attractive drooping branches. This variety, *Betula pendula youngii*, is always reliable

Cherries are very valuable flowering trees and Kanzan is just one of the many lovely forms available. It has a shuttlecock habit though as the trees age the branches tend to droop and spread more widely

Crab Apples

These are magnificent ornamental trees, some grown primarily for their spring flower display, others for their highly coloured fruits. All are hardy and easy to grow in a wide variety of soils, though they prefer reasonably good, well-cultivated, adequately drained soil and sunny, open places. All can be pruned at any time in autumn or winter as necessary.

Malus floribunda, the Japanese Crab, is one of the first to flower, opening its small but very abundant crimson and pink flowers in April. It makes a small, densely branched tree, 15 ft. or so high.

Malus lemoinei has deep wine-red flowers in April and May and grows to 20 ft. or thereabouts. *M. purpurea, M. aldenhamensis* and *M. eleyi* closely resemble it, but vary slightly in flowering time. *M. eleyi* also usually carries good crops of small red-purple fruits in autumn.

Dartmouth Crab has white flowers in spring followed by round red crab apples. Elise Rathke has white flowers, greenish yellow, red-striped fruits and a weeping habit. Golden Hornet has white flowers and yellow fruits. John Downie has white flowers and egg-shaped yellow and scarlet fruits. Red Siberian and Yellow Siberian are both white flowered and have cherry-size fruits, red and yellow respectively.

Cypresses

Cypresses are evergreen conifers, mostly conical in shape though varying considerably. Many make excellent hedges and windbreaks and all can also be planted as individual specimens.

Cypresses grow in a wide variety of soils, but prefer reasonably good, well-cultivated and adequately drained soil, the one exception being the Swamp Cypress (taxodium). All can be pruned in spring or early summer as necessary. Some kinds transplant rather badly and should be purchased in containers from which they can be taken without root injury, or with their roots bound in sacking.

Lawson Cypress (*Chamaecyparis lawsoniana*) is tall, green, pyramidal and very hardy. It has numerous varieties such as *allumii*, deep blue-grey; *columnaris*, dark blue-grey, columnar habit; *fletcheri*, light blue-grey, feathery leaves, slow growing; *erecta viridis*, light green, narrow pyramidal habit and *lutea*, golden leaved.

Leyland Cypress (*Cupressocyparis leylandii*) makes a fine, rather narrow, dark green pyramid and is one of the fastest growing of all evergreens.

The Arizona Cypress (*Cupressus arizonica conica*) makes a narrow, blue-grey column.

The Monterey Cypress (*Cupressus macrocarpa*) is bright green, fast growing but not very hardy. It has a beautiful golden-leaved form.

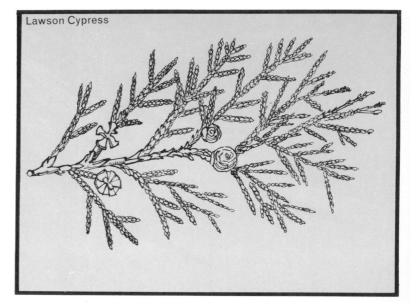
Lawson Cypress

The white blossom of the crab apple John Downie is followed by a striking display of fruit in the autumn. Crab apples are easy to grow given a reasonably good soil and a sunny, open position

Chamaecyparis obtusa is a Japanese cypress with numerous varieties of which this golden-leaved form named *crippsii* is one of the most attractive with its rich colouring

Magnolias

Many people call magnolias Tulip Trees, because of their tulip-shaped flowers, but this name belongs to the liriodendron.

Magnolias like good, well-cultivated soil, preferably free of chalk or lime, though some kinds will tolerate such soils. They thrive in sunny, sheltered places and benefit from an annual spring top-dressing of peat or leafmould and on chalky or limy soils may be fed with iron and manganese seque-strols. All have an open, branching habit and some spread widely.

The best evergreen kind is *Magnolia grandiflora*, with large, shining green leaves and fragrant white flowers, rather like water-lilies, from July to September, though usually few at a time. It is often grown as a wall shrub.

Magnolia soulangeana is the most popular deciduous magnolia. Its white, purple-flushed flowers are freely produced in late April and early May. *Alba* is a variety with pure white flowers; *lennei* has flowers white inside and purple outside; and both *rubra* and *nigra* are all purple and flower in May.

Magnolia sieboldii is a small, slender-branched tree with hanging, cup-shaped flowers each with a crimson central boss, produced from late May to July. *Magnolia wilsonii*, *M. sinensis* and *M. high-downensis* are similar, the last being particularly suitable for chalky or limy soil.

Maidenhair Tree and Others

The Maidenhair Tree or gingko, the Dawn Redwood or meta-sequoia and the Swamp Cypress or taxodium are all deciduous conifers, beautiful and rather uncommon.

The Maidenhair Tree is so called because its light green leaves are the shape of maidenhair fern leaves, but greatly enlarged. They turn yellow in autumn. The best variety, *fastigiata*, makes a tall but rather narrow column or pyramid and it is slow growing, for which reason it can be planted in relatively small gardens even though it may eventually reach 40 ft. or more.

The Dawn Redwood, by contrast, is very fast growing, sometimes adding 3 ft. or more each year, but it makes a fairly narrow pyramid of ferny, light green leaves which turn russet brown before falling in the autumn.

The Swamp Cypress closely resembles the Dawn Redwood in appearance but has even more feathery leaves, is much slower growing and turns a light cinnamon red in autumn.

All three thrive best in good loamy, well-cultivated soil, but will grow in most soils though the Swamp Cypress dislikes lime and chalk. It thrives in moist soil and is an excellent tree to plant beside a stream or lake.

Magnolia soulangeana

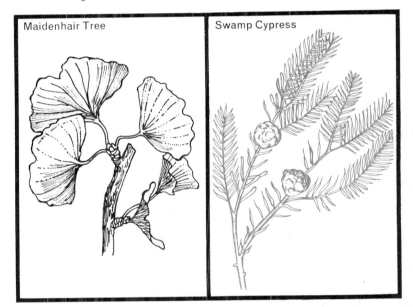

Maidenhair Tree

Swamp Cypress

Magnolias make excellent town trees and there are many kinds available. This one, *M. sieboldii*, is a small, slender-branched tree with pendant fragrant flowers from late May to July

The handsome bark and ferny foliage of the Swamp Cypress, *Taxodium distichum*. Though this will eventually make a large tree it is slow growing and very decorative when young

Maples

There are many different kinds of maple or acer including such familiar trees as the Norway Maple, *Acer platanoides*, and the Sycamore, *A. pseudoplatanus*, which are too large for the average-sized garden. By contrast the Japanese maples are very small, bushy trees or large shrubs and are very suitable even for small gardens.

All maples are deciduous and many colour well before the leaves fall in autumn. The Japanese maples are outstanding in this respect, the variety Ozakazuki turning scarlet and *lutescens* yellow. The leaves of *atropurpureum* are bronzy crimson from spring to autumn; those of *dissectum* are deeply cut into a lacy pattern and those of *dissectum atropurpureum*

are both lacily cut and coloured.

Acer negundo variegatum makes a tree of moderate size with light green leaves variegated with white. It grows well in towns.

Goldsworth Purple is a purple variety of the Norway Maple, a fine tree where there is space for it. *Brilliantissimum* is a slow-growing variety of Sycamore with coral-pink young leaves.

The Snake Bark Maples (*Acer davidii, hersii* and *pennsylvanicum*) have sage green bark, striped with light green and white.

All succeed in most soils and in sun or shade, but the Japanese maples prefer well-drained soils and rather sheltered places.

Plums, Snowy Mespilus

The ornamental plum most commonly planted in gardens is the Purple-leaf Plum, *Prunus cerasifera atropurpurea*. It is often sold as *Prunus pissardii*, and it has beetroot-purple leaves and small, pale pink flowers in late February or early March. A variety named *nigra* is similar, but has even darker purple leaves. Both make trees 20 ft. or so high which will grow almost anywhere.

Prunus blireiana is similar but makes a smaller, slower growing tree and has larger, semi-double rosy-pink flowers and copper-red leaves. It is the most beautiful plum but needs sun and a good, well-cultivated soil.

There are also ornamental varieties of the Blackthorn or Sloe,

Prunus spinosa. Purpurea, the Purple-leaved Sloe, has red young leaves which later turn purple, and small white flowers in March – April. *Rosea* is similar but has pale pink flowers. Both make big bushes or small trees and will grow almost anywhere.

The Snowy Mespilus, *Amelanchier canadensis*, makes a round-headed tree, 20 ft. or so high with bronzy young leaves turning crimson in autumn and masses of tiny white flowers in April. It will grow in any well-cultivated soil.

All these trees are deciduous and none needs regular pruning, though suckers should be removed. Trees can be thinned in August or September.

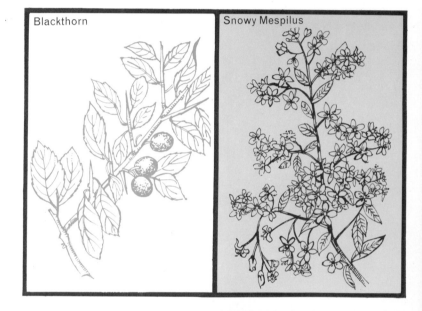

Japanese maples are very attractive foliage trees suitable for quite small gardens since they grow slowly. This is *Acer palmatum dissectum* with much divided purple leaves

Amelanchier canadensis, the Snowy Mespilus, is a graceful tree of medium size with abundant small white flowers in April. The foliage turns a brilliant crimson colour in the autumn

Rowans, Whitebeams

There are many kinds of sorbus, the Common Rowan or Mountain Ash being *Sorbus aucuparia*, and the Common Whitebeam, *S. aria*. They are excellent garden trees of small to medium size, thriving in almost any reasonably well-drained soil, and the whitebeams succeed particularly well on chalky or limy soils.

The Common Rowan or Mountain Ash makes a neat pyramidal tree 20 ft. or so high with rather ferny leaves and small white flowers in May and June followed by large clusters of orange-scarlet fruits. There are numerous varieties, one named *xanthocarpa*, with yellow fruits; another, *asplenifolia*, with even more fern-like leaves.

There is also the Chinese Mountain Ash, *Sorbus hupehensis*, with white fruits which turn pink, and the Japanese Mountain Ash, *S. matsumurana*, with very fine orange-scarlet fruits.

The Common Whitebeam also makes a neat, pyramidal tree, with leaves that are bright green on top and white beneath. The clusters of white flowers in May are followed by bunches of red fruits. Again there are several varieties, *pendula* having a weeping habit, and *lutescens* leaves which are creamy-white beneath. There is also the Swedish Whitebeam, *Sorbus intermedia*, with lobed leaves and the Chinese Whitebeam, *S. zahlbruckneri* (or *S. alnifolia submollis*), a very small, narrow tree.

Thorns

The thorns or hawthorns are small, densely branched deciduous trees, some of which are grown solely for their flowers and some for both flowers and berries. They are very hardy, growing almost anywhere, and will withstand pruning well so they can be thinned or cut back as necessary in autumn or winter.

The most showy flowering thorns are varieties of the Quick or Hawthorn, *Crataegus oxyacantha*. Paul's Double Scarlet Thorn (also known as *coccinea plena*) has clusters of fully double, light rosy-red flowers in May. *Rosea plena* has double pink flowers and *alba plena* double white, also in May.

Crataegus carrierei is a thorn without thorns, a neat tree 15 to 20 ft. high with white flowers in June, followed by large, orange-red berries which are not attractive to birds.

The Cockspur Thorn, *Crataegus crus-galli*, has white flowers, scarlet berries and leaves which turn yellow, orange and scarlet in autumn.

Crataegus prunifolia makes a rather broad, low tree, has white flowers in June followed by scarlet fruits and also gives fine autumn foliage colour.

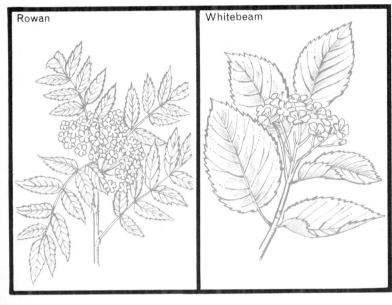

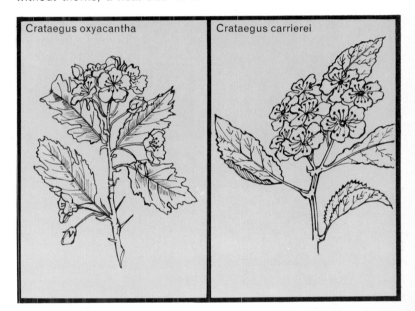

These handsome berries of *Sorbus aucuparia*, the Common Rowan or Mountain Ash, follow the white flowers. This tree is easily raised from seed sown in the spring and thrives on all well-drained soils

The thorns are small deciduous trees, some grown for the flowers alone and some also for berries. This variety of hawthorn, Paul's Double Scarlet Thorn, bears clusters of double flowers in May

Garden Hedges

Hedges serve both a decorative and a utilitarian role in the garden. They can be used to give privacy and to keep out intruders, to separate one part of the garden from another or to provide a fine background for a border of flowers or a handsome ornament. They can be clipped in simple or elaborate shapes or they can be permitted to grow freely, an informal mode of treatment that suits flowering shrubs, including shrub roses.

Formal hedges will need to be clipped from both sides so, if they are sited on the boundary, sufficient room must be left to give convenient access without trespassing on neighbouring property. It is not possible to insist that a neighbour trim a hedge for you, nor can he be compelled to permit access through his property to a hedge sited too close to the boundary.

All hedges cast some shade, interfere with the free movement of air and take food and moisture from the soil, sometimes for several feet on each side. Allowance should be made for this when siting hedges and planting other things near them. There are plenty of plants that enjoy shade, provided the soil is good and reasonably moist, but not so many that thrive in the dry shade found close to well-grown hedges. Often it is better to have a path or a lawn, rather than a flower border, immediately alongside a hedge to permit easy access for trimming and reduce interference with the roots of other plants. The roots of a hedge will grow quite happily beneath gravel, paving slabs or bricks.

On sloping ground hedges will break the flow of cold air down the slope which occurs during still, frosty weather. In consequence, cold air accumulates on the slope above each hedge and may cause injury to tender plants growing there. It is better to site hedges down, rather than across, slopes or to leave gaps in the bottom of the hedge through which cold air can trickle downwards.

In rose gardens, close encircling hedges may encourage mildew by restricting the natural movement of air, but there are other plants which are readily damaged by high wind and for which the shelter of a hedge is highly beneficial. Hedges give better protection against wind than either walls or fences of similar height, since they filter the wind rather than divert it and therefore cause far less air turbulence.

Though evergreen shrubs are most popular for garden hedge making, deciduous kinds can also be used. Hawthorn is the most widely used of all hedge-making plants, but for farm fields rather than for gardens. Beech, though a large tree, stands clipping well and when grown as a hedge retains its dead leaves all winter, making an excellent windbreak.

Planting

Like other shrubs hedges, once planted, will grow in the same place for many years without anything more than surface cultivation, so initial preparation should be thorough. If the ground has not already been well dug, take out a trench at least 2 ft. wide and 1 ft. deep for the whole length of the hedge, throw in some well-rotted manure or compost and break up the bottom of the trench with a fork, so working the manure or compost in.

Plant the hedge shrubs in this trench, if necessary first returning some soil to enable them to be placed at the correct depth. The soil mark on each plant, that is, the mark indicating where the soil came to in the nursery bed, should be about 1 in. below soil level. With container-grown hedging plants the top of the soil ball should be 1 in. below soil level.

Stretch a line tightly to mark the exact centre of the hedge and use this as a guide to planting, spacing the plants as recommended for the different kinds of hedging shrub. Return most of the soil around the roots and tread firmly, then scatter the remaining soil over the surface and level with a fork or rake.

When planting in spring, water for a few weeks if the weather is hot or dry until the plants are growing freely, especially if the hedge borders a drainage ditch.

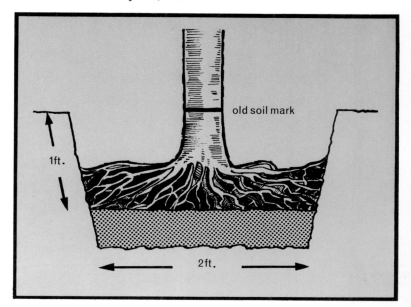

old soil mark

1 ft.

2 ft.

Berberis thunbergii atropurpurea makes a splendid hedge up to 6 ft. high with richly coloured, crimson foliage. Its densely branched habit and prickly stems make an impenetrable barrier

Care and Trimming

Do not neglect hedges after planting. They need care and feeding just like any other plants. Do not fork or dig near hedges as this destroys many of their roots. Keep the weeds down by hand weeding, shallow hoeing or the use of approved weedkillers such as paraquat or simazine but be careful to apply weedkiller as instructed and not in excess nor on the leaves of the hedging plants.

Feed each spring with well-rotted manure or garden refuse spread for a foot or so on each side of the hedge, or with a good compound fertiliser lightly peppered on the soil.

Trim young hedges three or four times each year from early June to late August to keep well furnished with growth right to the base. As they grow older one or two clippings each summer may suffice. Flowering hedges are best trimmed after flowering. Beech and hornbeam can be trimmed in summer or winter. Small-leaved shrubs such as privet, box, lonicera, cypress and yew may be trimmed with shears but larger-leaved shrubs, such as aucuba and laurel, are best pruned with secateurs so as not to disfigure the leaves.

When trimming, hold the shears so that the blades lie flat against the surface to be cut and the handles slope conveniently to the hands.

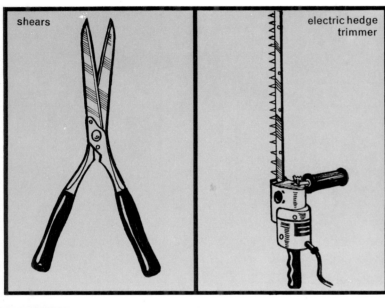

Conifer Hedges

The three principal kinds of conifer used for hedging are cypress, thuja and yew. All are evergreens which stand frequent clipping and yew, like box, is much used for topiary specimens.

The most popular hedging cypress, *Chamaecyparis lawsoniana*, (Lawson Cypress) with rather ferny, green foliage will make good hedges up to 10 ft. high. It is fairly quick growing, hardy and will grow in most soils. Plant 2 to 2½ ft. apart. There are numerous varieties of this cypress, some with lighter green foliage, some blue-green and some golden, all suitable for hedges either by themselves or in mixtures.

Leyland Cypress, *Cupressocyparis leylandii*, resembles Lawson Cypress but grows almost twice as fast.

Thuja plicata also resembles Lawson Cypress and has handsome dark green leaves. It grows well in heavy soils and may be treated as for Lawson Cypress.

Yew is available in dark green and golden-leaved varieties which may be planted separately or in mixture. It is slow growing and so does not need frequent clipping, is very durable and will grow in most conditions including chalk and limy soils. Plant 1½ to 2 ft. apart.

Chamaecyparis lawsoniana

Flowering hedges are especially attractive and *Pyracantha watereri* will also produce fine crops of scarlet berries in autumn and winter if trimmed after flowering to retain the faded flower trusses

The Golden-leaved Yew, *Taxus baccata aurea,* which makes a thick evergreen screen but is a slow grower. It is long-lasting and suitable for most soils, including chalk and lime

Deciduous Hedges

These are hedges made of shrubs that do not retain their leaves all the year. Their appearance changes with the seasons and this can add interest to the garden.

Beech is the most popular deciduous garden hedge. It grows rapidly, has such strong stems that it can be used to make a tall yet narrow hedge, and, when trimmed, retains its reddish-brown dead leaves throughout the winter. Plant shrubs 1 ft. apart for a good dense hedge. Beech grows in all well-drained soils, and especially well in chalky and limy soils. For a tapestry effect, Copper and Purple Beech may be mixed with green-leaved beech.

Hornbeam closely resembles beech and is better in clay and other wet soils. Plant in the same manner.

Myrobalan Plum has green leaves and small white flowers in April, and it makes a strong, quick-growing but not very ornamental hedge. Plant 1 ft. apart.

Prunus cistina is a purple-leaved plum which makes an excellent small hedge of up to about 4 ft. high. It is much neater and more decorative than Myrobalan Plum. Plant 18 in. apart and trim in April.

Quick, also known as Hawthorn and Whitethorn and commonly used by farmers as a hedging plant, makes a strong outer barrier and is very cheap. Plant 9 in. apart and cut back fairly hard the following winter to encourage a good branching habit.

Small-leaved Evergreens

Lonicera is the most popular small-leaved, fully evergreen hedge shrub. Two kinds are commonly used, *Lonicera nitida* with very slender stems and little round leaves and *L. yunnanensis* (or *L. nitida fertilis*) with stiffer stems. Both thrive in most soils and situations and will make good hedges up to 5 ft. high. Plant 1 ft. apart and prune tops immediately to encourage branching from base.

Box also has small, round, fully-evergreen leaves. It is stiffer in growth than lonicera, and thus much favoured for topiary specimens such as cones, peacocks, etc. Handsworth Variety, planted 2 ft. apart, is best for hedges up to 8 ft. high and for topiary; *suffruticosa*, purchased by the yard (enough when split up to plant a yard), is most suitable for low box edgings to beds.

Privet is only fully evergreen in mild winters. The best varieties are Oval-leaf, which is all green, and Golden which has bright yellow leaves and is slow growing. Both will grow practically anywhere and are excellent for hedges from 4 to 8 ft. high. Plant 1 to 1½ ft. apart and prune tops immediately to encourage branching from ground level.

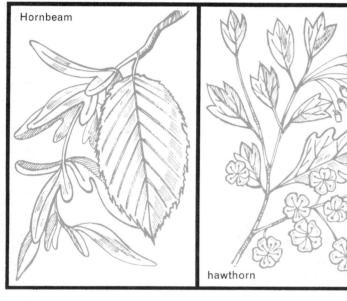
Hornbeam

hawthorn

box

privet

The Purple Beech, *Fagus sylvatica purpurea*, is, like the Common Beech, one of the best plants for a tall narrow hedge. These two and the Copper Beech, *F.s. cuprea*, can be mixed to give added interest

Lonicera nitida aurea, a golden-leaved form of this normally green-leaved shrub. Thriving in most soils, this lonicera will be well branched from the base if the tops are pruned immediately after planting

Large-leaved Evergreens

Common Laurel, (*Prunus laurocerasus*), has large, shining, dark green leaves, will grow well in most soils in full sun or dense shade and is excellent for large, broad hedges. It is a hungry shrub and not suitable for small gardens. Plant 2 ft. apart.

Portugal Laurel (*Prunus lusitanica*) has smaller, darker green leaves and is also excellent for a big, thick hedge, but is not recommended for small gardens. It will thrive in most soils in sun or shade.

Aucuba has large, light green leaves, heavily spotted with yellow in the most popular species, *Aucuba japonica*, sometimes called Spotted Laurel. It will grow anywhere, succeeding especially well in the shade even in grimy industrial surroundings, and is excellent for large hedges. Plant 2 ft. apart.

Holly makes a dense, impenetrable hedge. There are dark green-leaved, golden variegated and silver variegated varieties which may be planted separately or in combination. Holly succeeds in most soils in sun or shade and will make good hedges from about 5 to 10 ft. in height. It is very hardy and long lived, but rather slow growing. Plant 1½ ft. apart and trim in August.

Common Laurel

Shrub Hedges

Berberis darwinii

Spiraea arguta

Many flowering or fruiting shrubs make excellent informal hedges.

Berberis darwinii is neat, evergreen and prickly and has orange flowers in April; *B. stenophylla* is yellow flowered and less tidy. Both will make hedges to 6 ft. high and through. *B. verruculosa* resembles *B. darwinii* but is shorter and will make a good 4-ft. hedge. Plant all three 2 ft. apart and trim immediately after flowering.

Berberis thunbergii atropurpurea is deciduous, spiny and has small purple leaves and yellow flowers in early summer. Planted 2 ft. apart and pruned in March it makes a good 4- to 6-ft. hedge.

Cotoneaster simonsii is deciduous, stiffly erect and has scarlet berries in autumn and winter. Plant 1½ ft. apart and prune in March for a 4- to 5-ft. hedge. *C. henryana* is evergreen, scarlet berried, looser in habit and will make a 6- to 8-ft. hedge. Plant 2 ft. apart and prune in spring.

Laurustinus (*Viburnum tinus*) is a good evergreen, much like Portugal Laurel in leaf and habit, but slow growing with pink and white flowers in winter and spring. Plant 2 ft. apart and prune in spring.

Spiraea arguta is deciduous, twiggy, and has small white flowers in April. Planted 2 ft. apart and trimmed after flowering it makes a good 3- to 4-ft. hedge.

This fine holly with cream-edged leaves is named *Ilex aquifolium aurea marginata*. It is a female variety which will produce good crops of berries if a male holly is planted with it

Laurustinus (*Viburnum tinus*) makes a good dense evergreen hedge, 7 to 10 ft. in height. It has the added attraction of producing flowers from late autumn to early spring and it succeeds well in town gardens

Colourful Perennials

Planting

Plant small- to medium-sized plants with a trowel, large plants with a spade, being careful to make all holes sufficiently large to accommodate roots naturally spread out. Plant so that the crown, i.e. the point where leaves or stems join the roots, is ½ to 1 in. below the surface. Make soil firm around the roots.

Plant tall or fast spreading herbaceous plants about 2 ft. apart, plants of medium height or growth 15 to 18 in. apart and small plants 9 to 12 in. apart. When planting in groups of a kind, make each group an irregular shape and use an odd rather than an even number of plants, i.e. groups of 3, 5, 7, or more of each variety. Place the plants in each group a little closer than the recommended spacing and leave a rather greater space between groups, e.g. if the recommended spacing is 15 to 18 in. space plants in a group 15 in. apart and leave at least 18 in. between this and neighbouring groups. In this way, each group will grow together to form what appears to be one large plant clearly defined from neighbouring 'plants'.

March and April are good planting months and so is October for many kinds. Herbaceous plants grown in containers can be planted from these at almost any time, provided soil conditions are favourable.

Most herbaceous perennials, like trees and shrubs, live for many years and do not have to be frequently renewed from seed or cuttings like annuals or many bedding (temporary display) plants. Unlike trees and shrubs they have soft stems which in many kinds die down in the autumn and grow again the following spring, though a few have evergreen leaves and an even smaller number grow in winter and die down in the summer. Not all herbaceous perennials are hardy in Britain but here we are only concerned with those that are.

Hardy herbaceous perennials, to give them their full title (though they are often referred to simply as perennials or hardy plants) are very valuable in the garden since most are relatively cheap, grow quickly and can be readily increased by seed, division or cuttings. Many kinds grow so fast that it is desirable to dig them up every two or three years, divide them into smaller pieces and replant after digging the soil and enriching it with manure or fertiliser. Spring is usually the most favourable time to do this, though if herbaceous plants are quickly replanted and are well looked after subsequently, they can be moved at almost any time of the year. A few herbaceous perennials dislike root disturbance and are best left for many years. Examples of this kind are Japanese anemones, hellebores and peonies.

Most herbaceous plants will grow well in any reasonably good, well-cultivated soil. All enjoy moderate dressings of well-rotted manure or garden refuse and a sprinkling of bonemeal before planting and this feeding can be repeated each spring as a topdressing, lightly forked in.

Herbaceous perennials may be used in a variety of ways in the garden. Where space permits, whole borders or beds may be devoted to them or they can be used with shrubs, annuals or bedding plants or as isolated plants or groups of plants. An open, reasonably sunny position is best for beds or borders devoted exclusively to herbaceous perennials since this will suit the majority but there is no shortage of kinds that will grow in shade that is not too dense.

Most herbaceous plants flower for only three or four weeks each year, so if a bed or border devoted exclusively to them is to remain interesting for a long period plants with differing flowering periods must be selected and placed with due regard to their colour, height and flowering time. As a rule they are planted in irregular groups of a variety, the taller kinds at the back of a border or in the middle of a bed, shorter kinds in front or around the edge. It is better to make individual groups long and narrow rather than broad since they will be less conspicuous when out of bloom.

A summer border of hardy perennials which has been carefully planned and planted to include many herbaceous plants such as delphiniums, salvia, irises, campanula, golden rod and *Stachys macrantha*

Care and Feeding

Weeds must be kept down at all times by hoeing, hand weeding or the use of suitable weedkillers. Extra care, however, is required in using weedkillers in herbaceous beds and borders since the plants often have leaves right down to soil level and roots very near the surface. It is, therefore, sometimes difficult to restrict chemical applications to weeds alone and to keep them off the plants, to which they are likely to be equally fatal. Forking is not desirable because it disturbs surface roots.

If possible, apply an annual top-dressing of well-rotted manure or compost in spring and, at the same time, give a light scattering (about 3 oz. per sq. yd.) of a compound fertiliser. A second application of fertiliser at 2 oz. per sq. yd. may be beneficial about mid-summer.

Remove faded flower heads or stems and thin out growth where it is overcrowded. Water plants freely in dry weather, if possible by placing a sprinkler to play on them until the soil is well moistened to a depth of at least 2 in.

Water young plants individually from a watering-can until they are established and are growing well.

Staking

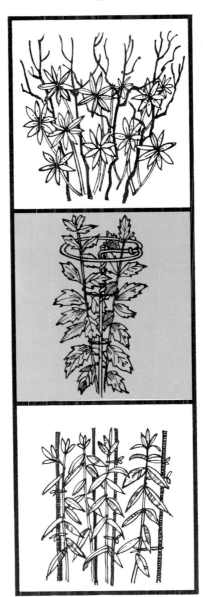

Herbaceous plants up to about 2 ft. in height are usually self-supporting, but taller kinds may require some extra support.

One simple and effective means of support is to use short bushy branches such as those sold as pea sticks and to thrust two or three of these firmly into the ground around each plant or group of plants when growth is still only a few inches high. The plants will grow through the twigs, obtaining support from them and at the same time concealing them from view.

Alternatively, squares of netting (string, nylon or wire) may be stretched between stakes about 18 in. above ground level so that the stems will grow through them and be held securely. Special wire supports are available which work in the same way and are both neat and durable.

A few plants with very long stems, e.g. delphiniums, hollyhocks and verbascums, may require staking with canes, one to each main stem. These should be thrust well down into the soil and should be sufficiently long to come to the base of the flower spike. The stems must be tied securely, but not too tightly. Make a double twist in the tie between stem and cane to allow for expansion.

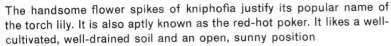

The handsome flower spikes of kniphofia justify its popular name of the torch lily. It is also aptly known as the red-hot poker. It likes a well-cultivated, well-drained soil and an open, sunny position

Verbascum vernale, a very useful herbaceous plant which thrives in dry soils and sunny positions. It has showy spikes of flowers during July and August and is not usually long lived

Lifting and Dividing

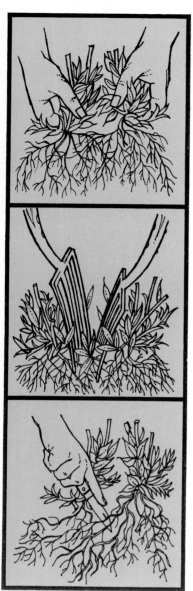

Many herbaceous plants spread outwards so that they progressively occupy more and more ground, and as they grow the centre portion of each plant gets more and more starved. To overcome this, plants are lifted, split up and replanted, i.e. divided.

Very fast growing plants, such as Michaelmas daisies and sunflowers, really need to be divided every second year for the best results, and most plants benefit from division at least every fourth year. Usually, the most convenient compromise is to re-make herbaceous beds and borders every third year, dividing as necessary.

March and April are good months for dividing most herbaceous plants, though it can also be done in October. Lift the plants carefully with a strong fork or spade and shake off as much soil as possible. Some plants can easily be divided with the fingers, but for tough old clumps thrust two forks (border forks or handforks, according to the size of the clump) back to back through the centre of the plant and lever them apart. Repeat as necessary to reduce plants to manageable size. Occasionally a knife may be needed to cut through tough crowns but it is better to rely on leverage only where this will work.

Discard the hard, starved centre portions and only replant the young pieces from the edges of the plants. Make sure that each piece which is retained has both shoots and roots.

Seed and Cuttings

Many herbaceous plants can be raised from seed and this is often the cheapest way of producing a large number of plants. However, seedlings usually take at least a full year to attain flowering size and do not always resemble their parents in every detail.

Seed may be sown in boxes or pots in a cool greenhouse or frame as soon as it is ripe in summer, or stored and sown the following spring. Most kinds can also be sown outdoors in May or early June. Seedlings are pricked out or are transplanted when sufficiently large to be handled and are usually grown on in a reserve bed until they have attained flowering size.

Some herbaceous plants can also be raised from either stem or root cuttings and this has the advantage that the plants produced do resemble their parents in every detail. Stem cuttings are usually prepared in March and April from firm young shoots and are rooted in sandy soil in a frame or cool greenhouse. Root cuttings are prepared from the thicker roots cut into short pieces and either inserted right way up in pots of sandy soil or strewn over the surface of sandy soil in seed boxes and covered with about ½ in. of the same mixture. Taken in winter or early spring, such cuttings will usually produce shoots by early summer when they can be transplanted to a nursery bed.

Beds of herbaceous perennials can be colourful for several months with the added interest of a good variety of leaf shapes and colours. Many kinds grow rapidly and need to be divided every few years

Solidago, popularly known as golden rod, is an easily grown herbaceous plant which readily seeds itself around. The branching sprays of tiny flowers appear in late summer and early autumn

Acanthus and Others

Acanthus mollis

Bergenia cordifolia

Bocconia cordata

Acanthus, bergenias and bocconias are plants which have leaves as decorative as their flowers and all are very easily grown.

The bear's breeches, or acanthus, has very large, shiny, green, deeply divided leaves, which were used by the ancient Greeks as models for the scrolls on their Corinthian columns. The flowers are hooded, light purple and white, carried in late summer in stiff spikes 4 to 5 ft. high and when cut and dried they can be used for winter decoration. In *Acanthus mollis* the lobes of the leaves are broad and waved, and in *A. spinosus* they are much narrower and spiny.

Bergenias are also sometimes called megaseas or giant-leaved saxifrages. They have big, rounded, rather leathery, shining green leaves and stiff, crowded sprays of pink or purple flowers on 1-ft. stems in spring. *Bergenia cordifolia* has light pink flowers; Silverlight is palest pink and Evening Glow reddish purple. All can be left undisturbed for years or can be divided if required.

Bocconia cordata is known as the Plume Poppy and also as macleaya. The leaves are large, rounded, deeply lobed and greyish and the little pinkish-buff flowers are borne in large sprays on 7-ft. stems in August and September.

All three plants spread steadily but need not be disturbed unless desired, when they can be lifted and divided.

Anemones, Globe Flowers

Japanese anemone

globe flower

Japanese anemones are good plants for herbaceous beds and borders, flowering in late summer. They have pink or white saucer-shaped flowers carried in small sprays on slender but rigid stems 2 to 3 ft. high.

These plants will grow in most soils in sun or shade but they do not transplant well, so it is wise to purchase small plants in pots or other containers from which they can be planted with roots unbroken. They should then be left undisturbed for as long as possible and will slowly spread outwards to form large clumps.

Some good varieties of Japanese anemone are: Alba, white; September Charm, soft pink; Louise Uhink, white and Profusion, deep rose.

The globe flowers are so called because their bright yellow or orange flowers are almost ball shaped. All are varieties of trollius and have attractive light green, deeply divided leaves, make neat clumps which do not spread too rapidly and enjoy moist places, though they will grow in any good, well-cultivated soil that does not dry out too rapidly in hot weather. They can be divided every three or four years. Most are 2 ft. high and flower in May, but Golden Queen is 3 ft. and has more open, orange flowers in June.

An early-flowering season and handsome, almost evergreen foliage make *Bergenia cordifolia* a fine garden plant. It is not fussy about soil and will grow in sun or shade

Globe flowers are excellent herbaceous plants for a moist situation. The yellow or orange blooms, which appear in May, resemble enormous buttercups and the foliage is deeply divided

Bergamots, Sages

monarda

salvia

These are related plants and they are among the most useful of medium height for the border, as they are easily grown in most places and make good masses of colour from July to September.

The bergamots, or monarda, grow 2½ ft. high with a bushy habit and carry their pink, scarlet or purple flowers in little clusters all over the top of the plants. There are several varieties differing mainly in colour. Representative examples are: Cambridge Scarlet, scarlet; Croftway Pink, rose pink and Blue Stocking, violet. All grow rapidly and should be divided every second or third year.

The best sage for the herbaceous border is *Salvia superba,* with slender violet-purple spikes from July to September. There are several good varieties differing mainly in height; Superba is 3 ft., Lubeca 2 ft. and East Friesland only 1½ ft. All will grow almost anywhere with a preference for good, well-drained soils and sunny places. They should be divided every second or third year.

Two other sages, sometimes planted in herbaceous borders, are *Salvia haematodes* with slender 3-ft. spikes of lavender-blue flowers in July and August and *Salvia uliginosa,* with short spikes of sky-blue flowers on wiry 4-ft. stems in September and October.

Bell and Balloon Flowers

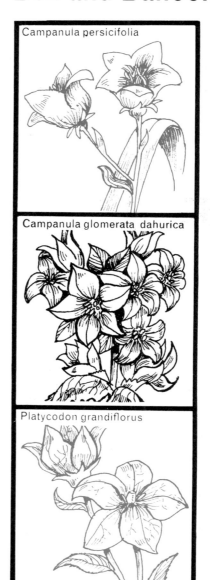

Campanula persicifolia

Campanula glomerata dahurica

Platycodon grandiflorus

There are many bellflowers or campanulas, some of which are rock plants. But there are also first-rate kinds for herbaceous borders and beds, all easily grown in almost any soil in sun or partial shade. They should be divided every third or fourth year.

Campanula persicifolia carries its flowers in slender 2- to 3-ft. high spikes in June and July. Telham Beauty is single and blue; Wirral Belle, double and deep blue and Fleur de Neige, double and white.

Campanula glomerata dahurica carries its violet-purple flowers in compact heads on 18-in. stems in June and July; *C. grandis* has 2-ft. spikes of blue flowers in June and July; and the tallest at 5 ft. with loose sprays of light blue flowers in July and August is *C. lactiflora,* of which Loddon Anna is a variety with mauve-pink flowers and Pouffe makes a 1-ft. high mound of lavender flowers.

The balloon flowers are varieties of *Platycodon grandiflorus,* very like bellflowers but slower growing, needing well-cultivated soil and not to be divided unless absolutely necessary. They are 18 in. high, flower in July and August and have inflated buds opening to cup-shaped flowers, commonly light blue, though there are soft pink and white varieties.

A refreshing corner of a garden which has been created by including many foliage plants of differing shapes and colours in and around a pool. The purple sage contrasts well with the surrounding plants

This bellflower, *Campanula glomerata dahurica,* flowers on 18-in. stems in early summer. Its rich colouring adds distinction to any herbaceous border and it is a valuable front row plant

Catmint, Heuchera

The Catmints or nepeta are grey-leaved plants with spikes of little lavender-blue flowers more or less continuously from June to September. The most popular kind is the Common Catmint, *Nepeta faassenii*, and since it only grows 18 in. high it is first rate for the edge of a bed or border. Six Hills Giant is a little taller and is a dark lavender-blue variety.

Catmints enjoy well-drained soils and sunny places, though they will grow almost anywhere. They spread rapidly and should be divided at least every third year. Bees are attracted by the flowers.

Heucheras are also primarily edging plants, but with small pink or red flowers in elegant sprays in June and July. The leaves are round, often with zones of different shades of green, and remain all the winter when the plants still make a good effect.

They need well-drained soil and succeed best in a sunny place, though they will grow in partial shade. They tend to get 'leggy' with age, and more soil can then be placed around them or the plants can be lifted, divided and replanted.

Representative varieties are: Coral Cloud, coral pink; Red Spangles, crimson-scarlet and Scintillation, bright pink.

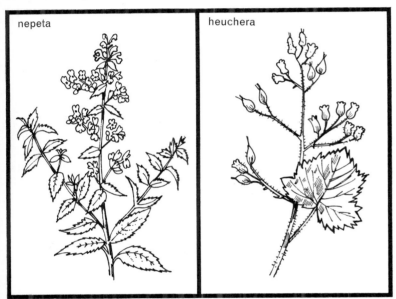

nepeta

heuchera

Christmas Roses and Others

Helleborus orientalis

Helleborus corsicus

Neither the Christmas nor the Lenten Rose are in any way related to true roses, but are herbaceous plants belonging to the buttercup family and known as helleborus or hellebores. The popular names have arisen because the flowers have a slight resemblance to single roses and appear in mid-winter or early spring. It is this early flowering that makes them so valuable in the garden. The plants in this group make slowly spreading clumps of dark green – more or less evergreen – deeply divided leaves which are themselves quite decorative. All thrive in shady places, enjoy good, well-cultivated soil and should be left undisturbed for as long as possible. It is best to start with fairly small plants.

The Christmas Rose, *Helleborus niger*, has white flowers on 1-ft. stems from December to February. There are several varieties, such as St Brigid and Potter's Wheel, with extra fine flowers.

The Lenten Rose, *Helleborus orientalis*, is $1\frac{1}{2}$ ft. tall, and has flowers varying from ivory white to deep maroon from March to April.

The Corsican Hellebore, *Helleborus corsicus*, has large clusters of yellowish-green flowers on 2- to 3-ft. stems in January and February. Its leaves are particularly decorative as are those of the Green Hellebore, *Helleborus foetidus*, with jade-green flowers at the same time.

Nepeta or Catmint is being grown here as an edging to formal beds for which purpose it is well adapted by reason of its neat grey foliage and long flowering season. It can be kept compact by fairly drastic clipping each spring

The Corsican Hellebore, *Helleborus corsicus,* has pleasant lime-green flowers carried on large heads in January and February and handsome divided leaves. It will thrive in sunny as well as shady places

Columbine, Monkshood

The columbines or aquilegias are delightfully graceful plants with ferny leaves and fragile-looking flowers, some with long spurs containing nectar poised on slender stems, and the varied colours are often as delicate as the shape.

Columbines grow readily from seed sown in a greenhouse or frame in March or out of doors in May and come into flower in the June of the following year. They range in height from 1 to 3 ft. They like well-drained soils and will grow in sun or shade. Although not usually long lived, they will often maintain themselves by self-sown seedlings. Double-flowered varieties are also available and the McKana Hybrids include a wide range of colours.

Monkshood or aconitums also have unusually shaped flowers, like little cowls, blue, white or yellow and carried in spikes. These plants thrive in any reasonably good soil and in sun or shade, and as they do not usually spread very fast they need dividing only every four or five years.

There are numerous varieties of which the following are representative: Bressingham Spire is violet blue, 3 ft., in July and August; Spark's Variety, indigo blue, 4 ft., June – July; Barker's Variety, deep blue, 5 ft., August – September; *Aconitum lycoctonum,* creamy-yellow, 4 ft., July – August; *Aconitum napellus bicolor,* blue and white, 3 ft., July.

Coneflowers

The coneflowers are closely allied to the sunflowers and they get their name because in some kinds the central disk, flat and button-like in the sunflowers, is raised into a cone. All are easily grown in most places. The yellow-flowered varieties are all rudbeckias, but the purple coneflowers are varieties of *Echinacea purpurea.*

Autumn Sun, also known as Herbstsonne, is one of the tallest of the rudbeckias, 6 or 7 ft. high with bright yellow flowers, each with a green central cone, in August and September. It is a fine plant for the back of a border, but needs staking.

Rudbeckia sullivantii Goldsturm is only 3 ft. high, stiff stemmed and self supporting. Its orange-yellow flowers have a black centre and are freely produced in August and September. *Rudbeckia speciosa* is similar but not quite so showy.

Goldquelle is 3 ft. high and has double, deep yellow flowers in September and October.

Golden Glow has double lemon-yellow flowers, is 5 ft. tall, and flowers in August and September.

The purple coneflowers are 3 to 4 ft. high, have rosy-purple flowers on very stiff stems in August and September. The King is a reliable variety.

All coneflowers grow fast and should be divided every second or third year.

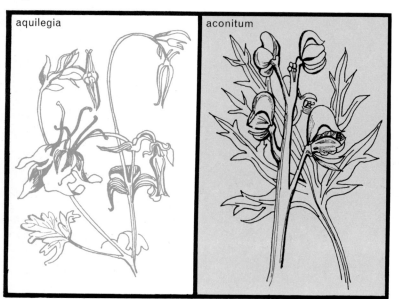

Long-spurred aquilegias. Many other colours are available and there are also short-spurred and double-flowered varieties as well as short kinds suitable for rock gardens

Rudbeckia sullivantii Goldstrum grows 3 ft. high and makes a handsome and accommodating border plant. It is ideal for cutting and arranging during August and September

Cornflowers, Scabious

The common cornflower is an annual but there are other useful kinds that are perennial herbaceous plants, quite hardy and easily grown in almost any soil and reasonably open situation. They vary greatly in size and in flower colour but all are fairly vigorous plants that are the better for being lifted and divided every three or four years.

The Mountain Cornflower, *Centaurea montana* has leaves that are silver-grey when young and blue flowers on 18-in. stems in May and June. *Centaurea dealbata* is 2 ft. high and has rosy-magenta flowers from June to August; *Centaurea macrocephala* is 3 ft. high, with big thistle-like yellow flowers in June and July and *C. ruthenica* is 4 ft.

high with lemon-yellow flowers in June and July.

The Caucasian Scabious (*Scabiosa caucasica*) makes an excellent cut flower, bearing its blue, purple or white flowers on good 3-ft. stems from July to October. It enjoys lime or chalk in the soil, and if these are lacking one or the other should be added before planting, and be given as an annual top-dressing each spring – say 4 oz. per sq. yd. of hydrated lime or 6 oz. per sq. yd. of finely ground chalk.

Plants should be divided every three years, but only in the spring as this scabious does not transplant well in autumn. Clive Greaves and Sarah Cramphorn are good blue varieties; Miss Willmott a good white.

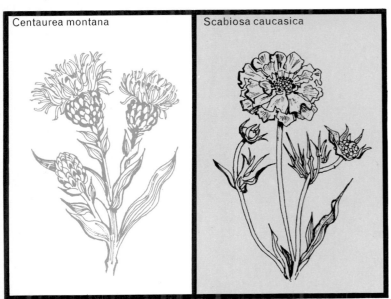
Centaurea montana
Scabiosa caucasica

Among the most attractive of all border flowers for cutting are the varieties of *Scabiosa caucasica*. In addition to the mauve and violet-purple kinds there are white varieties

Delphiniums

Delphinium elatum

Delphinium belladonna

Delphiniums are among the noblest of herbaceous plants, their tall spikes of flowers dominating beds and borders in June and July. They require good, fairly rich, well-cultivated and well-drained soil for in cold, wet soils they are apt to rot away in winter or be destroyed by slugs. They like open, sunny places.

Good delphiniums can be raised from seed, though the flowers may vary in colour and form. If sown in a greenhouse in March and planted out in June many seedlings will give small flower spikes in August and full-sized spikes the following June or July.

Cuttings can be taken of firm young shoots in March – April for rooting in a frame and planting out of doors in June or July. Old plants can also be divided in spring, but this is not so satisfactory.

There are two main types of delphinium, the Large-flowered or Elatum, 4 to 6 ft. high, with long spikes of bloom, and the Belladonna, about 3 ft. high, with smaller spikes or sprays of bloom. There are many varieties of the elatum type, single flowered, semi-double and fully double in colours from white, pale blue and lilac pink to bright blue and deep purple.

There are fewer belladonna varieties though the colour range is similar. Good seed strains are available of elatum delphiniums only.

A charming display of large-flowered delphiniums and anthemis. Delphiniums thrive in an open, sunny position and rather rich but well-drained soils. They are not usually very long lived

Day and Torch Lilies

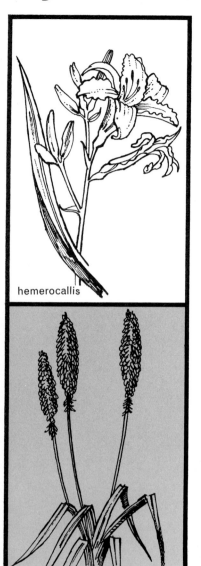

hemerocallis

kniphofia

The day lilies or hemerocallis are so called because each of their lily-like flowers only lasts for one day, though a succession of buds ensures a display for weeks. They make big clumps of narrow leaves and carry their flowers in July and August on stout, branched stems, 2 to 3 ft. high.

Day lilies will grow practically anywhere, though for the best results they should be planted in well-cultivated soil and be divided every second or third year. There are many varieties in a colour range from lemon yellow to deep orange and mahogany crimson.

Torch lilies or kniphofia are also known as red-hot pokers, both popular names referring to the close heads of typically scarlet flowers surmounting a stout stem. There are, however, many varieties differing in colour, height and flowering time. Representative varieties are: Gold Else, golden yellow, 2 ft., July and August; Maid of Orleans, ivory, 3 ft., July to September; Royal Standard, scarlet and yellow, 3 ft., July and *Kniphofia uvaria grandiflora,* coral and yellow, 4 ft., August and September.

All like well-cultivated, well-drained but not dry soil, and an open, sunny position. Only lift and divide when overcrowded. The stiff, grassy leaves are evergreen and may be tied together over each plant in autumn as a protection against frost. Untie again in the spring.

Dicentra, Polygonatum

The dicentras are very graceful plants with ferny, light green leaves and pendant heart-shaped flowers. The largest is *Dicentra spectabilis* or Bleeding Heart, 2 ft. high with arching stems and rose and white flowers in April and May. These plants will grow in most places, but like a reasonably good, well-cultivated soil and an open, sunny position.

Dicentra formosa is 18 in. high and has smaller, more clustered flowers very freely produced from April to June. There are rose-coloured and white varieties. This and the still smaller *D. eximea*, 1 ft. high, also available in white and pink varieties, are very adaptable and will grow in most places in sun or shade. All these plants can be divided every three or four years.

Solomon's Seal, *Polygonatum multiflorum,* enjoys shady places. It has creeping roots which send up long, arching, leafy stems from which the tubular green and creamy-white flowers hang in May and June. It will grow in most soils, is an excellent plant for woodlands as well as for shady town gardens, and can be left undisturbed for years. When it spreads too far the outer portions of each colony can simply be dug out.

Dicentra spectabilis

Polygonatum multiflorum

The handsome flowers of Black Prince, a variety of the day lily or hemerocallis. These are easily cultivated plants which will grow in almost any soil and a sunny or partially shaded position

The graceful arching stems and ferny foliage give added charm to *Dicentra spectabilis.* The pendant, heart-shaped flowers give this plant its common name, Bleeding Heart

Geums, Potentillas

Both geums and potentillas are sun-loving plants and both flower for most of the summer. They enjoy well-drained soils, and though geums in particular are very short lived in cold and damp places, both plants are extremely easy to grow.

Geum borisii has single orange-red flowers on 1-ft. high stems, but most garden varieties are 2 ft. high and have ruffled, semi-double flowers. Fire Opal, orange, Lady Stratheden, yellow, Red Wings and Mrs Bradshaw, scarlet, are typical varieties. Some of these can be raised fairly true to colour from seed, but for complete accuracy in reproduction plants must be divided and it is wise to do this every two or three years.

Potentillas resemble geums in many respects, though in general they are rather less neat in habit. Gibson's Scarlet is a sprawling plant, 1 ft. high, with single scarlet flowers all summer. Monsieur Rouillard, crimson, William Rollinson, orange and yellow, and Yellow Queen, yellow, are a little taller, more erect in habit and have double flowers. Master Floris is a delightful front-row plant, 1 ft. high, smothered all summer in single primrose and brick-red flowers.

Potentillas require the same conditions of well-drained soil and open, sunny positions that suit geums and, like them, they are best divided every second or third year.

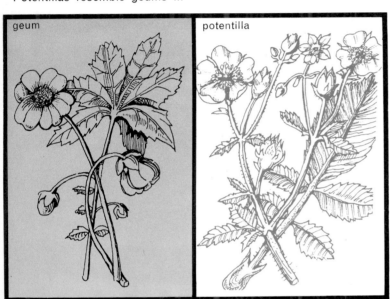

Golden Daisies

Three different kinds of herbaceous plant are included under this heading, the doronicum or leopard's-bane, coreopsis and anthemis.

Doronicums are the first to flower, opening their big yellow daisies in March and continuing into May. There are several kinds, two of the best being *Doronicum plantagineum* Harpur Crewe, 3 ft. high and excellent for cutting, and *Doronicum cordatum,* which is only 6 in. high and a good edging plant. Both will grow in almost any soil, in sun or partial shade, and should be divided every second or third year.

There are also several different kinds of coreopsis, all thriving in well-drained soils and sunny places. *Coreopsis grandiflora* has good-sized flowers on 3-ft. stems from June to August and makes an excellent cut flower. Mayfield Giant has even larger flowers and *auriculata* has a spot of crimson at the base of each petal. *Coreopsis verticillata* is very distinctive, being only 18 in. high and with narrow leaves and lots of little yellow flowers from June to August. It should be divided every three or four years.

Anthemis tinctoria is a bushy 2-ft. plant with ferny grey-green leaves; it flowers on long stems from July to August. Beauty of Grallagh is deep yellow and Mrs E. C. Buxton, light yellow. All like well-drained soils and sunny places and cannot be divided.

Flowering throughout the summer in a light, well-drained soil and sunny position, geums are gay but not as a rule long-lived herbaceous plants. This variety is Red Wings

Doronicum plantagineum Harpur Crewe is one of the showiest early-flowering perennials. The daisy-like flowers are excellent for cutting besides being highly decorative in the border

Erigerons, Geraniums

The erigerons look like low-growing Michaelmas daisies, but they start to flower in June and continue all summer. Most are very easy to grow in almost any soil and a fairly open place, but orange-flowered varieties such as B. Ladhams and *Erigeron aurantiacus* do not like wet soils and are liable to die in winter. Reliable varieties are: Charity, light pink, 2 ft.; Foerster's Liebling, cerise pink, 2 ft.; Merstham Glory, lavender blue, 2 ft. and Vanity, pink, 2½ ft. They should be divided every two or three years.

The herbaceous geraniums are quite hardy and not very like the bedding geraniums or pelargoniums to which they are related. There are numerous varieties, some with blue and some with magenta flowers. They are also easily grown in almost any soil in full sun or partial shade, and make good, bushy plants. They should be divided every two or three years.

Geranium armenum is 2 ft. tall with showy magenta flowers in June and July. *G. endressii* is 18 in. high, spreads rapidly and has pink flowers from June to September. Wargrave Pink is an improved variety.

Geranium grandiflorum has large blue flowers in June and July on a compact plant and is one of the best. Johnson's Blue has smaller light blue flowers from June to August on 18-in. stems. Russell Pritchard is crimson, 9 in. high and flowers from June to August.

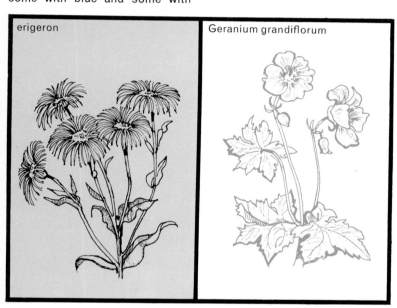

Grey Leaves, Everlastings

Grey and silver foliage is valuable in herbaceous beds and borders as a foil to brighter colours, and the wormwoods or artemisias are particularly good for the purpose. Nearly all tend to be a little woody, not quite shrubs yet not really true herbaceous plants either. Representative are: *Artemisia ludoviciana*, 2 ft.; *A. nutans*, 2 ft. and Silver Queen, 3 ft. Odd man out is *Artemisia lactiflora*, 4 ft. tall, which is green leaved and fully herbaceous, with creamy plumes of tiny flowers from July to September. It enjoys good, rich soil and can be grown in sun or shade, whereas the other varieties thrive in light, well-drained soils and like sunny places. All can be divided every two or three years.

The lavender cottons or santolinas are also half shrubby and do best in well-drained soils and sunny places. *Santolina incana* is 18 in. high and silver grey; variety *nana* is similar but under 1 ft. tall.

The herbaceous 'everlasting' flowers are mostly different kinds of anaphalis, and they, too, have grey leaves and are good border plants, liking sunny places and well-drained soils. Recommended kinds are: *Anaphalis margaritacea*, with silver flowers in August, 1½ ft.; *A. triplinervis*, creamy flowers in August, 1 ft. and *A. yedoensis*, creamy flowers in August, 2 ft.

Herbaceous geraniums have showy, saucer-shaped flowers which are freely produced in summer. This is *G. armenum*, one of the most strongly coloured kinds. There are others with blue or lavender flowers

Grey and silver foliage in the herbaceous border complements well the gay colours of other hardy plants. *Santolina incana* is an excellent example and it can be clipped each spring to keep a compact habit

Galega, Everlasting Pea

These are among the easiest plants to grow, and they are very useful for rough places, but since they grow very vigorously care must be taken to place them where there is no chance of their smothering weaker plants.

Goat's rue or galega makes a bushy plant 4 to 5 ft. high with little divided leaves and small clusters of vetch-like flowers very freely produced in June or July. There are several varieties, *hartlandii alba* with white flowers, Her Majesty, lilac blue and Lady Wilson, mauve pink. All will grow practically anywhere and should be divided every second or third year.

The Everlasting Pea, *Lathyrus latifolius*, resembles old-fashioned varieties of sweet pea and is a sprawling or climbing plant with stems 6 to 7 ft. long which die back in the autumn and grow again the following spring. There are both pink and white-flowered forms, blooming in July and August.

The Everlasting Pea will grow in practically any soil but likes warm, sunny places. It can be trained up walls, fences or tripods or allowed to sprawl over sunny banks. Division is not necessary and plants are easily raised from seed, though seedlings may vary in colour.

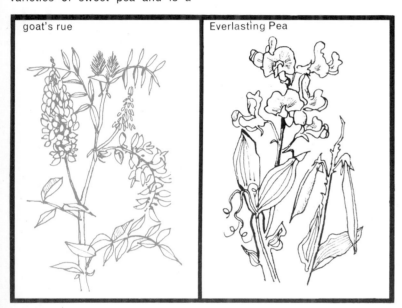
goat's rue   Everlasting Pea

Golden Rod, Yarrow

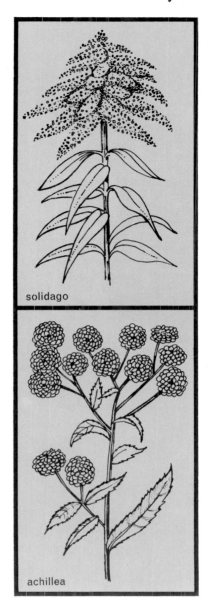
solidago

achillea

The golden rods (solidago) flower in summer and early autumn and all have dense sprays of very small yellow, daisy-type flowers. There are numerous varieties, differing in height and shade of yellow.

Representative varieties are: Lemore, primrose, 2 ft.; Goldenmosa, golden yellow, 3 ft. and Golden Wings, golden yellow, 4 ft. *Solidaster luteus* is similar but stiffer and is 2 to 3 ft., with light yellow flowers in August and September.

All will grow in almost any soil and place and are among the easiest of herbaceous plants to grow. They spread rather rapidly and should be lifted and divided every second year.

There are many yarrows (achillea); some dwarf plants for the rock garden, some larger plants for herbaceous borders and beds. These latter fall into three main groups as regards flower character, but all are equally easy to grow in almost any soil, though they prefer reasonably sunny, open places. They can be divided every third year.

Gold Plate has flat heads of yellow flowers on stiff 4-ft. stems in July and August. Coronation Gold is similar but smaller and flowers from June to September.

Cerise Queen has flat heads of carmine flowers on 2½-ft. stems from June to August.

The Pearl and Perry's White have sprays of little double white pompon flowers on 2½-ft. stems from June to August.

Lathyrus latifolius, the Everlasting Pea, is a delightful, climbing herbaceous plant which flowers in July and August. It can be allowed to scramble up wires, fences, tripods or over sunny banks

Achillea Coronation Gold is a very good plant for the herbaceous border, flowering throughout the summer in a well-drained, sunny place. It also makes an excellent cut flower

Gypsophila, Meadow Rue

When plants are massed together the effect can be heavy and wearying to the eye without the filmy texture provided by the gypsophilas and meadow rues.

The herbaceous *Gypsophila paniculata* is even lighter in effect than the annual gypsophila, with foaming masses of tiny white flowers from June to September in a 3-ft. dome over narrow, silvery-grey leaves and slender stems. It is most effective in its double-flowered forms, of which Bristol Fairy is typical. Flamingo repeats this effect in lilac pink and Rosy Veil, also pink, is more sprawling and only 1 ft. high. All varieties like sunny places and well-drained soils and are particularly happy on chalk and lime. The plants should be left completely undisturbed.

The meadow rues or thalictrums are equally slender and airy, with fern-like leaves and sprays of flowers. The loveliest is *Thalictrum dipterocarpum*, 5 ft. high, with very open sprays of little lavender and pale gold flowers in July and August. In Hewitt's Double each flower is a tiny, fully double pompon of lilac petals. *Thalictrum aquilegifolium* has closer, fluffy heads of purple flowers and is 3 ft. high and *T. glaucum,* 5 ft. high, is yellow.

The last two can be divided every three or four years, but *T. dipterocarpum* and Hewitt's Double should be left undisturbed. All like good, well-drained soils and sunny places.

Heleniums, Gaillardias

Both heleniums and gaillardias have daisy-type flowers but they produce a quite different effect when grown in the garden. Heleniums have quite stiff stems terminating in close-packed clusters of medium-sized flowers, so that when in bloom they make solid masses of colour in the borders. These flowers may be all yellow, yellow splashed with dull red, or entirely crimson or mahogany red. Heights, too, vary from 2 to 5 ft. and flowering time from July to September. All are easily grown in any reasonably well-drained soil and open position. They spread rapidly and should be divided every second or third year.

The flowers of gaillardia are much larger individually and are borne on more slender stems which are inclined to twist if not supported. Typically, the flowers are yellow with a broad central zone of red, but there are also all yellow varieties or all reddish-orange or reddish-bronze varieties. Heights vary from 2 to 3 ft. and the flowering period from June to September.

Gaillardias like well-drained soils and sunny places. They are apt to die in winter if the soil is wet and heavy and are seldom very long lived, though good strains can be raised quickly and cheaply from seed. The flowers are useful for cutting.

Thalictrum dipterocarpum, a lovely meadow rue that can be readily raised from seed. Its dainty flowers are borne on thin, wiry stems in large loose sprays and are as delightful cut as in the garden

The showy, daisy-like flowers of *Gaillardia* Wirral Flame. Unusual colours such as this are not reproduced entirely true from seed and so are propagated by division or root cuttings

Hostas, Rodgersias

Though hostas and rodgersias are grown largely for their handsome foliage, some also have very attractive flowers.

Hostas are also known as funkias and as plantain lilies. They make bold clumps of unusually broad, lance-shaped leaves, green in some varieties, blue-grey in others, variegated with silver or gold in others. The flowers, produced in July and August, are tubular and carried in spikes. Hostas will grow in either sun or shade, in almost any place, though for the best foliage effects they should be given good, well-cultivated soil.

There are numerous species of which the following are representative: *Hosta albomarginata* has leaves edged with white; *H. fortunei* has grey-blue leaves and lilac-blue flowers; *H. lancifolia* has rather narrow green leaves; *H. sieboldiana* has grey-green leaves and white flowers; *H. undulata variegata* has silver variegated leaves.

The rodgersias have rounded or deeply divided leaves, and the small flowers are produced in branched heads on stout stems. They like moist soils and shady places and look well near water. They should be left undisturbed and divided only if overcrowded.

Representative kinds are: *Rodgersia pinnata superba* with bronzy leaves and pink flowers in July and August; *R. tabularis*, with plate-like leaves and creamy-white flowers and *R. aesculifolia*, with divided leaves and white flowers.

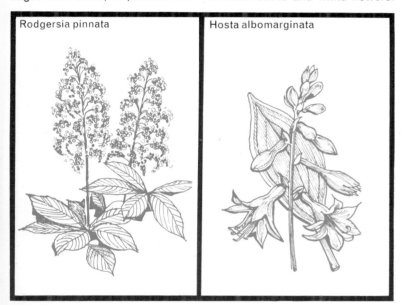
Rodgersia pinnata | Hosta albomarginata

Hostas are chiefly grown for their handsome leaves though a few species have a good display of flowers. They will thrive in damp, shady places and look especially attractive by water

Irises

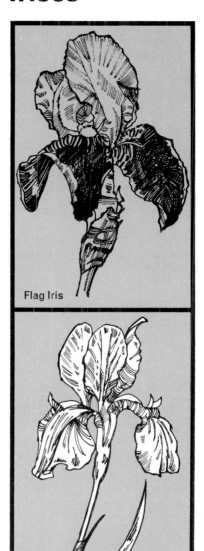
Flag Iris

Siberian Iris

Some irises have bulbous roots and some are plants for the waterside. However, the Bearded Iris (also known as German, June-flowering and Flag Iris) and the Siberian Iris are useful plants for herbaceous borders and beds.

There are a great many varieties of Bearded Iris, all flowering in May and June, with stout, branched flower stems each carrying several large flowers. Heights vary from 2½ to 4 ft. and the colour range is immense, including many shades and blends not commonly found in other plants.

These irises make rhizomes, i.e. fleshy stems lying flat on the ground from which the roots grow. Plants should be lifted every second or third year immediately after flowering and only a small portion of healthy young rhizome retained with each leaf cluster for replanting. Plant with the rhizome barely covered with soil and do not pile soil over it later. Bearded Irises thrive in good, well-cultivated and sunny places, and like chalky and limy soils.

The Siberian Iris *(Iris sibirica)* has taller, more slender stems, smaller more numerous blue, purple or white flowers in June and no rhizomes. It should be divided every second or third year.

The Algerian Iris *(Iris unguicularis)* has pale blue flowers on short stems in winter, likes a sunny place and well-drained soil and may be left undisturbed for many years.

There are a great many varieties of the Bearded Iris differing in height and colouring. This one is Snow Tracery which reaches a height of 3 ft. and flowers in late May and early June

Incarvillea, Penstemon

Incarvilleas are remarkable plants with trumpet-shaped flowers like those of the greenhouse gloxinia and an exotic appearance, but in fact they are quite hardy if planted in well-drained soil and an open, sunny place. They are slow starters, should not be disturbed unnecessarily and are best increased by seed, though the seedlings take a few years to reach flowering size.

Incarvillea delavayi is deep rose, 1½ ft. high and flowers in June. Bees' Pink resembles it, but has clear pink flowers, and *I. grandiflora,* only 1 ft. tall, has larger deep rose flowers. Bees' Pink must be increased by careful division in spring.

Penstemons also have trumpet-shaped flowers, but they are smaller, more numerous and carried in slender spikes continuously from July to October. There are many varieties differing in colour and flower size and not all are equally hardy, but it is very easy to root stem cuttings during the summer months and overwinter them in a frame to offset losses. Otherwise penstemons are easily grown in any reasonably good, well-cultivated soil, in sun or partial shade.

Representative varieties are: Evelyn, rose pink, 1½ ft.; Firebird, scarlet, 2½ ft. and Garnet, ruby red, 1½ ft. *Penstemon barbatus* has smaller, tubular, scarlet flowers in 4-ft. spikes. *P. heterophyllus* True Blue is 1 ft. high and has small, light blue flowers.

Liatris, Lobelia

Both liatris and lobelia are spike-flowered plants of medium size and striking colour, self-supporting and very useful for the middle positions in herbaceous beds and borders.

Liatris is sometimes known as blazing star, though the reason is not very obvious since the rather feathery purple flowers are crowded together in stout, stiff spikes with the peculiarity that they begin to open at the top and continue downwards. Gay feather, another popular name, seems more appropriate. Kobold is a particularly good variety with rosy-purple flowers in 2-ft. spikes in July and August.

These plants enjoy good, well-cultivated soils and sunny places, and can be left undisturbed for several years.

Some lobelias are annuals but several more are herbaceous plants, though not always fully hardy in all parts of the country. It is, however, very easy to lift them in autumn and transfer them to a frame for the winter, and in cold, exposed gardens this precaution should be taken with at least a few plants to maintain a reserve. Otherwise lobelias are easy to grow, enjoying good, well-cultivated soil and plenty of water in summer.

Lobelia cardinalis and *L. fulgens* both have slender 4-ft. spikes of brilliant scarlet flowers from July to October. *Lobelia vedrariensis* has deep purple flowers and a similar habit.

Incarvillea delavayi

penstemon

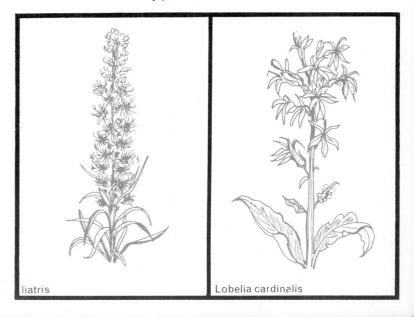

liatris

Lobelia cardinalis

The big gloxinia-like flowers of incarvillea have an exotic appearance and yet the plants are completely hardy when given good winter drainage and plenty of sunshine

The small flowers of liatris are crowded together on handsome, stiff, stout spikes and are peculiar in that they open from the top downwards. This kind is named *L. callilepis*

Loosestrife, Sidalcea

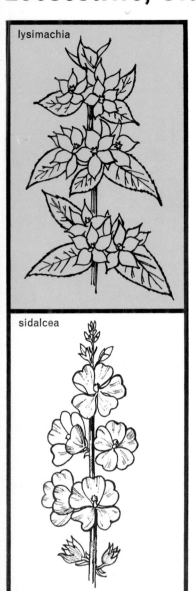

lysimachia

sidalcea

These are all spike-flowered plants, useful as a contrast to the flat or rounded heads of flowers that can easily dominate a herbaceous border.

The Yellow Loosestrife, *Lysimachia punctata*, has stiff 2- to 3-ft. spikes of bright yellow flowers in July and August and the Purple Loosestrife, *Lythrum salicaria*, has more slender 3- to 4-ft. spikes of rosy-carmine flowers at the same period. The Beacon is a deeper coloured variety and Robert a clear pink. Another kind of Purple Loosestrife, *Lythrum virgatum*, is shorter, 1½ to 2 ft. tall, and also has pink and carmine varieties.

All these will grow almost anywhere, and do not mind wet soils. They grow rapidly and should be divided every second or third year.

The herbaceous sidalceas have narrow, tapering 3- and 4-ft. spikes of pink, rose or mallow-purple flowers in August and September. There are numerous varieties differing in shade, representative examples being: Elsie Heugh, pale satin pink; Rev. Page Roberts, rose pink and Mrs Galloway, rose red.

All will grow almost anywhere, but prefer reasonably good, well-cultivated soil and open places. They should be divided every second or third year.

Lupins

lupin

The stout spikes of lupins are amongst the gayest flowers in the garden in June and if they are cut as soon as they fade, many plants will produce a few smaller spikes later in the season. It is, anyway, desirable to remove the faded flower spikes as they soon look untidy, also the heavy crops of seed they produce will weaken the plants, and if the seed is left to be naturally dispersed, seedlings of inferior quality may soon dominate the garden.

Lupins like deep, well-drained soils, but they do not thrive on chalky or limy soil on which their leaves turn yellow. Nor do they like much manure in the soil, though an annual dressing of a good compound fertiliser at about 3 oz. per sq. yd. in March will improve their quality.

Unlike many other herbaceous plants they cannot be divided and are increased either by cuttings or seeds. Cuttings of firm young shoots in spring provide the only means of raising plants exactly resembling the parents. Seedlings can be disappointing, but from commercially produced seed a good percentage of high quality plants will be obtained. Seed may be sown in a greenhouse or frame in February or March or outdoors in April or May. Early sown seedlings will often flower the same year, but they will be later than established plants.

Sidalcea is an excellent border plant, easily grown in any ordinary soil and reasonably open situation. The slender spikes of flowers are at their best in August. This variety is called Rev. Page Roberts

Lupins make a gay splash of colour in the herbaceous border in June and there is often a second flush of blooms later in the season. They are easily grown from seed or from cuttings of young shoots

Michaelmas Daisies

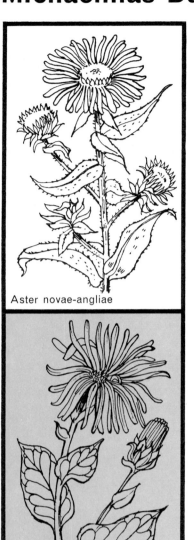

Aster novae-angliae

Aster amellus

Michaelmas daisies or perennial asters grow in any reasonably cultivated soil and in sun or partial shade. Because they grow so fast it is wise to lift, divide and replant at least every second year, though some gardeners do it annually.

The garden varieties may be divided into five main groups.

The Novi-belgii group is the most popular. Varieties have smooth shiny leaves, grow from 2 to 6 ft. high and have single, semi-double or double flowers in large sprays in September and October. Colour range is from white, pink and pale lavender to crimson and purple.

The Novae-angliae group is similar in general appearance but the leaves are slightly downy and not shiny. All varieties are tall (4 to 6 ft.) but colours only include the pink, rose and purple range.

The Dwarf or Dumosa group resembles the novi-belgii group except that no variety exceeds 2 ft. in height and most are 1 ft. or less. They are excellent for the front of a bed or border.

All varieties in the Amellus group have rather large, single flowers carried in broad, rather flat sprays. Most are 2 to 3 ft. high and flower in August and September. Colours are mauve, soft pink, blue and violet. Plant these in the spring; they do not transplant well in the autumn.

A miscellaneous group includes varieties with very small starry flowers freely produced in large sprays or clusters.

Peonies

Although one of the most sumptuous of flowers in late spring and early summer, peonies are rather slow to start and do not like interference. They should, therefore, be placed where they can remain undisturbed for years even when plants around them are being lifted. Peonies like rather rich, well-cultivated soil and rotted manure. Garden refuse can be worked in during preparation and applied each spring. These plants thrive best in a sunny, open place, but will grow in partial shade.

The common peony, *Paeonia officinalis*, flowering in May, has very full double blooms, crimson in the variety *rubra plena*, deep rose in *rosea plena* and white in *alba plena*. All are 2 ft. high.

The Chinese Peony, *Paeonia lactiflora*, flowers in June, is fragrant and has single, semi-double and fully double varieties. Representative of these are: Albert Crousse, double pink and crimson, 3 ft.; Bowl of Beauty, semi-double rosy-pink and lemon, 3 ft.; Duchesse de Nemours, double white, 3 ft.; Felix Crousse, double carmine red, 3½ ft.; *festiva maxima*, double white, 3 ft.; Lady Alexandra Duff, soft pink, 3 ft.; Sarah Bernhardt, double bright rose, 3 ft. and Solange, double soft salmon, 2½ ft.

Other fine peonies are Defender, single crimson, June, 3½ ft., Sunshine (also known as *P. peregrina* and *P. lobata*), single flame red, May, 3 ft. and *Paeonia mlokosewitschii*, single primrose, May, 2½ ft.

common peony

Chinese Peony

A variety of *Aster amellus*, an early flowering type of Michaelmas daisy with quite large single flowers during August and September. Plants are bushy and of medium height

The magnificent flowers of *Paeonia officinalis*. This single form is not as common as the fully double varieties which are great favourites with cottage gardeners

Phlox

These bear their honey-scented flowers in fine heads from July to September, and at that time are among the showiest plants in the garden. They will grow almost anywhere but enjoy good, well-cultivated soil into which decayed manure or garden refuse has been worked, and which is kept well watered in dry weather. They will grow well in full sun or partial shade.

Phlox are sometimes badly attacked by eelworms. These are almost microscopic pests which enter stems and leaves and feed within them. As a result, stems become swollen, leaves are contorted and plants make little or no growth. Healthy stocks of new plants can often be produced from infected plants by root cuttings, since the roots do not become infected by eelworms, but if these healthy plants are then planted on eelworm-infested land they will soon be attacked again.

Phlox spread fairly rapidly and should be divided every third or fourth year.

There are a great many varieties differing in height from 1 to 4 ft. and in colour from white, pink and lavender to crimson, purple and violet. Representative varieties are: Mia Ruys, white, 1 ft.; Caroline van den Berg, lavender, 3 ft.; Brigadier, bright orange-red, 3 ft.; William Kesselring, plum purple, 3 ft.; Border Gem, violet blue, 4 ft. and Windsor, carmine rose, 2½ ft.

Pinks, Campions

These are related plants, both thriving in open, sunny places and well-drained soils. Some kinds are not long lived but they are usually easily raised from seed or cuttings, and it is wise to maintain a stock of young plants to make good losses and to replace plants that have become straggly with age. Garden pinks, which are all varieties of the hybrids of *Dianthus plumarius,* have a special liking for limy or chalky soils.

The narrow, grey leaves of pinks are decorative in themselves and look well at the front of a bed or border. There are a great many varieties, those classed as Allwoodii flowering most of the summer and the ordinary garden pinks flowering mainly in June. Many are highly fragrant. Representative varieties are: Constance, bright pink; Doris, salmon pink; Mandy, cochineal pink; Inchmery, pale pink; Mrs Sinkins, white and White Ladies, white.

The Rose Campion, *Lychnis coronaria,* makes a well-branched plant 2 ft. high with grey leaves and magenta-crimson flowers from May to August. It is sometimes known as *Agrostemma coronaria,* and is readily raised from seed.

So is the Jerusalem Cross or Maltese Cross, *Lychnis chalcedonica,* a slightly taller less-branched plant, with heads of vivid scarlet flowers in July and August. Both will grow well in hot, dry places and in relatively poor sandy soils.

phlox

Dianthus allwoodii

Lychnis chalcedonica

Windsor, a typical variety of border phlox. Many other colours are available and varieties also differ in height and flowering time but all are sweetly scented

Lychnis chalcedonica, the Maltese or Jerusalem Cross, is a 3-ft. high herbaceous plant which is readily raised from seed. It prefers open, sunny positions and well-drained soils

Polygonums and Others

Polygonum campanulatum

Physostegia virginiana

Trandescantia virginiana

Polygonums, physostegias and tradescantias are useful for their ability to thrive in the more difficult places and to keep on flowering for a very long time.

The herbaceous polygonums all relish damp soils and most will grow in shady as well as open situations. *Polygonum bistorta superbum* and *P. amplexicaule* both have close little spikes of bloom, pink in the former, red in the latter, on slender 2- to 3-ft. stems from July to October. *P. campanulatum* creeps about on the ground and covers itself in filmy sprays of palest pink flowers, also from July to September.

Physostegia virginiana is called the Obedient Plant because its pink tubular flowers, carried in slender spikes, can be moved about as if hinged. The commonest form is rather tall and straggly, but a variety named Vivid is only 18 in. high, quite self-supporting and a good, deep rose colour. It flowers in September and October and is well matched by Summer Snow, a pure white, slightly taller variety. Both will grow almost anywhere.

Tradescantia virginiana, often called Spiderwort, is 18 in. tall and has clusters of three-petalled flowers from June to October, with rush-like leaves. There are several varieties such as J. C. Weguelin, light blue; Isis, dark blue; Osprey, white and blue and *rubra,* rosy-red. They will grow almost anywhere.

All these plants spread fairly rapidly and may be divided every two or three years.

Poppy, Evening Primrose

Some poppies are annuals or biennials but the Oriental Poppy, *Papaver orientale,* is a herbaceous perennial with large, immensely showy flowers in May and June. It likes deep, well-drained soil and a sunny place, and tends to rot in winter in heavy, wet, cold soil. Typically, the flowers are blood red with a black blotch at the base of each petal, but there are also scarlet-, pink- and white-flowered varieties, all about 3 ft. high. The Oriental Poppy is readily raised from seed sown outdoors in May and June but seedlings may vary in colour. Selected varieties can be increased by root cuttings.

The common evening primrose, *Oenothera biennis,* is a biennial but there are other perennial kinds, the best for herbaceous borders and beds being *Oenothera fruticosa* and *O. tetragona.* These produce rather fragile-looking yellow flowers on 18-in. stems from June to August. There are several varieties differing chiefly in the exact shade and size of the flowers; Fireworks has bronzy-red buds and deep yellow flowers and Yellow River has extra large yellow flowers. All grow readily in most soils, but prefer open sunny places. They should be divided every second or third year.

Oriental Poppy

evening primrose

The flowers of tradescantia, which are produced in succession from June to October, are unusual in that they only have three petals. Isis is one of several good varieties

The Oriental Poppy, *Papaver orientale,* is a herbaceous perennial easily raised from seed which it produces freely. Red, pink and white varieties are available as well as some with fringed petals

Sea Holly, Globe Thistle

The sea hollies or eryngiums have handsome leaves and sprays of distinctive teazle-like flowers, each surrounded by a stiff ruff of bracts often in distinctive metallic shades of blue. These plants are accustomed to sandy soils and throw long tap roots deep into the ground in search of water. In gardens they need good, well-drained soils and are apt to die in winter if at all waterlogged, but some kinds are more tolerant than others. One of the best and easiest is *Eryngium tripartitum*, 3 ft. high with wide sprays of small blue flowers in July and August. *E. oliverianum* has large metallic-blue flowers and Violetta is violet blue.

The globe thistles or echinopses are equally distinctive, with spheri-cal heads of blue or white flowers on stiff stems in July and August. They also push stout roots down into the soil and like well-drained, sunny places. Taplow Blue is a good variety, 3½ ft. high and light blue; *Echinops ritro* is 3 ft. high and steely blue; *E. humilis nivalis* is white flowered, 5 ft. tall and *E. sphaerocephalus* has grey-green leaves, silvery-grey flowers and is 6 ft. tall.

Neither sea hollies nor globe thistles can be divided easily and are best left undisturbed. They can be increased by seed and by root cuttings.

Shasta Daisy, Pyrethrum

Shasta Daisies, or Moon Daisies as they are often called, are big white daisies on 2- to 3-ft. stems. They are very useful for cutting in July and August, and make a fine foil to the brilliant colours of other garden flowers which are out then. They are all varieties of *Chrysanthemum maximum* and those with double flowers such as Esther Read and Wirral Supreme do slightly resemble some of the greenhouse chrysanthemums. There are a number of varieties, some single flowered, some semi-double, some fully double and a few with a slight flush of yellow.

All are quite hardy and easily grown in most places, though for the best results they should have well-cultivated soil and an open situation. They grow so rapidly that they should be divided every second year.

Pyrethrums resemble Shasta Daisies in flower shape and size, but differ in that they make clumps of ferny leaves, their main flowering season is May and June, and they have a colour range from white and pale pink to crimson. They are more difficult to grow as they need well-drained soil and a sunny situation, and may rot away in damp dark places in winter. They should be planted in spring or July and August, but should not be disturbed in autumn or winter. There are both single- and double-flowered varieties, all excellent for cutting.

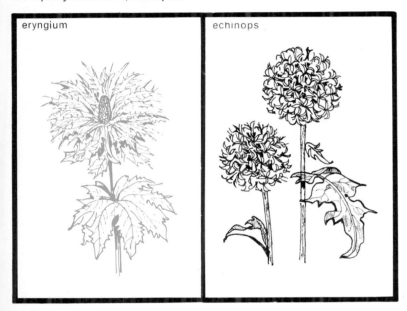

The distinctive flower heads of *Echinops ritro,* one of the globe thistles. They are carried on stiff stems in July and August. Self-sown seedlings often appear around these plants

Pyrethrums produce a first-class display in the garden and are excellent as cut flowers but they need very well-drained soil. This variety is Marjorie Robinson

Spiraea, Meadow Sweet

Spiraeas and meadow sweets enjoy cool, rather moist places, with peat or leafmould in the soil, growing well by streams and pools or in shady parts of the garden where they do not get scorched and dried out in summer. They can be divided every three or four years.

The herbaceous spiraeas are more correctly known as astilbes to distinguish them from the shrubby spiraeas. They make clumps of ferny leaves with elegant pyramidal plumes of white, pink or carmine flowers in June and July. Some of the numerous varieties, differing in colour and height, are: Ceres, rosy-lilac, 3 ft.; Fanal, ruby red, $2\frac{1}{2}$ ft.; Professor van der Wielen, white, $3\frac{1}{2}$ ft. and Red Sentinel, turkey red, $2\frac{1}{2}$ ft. *Astilbe simplicifolia* is only 9 in. high and has deep pink and pale pink varieties.

The meadow sweets or filipendulas are closely allied and enjoy similar conditions, but their plumes of flowers are more spreading or even flat topped. *Filipendula hexapetala plena* has little double, creamy-white flowers on 18-in. stems in June and July and is exceptional in growing well in quite hot, dry places. *Filipendula purpurea* has deep rose flowers on $2\frac{1}{2}$-ft. stems in July and August and *F. rubra* is similar but 4 ft. tall.

The Goat's Beard, *Aruncus sylvester*, grows 5 to 6 ft. high and produces large plumes of ivory flowers in June-July. It prefers moist soils but will grow almost anywhere.

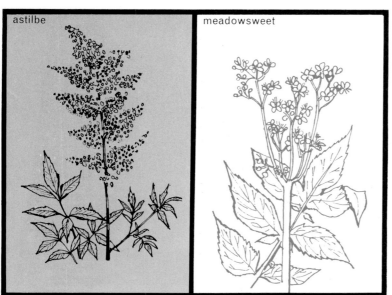

astilbe

meadowsweet

Spurges, Stonecrops

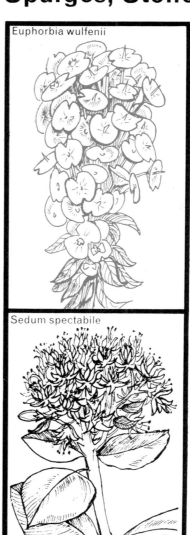

Euphorbia wulfenii

Sedum spectabile

There are many different spurges or euphorbias and in general they are not showy plants, but their foliage is often striking.

Euphorbia cyparissias has little narrow leaves, is 1 ft. tall and turns bright yellow in the autumn. It loves hot, rather dry places. So does *E. epithymoides* (also known as *E. polychroma*) which is 18 in. tall and has lemon-yellow flowers in April and May. *E. griffithii* is $2\frac{1}{2}$ ft. high and has reddish-orange flowers in May and June. *E. sikkimensis* is 3 ft. and produces a similar colour effect with its foliage. Both will grow in shady places. *E. wulfenii* is semi-shrubby, 3 ft. tall, with large heads of yellowish-green flowers in April and May. It is best left undisturbed, but most of the other varieties can be divided every three or four years.

The stonecrops or sedums also have good foliage. Many are rock plants, but the taller kinds are useful herbaceous plants for sunny places and well-drained soils. *Sedum spectabile* has fleshy grey-green leaves and flat heads of pink flowers on 18-in. stems in August and September. The hybrid Autumn Joy is similar in habit, but the flowers, in September and October, are reddish pink deepening to russet red. *Sedum maximum atropurpureum* has fleshy, beet-root-purple leaves and creamy flowers on 18-in. stems in August and September. All these plants can be divided every two or three years.

Meadow sweets are admirable plants for a cool, moist corner. The delicate plumes of flowers are accompanied by fern-like leaves. Above is *Filipendula purpurea*

Euphorbia griffithii was introduced into this country from the Himalayas. Its fiery flowers are produced mainly in May and June but side branches continue to flower throughout the summer

Sunflowers

helianthus

heliopsis

The true sunflowers are all helianthus, but here the name includes heliopsis which closely resemble sunflowers and have no popular name of their own. Both helianthus and heliopsis are vigorous, strong-stemmed, easily-grown plants thriving in almost all soils but preferring sunny places. All herbaceous perennial sunflowers have yellow flowers but they differ in height, flowering time, shape of bloom and shade of yellow.

Representative varieties of helianthus are: Capenoch Star, single deep yellow flowers on 4-ft. stems, August to October; Loddon Gold, full double yellow flowers on 5-ft. stems, July and August; Soleil d'Or, semi-double golden-yellow flowers on 4½-ft. stems, July to September and Monarch, very large single deep yellow flowers with black centres, on 7-ft. stems, September to November. The last is not very hardy and in cold or wet places some plants should be over-wintered in a frame.

Representative varieties of heliopsis are: Golden Plume, double golden-yellow flowers on 4-ft. stems, July and August and Incomparabilis, double orange-yellow flowers on 3-ft. stems, July and August.

Sunflowers should be divided every second year; the variety Monarch every year.

Verbascums, Veronicas

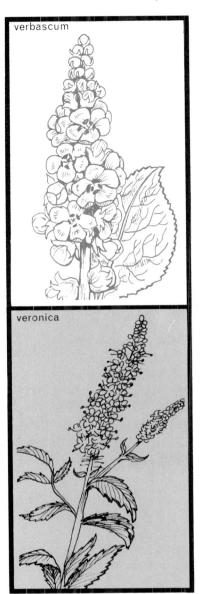

verbascum

veronica

Verbascums are also known as mulleins, and are valuable because of their long, slender spikes of flowers. Some are very tall and may require support in exposed gardens. Few are long lived, but many renew themselves by self-sown seedlings, particularly when grown in light, well-drained chalky or limy soils and warm, sunny places. They should be left undisturbed, and can be increased by root cuttings. Representative varieties are: Broussa, with leaves covered in white down and yellow flowers in a 6-ft. spike in June and July; Cotswold Beauty, biscuit and lilac, June – July, 4 ft.; Gainsborough, primrose, June – July, 4 ft.; Pink Domino, mauve-pink, June–July, 3 ft. and *Verbascum vernale*, yellow, July–September, 5 ft.

Veronicas also bear their flowers in spikes, but these are freely produced on bushy plants which are true perennials. Most kinds will grow almost anywhere, but prefer well-cultivated soil and an open situation. All can be divided every three or four years. Representative varieties are: Barcarolle, rose pink, 1½ ft., July to August; Minuet, grey-green leaves, pink, 1½ ft., June to August; Shirley Blue, clear blue, 1 ft., June to July; Wendy, silver grey leaves, deep blue, 1½ ft., July to August; *Veronica gentianoides*, light blue, 2 ft., April to May; *V. longifolia subsessilis*, deep blue, 1½ ft., July to August and *V. virginica alba,* white, 3½ ft., July to September.

Perennial sunflowers are excellent plants for the middle or back of the herbaceous border. This variety is Soleil d'Or and it flowers from July to September

Veronica gentianoides is one of the earliest of the herbaceous kinds and by mid-May it is fully out. The bright blue flowers are set off by shining green foliage

Practical Rose Growing

Roses are the most popular of all flowers. They captivate gardeners by the variety of their colours, shapes and perfumes, the ease with which they can be grown, the freedom with which they flower. A great industry has grown up in the production of rose bushes for gardens and also in the breeding of new roses both to meet the demand for novelty and also to replace old favourites that have become less satisfactory with age. The new roses, being raised from seed, start with a fresh lease of life whereas established varieties, which must be increased by cuttings or budding to keep them true to type, tend to become progressively debilitated by diseases which are passed on from one batch of plants to another. Nevertheless, it does not follow that the newest and most publicised roses are necessarily the best. Many old favourites show remarkable stamina and continue to delight successive generations of gardeners. There are even roses hundreds of years old that are still admired and planted and some of these have flower shapes and colours not commonly found in modern roses. However, few of these old-fashioned roses have the long flowering season of the new roses.

When planning a rose garden or border it is wise to bear in mind that some types, notably the wild roses (species), the ramblers and some of the shrub roses, flower only once each year, whereas other roses, often collectively known as bedding or display roses, flower for a much longer period, not as a rule continuously, but in two or three bursts or flushes from June to September. Each type has its place in the garden, but their uses are different and it is disappointing to plant, unwittingly, a non-repeat flowering rose in a place where one had expected a succession of blooms during most of the summer.

It is unwise to choose roses solely on the character of their flowers, however desirable these may seem. Some of the most magnificent blooms are produced sparingly on plants of deplorable habit. Flower shows are not, therefore, the best places in which to choose roses, nor are nursery gardens if all they have to show are the young plants being grown for sale. It is only in older plants that the true character of the plant can be seen; whether it is sufficiently well branched to cover a reasonable area of ground, whether it is of reasonable height and has abundant as well as attractive foliage. Many rose nurseries maintain display beds of older bushes, and these can also be seen in many public gardens and parks as well as in the gardens of friends and neighbours and those so frequently and generously opened to the public for charity. These are the best places in which to decide which varieties to buy and which to leave alone.

Types of Roses

For garden purposes, roses are divided into a number of different types, each with its own characteristics of growth and flower.

Hybrid Teas have large, shapely flowers produced singly or in small clusters from June to October, with peak-flowering periods in June-July and September.

Floribundas have smaller flowers in large clusters produced over the same period. They make more display in the garden, but the flowers are not individually so beautiful.

Hybrid Tea-type Floribunda is a rather clumsy name applied to varieties that are intermediate between hybrid teas and floribundas. They have medium-sized, shapely flowers, produced in fairly large clusters. They are becoming increasingly popular as the best all-purpose roses for garden and cutting. In America they are called Grandifloras, and, though that name is not officially recognised in Britain, it is sometimes used.

Dwarf Polyanthas are roses with small rosette flowers produced in large clusters from June to October. The first floribundas were produced from them.

Any of these types can be grown as standards, but usually nurserymen only offer the more vigorous kinds in this form.

For formal beds such as these, roses which flower freely from June to October are best. The floribunda or cluster-flowered roses have this quality and there are many varieties to choose from

The Site

climber

rambler

old-fashioned

Climbers have long, fairly stiff stems and medium to large flowers produced singly or in clusters. Some varieties flower from June to October with peaks in June-July and September, but some flower only once in June and/or July.

Climbing Sports resemble climbers in habit but are derived from bush varieties whose names they bear and which they resemble in every aspect except the greater length of their stems. Thus Climbing Étoile de Hollande has large, shapely, crimson flowers like those of Étoile de Hollande of which it is a 'sport'.

Ramblers are vigorous climbing or trailing roses with small flowers often of rosette type, carried in large clusters in July or August.

Shrub Roses are vigorous, bushy varieties, 5 ft. or more in height, usually with small- to medium-sized flowers produced in small or large clusters. They have various flowering times.

Old-fashioned Roses are varieties raised before the 20th century or with an appearance characteristic of these old varieties.

Miniatures are varieties which are 1 ft. or less in height with small flowers produced in clusters from June to October.

Species are wild roses, unaltered by hybridisation in the garden. They are extremely variable in appearance and habit, but nearly always have single flowers

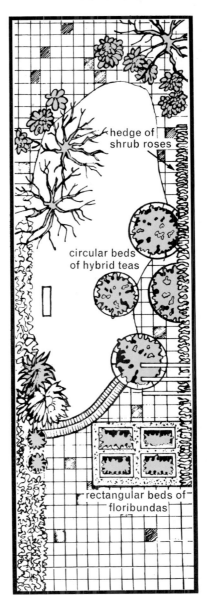

hedge of shrub roses

circular beds of hybrid teas

rectangular beds of floribundas

Roses thrive in most soils that are not very dry, very wet, very acid or very alkaline. They prefer good loamy soils, i.e. soils consisting of a mixture of clay, sand and decaying organic matter. In thin chalky soils, leaves are liable to become yellow through lack of green colouring matter; and in poorly drained soils some roots may die each winter, so weakening the plants and shortening their life.

The more open the situation the more suitable it is for roses. In enclosed places, where there is little movement of air, roses may suffer badly from mildew. Some varieties will grow in the shade, but most prefer sun for at least part of the day.

Roses are frequently given beds to themselves or even a section of the garden designed specially as a rose garden. This suits them well, but they can also be grouped with other plants. Floribunda roses look well with herbaceous perennials, and vigorous shrub roses may be associated with other shrubs.

Climbing and rambler roses require the support of walls, fences, pergolas, arches or poles. They do not climb of their own accord, but make long growths which will sprawl about if not tied in.

Rosa Nevada, one of the finest of all shrub roses. It is a vigorous variety, has attractive matt green foliage and produces a mass of flowers in early summer with usually a few more later in high summer

Baby Masquerade is a fine representative of the miniature type of rose suitable for edging or for massing in small beds such as these used to decorate a cobbled courtyard

The Plan

standard

half-standard

bush

trellis-work screen

rose pyramid

Everyone will have individual ideas on how a rose garden should be planned, but a few general suggestions may be borne in mind.

Since every variety of rose has its own distinctive habit it is better to give each variety a bed to itself rather than to make beds of mixed varieties. However standard roses look very effective planted among bush roses, so that they give a second tier of bloom. These standards may be of another variety to give contrasting colour.

Beds should be sufficiently large to make a good display but not so large that they cannot be looked after without walking on them. Beds from 3 to 6 ft. wide are most convenient and effective.

A pergola or screen covered with climbing roses can make a very pleasing background to rose beds. Rose covered arches, poles and pyramids (three or four poles lashed together at the top) can be used to break up the level of the rose garden.

Mown grass makes a delightful surround for rose beds, but in a small garden, paving will withstand the wear better.

Soil Preparation

Once planted, roses may occupy the same ground for many years, so the soil must be well prepared. Dig the site thoroughly and remove all perennial weeds, such as couch grass, bindweed, docks, thistles and nettles. Roses like a rich soil, so work in well-rotted manure or decayed garden refuse (compost) freely. One hundredweight (a good barrowload) of either of these to every 6 sq. yd. will not be too much. If possible, complete digging at least a month before planting. If neither manure nor compost is available, use substitutes such as peat, spent hops or shoddy at from 6 to 8 oz. per sq. yd. Hop manure, spent hops treated with fertiliser, is also suitable, but as brands differ, it must be used according to the manufacturers' instructions.

Leave ground rough after digging to 'weather', but immediately prior to planting give it a dusting of bonemeal, after which break down the surface with a fork and rake to leave a level, crumbly surface.

If water readily collects on the surface, improve drainage by laying pipe drains and connecting to a ditch or soakaway, or by working in coarse grit to improve the texture of the soil.

Chaplin's Pink Climber is a vigorous variety ideal for growing on a pergola. In a smaller garden it could be trained along a fence or screen or up a pillar

Brasilia, an attractive, large-flowered bicolor rose opening loosely with petals resistant to rain. It has abundant glossy foliage, which is crimson when young, and a vigorous upright habit

Planting Lifted Roses

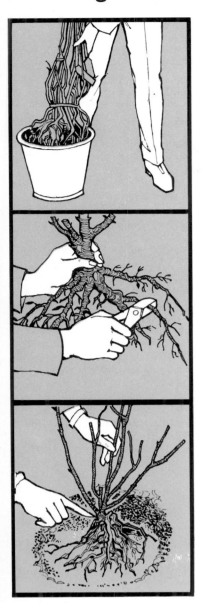

Plant roses lifted from the open ground at any time from mid-October until the end of March. If they arrive from the nursery when the ground is frozen or too wet for planting, open the bundle or bag sufficiently to expose the stems, but not the roots, place in a shed or garage and wrap sacking, straw or newspapers around the roots for additional protection. Plant at the first favourable opportunity.

If the roots appear dry, soak for a few minutes in a bucket of water. Cut off any damaged portions of root and the ends of long thin roots.

Plant bush roses from 18 to 24 in. apart according to the vigour of the variety. Plant standard roses 4 to 8 ft. apart, climbers and ramblers 6 to 10 ft. apart, and vigorous shrub roses at least 4 ft. apart.

Make each hole sufficiently large to accommodate all roots when naturally spread out and to allow the point of union between stems and roots to be $\frac{1}{2}$ to 1 in. below the surface. Break up the soil as it is returned, work it around the roots and make it thoroughly firm. Plant standards so that their uppermost roots are covered with 1 in. of soil and stake immediately.

The First Pruning

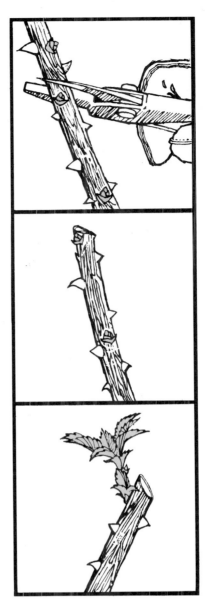

Roses that have been lifted for planting so that all or most of the soil has fallen from their roots must be pruned hard in the first year. Do this in March and cut each good stem down to within about 4 in. of soil level. Cut thin or damaged stems to about 1 in. or remove them altogether.

Prune with really sharp secateurs so as not to bruise the stems and make each cut just above a growth bud. These will appear as little swellings on the stems, each with a shallow semi-circular scar beneath it where a leaf stalk was attached.

It is from these buds that the new shoots will grow in April. Examine them towards the end of that month and if some stems have started to grow from the lower buds leaving the uppermost bud dormant, prune again to just above the uppermost of these shoots. If this is not done, the end of the stem, lacking new growth to draw sap through it, will die and the decay may continue down the stem.

This popular rose well deserves its name of Fragrant Cloud, for the large, well-formed flowers are particularly fragrant. They are borne on strong upright stems, with dark green, glossy foliage

Queen Elizabeth is a very vigorous rose which can become excessively tall unless carefully pruned. After planting it should be hard pruned like other roses that have suffered root disturbance

Container-grown Roses

Roses grown in containers, such as pots, polythene bags or tins, can be planted at any time of the year when the soil is in good condition, provided the plants are sufficiently established in the containers to be removed from them intact, with the soil around the roots.

Plant in holes sufficiently large to take the complete ball of soil as it comes from the container, with a little room to spare, so that some more fine soil can be worked in around it and also on top to a depth of about half an inch. Make this soil firm and if planting when the soil is fairly dry, water the plants in well.

Container-grown roses purchased in full growth in spring or summer need not be pruned until the following winter or spring, but container-grown roses planted in autumn or winter should be pruned the following March. It is not necessary to prune so severely as for lifted roses. Cut strong stems to 5 or 6 in.; thinner stems to about 2 in.

Pruning Bush Roses

After the first year, pruning of all bush roses can be done at any time between November and March inclusive. First remove any very old, weak, diseased or damaged stems. Old stems can be distinguished by their darker and rougher bark. Disease may show as purple or black spots or patches on the bark, or as cankers.

Prune the remaining healthy and vigorous stems according to variety and the purpose for which the roses are required. Naturally vigorous roses need lighter pruning than those that make less growth. Roses required for exhibition need harder pruning than those primarily required for garden display. Hybrid tea roses need more severe pruning than floribunda and shrub roses, and rose species.

For hard pruning shorten every strong stem to a length of about 4 in. and weak stems to 1 in. or remove them entirely. For medium pruning (applicable to most hybrid tea roses grown for garden display) prune strong stems to 6 in. and weaker ones to 2 or 3 in. For light pruning, shorten strong stems to about 10 to 12 in. and weaker ones to 4 to 6 in.

In all pruning, make each cut just above a growth bud and make clean cuts by using sharp secateurs.

Whisky Mac has fragrant, shapely deep yellow blooms, freely produced. Its dark green glossy foliage is tinted bronze when young. Like other popular varieties it can usually be purchased in containers for out-of-season planting

Frühlingsmorgen, a hybrid shrub rose, produces many delicate single blooms in May and June and a few later in the season. Growth is naturally vigorous and pruning should be relatively light

Pruning Climbers

Climbers and ramblers planted from the open ground, i.e. purchased with more or less bare roots and not in containers, must be hard pruned the first March after planting, just like bush varieties. Make an exception, however, for those varieties known as 'climbing sports'. These are always distinguished in catalogues by the word Climbing before their names, e.g. Climbing Étoile de Hollande, Climbing Ophelia etc. Only shorten strong stems of these by about one third, and weaker stems by half to two-thirds.

In subsequent years prune all climbing roses at any time after they have finished flowering. With rambler roses this may be as early as September, but with many modern perpetual flowering climbers it will be between November and March as for bush varieties.

First cut out all diseased or damaged stems and as much old wood as possible without sacrificing strong young stems. These can be retained at nearly full length or be shortened as necessary to fill the available space.

Some ramblers make so much young, cane-like growth from the base each summer that it is possible to cut out annually all the old stems that have just flowered and retain the young stems to flower the following year.

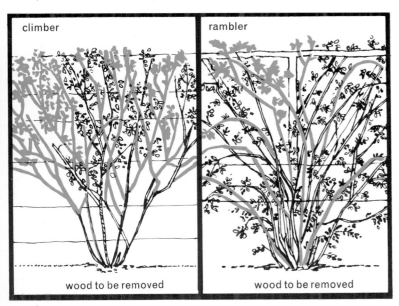

Pruning Standards

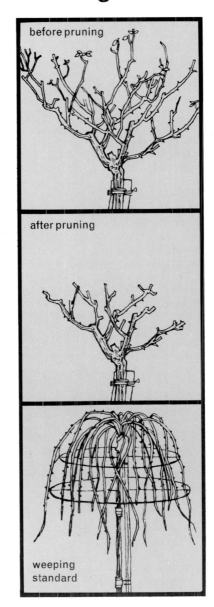

weeping standard

Standards are grown on a bare stem which may be anything from 2 to 4 ft. in height, with a head of branches on top so that the appearance is rather like that of a miniature tree. The main stem must be kept entirely free of growth at all times and if any shoots do appear they should be removed at once.

Prune the heads between November and March following the same general principles as those described for bush roses but pay greater attention to shaping the head. Make each cut immediately above a growth bud facing outwards from the centre of the head so that stems tend to grow outwards. Remove inward pointing stems and maintain a good balance of growth all round the head.

In April rub out any new shoots that are badly placed and likely to crowd the centre of the head or unbalance it.

Weeping standards are rambler roses budded on top of a 6 or 7 ft. stem from which stems cascade all round. Climbers can also be used, but these form stiffer growths and are not true weeping standards. Prune after flowering as for climbers and ramblers, but again pay particular attention to the balance of the head. A crinoline-like wire trainer can be attached to the top of the stake used to support the main stem and young growths can be tied down to it.

Flowering throughout the summer, the rambler rose New Dawn produces full, fragrant flowers on long stems. It can be pruned just as severely as is necessary to keep it within the available space

The floribunda rose Sarabande, grown here as a standard, is one of the most brilliant of vermilion varieties. Standards require careful pruning to keep the heads of branches well balanced all round

General Care

Keep rose beds free of weeds by hand weeding, hoeing or by using suitable weedkillers, such as simazine and/or paraquat.

For large individual flowers, thin out young shoots in spring, retaining the best two or three per stem. Later, when flower buds develop, thin these also to one per stem, retaining the central flower bud and removing the others (unless it is damaged when the best side bud should be retained). This thinning and disbudding is not necessary when roses are grown primarily for garden display and is never necessary for floribunda or climbing roses, which should be permitted to produce their flowers in clusters.

As flowers fade, cut them off with a short length of stem to encourage new growth and further flowering.

It is wise to spray roses as a matter of routine, whether or not pests and diseases are seen. Special combined insecticides and fungicides for use on roses can be purchased and should be used according to manufacturers' instructions about once a fortnight from May to September. Alternatively, use a mixture of a systemic insecticide, such as menazon, dimethoate or formothion, with a fungicide, such as thiram.

Feeding

mulching

feeding

applying iron sequestrol

It is the natural habit of roses to replace old growth with new, and much pruning is intended to assist this end. It can only be successful if the roses are growing strongly and to ensure this they must be well fed.

Each spring, spread well-rotted manure or garden compost over the surface of the bed at about 1 cwt. (a good barrowload) to 6 sq. yd. After pruning, scatter a compound fertiliser or a specially-blended rose fertiliser all over the surface of the rose beds, or for a couple of feet around each isolated rose bush, at the rate of 3 oz. per sq. yd. This fertiliser topdressing can be repeated at 2 oz. per sq. yd. at the end of May and again about six weeks later, but it should be well watered in if the weather is dry.

If leaves turn yellow in summer on chalk, limestone or other alkaline soils it is probable that the soil is deficient in iron and magnesium. To rectify this, apply iron sequestrols as recommended by the manufacturer and also sulphate of magnesium (epsom salts) at 1 oz. per sq. yd.

If neither manure or compost is available for spring application, use peat as a substitute and increase the spring fertiliser application to 4 oz. per sq. yd.

Escapade, a rather unusual colour in the floribunda range. The fragrant flowers are semi-double and are borne on well-spaced trusses. A vigorous grower with glossy foliage

Christian Dior, a large-flowered rose with full, shapely flowers borne on long stems. Like most of its kind it responds well to generous feeding coupled with fairly hard pruning

Suckers

Almost all commercially produced roses are budded on to a stock. The roots of the purchased plant are therefore of a different kind of rose from the stems, and if allowed to produce shoots these will bear flowers of a different and inferior kind (usually single, wild roses). Such shoots, growing direct from the roots or from the main stem below the head of branches, are referred to as 'suckers' and must be removed directly they are seen.

Suckers can be recognized by the fact that they come from below the main branches of the bush or standard and that they have a slightly different appearance. Usually they are thinner, with smaller leaves which are a different shade of green from the rest of the plant.

Thorns are also usually of a different character from those on the true garden rose stems. A comparison of the two shoots side by side usually reveals these differences quite plainly.

Cut off suckers at the place from which they grow. If they come straight from the roots, scrape away some soil with a trowel so that they can be cut off cleanly where they join the roots. Do not chop them off with a spade or a further crop of suckers will appear.

Any shoots arising part way up a standard rose stem are also certain to be sucker growths, and should be rubbed off immediately they appear.

Rose Hedges

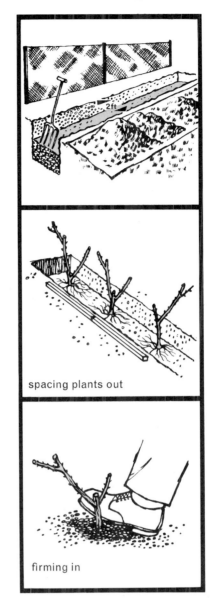

spacing plants out

firming in

Many vigorous varieties of roses make excellent ornamental hedges in good, well cultivated soil and open places, though few are suitable for close and regular clipping, which interferes with flowering. However the sweet-briar, *Rosa rubiginosa,* is grown mainly for the fragrance of its leaves and so can be pruned repeatedly. It makes a dense, thorny, impenetrable hedge to about 5 ft. Plant 1½ ft. apart and prune hard to encourage branching from ground level.

Any of the shrub roses may be planted 2 ft. apart to form informal hedges, which can be pruned to shape in winter or early spring and again in summer after each flush of flowers. According to their vigour they are suitable for hedges 4 to 6 ft. high and nearly as much through. Reliable varieties are Bonn, scarlet; Chinatown, yellow; Cornelia, pink; Heidelberg, red; Kassel, scarlet; Joseph's Coat, yellow and red; Nevada, creamy white; Uncle Walter, crimson.

Floribunda roses can be used in the same way. Plant vigorous varieties, such as Frensham, crimson; Queen Elizabeth, pink and Daily Sketch, pink and silver; 2 ft. apart. They will make good hedges of 4 to 6 ft. in height. Plant less vigorous varieties, such as Iceberg, white; Dorothy Wheatcroft, oriental red; Korona, scarlet; Masquerade, yellow and red and Shepherd's Delight, orange and yellow, 1½ ft. apart to make hedges 3 to 5 ft. in height.

The beautifully scented hybrid tea rose Wendy Cussons, a valuable asset to any garden. It produces many perfectly formed blooms, which are able to withstand rain

Extremely attractive rose hedges can be made by using vigorous varieties but careful pruning is required to preserve some regularity in shape without interfering with flowering

Roses on Walls

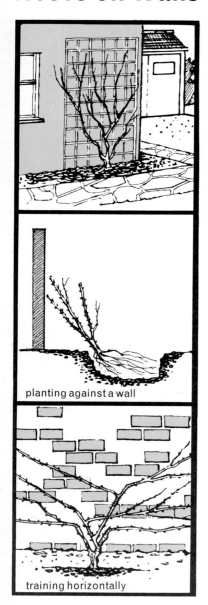

planting against a wall

training horizontally

Suitable roses can be found to be grown against walls whatever their aspect, even those facing north which get no direct sunshine. Since roses are not natural climbers some means of support must be provided. This may be wires trained between 'vine eyes' fixed in the masonry, trellis work or nylon-coated netting. Whichever method is chosen, make sure that it is securely fastened, for roses in full growth can be very heavy. Also, attach it 2 or 3 in. away from the wall so that it will be easy to tie the rose stems to it, for this will have to be done several times each summer to keep them tidy.

Plant at least a foot away from the wall, not close against it where the soil is sure to be dry. If plants do not make sufficient growth from low down to clothe the wall properly, cut one or two good stems back to within a foot of ground level at pruning time or train one or two shoots almost horizontally. This will check the rise of sap through them and encourage dormant buds to start into growth.

With climbing sports, retain the best of the older stems and shorten side shoots which have already flowered to about 1 in. to encourage fresh growth.

Underplanting

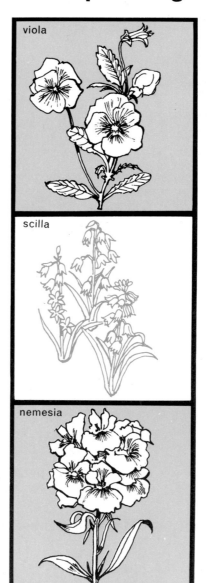

viola

scilla

nemesia

Though the less vigorous hybrid teas undoubtedly thrive best when planted in beds on their own, a great many modern roses, including most floribunda varieties, do not suffer from the competition of suitably chosen underplanting and this can be very useful to supplement the display made by the roses and continue it over a longer season.

Select plants not above 1 ft. in height, that are fairly shallow rooting and that will look attractive with the roses when they are in bloom. Violas and pansies are very suitable; the Lavender Cotton or santolina makes a good, silver-grey surround for scarlet and crimson roses. Most low-growing annuals and bedding plants may be used, particularly Sweet Alyssum, ageratum, lobelia, nemesia and verbena. Spring-flowering bulbs such as short tulips, hyacinths, crocuses, scillas and chionodoxas may be planted for a spring display.

Creeping rock plants, such as arabis, aubrieta and *Veronica prostrata,* may be used to carpet beds, and small herbaceous plants, such as *Hosta albo-marginata, Geranium* Johnson's Blue, variegated sage, nepeta (Catmint) and *Tiarella cordifolia* make excellent surround plants for rose beds.

Madame Gregoire Staechelin, a climbing rose, trained up the wall of a house. Plastic-coated netting attached to the wall provides support for the rose, and is soon hidden by the leaves and branches

A border of shrub roses, with Catmint, pinks and other perennials to prolong the flowering season. Vigorous roses accept this dual planting without ill effect provided they are well cared for

Pests

greenfly

leaf-rolling sawfly

leaf hopper damage

Greenfly may appear at any time from spring to autumn, and they will multiply very rapidly. The young shoots and leaves are attacked first and the green insects cluster around these, sucking sap from them. At the first sign of attack, spray with a greenfly insecticide and repeat as necessary.

Leaf hoppers are also known as frog flies. They live on the undersides of leaves, sucking sap from them, as a result of which the leaves become mottled with white. Empty white skin cases may be found sticking to the undersides of leaves. Spray as for greenfly.

Cuckoo spit is a mass of froth produced for protection by young froghoppers. It appears in spring with the cuckoo. When only a few, remove the insect inside the froth by hand, otherwise spray forcibly with malathion or lindane.

The grub of one kind of sawfly eats the surface of the leaves so that only a skeleton remains, while another causes the leaves to roll up. For either, spray at the first sign of attack with lindane.

Caterpillars of various kinds eat holes in rose leaves and can also be killed by spraying with lindane.

Thrips are small, narrow, active, yellowish or nearly black insects which attack leaves and flowers, particularly in hot weather. Leaves become mottled and flowers fail to open or are disfigured and petal edges turn brown. Spray as soon as damage is seen with lindane or malathion.

Diseases

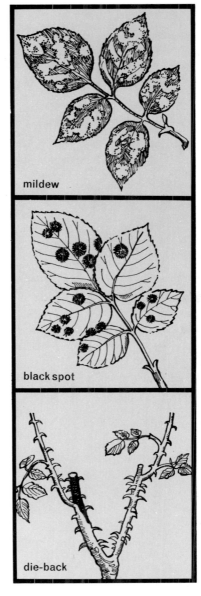

mildew

black spot

die-back

Mildew produces a powdery white coating on stems, leaves and flowers. Some rose varieties are more susceptible than others and the disease is particularly troublesome where there is little air movement. Spray with dinocap or thiram as a protection before the disease appears and repeat every few weeks.

Black spot produces roundish black spots on the leaves, which rapidly increase in size until the leaf falls prematurely. Some varieties are especially susceptible. Spray as a protection with captan or other recommended fungicide, starting in mid-April and continuing at fortnightly intervals until September.

Rust is identified by the small, orange-coloured pustules it produces on the lower surface of the rose leaves. Spray fortnightly as a preventive with zineb, thiram or colloidal copper, starting in June and continuing until September.

Stem canker attacks the stems, producing dark patches which eventually burst open to form large wounds. Cut out and burn all infected growth and spray frequently as for black spot.

Die-back attacks young stems in winter causing them to die back from the tip. Keep roses growing well by proper feeding and cultivation, spray in September with Bordeaux mixture or colloidal copper and cut out and burn diseased stems.

Vera Dalton is a particularly good pink cluster-flowered rose which seldom gives much trouble in the garden. However, it must be protected from greenflies, a universal rose enemy

This rose bush has been badly attacked by mildew, a disease which can be particularly troublesome where there is little movement of air. Effective fungicides are available to control it

Bulbs for Garden Display

Buying Bulbs

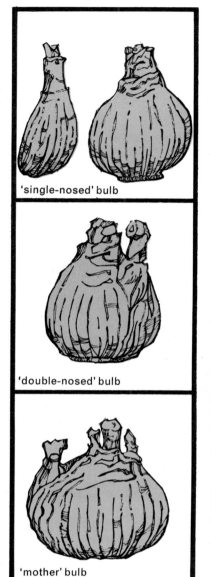

'single-nosed' bulb

'double-nosed' bulb

'mother' bulb

Bulbs, corms and tubers are all storage organs which enable plants to survive periods of drought or inactivity. Most can be kept dry for quite long periods in cool, airy frost-proof sheds or rooms and are usually sold in this condition by bulb merchants.

Many of the most commonly grown kinds, such as daffodils, tulips, crocuses and gladioli are usually carefully graded by size before sale. Some are sold according to the maximum circumference of the bulb, which is usually measured in centimeties. Tulip bulbs advertised as 11 to 12 cm. or gladiolus corms as 12 to 14 cm. would be a good size to buy.

Daffodils are graded according to the number of 'noses' or growing points they have. Thus a 'single-nosed' or 'round' has only one growing point and is unlikely to produce more than one flower, a 'double-nosed' bulb may produce two flowers and a 'mother bulb' will have more than two growing points. Large bulbs are worth more than small bulbs of the same variety, since in general they will produce better plants.

The two principal seasons for buying bulbs are in autumn for the hardy kinds and in spring for those that are more tender. There are also a few autumn-flowering bulbs that need to be planted in July or August.

Most plants that produce bulbs or other storage organs (collectively known as bulbs) become almost completely dormant at some time of the year. Foliage dies and the bulbs can then be dug up and stored for weeks or even months. It is not essential that this should be done, but it does provide a convenient method of marketing bulbs which can be sold 'dry' in shops. Those bulbs that flower in the spring or early summer mostly die down sometime between June and August and are then planted in the autumn. Bulbs that flower in late summer mostly die down in the autumn and are planted in the spring. Bulbs that flower in autumn die down in May or June and are planted in July or early August. Bulbs are of many different kinds and can be grown in various ways. Tulips and hyacinths are particularly useful for spring bedding displays and for cultivation in pots, window-boxes and other containers. Daffodils, crocuses and snowdrops are usually planted more informally and may be naturalised in grass, provided it is not mown until their leaves are beginning to ripen and turn yellow in May or June. Small bulbs such as grape hyacinths and scillas are often grown on rock gardens or used to make carpets of spring colour beneath taller plants.

A special tool can be obtained for planting bulbs in grass. It has a spade-like handle and a small circular blade which cuts out a neat core of turf just large enough to enable a bulb to be dropped in. Then the core is replaced, leaving little or no trace of the operation. Naturalised bulbs are usually permitted to grow undisturbed for years. They benefit from an annual early spring topdressing of a good compound fertiliser or bonemeal at 3 oz. to each square yard and this will also feed the grass.

Because spring-flowering bulbs die down in summer they can be used effectively with deciduous shrubs, which are bare of leaves when the bulbs are growing and flowering, or with herbaceous plants, most of which have hardly started to grow so early in the year. By such means a double display can be obtained from the same piece of ground without need for any extra work or replanting. Winter Aconite (eranthis), snowdrops, crocuses, scillas, chionodoxas, muscaris and daffodils are particularly recommended for this kind of two-tier planting since they do not have to be lifted annually but can be left undisturbed for years until they get overcrowded.

Bulbs that are dormant in summer are also sometimes useful in hot, dry situations since they are at rest when conditions are most unfavourable to growth. The thorough ripening the bulbs get under these conditions is often just what they need to make them flower freely.

Columbine, a primulinus gladiolus with upper petal curved over the flower like a little hood. Gladiolus corms are sold by size but it is not necessarily the largest that produce the best flowers

Increasing Bulbs and Corms

development of crocus corms

new corm forming

old corm

dividing dahlia tubers

increasing lilies from scales

Almost all bulbs can be increased by seed sown in spring in pots, frames or sheltered borders outdoors, but seedlings take several years to flower and often differ markedly from their parent plants in flower colour, form, etc. New varieties are raised from seed in this way.

Selected varieties are usually increased by division of the bulb clusters when these are lifted for cleaning and replanting.

Corms form new corms on top as the old corms wither away and also cormels (tiny corms) are formed around them. Both corms and cormels can be separated but cormels should be planted in a reserve bed to grow on as it is unlikely that they will flower for a year or more.

Tubers can be increased by careful division, which is best done when they start into growth and it can be seen just where the new shoots are. Each division must have both a portion of tuber and at least one shoot or growth bud. A sharp knife may be required to divide the tubers cleanly; dust wounds with quintozene.

Many lilies can be increased from mature bulb scales detached in autumn and kept in damp sand and peat in a frame or cool greenhouse. Some lilies, e.g. Tiger Lily, produce bulbils up the flowering stems. If collected when about to fall off in early autumn, and pressed gently into the surface of pans of seed compost, these root readily. Grow on as for cormels.

Allium, Ornithogalum

Allium ostrowskianum

Allium neapolitanum

Ornithogalum umbellatum

The onion and leek are both alliums and some of the ornamental species, grown for their handsome flower heads, have a similar odour when crushed. They are easily-grown plants in sunny places and reasonably good well-drained soils. Among the most decorative are *Allium ostrowskianum,* with globular heads of lilac-pink flowers; *A. neapolitanum* with looser heads of white flowers, *A. moly* with yellow flowers, *A. rosenbachianum* with very large heads of purplish flowers and *A. sphaerocephalum* with small heads of plum-purple flowers. All flower in summer.

Ornithogalum umbellatum has sprays of white flowers on foot-high stems in June, and is known as Star of Bethlehem. *O. thyrsoides* has 15-in. spikes of papery, white 'everlasting' flowers in May and June and is the South African Chincherinchee. The flowers are excellent for cutting and will last many months.

Plant all alliums and ornithogalums except the Chincherinchee in autumn 3 in. deep and 6 to 9 in. apart. Plant the Chincherinchee in April 3 in. deep and 4 in. apart in a specially warm and well-drained place or grow in pots, five or six bulbs in a 5-inch pot in a sunny, unheated greenhouse.

Poppy Anemones provide a riot of colour in the garden in spring or early summer and are also useful for flower arranging in the home. They can be increased from seed or by the small tubers they produce

Ornithogalum umbellatum, the Star of Bethlehem, is an attractive bulbous plant for June display. It can be allowed to grow for many years without disturbance and will often spread considerably

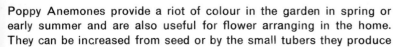

115

Amaryllis, Crinum

Crinum powellii

Some people call hippeastrum by the name of 'amaryllis', but here the name is used for the Belladonna or Jersey Lily, *Amaryllis belladonna*. It produces fine heads of trumpet-shaped pink and white flowers on stout 2-ft. stems in September. Plant the bulbs in autumn in well-drained soil and in warm, sunny, sheltered places, such as in a border near the foot of a south-facing wall. Only just cover the tip of the bulb, and in cold places, protect in winter with a covering of chopped straw or bracken. Leave undisturbed for years. Alternatively, plant one bulb in a 6- or 7-in. pot of John Innes No. 2 Potting Compost and grow in a frost-proof greenhouse in winter, standing the pots outdoors from June to September. Water moderately in winter, freely from March to June, and then keep the soil almost dry until flowering shoots appear in August.

Crinums have large, trumpet-shaped pink or white flowers on 3- to 4-ft. stems in summer, and are grown in the same way as the Belladonna Lily except that they should not be kept dry in summer as they are growing freely then, and not resting.

Anemone, Ranunculus

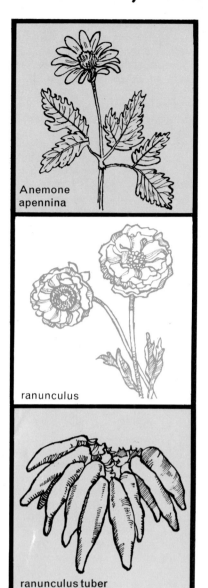

Anemone apennina

ranunculus

ranunculus tuber

Poppy Anemones produce showy flowers in shades of pink, red and blue in spring and early summer. They make first-rate cut flowers. St Brigid varieties have double flowers and De Caen varieties single flowers.

Plant from October to April for successive flowering in good, fairly rich, well-drained soil and a sheltered, sunny place. Soak tubers in water for a few hours before planting. Plant 2 in. deep and 4 in. apart and protect early plantings in winter with a scattering of peat or chopped straw. Lift tubers when foliage dies down in summer and store till planting time or leave undisturbed and protect in winter.

Other tuberous-rooted anemones are *A. blanda* with blue or pink flowers; *A. apennina* with blue flowers and *A. nemorosa* with white or pale blue flowers; all flower from March to May. They are suitable for cool, partially-shaded rock gardens, as edgings for beds, beneath thinly planted shrubs or for woodland. Plant 2 in. deep in rather leafy or peaty soil in September or October.

Giant-flowered ranunculus have showy double or semi-double flowers on foot-high stems from May to July.

Plant tubers claw-side downwards, 2 in. deep in specially sunny and sheltered places in rich, well-drained soil. Lift tubers when foliage dies down and store until planting time. They are not suitable for cold gardens.

Amaryllis belladonna, the Belladonna Lily, bears its magnificent, fragrant flowers on strong 2-ft.-high stems in late summer. If planted near a sunny wall, they will flower freely every year

Anemone blanda produces its pretty, star-like flowers early in the spring. It can take more sunshine than its ally, the British wood anemone (*A. nemorosa*) and is often planted in rock gardens

Chionodoxa, Muscari

Grape Hyacinth

Chionodoxa is known as Glory of the Snow, because its sprays of brilliant little blue and white flowers come so early in the spring, sometimes almost before the snow has gone. It is a fine plant for rock gardens, for edging borders or for planting under trees. Plant in autumn, 3 in. deep in reasonably good soil and leave undisturbed until overcrowded.

Muscari is known as Grape Hyacinth, because the little spikes of blue or white flowers look like tiny half-opened hyacinths or the newly-formed bunches of grapes. They spread rapidly and are excellent for rock gardens or beds or as edgings to paths. Plant in autumn, 3 in. deep in any reasonably good soil, and in a sunny or partially-shaded place. There are several different varieties, of which Heavenly Blue is one of the brightest and fastest growing. *Muscari tubergenianum* is known as the Oxford and Cambridge Grape Hyacinth because its spikes (8 in. high) are dark blue above and pale blue at the base. *M. botryoides album* is white-flowered. *M. comosum plumosum* is known as the Feather or Tassel Hyacinth because its blue flower sprays are loose and feathery. As they naturally flop about this plant looks best on a sunny ledge in the rock garden.

Crocus, Colchicum

Though crocus and colchicum are unrelated, their flowers have a superficial resemblance, and colchicums are often known as Autumn Crocuses. A better popular name is Meadow Saffron since there are true crocuses that flower in the autumn.

Both crocus and colchicum thrive in most soils, but the wild species of crocus prefer light, well-drained soils. All thrive in open, sunny places and colchicums will grow in partial shade.

Prepare ground by thorough digging. Work in some well-rotted manure or compost and scatter bonemeal at 3 oz. per sq. yd. over the surface.

Plant spring-flowering crocuses in September or October, autumn-flowering crocuses and colchicums in late July or August. Make holes for corms 2 to 3 in. deep; for colchicums 6 in. deep. Space crocus corms 3 to 4 in. apart; colchicums 6 to 8 in. apart.

Both crocus and colchicum can be naturalised in grass. Plant with a special bulb-planting tool, or remove turves, plant with a trowel or spade and replace the turves. Grass must not be cut until crocus and colchicum foliage has died down in May or June.

Leave plants undisturbed until overcrowded then lift as soon as foliage dies down. Divide the clusters of crocus corms or colchicum bulbs and replant at normal planting time. Feed each spring with bonemeal, 2 oz. per sq. yd.

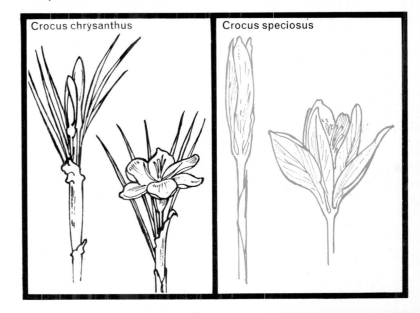

Crocus chrysanthus

Crocus speciosus

Muscari Heavenly Blue spreads rapidly to form a carpet of brightly coloured blooms which are attractive in bedding displays or in a rock garden. In the background is *Narcissus* Scarlet Elegance

Colchicum speciosum flowering in the autumn long before its broad leaves appear. The large bulbs are totally unlike the much smaller corms of crocus to which the flowers have a superficial resemblance

Cyclamen

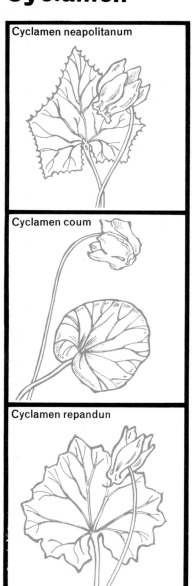

Cyclamen neapolitanum

Cyclamen coum

Cyclamen repandun

The fine greenhouse cyclamen are too tender to be grown out of doors, but there are also a number of small wild cyclamen that are quite hardy, and are delightful plants for cool, shady places in rock gardens, on banks or under trees. All like plenty of leafmould or peat and dislike disturbance. When the site is congenial they spread by self-sown seedlings.

All make flattish corms which are sold dry, or they may be purchased growing in containers. Start dry corms into growth in damp peat in a frame or greenhouse and plant out when they have a few leaves. Container-grown plants can be planted at any time, with the tops of the corms just covered with soil.

Cyclamen neapolitanum has indented, dark green leaves marbled with white. The pink flowers on 6-in. stems are produced from August to October. The variety *album* is white flowered.

Cyclamen orbiculatum has smaller, rounded, dark green leaves, sometimes with a silver zone or markings, and the flowers, on 3-in. stems, come from January to April. There are pink, crimson and white varieties, some of which may be sold as *C. coum, C. atkinsii* or *C. hiemale. C. repandum* has marbled, ivy-like leaves and pink, crimson or white flowers in March and April.

Daffodils

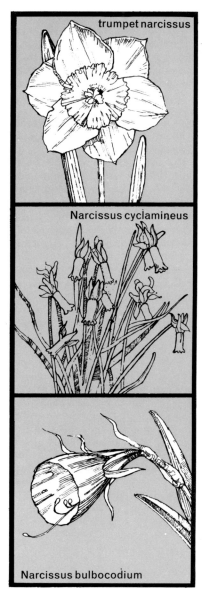

trumpet narcissus

Narcissus cyclamineus

Narcissus bulbocodium

Daffodils are botanically known as narcissus. In popular garden usage 'narcissus' is reserved for varieties with a cup or 'eye'-like centre to the flower, and 'daffodil' for those with a 'trumpet'-like centre.

For garden purposes daffodils are divided into 11 sections according to the character of the flower:

1. Trumpet Narcissi, e.g. Beersheba, Golden Harvest, King Alfred, Mount Hood, Queen of Bicolors, Rembrandt, Spellbinder, Unsurpassable.
2. Large-cupped Narcissi, e.g. Carbineer, Carlton, Eddy Canzony, Fleurimont, Fortune, John Evelyn, Rustom Pasha.
3. Small-cupped Narcissi, e.g. Chungking, Firetail, Matapan, Mystic, Verger.
4. Double-flowered Narcissi, e.g. Golden Ducat, Inglescombe, Mary Copeland, Van Sion, White Lion.
5. Triandrus Narcissi, e.g. Silver Chimes, Thalia.
6. Cyclamineus Narcissi, e.g. Beryl, Dove Wings, February Gold.
7. Jonquilla Narcissi, e.g. Lanarth, Trevithian, Waterperry.
8. Tazetta Narcissi, e.g. Cheerfulness (double), Cragford.
9. Poeticus Narcissi, e.g. Actaea, Pheasant's Eye (recurvus).
10. Species Narcissi (wild forms) e.g. *N. bulbocodium, N. pseudonarcissus* (English Wild Daffodil), *N. triandrus albus* (Angel's Tears).
11. Any other kind, e.g. Orchid-flowered, Butterfly-flowered.

Cool, shady corners of a rock garden can be filled to advantage with *Cyclamen repandum,* where pink, crimson or white flowers will develop amidst marbled ivy-like leaves

Verger is typical of the small-cupped type of narcissus. Not all varieties have a similar strong contrast between the colour of the cup or corona and the surrounding petals or perianth segments

Daffodils grow in most soils but prefer a rich, well-drained loam. They thrive in full sun or partial shade and many kinds can be naturalised in grass.

Prepare beds by thorough digging. Add rotted manure or garden compost and finish by scattering bonemeal over the surface at 3 oz. per sq. yd. Plant bulbs at least 6 in. apart in August, September or October (the earlier the better). Use a trowel and plant so that the bulbs rest firmly on the soil at the bottom of the hole, and are covered by their own depth of soil.

Daffodils can be lifted in late June when the leaves have died down, but it is not necessary to lift every year. Store lifted bulbs in shallow boxes in a cool, dry place until it is time to replant. Clusters of bulbs may be split into individual bulbs, but plant undersized bulbs in a reserve bed to gain size.

Daffodils also grow well in pots in unheated or moderately-heated greenhouses, frames, etc. Pot in August or September, shoulder to shoulder, in 6- or 7-in. pots or place two layers of bulbs staggered one above the other in an 8- or 9-in. pot. Plunge pots beneath 2 in. of sand, peat, or sifted ashes in a shady place and leave for at least ten weeks. Then take the pots into a greenhouse or under other protection and keep well watered. After flowering allow bulbs to complete their growth, then shake away the soil and store ready to plant out in the autumn. Do not force bulbs a second year.

Eranthis is a delightful little plant with yellow, buttercup-like flowers each surrounded by a green ruff. They appear in mid-winter when little else is in flower, and the plant is popularly known as Winter Aconite. It will grow in shade, and can be used to carpet the ground beneath shrubs or as an edging to a shady border. Plant in autumn 2 in. deep in good, rather moist soil and leave undisturbed for years to spread into a low carpet of growth which dies down completely in summer but reappears in January.

Erythronium is equally delightful, and because the commonest kind, *E. dens-canis,* has little mauve-pink nodding flowers in early spring it is known as Dog's Tooth Violet, though it is really more like a cyclamen. There are several other kinds; one named Pagoda has yellow flowers on foot-high stems.

Erythroniums will also grow in shade, but not such dense shade as Winter Aconite. A north-facing rock garden or bank suits them well.

Plant erythroniums in autumn 2 in. deep in soil with which plenty of peat or leafmould has been mixed, and leave undisturbed for years.

correctly-positioned bulbs

storing bulbs

bulbs planted in a double layer

Dog's Tooth Violet

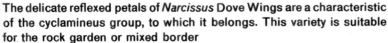

The delicate reflexed petals of *Narcissus* Dove Wings are a characteristic of the cyclamineus group, to which it belongs. This variety is suitable for the rock garden or mixed border

Eranthis tubergenii, a charming hybrid form of Winter Aconite. If left undisturbed these plants will in time make a carpet beneath trees or shrubs that are not too closely planted

Fritillaries

Crown Imperial

The Snake's-head Fritillary or *Fritillaria meleagris* is so called because its nodding, bell-shaped flowers carried on slender foot-high stems, are spotted and chequered rather like the skin of a snake. They are in shades of purple and white and are produced in April and May. This fritillary thrives in good, loamy soil and partially-shaded places and can be naturalised in grass that is not cut until about mid-summer. Plant in autumn 4 in. deep and 6 in. apart and leave undisturbed for many years.

The Crown Imperial is also a fritillary, named *Fritillaria imperialis,* but it is very different in appearance. It makes a stout stem 3 ft. high, terminating in a cluster of nodding yellow or reddish-orange bell-shaped flowers surmounted by a tuft of green leaves. It thrives in rich, loamy, but well-drained soils and open, sunny places and is not suitable for naturalising in grass. Plant the bulbs in autumn in holes 6 to 8 in. deep and 12 in. apart and leave undisturbed. Alternatively, the bulbs may be planted on their sides to prevent water collecting in the hollow on the top, and causing decay. This is a useful precaution on damp, heavy soils and in wet districts.

Galtonia, Camassia

Camassia cusickii

Camassia esculenta

Galtonia candicans is known as the Summer Hyacinth because its 4-ft. spikes of nodding ivory-white flowers do look rather like a greatly enlarged hyacinth and they are produced in late summer (August and September). Plant the bulbs in autumn or early spring 6 in. deep and at least 1 ft. apart in fairly rich soil and a sunny position. Plants may be left undisturbed until overcrowded, or may be lifted, separated into single bulbs, and replanted in autumn or spring.

Camassias produce their starry, blue or white flowers in long, narrow spikes 2 to 3 ft. high in early summer, and are good plants for a sunny border. They associate well with other early-flowering herbaceous perennials and are not fussy about soil so long as it is reasonably well-drained.

Plant the bulbs in autumn 3 in. deep and about 12 in. apart in an open or partially-shaded bed or border. Lift and divide in autumn when overcrowded.

Recommended kinds are *Camassia cusickii*, lavender, 2 ft.; *C. esculenta,* deep blue, 2 ft.; *C. leichtlinii*, blue, 3 ft.; *C. leichtlinii alba*, white, 3 ft.

The Snake's-head Fritillary, *Fritillaria meleagris* with its spotted petals reminiscent of a snake's skin, will naturalise well in shady places. White-flowered forms are also available

Galtonia candicans produces spikes of bell-like, fragrant flowers in August and September on 4-ft. high stems. The bulbs should be planted in rich soil and a sunny position

Hyacinths

Roman Hyacinth

Hyacinths are sold either as 'ordinary' or 'specially prepared' bulbs, the latter having been given special treatment to make them grow rapidly. Such bulbs are useful for forcing in greenhouses or indoors, but only ordinary bulbs should be planted outdoors.

Cynthella Hyacinths (also known as Roman Hyacinths) and Miniature Hyacinths have smaller, looser flower spikes and are most useful for indoor and greenhouse culture.

Prepare soil by thorough digging and working in some well-rotted manure or compost. Finish off with a scattering of bonemeal at 3 oz. per sq. yd. Improve drainage if soil is liable to lie wet in winter. Hyacinths succeed best in moderately rich, well-drained soils in sunny, sheltered places.

Plant in September or October with a trowel, making holes twice as deep as the bulbs, and spacing them 6 to 8 in. apart. Scatter peat, chopped straw or dead leaves over the surface of the bed in winter as a protection against frost.

Lift bulbs in June when the foliage has died down and store in shallow trays in a cool, dry place until re-planting time.

Hyacinths for greenhouse and indoor culture may be grown in drained pots in ordinary potting soil, or in undrained bowls in special bulb fibre.

Bulbous Irises

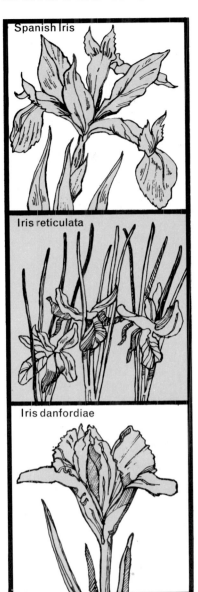

Spanish Iris

Iris reticulata

Iris danfordiae

There are numerous kinds of iris with bulbous roots, and all should be planted as dry bulbs in September or October. They like good, well-drained soil and an open, sunny position.

Prepare ground by thorough digging and work in a moderate quantity of well-rotted manure or garden compost. Scatter bonemeal over the surface at 3 oz. per sq. yd.

Plant with a trowel 3 in. deep and 4 to 6 in. apart. When overcrowded, lift in summer as soon as the foliage has died down, separate bulb clusters and store in a cool, dry place until normal planting time.

English, Dutch and Spanish Irises all produce fine flowers on long stems in May and June. There are white, blue, yellow, orange and bronze-purple varieties and all make excellent cut flowers.

Iris histrioides has blue flowers on 4-in. stems in January to February; *I. reticulata,* violet-purple flowers on 6-in. stems in February to March; *I. danfordiae,* yellow flowers on 4-in. stems in January to February. All are best planted in the rock garden or in sheltered borders as their flowers are easily damaged by frost and rain. *I. danfordiae* requires particularly rich, light, well-drained soil and is more difficult than the other two.

Mixed hyacinths used as bedding plants are well suited to the formality of this paved garden. After flowering the bulbs should be lifted and planted in a less conspicuous place until the leaves have died

The Spanish Iris flowers well in a sunny border in May and June. It is an excellent flower for cutting and arranging, as well as being very decorative in the garden

Lilies

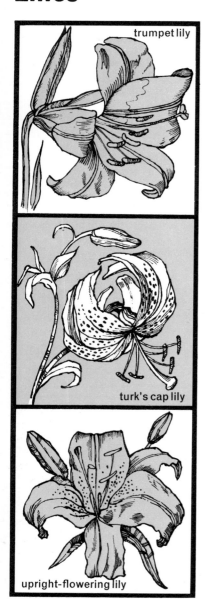

trumpet lily

turk's cap lily

upright-flowering lily

Lilies may be classified according to the shapes of their flowers and the way in which they are borne.

Trumpet Lilies have long funnel-shaped flowers usually produced in clusters, e.g. Black Dragon, white and purple, 6 ft.; Golden Clarion, yellow, 4 ft.; Limelight, lemon, 4 ft.; *Lilium longiflorum*, white, 3 ft.; L. candidum, white, 3 ft.; Olympic Hybrids, cream to pink, 4 ft.; Pink Perfection, pink, 4 ft.; *L. regale,* white and yellow, 4 ft.

Turk's Cap Lilies have pendant flowers, the petals of which are curved back. They are usually borne in large sprays, e.g. Bellingham Hybrids, yellow to red, 6 ft.; Bright Star, orange and white, 4 ft.; Fiesta Hybrids, yellow to maroon, 3 ft.; L. hansonii, yellow, 4 ft.; L. henryi, orange, 4 ft.; *L. martagon,* white to maroon, 4 ft.; *L. pardalinum,* orange and maroon, 4 ft.; *L. speciosum,* pink and white, 4 ft.; *L. tigrinum,* orange, 4 ft.; *L. davidii willmottiae,* orange-red, 4 ft.

Bowl-shaped lilies have large, widely-opened flowers which may be broadly funnel-shaped or nearly flat, e.g. *L. auratum,* white and gold, 5 ft.; Green Dragon, green and white, 3 ft.; Jamboree Strain, white and red, 5 ft.

Upright-flowering lilies have clusters of flowers facing upwards and outwards, e.g. Cinnabar, maroon, 2½ ft.; Mid-century Hybrids, lemon to crimson, 2 to 3 ft.; *L. hollandicum,* yellow to blood red, 12 to 18 in.

Lilies prefer deep, moderately rich, well-drained soil, and dappled shade. They associate well with rhododendrons and azaleas.

Prepare soil by thorough digging; work in some well-rotted manure or garden compost. Peat may also be used freely, especially on light sandy and heavy clay soils. Plant dry bulbs in September or October, (but *Lilium candidum* in August); growing bulbs can be lifted and transplanted carefully in March. Bulbs delivered after October should be potted and grown in a frame until spring when they can be planted out.

Plant with a trowel or spade making holes amply large enough to contain the bulbs and sufficiently deep to allow bulbs to be covered with 3 in. of soil (*Lilium candidum* and *L. testaceum* ½ in. only). Place a handful of sharp sand and another of peat under and around each bulb.

Do not hoe or fork around growing lilies. Remove weeds by hand or spread peat or leafmould over the surface to smother weeds. Stake tall varieties individually.

Do not disturb after flowering. Lilies establish themselves slowly and give their best display after several years. Lift only when overcrowded and then do so in September or October, replanting as quickly as possible.

Feed lilies each spring by spreading well-rotted manure or garden compost around them, or peat supplemented by hoof and horn meal at 2 oz. per sq. yd.

Lilium auratum is known as the Golden-rayed Lily of Japan. It reaches a height of 5 to 7 ft. and carries several of its large heavily scented flowers on each stem

Lilium Honeydew is a hybrid trumpet lily which can produce 15 or more of its funnel-shaped blooms on each 5-ft. stem. It is suitable for growing in pots or in a partially shaded place out of doors

The Montbretias

Curtonus paniculatus

Tritonia crocata

The common montbretia is a very familiar plant with branched spikes of orange-red flowers on stiff but slender 2-ft. stems in late summer. It will grow in a great variety of soils and situations including quite poor, sandy soils and hot, sunny places. Improved varieties with larger flowers in various colours from yellow to coppery-red are available, but they are not so hardy or so vigorous. Plant all montbretias 3 in. deep in spring, the choicer kinds in good, well-drained soil and a sunny position. In cold gardens, lift the choice kinds in late October and place in a frame for the winter, planting out again in the spring.

Crocosmia masonorum looks like an extra-fine montbretia with larger, redder flowers and more handsome leaves. It needs the same treatment as the common montbretia and will grow in any good, well-drained soil and sunny place.

Curtonus paniculatus was once known as Antholyza, from which it derived the popular name of Aunt Eliza. It is like a taller montbretia with smaller, almost scarlet flowers and needs the same treatment as the common montbretia.

Tritonia crocata is also allied to montbretia, but it is much smaller and more tender. The orange cup-shaped flowers are borne on 12-in. stems in summer. Plant the corms in spring 2 in. deep in sandy soil and a sunny, sheltered place or put six corms in a 5-in. pot and grow in a sunny greenhouse or frame.

Scillas, Bluebells

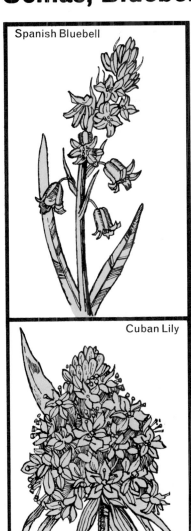

Spanish Bluebell

Cuban Lily

The scillas are quite a varied group, ranging from the little Siberian Squill, *Scilla siberica*, with 4-in. sprays of deep blue flowers in February and March, to the bluebells, the English Bluebell, *Scilla nonscripta*, too well-known to need description and the Spanish Bluebell, *Scilla hispanica*, with larger, stiffer flower spikes which may be blue, pink or white. Yet another fine species is *S. peruviana*, sometimes known as the Cuban Lily, with big heads of blue flowers on 9-in. stems in May and June.

Because the scillas and the bluebells are so varied they do not all need the same treatment, but all should be planted in autumn.

Plant the squills, including *S. siberica*, *S. bifolia*, and *S. tubergeniana* 3 in. deep in good, reasonably well-drained soil in sunny places. They are excellent for rock gardens, as edging to borders or as a carpet beneath taller plants.

Plant English and Spanish Bluebells 4 in. deep, in any reasonably good soil and a sunny or shady place, and leave undisturbed for years. These are excellent plants to naturalise in grass or to grow in wild gardens and woodlands.

Plant *Scilla peruviana* 4 in. deep in good, well-drained soil and a warm, sheltered, sunny place.

Crocosmia masonorum is a fine summer-flowering plant for warm, sunny places. It looks much like a montbretia but the flowers are larger and set closer together so that they make an even better display

The common bluebell is an excellent bulb for planting in shady places. It often grows wild in woodlands and spreads more rapidly than the large-flowered Spanish bluebell

Snowdrops, Snowflakes

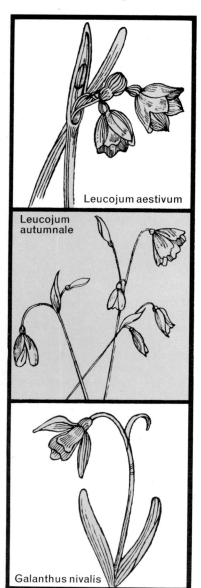

Leucojum aestivum

Leucojum autumnale

Galanthus nivalis

Snowdrops belong to the genus *Galanthus* and have small, white and green nodding flowers in winter and early spring. Snowflakes belong to the genus *Leucojum* and have more bell-shaped flowers. There are several kinds, e.g. the Spring Snowflake, *L. vernum,* with white and green flowers on 6-in. stems in early spring; the Summer Snowflake, *L. aestivum,* with similar but larger flowers on 18-in. stems in May; and the Autumn Snowflake, *L. autumnale,* with white and pink flowers on 6-in. stems in autumn.

The Common Snowdrop grows best in shade, snowflakes in shade or sun, but not in hot, dry places and the large-flowered mediterranean snowdrops prefer sunny places. All like good, rich, slightly moist soil.

Prepare by thorough digging and work in well-rotted manure or compost freely. Sprinkle bonemeal over the surface at 3 oz. per sq. yd.

Plant dry bulbs in September or October 4 in. deep. Alternatively lift, divide and replant growing plants in March (snowdrops directly they have finished flowering).

Leave plants undisturbed until overcrowded then lift in summer when leaves have died down or in March as stated above. Divide bulb clusters before replanting.

Bulbs may also be naturalised in grass but this cannot be mown until the bulb foliage has died down.

Tulips

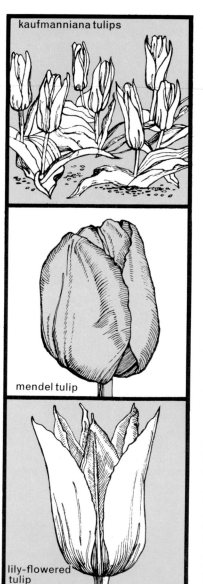

kaufmanniana tulips

mendel tulip

lily-flowered tulip

Tulips are classified according to their time of flowering and type of flower.

Kaufmanniana Tulips flower in March, and have widely-opened flowers on short stems. They are also called Water-lily Tulips, e.g. César Franck, Heart's Delight.

Greigii Hybrid Tulips flower in April and have cup-shaped flowers on short to medium stems and chocolate-striped leaves, e.g. Oriental Splendour, Red Riding Hood.

Early Single Tulips flower in April and have cup-shaped flowers on short to medium stems, e.g. Bellona, De Wet, Pink Beauty.

Early Double Tulips flower in April and have double flowers on short to medium stems, e.g. Maréchal Niel, Murillo, Orange Nassau.

Mendel and Triumph Tulips flower in late April and have single flowers on medium stems, e.g. Elmus, Garden Party, Krelage's Triumph, Sulphur Glory.

Darwin, Darwin Hybrid and Cottage Tulips flower in May and have single flowers on long stems, e.g. Beauty of Apeldoorn, Carrara, Golden Age, Gudoshnik, Holland's Glory, Mrs Moon, Ossi Oswalda, Pride of Haarlem, Queen of Bartigons, Queen of Night, The Bishop.

Lily-flowered Tulips flower in May and have single flowers with pointed reflexing petals on long stems, e.g. Mariëtte, Queen of Sheba, White Triumphator.

Peony-flowered Tulips flower in May and have double flowers on long stems, e.g. Mount Tacoma.

Leucojum vernum, the Spring Snowflake, looks rather like a very large snowdrop but the flowers produced in February and March are more bell shaped. It is suitable for a sunny or shady position

Darwin hybrid tulips providing a gay splash of colour in a small paved garden. Flowering during the month of May, they are especially effective when planted in groups of a colour

Bulb Hygiene

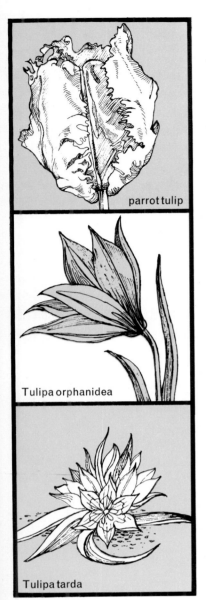

parrot tulip

Tulipa orphanidea

Tulipa tarda

Parrot Tulips flower in May and have very large single flowers, the petals of which are wrinkled and frilled, e.g. Blue Parrot, Fantasy.

Multi-flowered Tulips flower in May and have long branching stems carrying several flowers, e.g. Claudette, Georgette.

Viridiflora Tulips flower in May and have medium to long stems and single flowers, the petals of which are marked with green, e.g. Artist, Greenland.

Species Tulips are wild kinds, varying greatly in character, and suitable for rock gardens, e.g. *T. clusiana* (Lady Tulip), *T. orphanidea*, *T. praestans* Fusilier, *T. tarda*.

Tulips prefer a good, loamy soil and an open, sunny position. Prepare ground by thorough digging Work in plenty of well-rotted manure or garden compost and finish with bonemeal at 3 oz. per sq. yd.

Plant bulbs at least 4 in. apart in September, October or November with a trowel, in holes 4 in. deep and large enough to allow each bulb to sit firmly on the soil.

Lift tulips in June or July when leaves have died down and store in shallow trays in a cool, dry place until replanting time. If beds are required for summer flowers, lift tulips as soon as they have finished flowering and replant close together in any convenient place to complete growth before final lifting and storing.

Separate bulb clusters into individual bulbs before replanting, but plant undersized bulbs in a reserve bed.

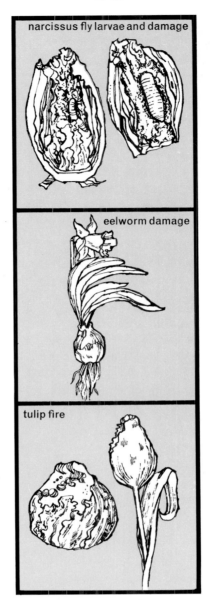

narcissus fly larvae and damage

eelworm damage

tulip fire

Apart from the ordinary pests and diseases that attack most plants, e.g. greenfly, caterpillars, slugs, mice, grey mould, etc., bulbs suffer from some troubles of their own. In particular the bulbs, corms or tubers are themselves liable to become infected with disease and should be carefully examined when lifted.

If any exhibit dark patches or spots, or appear scabby, or show any signs of decay or are wounded, dust them thoroughly with quintozene or dip in a thin paste of 4 per cent. calomel dust and water.

Daffodil bulbs may be hollowed out by maggots of the narcissus fly. Destroy such bulbs or soak in lindane solution prepared as for spraying. Sprinkle lindane dust around necks of growing plants during May and June to prevent the flies from laying their eggs.

Tulips may be damaged by a disease known as tulip fire, which causes leaves, flowers and stems to wither as if burned. If this disease is troublesome, spray with thiram every 10 to 14 days from March to May, except while plants are flowering.

Eelworms sometimes infest bulbs causing distortion of leaves and stems. Such plants should be burned and the site not used for bulbs for several years.

Tulipa tarda is a charming little species suitable for the rock garden. In April each stem will carry up to six of the distinctive star-shaped flowers. Also growing here is aubrieta

Darwin tulips, wallflowers and forget-me-nots in a delightfully informal garden. By underplanting the tulips with other plants the rather stark stems of the tulips are concealed

Making a Rock Garden

Most rock plants are relatively small and so a considerable variety can be grown in quite a limited space. They are immensely varied in character, some being tiny shrubs, some herbaceous plants, some bulbs, corms or tubers. Though the majority enjoy open sunny places and well-drained soils, suitable rock plants can be found for almost any situation in the garden, including those that are moist and shady. They are mostly wild plants introduced from many different lands and it is this ability to enjoy, in small compass, such a varied and interesting range of plants that accounts for much of the fascination of rock plants.

It is not essential to have a rock garden in order to grow rock plants. Many will grow just as well in ordinary beds, provided the soil is suitable and they are not overrun by larger plants. Dry walls and raised beds are also satisfactory substitutes for rock gardens and may fit more appropriately into the design of small gardens, even those of mainly formal design.

Yet another possibility is to grow rock plants in pots, pans or other containers. Old stone troughs and sinks are excellent for this purpose provided they have adequate drainage holes through which surplus water can escape. Trough or sink gardens can make beautiful and interesting ornaments for terrace and patio gardens and if each container is restricted to plants with similar requirements, exactly the right kind of soil can be supplied and the best aspect chosen. To carry this system of individual treatment a stage further, a rock plant grown in a pot or pan can have its special soil mixture, can be placed in a frame when normally in its mountain home it would be protected by a deep carpet of snow, and can be brought into a light, airy greenhouse when it is about to flower so that its blooms are not damaged by rain.

Some rock plants prefer acid soil and can be grown most successfully in special peat beds built in shallow terraces and retained by low walls of peat blocks. A cool, partially shaded position is best and it is usually necessary to mix some coarse sand with the peat filling to improve its porosity. Provided the peat beds are built above the surrounding level, lime-hating plants can be grown even in chalk or limestone districts.

Some gardeners value rock gardens more for the beauty of the stone than for the individual qualities of the plants growing in them. There is no doubt that well-laid stone can be very attractive, but the natural type of rock garden can be a trifle incongruous in a too-sophisticated setting, cheek by jowl with trim lawns and well-kept flower beds. It is a feature for the wilder parts of the garden and one that can often be combined effectively with an informal pool or stream.

Making a Rock Garden

Buy approximately 1 ton of rock for every 10 sq. yd. of rock garden. Pieces weighing from ½ to 1 cwt., each are best, though larger pieces are useful if help is available for placing them.

Unless the soil is naturally well drained, prepare the site by excavating to a depth of about 1 ft. and placing broken bricks or other hard rubble in the bottom as drainage. Return the soil, mixing in sand and coarse peat in the process. The finished bed may be flat, sloped or contoured according to personal taste and the size and nature of the garden planned.

Set each stone on its broadest face and let it well into the soil so that it appears firm and as if part of a larger underground formation exposed here and there to natural weathering and erosion. Place stones to form more or less level shelves or terraces, but of varying shape and size so that they do not look artificial, like a wall.

Slope the stones slightly backwards into the soil and follow the same tilt throughout the construction. A brief study of natural rock outcrops on hillsides will show what is required.

Fill in behind all stones with prepared soil mixture, and leave no empty or loose pockets in which water might collect or which would permit subsidence.

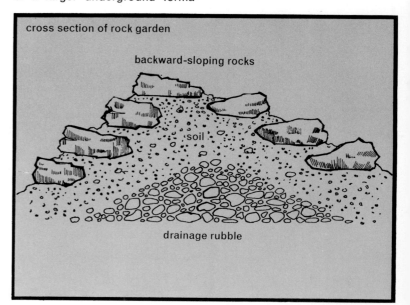

cross section of rock garden

backward-sloping rocks

soil

drainage rubble

Simple but effective rock garden construction with blocks of sandstone placed to retain shelves of relatively level soil on which the major planting is carried out

Building a Dry Wall

A dry wall is one built without mortar or cement. Such walls may be used to contain rock beds, hold up terraces and banks, or may be built as divisions or boundary walls. Any kind of stone may be used, rough hewn or faced, as well as special building blocks or bricks.

Start by excavating the foundation of the wall to a depth of at least 6 in. and ramming the bottom firmly. Set a layer of the largest available stones in this trench and spread soil over them. Place more stones on top, adding soil where necessary and ramming it in firmly between stones so that there are no loose places. Build terrace walls with a very slight backward slope or 'batter' for stability.

Continue to build the wall up in the same way taking care that vertical courses do not coincide. With terraces, ram soil between the wall and the bank behind as work proceeds, and set an occasional long stone back into the bank for greater security. High walls may require buttresses to be built out every 10 or 12 ft.

If boundary or division walls are to be used for plants, build them double with a core of at least 9 in. width of soil between in which plants can root.

A Raised Rock Bed

This is a method of growing rock plants which can be used without incongruity even close to a building. The bed can be of any size and shape but as a rule it is inconvenient to exceed a height of 3 ft. or a width of 6 ft. The bed is retained by dry stone walls built without mortar. Roughly dressed sandstone is an excellent material.

Begin by excavating soil and placing drainage rubble as for a rock garden. Fill up the hole with prepared soil almost to ground level and then place a course of stones around the bed, making them thoroughly firm.

Fill in with the soil mixture to just cover this first course and then set another, taking care that the vertical crevices between

stones in successive courses do not coincide.

Continue building up the bed in the same way until it is completed, finishing off by half burying a few large blocks of similar stone on top and scattering stone chippings over the surface.

Plant both in the bed itself and in the surrounding walls. It is helpful to place some of the plants in position while the walls are being built.

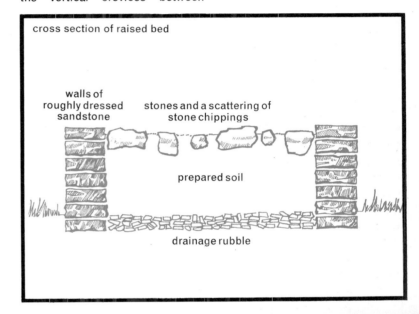

cross section of raised bed

walls of roughly dressed sandstone

stones and a scattering of stone chippings

prepared soil

drainage rubble

A well-made dry wall can be as good a place for rock plants as a conventional rock garden. Such a wall is most effective when it is used to support a bank of soil which provides ample root run for plants

Rock plants in a raised bed. This feature can often be used effectively in the more formal places as here, in the angle of a house wall, where a rock garden might appear out of place

Making a Scree

Some rock plants require a much more porous soil than that normally used for rock gardens. In nature they grow on the accumulations of rocky debris often found at the foot of steep mountains.

In gardens similar screes can be constructed either as a part of a rock garden, perhaps on the flatter part in front of the major outcrops, or as a separate feature.

Prepare a mixture for the scree bed with 4 parts of stone chippings $\frac{1}{4}$ to $\frac{3}{8}$ in. size, 2 parts loamy soil, 2 parts coarse sand and 1 part peat. Excavate the site as for a normal rock garden but place at least a 9-in. depth of rubble in the bottom for drainage. On this place 6 to 9 in. of the prepared mixture, and set a few large, flat-tish stones on the surface, sinking them in for stability and a natural appearance. Scatter more of the same stone chippings all over the surface and plant solely with non-rampant rock plants.

For some ericaceous plants and gentians two or three times as much peat and less soil will give even better results. Do not use limestone for these plants.

Plants in Paving

Many small tufted or creeping plants will grow in the crevices between paving slabs provided they can root uninterruptedly into the soil below. If the paving is set in concrete it will be necessary to leave holes in the concrete to let the roots through. Paving plants can be considered in two groups, those that will stand a certain amount of wear and those that should be placed where they will not be walked on.

Prostrate plants that can be walked on are *Acaena buchananii, A. microphylla, Achillea rupestris, A. tomentosa, Arenaria balearica, A. caespitosa, A. purpurascens; Cotula squalida; Erodium chamaedryoides roseum; Geranium sanguineum; Linaria aequitriloba; Mazus reptans;* *Potentilla nitida; Raoulia australis, R. glabra; Sedum dasyphyllum, S. lydium, S. spurium, Stachys corsica; Thymus serpyllum* and *Veronica rupestris.*

Tufted plants and others which should not be much walked on are *Antennaria dioica, Armeria maritima, Campanula cochlearifolia, C. garganica, Dianthus alpinus, Gypsophila repens, Phlox douglasii, P. subulata, Saxifraga muscoides, Sedum spathulifolium* and *Silene acaulis.*

cross section of scree bed

stones and a scattering of stone chippings

prepared soil

drainage rubble

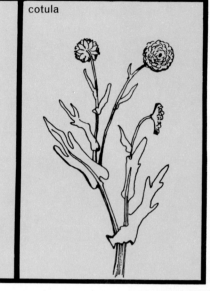

cotula

Antennaria dioica

A scree garden can be made on level or sloping ground, does not require much rock, and will provide congenial conditions for many lovely mountain plants

Many small tufted or creeping plants will grow well in the crevices between paving slabs provided they can root easily into good soil below. It may be wise to leave relatively plant-free areas for walking on

Planting Rock Plants

Most rock plants can be planted just like any other small plants, but when they are to be established in narrow crevices between large rocks or in a wall it is not easy to plant them with an ordinary trowel. Either use a very narrow-bladed trowel, such as a bulb-planting trowel, or a sharpened stick to scrape out the soil. Insert the roots carefully, pushing them well back with the fingers or a stick and then push soil in around them. Alternatively, build the plants into position while the rock garden or wall is being made, first setting one stone in place, then spreading a little soil over it, laying the plant roots on this, covering with more soil and finally setting the next stone to hold everything firmly in place.

If rock plants are purchased in pots or other containers, remove them carefully by inverting each pot and rapping its rim smartly on some firm surface, such as a rock or a tool handle. If possible plant without disturbing the root ball and see that this is just covered with soil.

Rock plants in pots and containers can be planted at any time of the year, even when in flower, but when lifted from the ground they are best planted in spring or immediately after flowering.

Care of Rock Plants

The greatest dangers with rock plants are that the more vigorous kinds may overrun the smaller and weaker ones or that fallen leaves may smother them. For these reasons examine them frequently, cut back or remove any plants that are spreading too far, and also collect all fallen leaves and place on the compost heap.

Remove weeds as they appear either by pulling them out or by cutting them off just below ground level. Do not use this latter method for vigorous perennial weeds such as dandelions and thistles as they will simply grow again from the severed root and make several crowns where formerly there was only one.

Some straggly rock plants, such as sun roses (helianthemum), arabis, aubrieta and yellow alyssum, are improved by annual trimming with scissors or secateurs. Do this as soon as the plants finish flowering.

Most rock plants like plenty of water while they are growing, but tend to get too much water in winter. At this season protect choice plants, especially those with downy or hairy leaves, with panes of glass supported on notched sticks or bent wires 6 to 8 in. above the plants. Do not close in the sides of these rain shelters as circulation of air is essential.

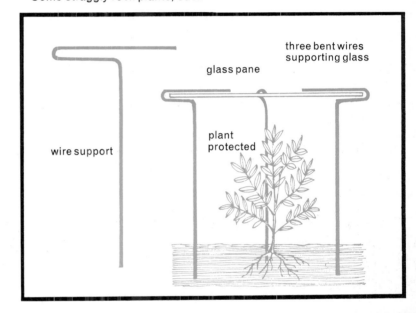

three bent wires
supporting glass

glass pane

wire support

plant
protected

A well-planted rock garden in which there is plenty of variety in colour and form. Care must be taken not to allow any vigorous plants to dominate the whole

An old stone trough filled with rock plants. One advantage of this method of cultivation is that the plants can be given more individual attention than is possible in a rock garden

Achillea, Armeria

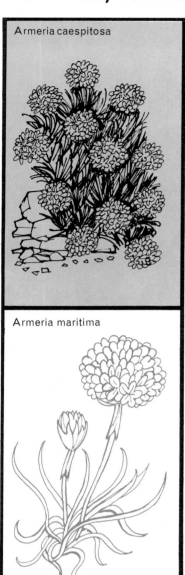

Armeria caespitosa

Armeria maritima

Achilleas are also known as yarrows. Some of them are herbaceous plants but there are also small varieties suitable for the rock garden and very easily grown in any reasonably open space and well-drained soil. Some of them spread rather rapidly, but if they grow too large they can be lifted, divided and replanted.

Achillea ageratifolia is 9 in. high and makes a mat of silvery leaves studded with white flowers; *A. clavenae* is 6 in. high, also with silvery leaves and white flowers; *A. tomentosa* has grey-green leaves and light yellow flowers and King Edward is very similar but cream in colour. All varieties flower in summer.

Armerias are called thrifts or sea pinks and will grow in the poorest soils and driest places. They make close mounds of short, spiky, dark green leaves and in May and June the flowers are crowded in little ball-like heads on 4-in. stems. In *Armeria maritima*, the Common Thrift, they are pink, but Vindictive has deep carmine flowers. There is also a white variety named *A. m. alba*. *Armeria caespitosa* is a smaller plant with pale pink flowers. Bevan's Variety is a deep rose form of it, but both are more difficult to grow than the Common Thrift, requiring a very gritty soil with a reasonable water supply in late spring and summer.

Aethionemas, Androsaces

Aethionemas are little bushy plants 6 to 12 in. high with narrow blue-grey leaves and heads of small pink flowers in May and June. They need plenty of light and first-class drainage, and they like gritty soils that contain some lime or chalk. They can be raised from seed but seedlings may vary slightly in quality, so the best varieties, such as Warley Rose with rose-pink flowers and a particularly compact habit, are increased by summer cuttings.

Aethionema grandiflorum, 12 in. high, and *A. pulchellum*, 9 in., are lighter coloured and sometimes shorter lived.

Androsaces make carpets or hummocks of densely downy leaves which catch the damp and can rot if not protected in winter, They, too, like sunny, open places and first-rate drainage. They should be divided and replanted every three or four years.

Androsace lanuginosa is the easiest to grow, a creeping plant with little pale pink, red-eyed flowers in clusters on 6-in. stems in June and July. *A. sarmentosa* makes a number of close rosettes of leaves and is more sensitive to damp. The deeper pink flowers on 4-in. stems come in May and June. *A. villosa* is still more rosetted in habit, with very downy leaves and white flowers on 3-in. stems in May and June. It requires protection in winter.

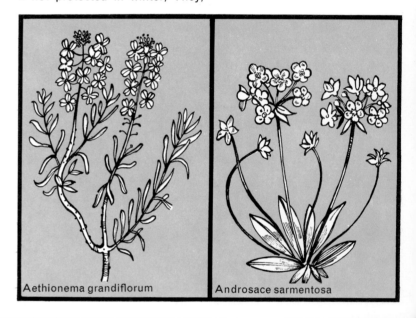

Aethionema grandiflorum

Androsace sarmentosa

Armeria maritima Vindictive, a strongly coloured variety of the Common Thrift. All the thrifts will give a good account of themselves in the poorest soils and the driest places

Displaying distinctive blue-grey leaves and rose-pink flowers in May and June, *Aethionema* Warley Rose is a welcome plant in any rock garden, especially as it is compact in growth

Antennaria and Others

All these are carpeting plants, useful in the rock garden as ground cover over small bulbs. *Antennaria dioica* has little grey, pointed leaves and pink or white flowers on 4-in. stems in April and May. It does not mind hot, dry places and is an excellent plant for walls.

Arenaria balearica makes a close carpet of tiny green leaves studded all over in June and July with tiny white flowers. Unlike many rock plants it grows best in cool, rather moist soil in a partially shaded place. It is just the plant with which to create the illusion of a little alpine meadow, and all manner of small bulbs such as crocuses and scillas can be planted under it to heighten the effect.

Arenaria caespitosa is more rounded and moss-like in growth, and there is a good golden-leaved variety named *aurea*.

Arenaria montana is more sprawling in growth, with quite large flowers freely produced in May and June. It will thrive in full sun or partial shade.

Erinus alpinus forms its carpet with tiny rosettes of leaves on which 4-in. flower stems stand in May and June. The common form has heather-purple flowers, but there are several varieties: Dr Hanelle, with carmine flowers; Mrs Charles Boyle, pink and *albus*, white. All will grow with very little soil and often establish themselves on walls.

Arenaria balearica

Aquilegias and Others

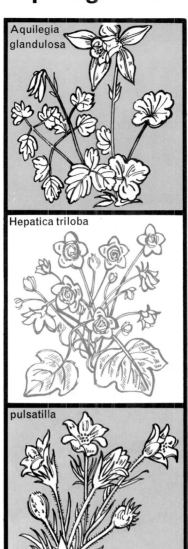

Aquilegia glandulosa

Hepatica triloba

pulsatilla

Although from a casual inspection it might seem improbable, aquilegias, hepaticas and pulsatillas are all related plants.

Many aquilegias or columbines are herbaceous plants, but *Aquilegia glandulosa* is a beautiful rock plant, easily grown in a cool place, shaded from the hottest sun in soil containing plenty of leafmould or peat. It has light blue and white flowers on 9-in. stems in June and July, and, though not usually long lived, produces seed freely which often germinates around the plants.

Hepaticas also enjoy cool places in partial shade and leafy or peaty soil. They make slowly spreading clumps of lobed leaves and bear their blue, anemone-like flowers on 3-in. stems in February and March. *Hepatica transsilvanica* is lavender blue; *H. ballardii* is a deeper blue and *H. triloba* a smaller plant with blue, pink and white varieties in single- and double-flowered forms.

Pulsatillas are known as Pasque Flowers because they usually bloom at Easter. The leaves are covered in silky-grey hairs and the mauve- to wine-coloured flowers on silky foot-high stems are followed by fluffy white seed heads. The plants like sunny, open places and plenty of lime or chalk. They are easily raised from seed, giving attractive variations in colour.

Erinus alpinus is a useful plant for wall decoration, growing well in very little soil. The purple, carmine or white flowers, on their slender stems, have a quiet charm and appear in May and June

Pulsatilla vulgaris is called the Pasque Flower because it blooms at Easter. Give this plant a sunny, open position and chalky soil and it will be entirely happy

Alyssum, Iberis

Alyssum saxatile

iberis

The alyssum to grow in rock gardens is not the annual Sweet Alyssum, but a perennial kind named *Alyssum saxatile*. It loves open places and is just the plant to grow on a sunny ledge or terrace wall. It has grey leaves and from April to June close sprays of bright yellow flowers are so freely produced that the popular name for this plant is Gold Dust. There is a lemon-yellow variety called *citrinum* and the pale yellow Dudley Neville is another attractive variety; *flore pleno* has double flowers and makes an even better display. The single-flowered varieties usually produce a lot of seed and self-sown seedlings may appear freely, but the double-flowered variety produces no seed and is increased by spring and summer cuttings.

There are annual kinds of iberis or candytuft but there are also several perennial kinds suitable for rock gardens and thriving under exactly the same conditions as *Alyssum saxatile*. All can be raised from seed or from summer cuttings.

Iberis sempervirens has dark green evergreen leaves and makes a sprawling bush 9 in. high, with abundant clusters of white flowers in May and June; Little Gem is a shorter variety and *Iberis saxatilis* is also no more than 6 in. high and produces its white flowers from February to June. *I. gibraltarica* is taller, more open, with lilac-pink flowers in May.

Arabis, Aubrieta

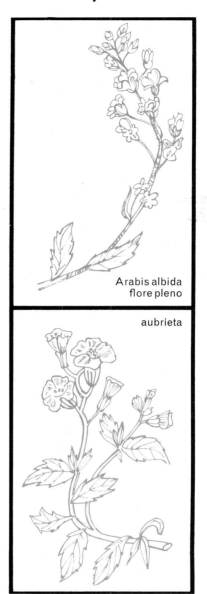

Arabis albida
flore pleno

aubrieta

Both these plants make carpets of growth and are seen at their best planted where they can hang down a wall or shower themselves over rocks. They both flower in April and May and make admirable companions because of the similarity of their growth and the contrast of their flower colours.

Arabis albida is pure white and it has a fine double-flowered variety named *flore pleno*. There are also single-flowered pink varieties, one named *rosea*, very pale pink, and another *coccinea*, a brighter rose pink.

Aubrietas come in all shades from lavender to crimson but there are no white varieties. Representative varieties are: Bressingham Pink, clear pink double flowers; Church Knowle, grey blue; Crimson Queen, deep carmine; Dr Mules, violet purple; Gloriosa, satin pink; Godstone, purple and Wanda, double, red.

Single-flowered arabis and aubrieta can easily be increased by seed and self-sown seedlings often appear in the garden, but seedlings are likely to differ in flower colour from their parents. Double-flowered varieties cannot be raised from seed and so they and selected varieties are increased by cuttings in the summer.

The look of established plants is improved by annual trimming with scissors or shears after flowering.

Alyssum saxatile has earned the name Gold Dust because of the brilliance of its small yellow flowers and the freedom with which they are produced. There are also double-flowered varieties which make an even greater display

Aubrietas, those gay flowers of April and May, can be easily raised from seed. Self-sown seedlings often appear in the garden, though these may well be different in colour from their parents

Campanulas

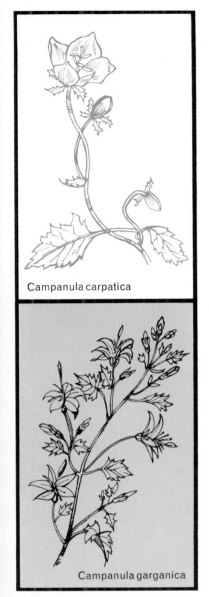

Campanula carpatica

Campanula garganica

The campanulas are known as bellflowers because most of them have bell-shaped flowers. Some kinds are large plants for herbaceous borders but there are also a great many dwarf kinds which make excellent rock plants. All thrive in open places and the more vigorous kinds will also put up with quite a lot of shade. Some spread rapidly and may need to be restricted. They can be divided in spring or after flowering.

Campanula carpatica is one of the tallest of the dwarf kinds, 9 in. high, and suitable for the front of a bed or border as well as for the rock garden. The fine blue or white flowers, appearing in July and August, are cup-shaped and face upwards. *C. turbinata* is similar, but shorter.

Campanula garganica spreads almost flat and has starry blue or white flowers in June and July. W. H. Paine is a good variety, blue with a white eye.

Campanula posharskyana is a rampant grower, spreading rapidly, with long slender stems, only about 6 in. high. The flowers are pale blue and appear in June and July.

Campanula portenschlagiana is also known as *C. muralis*. It is one of the best rock plants, compact in habit with abundant bell-shaped blue flowers from June to August.

Campanula pusilla, also good, has slender stems and from June to August dainty hare-bell flowers in shades of blue and also white.

Cerastium and Others

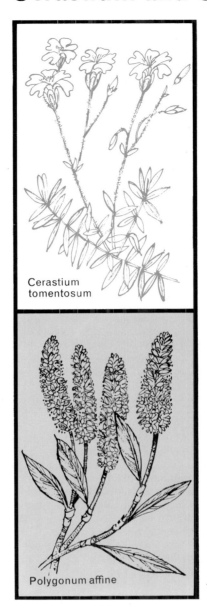

Cerastium
tomentosum

Polygonum affine

These plants are of rampant growth, useful for covering banks and other open sunny places quickly, but not to be planted near choice rock plants which they may overrun. They will grow practically anywhere, are not in the least fussy about soil and, when they get too big, can be lifted, divided and replanted. But the underground stems of cerastium tend to get under rocks and into the crevices of walls and can be very difficult to remove once this plant is introduced.

Cerastium tomentosum is known as Snow in Summer, because it has silvery-grey leaves and abundant white flowers in June. *C. biebersteinii* is very like it, but not quite so invasive.

Saponaria ocymoides will also make spreading mats of slender stems but it keeps these above ground, and so is not difficult to curb if it gets too big. The flowers, which are borne in succession from May to August, are rose pink in the common form, but carmine in the variety *splendens.*

The two best rock-garden polygonums also spread rapidly but are easily kept in control. *Polygonum affine* has close, stubby spikes 6 in. high of rose pink flowers (red in the variety Darjeeling Red) and *P. vacciniifolium* has more slender spikes of pale pink flowers. Both flower from August to October and have good autumn foliage colour.

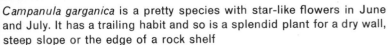

Campanula garganica is a pretty species with star-like flowers in June and July. It has a trailing habit and so is a splendid plant for a dry wall, steep slope or the edge of a rock shelf

Saponaria ocymoides growing in association with the yellow *Linum* Gemmell's Hybrid. Both plants are very free flowering during the summer months and prefer sunny positions and well-drained soil

Dianthus

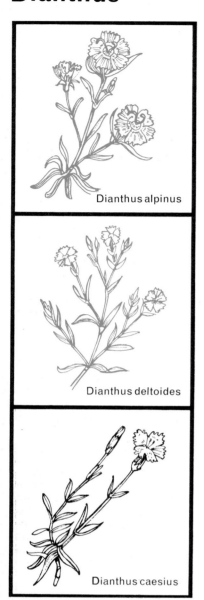

Dianthus alpinus

Dianthus deltoides

Dianthus caesius

Dianthus is the all-embracing name for pinks, carnations and Sweet Williams. Many of them are unsuitable for the rock garden, but that still leaves a goodly number of fine rock plants for sunny places. Most, but not all, enjoy lime or chalk in the soil, though they can get on without it.

Dianthus alpinus is one of the 'tinies', only 3 in. high, with deep rose flowers in May and June. It can easily be overrun by more vigorous plants, such as *Dianthus deltoides*, the Maiden Pink, a tumbling mass of thin stems and small leaves covered in July and August with carmine flowers. It is a fine plant for a ledge or as a cascade down a wall.

The Cheddar Pink, *Dianthus caesius*, looks just like a small garden pink with tufted grey-green leaves and good pink flowers on 6-in. stems in June.

Dianthus neglectus makes a neat, tufted plant with quite large deep rose flowers sitting close down on it from June to August. It dislikes lime or chalk and needs a very gritty, well-drained soil.

There are also a lot of hybrid pinks with garden names that are just the right size for the rock garden. La Bourbrille, pink and crimson; Little Jock, pink; Mars, crimson, are typical, but in poorly drained soils or shade some of these may prove short lived.

They can be readily increased by cuttings in summer, and the wild pink by seed.

Geraniums, Erodiums

These rock garden geraniums have only a slight connection with the geraniums (more correctly, pelargoniums) which are grown in greenhouses or bedded out in summer. They are perfectly hardy plants, low growing and perennial, and are very easy to grow in quite ordinary soil, in full sun or partial shade. When they spread too far they can be lifted and divided, preferably in spring. Their popular name is cranesbill, because their seed pods look like a crane's long beak.

Geranium sanguineum has deep magenta flowers from June to August and is 9 in. high. A variety named *lancastriense* is pink, only 6 in. tall and is a better plant. *G. subcaulescens* is more tufted, standing 9 in. high, with rosy-magenta flowers from June to August.

The erodiums are closely related and are called Heron's Bill because of the similar shape of their seed pods. They thrive in exactly the same conditions as geraniums. One of the best is *Erodium chamaedrioides roseum*, which makes carpets of soft green leaves studded with pink flowers from May to October. It is also sold as *E. reichardii roseum*.

Erodium chrysanthum has grey leaves and sulphur yellow flowers on 6-in. stems in June and July. *E. macradenum* has pale violet flowers on 4-in. stems, also in June and July.

Erodium chrysanthum

Dianthus La Bourbrille, an attractive pink which grows about 3 in. tall. Given a sunny position in good soil this is one of numerous hybrids which grow well in a rock garden

The hardy herbaceous geraniums include many well suited to rock garden cultivation, one of the finest being *Geranium sanguineum lancastriense*. This is quite prostrate and flowers in summer

Gentians

Gentiana sino-ornata

Gentiana septemfida

Gentiana acaulis

The gentians, or *Gentiana*, vary in their ease of cultivation; some are easy, and some more difficult. All like plenty of peat or leafmould in the soil, good winter drainage but plenty of moisture in summer. The autumn-flowering kinds, *G. sino-ornata*, *G. farreri*, *G. macaulayi* and others, all dislike lime or chalk in the soil and need shade from the sun around mid-day. These have brilliant blue trumpet flowers on carpets of narrow green leaves.

The Willow Gentian, *G. asclepiadea*, will grow in shade and ordinary soil. It bears its deep blue flowers on 18-in. stems from June to August. Other easily grown summer-flowering kinds are *G. septemfida* and *G. lagodechiana*, with clusters of deep blue flowers on 6- to 9-in. stems from July to September. They succeed best in open, sunny places.

So do the spring-flowering gentians, of which the most popular two are *G. verna*, with small, intensely blue flowers on 2-in. stems and *G. acaulis* with large, deep blue, stemless trumpets on low mounds of leaves. *G. verna* is often short lived, but can be fairly easily renewed from seed. *G. acaulis* likes rich soil and a sunny place, and should be fed annually with a sprinkling of bonemeal. It is sometimes shy to flower for no obvious reason.

Gypsophila and Others

Tunica saxifraga

Silene schafta

These plants are related, and gypsophila and tunica are similar in appearance with slender, sprawling stems and little flowers in loose, graceful sprays. There are large gypsophilas suitable for borders and cutting, but *Gypsophila repens* is perfectly suited to the rock garden or may be planted on a wall down which it will cascade. It is only a few inches high, but will spread for a foot or more. There are pink and white forms which flower from May to July. *G. fratensis* is very similar and *G. cerastioides* is smaller with white flowers flushed with pink.

Tunica saxifraga, which also has tiny pink or white flowers produced during July and August, is about 9 in. high and spreading. It has two very attractive varieties with double flowers, *alba plena*, white and Rosette, pink.

Silenes are more varied in habit but thrive in similar sunny places. *Silene alpestris* is tufted in habit and bears little white flowers on 4-in. stems in May and June. It has a double-flowered variety named *flore pleno* which is an even better rock garden plant.

Silene maritima flore pleno is a double-flowered variety of the Bladder Campion, with slender flopping stems and white flowers which bloom from May to July. *S. schafta* also makes a wide-spreading plant 9 in. high, smothered in deep rose flowers in August and September.

Large, stemless, intensely blue trumpets on low mounds of leaves are the distinctive features of *Gentiana acaulis*. It thrives in rather rich soil, and should be divided and replanted every three or four years

An ideal plant for clothing a wall is *Gypsophila repens*, which varies from white to pink. Though only a few inches in height, it will spread for a foot or more and is trailing in habit

Helianthemums

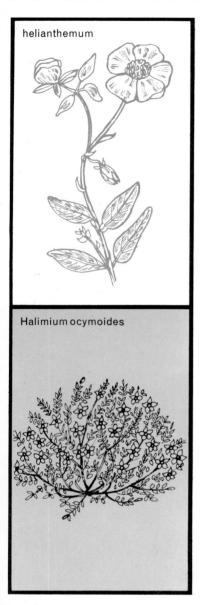

helianthemum

Halimium ocymoides

Helianthemums are known as sun roses, or rock roses, though the last name belongs to the larger cistus. They are sprawling, shrubby plants with narrow ever-green leaves and rather fragile flowers produced with great abundance in May and June. They like open, sunny places and well-drained soils and thrive particularly well on limy or chalky soils.

They can be readily raised from seed, but seedlings are likely to differ in flower colour and habit so selected varieties are best increased by summer cuttings. As plants age they tend to get straggly, a fault that can be corrected by trimming them annually with scissors or shears as soon as they have finished flowering.

Representative varieties are: Ben Afflick, orange; Ben Dearg, deep copper-orange; Ben Nevis, orange-yellow; *chamaecistus*, crimson; Cerise Queen, cerise double flowers; Fireball, red double flowers; Jubilee, yellow double flowers and *Rhodanthe carneum,* grey leaves with pink flowers. *Helianthemum lunulatum* is neater and more compact, 6 in. high, grey leaved with yellow flowers in June and September.

Halimium ocymoides is closely allied and sometimes called *Helianthemum algarvense*. It is a little shrub, 2 ft. high, with yellow, maroon-blotched flowers in June.

Hypericums, Potentillas

Hypericums are known as St. John's Worts. Some of them are quite large shrubs but there are also numerous kinds suitable for the rock garden, all yellow flowered and all very easily grown in any reasonably well-drained soil and open place.

Hypericum coris is one of the smallest, a neat, tufted plant 6 in. high, with narrow leaves like a heather and bright yellow flowers in June. *H. polyphyllum* is about the same height but more vigorous and spreading, and there is a pale yellow variety named *sulphureum*. *H. olympicum* is more upright in habit and 1 ft. high, and it also has a pale yellow variety named *citrinum*. *H. reptans* is completely prostate and flowers from July to September.

There are shrubby potentillas and herbaceous kinds as well as creeping plants for the rock garden. All are easily grown in well-drained soils and sunny places. *Potentilla alba* has white, strawberry-like flowers from June to October and spreads rather rapidly. *P. nitida* has silvery leaves and rose-pink flowers in June and July. It does not always flower well and seems to succeed best in rather poor, gritty soils. *P. tonguei* trails about; an outstandingly good plant, it has orange flowers from June to August.

All these kinds can be divided when they get too big.

Potentilla nitida

Helianthemums, the colourful and popular sun roses, are a delight in May and June when they carry their flowers with great freedom. These shrubby plants are easily raised from seed or from summer cuttings

The free-flowering *Hypericum polyphyllum* finds a congenial home on a dry stone wall. An open position and well-drained soil are the principal needs of this and other rock-garden hypericums

Phlox, Thyme

Phlox douglasii

Thymus serpyllum

In addition to the showy herbaceous phlox there are some very useful mat-forming kinds suitable for a rock garden, terrace, or walls. They are easily grown in moist soils and open places.

Phlox subulata is the most vigorous kind, making wide carpets of narrow leaves covered in flowers in May and June. Vivid and Camla are rose-pink, Betty is soft pink, G. F. Wilson light blue and Temiscaming, light crimson.

Phlox douglasii is more compact, but otherwise very similar. May Snow, also known as Snow Queen, is pure white; Effuse, also known as Boothman's Variety, is mauve and Rose Queen is soft rose.

Phlox divaricata laphamii is a taller plant, like a miniature herbaceous phlox, with lavender blue flowers on 1-ft. stems in May and June.

Thymes are grown both for the fragrance of their leaves and for their flowers. *Thymus serpyllum* is completely prostrate. The flowers of the common form are heather pink; those of *albus* are white; *coccineus*, crimson and *lanuginosus* has grey, hairy leaves and pink flowers. All bloom in June and July.

Thymus nitidus makes a neat bush 18 in. high, covered in mauve flowers in May; and *T. citriodorus*, a little lower, is spreading and has lemon-scented leaves. Silver Queen has silver variegated leaves and *aureus* has yellowish-green leaves. All like open sunny places and well-drained soils.

Saxifrages

mossy saxifrage

cushion saxifrage

London Pride

There are a great many saxifrages, (saxifraga) and only the easiest to grow are included here.

The Mossy Saxifrages are so called because their deeply divided soft green leaves make low rounded mounds which at a distance look a little like moss. The flowers, carried on slender stems, come in April and May, and make a great display. These saxifrages like good, rather moist soils and half-shady places though they can be grown almost anywhere. If dried out they go brown in the centre. They can be lifted and divided when they grow too large. Representative varieties are: James Bremner, white, 9 in.; Pompadour, crimson, 6 in. and Winston Churchill, pink, 6 in.; but there are many more.

Cushion or Kabschia Saxifrages make much harder, tighter cushions of leaves, often silvery-grey and spiky. They flower in March and April, and must have well-drained soil and an open, sunny place. Representative varieties are: Cranbourne, lilac pink; His Majesty, white; *elizabethae,* soft yellow; *jenkinsae,* soft pink and *burseriana,* white.

The London Prides make rosettes of green leaves and have loose sprays of small pink flowers. They will grow almost anywhere and do not mind shade. The Common London Pride, *Saxifraga umbrosa,* is 1 ft. high and flowers in June and July. *S. primuloides* Elliot's Variety is only 6 in. high and flowers in April and May.

Phlox subulata makes carpets of colour in the rock garden in May and June. Shown above is the soft-pink variety, Betty, but there are many others ranging from white to purple

Saxifraga burseriana, one of the best cushion or kabschia saxifrages, has large flowers on slender red stems in March and April. This is a plant for sunny places and well-drained soils

Primulas

The primrose and polyanthus are typical primulas, but not the best kinds for rock gardens. There are a great many of these and they differ so much that specialists divide them into 13 sections, but for general garden purposes they may be considered in two main groups: those that like open, sunny places and good, well-drained soil, and those that like partially shaded places and moist soil.

The auricula, *Primula auricula*, is typical of the first group. It has rather leathery leaves, more or less covered in white meal, for which reason it is called Dusty Miller. The primrose-like flowers are borne in clusters on 6-in. stems in May and June. There are many colours including rich purple and mixtures of green, white and yellow.

Primula pubescens is very similar, but smaller and neater, with violet, blue, rose, milky white or dull red flowers. *P. viscosa* is also closely allied, and also has a range of rich colours.

Primula juliae makes low mounds of neat, rounded leaves with almost stemless magenta flowers in March and April. There are a number of excellent hybrids between this and the primrose, with longer stems, larger leaves and pink to crimson flowers. They are known collectively as *P. juliana*, and grow best in well-cultivated soil, in sun or shade.

Some kinds are called Candelabra Primulas because they carry their flowers in successive whorls up a long stem, rather like a candelabra. *Primula japonica* and *P. pulverulenta*, both with magenta-crimson flowers on 18-in. stems in May and June, are typical, and easily grown in damp soil containing plenty of peat or leafmould. They are excellent waterside plants.

The Bartley Hybrids are similar and in various shades of pink, carmine and crimson. *P. helodoxa* is a yellow, and *P. bulleyana* deep yellow to bronze-red.

Primula sikkimensis and *P. florindae* both carry their yellow flowers in big heads rather like giant cowslips. They thrive in damp places, and so does *P. rosea* with 6-in. clusters of brilliant rose flowers in April and May.

Primula denticulata is called the Drumstick Primrose because it carries its lavender, violet, rose or white flowers in globular heads on stiff 8- to 12-in. stems like drum sticks in March and April. It will grow almost anywhere, in sun or shade, in moist or well-drained soil. *P. capitata* and *P. mooreana* with flatter heads of violet-purple flowers are not quite so easy and should be given plenty of leafmould or peat, and a partially shaded place. These conditions also suit *P. sieboldii* with soft green, crinkled leaves and loose heads of pink or white flowers on 6-in. stems in April and May.

Primula pulverulenta

Primula denticulata

Primula auricula

Primula rosea

Primula pubescens Mrs J. H. Wilson breaks into colourful heads of flowers in May. Increase this attractive plant by division in July, or by sowing seed when ripe, but seedlings may vary in colour

Moist, peaty beds of soil in rock gardens can become cheerful splashes of colour in May, when planted with *Primula sieboldii*. There are numerous forms differing in flower colour

Sedums, Sempervivums

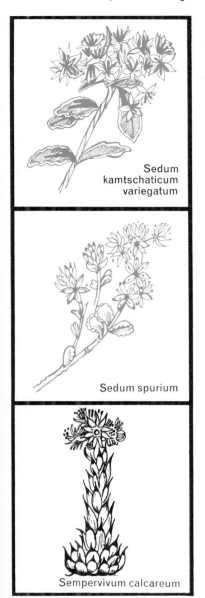

Sedum
kamtschaticum
variegatum

Sedum spurium

Sempervivum calcareum

Sedums, sometimes known as stonecrops, have fleshy leaves which enable them to survive periods of drought. *Sedum dasyphyllum* and *S. lydium* make close hummocks of very small leaves, grey in the former, bronze in the latter. *S. spathulifolium* makes rosettes of fat spoon-shaped leaves, dull purple in *purpureum*, grey in Cappa Blanca. *S. kamtschaticum variegatum* has golden variegated leaves and sprays of yellow flowers on 6-in. stems. *S. cauticolum* has bluish-grey leaves and purplish pink flowers on 4-in. stems; *S. rupestre* has narrow grey leaves and curling heads of yellow flowers on 9-in. stems. *S. spurium* is a rampant grower with sprays of pink flowers but its variety Dragon's Blood with wine-red flowers spreads less rapidly.

Closely related to the sedums is *Cotyledon simplicifolia,* with 6-in. drooping sprays of yellow flowers.

Sempervivums, known as house leeks, make rosettes of stiff leaves which may be small and covered with grey hairs like cobwebs in *Sempervivum arachnoideum* and *S. doellianum,* or large and shiny, green, tipped purple in *S. calcareum* and green in *S. tectorum.* The flowers are borne in stiff sprays on short, stout stems.

All like sunny places and well-drained soil containing lime and chalk. Both sedums and sempervivums can be divided when they become too large.

Violas, Veronicas

Any violas can be planted in rock gardens, but the large-flowered bedding varieties are rather too sophisticated to look in place. Far better are the wild kinds such as the Horned Violet, *Viola cornuta,* which makes low, tumbled masses of growth covered in small, light blue flowers from April to July. A white variety is *alba* and *purpurea* is violet-purple.

Viola gracilis is neater in habit with smaller deep blue flowers. *V. g. lutea* is a yellow-flowered variety and Grandeur is a violet-purple.

Viola labradorica purpurea is an attractive violet with deep purple leaves. Like the other violas it will grow anywhere, enjoys semi-shady places with cool, slightly moist soils and can be lifted and divided when it spreads too far.

Some of the rock garden veronicas are also trailing plants that can be grown almost anywhere, but they all prefer sunny open places. *Veronica prostrata,* also known as *V. rupestris,* makes a wide carpet of green leaves covered with short spikes of blue flowers in June and July. A pink-flowered variety is *rosea.* *V. teucrium* has longer, 6-in. spikes of blue flowers and Trehane has similar flowers contrasted with soft yellow leaves. By contrast *V. catarractae* makes a little spreading bush about 9 in. high with neat leaves and white, lilac-veined flowers from June to September.

Viola cornuta alba

The colourful *Sedum spurium* Dragon's Blood is an unusually attractive stonecrop for the late summer garden. It is sprawling in habit and needs an open sunny position where it will spread rapidly

A beautiful sprawling plant for the rock garden is *Viola gracilis*, a species which grows 4 to 6 in. tall. It flowers profusely over a long period if planted in good soil and a cool place

Annual Flowers

These are plants with a short life but a merry one. In the compass of a few months they grow, flower and die, leaving the ground free for further cultivation, if necessary, and for other plants. They are among the cheapest flowers to grow and the quickest to give a return. They are invaluable for furnishing new gardens before more permanent plants have been put in or have become sufficiently established to require all the space. They are also excellent for filling any vacant spaces that may occur in the flower beds, and since few of them make any great demands on the soil, they can often be grown with, or close to, other plants without robbing them unduly.

There are many different kinds of annuals and innumerable varieties of some of the most popular ones, such as marigolds and petunias. They vary greatly in height and habit as well as in the colour and form of their flowers. Some sprawl over the ground and make colourful flower carpets beneath taller plants. Some are bushy, some erect and a few, such as the sweet pea, the canary creeper, the large nasturtium and the Morning Glory, are climbers. There are also annuals, such as mignonette, stocks and nicotiana, with sweetly scented flowers though most rely more on their colour than on their fragrance to attract the insects that pollinate their flowers.

Some annuals make themselves so completely at home that once grown they continue to renew themselves year after year by self-sown seed with no help at all from the gardener. However, this is not usually a very desirable way of growing annuals, particularly the more highly developed garden varieties, which tend to deteriorate in quality rather rapidly unless grown in isolation and with careful selection to eliminate inferior forms. Seed of a few kinds can be saved and sown at home, but as a rule it is better to purchase fresh seed each year from a reliable source. This is essential in the case of those special hybrids known as F_1 or F_2 hybrids, since they have to be remade each year by crossing different parent varieties which are retained by the raiser and not sold or otherwise distributed to other producers. Often these F_1 or F_2 hybrids are superior in uniformity and vigour to ordinary varieties, but they are more costly to produce and more expensive to purchase.

Because of their relatively short life and frequent renewal from seed, annuals suffer very little from pests and diseases and are amongst the most trouble-free plants in the garden. They are usually favourites with children who enjoy growing them from seed and watching the seedlings develop so rapidly into flowering plants, and who so delight in their gay colours.

African Daisies

Several beautiful African daisies can readily be raised from seed for flowering during the summer months in open, sunny places and reasonably good well-drained soils. All are half-hardy annuals, seed of which should be sown in March in a greenhouse or frame in a temperature of 15 to 18°C. (60 to 65°F.), pricked out and hardened off for planting outdoors in late May or early June.

African daisies cover a very wide range of colours. *Arctotis grandis* has silvery white and pale blue flowers and there are also several hybrid strains with flowers in light or rich colours including yellow, orange, red and wine-purple. Heights vary from 1 to 1½ ft.

The Swan River Daisy or brachycome has blue, pink or white flowers and is 12 to 15 in. high.

The Star of the Veldt, or dimorphotheca, is also 12 to 15 in. high and includes unusual shades of beige, buff and apricot as well as yellow and orange.

Ursinia is brilliant orange and 12 to 15 in. high. Venidium has large orange flowers with a nearly black central zone and is 2 to 3 ft. high.

Space all plants 1 ft. apart, except venidium which needs 18 in.

This variety of dimorphotheca, Goliath, is one of many beautiful African daisies. It is very free flowering and makes a good cut flower. When growing in the garden, flowers close in the evenings

Antirrhinums

In mild districts with well-drained soils antirrhinums can sometimes be kept for several years, for they are strictly perennials. However, since the plants tend to become straggly with age, and some are likely to die, they are best if treated as half-hardy annuals and renewed each year from seed.

Sow seed in February or March in a greenhouse or frame, at a temperature of 15 to 18°C. (60° to 65° F.). Prick out the seedlings and give increasing ventilation, so that by early May at the latest the plants can begin to be hardened off for planting out of doors in late May or early June.

There are dwarf, intermediate and tall varieties, each in the complete colour range except blue.

The dwarf varieties should be spaced 6 to 8 in. apart; the intermediate, 12 in. apart and the tall ones about 15 in. apart.

Antirrhinums will grow in almost any soil and situation, but thrive best in reasonably good, well-drained soil and open, sunny places. In hot, dry places, some varieties are liable to suffer from rust disease (orange spots on the underside of leaves causing withering of the whole plant), but rust resistant varieties can be obtained.

Antirrhinums are excellent for filling beds on their own, in mixed or separate colours or in patterns of contrasting colours. The low-growing varieties are also very useful as carpets beneath taller plants, or as edging plants.

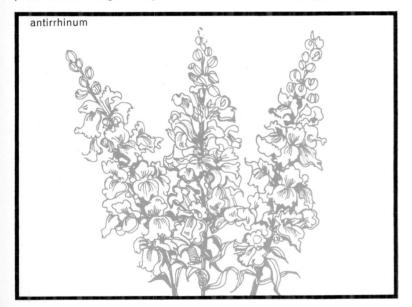

antirrhinum

Intermediate antirrhinums planted in borders of mixed perennial and annual flowers. Many colours are available and also different heights and flower forms

Asters

The annual asters or callistephus must not be confused with the perennial asters which include Michaelmas daisies since, though they are related, they need quite different treatment.

The annual asters are all half-hardy annuals flowering from mid-summer until early autumn. There are many different types and varieties, some with single and some with double flowers. The doubles may have large, rather shaggy flowers (Ostrich Plume); slightly smaller, more regularly-formed flowers (Comet) or still smaller, neater flowers (Pompon). Heights range from 1 to 3 ft. and there is a good colour range from white, lavender and pale pink to violet, purple and crimson.

Sow seed very thinly in March or early April in a frame or greenhouse in a temperature of around 15°C. (60°F.). Prick out as soon as the seedlings are big enough, giving good ventilation, and harden off for planting out 1 ft. apart in late May or early June. Alternatively, sow outdoors in early May where plants are to flower, and thin seedlings to 9 in. apart. Single asters are best for outdoor sowing.

Asters will grow in most places but prefer good, loamy soils and open, sunny or only lightly-shaded places.

callistephus

Comet asters providing a riot of colour during the summer and autumn months. Other types have more loosely formed or single flowers and all are available in a wide colour range

Clarkia, Godetia, Mallow

clarkia

lavatera

These are amongst the easiest of hardy annuals to grow. They will do well either in the open in full sunlight or in partial shade and either in poor sandy soils or in good rich loams.

Clarkia carries its white, pink, salmon or carmine single or double flowers on slender 2- to 2½-ft. spikes. Some varieties of godetia have a similar habit, but with larger flowers and spikes to 2½ ft. There are also shorter, bushier varieties known as azalea-flowered because of the slight resemblance of the flowers to those of an azalea. They may be single or double and have a similar colour range to clarkia with some especially good pink and salmon pink varieties. All are first rate for beds or for the front of borders.

The two annual mallows are lavatera and malope. Both have flaring, funnel-shaped flowers, rose pink in lavatera, deep magenta red in malope, which are carried on well-branched 3-ft. tall plants.

Sow seed during March, April or May or in early September outdoors where plants are to flower. Thin clarkia and godetia to 8 in. apart, lavatera and malope to 18 in. The taller varieties should be supported by short pea sticks (bushy hazel branches) or they may blow down in strong wind.

Cleome, Cosmea

Cleome is an attractive and rather unusual half-hardy annual known as the Spider Flower because of the spidery shape of its pink or white flowers which are carried in loose heads on 3 to 4 ft. stems in summer. Because of its height and striking appearance, it is very suitable for planting in groups towards the back of a border or in the middle of a bed.

Cosmea, also known as cosmos, is a graceful half-hardy annual which has narrow ferny leaves and daisy-type flowers in late summer and early autumn. The commonest kinds have white, pink, rose or purplish-red flowers on 3 to 4 ft. stems, but there are also varieties with orange flowers on 2½ ft. stems.

Sow seed of all varieties during March in a greenhouse or frame at a temperature of 15 to 18°C. (60 to 65°F.). Prick out and harden off, and plant outdoors in late May or early June, 1 ft. apart.

Cosmeas will grow in most places but thrive best in reasonably good soil and an open, sunny place. In shade they tend to become tall and leafy with fewer flowers.

cleome

cosmos

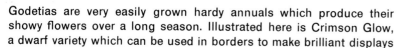

Godetias are very easily grown hardy annuals which produce their showy flowers over a long season. Illustrated here is Crimson Glow, a dwarf variety which can be used in borders to make brilliant displays

Cosmos bipinnatus is also known by its old name of cosmea. It is a colourful garden plant for the late summer and early autumn and the ferny foliage is highly decorative

Cornflower, Sweet Sultan

cornflower

Sweet Sultan

Both these plants are hardy annuals and are related, the latin name of the cornflower being *Centaurea cyanus* and of the Sweet Sultan, *Centaurea moschata*. Both are useful cut flowers as well as being good garden plants.

Cornflowers are commonly blue though there are also white- and pink-coloured varieties. They are so tall (3 ft. or more) that they need the support of pea sticks or something similar to hold them up. However there are dwarf kinds (9 to 12 in.) which need no staking and can be used as edging plants.

Sweet Sultans are about 18 in. high and are similar to cornflowers in shape. The colour range, however, also includes yellow, mauve and purple but not pure blue.

Sow seed in March or April outdoors where plants are to flower. Thin seedlings to 9 in. apart but 12 in. apart for tall cornflowers.

Cornflowers will grow almost anywhere, though they prefer well-drained soils and open, sunny places.

Sweet Sultans like rather good, well-cultivated and well-drained soil and a warm, sunny, sheltered position. They are not as easy as cornflowers to grow successfully.

Daisy Flowers

The annual chrysanthemum, coreopsis and gaillardia all have perennial relations with which they must not be confused as they need quite different treatment.

Annual chrysanthemums are 18 to 24 in. high and have variously-coloured flowers which are like large single or double daisies. There may be several colours in one flower in concentric rings or the flowers may be entirely lemon or yellow.

The annual coreopsis is often known as calliopsis. Its daisy-type flowers have big petals and small central discs and are yellow, usually splashed at the base with crimson or maroon. They are carried in sprays on slender 2 to 3 ft. stems.

The annual gaillardia has very showy flowers which are deeply frilled. They are either yellow and red or all red and grow to about 18 in. high.

Sow seeds of annual chrysanthemum and annual coreopsis outdoors in March or April where plants are to flower and thin seedlings to 9 in. apart. Sow annual gaillardia during March or early April in a greenhouse or frame, prick out, and harden off for planting outdoors in late May or early June, 9 in. apart. All like reasonably good soils and open, sunny places.

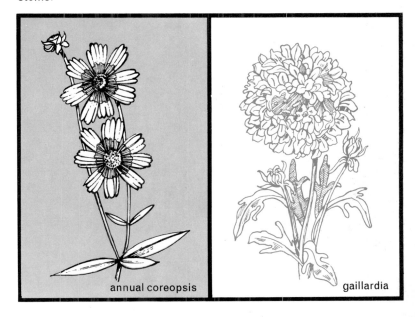

annual coreopsis   gaillardia

Polka Dot, a charming strain of *Centaurea cyanus*, the cornflower. It makes a dwarf, compact plant with a bushy habit and the flowers cover a very wide colour range

Chrysanthemum segetum, one of the annual chrysanthemums, is showy in the garden and useful also as a cut flower. Commonly called the Corn Marigold, it grows to about 18 in.

Edging Plants

Alyssum, ageratum, candytuft and lobelia are four of the most popular edging and carpeting plants since they are quite short and soon cover the area of a dinner plate or more.

The annual alyssum is also known as Sweet Alyssum because of its honey fragrance. It must not be confused with the yellow *Alyssum saxatile*, a perennial requiring quite different treatment. The Sweet Alyssum has white or purplish flowers and is 6 to 8 in. high.

Ageratum has fluffy little heads of soft blue or lilac flowers and is from 4 to 9 in. high.

Candytuft has white, lavender, rose and carmine flowers and is from 9 to 15 in. high.

Lobelia varies in colour from light to deep blue and white to purple. There is also a trailing kind, *Lobelia tenuior*, which is especially suitable for hanging baskets and window-boxes.

Alyssum and candytuft are hardy annuals. Sow during March, April, May or early September outdoors where they are to flower and thin seedlings to 6 in. apart.

Ageratum and lobelia are half-hardy annuals. Sow in March or early April in a greenhouse or frame, in a temperature of around 15°C. (60°F.); prick out and harden off for planting out in late May or early June, 6 to 8 in. apart.

All will grow well almost anywhere, but prefer reasonably good soils and open, sunny places.

candytuft

Lobelia tenuior

Annual Grasses

Avena sterilis

Briza maxima

Lagurus ovatus

Agrostis nebulosa is a 1-ft. high hardy annual known as Cloud Grass with sprays of small flowers.

Avena sterilis is a 3-ft. high hardy annual known as the Animated Oat because the flowers move as the humidity varies.

Briza maxima and *B. minor* are known respectively as the Large and Small Quaking Grasses, because their nodding, heart-shaped flowers are hardly ever still. They are hardy annuals 12 to 18 in. high.

Coix lachryma-jobi is called Job's Tears because of its pearly-white flower clusters. It is a 2-ft. perennial usually grown as a hardy annual.

Eragrostis tenella, also known as *E. elegans*, is a 2-ft. hardy annual with sprays of tiny flowers.

Hordeum jubatum, called Squirrel-tail Grass because its flowers hang in close, tail-like trails, is a 1-ft. hardy annual.

Lagurus ovatus, known as Hare's-tail Grass, has rounded fluffy flower heads and is a 1-ft. tall hardy annual. Cut in dry weather for winter decoration.

Panicum violaceum has silky green and purple flower plumes and is a 3-ft. hardy annual.

Pennisetum villosum (*P. longistylum*), has feathery flower spikes on 2-ft. stems. It is grown as a half-hardy annual.

Zea mays is the maize of commerce. Ornamental varieties are about 4 ft. tall and grown as half-hardy annuals, or seed may be sown out of doors in early May where the plants are to grow.

Dwarf varieties of ageratum are ideal annuals to use for the groundwork of bedding schemes, for edging, or for furnishing window-boxes. Taller varieties are also available up to 18 in. in height

Briza maxima, the Large Quaking Grass, is a handsome annual grass with nodding, heart-shaped flowers which are hardly ever still. It reaches a height of 12 to 18 in.

Larkspurs

annual larkspur

There are both annual and perennial larkspurs, all of which are delphiniums, but in gardens the name delphinium is usually reserved for the perennial kinds, and the annual varieties, derived from *Delphinium ajacis,* are known simply as annual larkspur. The two groups need quite different treatment.

Annual larkspurs carry their flowers in slender 2- to 3-ft. spikes. They have a good colour range from white, pale blue, lavender and pink to scarlet and violet.

Sow seed during March, April or in early September outdoors where plants are to flower and thin seedlings to about 12 in. apart. Support the flower stems as they appear by pushing short pea sticks into the soil around them.

Larkspurs like well-cultivated soil and an open, sunny position. For a September sowing the position chosen must be well drained. Plants from this sowing should commence to flower in May.

Annual larkspur is a good cut flower and is also excellent for large beds or for making groups among lower-growing plants or at the back of borders.

Marigolds

The Pot Marigold or calendula is a hardy annual with yellow or orange flowers which in good garden varieties are always double, though self-sown seedlings may revert to single flowers. They will grow in almost any soil and situation but prefer it to be open and sunny. Sow during March, April, May or September outdoors and thin seedlings to 9 in. apart.

French and African Marigolds are half-hardy annuals derived from various tagetes. Typically the French Marigolds are shorter and have smaller orange and chestnut red flowers, the African Marigolds are taller and have large, almost globular yellow or orange flowers. However, they have been much interbred so that the distinction between the two types is becoming blurred. All are fine plants for beds and borders, and like well-cultivated soils and open, sunny places. Sow during March or early April in a greenhouse or frame, in a temperature of about 15°C. (60°F.). Prick out seedlings and harden off for planting outdoors in late May or early June; dwarf varieties, which reach a height of 6 to 12 in., 9 in. apart; tall varieties 12 in. apart.

The Dwarf Marigold, *Tagetes signata,* makes a dome-shaped plant about 9 in. high covered in small, single yellow or orange flowers. It is a half-hardy annual, likes the same conditions as the French and African Marigolds, and is excellent for edging beds and borders. Space 6 to 8 in. apart.

Pot Marigold

Larkspur is a favourite annual for bedding and cutting. This strain, Giant Imperial, produces double flowers on slender spikes 4 ft. high. Other shorter varieties are available

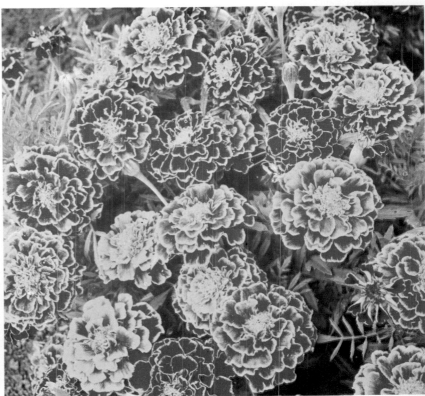
Excellent annuals for beds and borders, the French and African Marigolds continue to flower well into the autumn. Fiesta is a typical example of the French type with bicolor flowers

Mesembryanthemum etc.

These are creeping, half-hardy annuals with fleshy leaves which enable them to grow in very hot, sunny places.

The annual mesembryanthemum (*Mesembryanthemum crini-florum*) is also known as the Living-stone Daisy because it comes from Africa and has daisy-like flowers, though it is not a true daisy. There is a wide range of brilliant colours. There are also perennial mesembryanthemums which need different treatment.

Portulacas also have very showy flowers in a wide range of brilliant colours and they may be either single and cup shaped or double and ball like.

Sow seed during February or March in a greenhouse or frame, at a temperature of 18°C. (65°F.), prick out seedlings and harden off for planting outdoors in late May or early June. Space mesembryanthemums 9 in. apart, portulacas 6 in. apart in a warm, sunny place and well-drained soil.

Mignonette thrives best of all in chalky or limy soils, though it will grow in any reasonably good, well-drained soil and open, sunny position. Sow during March, April or early May outdoors where the plants are to flower and thin seedlings to about 6 in. apart. The heads of green and dull red flowers on foot-high stems are not very showy, but make a useful contrast to more brilliant flowers, and are very fragrant.

Nasturtium, Morning Glory

The nasturtiums are varieties of tropaeolum which are treated as if they were hardy annuals, even though they are killed by frost. However they grow so rapidly that if sown outdoors in April or May, they will escape all but exceptionally late frosts and yet be in flower from about mid-summer. There are dwarf and trailing or climbing varieties, the first suitable for beds, borders and edging, the second for covering trellis work, fences, sheds etc. Colours are in various shades of yellow and red. All flower most freely in rather poor soils and warm, sunny places. Sow seeds separately 1 in. deep and 6 to 8 in. apart where plants are to flower.

Morning Glory (ipomoea) is a twining plant with blue funnel-shaped flowers, easily grown as a half-hardy annual. Sow during March or early April in a frame or greenhouse, temperature 15 to 18° C. (60 to 65°F.), two seeds in each 3-in. pot and harden off for planting outdoors in late May or early June against warm, sunny walls or fences. Place strings or wires for the plants to twine around.

The annual convolvulus is closely related and has similar but smaller blue, purple, pink or cherry red flowers, but the sprawling plants are only about 1 ft. high and are suitable for beds, borders and edging. Sow seeds during March or April in good well-drained soil and a sunny place and thin seedlings to 9 in. apart.

mesembryanthemum

nasturtium   annual convolvulus

Portulaca is a showy annual for a sunny bank, rock garden or the top of a dry wall. It offers a wide range of brilliant colours, on both single- and double-flowered forms, the latter shown above

Morning Glory is a vigorous twining plant which is grown as a half-hardy annual though it is truly perennial but not winter hardy. It will flower throughout the summer in a warm, sunny place

Nemesia, Nicotiana

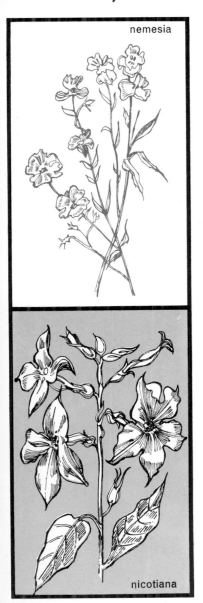

nemesia

nicotiana

Nemesia makes a neat half-hardy annual 8 to 12 in. high with flowers in a wide range of colours, including white, yellow, orange, red, lavender and blue. It likes rather rich, well-cultivated soil and open, sunny places, though it can be grown almost anywhere. It is excellent as an edging, for filling small beds or for growing in groups among other plants.

Sow seed during March or early April in a greenhouse or frame, in a temperature of about 15°C. (60°F.) prick out seedlings and harden off for planting outdoors in late May or early June. Space plants 6 in. apart.

The garden nicotiana is a relation of the tobacco plant and is also known as sweet-scented or jasmine tobacco, because of its sweet scent which is most noticeable in the evening. Flowers of some varieties do not open until evening, but day-light opening varieties are available and are to be preferred. Plants are 3 to 4 ft. high and have white, lime green, rose or carmine flowers. They like good, rich soil and will thrive in partial shade as well as in the open.

Sow seeds during March or early April in a greenhouse or frame, temperature 15 to 18°C. (60 to 65°F.) prick out seedlings and harden off for planting outdoors 1 ft. apart in late May or early June.

Nigella, Scabious

Love-in-a-Mist or nigella is a very elegant hardy annual about 18 in. high, with fine, ferny leaves and blue, rose, purple or white flowers a little like cornflowers but nestling amongst their leaves. It will grow in any reasonably good soil and open position. Sow seeds during March, April or early September outdoors where plants are to flower and thin seedlings to 9 in. apart.

The annual or Sweet Scabious must not be confused with the Caucasian Scabious which is a hardy perennial requiring different treatment. The annual scabious, despite its name, is not a true annual, but a perennial too tender to overwinter outdoors in most parts of Britain, and so readily raised from seed that it is always treated as an annual. The pin-cushion-shaped, fragrant flowers are in various colours from white, pink and lavender to crimson and purple. It grows about 3 ft. high.

Sow seed during March in a frame or greenhouse, temperature about 15°C. (60°F.), prick out seedlings and harden off for planting out 1 ft. apart in May or early June. Push some short, bushy twigs into the ground around the plants for support.

Alternatively, sow during April or early May outdoors where the plants are to flower and thin seedlings to 9 in. apart.

The annual scabious likes good, well-drained soil and an open sunny position.

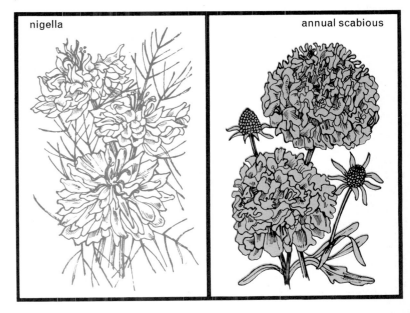

nigella

annual scabious

A delightful planting of mixed petunias and nicotianas which, together with fuchsias, brighten a shady corner and hide a dark wall. White nicotianas are usually the most fragrant

An accommodating hardy annual with a charming name is Love-in-a-Mist or nigella. It is well loved by flower arrangers who use the curious inflated seed heads in dried arrangements

Petunias

These immensely showy, half-hardy annuals succeed best in rather light, well-drained soils and warm, sunny places, though they can be grown almost anywhere. There are a great many varieties, some with medium-sized, single flowers, some with larger, single flowers and some with big double flowers. All are available in a wide range of shades of blue, purple, red and pink together with white and pale yellow. The single-flowered kinds are first-rate plants for filling beds and borders or for associating with other plants, also for growing in window-boxes, tubs etc. The double-flowered varieties are less satisfactory in beds, but make good pot, tub or window-box plants.

Sow seed in February or March in a greenhouse or frame, temperature 18°C. (65°F), prick out seedlings and harden off for planting outdoors in late May or early June. Space plants about 9 in. apart or, if grown throughout in pots, have one plant in each 5 in. pot in John Innes potting compost or one of the peat potting mixtures.

Petunias do not grow so well in cool, wet districts, though rain-resistant varieties are available and should be used in such places.

petunia

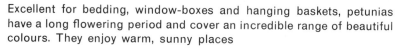

Excellent for bedding, window-boxes and hanging baskets, petunias have a long flowering period and cover an incredible range of beautiful colours. They enjoy warm, sunny places

Phlox, Pinks, Carnations

The annual phlox are very different in appearance from the perennial phlox though individually the flat, round flowers in a variety of rich and brilliant colours are similar. The plants are sprawling and good for carpeting in sunny places.

Sow seed during March or early April in a greenhouse or frame, temperature 18°C. (65°F.). Prick out and harden off for planting outdoors in late May or early June, 9 in. apart. Keep trailing stems pegged to the soil to prevent them being blown about and broken.

There are a great many annual pinks and carnations, many rather similar in appearance to the perennial pinks and carnations, but requiring quite different treatment. Particularly recommended are the Indian Pinks (*Dianthus heddewigii*), 6 to 12 in. high, with single or double-fringed flowers in many shades of pink, carmine and crimson with white, and the Chabaud Carnations, 18 in. high with large, double flowers in a variety of colours, which are excellent for cutting.

Sow seed during March or early April in a greenhouse or frame, temperature around 15°C. (60°F.) prick out and plant out in May or early June, 9 in. apart. Alternatively, sow annual pinks in April or early May outdoors where they are to flower and thin seedlings to 6 in.

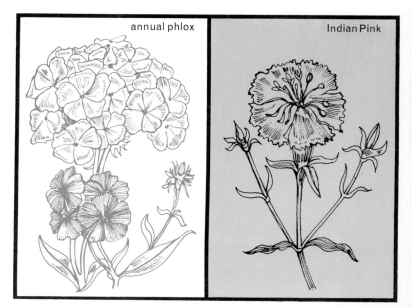

annual phlox

Indian Pink

An enchanting strain of the annual phlox is Twinkle, Dwarf Star Mixed. Growing no more than 8 in. high, it has dainty star-like flowers which are carried in great profusion well above the foliage

Poppies

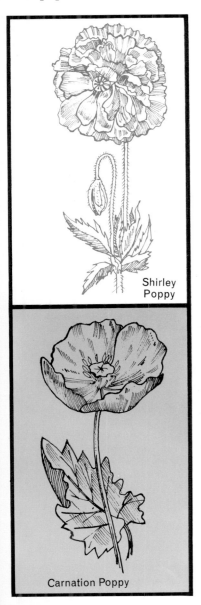

Shirley Poppy

Carnation Poppy

The annual poppies must not be confused with the Oriental Poppy (*Papaver orientale*) which is a perennial and needs quite different treatment.

There are three main groups of annual poppies. The Shirley Poppies (*Papaver rhoeas*) are 18 to 24 in. high, slender, green leaved, with mainly pink and white, rose or red flowers. The decorative Carnation Poppies (*Papaver somniferum*) are 2 to 3 ft. high, stouter stemmed with blue-grey leaves and larger flowers in a wide range of colours. The Californian Poppies (*Eschscholzia californica*) are more sprawling in habit, about a foot high, with flowers mainly cream, yellow, apricot, orange or coppery red.

All the annual poppies are available in single- and double-flowered varieties. They all like warm, sunny places and well-drained soils, but will grow practically anywhere.

All are hardy annuals. Sow seed during March, April, May or September outdoors where the plants are to flower. Thin seedlings to 9 in. apart (12 in. is probably better for Carnation Poppies). Do not retain self-sown seedlings which are liable to produce flowers that are of inferior quality.

Sweet Peas

Sweet peas are hardy climbing annuals which can be sown out of doors in March or April where they are to flower in summer. Sow the seeds 1 in. deep and 2 to 3 in. apart in a sunny, open place in good, well-cultivated soil. Sow in double rows 1 ft. apart with at least 4 ft. between each pair of rows, or in circles or groups. Place pea sticks (hazel branches are best) or netting to support the plants to a height of at least 5 ft., then allow the sweet peas to grow naturally. Pick the flowers regularly.

Finer flowers with better stems for cutting are obtained by growing on a single stem. For this method sow in late September or early October three or four seeds in 3-in. pots in John Innes or peat-based seed compost, and germinate them in a frame. Early in January pinch out the tip of each seedling and, keeping the best shoot on each plant, in March remove all the others.

Harden off the seedlings in late March or early April for planting out in ground that has been well manured. They should be planted 9 in. apart in a double row 1 ft. apart with 5 ft. between each pair of rows. Each plant should be supported by an 8-ft. cane lashed to horizontal wires strained between posts. Remove all side-shoots and tendrils, so restricting each plant to a single stem. Feed the plants occasionally with a compound fertiliser and keep them well watered in dry weather.

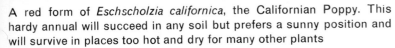

A red form of *Eschscholzia californica*, the Californian Poppy. This hardy annual will succeed in any soil but prefers a sunny position and will survive in places too hot and dry for many other plants

Sweet peas are strongly recommended as flowers for cutting, for the more often they are picked, the more flowers they will produce. This variety is Lavender Lace

Salvias

Scarlet Salvia

The annual salvias are sages but they must not be confused with culinary sage, which is a small shrubby plant requiring quite different treatment.

The two most popular annual salvias are *Salvia splendens* (the Scarlet Salvia) and *Salvia horminum*. The first is actually a perennial but is almost invariably grown as a half-hardy annual, the second is a hardy annual.

The Scarlet Salvia makes a well-branched plant 12 to 18 in. high, with long slender spikes of scarlet flowers. It is a fine plant for filling beds or borders or for making bold splashes of colour with other plants. It likes good, well-cultivated soil and warm, sunny places. Sow during January or February in a greenhouse, temperature 18°C. (65°F.), prick out seedlings and later pot singly in 3-in. pots. Harden off for planting outdoors in late May or June. Pink and purple varieties are available.

Salvia horminum grows 18 in. high and has long violet-purple or rosy-purple spikes. It thrives in any reasonably good soil and open position. Sow during March, April or early May outdoors where plants are to flower and thin seedlings to 9 in. apart.

Stocks

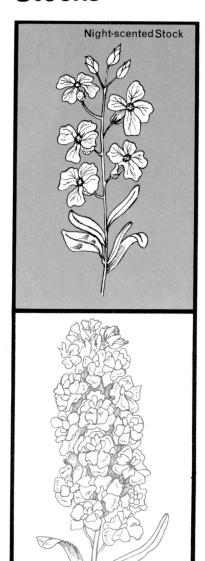

Night-scented Stock

Ten-week Stock

There are several different types of stock and all have scented flowers. The Ten-week Stocks are the most popular, 1 to 2½ ft. high with a good percentage of double flowers and a colour range from white, cream, mauve and pink to crimson and purple.

Brompton Stocks are 2 to 3 ft. high and are grown as biennials to flower in spring and summer before the ten-week stocks. Colours are mainly shades of pink, rose, red and purple with white.

Night-scented Stock is a small plant 9 to 12 in. high with insignificant flowers which are shut by day and which are intensely fragrant at night.

Virginian Stock is also a small plant with many-coloured small flowers, rather like confetti.

Sow Brompton stocks outdoors in late June or early July. Transplant seedlings to 6 in. apart and plant in flowering beds in September 12 in. apart. Choose good, well-drained soil and a sunny, sheltered place.

Sow seed of night-scented and Virginian stock thinly during March, April or May outdoors where the plants are to flower in sun or partial shade and ordinary soil. Do not thin seedlings.

Salvia splendens, a tender perennial treated as a half-hardy annual. It is an excellent bedding plant. This popular early variety, Blaze of Fire, grows 1 ft. tall and has a compact habit

One of the best known annuals is Virginian stock. It is very hardy and easy to grow with small flowers on 6-in. stems and is popular with children since it quickly produces a colourful display

Sunflowers, Coneflowers

There are both annual and perennial sunflowers and coneflowers, some annual kinds looking much like the perennial kinds, though they need quite different treatment. All have big, showy, daisy-type flowers, single or double, mainly yellow or orange though in some varieties splashed or ringed with crimson or maroon. The coneflowers are sometimes called Gloriosa Daisies and are mainly derived from *Rudbeckia hirta*. There are numerous varieties differing in colour and in height from 1 to 3 ft.

The annual sunflowers are all derived from *Helianthus annuus* and range in height from 3 to 7 ft. All grow almost anywhere, but thrive best in reasonably good, well-drained soil and an open, sunny place.

Sow the coneflowers during February or March in a greenhouse or frame, prick out and harden off for planting outdoors in May about 18 in. apart. Alternatively sow outdoors in July and plant out in September in a sunny, sheltered and particularly well-drained place.

Sow annual sunflowers during March and April outdoors where they are to flower, spacing them 6 in. apart and thin seedlings to at least 18 in. apart.

coneflower · sunflower

Verbena, Zinnia

verbena

Verbenas are really perennial plants, but they are too tender to survive the winter in most parts of Britain and are so readily raised from seed that they are usually treated as half-hardy annuals. They are trailing plants with clusters of flowers in many shades of blue, pink and red.

Sow during February or March in a greenhouse or frame, temperature 18°C. (65°F.). Prick out and harden off for planting outdoors in late May or early June, 9 in. apart, in good, well-cultivated soil and an open, preferably sunny position. Shoots may be pegged to the ground to cover it completely with a carpet of growth.

Zinnias are erect-growing plants with large, single or double daisy-type flowers in a variety of colours, including yellow, orange, pink, salmon, scarlet and purple, some varieties having quilled petals like those of a chrysanthemum. Heights range from 1½ to 3 ft.

Sow in March or April in a well-ventilated greenhouse, in a temperature of 15°C. (60°F.). Prick out and harden off for planting out, 1 ft. apart, in late May or early June in good rich soil and an open, sunny place. Alternatively, sow in early May outdoors where they are to flower, and thin the seedlings to 1 ft. apart.

zinnia

The familiar sunflower, *Helianthus annus,* is a great favourite for cottage gardens. It is a hardy annual preferring an open, sunny place and well-drained soil

Zinnias are half-hardy annuals which often succeed best when sown in May where they are to flower. They do not then suffer the check of being transplanted

A Selection of Biennials

What is a Biennial?

Biennials are plants which must be renewed annually from seed, since they die after they have flowered and set seed. In this they resemble annuals, but unlike them biennials take over a year to complete their cycle of growth. Seed sown one year will produce plants which will flower the next year, ripen their seed and die before the second winter.

Some plants that are not truly biennials are usually grown as such in gardens because this is the way to see them at their best. For example wallflowers will live for years in poor, well-drained soil, but they get straggly with age. Their flowers are of better quality in good, rich soil in which their softer growth is likely to die in the course of the second winter.

It is also true that some plants which are really biennials can be treated as annuals, that is, induced to flower the first year, if the seed is sown very early in a greenhouse and the seedlings are later planted out.

But the general rule with biennials is to sow seed in a frame or out of doors in May or June, transplant the seedling to a reserve bed in July, spacing them a few inches apart each way, and finally plant them in September or October where they will flower the following spring or summer.

Many biennials flower in May and June, thus usefully filling an awkward gap that can occur between the spring and summer flowers. Like annuals, they are temporary plants which should be pulled up and burned or put on the compost heap when they have finished flowering. Also, as with annuals, though it is easy enough to save seed of most kinds it is usually impossible to prevent cross fertilisation of different varieties, as a result of which home-saved seed produces only a mongrel population. The distinction between annuals, biennials and herbaceous perennials is not always clear cut since sometimes varieties of one group can be treated as if they belonged to one of the other groups e.g. hollyhocks can be grown as annuals, biennials or short-lived perennials. However, to be sure of a regular succession of biennials it is necessary to sow seed every year at the correct season.

Since biennials must, as a rule, spend one winter out of doors, they run more risks and require a little more thought than annuals. Excessive wet often causes more losses than cold, though it is a combination of the two that can do the greatest damage. Good soil drainage is very helpful to most biennials and it also pays to get them well established before the winter. A common routine is to plant biennials in the beds used for annuals or other temporary summer flowers such as dahlias and geraniums (pelargoniums). Because some of these may go on flowering well into October, there is a temptation to delay the planting of biennials until late October or even November. In cold districts or on poorly drained soils this is asking for trouble. Far better results are obtained by letting the biennials follow those summer flowers that finish, and so can be cleared away, relatively early, leaving the later flowers to be followed by such spring-flowering bulbs as tulips and hyacinths which do not suffer from being planted in late October.

Similar forethought will prevent another difficulty that can occur with biennials – what to put in their place when they finish flowering in July. This need present no problem if some annuals are sown late, the young plants being grown on in seed trays or small pots until they are required to fill up the gaps left by the biennials. Outdoor chrysanthemums are also excellent for the same purpose, since they can be grown, if desired, in a reserve bed and then be moved to the ground in which the biennials have been flowering, even if by that date the chrysanthemums themselves are already coming into bloom. It is by such devices as these that resourceful gardeners will maintain a constant supply of flowers where others with less forethought have only a spasmodic display.

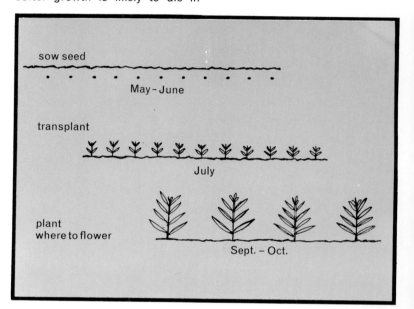

The large, bell-shaped flowers of the Canterbury Bell *(Campanula medium)* are produced in June and July on 2½-ft. stems. Seed should be sown in May or June, to flower the following summer

Daisies, Forget-me-nots

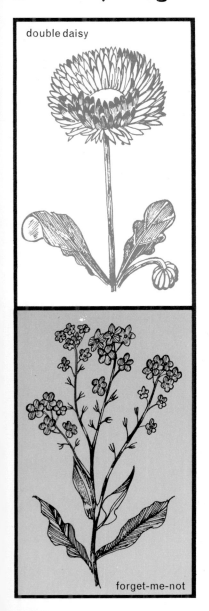

double daisy

forget-me-not

The showy white, pink or red double-flowered daisies so popular for a spring display are giant varieties of *Bellis perennis* the familiar daisy of lawns and meadows. These fine double-flowered varieties are excellent for interplanting in beds of tulips, hyacinths and other spring bulbs.

Sow seed in May or June in a frame or out of doors, transplant seedlings 3 or 4 in. apart in a sunny place and well-cultivated soil and transfer plants in September or October to where they are to flower, spacing them 6 to 8 in. apart. They can be lifted, split up and replanted after flowering, but it is more satisfactory to raise anew from seed each year.

Forget-me-nots or myosotis are the favourite blue-flowered plants for interplanting in spring beds of tulips. They also make good beds on their own and may be grown under shrubs and in woodlands as they do not mind shade. In addition to blue there is also a pink-flowered variety.

Sow seed in June or early July out of doors in well-broken soil. Transplant the seedlings 3 in. apart in rows 6 to 8 in. apart in a cool, partially shaded place, keep well watered and transfer to flowering beds in October or November, spacing the plants 6 to 9 in. apart.

After flowering, pull up the plants and scatter some over a prepared seedbed on which they will shed their seeds and give a new crop of seedlings.

Foxgloves, Hollyhocks

hollyhock

Foxgloves, or digitalis, carry their tubular flowers in tapering 4- to 6-ft. spikes in July and August. In the ordinary varieties the flowers droop and are all on one side of each spike, but in the Excelsior varieties they are held outwards all round the spike. Both types are available in a range of colours from white, cream and pink to rose red. All grow well in any reasonably well-drained soil in the open or in shade.

Hollyhocks carry their large flowers in stout spikes 6 to 8 ft. high. The flowers may be single, like little plates, or double like rosettes, in a range of colours from white, cream and pink to salmon and crimson. They flower in July and August and like well-drained soils and sunny places. In some places they suffer severely from a disease which produces rusty pustules on the leaves and where this is troublesome plants should be sprayed frequently from May to August with Bordeaux mixture or thiram. Rust-resistant varieties are available.

Sow seed of foxgloves and hollyhocks out of doors in May or June; transplant seedlings 6 in. apart in rows 9 in. apart in well-cultivated soil and transfer plants to their flowering positions in September or October, spacing foxgloves 1 ft. apart and hollyhocks 2 ft. apart.

Varieties are also available which can be sown in a greenhouse in February or March to flower the same year.

The popular double daisies, available in red, pink or white are decorative on their own or they can be used as groundwork beneath the taller spring-flowering bulbs

Excelsior Hybrids are especially attractive foxgloves with flowers held outwards all round the stems. Foxgloves of all kinds are equally at home in sunshine or shade

Pansies, Violas

There is very little difference between pansies and violas, but in general violas are a little more tufted and less straggly in habit of growth and the flowers of pansies are almost always of two or more colours, one prominently blotched on the other. Nowadays it is customary to treat both as biennials, but the small-flowered violas are much easier to keep from one year to another. Both are available in a wide range of colours and seed can be purchased to give mixed or separate colours. Both flower in spring and summer and some varieties of viola are available which flower from late winter.

Sow seeds in May or June in a frame or greenhouse or a sheltered place out of doors in soil with which plenty of peat or leaf-mould has been mixed. Prick off the seedlings 2 in. apart in boxes or beds of finely broken soil, keep them well watered and plant them in September or October 6 to 9 in. apart where they are to flower.

Alternatively, sow seed in a greenhouse with a temperature of 15°C. (60°F.) in February or March, prick off the seedlings into boxes and plant them out in May to flower the same year. Seedlings raised in this way are on sale each spring.

Pansies and violas like fairly, rich, well-cultivated soil and will grow in sunny or shady places. The flowering season is extended by removing dead flowers.

Primroses, Polyanthuses

The main difference between primroses and polyanthuses is that whereas the former carry only one flower on each slender stem, polyanthuses have stouter stems each bearing a cluster of flowers. Primroses are more graceful but polyanthuses make a more solid display. Both are available in a great range of colours from white, cream, pale pink and lavender to deep orange, crimson and deep blue and all flower from March to May. Seed can be purchased to give separate or mixed colours.

Sow seed in a frame or greenhouse in March or April or out of doors in May or June using soil in which plenty of peat or leaf mould has been mixed. Prick out frame- or greenhouse-raised seedlings 1½ in. apart in shallow boxes filled with John Innes No. 1 Potting Compost and plant out of doors when the seedlings are filling the boxes.

Grow on in a partially shaded place in good, well-cultivated soil with which plenty of leaf mould or peat and some rotted manure or garden refuse has been mixed. Transfer the plants to their flowering beds in September or October, spacing them about 9 in. apart. After flowering, the plants can be lifted, divided and replanted, but the best results are obtained by raising from seed each year.

Primroses and polyanthuses will grow in sunny or shady places.

Pansies are available in a great range of colours and sizes but most have the cheerful 'faces' with central streaks or blotches seen in this early flowering variety

Many delightful colours are available in the polyanthus. Shown here is a selection of the Pacific strain which is notable for the large size of its individual flowers carried on very fine trusses

Sweet William and Others

Canterbury Bell

Canterbury Bells are varieties of *Campanula medium*. They carry their large, bell-shaped flowers in broad spikes 2½ ft. high in June and July. The cup-and-saucer varieties have an extra ring of flat petals behind each bell and the double varieties have several bells one inside the other. All are available in white, pink, rose, mauve and blue varieties.

Sweet Williams are varieties of *Dianthus barbatus* and they carry their brightly coloured flowers in large, flattish heads in June and July. There are many varieties, in heights ranging from 6 in. to 2 ft. in separate or mixed colours. The auricula-eyed varieties all have a conspicuous white eye to the coloured flower.

Brompton Stocks resemble other stocks but are taller, more branching and flower from March to May. The colour range is from white, lavender and pink to crimson and violet.

All these plants like sunny places and well-drained soil and Brompton Stocks are sometimes difficult to overwinter out of doors in heavy soil or in cold gardens. Sow seeds of Sweet Williams in May or June, or of Brompton Stocks in July, in a frame or outside in well-prepared soil. Transplant seedlings 6 in. apart in good soil and an open, sunny position, and transfer to flowering beds in September or October. Brompton Stocks may also be grown in an unheated greenhouse.

Wallflowers

cheiranthus

Wallflowers are among the most richly scented of spring flowers, and are available in a fine range of colours. Dwarf varieties are about 1 ft. high and normal varieties 18 in. high. Representative varieties are: Blood Red; Cloth of Gold; Eastern Queen, chamois flushed pink; Fire King, orange-red; Primrose Monarch; Ruby Gem, ruby violet; Golden Bedder, Orange Bedder, Primrose Bedder and Scarlet Bedder, all dwarf and Vulcan, dwarf crimson. The Siberian Wallflower, *Cheiranthus allionii*, has vivid orange flowers on foot-high plants and continues to flower into June, but the flowers are not scented.

Sow seeds in April or early May out of doors in drills ½ in. deep. Transplant the seedlings when about 3 in. high to a reserve bed of well-cultivated soil in an open, sunny position, planting them 6 in. apart. After a fortnight pinch out the top of each plant to encourage branching from low down. Keep down weeds all the summer.

In September or as early as possible in October, transplant to where they are to flower, spacing the plants about 1 ft. apart. They can be grown with the colours mixed, in beds or blocks all of the same colour, or patterns of different colours can be arranged.

After flowering, remove the plants and either put them on the compost heap or burn them.

The Sweet Williams are welcome border plants for early summer colour. They are available in separate and mixed colours in heights from 6 in. to 2 ft. but all are derived from *Dianthus barbatus*

Wallflowers and forget-me-nots combined with tulips bring all the gaiety of spring to this attractive garden. The first two are grown as biennials for best results, although both are really perennials

Garden Pools

Water can be used in many ways in the garden. It provides a medium in which plants of a special kind, the aquatics, can be grown. It can also be stocked with fish which bring life and movement to the garden. Plants and fish combine well, as the latter benefit from the protection which floating and submerged leaves provide. But if the fish are to be enjoyed to the full, planting must not be too dense or they will be screened almost completely from view. One advantage of having both fish and plants in a pool is that they will assist in keeping the water fresh. However, if crystal clear water is required it will be best to have no living things in it and to rely on chemicals to prevent growth of weeds and scum.

The smooth surface of water provides a texture quite different from anything else in the garden and also acts as a mirror, capturing the changing colour of the sky and reflecting the plants, ornaments or buildings placed sufficiently close to it. Fountains and cascades bring both movement and the pleasant sounds that falling or rushing water can create. But it is only still water that reflects clearly, so if the mirror effect is uppermost in the garden maker's mind, fountains and cascades must either be banned altogether or be kept sufficiently far away to prevent disturbance of that part of the water which is to provide reflections.

Almost any moving-water effects are possible, even in quite a small garden, by the use of an electrically operated pump which can be submerged in the pool to circulate water from it through fountains or pipes. If plants are to be grown in the water or it is to be stocked with fish this is far better than using water from an outside source, such as the mains, since this will constantly change the temperature of the pool, as well as robbing it of valuable nutrients and possibly introducing chemicals harmful to the life in the pool.

Fountains can be of many different types, single jet, multiple jet or simply bubbling up a few inches above the surface of the water. It is even possible to obtain fountains which produce changing patterns by a simple mechanism operated by the pressure of the water passing through the fountain.

If water is used in formal parts of the garden, the shape of basin or pool should contribute to the design. By contrast an informal pool should appear as natural as possible, with plants, turf or rocks concealing any concrete, glass fibre or plastic sheeting used in its construction.

One other possible use of water is as a fine spray over statues, ornaments or stones to keep parts or the whole moist, so producing a gleaming, in place of a dull, surface.

Siting and Planning

Water gardens in which water-lilies are to be grown should be sited in a reasonably open place where they at least get the afternoon sun which is so necessary to open the flowers effectively. Fish, on the other hand, benefit from some shade and the green, scummy growth which sometimes obscures water is less likely to prove troublesome in pools that are not fully exposed to the sun.

A happy compromise is to provide some shelter to the north and east, but to leave pools fully open to the south and west. However, if the purpose of the water is purely ornamental and there is no intention to stock it with plants or fish the aspect is immaterial.

Water gardens may be formal or informal. The first-mentioned may take the form of circular, rectangular or other symmetrical shapes, usually clearly defined by flagged or otherwise paved edges; alternatively, they may be bowls or basins of water raised above the level of the soil. They may contain fountains or be fed by dripping wells or other architectural features.

Informal pools will usually, though not invariably, be of irregular outline with grass or soil to water level. They may be features on their own or form part of a rock garden. They may be combined with streams, cascades or other natural-looking features.

formal pool

informal pool

This small informal pool makes a delightful feature. Water brings a completely new element into the garden and allows for the introduction of many water-loving plants

Construction

Informal pools can sometimes be made by damming a stream and allowing it to flood the surrounding land, but more usually they are excavated and lined with some impervious material, such as glass fibre, plastic or rubber sheets or concrete.

For dish-sided pools concrete is laid in much the same manner as for paths. If the sides slope fairly steeply it will help if one spreads reinforcing wire or ordinary wire netting over them first to hold the concrete and strengthen it.

For vertically-sided pools a different method is required. Erect wood shuttering made of planks nailed to uprights or otherwise supported. Place this shuttering at least 4 in. from the excavated sides of the pool (or if the pool is being built above ground level, 4 in. apart), and shovel the concrete into the space between, tamping it down well to make certain that no holes or loose places remain. When the concrete is dry, remove the shuttering and spread more concrete to a depth of at least 6 in. all over the bottom of the pool.

Concrete can be coloured with powdered dyes which are available from most builders' merchants. It can also be made waterproof with special powders or liquids. Both colourants and waterproofing compounds must be mixed with the cement and aggregate before water is added.

Fill and empty concrete pools several times before placing plants or fish in the pool, or alternatively, paint the concrete with bituminous paint or waterglass before filling to prevent chemicals in the concrete from dissolving into the water.

Glass fibre pools can be bought ready made in a variety of shapes and sizes. All that is then necessary is to excavate a hole large enough to accommodate the pool, set the mould in place, and fill in with soil around it so that it is firmly supported. Such pools are very durable and when well installed and properly planted their artificial nature can be concealed so well that they appear natural.

Special plastic or rubber sheets can be purchased as pool liners. They must be welded together by the manufacturer to provide a single sheet that will completely line the bottom and sides of the pool and just overlap the edges where it can be held down by soil and/or rockery or paving stones. All large stones and other hard, sharp objects should be removed from the bottom of the excavation. A layer of sand is an advantage to provide a smooth bed for the sheet.

Fountains and Cascades

Moving water adds greatly to the attractiveness of many water gardens. If mains electricity is available, fountains, cascades and the rest are best operated by small electrically operated pumps. The pump may either be installed close to the pool, the best method if a large volume of water is to be used, or it may be actually submerged for which purpose special units are available in which all the electrical parts are completely watertight. By either system, the water is constantly circulated from the pool and returned to it so that the only loss is by evaporation, requiring a minimum of topping up. This is also better for fish and plants than frequent renewal by mains water which is usually chemically treated and may be at a different temperature.

Fountains are available in many patterns either on their own or combined with ornaments or statues. Cascades can be lined with concrete or with plastic or rubber sheets like the pools themselves. Glass fibre cascades can be obtained in sections, but it is rather hard to screen the artificiality of these. The best results are often obtained by forming cascades of large rocks embedded in concrete, but with no concrete actually showing.

Constructing an informal pool. The shape has been well marked out and is being excavated. Note the polythene liner which will be used to cover the bottom and sides of the pool completely

This illustrates well the construction of a pool, with a cascade, using glass fibre sections. This is a comparatively easy method but it is often difficult to mask the artificiality of the glass fibre

Planting and Stocking

From mid-April to the end of May is the best period for planting in water, but the surrounding beds can be planted earlier or even in summer if plants are obtained in containers.

The easiest and cleanest way to grow aquatics is in special plastic baskets which can be purchased for the purpose. Each plant is given a basket to itself and is planted in good garden soil with which bone-meal has been mixed at 2 oz. per 2 gall. bucket of soil. Fill the baskets to the brim and plant so that the crowns are just level with the surface of the soil. Then stand the baskets in the pool where they are to grow. Most water-lilies thrive in about 1 ft. depth of water, but most marginal plants prefer only an inch or so of water over the roots. Pools may be made with a shelf around the edge for these shallow water plants or, alternatively, the baskets can be stood on bricks to bring them to any required level.

If fish are to be kept in the pool there should be some oxygenating plants to keep the water sweet and provide shelter. These are free-floating plants and they can simply be dropped into the water without any soil, or a small stone can be tied to the bottom of each to sink it where it is required.

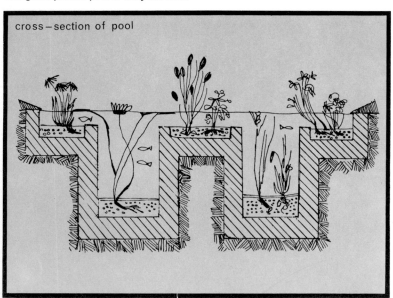
cross—section of pool

Floating Leaves

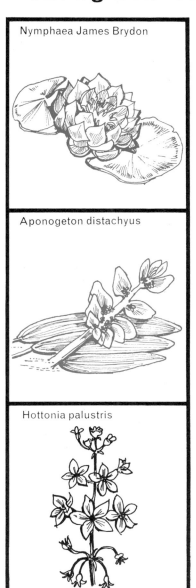
Nymphaea James Brydon

Aponogeton distachyus

Hottonia palustris

There are numerous varieties of water-lily or nymphaea, all flowering in summer and differing in vigour as well as in the size and colour of their flowers. All have floating leaves and display their flowers just above these. Most suitable for pools of medium size with from 1- to 2-ft. depth of water are the varieties of *Nymphaea marliacea*, with pink, crimson or yellow flowers, varieties of *N. lay-dekeri* with pink or crimson flowers, and such varieties as Escarboucle, crimson; James Brydon, red; Rose Arey, scented and Mrs Richmond, pink. For very small pools with only 5 to 8 in. of water, varieties of *N. pygmaea* and *N. tetragona* may be used.

Aponogeton distachyus is known as the Water Hawthorn and has little spikes of sweetly-scented, white flowers from late spring to early autumn. It thrives in water up to 18 in. deep. *Menyanthes trifoliata* is known as the Bog Bean. It has three-part leaves and clusters of white or pale pink flowers. It likes 4- to 6-in. depth of water.

Nymphoides peltatum has clusters of bright yellow flowers with fringed petals. It likes water up to 18 in. deep.

Elodea, hottonia (Water Violet), myriophyllum and utricularia are oxygenating plants.

Planting a water-lily in a special plastic basket designed for aquatics. Good garden soil to which bonemeal has been added is used and a coarse hessian liner helps to retain this mixture

The water-lily Mrs Richmond. The immense flowers of this variety colour to deep rose as they age. It is a handsome subject for pools with 1- to 2-ft. depth of water

Marginal Plants

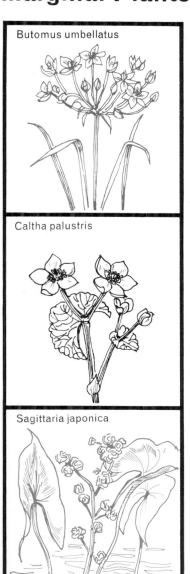

Butomus umbellatus

Caltha palustris

Sagittaria japonica

Alisma (Water Plantain) has 2-ft. sprays of small pink flowers in summer. It likes 2 or 3 in. of water over its roots. Butomus (Flowering Rush) has heads of pink flowers on stout 3-ft. stems in late summer. It likes 3 to 4 in. of water.

Calla palustris (Bog Arum) has little yellow and green arum lily flowers in early summer. It can be planted outside the pool or in up to 2 in. of water. *Caltha palustris* (Kingcup or Marsh Marigold) has large buttercup-like flowers in spring. A double-flowered variety is named *flore pleno*. Treat like calla.

Iris laevigata and *I. kaempferi* have large, showy white, violet or purple flowers in May and June. The first likes an inch or so of water, the second prefers to be just outside the pool.

Lysichitum (Skunk Cabbage) has large yellow or white flowers like arum lilies in spring. Treat like calla. *Mimulus luteus* (Musk) has yellow- or red-blotched flowers in summer. Treat like calla.

Pontederia has spikes of light blue flowers in summer and likes 2 to 3 in. of water. Sagittaria (arrowhead) has stiff sprays of white flowers in summer. There is a double-flowered variety and both like 3 to 4 in. of water. *Scirpus tabernaemontani zebrinus* has quill-like leaves banded yellow and white. It likes 2 to 4 in. of water.

Typha (reed mace) has cigar-like flowers in late summer. The best garden kinds are *Typha angustifolia* and *T. minima*. Both like 3 to 4 in. of water.

Keeping Water Clean

It is only possible to have crystal clear water in pools that have no living things in them. Wherever plants are grown and fish breed and feed there will be some discolouration of the water and some growth of weed which must be removed if it gets too thick.

Much weed can be removed with a garden rake or a sieve drawn through the water or by fixing a piece of wire mesh over the tines of a garden fork. Green scum and blanket weed, a dense growth like green cotton wool, are most likely to be troublesome in hot summer weather in pools that are fully exposed to the sun.

Chemical treatment with copper sulphate, simazine or other weed-killers is not recommended in stocked pools because of the danger of killing plants and fish.

Pools should be emptied, cleaned and refilled every second or third year. Fish can be placed in buckets of water and plants stood on one side for a few hours while the pool is scrubbed and flushed with clean water. Do not use chemicals or detergents during the cleaning process.

A fine display of well-contrasted marginal plants around a charming natural pool in late spring. The double-flowered kingcup, *Caltha palustris flore pleno*, is prominent in the foreground

An attractive feature of this well-kept pool is the Water Hawthorn with its little spikes of sweetly scented flowers. Well-balanced planting and correct stocking with fish can help to keep the water clean

Patios and Plants in Containers

Planning

A patio is virtually an outdoor room, a part of the garden which can be frequently used as a place in which to sit, eat and meet one's friends. For these reasons it must be private and sheltered, and it must be well paved so that it can be used with comfort and without danger of bringing dirt into the house, even after heavy rain.

The natural place for a patio is adjacent to the house, indeed the original Spanish patio was always an inner courtyard surrounded by the house. But the term has been given a wider meaning, and is now used to describe any small, formal, and to some degree enclosed, garden.

The actual size, shape and design of the patio is a matter for individual taste and may be determined to a considerable degree by the site itself. In very small, town gardens it may be best to treat the whole area as a patio, but in larger or country gardens it is more probable that the patio will be a small part of the whole, possibly looking out on to the rest of the garden, though it may be entirely separated from it.

Whatever the size and character of the patio, firm lines and a strong sense of design are desirable.

Fashions have a habit of going full circle, though they may take a long time to do so. That is precisely what has happened in gardening. In mediaeval times all gardens were small and enclosed, mainly because the world outside was a dangerous place and private property had to be well protected by walls. As the power of central authority and the wealth of the nation increased, gardens grew in size, discarded their walls and hedges and eventually developed into landscapes encompassing the surrounding countryside or such parts of it as seemed desirable. Now, in the twentieth century, gardens are again small, though for very different reasons. It is the immense value of land in and near great cities and centres of industry that has progressively reduced the size of building plots, until now the house often occupies more ground than the garden. The effective planning of such tiny spaces presents special problems to which two quite different approaches have been made. In Canada and the U.S.A., where living conditions are very similar to our own, open-planned gardens have been seen as the major solution. Walls, hedges, fences, and even simple rails or chains to mark the boundary between one plot and another, have been swept away and all the gardens in a street or block have been planned as one. This can produce a remarkable impression of spaciousness but it does tend to destroy privacy and prevent an individual approach to plants and planning.

In Britain open planning has only proved moderately acceptable. Instead, there has been a return to the mediaeval conception of the garden as an extension of the house; a courtyard or outdoor room in which leisure can be spent and friends entertained. Early in this century such concepts were already being used to break up large gardens. Gertrude Jekyll, who at this period influenced garden styles greatly, often divided gardens into several compartments. At Hidcote, near Chipping Campden in Gloucestershire, Major Lawrence Johnston made a garden which is virtually a whole succession of outdoor rooms differing in size and treatment. This garden is now the property of the National Trust, as is Sissinghurst Castle, another fine compartmented garden made by Victoria Sackville-West and her husband, Sir Harold Nicholson, and both provide many object lessons for those who wish to design small gardens in this modern and intimate style. Even without any soil at all plants can be grown successfully in containers of peat compost and by such means balconies and rooftops can be filled with colour and fragrance. The advantage of peat compost here is that it is much lighter than soil and so places less strain on rafters or balcony supports.

An attractive patio garden is an asset to any house, as it can be used as an outdoor room. Flowering plants give a touch of colour, and shrubs give privacy and protection from wind

Paths and Terraces

Though grass need not be excluded from a patio it should not form the main paths or sitting places, which should be well paved so that they remain clean and usable. Rectangular paving slabs are ideal since they accord with the formal style of a patio, are comparatively easy to lay, and can be obtained with a good, non-slippery surface. Bricks look nice but become dangerously slippery in wet weather. Crazy paving is rather too rustic in appearance for most patios and is difficult to lay well. Gravel is apt to pick up on the feet and asphalt has a poor appearance. Concrete is probably the best substitute for paving slabs. It can be tinted to give it a better appearance, and scored with the point of a mason's trowel to simulate the joints between paving slabs.

If paving slabs are used they should be bedded in concrete so that they are completely secure and cannot ride up and cause accidents. If creeping plants are to be grown between the slabs, leave planting spaces for these when the slabs are laid. They must be able to root down freely into the soil below.

Patterns in paving can be created by using specially-shaped paving slabs designed for pattern making, or by making panels of pebbles set in concrete. It is even possible to use pebbles of different colours to produce designs.

Walls and Screens

Patios require shelter to give protection from winds and hot sunshine, and also to give privacy. This can be provided with wooden or metal screens of various kinds, by building walls of brick, stone or special walling blocks, or by evergreen plants.

Probably the cheapest form of screening available is woven wooden panels. Various patterns of closeboard fence are a little more expensive, while some of the most attractive effects in wood can be obtained with either close or open horizontal boarding.

If more money is available, wrought-iron may be considered either as a complete screen or in panels inserted in walls.

Equally attractive effects can be obtained with concrete screen blocks available in a variety of patterns. The openwork blocks can be clothed with clematis, honeysuckle, jasmine, ornamental vines or a thornless rose, such as Zéphirine Drouhin. These will grow through the blocks and find their own support.

Part of the patio may be covered with beams in the manner of a pergola and wisteria or laburnum may be trained so that the flower trails hang down inside.

If evergreens are used choose kinds that will grow fast so that they give the required protection rapidly, and yet can be kept at whatever dimensions are necessary. Leyland Cypress has precisely these qualities.

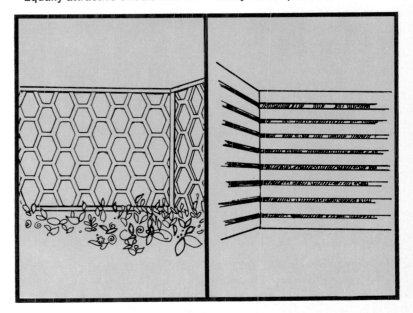

A wide range of paving materials are now available from garden centres and paving specialists. Here, concrete paving slabs in varying colours have been used to make an abstract design

Wooden beams and plastic sheeting are used to protect this patio and make it a really sheltered place both for sitting in and for cultivation of plants that enjoy some protection

Water

Water can be a great asset in a patio since it introduces a new texture and the possibility of using sound as an additional attraction. It also means that one can enjoy a further range of plants, the beauty of reflections and the movement and colour of fish.

As a rule the patio pool will be formal in design; perhaps a simple rectangle or a circle, either placed in a central position or set against a wall, with a dripping fountain trickling into it. The pool need not be deep; six inches of water is sufficient for miniature water-lilies, such as *Nymphaea pygmaea* and its varieties, and twelve inches will grow almost anything. Plants are best grown in pots or plastic baskets which will restrict their growth to some extent and make it easy to lift, divide and re-plant them when they grow too large. Very pleasing effects can be obtained by covering the bottom of the pool wholly or partially with large pebbles.

Fountains can be operated by small electric pumps and can be of many different types from single jets to multiple sprays, or a gentle water jet may simply be used to disturb the surface or bubble up through a bed of pebbles.

Hardy ferns grown in pots or a soil bed can make an attractive surround for the pool.

Planting

It is quite possible to make an attractive patio with very few plants, or it can be more or less filled with plants if desired. Often, comparatively tender plants will thrive in sheltered patios.

Unless evergreen shrubs are used to screen the patio it will be wise to include one or two in the planting so that it still looks attractive in winter. Some of the low-spreading junipers may be used or flowering evergreens with an interesting shape of leaf, such as mahonias and yuccas. Camellias, the smaller rhododendrons and evergreen azaleas, lavenders and rosemaries are also excellent, and amongst deciduous shrubs, Japanese maples and hydrangeas.

Herbaceous plants with good foliage look attractive for months. *Acanthus mollis,* astilbes, dicentra, heucheras, hostas, irises, incarvilleas, rodgersias and *Tiarella cordifolia* are a few that may be used with excellent effect.

Creeping plants in the crevices between flagstones or encroaching on paths from the edges of beds should be really prostrate, such as acaenas, arenarias, *Mazus pumilio* and *Mentha requienii.*

To maintain colour, bulbs and bedding plants in season are invaluable. Some fragrant varieties should be included, such as heliotropes, nicotianas and stocks, and also plants with a long-flowering season, such as antirrhinums, *Begonia semperflorens,* fuchsias, pelargoniums and petunias.

A simple pool with a fountain makes an interesting feature in this paved garden. The pebbles which line the pool form a further attraction and give a clean finish appropriate to the whole design

Green foliage plants have a refreshingly cool appearance and make a pleasant change from vivid flowering plants. Included here are *Rodgersia aesculifolia*, epimediums, rheums and ornamental grasses

Plant Containers

Pots, vases, tubs, troughs and other containers can be most useful in patios, both because they can themselves be ornamental and also because they can be filled with permanent or bedding plants to further the display. If room is available elsewhere in the garden, it may even be possible to have a reserve of containers which can be moved on to the patio when the plants growing in them are capable of making their greatest effect.

The choice in ornamental containers is very wide, ranging from simple wooden tubs to elaborate reproductions in plaster or glass fibre of antique lead or stone vases and troughs. Excellent modern designs in concrete or asbestos cement are also available and lovely pottery vases and jars, some of the best being imported from Provence.

Containers may either stand on the ground or be raised on pedestals or walls. Whichever method is chosen, they should stand on a hard surface with a free outlet for surplus water and no likelihood that worms will enter from below.

Hanging baskets can also be used with excellent effect in patios. They should be suspended from beams or from brackets.

Care of Container Plants

Plants grown in window-boxes, hanging baskets, vases, tubs, troughs and other containers are almost completely dependent on the gardener for water and food. The rainfall they receive will certainly not be adequate for their needs, since much of it will drain away or be evaporated. Dryness and starvation are the two commonest causes of failure with container-grown plants of any kind.

In hot weather, such plants are likely to need daily watering and even in dull, showery weather they may need watering two or three times a week. When watering, apply direct from the spout of the can or through a very coarse rose and give enough to soak right through the soil and begin to trickle out at the bottom.

If good fresh potting compost is used, plants should not need feeding for the first six weeks of their container life. After this time, feed once a fortnight with seaweed extract fertiliser or a liquid fertiliser, used as directed by the manufacturers.

The only pests that are likely to be troublesome are greenflies and capsid bugs. Occasional syringing with a good insecticide will get rid of these.

Faded flowers should be removed as they appear, not only for the sake of tidiness, but also because this helps to prolong the flowering life of the plants.

Containers are often as decorative as the plants themselves. They should be chosen so that they enhance the plants, provide good growing conditions and fit in with the style of the garden

A delightful planting of summer flowers used to decorate a back yard. Standard fuchsias and hanging baskets of pelargoniums give an added dimension to the scene

Hanging Baskets

Hanging baskets are usually made of wire or plastic, are bowl shaped and from 12 to 18 in. in diameter. They are filled with growing plants and suspended by chains from greenhouse rafters, or in verandahs, loggias, garden rooms, porticos or other places where they will add to the decorative display. Though it is possible to use hanging baskets at any time of the year, they are most useful in summer and the usual practice is to make them up in May or early June and to empty them in October.

Almost any of the plants commonly used for summer bedding may be used for hanging baskets, but pelargoniums, fuchsias, dwarf nasturtiums, lobelias and petunias are particularly suitable. *Campanula isophylla*, a slightly tender, trailing, perennial bellflower with blue or white flowers is also very useful and so are the various ornamental forms of asparagus, ivy, tradescantia and zebrina.

There are also pendulus varieties of begonia which are ideal for hanging baskets in greenhouses, loggias and other similar protected places.

Before filling hanging baskets, they should be lined with a thick layer of moss to prevent the compost from being washed out. The plants are then placed in position with John Innes or a peat-based potting compost around their roots.

An upright growing plant such as a zonal pelargonium or a fuchsia may be placed in the centre of each basket with a few trailing or spreading plants around to fill it comfortably. The basket must not be overfilled at the start as the plants will grow considerably during the summer and will become overcrowded.

Fill each basket almost to the rim with potting compost, then water thoroughly and hang up to drain. It is an advantage if baskets can be kept in a greenhouse for a week or ten days after they have been made up, so that the plants may become a little established before they are taken to colder and more exposed places.

As the plants grow, peg some of the trailing varieties to the outside of the baskets with pieces of bent wire so that they are more or less completely covered.

Hanging baskets should be watered daily in warm weather, as they tend to dry out rapidly.

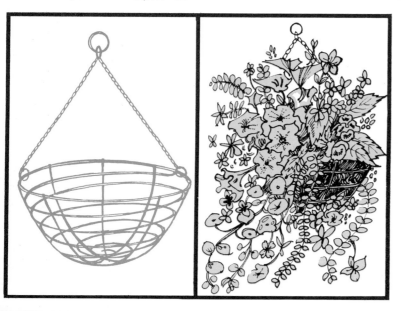

A fine example of *Fuchsia* Swingtime, growing in a hanging basket. Often these baskets are more effective if they are planted with just one particular variety

A hanging basket giving added interest to a plain brick wall. Among the plants are several types of pelargoniums, including some grown for their coloured leaves, lobelias and fuchsias

Vases, Tubs, Troughs

Vases, tubs and troughs of many kinds can be used both as ornaments in the garden, and to be filled with flowers in season to add still further to the display. Vases and troughs may be of stone, pottery, concrete, metal or plastic. Lead was once largely used, beaten or cast in elaborate designs, but this is too expensive a material to be used much nowadays. Instead, excellent reproductions of old lead vases and troughs in glass fibre or plastic can be purchased, and have the merit of being both light and durable. Wooden troughs are also available, and tubs are normally made of wood, often being barrels sawn in half, and provided with extra metal bands for strength.

Whatever kind of container is used, if plants are to be grown in it, it should be provided with drainage holes to allow surplus water to escape. If these holes are at the bottom of the sides, the containers may stand directly on the ground, but if the holes are in the bottom itself, it will be better to raise the container on slates, tiles or battens so that there is a space through which water can escape freely.

Wooden containers of all kinds, including window-boxes, must be either charred inside or treated with a wood preservative, such as copper naphthenate, which is harmless to plants. Creosote should not be used as a preservative, as this gives off fumes which are toxic to plants.

Containers should be filled with John Innes or a peat-based potting compost before planting takes place. If it is possible, this compost should be changed once a year, but if not, feed the compost when plants are renewed with John Innes Base Fertiliser at the rate of 4 oz. per bushel of soil.

Any of the plants that are used for spring and summer bedding may be used for ornamental containers. Pelargoniums (geraniums), fuchsias, petunias, lobelias, gazanias and mesembry-anthemums are particularly suitable for summer displays and wallflowers, polyanthuses, tulips and hyacinths for spring.

In addition, there are other plants which make good permanent occupants for containers, including the African Lily or agapanthus, hydrangeas, camellias, many of the smaller kinds of rhododendrons and evergreen azaleas, clipped bay and box, both green and variegated, and the slower-growing varieties of cypress, juniper and thuja. African Lilies are not completely hardy, so they should be moved to a greenhouse or shelter in winter, if possible in the containers in which they are growing.

Fuchsias, pelargoniums, lobelias and various foliage plants in an old lead trough. These troughs are fairly hard to come by, but glass fibre copies are readily available

These stone troughs blend well with the surrounding paving and wall, making an ideal background for the gay flowers. Similar troughs can be obtained made from concrete suitably prepared and coloured

Window-boxes

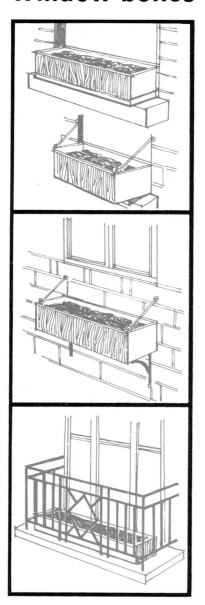

Even in town houses without gardens it is still possible to grow plants by using window-boxes. If the windows are of the sash type the boxes should stand on the the window-ledges, raised an inch or so on blocks so that surplus water can escape, but secured with bolts, metal straps or bars so that they cannot be dislodged accidentally. For casement windows, boxes must be fixed a few inches below the ledge so that the windows can be opend over the tops of the plants. This may be done with metal straps fastened to the ledge or the boxes may be supported on brackets firmly fixed to the wall.

Window-boxes may be made of wood, plastic or metal. They should not normally be less than 8 in. wide and 6 in. deep and must be well supplied with drainage holes to allow surplus water to escape.

Either John Innes No. 3 Potting Compost, or better still one of the lightweight peat composts, may be used to fill the boxes. If possible, it should be renewed each year, but if not, John Innes Base Fertiliser should be added to the soil at the rate of 4 oz. per bushel of soil before new plants are put into it.

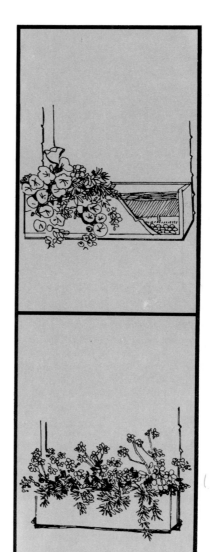

Almost any of the kinds of plants that are used for spring and summer bedding, including annuals and bulbs, may also be used for window-boxes, but the shorter varieties are to be preferred.

For spring, dwarf wallflowers, primroses, polyanthuses, violas, pansies and double daises are particularly suitable, also crocuses, tulips up to 1 ft. high and hyacinths.

For a summer display, violas and pansies may also be used with Sweet Alyssum, dwarf begonias, lobelias, dwarf French and African Marigolds, petunias (the double-flowered varieties particularly), Tom Thumb nasturtiums and verbenas. *Lobelia tenuior* and *Campanula isophylla* in blue and white varieties are useful trailing plants to hang over the edges of boxes, and ivy-leaved pelargoniums can be used in the same way. Zonal pelargoniums and short or weeping fuchsias, such as Tom Thumb and Alice Hoffman, Molesworth and Cascade may also be used.

Even in. winter, window-boxes can be made attractive with a variegated variety of periwinkle (*Vinca minor*), dwarf conifers, *Hebe pageana* and other small evergreen shrubs.

An attractive wooden window-box filled with fuchsias, begonias, pelargoniums and ivy-leaved geraniums. In the autumn, these summer-flowering plants can be replaced by spring-flowering bulbs

In this gay window-box, the trailing stems of Creeping Jenny, *Lysimachia nummularia*, unite the flowers with the branches of *Cotoneaster horizontalis* spreading up the wall below

Furniture

Plants can be removed from window-boxes or added to them as required so that a constant succession of interest is maintained. One of the advantages of using a peat-based potting compost is that these changes can be made more easily than with a soil-based compost since it does not become so consolidated.

When moving the plants, always lift them carefully with a handfork and plant equally carefully with a trowel. During this operation, avoid breaking or disturbing the roots of neighbouring plants unnecessarily. Immediately after planting water well and subsequently inspect the boxes daily, watering thoroughly as soon as the soil begins to dry.

From June to August feed every week with a seaweed-based fertiliser or any other suitable liquid fertiliser used in a very diluted state. Stake where necessary.

Pick off all faded flowers regularly and also remove discoloured or dying leaves. In hot weather, syringe the plants daily with water, increasing this to two or three times a day if it is really hot. Plants enjoy a moist atmosphere as this prevents them from wilting, and the moisture also helps to keep some pests away.

When planting a combination of bulbs and plants, place an inch or so of compost or peat in the bottom of the box, space out the bulbs on this, add a little more compost, then put the plants in position and fill in with compost.

Chairs or benches of some kind will almost certainly be required for a patio, and also possibly tables and a barbecue. All should be chosen and placed with as much care as ornaments, since they can serve an ornamental as well as a utilitarian role.

There is no shortage of good design in furniture from which to choose, and a variety of materials is also available. For the traditional style of patio, wrought-iron furniture may be preferred. It can be obtained with a natural finish, painted or nylon coated, the latter giving the greatest durability.

Modern furniture may be constructed of one of the African hardwoods, such as sapele or teak, or be of lightweight metal. Alternatively, folding or stackable furniture may be used, but this seldom adds much to the appearance of a patio.

Soft furnishings should be of nylon or some other waterproof and readily washable material. Colours should be considered not only in relation to the house and the permanent features of the patio but also in relation to the flowers which are to be grown.

Gardening without a garden. All the plants contributing to this medley of colour are growing in containers of some kind including window-boxes, tubs and flower pots

These metal-work chairs are ideal for a patio garden, for not only are they able to withstand sun and rain, but they are also attractive to look at. An annual coat of paint will keep them looking new

Bedding Plants

Bedding out means putting plants in the garden for a limited period only, while they are able to contribute most to the display, and then replacing them with other plants. Spring bedding plants are those that make this display from March to May; summer bedding plants those that continue from June to September. There are also some plants that make their peak display in May and June and so provide a useful link between spring and summer. In public parks and large gardens, winter bedding with evergreen plants is also occasionally practised, but this is seldom attempted in small gardens.

To maintain a constant display from spring to autumn necessitates several changes and a considerable reserve of plants. Most amateur gardeners are satisfied with a simpler programme consisting of two main changes, one made in late May or early June, when the summer plants are put out and the other in September or October, when the spring bedding is planted. Bedding out may be used in any way in conjunction with any other type of planting. However, traditionally it is done in clearly defined patterns which may be simple or complex according to taste. Beds, as well as the patterns created by the plants in them, are usually in regular, geometric shapes and so this kind of planting is specially suitable for formal gardens.

Carpeting plants are those that are naturally low growing or can be kept so by pinching, clipping or pegging to the soil. Taller plants may be used above these to produce a second or even a third tier of flowers, but this can involve considerable expense. Less costly is to use dot plants, that is taller plants well spaced out amongst the lower growing varieties. Standard plants, like little formal trees 3 or 4 ft. high, may be used in the same way but may take several years to form since they must be carefully trained and pruned to get the desired effect and this takes time. Because most summer bedding plants are not fully hardy these prepared standards must be overwintered in a frost-proof greenhouse or suitably light yet sheltered place.

Beds may be simple or elaborate according to taste and the patterns may be given permanent form by being edged with small shrubs, such as box, lavender, rosemary or rue, kept close trimmed. A special form of box, known as edging box, is used for this purpose and is sold by the yard of edging. The best rue for edging is Jackman's Blue and the best lavender, a dwarf variety such as Hidcote. All may need to be clipped three or four times each summer to keep them sufficiently neat. One advantage of this kind of edging is that it looks attractive at all seasons even when there are no flowers or coloured leaves to fill in the patterns.

Begonias

Begonia semperflorens

tuberous-rooted begonia

Begonias are perennials, but *Begonia semperflorens*, a fibrous-rooted type, is always grown as a half-hardy annual, and is much used in summer bedding because of its neat habit and continuous flowering. Plants are from 4 to 8 in. high, have slightly fleshy leaves which may be green or bronze and clusters of white, pink or red flowers. Organdy, with green leaves and Galaxy, with bronze leaves are good varieties to give a mixture of colours, but separate colours can also be obtained.

Sow seed in late January or February in a temperature of 15°C. (60°F.), prick out seedlings and grow on in boxes or pots until late May or June when the threat of frost has passed and it is safe to plant out of doors. The plants like good, well-cultivated soil and plenty of water.

The large-flowered tuberous-rooted begonias can also be raised from seed in the same way as fibrous-rooted types, or tubers can be obtained and started into growth in the spring in a greenhouse.

These large-flowered kinds are not so adaptable for bedding as *Begonia semperflorens* but look attractive in beds on their own.

Begonia multiflora is intermediate in habit between the tuberous-rooted begonias and *B. semperflorens*. It can be raised from seed or grown from tubers and is a useful alternative for bedding. The plants reach a height of about 10 in.

The scarlet in this summer display is provided by *Begonia* Indian Maid with the deep blue of lobelia as a surround and the silver of *Centaurea gymnocarpa* as dot plants for contrast

Dahlias

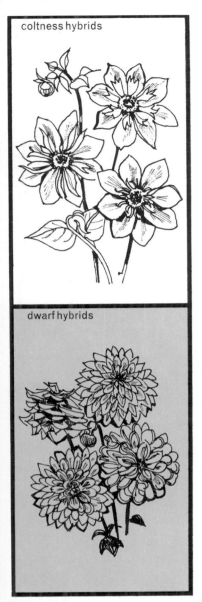

coltness hybrids

dwarf hybrids

Dahlias of all kinds can be used for summer bedding, but the most useful and adaptable are the bedding varieties, such as the single flowered coltness hybrids and various other strains of dwarf hybrids, 1½ to 2 ft. high, with semi-double or double flowers in mixed colours. These types are readily raised from seed.

Sow in a greenhouse, at a temperature of 15 to 18°C. (60 to 65°F.) in February or March, and prick out as soon as possible at least 2 in. apart as the plants grow rapidly. Alternatively, they may be potted singly in 3-in. pots in John Innes or a peat-based compost. Keep the plants well watered and harden off for planting out in late May or early June. Space the plants 1½ ft. apart in good, well-cultivated soil and an open sunny place.

There are also a number of dwarf dahlias which can be grown from tubers, and are propagated by cuttings in the spring. These cuttings will produce flowers that are identical in colour and shape to the parent, and are ideal for use in bedding schemes where colour patterns are required. The tubers that are produced during the growing season can be lifted in the autumn, stored, and used again the following year.

Balsams, Heliotropes

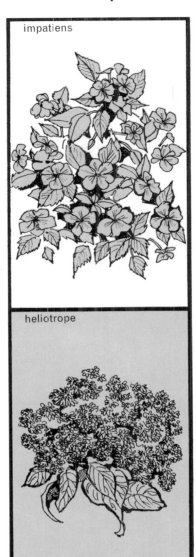

impatiens

heliotrope

The balsams or impatiens are commonly grown as pot plants, but dwarf varieties of *Impatiens sultanii*, such as Imp, available in white, rose, carmine, scarlet, orange, purple and in mixtures of these colours, and growing to a height of 9 in., make excellent summer bedding plants.

Sow seed in a greenhouse, at a temperature of 21°C. (70°F.) and do not shade the seed pans. Prick out and harden off for planting out of doors in late May or June in a sunny or partially shaded place. Space the plants 9 to 12 in. apart.

Heliotropes are also popular pot plants which are excellent for summer bedding. Marine is an excellent variety with violet-purple flowers, compact, well branched and 15 in. high. It can be grown from seed, or plants can be raised from cuttings in spring or August.

Sow seed in February or early March in a greenhouse, at a temperature of 18°C. (65°F.), prick out the seedlings and later pot them singly in 3-in. pots. Harden them off gradually for planting out in late May or early June, in good, well-cultivated soil and a sunny position. Space dwarf plants 1 ft. apart, standards 2 to 3 ft. apart. Plants can be lifted in late September or early October, potted singly and kept in a greenhouse with a minimum temperature of 7°C. (45°F.) for another year or to give spring cuttings.

Bedding dahlias are easily raised from seed. They produce a very rewarding crop of flowers, continuing to do so until the plants are cut back by frost. This is a typical Coltness Hybrid

Impatiens sultanii Orange Baby is one of the many varieties of dwarf balsam which are now available. The popular name of these plants is Busy Lizzie

Fuchsias

Many varieties of fuchsia make excellent summer bedding plants. They can be grown as bushes or trained as standards, and can be raised from cuttings, or plants can be purchased in May or early June ready for planting out.

Bush fuchsias are best planted on their own in beds or blocks of one variety but standard fuchsias may be associated with almost any other summer bedding plants. They look particularly attractive over a groundwork of *Begonia semperflorens* or antirrhinums.

Space bush plants 1½ ft. apart and standards at least 3 ft. apart. Give them a good, well-cultivated soil and water the plants freely in dry weather. Stake standard fuchsias straightaway with 1 in. by 1 in. stakes as the heads become very heavy and are easily snapped off by wind.

In October, lift the plants carefully and either pot them separately or pack them close together in boxes with some old potting soil or peat around the roots. Bring them into a reasonably frost-proof greenhouse (they are nearly hardy and will survive a degree or two of frost) or place them in a light shed for the winter. Water very sparingly until March, then shake out the soil, prune off any damaged roots, re-pot in a size smaller pot and water more freely as growth re-starts.

Geraniums

The geraniums used for summer bedding are correctly named pelargoniums. There are two main types; Zonal-leaved with round, slightly downy leaves and strong stems and Ivy-leaved with smooth, angular leaves and weak stems.

All pelargoniums like warm, sunny places and well-drained soil though they will grow almost anywhere. They can be raised from cuttings, or plants can be purchased in May or June.

Plant zonal pelargoniums 12 to 15 in. apart, ivy-leaved pelargoniums 18 in. apart. Either peg the stems of the ivy-leaved varieties to the soil, spreading them out so that eventually they completely cover it, or tie them to short canes to make columns. The plants can be lifted in September or October and brought into a greenhouse with a minimum temperature of 7°C. (45°F.) for the winter.

Some good bedding zonal pelargoniums are: Gustav Emich, double scarlet; King of Denmark, semi-double pink; Maxim Kovalevski, single vermilion; Paul Crampel, single scarlet; Queen of the Belgians, double white and Vera Dillon, single magenta.

Good ivy-leaved varieties are: Abel Carrière, soft purple; Galilee, pink; Jeanne d'Arc, white; Mrs W. A. R. Clifton, scarlet.

Ornamental leaved varieties are: Chelsea Gem, green and silver; Crystal Palace Gem, green and gold; Mrs Henry Cox, green, yellow and red.

Standard fuchsias make particularly attractive plants with their large heads of dangling flowers. A plant such as the one shown here would take two or three years to develop from a cutting

Zonal pelargoniums (geraniums) are always popular bedding plants. Here they are mixed with stocks and the silvery foliage of *Senecio cineraria* and set off beautifully by the well-kept grass verge

Silver and Grey

Senecio cineraria

Centaurea candidissima

Kleinia repens

Plants with silver or grey leaves are useful in summer bedding schemes as a foil to the colours of the flowers. They are often used as dot plants.

One of the most popular is *Senecio cineraria*, also known as *Cineraria maritima*, a bushy, fairly hardy perennial with deeply-divided silvery-white leaves. It can be grown from seed sown in a warm greenhouse in February–March, or by cuttings inserted in a frame or greenhouse in August–September and protected until the spring. *Senecio leucostachys, Centaurea gymnocarpa* and *C. rutifolia* (*C. candidissima*) are similar in appearance and are grown in the same way.

Calocephalus brownii, also known as *Leucophyta brownii*, is even more silvery, with wiry stems and narrow leaves. It can be grown as a small column, about a foot in height, and used as a dot plant, or the growing tips can be pinched out frequently so making it into a dwarf, spreading plant suitable for carpet bedding.

Kleinia repens, also known as *Senecio repens*, is a creeping plant only an inch or so high, with blue-grey leaves. It is useful for outlining the finer details of carpet bedding or for forming letters or figures in floral clocks, etc. in public parks. It is grown from cuttings taken in spring or summer and rooted in a warm greenhouse.

Coloured Leaves

kochia

abutilon

Coloured foliage can be as useful as silver and grey foliage in diversifying the effects in summer bedding displays. Kochia is an annual known as Summer Cypress, because it makes a 2-ft. column of fine leaves and looks like a miniature conifer; these are green at first turning to purplish-red in late summer. Sow seed in a warm greenhouse in March and harden off seedlings for planting out in late May or early June as dot plants.

Abutilon thompsonii is a shrubby plant with light green leaves heavily mottled with yellow, and with orange, drooping, trumpet-shaped flowers. It will quickly grow to a height of 3 ft. and can be used as a background or a centrepiece. The plants can be bought in May or June or raised from summer cuttings which are kept in a frost-proof greenhouse in winter.

Chrysanthemum parthenium aureum (Pyrethrum parthenifolium aureum) is known as Golden Feather because it has bright yellow feathery leaves. It is grown like kochia from seed and planted out 6 in. apart to form a carpeting or groundwork plant 4 to 6 in. tall.

Alternantheras and iresines are used for carpet bedding in a similar manner, but are pinched or clipped to keep them short and compact. Varieties are available with leaves in various combinations of green, yellow, cerise and crimson. Plants can be purchased in late May or June, or raised from cuttings in a warm greenhouse in spring.

Grey foliage plants, such as *Centaurea gymnocarpa* add further interest to a border, both in colour and in texture, and help to set off other plants. Also shown are geraniums in the background and heliotropes

The bright red leaves of *Iresine brilliantissima* are as colourful as flowers. *Fuchsia* Golden Treasure beyond has golden foliage, and *Ruta graveolens*, in the foreground, has feathery blue-grey leaves

Plants for Special Purposes

A Child's Garden

The first essentials for a child's garden are that the plants must be easy to grow and give a reasonably quick result.

Many annuals and bulbs fulfil both requirements and bulbs have the additional merit that good ones are almost certain to flower the first year. Narcissi (daffodils), crocus, chionodoxa, muscari (Grape Hyacinths) and *Scilla siberica* are likely to continue for years with minimal attention. Hyacinths and tulips, though highly reliable the first season, are less certain in subsequent years.

Among the most suitable hardy annuals which can be sown where they are to flower are: Sweet Alyssum, calendula, clarkia, coreopsis, eschscholzia, godetia, gypsophila, lavatera, malope, Mignonette, nasturtium, nigella and annual poppies. A few plants of antirrhinums, double daisies, pansies and petunias put in when they are just coming into flower are valuable, and perennials such as dicentra (Bleeding Heart), polygonatum (Solomon's Seal) and lupins are liked for their flower shapes. So is the miniature rose Cécile Brunner.

Many children enjoy growing radishes and lettuces and even sweet-scented herbs such as sage and thyme.

Beds for children should be not more than 3 ft. wide with access from both sides, and mown grass is the ideal surround.

However difficult a soil or situation may be it is usually possible to find some plants that will grow in it. But this is only one way of dealing with this problem. Another is to improve the condition that is causing the difficulty and so widen the selection of plants that can be used successfully. Chalk soils are limiting because they are often deficient in iron and manganese which suffer chemical changes that render them insoluble and therefore unavailable as plant food. Special preparations of these chemicals, known as sequestrols, can be used to make good the deficiencies and the soil can be made less alkaline by giving it heavy dressings of acid peat or leafmould.

Heavy clay soils are difficult because they retain too much water, are poorly aerated and tend to become sour. Generous liming will improve their texture and correct sourness, but it can make it difficult to grow lime-hating plants such as rhododendrons, pieris and many heathers. Peat, well-rotted garden compost, stable manure and coarse sand will all help to improve the texture of clay soils.

Plants growing in seaside gardens are often battered by gales which may bring salt spray as an added hazard. Here the remedy is to provide a substantial windbreak on the seaward side. There is nothing better for this than *Cupressus macrocarpa*, which grows rapidly and is evergreen. The yellow-leaved variety is even more salt resistant than the green. *Pinus radiata* is a fast-growing pine that does well by the sea and makes a tall and substantial windbreak. While such plants are growing temporary shelter can be provided with wattle hurdles or interwoven fencing.

In very hot sunny places improvement can be effected by planting trees to give some shade, but since in such places dryness is often as damaging as the intensity of the sunlight, the trees must be planted sufficiently far away not to fill the flower beds with their roots. Some kinds such as the cypresses do not make very extensive root systems, and some such as oak push their roots downwards rather than outwards and these are to be preferred as shade givers in such places. Water sprinklers permanently installed can also transform the planting possibilities in a hot, dry garden. Sprinklers that give a fine, rain-like spray are the most satisfactory as the water then has time to soak in.

Plants that spread densely over the surface of the soil are often recommended as ground cover to smother weeds and so save labour. This works well provided the soil is well cleared of weeds first and any perennial weeds that appear later are removed promptly. But if weeds are allowed to become established under the ground cover it can be a major operation to get rid of them.

lupin

Plants for a child's garden must be easy to grow and give quick results. *Scilla siberica*, primulas and muscari are ideal for this purpose since they will look very attractive for many years with minimal attention

Chalk

Chalk and limestone soils are normally alkaline, and being usually porous and quick draining they are slow to accumulate humus. The plants listed are those which are known to do well on chalk, but many others will grow well if kept moist. Humus is best added in the form of peat.

Good hardy perennials for chalk and limestone soils are achillea, aster (Michaelmas daisies); campanulas, centaurea (perennial cornflowers), centranthus (valerian), *Chrysanthemum maximum* (Shasta Daisies), coreopsis; delphiniums, dianthus (pinks, Sweet Williams and carnations), doronicum; eremurus; gaillardias, hardy geraniums, geums, gypsophila; helenium, helianthus, (sun-flowers), helleborus; iris; *Papaver orientale* (Oriental Poppy), phlox, pyrethrum; rudbeckia; *Salvia superba, Scabiosa caucasica*, sedum, sidalcea, solidago; thalictrum and verbascum.

Good rock plants are aethionema, alyssum, arabis, armeria, aubrieta, campanula, dianthus, erodium, gypsophila, helianthemum (sun rose), hypericum, iberis (candytuft), linum, phlox, potentilla, sedum and thymus (thyme).

Good annuals and bedding plants are antirrhinum, aster, candytuft, coreopsis, dianthus, gypsophila, lavatera, linum, Mignonette, nasturtium, pansies, poppies, rudbeckias, scabious, violas and wallflowers.

Good shrubs for chalk or limestone soils are berberis, buddleia, bupleurum, buxus (box); caryopteris, cistus (rock rose), chaenomeles (cydonia or Japanese Quince), colutea, *Cornus alba* and varieties, cotoneaster (all varieties), *Cotinus coggygria* (Smoke Tree), cytisus (broom); deutzia, escallonia; forsythia, fuchsia; genista (broom); hypericum, hebe (shrubby veronicas); lavandula (lavender), ligustrum (privet); philadelphus (mock orange), *Potentilla fruticosa*; rhus (sumach), rosmarinus (rosemary); sambucus (elderberry), santolina, *Senecio laxifolius*, spartium (Spanish Broom), syringa (lilac); ulex (gorse); viburnum, vinca (periwinkle) and weigela.

Good trees are carpinus (hornbeam), crataegus (thorns), fagus (beech), ilex (holly), laburnum, malus (apple), prunus (almond, cherry, peach and plum), sorbus (Mountain Ash or Rowan, Whitebeam) and taxus (yew).

Good climbers are clematis of all kinds, honeysuckles, pyracantha and ornamental vines.

Conifers that do well on chalk are cedrus (cedar), cupressus, chamaecyparis and cupressocyparis (cypresses), gingko (Maidenhair Tree), juniperus (juniper), larix (larch), metasequoia, *Pinus sylvestris* (Scots Pine), taxus (yew) and thuja.

Good bulbs are alliums, crocus, erythronium, iris, narcissi (daffodils) and tulips.

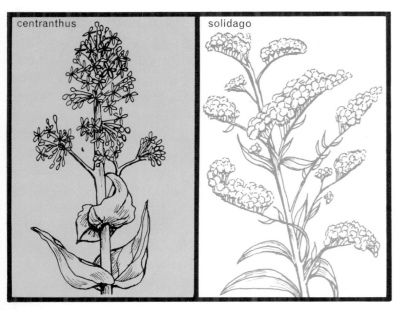

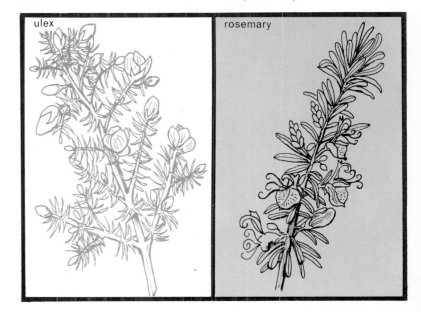

Michaelmas daisies and golden rod are two very useful herbaceous plants for a chalky soil. They will flower well together in the September border and are best divided and replanted fairly frequently

Among the conifers which will thrive in a chalky soil is *Thuja occidentalis* here shown in its slow growing variety *ellwangeriana*. Also shown is *Campanula carpatica*, in blue and white varieties

Shady Places

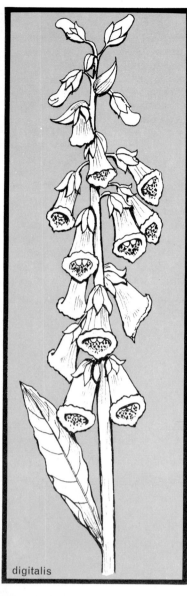
digitalis

Shade or low light intensity varies from the shadow thrown by fences or buildings where the plant receives little or no direct sunlight but is open to the sky and normal rainfall, to deep shade under trees where the plant also has to compete with the tree roots for water and food. In such conditions it is well worth feeding and watering it.

Good hardy perennials for shady places are acanthus, aconitum, *Anemone japonica,* aquilegia, *Artemisia lactiflora, Aruncus sylvester,* astilbe, astrantia; bergenia, *Brunnera macrophylla;* campanula, convallaria (lily of the valley); dicentra, digitalis (foxglove); *Helleborus niger* (Christmas Rose), *H. orientalis* (Lenten Rose), hemerocallis, hosta; lysimachia; mertensia; phlox, polygonatum (Solomon's Seal), primroses, polyanthus, pulmonaria; thalictrum, tiarella, *Tradescantia virginiana,* trollius and violas.

Good rock plants are arenaria, campanula, epimedium, *Gentiana asclepiadea,* haberlea, meconopsis, omphalodes, *Primula denticulata, P. juliae, P. juliana,* ramonda, sanguinaria, *Saxifraga umbrosa* (London Pride), mossy saxifrages and rock violas.

Bulbs and tubers for shady places are *Anemone apennina, A. blanda, A. nemorosa,* colchicums, hardy cyclamen, eranthis (Winter Aconite), erythronium (Dog's Tooth Violet), *Fritillaria meleagris,* lilies, narcissi, scilla and snowdrops.

Good shrubs for shady places are azaleas, aucuba; bamboos, *Berberis darwinii, B. stenophylla,* buxus (box); camellias; *Danae racemosa* (Alexandrian Laurel); enkianthus, *Euonymus japonicus, E. fortunei (E. radicans);* forsythia; gaultheria; hydrangea, hypericum; ilex (hollies); kerria; ligustrum (privet); pernettya, *Prunus laurocerasus* (Cherry Laurel), *P. lusitanica* (Portugal Laurel), pyracantha; *Ribes sanguineum* (Flowering Currant), *Ruscus aculeatus* (Butcher's Broom); sarcococca, skimmia, symphoricarpos (Snowberry); *Viburnum tinus* (Laurustinus) and vinca (periwinkle).

Climbers for shade are chaenomeles (cydonia or Japanese Quince), clematis, *Forsythia suspensa,* hedera varieties (ivies), *Hydrangea petiolaris, Jasminum nudiflorum, Kerria japonica flore pleno,* lonicera (honeysuckles), pyracantha and *Schizophragma hydrangeoides.*

Annuals and bedding plants to grow in shade are annual asters, begonias, *Bellis monstrosa* (double daisy), *Calceolaria integrifolia,* impatiens, *Matthiola bicornis* (Nightscented Stock), *Mimulus tigrinus* (musk), myosotis (forget-me-not), nicotiana, pansies, *Saponaria vaccaria* and violas.

symphoricarpos

A charming collection of naturalised bulbs under the shade of trees. Narcissi, erythroniums, muscari and scillas combine to provide this delightful spring scene

There are many beautiful species and varieties of clematis like this one which is named Lasurstern and has very large flowers

Ground Cover

Some plants will cover the ground with such a dense growth that weed seeds have little chance to germinate. Such plants are known as ground-cover plants. Provided the soil has been cleared of perennial weeds before the ground cover is planted, subsequent maintenance will be reduced to a minimum. It is important that the plants chosen are reasonably sturdy but not so vigorous that they become almost as great a nuisance as the weeds they are replacing.

Some ground-cover plants make such a low carpet of growth that bulbs can be planted to grow through them. Others are too vigorous for this but are quite suitable as ground cover beneath shrubs and trees.

Good plants for ground-cover purposes are *Acaena buchananii, A. microphylla, Arenaria balearica, A. caespitosa, A. purpurascens; Cotula squalida; Erodium chamaedryoides roseum; Linaria aequitriloba; Mazus reptans; Raoulia australis, R. glabra; Sagina glabra* and its golden-leaved variety, *Saxifraga muscoides, Sedum dasyphyllum, S. lydium; Thymus serpyllum*, some of the veronicas such as *Veronica rupestris* and *Waldsteinia sibirica*.

Plants of moderate vigour suitable for growing with shrubs are *Ajuga reptans, Alchemilla mollis, Arisarum proboscideum, Arundinaria pumila, Asperula odorata*, astrantia; bergenia; *Calluna vulgaris* (heather), *Cornus canadensis, Cotoneaster dammeri; Doronicum cordatum;* epimediums, low-growing ericas such as *Erica carnea, E. darleyensis* and *E. vagans, Euonymus fortunei radicans, Euphorbia cyparissias:* '*Fragaria indica; Gaultheria procumbens;* small varieties of *Hedera helix* (ivy) such as *cristata,* Jubilee and *tricolor, Heucherella tiarelloides, Hosta lancifolia, H. undulata; Lamium galeobdolon, L. maculatum; Myosotis dissitiflora* (forget-me-not); *Omphalodes verna; Pachysandra terminalis,*

Polygonum affine, Prunella grandiflora, pulmonarias; *Sarcococca humilis,* mossy saxifrages, *Sedum spurium; Tellima grandiflora, Tiarella cordifolia, Tolmiea menziesii; Viola labradorica* and *Vinca minor* (periwinkle).

Vigorous ground-cover plants, best planted on their own, are *Cerastium tomentosum, Gaultheria shallon, Hedera helix* (ivy, common kind and vigorous varieties), also *Hedera colchica dentata variegata, Hypericum calycinum, Polygonum campanulatum,* Rose Max Graff, *Stachys lanata* and *Vinca major* (periwinkle).

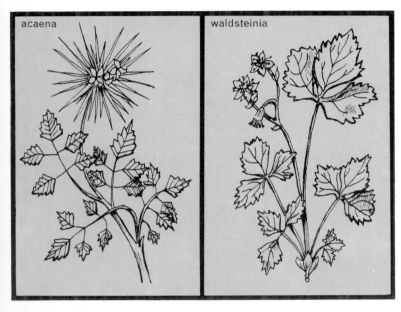

acaena

waldsteinia

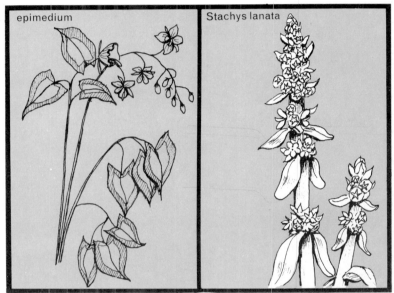

epimedium

Stachys lanata

There are several species of veronica which will make delightful ground-cover plants and provide a carpet of blue to set off other plants such as the variously coloured primroses seen here

The attractive leaf colouring of *Lamium galeobdolon variegatum* contrasts well with the red brickwork. Known by the common name of Variegated Yellow Archangel, it is a rapidly spreading ground-cover plant

Hot, Dry Places

Hot, dry soils mean those which, because of their aspect and rapidity of drainage, become arid for weeks or months in summer. They are excellent for bulbous plants such as tulips or nerines, which benefit from a good baking. Grey-leaved, many fleshy-leaved plants (succulents) and some with spiny leaves are adapted to survive periods of drought, and mulching after rain or watering will help to conserve moisture. Plant at the beginning of a rainy period, such as autumn, rather than spring.

Good hardy perennials for hot, dry places are achillea, anaphalis, anchusa, anthemis; catananche, centaurea, centranthus, coreopsis; dianthus, echinops, erigeron, eryngium, gaillardia, galega, geum, gypsophila; linum, lupinus; nepeta; oenothera; *Papaver orientale*, potentilla; schizostylis, sedum and verbascum.

Good rock plants are alyssum, arabis, armeria, aubrieta, cerastium, dianthus, erodium, *Geranium sanguineum,* gypsophila, helianthemum, linum, othonnopsis, oxalis, *Polygonum affine,* sedums, sempervivums and zauschneria.

Good annuals and bedding plants are Sweet Alyssum, anagallis, antirrhinum, clarkia, coreopsis, dianthus, dimorphotheca, eschscholzia, gaillardia, gazania, godetia, gypsophila, lavatera, linum, lupin, malope, mentzelia, mesembryanthemums, nasturtiums, poppies, portulaca, ursinia and venidium.

Good shrubs for hot, dry places are abelia, *Acacia hispidissima,* atriplex; buddleia; caryopteris. ceratostigma, cistus, colutea, cytisus (broom); genista (broom); halimium, hedysarum, *Hibiscus syriacus, Hypericum calycinum;* indigofera; lavandula (lavender), *Lupinus arboreus* (Tree Lupin); *Olearia scilloniensis;* perovskia, phlomis, phormium, piptanthus, *Potentilla fruticosa;* romneya, rosmarinus (rosemary); santolina, *Senecio laxifolius,* spartium; *Teucrium fruticans; Ulex europaeus plenus* (double-flowered gorse) and yucca.

Climbers for hot, dry places are *Campsis grandiflora, C.* Madame Galen, *Ceanothus impressus, C. rigidus, C. thyrsiflorus, Cotoneaster horizontalis;* hedera varieties (ivies); *Magnolia grandiflora; Passiflora caerulea* (passion flower), *Polygonum baldschuanicum* (Russian Vine); *Solanum crispum, S. jasminoides* and ornamental vines (including ampelopsis, parthenocissus and vitis).

Bulbs suitable for hot, dry places are agapanthus, alstroemeria, allium, *Amaryllis belladonna;* babiana, brodiaea (triteleia); camassias, *Crinum powellii, Crocosmia masonorum, Curtonus paniculata (Antholyza paniculata);* ixias, ixiolirion; lapeirousia; montbretias, *Nerine bowdenii;* sparaxis, *Sprekelia formosissima;* tigridia, tulips and zephyranthes.

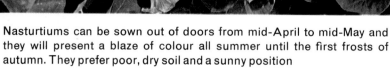

Nasturtiums can be sown out of doors from mid-April to mid-May and they will present a blaze of colour all summer until the first frosts of autumn. They prefer poor, dry soil and a sunny position

Passiflora caerulea is a fairly hardy passion flower, a vigorous quick growing climber than can be grown successfully in many parts of the British Isles against a sunny sheltered wall

Seaside Gardens

In seaside gardens temperatures tend to be less extreme, so that many less hardy plants will survive most winters. But seaside gardens are frequently exposed to salt, gale-force winds and blown sand, and a windbreak is usually needed for the more tender plants.

Trees and shrubs which form an outer windbreak resistant to salt spray are *Atriplex halimus, Euonymus japonicus*, griselinia, *Hippophae rhamnoides* (Sea Buckthorn), *Lycium chinense, Olearia albida, O. haastii, O. oleifolia, O. traversii* and tamarix.

In the milder parts of the South and West may be added *Cupressus macrocarpa, Olearia macrodonta, Pinus radiata*, pittosporum and *Senecio rotundifolius*.

Good shrubs to plant within such a sheltered belt are abelia, arbutus; berberis, buddleia; callistemon (bottle brush) in mild districts, calluna, camellia, caryopteris, ceanothus, ceratostigma, choisya, cistus, clerodendrum, colutea, *Convolvulus cneorum, Corokia cotoneaster, Coronilla glauca,* cotoneaster, cytisus; daphne; erica, escallonia; fatsia, fuchsia; genista, hebe, *Hibiscus syriacus,* hydrangea, hypericum; lavender, leptospermum, *Lupinus arboreas* (Tree Lupin); mahonia, myrtus; perovskia, phlomis, phormium, potentilla; romneya, rosmarinus, ruta (rue); *Salvia grahamii;* teucrium, tricuspidaria (mild districts only); *Viburnum tinus;* weigela and yucca.

Good trees for mild districts are *Acacia dealbata* (Mimosa), *Cordyline australis* (New Zealand Cabbage Palm), embothrium, hoheria, paulownia and *Trachycarpus fortunei* (hardy palm). Laburnums do well by the sea and are completely hardy.

Good hardy perennials are achillea, agapanthus, anthemis, armeria, *Aster pappei;* catananche, crambe, *Cynara scolymus* (Globe Artichoke); dianthus (pinks, carnations and Sweet Williams), dierama, dimorphotheca; echinops, eryngium, euphorbia; kniphofia; limonium (statice), lupin, lychnis; sedum, stachys and zantedeschia (Arum Lily) mild districts only.

Good bulbs and tubers to grow are *Amaryllis belladonna*, babiana, brodiaea (triteleia), cannas, crinum, dahlias, gladiolus, hyacinths, iris, montbretia, muscari (Grape Hyacinth), narcissi (daffodils), nerine, scillas (bluebells and squills) and tulips.

Good annuals and bedding plants are Sweet Alyssum, anagallis, arctotis, annual asters; *Begonia semperflorens;* calendula, clarkia, convolvulus; dianthus (annual pinks and carnations), dimorphotheca; eschscholzia; gazania, godetia; lavatera, limonium (annual statice), *Linum grandiflorum;* malope, mesembryanthemum; nemesia; annual poppies, petunias; stocks; tagetes (marigolds); ursinias; venidium, wallflowers and zinnias.

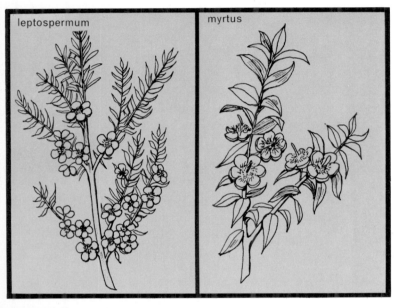

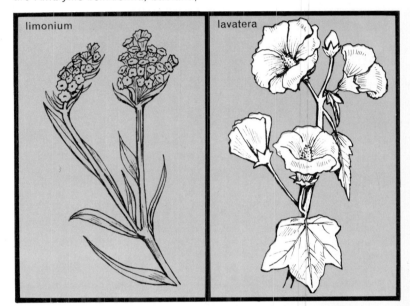

Seaside gardens face a special problem with salt-laden winds. *Fuchsia magellanica riccartonii*, which flowers all summer, is one of the plants which does well in such conditions

All the brooms make good seaside shrubs. This one, *Cytisus praecox,* is covered in flowers during April and here it has been planted with aubrieta and *Alyssum saxatile* which also do well by the sea

Flowers for Cutting

Hardy Annuals

preparing seed drills

sowing seed

covering seed

Any flower can be cut but not all flowers are equally good for the purpose. Many do not last well in water and some have unsuitable stems or an unpleasant smell. Equally not all flowers that are good for cutting are satisfactory for garden display. Some continue to flower for months but never make much of a show at any one time and some have flowers that quickly look shabby if left uncut. All these points must be considered when choosing flowers for the garden that will be suitable for cutting.

It must be decided, too, whether cut flowers are to be taken from the ordinary flower borders or whether special beds are to be set aside for them in a concealed part of the garden. The latter course is preferable if space permits since the plants can be given the special attention they may need and the flowers cut without denuding the ornamental garden. But in small gardens there may be no room for special beds and then flowers must be selected for cutting by thinning carefully rather than by stripping plants completely.

Most flowers last best if they have been cut from plants that have grown vigorously and fast. Good feeding and adequate watering will help to produce the soft, succulent stems which take up water readily. Rose bushes that are to be used for cutting need to be pruned rather more severely than those grown for garden display only. This will reduce the number of flowers but increase the length of flower stems. When the roses are cut a fair length of stem should be taken, each cut being made just above a well-developed leaf, since where the leaf joins the stem there will be a growth bud which may produce another stem and more bloom. Similar hard pruning often helps shrubs used for cutting by improving the length of stems, making them stouter and more succulent and also increasing the size of the flowers.

However well grown they may be there are some flowers that take up water badly. It always helps to carry a bucket of water round while cutting flowers and place them directly in this before air has entered the base of the stem and perhaps caused an air lock. If this cannot be done it will pay to cut off a little from the bottom of each stem when it can be put into water and perhaps to slit the stem vertically. It is also wise to change the water in vases daily. Foliage is also of great value to flower arrangers and provision should be made for this in sufficient variety and quantity at all times of the year. With bulbs it is never wise to take too many of their leaves since the bulbs are then starved and may not produce flowers the following year. The removal of the flower is, on the whole, beneficial since it prevents any possibility of seed production which always puts a considerable strain upon a plant.

The following annuals can be grown from seed sown out of doors in spring where the plants are to flower. All like moderately rich, well-cultivated soil and an open, sunny position. Sow the seeds thinly in straight drills $\frac{1}{2}$ in. deep and 1 ft. apart, thin out the seedlings to about 6 in., and discard after flowering.

Calendula (Pot Marigold): orange or yellow daisy flowers. Best in double-flowered varieties such as Pacific Beauty, Pacific Gold and Radio.

Coreopsis (calliopsis): yellow daisy flowers with chestnut-red centres.

Chrysanthemum: there are several annual kinds, some with single, some double flowers. Tricolor, with rings of different colours, is particularly useful for cutting.

Cornflower: the tall varieties, in blue and pink, are best for cutting but need support when growing.

Gypsophila: the annual gypsophila has larger flowers than the perennial kind but not such big sprays. There are white and pink varieties.

Larkspur: slender spikes of white, blue, pink or scarlet flowers.

Mignonette: valued for its fragrance, it likes a limy soil.

Nigella (Love-in-a-Mist): rather like a cornflower, but with feathery foliage.

Sweet Sultan: another cornflower-like plant with a good range of colours.

Chrysanthemum spectabile Cecilia, an attractive annual chrysanthemum which produces its flowers very freely over a lengthy period. The single blooms may reach 4 in. in diameter

Half-hardy Annuals

Half-hardy annuals are best sown in February or March in a moderately heated greenhouse or frame. Prick seedlings out into boxes of John Innes No. 1 or peat-based potting compost and harden off for planting outside in late May.

Arctotis: single daisy-type flowers in a good range of colours, including silvery blues and wine reds.

Antirrhinums (snapdragons): the tall varieties are particularly good for cutting.

Asters: there is great variety in the character of the flowers – some are single, some ball-like, some shaggy.

Carnations: the annual or Chabaud carnations are readily raised from seed and have a good colour range. Some are scented.

Cosmos: elegant single daisy flowers in white, pink, crimson and orange with ferny foliage.

Marigolds: the tall, double-flowered African F_1 hybrid varieties are best for cutting.

Molucellas (Bells of Ireland): green flower spikes. They require a temperature of 18 to 24° C. (65 to 70°F.) for germination.

Rudbeckia: bold yellow, orange or mahogany-red daisy flowers, single and double.

Ten-week Stocks: Hansen's 100% Double Column Stocks are best for cutting.

Zinnia: the tall, double-flowered varieties are fine cut flowers, both flat-petalled and quill-petalled varieties.

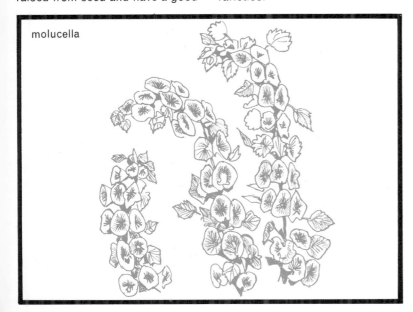

Molucella laevis, Bells of Ireland, is an unusual-looking plant often used for flower arrangements. The small white flowers are usually removed as it is the bell-shaped calyces that are most decorative

Biennials

Biennials are plants that must be sown one year to flower the next, after which they are discarded. Most can be sown out of doors in May or June and planted in September where they are to flower.

Brompton Stocks: the 100% double varieties should be grown for cutting in May and June before the annual stocks. They need well-drained soil and a fairly sheltered position and are excellent for sea-side gardens.

Canterbury Bells: the tall, single-flowered and cup-and-saucer varieties are best for cutting. They flower in June and July.

Honesty (lunaria): this is grown primarily for the oval, parchment-like seed heads which last all the winter, but the purple flower sprays are also decorative and there is an attractive variety with variegated leaves.

Iceland Poppies: these are the most useful for cutting because of their good colour range, including yellow, orange, apricot, salmon, pink, rose and red. As soon as cut the stems should be stood for half a minute in 1 in. of boiling water to prevent air entering and so enable them to take up water.

Sweet Williams: fine, flat heads of flowers in pink, scarlet, crimson and white. The auricula-eyed varieties have a white eye.

Wallflowers: tall varieties such as Blood Red, Cloth of Gold, Fire King and Eastern Queen are best for cutting.

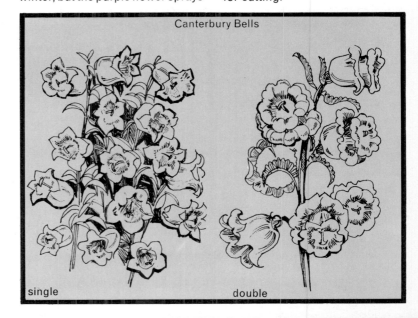

Canterbury Bells

single   double

Sweet Williams *(Dianthus barbatus)* are always popular garden flowers, and are also suitable for cutting. They are easily raised from seeds sown in May or June

Flowering Perennials

A great many hardy herbaceous perennials can be used for cutting and the following are only a few of the most useful.

Achillea, The Pearl: small, double white flowers freely borne in sprays most of the summer.

Alstroemeria, Ligtu Hybrids: elegant heads of pink or salmon flowers in July – August. Grow in a warm, sheltered place where the plants can remain undisturbed.

Chrysanthemum maximum (Shasta Daisy): large, white daisies on long stems in July and August.

Doronicum, Harpur Crewe: large yellow daisies in May.

Gypsophila, Bristol Fairy: large sprays of small, double white flowers in July and August which look excellent with sweet peas. Do not disturb the plants.

Gaillardias: large yellow, bronze-red or red and yellow daisies from June to September.

Heucheras: sprays of small pink or red flowers from June to August.

Peonies: single, semi-double and double varieties are all excellent. Leave them undisturbed.

Pyrethrums: large single or double daisy-type flowers, white, pink or red in June. They need well-drained soil.

Scabiosa caucasica: lavender or white flowers from July to October. They like lime.

Solomon's Seal (polygonatum): useful for foliage as well as for its pendant green and white flowers appearing in May. It likes shade.

Foliage Perennials

Good foliage can be cut from many hardy herbaceous perennials, but the following plants have particularly distinctive leaves.

Acanthus (bear's breeches): large, divided, deep green leaves, broad lobed in *A. mollis*, narrow lobed in *A. spinosissimus*.

Arum pictum: arrow-shaped leaves, dark green, veined white.

Bocconia (Plume Poppy): large, rounded, grey-green leaves sometimes shaded with bronze.

Cynara: more familiar as the cardoon and globe artichoke of the vegetable garden. Long, deeply divided, silvery-grey leaves. It may need protection with straw and dry bracken in winter.

Hostas: there are several kinds, all with fine leaves broadly lance shaped in some, heart shaped in others; shining green, blue-grey or green and cream according to the variety. They do well in shade.

Rodgersia: there are several species, all with large, deeply divided or finger-like leaves, green or bronze. All like rich, damp soil.

Sedum (stonecrop): *Sedum spectabile variegata* has cream and light green leaves, *S. maximum atropurpureum* purple leaves, and the variety Autumn Joy bronze leaves.

Thalictrum: several kinds have leaves like the maidenhair fern. *T. glaucum* and *T. dipterocarpum* are especially attractive, the latter with sprays of small amethyst-like flowers in July – August.

alstroemeria

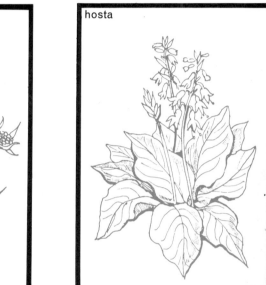

Scabiosa caucasica

hosta

rodgersia

Paeonia Felix Crousse, a magnificent fully double variety. Peonies do not like to be disturbed, and will not flower freely until they have become well established

Rodgersia pinnata is a handsome foliage plant for damp, peaty places. Delicate sprays of flowers are produced in the summer and provide an added attraction

Flowering Shrubs

Flowers can be cut from most flowering shrubs but the following varieties are especially recommended for cutting. Keep these shrubs well fed and watered so that they make strong growth which is able to take up water readily. Slit the bottoms of the stems after cutting or crush them to help them take in water.

Flowering in March, forsythia can be cut in bud and allowed to open indoors. Lynwood is a fine variety.

Spiraea arguta, sometimes known as Bridal Wreath because of its abundant, small white flowers and *S. thunbergii* also flower at about the same time.

Chaenomeles, another March-flowering shrub, may be grown against a wall or as a bush. There are red, pink and white varieties.

Camellias flower from February to May. The varieties of *C. williamsii*, including the double-flowered Donation, are particularly good for cutting.

Deutzia elegantissima has long sprays of mauve-purple flowers in April – May.

Choisya ternata (Mexican Orange Blossom) has good, shining, evergreen foliage and the fragrant white flowers appear in May.

Lilacs of all kinds also come out in May. If they are to be used for cutting they must be fairly hard pruned.

Philadelphus (mock orange) flowers in June. Many varieties are highly fragrant.

Foliage Shrubs

The following shrubs are worth growing specifically for the value of their foliage for cutting.

Acer japonicum aureum: a Japanese maple, rather slow growing, with soft, yellow leaves which last quite well in water.

Chamaecyparis and cupressus: various kinds of cypress, particularly the grey and the golden-leaved varieties, all of which are evergreen.

Cryptomeria japonica elegans: an evergreen with feathery leaves which turn russet red in autumn.

Cytisus scoparius: the Common Broom, valuable for the highly stylised effects that can be obtained with its whippy, evergreen branches.

Danae racemosa: the Alexandrian Laurel, with narrow green leaves, will thrive in dense shade.

Elaeagnus pungens aureo-variegata: shining evergreen leaves splashed with gold.

Eucalyptus: fast growing and handsome, usually with blue-grey leaves, they should be pruned fairly hard each March for the best foliage. *E. gunnii* is one of the hardiest varieties.

Euonymus fortunei Silver Queen: shining evergreen leaves bordered with silver.

Hollies: all kinds, but especially *Ilex aquifolium* Golden Milkmaid, gold edged with green.

Pittosporum tenuifolium: slender black twigs with waved pale green evergreen leaves. Silver Queen has silvery-green leaves.

Camellia williamsii

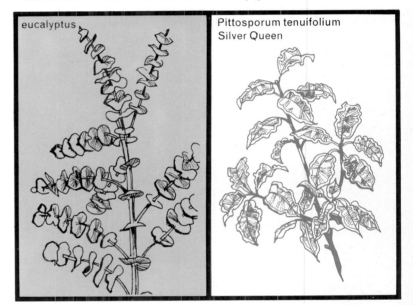
eucalyptus

Pittosporum tenuifolium
Silver Queen

A fine example of Japanese quince (chaenomeles) growing on the wall of a house. The angular, branched stems look well in a Japanese-style decoration and the large fragrant fruits are also decorative

A foliage border containing shrubs with pleasing leaf colour and shapes can provide much material. This attractive grouping includes *Cornus alba spaethii*, variegated sage, Golden Marjoram and hosta

Spring-flowering Bulbs

Daffodils of all kinds are excellent as cut flowers. They are easily grown in the garden in sun or shade and in any reasonably good soil. By making a careful selection it is possible to have flowers from February to May.

The earliest to bloom are the cluster-flowered varieties such as Scilly White and Soleil d'Or. These are followed rapidly by cyclamineus daffodils such as February Gold and Peeping Tom. Then come hundreds of varieties of many types and the last to flower is the Old Pheasant Eye daffodil, *Narcissus poeticus recurvus*, in May.

Tulips do not last as cut flowers so well as daffodils and are not usually quite so permanent or so ready to increase, but the tall ones, particularly the darwin, cottage, lily-flowered and viridiflora tulips are all beautiful flowers for cutting, blooming in late April or May. The early-flowering tulips are mostly rather short stemmed, but the mendel and triumph varieties, flowering in April, have excellent stems for cutting.

Tulips prefer open, sunny places and when grown for cutting should be lifted each July and be replanted in October 4 in. apart in rows 1 ft. apart. They need well-cultivated, well-drained soil which should be dressed with bonemeal at 4 oz. per sq. yd. before planting.

Lilies of the Valley

Lilies of the valley, excellent for cutting in May, can be produced from a permanent bed in the open. Plant single roots, known as crowns, in October or March 4 in. apart in well-cultivated soil and a partially shaded place, only just covering the crowns. If the soil is of clay, sand or chalk work in plenty of leafmould or peat before planting. Keep the bed clear of weeds and water freely in dry weather.

Beds can remain undisturbed for years until a falling off in the quality and number of the flowers indicates that the roots are overcrowded and starved. Lift the roots in October, split up into single crowns and start again.

For winter and early spring blooms, lilies of the valley must be grown in a greenhouse. For earliest flowering, purchase specially retarded crowns in early autumn, potting 8 or 10 in each 5- or 6-in. pot in John Innes No. 1 or peat-based potting compost. Keep in a dark place in a temperature of 18 to 21°C. (65 to 70°F.) and water freely. After 7 to 10 days bring the pots into the light, reducing the temperature a little, and the flowers will be produced in about one month.

For later flowering use ordinary crowns potted in the same way, keeping them in an unheated frame for five or six weeks then bringing them into a greenhouse at 13 to 18°C. (55 to 65°F.).

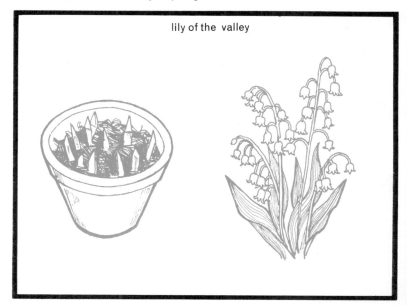
lily of the valley

Few flowers are more welcome in spring than the daffodils. Shown here is Harrier, a large-cupped variety, but there are hundreds to choose from differing in colour, size and flower form

The fragrant scent of the lily of the valley (convallaria) makes it a delight to grow. It prefers a shady spot if grown out of doors, but for early flowers it can be grown under glass

Summer-flowering Bulbs

Nerine bowdenii

The most useful summer-flowering bulbs for cutting, apart from gladioli are the Dutch, Spanish and English Irises. All three are very similar in appearance and differ mainly in their time of flowering. The Dutch are the first to open in June, the Spanish following a week or so later and the English in July. The widest selection of colours is in the Dutch group.

Plant irises in September 3 or 4 in. deep and 4 in. apart in rows 1 ft. apart in well-cultivated soil and an open, sunny position. Lift, divide and replant the bulbs every third or fourth year.

For earlier flowers plant the bulbs in pots or boxes in John Innes No. 1 or peat-based potting compost, keep them in a frame for 6 or 8 weeks and then bring them into a light greenhouse, with a temperature of 10 to 15°C. (50 to 60°F.). Even earlier flowers can be obtained by growing *Iris tingitana* and Wedgwood (a hybrid variety) in the same way.

Other summer-flowering bulbs useful for cutting are montbretias, particularly the large-flowered Earlham Hybrids; *Crocosmia masonorum*, and in sheltered places *Nerine bowdenii* and *Amaryllis belladonna*. All like sunny places and well-drained soil. The Earlham Hybrid montbretias are best lifted and placed in a frame each October.

Gladioli

planting gladiolus corms

staking

tying

Gladioli are slightly tender, but since the corms of the popular summer-flowering kinds can be stored dry in winter, this is no disadvantage. However, the early-flowering or nanus varieties must be planted in October and, except in very mild districts, must be grown in a frost-proof greenhouse in pots, boxes or beds of fairly rich, porous soil.

Plant summer-flowering gladioli in succession from mid-March to mid-May, 3 to 4 in. deep and 6 in. apart in good, well-cultivated soil in an open, sunny position. Water freely in dry weather and feed in June and July with a sprinkling of a good compound fertiliser. Place a 3-ft. cane to support each flower spike of tall varieties and tie twice, once low down and again just below the bottom flower bud. Cut the flower stems as soon as the bottom flower buds begin to show petal colour, but leave some leaves to feed the corm.

Lift the plants about six weeks later, cutting off all top growth 1 in. above the corm. Remove the old, withered corm from the base of the plant and store the new corms in a dry, frost-proof place until the following spring. Tiny corms (cormels) clustered round the large corms may also be kept and planted in spring $\frac{1}{2}$ in. apart to grow on to flowering size in a year or so.

Dutch Irises flower in June, producing their interestingly shaped blooms on long stems. If the flowers are cut, the leaves should be left to return food to the bulb for the following year's crop

The distinctive spikes of summer-flowering gladioli are always popular for cutting. For this reason they are often planted in a separate part of the garden so that the main flower display is not spoilt

Sparaxis, Ixia

ixias

These are natives of South Africa and are accustomed to a warmer climate than our own. They can be grown successfully outdoors in the south and west and in some sheltered gardens elsewhere, but in cold districts they are better grown as pot plants in an unheated or slightly-heated greenhouse.

The flowers of sparaxis are very gay, usually in two contrasting colours such as red, purple or maroon with white or yellow, and for this reason it is known as the Harlequin Flower. The flowers come in spring in sprays on 9-in. stems.

The flowers of ixia are also in many colours from white, yellow and pink to orange, scarlet and magenta, and are produced in May and June on wiry, arching 18-in. stems.

Plant both sparaxis and ixia in early autumn 3 in. deep and 4 to 6 in. apart in light, well-drained soil and a sunny, sheltered position. They succeed well on rock gardens, raised rock beds and terraced walls. Leave undisturbed until overcrowded.

Alternatively place five or six bulbs in a well-drained 5-in. pot filled with John Innes No. 2 Potting Compost and water moderately at first and fairly freely in spring, but allow to dry off in July. Keep in a greenhouse or frame in winter, but stand outdoors in summer.

Roses for Cutting

All well-grown roses can be cut and used for decoration in the house but some are better for this purpose than others. Old-fashioned roses look lovely but do not usually last as well as the more closely formed hybrid tea varieties. Cut all roses just as the buds start to open. This is particularly important with semi-double and single varieties.

Cut roses in the early morning and not in the middle of the day when the sun will have been shining on them for several hours. Immediately place cut roses in water deep enough to come to within an inch or so of the flowers and leave them in the water in a cool place for at least an hour before arranging them. Change the water daily and cut a little from the bottom of each stem when doing so.

Hybrid tea roses which are particularly suitable for cutting include Baccara, Fragrant Cloud, Mischief, Miss Ireland, Peace, Perfecta, Spek's Yellow, Stella, Sterling Silver, Super Star, Virgo and Wendy Cussons.

Among the floribundas suitable for cutting are, Dearest, Elizabeth of Glamis, Evelyn Fison, Iceberg, Queen Elizabeth and Violet Carson.

Peace

Ixias or African Corn Lilies are natives of South Africa, and should be grown in a warm, sheltered position. They produce their gaily coloured flowers on slender but wiry stems

Roses make admirable cut flowers and if care is taken in cutting and arranging them they will last for many days in water. The large-flowered varieties, such as Mischief, shown here, are especially suitable

Border Carnations

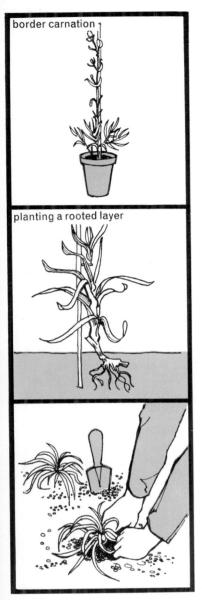

border carnation

planting a rooted layer

Border carnations are hardy and may be grown out of doors all the year, though they are often grown in pots and kept in a cool greenhouse during the winter, sometimes until they have flowered in summer, after which they may be stored out of doors or transferred to a frame.

Border carnations like a sunny, open position and fairly rich, well-dug soil containing plenty of lime or chalk. Plant or pot them in spring or early autumn and, if they are to be placed in beds, space them at least 18 in. apart each way. Tie the flowering stems to 2-ft. canes and reduce the flower buds to one per stem, retaining the topmost bud. Water them freely in dry weather and feed each March with a compound fertiliser, repeating at half rate in early June.

In July, layer non-flowering stems to produce young plants. Choosing healthy stems only, make a slanting incision through a joint where it can easily be brought to ground level, scrape away a little soil, peg the layer into a depression with a piece of wire, bent like a hairpin, and cover it with a mixture of good soil and sand. Keep it well watered, and by September the layer should be well rooted. Then sever the young plants from the parents and a week later lift and either plant or pot them as before. Old plants are usually best discarded after two or three years.

Everlastings

The name 'everlasting' is given to flowers with a papery texture which can be easily dried and used for winter decoration.

Cut the flowers just before they are fully open, tie them in small bunches and suspend them head downwards in a dry, airy place but not in direct sunshine. When dried, the stems of many kinds may have to be strengthened with florists' wire.

Acroclinium (*Helipterum roseum*) is a hardy annual to be sown out of doors from March to May where it is to flower. The double, daisy-like flowers vary from white to rose. Rhodanthe (*H. manglesii*) has small pink or white flowers on slender 12 in. stems.

Helichrysum monstrosum has larger flowers in a wider range of colours. A hardy annual, it can be sown outside but does better if raised in a greenhouse or frame and planted out later.

Give similar treatment to *Statice sinuata* (*Limonium sinuatum*) which has blue, pink or yellow flowers. *Statice latifolia* (*Limonium latifolium*), with larger sprays of smaller lavender flowers, is a perennial. Plant in a sunny place in good, well-drained soil and leave alone.

Honesty (*Lunaria biennis*) is a biennial grown for its parchment-like fruits. Sow in May or June for cutting the next year and discard the plants after cutting.

Physalis is a perennial grown for its inflated orange fruits. Plant in good, well-drained soil.

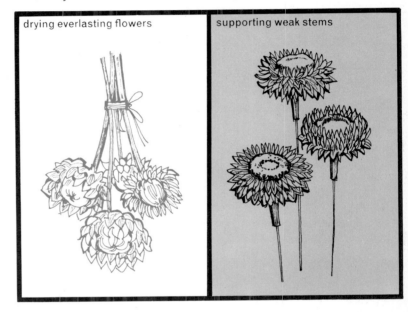

drying everlasting flowers

supporting weak stems

A selection of border carnations, showing the clearly defined colourings. These plants are hardy, but may be protected to improve the quality of the flowers

Helichrysum monstrosum, one of the best of the everlasting flowers, ranges in colour from white, yellow and orange to red. It is a half-hardy annual

Dahlias

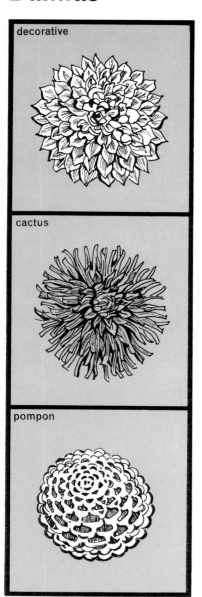

decorative

cactus

pompon

Many kinds of dahlia make admirable cut flowers, of which the best are those with small or medium-sized double flowers carried on long stems. Many of the so-called water-lily dahlias are excellent as they have not too many petals, take up water well and look delightful in floral arrangements. Small decorative, small cactus and the pompons are also very good types.

For cutting it is essential to thin the plants well, so that they are not overloaded with flowers at any time. Each stem should be restricted to one flower, the terminal one, with all side buds and side-shoots removed at an early stage, and the plants must be watered and fed well.

Cut dahlias when they are about three-quarters open, with some of the centre of the flower still closed. Choose good long stems and cut just above a pair of leaves, since new flower stems will then grow from the axils to continue the crop. Stand dahlia stems in water immediately they are cut, carrying a bucket around the garden for this purpose.

Chrysanthemums

Chrysanthemums are usually grown from cuttings which are taken from plants cut right down after flowering and kept through the winter in pots or packed close together in boxes. These old plants, kept specifically to provide cuttings, are called 'stools'. Cuttings are taken from them any time between January and April or even May.

The best cuttings are prepared from shoots growing through the soil directly from the roots of the stools. Cut them off just below soil level when about 3 in. high, sever each cleanly with a razor blade just below a leaf joint, remove one or two of the lower leaves and dip the base of each cutting in hormone rooting powder. Insert the cuttings in John Innes, or a soil-less seed or potting compost in pots, boxes or in a bed, whichever is most convenient. The essential thing is that they must be kept moist and in still air at a temperature of 10 to 15°C. (50 to 60°F.). For early cuttings (January to March) a propagator or propagating frame inside the greenhouse is convenient.

After insertion, water the cuttings well, place them in the propagator or frame if available, and shade them for three weeks from strong sunshine. Continue to water sufficiently to keep the soil or peat moist but not sodden. Cuttings should root in 3 to 5 weeks, which will be evident when they start to grow.

Dahlias, especially those with small- to medium-sized flowers such as this Border Prince are excellent for cutting as well as making a splendid show in the garden

Goya, an early-flowering chrysanthemum belonging to the reflexed decorative group. It has flowers of medium size which reveal their best qualities when restricted to one per stem

Violets

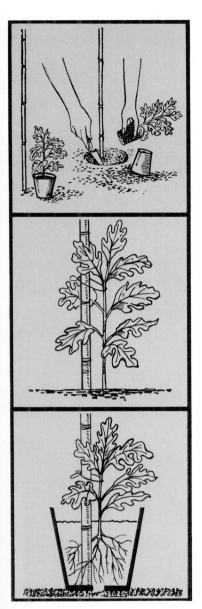

Provided they have been properly hardened off in a frame or sheltered place out of doors, early-flowering chrysanthemums can be planted out between late April and mid-May.

Select an open, sunny place for them and prepare the soil by thorough digging or forking. Work in manure or well-decayed garden refuse at 1 cwt. to 10 sq. yd. and give a dusting of a well-balanced compound fertiliser before breaking down the surface of the soil to a crumbly condition.

Plant at least 15 in. apart and, if planting in rows, leave a 30-in. alleyway between each pair of rows. Drive a 4-ft. cane into the soil to support each plant and tie it to this at once. Water well.

Stopping means pinching out the growing tip of a plant or shoot to make it branch. The time of stopping has some effect on the time of flowering and plants that are stopped twice tend to produce flowers with fewer petals than those that are stopped only once.

Left to their own devices chrysanthemums will produce flowers in clusters or sprays. To obtain larger flowers, one per stem, they must be disbudded. Watch for the tiny flower bud appearing at the top of each stem some time between July and October, according to variety and carefully remove any other flower buds or shoots around or below it.

Spray the plants occasionally with an insecticide to kill green-flies and capsid bugs.

single

double

Both Parma violets, with double flowers, and single violets may be grown, but the latter are hardier, freer flowering and, if the right varieties are chosen, have longer stems. Princess of Wales is one of the best.

Violets can be grown out of doors all the year in rich, well-cultivated soil in a position shaded from the hottest sunshine. Excellent spring flowers can be obtained in this way, but for winter flowers it is necessary to grow plants in frames from September onwards.

Raise new stock annually by removing rooted offsets from old plants in March or early April. Plant single varieties 1 ft. apart in rows 18 in. apart, double varieties 6 in. apart in rows 1 ft. apart. Water freely in dry weather and spray occasionally with malathion or derris to kill red spider mites. Remove all runners thrown out from the main plants and feed with a good compound fertiliser in June and July.

Lift the plants with as much soil as possible in September and replant them side by side in a frame, watering them in well. Ventilate freely at first but sparingly from November onwards and keep the soil moist but not sodden. Pick the flowers regularly.

Spray chrysanthemums are becoming increasingly popular due to the fact that they require less attention than disbudded types. This attractive variety, Pinnochio, has reflexed petals

Violets flowering in a shady spot are a delightful sight in spring. They may be allowed to grow naturally in a woody area, or can be cultivated in frames specially for picking early

Winter Flowers

The following plants can be grown out of doors without protection and are excellent for cutting.

Garrya elliptica: an evergreen shrub with long, grey-green catkins, of which the male form is the more effective. It will flower extra early if trained against a sunny wall.

Hamamelis mollis: the witchhazel, with fragrant yellow flowers. A variety named *pallida* is sulphur yellow.

Helleborus niger: the Christmas Rose. It will grow in sun or shade, and if the plants are covered with cloches or frame lights the white flowers will be cleaner and appear earlier.

Iris stylosa: the Algerian Iris. It grows best in fairly poor soil in a warm, rather dry position such as near the foot of a south-facing wall, and should be left undisturbed. Cut while in bud.

Mahonia japonica: a handsome, evergreen shrub with sprays of pale yellow flowers scented like lily of the valley appearing from February to April.

Prunus subhirtella autumnalis: an ornamental cherry with small, pale pink flowers produced freely from November to March whenever the weather is mild. It opens well indoors.

Viburnum fragrans: small clusters of white and pink flowers, very fragrant. *V. bodnantense* is similar but is a deeper pink and the branching habit is more angular. Both open well indoors.

Berries, Fruits

All berries and fruits can be used in flower arrangements but the following shrubs and small trees are specially recommended.

Berberis jamesiana: long arching branches carrying pendulous clusters of coral-red berries.

Callicarpa: several kinds, with clusters of small violet berries. They need a warm, sunny position.

Crataegus prunifolia: a thorn with quite large scarlet fruits which last well into the winter.

Cotoneaster: most varieties, but particularly *C. wardii* and *C. watereri* with their arching stems.

Cydonia oblonga: the Common Quince with golden yellow, scented fruits the size of small pears.

Decaisnea fargesii: vigorous deciduous shrub with hanging blue-grey fruits, cylindrical in shape.

Euonymus europaeus: the Spindle Tree, a vigorous deciduous shrub with rose-coloured fruits splitting to reveal orange seeds.

Malus: any of the crab apples, such as Siberian Crab, Dartmouth, Golden Hornet and John Downie.

Pernettya mucronata: an evergreen with white, pink, lilac or purple berries.

Pyracantha (firethorn): all varieties. The leaves are evergreen and the berries scarlet, orange or yellow.

Sorbus aucuparia: the Mountain Ash or Rowan, with scarlet fruits.

Symphoricarpos racemosus: the Snowberry with round, white, berries.

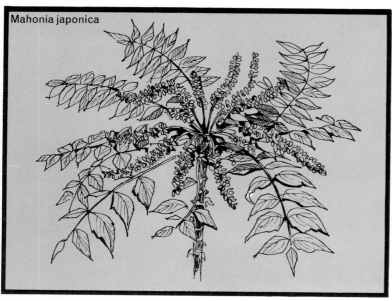

Mahonia japonica

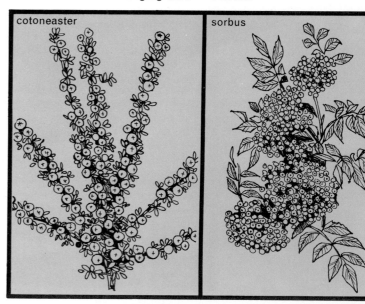

cotoneaster — sorbus

Garrya elliptica, with its decorative male catkins which are produced during the winter. It is particularly effective when trained against a sunny wall but will make a bush in the open

The thorns are all very hardy small trees growing well in town gardens. This is one of the most decorative, *Crataegus prunifolia*, with large, persistent berries and shiny leaves which follow in autumn

Indoor and Greenhouse Plants

Indoor and Greenhouse Plants

Four centuries ago gardeners invented the orangery as a means of keeping the newly introduced orange trees alive in climates too cold for them to survive out of doors in winter. By comparison with modern greenhouses orangeries were inefficient structures in which to grow plants, but they were usually handsome buildings adding materially to the appearance of many a fine estate and they performed their limited function satisfactorily. Well built with solid stone or wooden walls and tiled, slated or leaded roofs, they were, as a rule, provided with windows on one side only, that which received most sunshine. If they were heated at all, it was by flues constructed in the walls, and the amount of heat lost must have been very great, but then it was only the wealthy who could afford to contemplate growing oranges.

We have moved a long way since those days. As exotic plants more tender and exacting than the orange were introduced, gardeners had to devise better structures that would admit more light and could be heated and ventilated more efficiently. They were assisted by structural innovations such as wrought-iron glazing bars and cast-iron water pipes, and in the 19th century they constructed many large and often beautiful winter gardens, conservatories and greenhouses in which the largest and most exacting plants could be grown to maturity. These houses were warmed by water flowing to and from boilers by the natural tendency of hot water to rise and of cold water to sink. To this day this thermo-siphon principle is still used to heat many privately owned glass-houses, though for commercial purposes it has been superseded by more efficient systems, such as pump-circulated water, high pressure steam and various systems of warmed (and sometimes humidified) air blown into the houses.

Electrical heating systems have also been developed and, though usually considerably more expensive to run than those operating on solid fuels or oil, they are often relatively cheap to install and are always extremely easy to control. They have been of major importance to amateur gardeners with small to medium size greenhouses in which convenience rather than cost effectiveness is the first consideration. The owner of an electrically heated greenhouse does not have to order fuel, has no fire boxes to clean or chimneys to sweep and the whole system can be made completely automatic by fitting a simple thermostatic control.

Now electricity, so long supreme as a labour-saving source of heat, is being challenged by natural gas which, unlike the gases produced from coal and oil, gives off no harmful fumes when burned. The waste products of natural gas – water and carbon dioxide – are positively beneficial to plants and so it can be burned within the greenhouse with every unit of heat trapped where it will do most good. Gas heating is as easily controlled by thermostat as electricity, the average cost of installation is certainly no greater and running costs are considerably lower. The limiting factor, as it always has been with electricity, is the availability of supply, but at least gas

has the advantage that it can be bottled under pressure and distributed to remote places.

What the future holds one can only guess, but there may well be developments in the use of nuclear heat, or in tapping the vast latent sources of heat in the earth itself. On the structural side it may well be that we shall see the natural light abandoned in favour of artificial light, on the grounds that it is cheaper to illuminate than it is to heat, and that it is cheaper to warm a building with well insulated walls than one made largely of glass or translucent plastic. Plant houses in which all windows have been eliminated are already in use and have proved their practicability, and some are also heated from natural sources thus effecting ever greater economies. Even the amateur can share in these new techniques by investing in a plant cabinet, a kind of miniature plant house designed to stand inside a room and to provide, under complete control, any type of climate that particular plants may require. It may all seem a far cry from the 17th-century orangery, yet in one way the wheel may be said to have turned full circle for the orangery was primarily an efficient insulator against outside cold and that is the major function of the 20th-century plant house and plant cabinet. The main deficiency of the orangery, its lack of light, has been rectified by developments in illumination undreamed of then.

There is also a similarity between present-day interest in garden rooms and house extensions and the old-time winter gardens and conservatories, for all have the dual purpose of being made for the use of both people and plants. We also bring plants right into our homes and, since these are usually better lighted and are almost invariably better heated than the 17th-century orangeries, we are constantly discovering that we can grow indoors a much greater variety of plants than at one time seemed probable. In most rooms it is neither lack of light nor lack of warmth that is the major limiting factor but rather lack of humidity since our requirements for comfort and those of many plants for health do not coincide. The indoor plant cabinet, its elegant predecessor the Wardian case, and that decorative oddity, the bottle

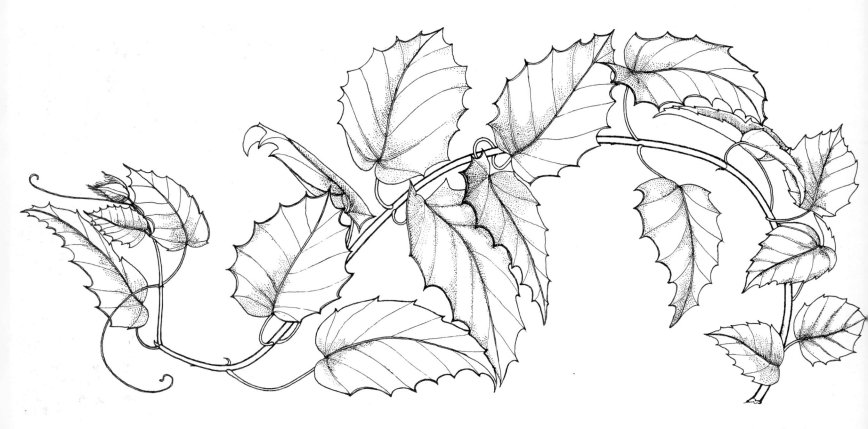

garden, are all means of overcoming this difficulty and bringing a greater variety of plants even more closely into the daily pattern of our lives.

Another invention that is having a similar effect is the humidifier. This device, essential in some manufacturing processes, is now widely used in hospitals and is creeping into offices and private houses as it becomes increasingly apparent that the very dry air induced by central heating is neither as comfortable nor as good for health as we have supposed. The day is probably not far distant when indoor humidity will be as much under finger-tip control as heating and lighting are today, and though we shall never want to live in the moisture level of a tropical forest we may well find that the ideal conditions for human beings and a vast range of temperate and sub-tropical plants are not so very different.

That the interest in house plants has come to stay is evident. It is all part of urban man's attempt to re-forge his links with nature and architects and builders are already taking it into account. The picture window, which did so much to bring house plants into favour, was developed for people rather than for plants, but the extra wide window-sill, tiled and dished or channelled to conserve moisture, is a refinement for the benefit of plants and one which could no doubt be extended in many ways. Some architects are considering the possibilities of hydroponics or other systems of soilless cultivation to extend the growth of plants in buildings, and are making provision for such installations in their designs. Lightweight materials such as vermiculite and expanded polystyrene have already proved their worth in the cultivation of some plants and could be more widely used if the supply of plant nutrients to such sterile rooting media could be made sufficiently reliable and foolproof.

Gardeners often talk as if temperature, moisture and light intensity were the only three considerations that matter when providing artificial climates in which to grow plants. In fact there is a fourth which for certain plants is just as vital. This is the relative length of day to night, for this controls the growth and flowering sequences of many plants. In a broad way plants can be divided into three groups: short-day plants which keep growing until nights exceed a certain length when they begin to produce flower buds; long-day plants which mainly grow when days are of medium length and start to flower only when they become long; and plants which have no clear photoperiodic pattern (the scientific name given to this phenomenon). The chrysanthemum is a typical short-day plant, the fuchsia a long-day plant, but temperature can complicate matters. The popular Christmas Cactus (page 209) is a short-day plant in fairly warm temperatures, but is unaffected by day length in temperatures below 10° C. (50° F.). If it is grown in a normally heated room which is artificially lighted most evenings in autumn and winter it may not flower at all, since the night is shortened (or the day lengthened) by the lighting. But if it is covered each evening and left in the dark for at least 12 hours it will flower quite normally. Similar effects of inducing growth or flowering at will can be produced by changing the colour of the light and again all kinds of exciting developments appear possible as our knowledge of plant behaviour increases.

To conclude on a less technical note, it is worth observing that the success of the orangery was dependent on the fact that the orange bushes only needed protection in winter. During the summer, when they were making their growth and needed much more light than the orangery could provide, they stood out of doors as objects of beauty as well as proof of their owner's wealth and horticultural skill. Today some house plants are placed out of doors in summer and many more would be if their owners only realised the improvement this could make to their health. Like the oranges of old, many house plants would make handsome specimens to decorate a patio or sheltered terrace from June to September. Provided they were assured such an annual vacation outdoors, many more species could be added to the already extensive list of plants to be grown indoors. Many of the popular grey-leaved plants, such as the various species of euryops, numerous very beautiful artemisias, silvery helichrysums and slightly tender olearias, fit perfectly into such an in-and-out routine since they are plants that appreciate dry air in winter but welcome all the light and warmth that is available in summer.

House Plants

Care of House Plants

The leaves of evergreen pot plants should be sponged occasionally, using either one of the proprietary preparations or a home-made mixture of milk and water

As the interest in house plants increases so the range of available plants grows. In part this is due to the competition of commercial growers anxious to cash in on the potentially highly profitable market. The more enterprising of these are constantly searching for new plants that have the necessary toughness to survive the conditions of an average living room, office or shop. Sometimes these discoveries are really new in the sense that they are plants not previously cultivated, or grown on so limited a scale as to be virtually unknown. More often the discovery is simply that a plant previously believed to be unsuitable for room cultivation can be so grown provided it is given the right treatment.

But there is another reason why the list of house plants is now so much longer than it used to be and is constantly growing. This is that rooms are on average much better lighted and warmed than they used to be. Big picture windows and central heating have done more for house plants than anything else though they do bring new problems of their own, the windows actually encouraging an excessive amount of heat on sunny days and the heating aggravating the already over-dry atmosphere of living rooms. Decorative Venetian blinds can take care of the first problem and automatic humidification can look after the second. Already the use of both these devices is increasing rapidly and they may soon be taken as much for granted in the modern home as central heating is today. A few architects make positive provision for house plants when preparing plans for new buildings and this may well prove popular and be more widely practised.

The qualifications of a first-rate house plant are that it must be able to grow and look happy in a relatively dry atmosphere and poor light, and that it must be suitable for cultivation in pots of reasonable size. For special places one can go outside these limits but they remain essential for the really big sellers.

Plants that fulfill these conditions may be further grouped under three headings: one, the very easy plants that can be grown in rooms in which the temperature sometimes falls as low as 7° C. (45° F.); a second, those requiring a rather higher temperature, rarely falling below 13° C. (55° F.), and the third, tropical plants which enjoy temperatures of 18° C. (65° F.) or more all the year. It will be observed that even the last come well within the range of what would be regarded as average temperatures in any centrally heated room. Most house plants will appreciate being grown in the lightest part of the room, though not necessarily in a window where they will get a great deal of direct sunshine. A few will survive even far removed from windows in poorly lighted corridors. All dislike being placed near fires or stoves which are only used intermittently or in a position exposed to draughts.

House plants may be grown in John Innes or a peat-based potting compost. Commercial growers are tending increasingly to use peat composts and it is in these that plants are likely to be growing when purchased. When potting on into a larger pot as the plant increases in size it is wise to use compost of a similar type to that in which it is already growing.

Water house plants whenever the soil shows signs of drying out, which may be daily in warm rooms when the plants are growing, and feed once every two or three weeks from May to August with a liquid plant food. Large evergreen leaves should be sponged with water two or three times a week in spring and summer, with a little white oil emulsion added if red spider mites are troublesome.

If it can be managed, pack damp sphagnum moss around the pots or plunge them in containers of moist peat, both to keep the air around the plants moister and to slow the drying of the soil. Moss or peat can be watered daily to keep it moist.

Only re-pot when pots become overfilled with roots and then into a pot which is only slightly larger. This should be done in spring and some of the old compost removed and replaced with fresh.

Plant Cases

Plant cases provide a greater control of growing conditions and they can, therefore, be used to grow a much wider range of plants than would be possible in the atmosphere of a room

The Wardian case was popular in the 19th century as a means of growing ferns and some other moisture-loving plants indoors. It is really a miniature greenhouse in which a stable atmosphere can be maintained and is small enough to be stood on a table.

Wardian cases are still occasionally seen as period pieces, but their place has largely been taken by more elaborate cabinets of various sizes and designs, usually equipped with their own electric heating and lighting. Because temperatures, humidity and illumination can all be controlled, a much wider range of plants can be grown than would be possible in the atmosphere of the room itself, and really the main limitation

is imposed by the size of the case and what it can conveniently contain. Such cabinets are excellent for cultivating small flowering plants such as saintpaulias and impatiens and may also be used for some small-growing kinds of orchids.

Plants growing in plant cabinets should be treated in much the same way as plants in greenhouses.

Do not use artificial lighting in winter to extend day length to more than 12 hours unless it is known that the plants grown will respond well to this. The growth and flowering periods of some plants are controlled by the ratio of day to night length and variations can be upsetting.

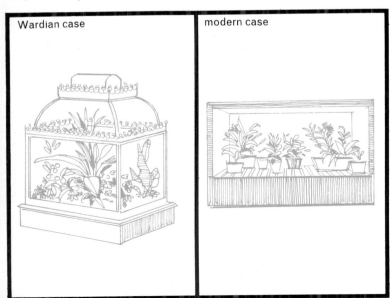

Wardian case   modern case

Bottle Gardens

If care and patience are exercised in creating bottle gardens, they will make very attractive features which will require little attention for several years

Bottle gardens are usually created in large carboys or specially made bottles of a similar globular shape. Place two or three inches of moist peat-based compost in the bottom of the bottle, running it through a paper funnel to avoid soiling the sides, and insert small house plants through the neck, planting them with the aid of long sticks or specially made wooden tongs. It is best not to stopper the mouth of the bottle as a slight circulation of air is desirable to prevent condensation forming, though the rate of drying out will be very slow. Under normal room conditions watering will only be necessary three or four times a year. However, the soil must not be allowed to dry out and a moderate quantity of water should be applied as soon as it shows signs of doing so.

Provided suitable slow-growing plants are chosen and they are not fed in any way, a bottle garden can remain in good condition for several years. Eventually, however, plants will become overcrowded or some will fall into ill health and then the bottle will have to be emptied and the process started again.

Some of the smaller ferns grow well in bottle gardens, suitable kinds being *Adiantum cuneatum*, a maidenhair fern; *Pellaea rotundifolia*, and silver-variegated varieties of *Pteris* such as *argyraea* and *victoriae*. Other good plants are the variegated acorus, cryptanthus, fittonia, maranta, peperomia and sonerila.

Bulbs in Bowls

Mixed hyacinths growing in a pottery bowl are a bright addition to the home in the winter months, and will quickly fill a room with their 'heady' scent. Specially prepared bulbs will flower at Christmas

It is convenient to grow bulbs for the home in bowls without drainage holes, so that no water can trickle out to damage furniture, fabrics, etc. Ordinary soil and potting composts quickly become sour in such bowls and special bulb fibre must be used. This can be purchased ready for use or prepared at home with 6 parts by bulk of medium grade horticultural peat, 2 parts crushed shell and 1 part crushed charcoal, well mixed.

Thoroughly moisten the bulb fibre before use. Place a layer of fibre in the bottom of the bowl, set bulbs shoulder to shoulder on this and barely cover with more fibre. Water well, and place in a cool, dark place (such as a cupboard, but not an airing cupboard which will be too hot) for from eight to ten weeks so that roots may be formed freely. Then bring bowls into a light, moderately-warm place. If in a window, give each bowl a quarter turn daily so that the growing plants receive equal illumination all round. Support flower stems with split canes or thin stakes placed around them with encircling ties of green twist.

After flowering, plant bulbs carefully outdoors where they can complete their growth. Do not use the same bulbs in bowls for two years running.

All hyacinths, including, 'prepared' ones, and some daffodils such as Cragford and Geranium succeed especially well in bowls.

Popular Flowering Plants

Impatiens or Busy Lizzie is a popular indoor flowering plant which will do well when grown in a light sunny window, though it should not be allowed to dry out as the buds will drop

Some flowering plants, dealt with more fully elsewhere in this book, make good pot plants for well-lighted rooms. These include cyclamen, impatiens (Busy Lizzie), greenhouse azaleas, pelargoniums, hibiscus and anthurium.

Of these, impatiens and anthurium are best fitted to remain indoors permanently. Impatiens grows quite well in shade, is not too seriously affected by the rather dry air of most rooms, and is capable of flowering all the year.

Cyclamen need a marked rest in summer and are then much better stood outdoors, preferably shaded from direct sunshine. They need not be brought inside again until late September.

Azaleas are also much better out of doors from May to October. They dislike dry air while making their growth and flower buds and should be well watered, frequently syringed with water and occasionally fed with weak liquid fertiliser while outside.

Pelargoniums of all kinds need more light, especially in summer, than is normally available in rooms and may be stood out of doors from June to September in a sunny place. Hibiscus can be treated in the same way.

The best anthurium for rooms is *A. scherzerianum*, the Flamingo Flower, as it puts up with dry air better than the larger-flowered *A. andreanum*. It should be grown in a light window but not in full sun and should never be put outdoors.

Hibiscus rosa-sinensis

Aglaonema and Others

Aphelandra and Others

The attractive flowers of *Spathiphyllum wallisii* have given it the popular name of White Sails. It should be protected from direct sunlight and should not be allowed to dry out

Codiaeums (top left) will make handsome house plants for short spells provided these are followed by periods of recuperation in a warm greenhouse. The leaves vary greatly in shape and colour

Aglaonema and spathiphyllum belong to the arum family and may produce arum-like flowers which add to their attractiveness. *Aglaonema treubii*, the kind usually grown as a house plant, has spear-shaped leaves, dark green splashed and banded with lighter green and the flowers are white. It likes a warm, rather moist atmosphere, a minimum temperature of 15° C. (60° F.), a fair amount of water in spring and summer but the soil only just moist in autumn and winter.

Spathiphyllum wallisii also has white flowers which are produced much more regularly and freely so that the popular name of the plant is White Sails. The leaves are similar in shape to those of the aglaonema but dark shining green without other colouring. It will succeed in temperatures 2 to 5° C. (5 to 10° F.) lower than *Aglaonema treubii*, likes shade, requires regular feeding from May to August and is best divided and re-potted each spring as it grows rapidly and soon exhausts the soil. Re-pot in John Innes or peat-based potting compost.

Related to these, though totally different in appearance, is *Acorus gramineus variegatus*. This has narrow rush-like leaves banded with white. It is hardy and can be grown out of doors in damp soil, but is also a splendid little plant for a bottle garden, preferably planted in peat-based potting compost.

Aphelandra squarrosa louisae is known as the Zebra Plant because of the pattern of striping on its leaves, white transverse veins on a dark, shiny green leaf. The spikes of closely packed yellow flowers have a curiously wooden look and are handsome but the plant is chiefly valued for its leaves. It likes a fairly light position and a minimum winter temperature of 13° C. (55° F.).

Pachystachys lutea has similar flower spikes but its leaves are plain green. It is treated in the same way, although it is really better grown in an intermediate or warm greenhouse.

Sanchezia nobilis is also related and has varieties with yellow- or white-veined leaves. It requires similar treatment to aphelandra.

Crotons, also known as codiaeums, are also grown for their coloured leaves which may be broad or narrow, smooth or twisted in a great variety of colours, including green, yellow, rose, red, copper and bronze. They are amongst the most beautiful of foliage plants and grow well in warm, well-lighted greenhouses, but are not so easy to manage in rooms, though they make excellent house plants for short periods, interspersed with periods of recuperation in a greenhouse. They like light, fairly warm conditions and dislike widely fluctuating temperatures and draughts. They should be fed regularly from May to August and be well watered.

aglaonema

Spathiphyllum wallisii

Aphelandra squarrosa louisae

codiaeum

Aralia and Others

House plants flourish in a moist atmosphere, and many plants will benefit if sprayed lightly with water from time to time. Here, *Fatsia japonica* is being given this treatment

Aralia elegantissima is sometimes called the Spider Plant because of the spidery appearance of its very narrow, toothed, almost black leaves arranged in a fan like those of a Horse Chestnut. The young leaves are coppery red. It needs a light place and a minimum winter temperature of 13° C. (55° F.). Red spider mites are partial to it and since sponging of these narrow-toothed leaves is difficult they should be sprayed occasionally with derris or white oil emulsion. The plant is also known as *Dizygotheca elegantissima*.

Fatsia japonica is known as the False Castor Oil Plant, and is occasionally called *Aralia sieboldii*. It has large, shining, laurel-green leaves cut into broad lobes and it can be grown in quite unheated rooms – even out of doors – and in very poor light. There is a variety with leaves bordered with cream, but it is not quite so easy to manage.

Fatshedera lizei is a hybrid between fatsia and an ivy (hedera). It has leaves very like those of *Fatsia japonica* but smaller, and the plant makes long, flexible stems which need to be trained to a stake or trellis. There is a variety with cream-edged leaves. Treatment is the same as for fatsia.

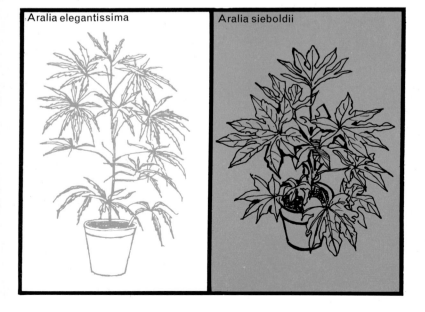

Araucaria and Others

Araucaria excelsa, the Norfolk Island Pine, is a delightful and easy-to-grow house plant. If near a window it should be turned occasionally to prevent uneven growth

Araucaria and aspidistra are old-fashioned and easily grown house plants. *Araucaria excelsa* is known as the Norfolk Island Pine, but is more like a stiffly branched fir tree. It has dark green, needle-like leaves on horizontal branches arranged in regular whorls to form a pyramid and in this it resembles the Monkey Puzzle Tree, *Araucaria imbricata*, to which it is related. It likes a light position and does not mind a minimum temperature of 7° C. (45° F.). If grown near a window it should be turned periodically to prevent uneven growth.

The aspidistra has broadly lance-shaped deep green leaves, which are striped with white in the variegated variety. It will grow in quite poorly lighted rooms and will withstand a lot of mismanagement. It can be grown in soil or peat composts and should be watered fairly freely in spring and summer, moderately in autumn and winter. The shine of the leaves is improved by regular sponging with water containing a few drops of milk. Overgrown plants can be split into several pieces in spring, each of which can be re-potted and will soon make a good plant.

Ardisia crispa, described more fully on page 272, is sometimes grown as a house plant and is useful for its shiny evergreen leaves, even if, under room conditions, it fails to produce good crops of scarlet berries. It should be given all the light possible.

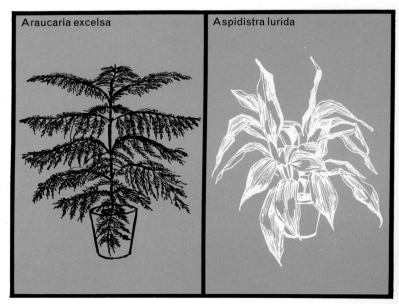

Beloperone and Others

Hoya carnosa is very reluctant to flower when grown indoors but in its variegated form it makes an attractive foliage plant. It needs to be trained against a stake or trellis

Hoya carnosa

Beloperone guttata is known as the Shrimp Plant because of the vaguely shrimp-like appearance of its curling russet-pink flower heads. It is one of the few flowering plants that will do well indoors and it flowers for a long period in summer and autumn. It will thrive in any room with a minimum temperature of 7° C. (45° F.), but is best placed in or near a window as it likes light. Keep moderately watered at all times, more freely in summer, and feed from May to August.

Hoya carnosa is known as the Wax Plant because the little clusters of fragrant white flowers look as if they are made of wax. However, the flowers are not freely produced indoors and this plant is usually grown in one of its variegated forms for the fleshy dark green leaves margined with cream or with a yellow centre.

Hoya carnosa will grow in a room with a minimum temperature of 18° C. (65° F.). It is a climber which should be trained around a stake or over a little trellis and it needs a fairly light position.

Grevillea robusta, described more fully on page 245, is often grown as a house plant. It tends to grow too fast and may have to be discarded after a while, but young plants are readily raised from seed. It should be given a reasonably light place.

Bromeliads

Despite its exotic appearance neoregelia is an easy and thoroughly reliable house plant to grow. The central cup or 'vase' should be kept filled with water

The pineapple is a bromeliad and it is occasionally grown for ornament in well-heated greenhouses, but there are other more decorative members of the family. All have stiff, strap-shaped or sword-like leaves arranged in rosettes often around a central cup, referred to as a 'vase', which collects water and helps to sustain the plant. Among the best are: aechmea with mottled leaves and stiff pink and lavender or scarlet flower heads; cryptanthus with flat, starfish-like rosettes of cream, green or golden-brown leaves; neoregelia and nidularium with green and cream leaves turning to pink or scarlet around the vase and vriesia with banded leaves and quill-like scarlet flower spikes.

Grow bromeliads in the smallest pots that will contain their roots. Pot them in a mixture of equal parts sphagnum peat, sharp sand and osmunda fibre. Grow in a temperature of 18° C. (65° F.) or more, which may drop occasionally in winter to 13° C. (55° F.) but no lower, and keep away from direct sunshine. Maintain as moist an atmosphere as possible. Water freely in spring and summer, moderately in autumn and winter, always keeping the central cup or vase filled with water, and feed with very weak liquid manure about once a fortnight in summer. Increase by removing offsets in May.

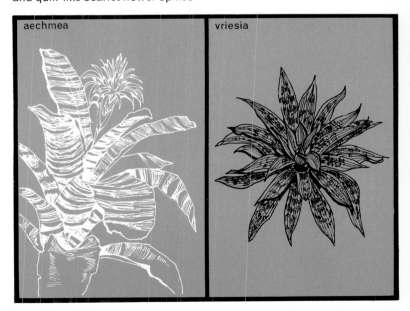

aechmea

vriesia

Calathea, Maranta

Warm, humid conditions are ideal for marantas. To maintain the humidity around the leaves it is often necessary to pack damp moss or moist peat round the pots. Keep the plants out of direct sunshine

These are related plants, grown for their attractively marked foliage. All are fairly small, compact plants thriving in warm, rather humid conditions, for which reason they are excellent plants for bottle gardens. However, they can also be grown in rooms in which the temperature does not fall below 13° C. (55° F.). It is desirable to pack damp moss around the pots or to plunge them in moist peat to maintain humidity around their leaves. Keep them out of direct sunshine which may scorch the leaves and water moderately at most times, but a little more freely in summer.

The leaves of calatheas are oval or oblong in various shades of green on top, regularly blotched with darker green, and shades of purple beneath. *Calathea makoyana,* also known as *Maranta makoyana,* is one of the most beautiful and is often known as the Peacock Plant.

Maranta leuconeura is a shorter plant, very variable in the colour of its leaves which may be light green with dark green or red blotches and with white or crimson veins.

All calatheas and marantas thrive in peat-based potting composts.

Calathea makoyana

Chlorophytum and Others

Tradescantia is an excellent plant to grow round the edge of a container from which it will hang attractively. It grows almost anywhere and does not require much attention.

Chlorophytum comosum variegatum

Rhoeo discolor

Zebrina pendula

These are among the easiest of house plants to grow. They will thrive with little light and quite low temperatures, certainly down to 7° C. (45° F.) or even a little less.

Chlorophytum comosum variegatum makes a large tuft of long narrow leaves banded with creamy white and the plant produces long, arching stems bearing plantlets which can be used for propagation. The leaves and stems of *Rhoeo discolor* are purple and the habit of the plant sprawling.

Setcreasea purpurea is allied and is known as Purple Heart. It has purple leaves and stems, grows upright, and can be cut hard back if it becomes untidy.

Tradescantia fluminensis and *Zebrina pendula* are so much alike that they share the same popular name, Wandering Jew. They are trailing plants with oval, light green leaves striped with silver, cream and pink. In zebrina the leaves are purple underneath. They are excellent plants to grow round the edge of a container, over which they will hang, but they can be grown almost anywhere in John Innes or peat-based potting compost, and it is almost impossible to kill them even by over or underwatering.

Water freely in spring and summer, moderately in autumn and winter. Divide the plants when they get too large or take cuttings of firm young stems. Raise young plants of chlorophytum by pegging down the plantlets to the soil.

Cissus and Others

Cordyline and Others

The rhoicissus (right) is a fine house plant which will tolerate all but the worst conditions. The leaves are made up of three leaflets which are bronzy when young becoming deep green as they age

The narrow sword-like leaves of cordyline (right) may be coloured green to deep purple and are sometimes handsomely variegated with cream or white. They thrive in a minimum temperature of 10° C. (50° F.)

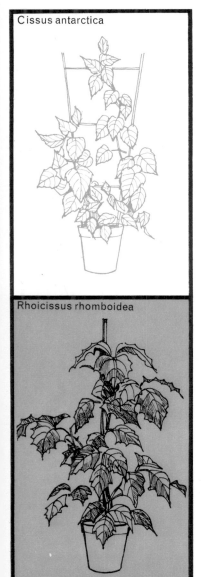

Cissus antarctica

Rhoicissus rhomboidea

These are climbing plants with something of the character of vines – indeed, the popular name of *Cissus antarctica,* the Australian kind commonly grown as a house plant, is Kangaroo Vine and of *Rhoicissus rhomboidea*, Natal Vine. Both support themselves by means of tendrils and should be given stakes or a little trellis up which to climb.

The leaves of *Cissus antarctica* are heart shaped, often toothed and lustrous green, and the stems are reddish purple. Each leaf of rhoicissus is made up of three leaflets, bronzy at first but turning deep shining green as they age.

Allied plants are *Cissus striata* and *C. sicyoides*, both of which have leaves composed of several separate leaflets, quite small and densely produced in the first named, and *Tetrastigma voinieria-num,* also with compound leaves but composed of very large leaflets. It grows very vigorously and is only suitable for growing where there is ample space.

All these plants can be grown in rooms with a minimum temperature of 7° C. (45° F.). They will tolerate poor light, but can also do well grown near or around windows. They should be watered fairly freely in spring and summer, only moderately in autumn and winter. Tips of growing shoots can be pinched out occasionally in summer if a more bushy habit is wanted.

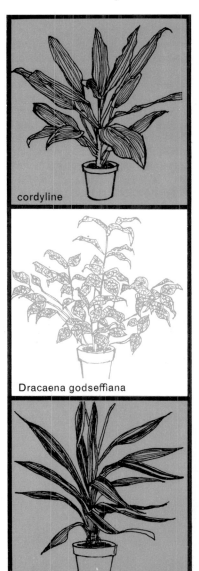

cordyline

Dracaena godseffiana

Pandanus veitchii

These are all plants which may be referred to popularly as 'palms', though they are not really palms nor related to the palm family. But their large rosettes of long, narrow, strap-shaped leaves give them an exotic and slightly palm-like appearance. They make distinctive and decorative pot plants for the house.

There are numerous varieties of cordyline with leaves differing in colour from green to deep purple, sometimes variegated with cream or white, but all will thrive in rooms with a minimum temperature of 10° C. (50° F.).

Dracaenas are also numerous and differ not only in the colour but also in the width of their leaves. All are known by the popular name of Dragon Plant but some require more warmth than others. *Dracaena deremensis warneckii* and *D. fragrans massangeana* enjoy a minimum temperature of 15° C. (60° F.), whereas *D. godseffiana* and *D. sanderiana* will be quite content with a minimum of 13° C. (55° F.).

Pandanus veitchii is popularly called the Screw Pine (after the pineapple, not the pine tree). The leaves are fairly broad, green with a white margin, and it prefers fairly warm conditions and a minimum temperature of 15° C. (60° F.).

Pleomele reflexa has yellow leaves striped with green.

All these plants like fairly light places, should be watered freely in spring and summer, but very moderately in autumn and winter.

Dieffenbachia, Syngonium

Dieffenbachia demands a minimum temperature of 15° C. (60° F.) and prefers a shady position in the room. The leaves should be sprayed with water frequently in the summer

Dieffenbachia picta, the kind commonly grown as a house plant, has large leaves carried around a central stem in a somewhat tree-like fashion. The leaves are variously blotched with cream or yellow according to the variety; indeed, in some there is more variegation than basic green colour. All like shade and need warm rooms with a minimum winter temperature of 15° C. (60° F.). They should be watered rather freely in spring and summer, just sufficiently to keep the soil moist in autumn and winter, and should be fed from May to August. Leaves should be sprayed frequently in summer.

Syngoniums, like dieffenbachias, belong to the arum family, but are climbing plants. The leaves are shaped like an arrowhead and are either dark, shining green or variegated with lighter green along the veins. All kinds require the same conditions as dieffenbachias but must be provided with some support to which their long stems can be tied, the best choice being moss-covered wire or cork that can be kept moist. The popular name for this plant is Goosefoot Plant and syngonium is often sold as nephthytis.

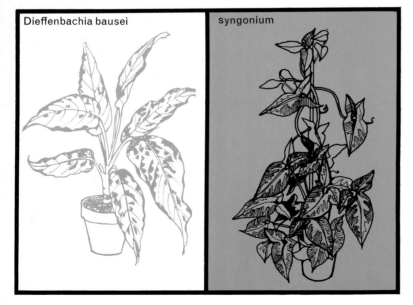

Dieffenbachia bausei

syngonium

Ferns

Asplenium bulbiferum has finely divided fronds which carry tiny plantlets on the upper surface. This is a good fern for the home provided the air does not get too dry

By no means all ferns make good room plants as the atmosphere is too dry for them, but some kinds will survive for long periods, especially if damp moss is packed around the pots to keep the air moist.

Among the most satisfactory kinds are the Bird's Nest Fern, *Asplenium nidus,* with broad, shining dark green fronds; the Holly Fern, *Cyrtomium falcatum,* with rather large holly-green segments to its fronds; and the Ribbon Fern, *Pteris cretica,* with long, narrow, ribbon-like segments which in some varieties are crested, divided or waved. Others that may be tried provided the air is not too dry are the Mother Spleenwort, *Asplenium bulbiferum,* with finely divided fronds carrying tiny plantlets on the upper surface, and the Ladder Fern, *Nephrolepis exaltata,* with ladder-like fronds and a great many varieties.

The Stag's Horn Fern, *Platycerium bifurcatum,* is peculiar in that it obtains its food from water and the air, not from the soil. For room cultivation it is grown in peat in a pot so that it can be kept moist, but the pot must be placed on its side except when being watered. Plants can be suspended on walls where their large greyish green, antler-like fronds look very handsome.

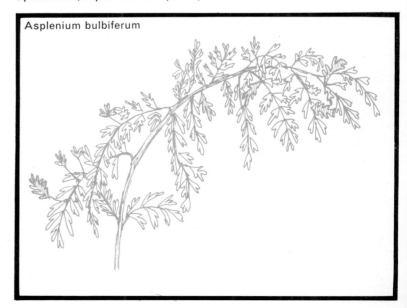

Asplenium bulbiferum

Ficus

Ficus elastica decora, an improved form of the India-rubber Plant, is a very popular house plant. Care should be taken not to overwater which can cause the loss of the lower leaves

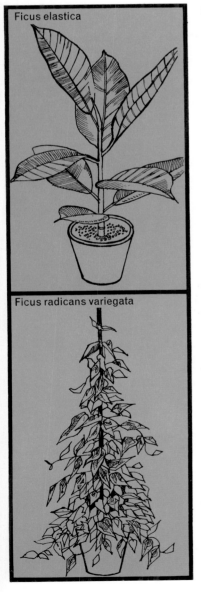

Ficus elastica, the India-rubber Plant, is one of the most hard-wearing plants and one of the few which will grow in quite poorly lit places. It has large, dark green, shining, leathery leaves; but there are also variegated varieties, one mottled with cream, another with cream and light green. All are best grown in rooms with a minimum temperature of 13° C. (55° F.), though the green-leaved variety will stand slightly lower temperatures. All should be watered fairly freely from April to September, sparingly from October to March and should be fed regularly from May to August.

Ficus pendula and *F. radicans* are creeping plants which will climb like ivy with the aid of clinging aerial roots. Both have small rounded leaves and there is a pretty variegated variety of *F. radicans* with cream-edged leaves. Of the two, *F. pendula* is the hardier, thriving in a minimum temperature of 7° C. (45° F.) whereas *F. radicans* prefers 10 to 13° C. (50 to 55° F.). Both like shade and should be watered throughout the year sufficiently to keep the soil moist.

The variegated variety of *F. radicans* is particularly sensitive to dry air. It can be grown in a bottle garden or plant cabinet or be allowed to climb up a pillar made of wire netting packed with sphagnum moss and kept moist.

The giant of the family, *F. lyrata*, is known as the Banjo or Fiddle-leaved Fig. It is grown like *F. elastica* but needs plenty of room.

Fittonia and Others

Fittonia argyroneura has handsomely marked leaves. In common with other fittonias it enjoys warmth and humidity and is an excellent plant for the bottle garden or plant cabinet

Fittonias are low-growing perennials with ornamentally veined leaves, white on green in *Fittonia argyroneura*, pink on purple in *F. verschaffeltii*. Both enjoy warmth and moisture and are more suitable for growing in bottle gardens, Wardian cases or plant cabinets than in a drier room atmosphere. Both can be grown in J.I.P. No. 2 or peat-based potting compost, should be watered normally and kept out of strong sunshine. They can be increased by division in spring, the best season for repotting, but this is seldom required. Both can also be grown in a shady part of an intermediate or warm greenhouse.

Sonerila margaritacea is another tender perennial grown for its intricately coloured leaves, which in some forms are so heavily flecked with silver as to appear more silver than green. Underneath they are purple. It requires similar conditions to the fittonias. Increase is by cuttings of young shoots in a warm propagator or from seed sown at 20 to 24° C. (70 to 75° F.).

Hypoestes sanguinolenta is called the Polka Dot Plant because its leaves are covered in pink spots. It is easily grown from seed sown in a temperature of 15 to 18° C. (60 to 65° F.) in spring in J.I.S. or peat-based seed compost. The seedlings should be potted singly in J.I.P. No. 1 or peat-based potting compost and grown on in any reasonably light place with normal watering.

Gynura and Others

Hedera

The velvety purple leaves of *Gynura sarmentosa* make it a most distinctive trailing plant. However, the ragged orange flowers are most unattractive and should be removed at bud stage

Ivies are very accommodating house plants for they are easy to grow and can be put to many different decorative uses. They are readily increased from cuttings

Gynura sarmentosa is a trailing perennial with soft violet-coloured stems and young leaves, the colour persisting on the underside of the old leaves. It will grow in any reasonably light place in J.I.P. No. 1 or peat-based potting compost, but should not be overwatered, particularly in winter. It can be increased by cuttings in spring or summer in a warm propagator.

Hypocyrta glabra is known both as the Clog Plant and the Goldfish Plant because of the shape and colour of its little orange flowers produced in summer. The rounded leaves are closely set on the stems, rather thick, glossy and dark green. Altogether, this is a distinctive little plant and one that can be grown in any reasonably light place, even in a window with direct sunshine. It should be grown in J.I.P. No. 1 or peat-based potting compost with normal watering and can be trimmed or pinched in spring or late summer if it gets too large. Increase is by cuttings of firm young shoots in summer in a propagator. It does not need much warmth and can also be grown in a cool or intermediate greenhouse.

Plectranthus oertendahlii is a perennial grown for its leaves, veined white on a bronze and green ground colour, and its sprays of small purplish-white flowers in summer. It requires similar treatment to hypocyrta except that it is best kept out of direct sunshine. Increase by division when re-potting in spring.

Plectranthus oertendahlii

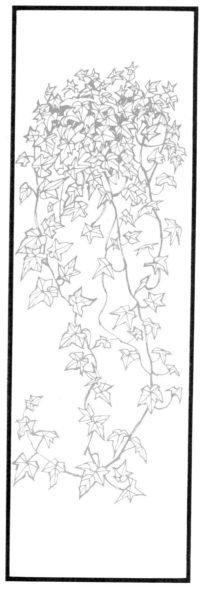

Ivy (or hedera) is one of the most easily grown plants for indoors, and can be used in many decorative ways. Ivies can be collected in the country, potted in John Innes or peat-based compost and used in the home but more decorative varieties are available in the shops. Some have small leaves which may be variegated with grey, silver, cream or yellow. Others have larger leaves or leaves of unusual shape or which change shape as they age. Yet others branch and make little bushes which need no support.

All ivies can be grown in unheated rooms. They will grow in sun or shade in John Innes or peat-based potting compost. They should be watered throughout the year, freely in spring and summer, moderately in autumn and winter. Most can be readily increased by cuttings in summer.

The Cape Ivy is a quite different plant belonging to the groundsel family. Its name is *Senecio macroglossus;* it has ivy-like leaves with a cream edge in the most popular variety, and in a light place it may produce yellow, daisy-like flowers. It requires a minimum temperature of 7° C. (45° F.), otherwise treat as for ivy. *S. mikanioides* is very similar and requires the same treatment. There is a good cream-variegated variety of *S. macroglossus*.

Monstera and Others

The distinctively cut leaves of the monstera make it the dominant plant in this arrangement. The other plants are *Begonia rex*, impatiens, dracaena and *Scindapsus aureus*

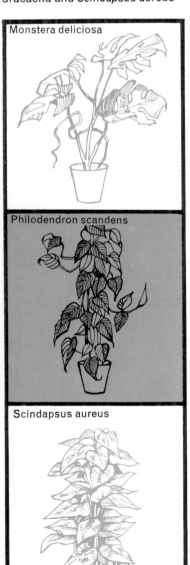

Monstera deliciosa

Philodendron scandens

Scindapsus aureus

These are all related and easily grown plants, mostly climbing, which will thrive in quite poor light. Monstera is the most striking in appearance with big leaves cut and divided in a curious way which makes them appear perforated with large holes. As they grow they produce hanging aerial roots which increase the appearance of jungle-like profusion.

There are several different kinds of philodendron of which *Philodendron scandens* is the most popular. It has green heart-shaped leaves and is a climber. So is *P. hastatum* with broadly arrow-shaped leaves, but *P. bipinnatifidum,* with very large, doubly divided leaves is a bushy, non-climbing plant.

Scindapsus aureus is much like *Philodendron scandens* but its leaves are blotched with yellow.

All these plants can be grown in rooms with a minimum temperature of 13° C. (55° F.) and monstera, *Philodendron scandens* and *Scindapsus aureus* in temperatures 3 or 6° C. (5 or 10° F.) lower. All should be watered fairly freely in spring and summer, moderately in autumn and winter and should be fed from May to August.

Palms

Howea belmoreana is one of the popular palms, and will live for many years provided it is given plenty of water during the summer months and is potted on regularly

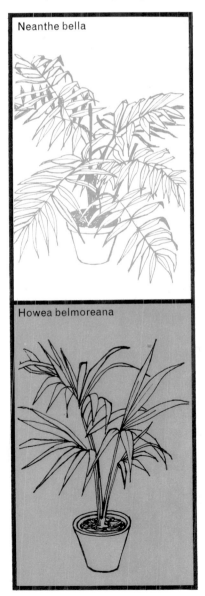

Neanthe bella

Howea belmoreana

There are many different kinds of palm, most of which can be grown as pot plants, but many are so large that they are only suitable for large rooms and halls. Most succeed better in a shady greenhouse than in a room since they enjoy a moist atmosphere, but all can be used for room decoration for periods of a few weeks or even months.

The best kind for permanent cultivation indoors is *Neanthe bella,* the Dwarf Palm. This is so slow growing that it can be planted in a bottle garden, and it will grow in sun or shade. Water freely in spring and summer, sparingly in autumn or winter. Sponge the leaves occasionally to keep them glossy and if they are attacked by scale insects (like minute limpets) sponge or spray the leaves with white oil emulsion.

Phoenix roebelinii, a dwarf relation of the Date Palm, also makes a useful pot plant most suitable for light rooms or greenhouses.

Others are *Howea* (or *Kentia*) *belmoreana* and *Trachycarpus fortunei,* the last sufficiently hardy to be planted outdoors in areas where frosts are not severe or prolonged when it becomes too large for room or greenhouse cultivation.

Cocos weddeliana is a small palm with very graceful leaves. It is so slow growing that it is often planted in bottle gardens and since it enjoys a warm damp atmosphere is really better there than in the open room.

Peperomia, Pilea

These two peperomias, *P. rotundifolia* and *P. tithymaloides* (in foreground), are recent introductions as house plants, the former producing unusual flowers

There are several different kinds of peperomia, all small plants with rather fleshy, ornamental leaves. *Peperomia caperata* has wrinkled, velvety looking green leaves marked with purple and grey. *P. hederaefolia* has grey-green leaves with white veins; *P. sandersii,* also known as *P. argyreia,* has silvery leaves veined with dark green; *P. magnoliaefolia* is cream or pale yellow with a central splash of grey-green which widens as the leaves age.

All need rather careful watering as they are inclined to rot if kept too wet, but they like a moist atmosphere and shade. They enjoy a minimum temperature of 13° C. (55° F.) and seldom need re-potting as they make little root,

getting much of their food from the air. All are good plants for bottle gardens.

Pileas are also small but less decorative. *Pilea cadierei nana* is the best, with dark green leaves streaked with silvery grey, for which reason it is known as the Aluminium Plant. *P. microphylla* is also known as *P. muscosa* and its popular name is Artillery Plant because if it is disturbed when in flower it emits puffs of pollen. The leaves are small and crowded making the plant look like a fern or moss.

Both these plants are very easily grown in any room with a minimum temperature of 7° C. (45° F.) in sun or shade.

Peperomia caperata

Pilea cadierei

Pineapple and Others

The variegated pineapple, *Ananas comosus variegatus*, is a most effective plant for the house but it likes warm conditions and must not be exposed to draughts

citrus

It is the variegated pineapple, *Ananas comosus variegatus*, that is grown as a house plant. When in good condition it is very handsome, with rosettes of narrow, serrated, cream-edged leaves. Unfortunately these leaves easily spot if water lodges on them so the plant should be watered carefully. Do not let plants stand in saucers of water, the soil should be nicely moist throughout, no more. Grow it in J.I.P. No. 2 compost mixed with an equal bulk of peat. Maintain a minimum temperature of 15° C. (60° F.) and keep in a light window. Pineapples grown in rooms are unlikely to fruit, but if grown in a warm greenhouse they should fruit after about four years. Plants are increased either by detaching offsets (slips) from the base when re-potting in spring or by cutting off the top rosette of leaves from the fruit and rooting this in a warm propagator.

Any of the oranges, lemons or grapefruits (citrus) can be grown as pot plants, but the best for the purpose is the Calamondin Orange, *Citrus mitis,* because of its compact habit and ability to fruit when quite small. Its cultivation is described on page 255. Indoors put it in a well-lighted window and, if possible, stand the plant outdoors in a warm sunny place from June to September.

The Avocado Pear, *Persea gratissima,* described on page 255, makes a handsome house plant if the tips of the shoots are pinched occasionally to make it branch.

Sansevieria, Saxifraga

The fleshy, strap-shaped leaves of the sansevieria form an effective background and they contrast well with the other house plants in this easily imitated arrangement

There are several different kinds of sansevieria but by far the most popular is *Sansevieria trifasciata laurentii,* known as Mother-in-law's Tongue. It has fleshy, strap-shaped, slightly corkscrewed leaves banded and striped with yellow. It is an extremely hard-wearing plant which will grow in sun or shade and will survive in a room with a minimum temperature of 7° C. (45° F.) though it prefers a little more. It should be watered rather sparingly at all times and should be fed monthly from May to August.

The saxifrage that is grown as a room plant is *Saxifraga sarmentosa,* also known as *S. stolonifera,* popularly called Mother of Thousands because of the slender runners it produces, each carrying numerous plantlets which can easily be rooted if in contact with soil. It has sprays of small pink flowers and there is an attractive variety named *tricolor* in which the leaves are splashed with cream and rose. These plants should be grown in fairly light places, near a window. They are virtually hardy, do not need artificial heat and should be watered freely in spring and summer, moderately in autumn and winter.

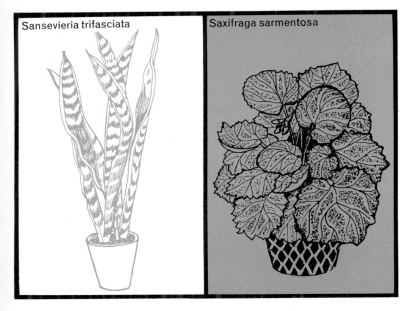

Schefflera and Others

Elettaria cardamomum is a native of India and is one of the chief sources of cardamom. This variegated form makes an especially attractive foliage plant

Schefflera actinophylla (also known as *Brassaia actinophylla*) is an evergreen tree which can reach a height of 10 ft. or more in a tub, but it is slow growing and can be kept for years at much more reasonable dimensions in a 6- or 7-in. pot. It makes a single stem with long leaf stalks carrying leaves composed of numerous large green leaflets arranged in a fan. Grow it in J.I.P. No. 2 compost in a light place but not in direct sunshine. Water normally and maintain a temperature above 10° C. (50° F.). Increase by seed sown in a warm propagator in spring.

Elettaria cardamomum is a herbaceous plant with firm stems and broad dark green leaves which are cinnamon scented. It can be grown in J.I.P. No. 1 or peat-based potting compost and does not mind a considerable degree of shade; it should always be kept away from direct sunshine. Water fairly freely from spring to autumn but very sparingly in winter. Increase by division when re-potting in spring.

Almost any kind of pittosporum can be grown as a house plant, but the best for the purpose are *Pittosporum eugenioides* and its variegated variety and *P. tobira.* All are shrubs or trees grown primarily for their shining evergreen leaves, but *P. tobira* also produces clusters of scented white flowers. They are easily grown in pots in the same way as schefflera but are hardier. Increase by summer cuttings in a propagator.

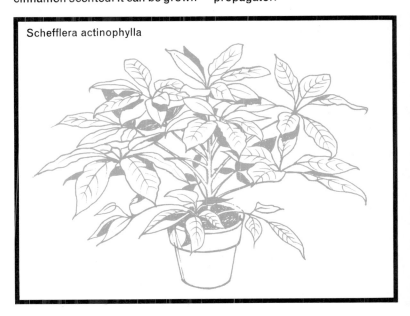

Cacti and Succulents

Succulents are plants with very fleshy leaves or stems which enable them to store considerable quantities of water and so survive periods of drought. Many of them are natives of hot countries and must be grown in greenhouses or well-lighted rooms in countries where frosts are severe or prolonged, but some, such as many sempervivums and sedums, are quite hardy.

Cacti are a family of succulents most of which have no leaves, or only minute leaves, their function being taken over by the swollen body of the plant. The shapes of these plants are often very strange; they are frequently spiny and the flowers are borne on the main body of the plant. In some, especially the epiphyllums and some allied kinds, these flowers are very showy. Most cacti are easy to grow but many are too large to be conveniently accommodated except as young plants. Since all are accustomed to dry air many make excellent room plants if they can be given sufficient light.

Succulents other than cacti are so numerous and varied that few generalisations can be made about them. Most are as easy to grow as cacti.

It is the enormous variety to be found in cacti and other succulents that is one of their great attractions. Large collections can be built up of many different genera and species from all parts of the world. Because of this wide distribution in nature, cacti and succulents differ greatly in the temperature range to which they are accustomed, some being completely hardy and some injured by the slightest frost. Yet in this respect they are exceedingly adaptable and there is certainly no need to group them into different temperature groups as recommended for other greenhouse plants. Most cacti will thrive in any place with a minimum winter temperature of 4° C. (40° F.) and even the more tender succulents are quite content with a minimum of 10° C. (50° F.) provided they are kept fairly dry in winter.

Since they are able to live without water for quite long periods, cacti and succulents can be very convenient plants for gardeners who have to be away from home a great deal. For a similar reason they do not present any special problems when short holidays are taken. All the same it is a mistake to think of them as plants which need to be watered sparingly at all times. Most come from places where periods of drought alternate with rainy seasons when they are able to replenish their reserves, make their growth and complete their flowering.

Cacti and succulents can be grown in pots and pans like other greenhouse plants or they can be planted in little indoor gardens made with beds of suitably gritty soil, perhaps worked into irregular mounds with a few stones half buried in the soil. Such gardens should not be overplanted since cacti and succulents do not look their best when huddled together. Much of their charm lies in their highly individual shapes and they must always have sufficient space for these to be appreciated clearly.

Care of Plants

Aporocactus flagelliformis bears the imaginative common name of the Rat-tailed Cactus. As with all cacti that are grown in the home it needs careful watering

Contrary to popular belief, cacti and succulents should not be kept dry for most of the time. While they are growing they may need watering as frequently as non-succulent plants since the porous soil in which they are grown tends to dry out quickly. From April to September examine the plants daily and water any that appear dry. Give sufficient water so that it soaks right through the soil and starts to trickle out at the bottom, then do not re-water until the soil is dry again. From October to March it will be enough to examine the plants once or twice a week. Apply the water direct to the soil, and not to the plants. A few kinds, notably the stone mimics (page 29), resent any water lodging in them and are better watered by standing the pots for a few minutes in water almost up to their rims.

No artificial heat is usually required from April to October, but in winter frost must be excluded for all tender kinds. A minimum winter temperature of 7°C. (45°F.) suits most tender cacti and succulents. High temperatures in winter are undesirable.

Most cacti and succulents enjoy sunshine, but some prefer a degree of shade in summer. This is specially true of the epiphyllums and their allies, and also of haworthias and gasterias.

Potting and Handling

This varied collection of cacti and succulents provides an unusual decorative feature for the home. The container used must have ample outlet for surplus water

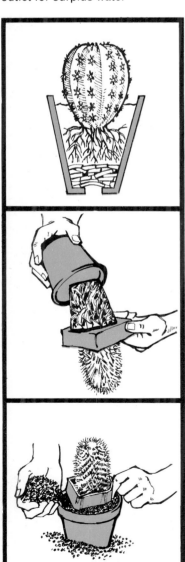

Cacti and succulents can be grown in any reasonably good soil that is sufficiently porous. John Innes No. 2 Potting Compost with the addition of 1/6th its own bulk of very coarse or sharp grit suits most kinds of cacti and succulents, and they can be grown in ordinary clay or plastic flower pots or in any container that has ample outlet for surplus water.

Pot cacti and succulents in March or April or when they are just starting to grow. Place some pieces of broken clay pot or a few small pebbles or stone chips in the bottom of the container to improve drainage, and, without disturbing the roots, place the plant in the pot and carefully work the new soil around the old.

Some cacti are so spiny that it is difficult to hold them. One way of dealing with the problem is to take a sheet of paper and fold it several times to form a thick band. Wrap this round the body of the plant and grip the two ends so that the paper holds the plant without the fingers coming into contact with it.

Take care not to break off the spines when handling cacti as they will not grow again and the damage spoils the appearance of the plant.

Increasing Plants

The enormous and beautiful flowers of epiphyllums appear from April to June. Like most cacti and other succulents, they are very easily propagated from cuttings

Many cacti and succulents can be increased by division when re-potting. Some make numerous offsets which can be detached easily and even if they have no roots they will generally form them readily if placed in very gritty soil and kept moist.

Many succulents can be grown from individual leaves treated like cuttings and pressed into gritty soil. Some varieties do this naturally, the leaves falling off and rooting where they lie on the damp soil. Bryophyllums, for instance, form plantlets on the edges of the leaves, which fall off and subsequently root and grow.

Branching succulents can usually be increased by inserting short pieces of stem as cuttings and with some cacti which do not make offsets, pieces of the plant can be severed and treated as cuttings.

Many cacti and succulents can also be grown from seed and some firms offer packets of mixed seeds which provide a cheap and interesting way of starting a collection. Sow the seeds in February or March in John Innes Seed Compost, do not cover them at all or at the most sprinkle coarse sand over them and germinate at 21° C. (70° F.). Allow the seedlings to make tufts of roots before pricking them out, using similar compost, and later pot them singly.

Keeping Plants Healthy

The genus *Notocactus* provides many easily grown plants with striking flowers. A watch should be kept for pests and diseases but these are not usually a major problem

Cacti and succulents are not, as a rule, greatly troubled by pests or diseases.

Mealy bug, a small bug-like creature protected by a covering of a white waxy substance, may attack the plants above or below ground. Above the surface it can be seen and picked off with a pointed stick or the plants can be sprayed with malathion, but below ground it may well be overlooked. Watch for it when re-potting and, if present, wash it off with malathion.

Scale insects attach themselves to plants like minute limpets but they too can be killed with malathion.

Red spider mites are so tiny that they can scarcely be seen without a hand lens, but small brown spots towards the tips of plants are a warning to look out for them. If present, spray with malathion or fumigate with azobenzene.

Slugs and snails can be controlled with metaldehyde bait, woodlice and ants by dusting with an insecticide, and mice can be trapped or poisoned.

Rot may be due to various fungi encouraged usually by overwatering. Cut out all the infected growth, dust the area with flowers of sulphur or quintozene and keep the plant rather dry for a time.

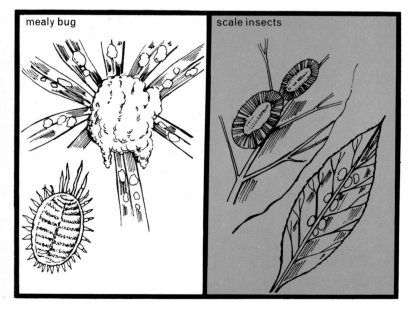

Small Cacti

Rebutias are dwarf-growing cacti which flower readily. They are very easy to grow and when properly cared for they may even produce flowers as one-year-old seedlings

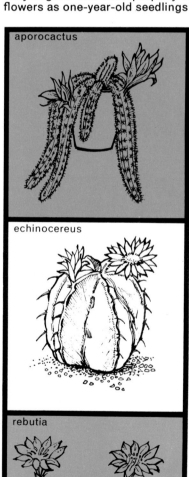

Aporocactus flagelliformis: the Rat-tailed Cactus, so called from its long, narrow, trailing stems. The flowers are cerise.

Astrophytum: known as the star cacti, the plants of this group are globular with star-like ribs and red and yellow flowers on top.

Chamaecereus: clusters of small, spiny, cylindrical stems with scarlet flowers in early summer.

Echinocereus: a varied group, some upright, some sprawling, with attractive flowers in many colours. Even tiny plants will flower.

Echinopsis: barrel-shaped plants markedly ribbed with white or creamy flowers on top. There are numerous kinds.

Gymnocalycium: small globular plants with quite showy flowers on top. All kinds like some shade in summer and free circulation of air.

Lobivia: usually globular or cylindrical plants which flower while still quite young. There are many kinds with flowers ranging from golden yellow and orange to pink and carmine.

Mammillaria: globular or cylindrical plants with spines and some with wool also. Small flowers are borne in circles around the tops of the plants ranging from white and yellow to pink, crimson and green. There are more than 200 kinds.

Notocactus: globular, usually flat-topped plants, ribbed, with red and yellow flowers on top. They are very easily grown.

Rebutia: almost globular plants with flowers around the bottom in yellow, salmon, pink and carmine.

Large Cacti

The golden spines and globular shape of *Echinocactus grusonii* give it the common name of the Golden Barrel Cactus. It can grow to nearly 3 ft. across

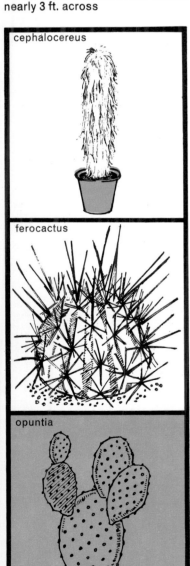

cephalocereus

ferocactus

opuntia

Cephalocereus: tall cylinders covered in long hairs. This characteristic is most marked in *C. senilis*, known as the Old Man Cactus, a great favourite.

Cereus: tall columns of growth with fine flowers, usually white, which open at night. Only quite old plants flower.

Cleistocactus: tall columns with small red flowers on the side.

Echinocactus grusonii: a globular-shaped cactus with golden spines known as the Golden Barrel Cactus or Mother-in-law's Chair.

Ferocactus: a group known as the barrel cacti because of their shape. All kinds have long, often brightly coloured spines.

Harrisia: plants with long thin growths which sprawl about unless tied to some support. The white flowers, which are scented, open at night.

Lemaireocereus: allied to cereus, with smooth, ribbed stems. This group needs warmth and light.

Opuntia: large circular, flat 'pads' built one on top of another which often produce very large plants. The Prickly Pear, a troublesome weed in some hot countries, is an opuntia.

Trichocereus: another group allied to cereus and easy to grow. They make long, branching plants with showy white flowers, but these are likely to be produced only by mature plants.

Epiphytic Cacti

Schlumbergera buckleyi, the Christmas Cactus, was formerly known as zygocactus and may still be listed under that name. It is a very popular plant and is widely grown

An epiphyte is a plant which receives most of its food from the air. In nature such plants often live in the branches of trees or on damp rocks. A number of cacti have these characteristics and nearly all of them are remarkable for the size and beauty of their flowers. In summer most of these cacti prefer a certain amount of shade and from June to September they can be grown in a shelter made of lath slats allowing the free circulation of air, or suspended from a small tree.

The principal kinds are epiphyllum, schlumbergera (zygocactus) and rhipsalidopsis. There are many hybrids in various colours including shades of pink and carmine.

Schlumbergera buckleyi (formerly zygocactus) is known as the Christmas Cactus because it starts to flower in December, continuing until February. The flattened stems have a graceful arching habit. *Rhipsalidopsis gaertneri* (formerly *Schlumbergera gaertneri*) has a similar habit but flowers in March and April. It is known as the Easter Cactus.

Epiphyllums themselves are usually stiffer and more erect in habit. They flower from April to June and rest in December and January, at which period they require little or no water. From March to June water fairly freely, sparingly for a few weeks after that, then more freely as they start into growth again.

schlumbergera

epiphyllum

Agave, Aloe

Agave americana is chiefly grown for its large rosettes of striking foliage. There are several varieties with banded or striped variegations, this one being *Agave a. marginata*

These plants with stiff, fleshy leaves, usually arranged in rosettes, are all easy to manage, though some are too large to be conveniently grown in pots except while young. They should be watered fairly freely in spring and summer, moderately in autumn and winter and grown in a light, sunny place.

Agave americana is known as the Century Plant because it is so slow in coming into flower. The very tall spikes are striking rather than beautiful and the plant is grown for its large, blue-grey, spine-tipped leaves which in some varieties are striped or banded with cream or white. It can be grown out of doors in some mild seaside gardens and can be planted out from May to October almost everywhere. Other smaller kinds are *Agave filifera*, with threads along the edges of the leaves, and *A. victoriae-reginae*, with dark green leaves decorated with white lines and hairs.

The most popular aloe is *A. variegata*, a neat plant known as the Partridge Aloe because of the grey and white markings on the leaves. So is *A. plicatilis*, the Fan Aloe, so called because the stiff, blue-grey leaves are arranged in a fan, not a rosette. *A. striata*, the Coral Aloe, has leaves edged with pink.

Gasteria and haworthia are allied to the aloe, but enjoy more shade and can be used as house plants. They are small plants with tapered leaves, often striped or spotted with white like the Partridge Aloe.

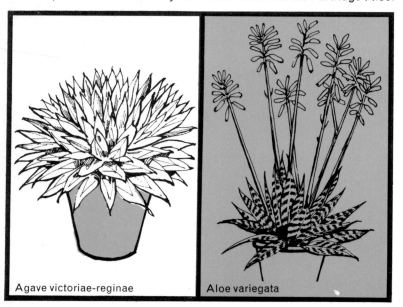

Agave victoriae-reginae

Aloe variegata

Crassula and Others

Kalanchoes are often sold by florists and greengrocers as house plants at Christmas. They should be watered carefully and kept at a minimum of 13° C. (55° F.) in winter

Crassulas, kalanchoes and rocheas are closely related plants with fleshy leaves which are sometimes confused with one another. The most useful as pot plants are *Crassula falcata*, with fleshy grey leaves and scarlet flowers in summer; *Kalanchoe blossfeldiana* with little sprays of scarlet or yellow flowers in winter, and *Rochea coccinea* (it is sometimes called *Crassula coccinea*) with close-packed leaves and tight clusters of scarlet flowers in summer. There are many other good crassulas, including *C. arborescens* which in time makes a big plant, *C. lycopodioides* and *C. tetragona*, both like tiny trees.

Pot these plants in spring in the smallest pots that will accommodate the roots comfortably. Water them fairly freely in spring and summer; sparingly in autumn and winter in the case of crassula and rochea, but more generously for kalanchoe which is then in its growing period. Keep them in a light, sunny place without shading and with a minimum winter temperature of 7° C. (45° F.), though 13° C. (55° F.) will be better for kalanchoe as it will then be in flower.

Raise kalanchoe from seed sown in March or April for winter flowering, prick off into boxes and later pot singly in 3-in. pots.

Raise crassula and rochea from cuttings of firm young shoots in very sandy soil in May, June or July.

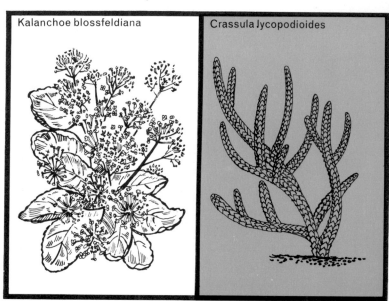

Kalanchoe blossfeldiana

Crassula lycopodioides

Euphorbia

Lampranthus

There are lots of succulent euphorbias and many of these differ greatly in appearance. This one, *Euphorbia obesa*, needs very good drainage and little or no water in winter

Lampranthus roseus has cheerful pink flowers and is one of the taller-growing kinds in this group. It can be planted out in a sunny border from June to September

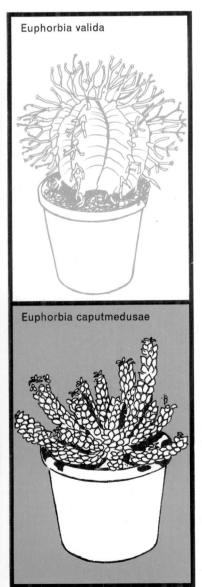

Euphorbia valida

Euphorbia caputmedusae

Not all euphorbias are succulents. Some are hardy herbaceous plants and one, the Poinsettia (*Euphorbia pulcherrima*) is a popular greenhouse shrub grown for its scarlet bracts which appear in winter. But there are also many succulent kinds of euphorbia, many of which differ greatly in appearance. Some, such as *Euphorbia abyssinica* and *E. grandidens,* are branched and tree-like, others such as *E. clava* and *E. clandestina* have a single stem with leaves on top like a little palm tree. Yet others, such as *E. meloformis, E. obesa* and *E. valida*, have very swollen stems like cacti. Then there is *E. caputmedusae*, which means Medusa's Head, an allusion to the grey-green snake-like branches which radiate from a ball-like central stem. Very popular, too, are those with vermilion bracts, like flowers, such as *E. splendens* and *E. bojeri*, both of which are known as Crown of Thorns or Christ's Thorn, because they are so spiny.

Even the largest of the euphorbias can be grown in pots when young. Give them a minimum temperature of 13° C. (55° F.) and water most of them moderately in spring and summer, sparingly in autumn and winter, but hardly at all for *E. splendens* and *E. bojeri* in January and February. Prune these two in May to keep them bushy.

Cultivation of euphorbias under greenhouse conditions is given on pages 260 and 261.

Most of the plants which are commonly called mesembryanthemum have been renamed lampranthus by botanists. Most are sprawling plants with small, fleshy leaves, but some make stiffer, more bushy growth. Many have showy flowers opening fully only in bright light. They are easily grown in J.I.P. No. 1 compost in a cool greenhouse without shade, watered moderately in spring and summer, then sparingly.

Water all kinds freely in spring and summer, sparingly in autumn and hardly at all in winter. Cuttings of firm young stems root readily in summer and make good flowering plants the following year.

Among the showiest kinds are: *Lampranthus aurantiacus*, bushy to 1½ ft., orange-red flowers; *L. blandus*, similar, but pink flowers; *L. brownii*, to 1 ft., smaller orange-red flowers; *L. coccineus*, sprawling scarlet flowers; *L. falcatus*, sprawling, pink, scented flowers; *L. roseus*, bushy to 2 ft., pale pink.

Cryophytum crystallinum is closely allied but is grown for the decorative effect of the shining watery spots which cover its leaves and prostrate stems, giving it the popular name Ice Plant. It is an annual readily raised from seed sown in a temperature of 15 to 18° C. (60 to 65° F.) in March and grown on as for Lampranthus. Similar culture suits *Dorotheanthus bellidiflorus* (often called *Mesembryanthemum criniflorum*), the Livingstone Daisy.

Sempervivum and Allies

There are numerous species and varieties of sempervivum, the popular houseleek. These massed rosettes belong to *Sempervivum tectorum calcareum* Mrs Guiseppe

Sempervivum Commander Hay

The true sempervivums or house-leeks are hardy and can be grown out of doors successfully provided they do not get too wet, especially in winter when they can easily rot away. But their near relatives, the aeoniums and aichrysons, are tender except in very mild places. All are excellent plants for growing in sunny greenhouses in pots or pans, the hardy kinds with just sufficient heat to keep out frost. All enjoy a very freely drained, fairly rich soil with plenty of coarse grit or sand. J.I.P. No. 2 compost with the addition of half its bulk of extra sand will suit them well and pots or pans can be filled to a quarter of their depth with broken crocks or gravel to ensure that soil is never sodden. They all enjoy full exposure to light and sunshine at all times as this improves the colour of the leaves, and they should also be ventilated freely, subject to the necessity to protect species of aeonium and aichryson from frost.

Species and varieties of sempervivum are numerous and names are often confused. They range from the tiny, filament-covered rosettes of *Sempervivum arachnoideum minimum* to the 6-in. plum-purple rosettes of Commander Hay. The aeoniums are much bigger, sometimes branched and almost shrub like. *Aichryson domesticum* has much smaller leaves heavily variegated with white in some forms. It is freely branched and is an excellent house plant, which will put up with some shade.

Stapelia and Allies

The exotic flowers of the stapelias have an attractive star-like shape and are handsomely marked. In some species, however, they have an unpleasant smell

Stapelias have fleshy stems, ribbed and notched, but it is the strangely marked flowers which make them so attractive. These are shaped like a star-fish and are striped, speckled and mottled in the oddest way with brown, purple, maroon and yellow. Some, but not all, have an unpleasant smell and stapelias are sometimes called the carrion flower. There are many different kinds but the best known is *Stapelia variegata* and its varieties with yellowish flowers, variously speckled with brown, maroon and crimson.

Allied to stapelia is caralluma, with more bell-shaped flowers; duvallia, a smaller plant; echidnopsis, stiffer and more branched; hoodia with cup-shaped flowers and tavaresia, whose stems are covered with bristly hairs.

All these plants should be grown in soil with a little more coarse sand or grit than recommended for most succulents. Water them freely in spring and summer, sparingly in autumn and winter, especially hoodia and tavaresia, and maintain a minimum winter temperature of 10° C. (50° F.). Re-pot them each spring and keep up a succession of young plants by severing the stems in summer and rooting them as cuttings.

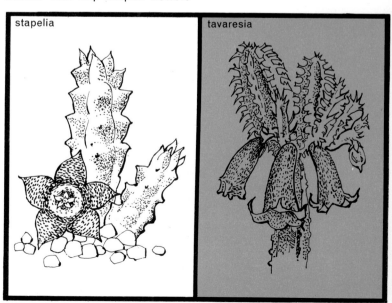

stapelia

tavaresia

The Stone Mimics

The stone mimics are very interesting subjects to grow. Lithops are the most pebble like of all and there are many kinds, differing in their colour and markings

fenestraria

gibbaeum

lithops

Some succulents protect themselves in the wild by contriving to look almost exactly like the stones among which they grow. They are all small plants very suitable for cultivation in pots and though they may not be beautiful they are of great interest and variety.

Argyroderma consists of two segments like a pebble neatly sliced in half. The small flower is produced in the centre.

Conophytum has growths like fat buttons complete with a depression in the top from which the quite large flowers develop. There are many kinds, differing in shape, colour of growth and flower.

Fenestraria has a little transparent 'window' on top of each growth to let in the light, since in its natural state it grows embedded in sand with only the 'window' uncovered.

Gibbaeum has cleft growths like the mouths of some fish, for which reason it is called shark's head.

Lithops are the most pebble-like of all and are available in a variety of kinds, differing in their colour and markings.

Pleiospilos has pairs of leaves forming on top of one another but as the new leaves grow the old ones wither away.

All these plants like an extra ration of coarse sand or grit in the soil. Sink the pots in gravel or sand, give them the lightest possible position, and water them fairly freely from May to November, but very little for the rest of the year.

Other Kinds

Echeverias are handsome succulents. There are about 100 species and numerous hybrids and this one, *Echeveria retusa*, makes an excellent house plant which will grow to 2 ft.

The bryophyllums have leaves of various shapes and colours, with little plantlets on them which drop off and soon grow into new plants. Bryophyllums are now regarded as species of kalanchoe.

Cotyledons are branching plants with variously shaped leaves. One of the best is *C. orbiculata* with grey leaves and clusters of hanging yellow flowers.

Most echeverias make neat rosettes and the fleshy leaves are of various colours – pale green, blue-grey and bronze, sometimes marked with pink. *E. harmsii*, also known as *Cotyledon* and *Oliveranthus elegans*, is a branching plant with narrow grey leaves and large, scarlet and yellow flowers.

Kleinia articulata is known as the Candle Plant because of the shape of its stems, which are like old-fashioned tallow candles.

Many sedums (stonecrops) are hardy, but some are tender and make good pot plants. *S. morganianum* carries its silvery-green leaves in long tassels and can be suspended in a basket. *S. sieboldii* has blue-grey leaves with pale yellow centres in the variegated variety.

All these are easy plants to grow in J.I.P. No. 1 or equivalent compost in a cool greenhouse without shade or in a sunny window.

Echeverias are often used for bedding outdoors in summer, but in winter need to be watered with special care as the leaves may spot if water lies on them.

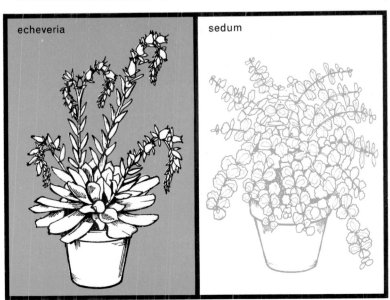

echeveria

sedum

Bonsai

Bonsai is the Japanese name for dwarfed trees. These are quite different from topiary specimens, which are trees or shrubs clipped to artificial shapes. Bonsai reproduce the natural shape of each kind of tree, though they are usually modelled on ones which are very old or which have grown in exposed places and so developed romantic and interesting shapes. Bonsai may be single specimens or groups of small trees growing like a little grove or copse. They can be grown in ordinary flower pots but are usually put in special ornamental bowls made with proper drainage holes and small feet to raise the bowl off the surface, thus discouraging roots from forming a mat beneath the pot. The more light bonsai receive the better, as this helps to keep them dwarfed. They can be used for short periods for room decoration but should not be kept for long in poor light.

When purchasing ready formed bonsai specimens it is important to remember that the oldest plants are the most valuable provided they are well formed and in good health. This is in contrast with other kinds of nursery stock where old plants are usually to be avoided and it is young specimens with plenty of growth ahead of them that are most desirable. It is age which gives a bonsai tree its peculiar charm but very old specimens are inevitably rare and commercial producers of bonsai, not unnaturally, attempt to mimic the appearance of antiquity in young plants.

When choosing a bonsai tree examine it as follows. Its shape, however romantic, must be characteristic of its species and not so distorted as to look like some different kind of tree. The trunk must be substantial and well formed, tapering from base to top and not overburdened by its branches, which should be well spaced and must not arise so low down as to give the appearance of a bush. Some roots should appear on the surface, dipping naturally into the soil after a few inches but conveying the idea of an ancient tree with surface roots eroded by wind and rain. The soil must be kept high in the container so that the root formation is clearly visible viewed from the side. Neither roots nor branches should cross or rub, and the branches must not give a mop-headed appearance. A specimen representing a wind-blown tree, with most branches going one way, is better if it is set towards one end of a fairly long container so that the branches can extend over it, otherwise the effect will be unbalanced.

Many specimens have one specially attractive side, but all should be reasonably good viewed from any side. Late removal of a training wire may have chafed or ridged a stem, and removal of a large branch, which would not have been necessary had constant attention been given to the pinching of young shoots, can have left a large scar. Freedom from large scars or other blemishes is particularly important in deciduous specimens since the branches are so very open to inspection in winter.

Making Bonsai

Bonsai is the Japanese name for dwarfed trees grown, sometimes to a great age, in a handful of earth in a shallow container. A collection of these trees is shown above

Many useful specimens for bonsai can be found growing wild, particularly in rocky and exposed places. Look for seedlings that have been stunted or restricted by poor soil and lack of room to spread their roots, and have already acquired an interesting shape. Lift such plants with great care, preserving as much of the root system as possible, and pot them up at once. They will require shading and frequent overhead syringing for a few weeks while recovering from the shock of transplanting. Spring and autumn are the best seasons for moving such natural specimens.

Alternatively, bonsai can be grown from cuttings or seed, but seed is better as it is easier to train the seedlings in a natural manner. Sow the seed in spring in J.I.S. or peat seed compost, preferably in twos or threes in peat pots (to be singled later), and germinate them in an unheated greenhouse or frame.

If grown in peat pots it is easy to prune the roots when they penetrate the soft walls of the pots, and so growth can be restricted from the start. If grown in seed pans and transplanted singly to ordinary pots in John Innes No. 1 compost, it will be necessary to tap them out occasionally to cut off any coarse roots on the outside of the soil ball. As the seedlings grow some side buds should be rubbed out, so ensuring that branches only grow where needed.

Suitable Plants

This bonsai is *Juniperus sargentii*. Bonsai need the maximum amount of light to keep them dwarfed and they should be used as room decorations for only a short while

A distinctive habit and branch pattern are points to look for when choosing a small tree or shrub for bonsai. A low-growing cotoneaster is one of many suitable shrubs

Bonsai must not be starved but be grown in J.I.P. No. 1 or equivalent. Vigorous kinds are re-potted annually, less vigorous ones every second or third year. When re-potting, tease out much of the old soil with a pointed stick and shorten or remove some of the coarser roots so that the tree can be returned to the same size container.

Start to restrict non-flowering bonsai just before they begin to grow each spring, when the growth buds likely to produce unwanted shoots should be carefully nipped out. Later, in spring and summer, shoots that are misplaced or those that are growing too big can be shortened or cut out where they join another stem. Prune all flowering bonsai when flowers fade but so as to keep the shape. Deciduous trees can be checked by carefully picking off all the young leaves. New ones will grow giving shorter, weaker growth and smaller leaves.

Keep the soil moist at all times, especially in spring and summer.

Young stems can be trained in any direction using soft fillis and temporary canes. Start with a slight pull and shorten the tie as the stem stiffens. Or use copper wire which can be progressively bent to force the stem into the required shape. Do not wire young or newly potted trees and keep constant watch that the bark is not chafed. Although the wire must be left on until the stem is woody, make sure it is not cutting into the bark as wounds are difficult to hide.

pine

maple

dwarf azalea

Any small trees and some shrubs can be used for bonsai, but preference should be given to those with a distinctive habit and branch pattern. Pines of many different kinds are suitable and so are some species of spruce. Junipers are good; a favourite with Japanese bonsai artists is the naturally spreading, almost prostrate form of *Juniperus chinensis* known as *sargentii*. *Cryptomeria japonica*, cedars, larches and *Ginkgo biloba*, the Maidenhair Tree, are other good conifers for dwarfing.

Japanese maples are first favourites, but *Acer palmatum* may get die-back and may lose whole branches. Beeches and hornbeams both dwarf well, and zelkova is much used in Japan. Suitable flowering trees include plum, cherry, crab apple, hawthorn, Judas Tree and mulberry.

Fruiting trees should be chosen for the smallness of their fruit to maintain a sense of scale.

Good shrubs with which to form bonsai include dwarf forms of azaleas and rhododendrons, camellias, prostrate or low-growing cotoneasters, pomegranate (*Punica granatum*), pyracantha and various spindle trees. The bush form of ivy is also sometimes used and so are various hollies. Other possible evergreens are box and yew, but care must be taken to develop their natural habit and not merely to clip them into artificial shapes.

Greenhouse Management

Types of Greenhouse

Spring is a very attractive time in the cool greenhouse when many brightly coloured plants can be grown. Included here are narcissi, cyclamen, primulas, veltheimias and cinerarias

Lack of a clearly defined management policy is often the main difficulty in greenhouses devoted to a variety of ornamental plants. Each plant has its own requirements and, though there may be a considerable measure of elasticity in these, it may be impossible to decide on any overall management policy for the house that will not spell disaster for some of its occupants.

It is sometimes suggested that differences of requirement can be met by segregating plants with like needs within the greenhouse. Some plants, we are told, should be grown at the warm end, others near the door where it is presumably cooler (and incidentally probably a lot draughtier) and so on. But the whole essence of good greenhouse management is to eliminate as far as possible variations of temperature within the house and to secure as even a distribution of air, whether warm or cool, wet or dry, as is possible.

It is wise, therefore, when choosing plants to eliminate any which have such very different requirements that they cannot be fitted in comfortably to an overall management routine. With this idea in view I have adopted in this book a system of greenhouse classification according to temperature, and have used this instead of repeating detailed instructions for temperature control throughout the year. Four basic regimes are considered as follows:

Cold greenhouse. No artificial heat used at any time of the year. In such a greenhouse winter temperatures may be little or nothing above those outside and in cold districts such houses are unsuitable for any plants that are injured by frost.

Cool greenhouse. In this, a minimum winter temperature of 7° C. (45° F.) is maintained with an average from autumn to spring of 10 to 13° C. (50 to 55° F.) rising in summer to 13 to 18° C. (55 to 65° F.).

Intermediate greenhouse. Minimum winter temperature of 13° C. (55° F.) with average autumn to spring temperatures of 13 to 16° C. (55 to 61° F.) rising in summer to 16 to 21° C. (61 to 70° F.).

Warm greenhouse. Minimum winter temperature of 18° C. (65° F.) with an average autumn to spring of 18 to 21° C. (65 to 70° F.) rising in summer to 21 to 27° C. (70 to 80° F.).

If plants are watered individually it is possible to vary the quantity for each according to its requirements at the moment. But in many modern greenhouses some system of automatic or semi-automatic watering is installed to save labour and then it does become necessary to keep plants with the same water requirements together. Fortunately a great many plants have similar needs, which may be briefly described as water applied freely from April to September while they are making their growth, but only moderately from October to March when they are resting. To avoid repetition I have called this 'normal watering' and have only given more detailed instructions where it is necessary to depart from this norm.

Greenhouses may be either span-roofed or lean-to. In the former type the roof is usually, though not always, double-sided with an equal slope on each side, whereas the lean-to house has a one-sided roof. It is intended to stand against a wall, whereas the span-roofed greenhouse is free standing.

Either type of greenhouse may be glazed to ground level or to only about 2½ ft. above the ground with a wood, brick or concrete wall below that. Fully glazed houses are useful for plants grown in beds at ground level, such as shrubs and climbers; and also for tall plants such as greenhouse chrysanthemums. Greenhouses built on low walls are useful for pot plants that are to be grown on stages, also for raising seedlings and rooting cuttings where it is convenient to have plants at about waist level. The comparatively ill-lighted space under the staging can be used for storage, and also for shade loving plants such as *Begonia rex* and ferns.

Greenhouse framing may be of wood or metal. Wood is in general cheaper, but sash bars usually need to be rather thicker and so exclude some light. Western red cedar is much more rot resistant than deal and aluminium alloy framing is durable and requires little maintenance.

Either glass or plastic may be used for glazing, but some plastics deteriorate fairly rapidly, so they must be selected with care.

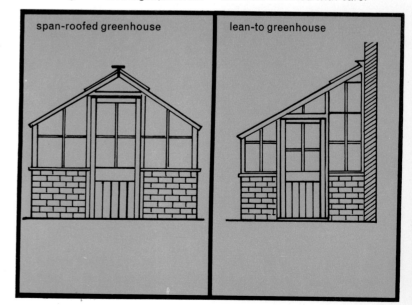

span-roofed greenhouse   lean-to greenhouse

A conservatory extension to the house has a dual purpose as it is made for the use of both people and plants. Ideally, conservatories should be used for the display of plants when they are at their best

Even where space is limited it is often possible for a small lean-to greenhouse to be built. This type of house can often be heated by an extension of the home heating system

Occasionally greenhouses of other shapes may be preferred. Circular or octagonal greenhouses can fit compactly into some awkward places and the interiors can be very economical of space. Dome-shaped houses have been constructed and also tunnel-shaped houses which in section may be either semi-circular or have six or eight separate faces. Such houses let in a lot of light, but can be more costly to construct than the conventional types.

Commercial gardeners have been making increasing use of readily portable greenhouses covered with stout plastic sheeting. The basic forms are often tunnel shaped and the plastic usually needs biennial renewing.

Portability is generally of less interest to private gardeners and greenhouses covered with rigid plastic sheets, usually of the corrugated type, have a wider appeal, especially as they are easily constructed at home on a simple wooden frame.

Conservatories are intended primarily for the display of plants when they are at their best in flower, fruit or leaf. They are often attached to the house from which they may be entered directly by french windows or a door. As a rule conservatories are supplied from other greenhouses or frames in which the plants are grown to maturity.

With the exception of those to be used for ferns or other shade-loving plants, always place greenhouses in as sunny a position as possible. It is easy to exclude light, if necessary, by shading; much more difficult to provide extra illumination when light is lacking.

Place lean-to greenhouses against walls with a southerly aspect and span-roofed greenhouses in the open well away from the shade of trees, but if heating is to be installed do not overlook the possibility that a supply of hot water or electricity may be required from the dwelling house. If so it may be necessary to compromise and place the greenhouse near the main building even if this means some loss of light.

Make sure that the greenhouse is securely placed on substantial foundations and that it is level. It is important to select a spot where surface water is not likely to drain into it and to provide good access to the greenhouse in all weathers, preferably by means of a paved, gravelled or asphalted path.

If possible, arrange for a water supply inside the greenhouse. It is also convenient to have electric lighting, even if electricity is not used as a means of heating.

The situation of a conservatory is often determined by the room to which it is attached. Since flowering plants are unlikely to remain in it for long it is not essential for it to be in the sun.

conservatory

roller blinds

Heating

A paraffin oil heater designed specially for use in a greenhouse. Such heaters are simple and inexpensive to run, and greatly increase the range of plants that can be grown

Burning natural gas is an ideal way of heating greenhouses as it not only provides even, all-round heat but also is very economical to run. Portable heaters, as shown here, are readily available

Without some form of heating it will be impossible to exclude frost from the greenhouse at all times, and this will limit the range of plants that can be grown. Many of the most popular, useful or beautiful greenhouse plants are easily injured or killed by frost.

Heating may be by hot air, hot water, electric radiator, paraffin oil stove or gas. Hot-air heaters are frequently used in large greenhouses and can be economical and satisfactory, but they have not yet been much used in small greenhouses.

Hot water provides evenly distributed heat. The water may be heated by a solid-fuel boiler, a gas or oil-fired boiler or an electric immersion heater. All these are satisfactory, but solid-fuel boilers will need the most attention. If the dwelling house has central heating the possibility of extending the system to the greenhouse should be considered.

Ordinary electric radiators do not provide a sufficiently well-distributed source of heat. They must either be equipped with fans to blow the hot air around the greenhouse or be of the low-temperature type with a large radiating surface, such as tubular or panel heaters.

Oil stoves burning directly in the greenhouse are cheap to install and simple to run, but must be carefully cleaned and tended, as if they overburn, their fumes can be very damaging to plants.

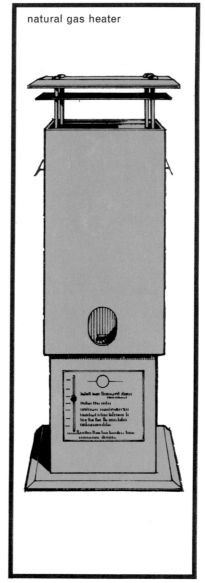

natural gas heater

Boilers heated by coal gas can be used in place of solid-fuel or oil-fired boilers. However, care must be taken to site them so that there is no danger of fumes from the consumed gas entering the greenhouse as the sulphur compounds they contain are harmful to plants. This danger does not apply to natural gas as the by-products of burning this are carbon dioxide and water vapour, both beneficial to plants. In consequence free-standing stoves burning natural gas will allow the maximum use of heat with the minimum cost of installation.

North Sea gas is a natural gas of this type and stoves specially adapted for greenhouse use are available for use with it. There is no theoretical limit to the size of such stoves, but since the heat in a greenhouse needs to be distributed as evenly as possible, it is usually better to use several stoves spaced out in a large greenhouse rather than one big stove.

One of the most popular types is designed to give a 10° C. (50° F.) rise in temperature in a greenhouse of 100 sq. ft. area and in most parts of Britain one such stove would probably exclude frost from a house double this size. These stoves are thermostatically controlled and require a minimum of attention.

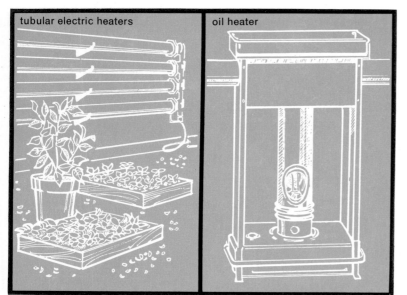

tubular electric heaters

oil heater

Ventilation

Good ventilation is extremely important. This greenhouse is well equipped with ridge ventilators and slatted blinds, so that the inside environment can be well controlled

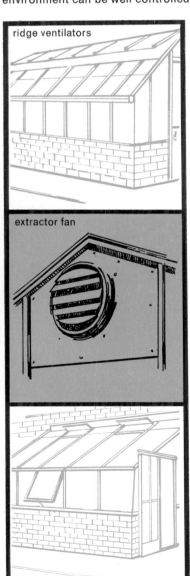

ridge ventilators

extractor fan

In sunny weather the air inside a greenhouse warms rapidly and can soon become too hot. Ventilation is essential to let this hot air escape and cooler air enter and, if required, to allow damp air to be replaced by drier air.

Ventilation may be effected by opening ventilators or by using extractor fans, both of which methods can be made automatic. The most important ventilators are those which are at or near the ridge of the greenhouse, since hot air rises and will escape most readily from the highest point. Ideally, ventilators should be equivalent to the length of the ridge and be placed half on one side, half on the other in a span-roofed house, so that they can be opened away from the prevailing wind. Strong draughts can be harmful to plants.

Extractor fans should be placed as high as possible, usually in the end panels of the greenhouse, and must be sufficiently powerful to change the air within the house every three or four minutes.

Ventilators in the sides may be useful in very hot weather to ensure a through current of air but they can create draughts if they are incorrectly used. The greenhouse door may also be left open on very hot days as additional ventilation.

The aim in ventilation should always be to maintain a reasonable temperature, a little higher during the day than at night.

Automation

Temperature control is a major factor in greenhouse management and many automatic devices are available to assist with this. Shown here is a thermostatically-controlled extractor fan

Greenhouses are affected by every change in the weather, small houses more rapidly than large ones because of the smaller volume of air they contain. Therefore anything that can be done to control automatically temperature, ventilation and humidity will greatly reduce the amount of time that must be devoted to the house.

Temperature control in winter depends mainly on controlling the supply of artificial heat. This can be done by a thermostat, which is now almost standard equipment incorporated with electric and natural gas heaters as well as oil-fired boilers and can be applied to some free-standing paraffin heaters. If a separate thermostat is used it should be placed as centrally as possible and be screened from direct sunshine.

In summer, temperature control depends mainly on ventilation and shading. Though various ingenious methods of automatic shading have been used none has yet caught on with the public. Automatic ventilation is a different matter since extractor fans can also be thermostatically controlled. Alternatively, ventilators can be automatically opened by a device operated by a very heat-sensitive fluid inside a cylinder. The cylinder contains a piston which is pushed outwards by the expanding fluid and in so doing lifts the ventilator.

Extra humidity is most likely to be required in summer and can be provided by a humidifier.

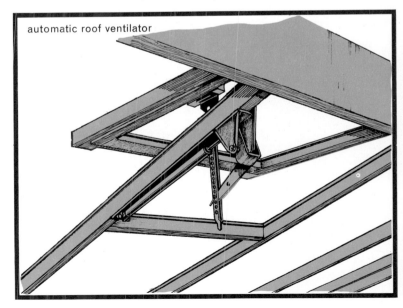

automatic roof ventilator

Watering

Plants in a greenhouse should be watered individually if possible. Care must be taken to direct the water at the soil, and not to splash the leaves or stems

Different plants require water in different quantities at different times of the year, three variables which make generalisation difficult. In general, the rule should be to keep soil moist throughout each pot or bed, but not to allow it to remain saturated for any length of time.

Provided soil is of the correct texture and drainage is adequate, surplus water will run away fairly quickly. So give sufficient water to soak the soil right through and then give no more until it begins to dry out. This can usually be decided by examining or feeling the surface of the soil, but when in doubt pick up a pot and feel its weight. Dry soil is lighter than wet and experience is soon gained in gauging the rela-

tive weights. In the case of beds, scrape away a little soil with the forefinger and see how moist it is an inch or so below the surface, where the roots are.

In spring and summer examine plants daily to see which ones require water and in autumn and winter examine them every third or fourth day. In very warm weather pot plants may require watering both morning and evening.

Apply water direct to the soil, not to the leaves or stems. Some plants like to have damp leaves, but these can be separately syringed overhead.

Automatic Watering

Some system of automatic watering, such as the capillary bench shown in the foreground above, is useful in the larger greenhouse or when the owner is absent for long periods

Various systems of automatic or semi-automatic watering are available, some electrically operated, others purely mechanical. One of the simplest is the capillary bench, which is a bed of sand or gravel kept constantly moist. Pot plants are placed on this and draw water from it by capillary attraction as the soil or peat they contain becomes drier than the bench. This bench must be quite level. It can be covered with asbestos cement sheets or polythene sheeting or the sand or gravel can be contained in shallow plastic trays. About an inch thickness of aggregate is required. Water can be supplied from a small tank fitted with a ball valve, by periodic trickle irrigation, or direct from the mains

supply via a special control unit. Various proprietary kits are available.

Plastic pots without drainage crocks are best for use on capillary benches since they are thin and the soil inside them comes readily into contact with the moist sand or gravel on the bench. The capillary action must be started by watering each pot well after it has been placed in position.

Another system uses fine bore plastic pipes to convey water individually to each pot. Yet another uses a siphon tank to deliver water through rubber tubing fitted with drip nozzles, which can either be placed to discharge directly into the plant pots or on to a capillary bench.

capillary bench

Damping Down, Shading

Damping down a greenhouse with a watering-can fitted with a fine rose. This is an important job in the summer time, for it keeps the atmosphere of the house moist

In hot or dry weather gardeners spray or splash water about inside their greenhouses to evaporate and so cool the air and keep it moist. This is known as 'damping down' and is very important for some tropical and sub-tropical plants that originate from places with a humid atmosphere. It also helps to control red spider mites.

Damping down may be done with a syringe or with a watering-can fitted with a fine rose. Use clear water and thoroughly wet the floor of the house and the staging, especially if this is of a solid type covered with sand, gravel or ashes. Damp down in the morning and again at mid-day and in the evening too if conditions need it.

A hygrometer can be purchased

to record the relative humidity of the air, but usually the look of the plants and the feel of the air on the skin is sufficient guide.

Shading is required to prevent direct sunshine from over-heating the air or damaging plants. It is more important for some plants than for others – hence the advantage of shading by means of roller blinds which can be readily raised or lowered as required. Alternatively, the glass can be sprayed or painted with lime-wash or a special shading compound. This is usually done in May and the shading is washed off at the end of September.

damping down

shading

Staging and Beds

Gravel on greenhouse staging provides an attractive, moisture holding background for plants. Collect up leaves and other debris that fall on to the gravel or infection may be started

slatted staging

solid staging

greenhouse beds

Plants may be grown either in pots, boxes or other containers or in beds of soil. If grown in containers it is usually most convenient to keep them on staging at about the level of an ordinary table, so that they can be examined and handled easily.

Staging may be either of open slat or of solid construction. Open staging is usually made of slats about 2 in. wide, spaced an inch apart. It can be made portable so that it can be removed quickly if the greenhouse is required for plants grown from floor level. Open-slat staging is best for those plants that require a fairly dry atmosphere, such as carnations and succulents.

Solid staging is often of asbestos cement sheets which rest on trestles and are covered with sand, small (pea) gravel, ashes or peat. These materials can be kept moist if desired and so this kind of staging is best for plants that appreciate a rather moist atmosphere, such as begonias and gloxinias.

Beds of soil for greenhouse plants can be constructed on solid staging, but are usually made at floor level. They should be at least 9 in. deep and may be separated from the natural soil with a sheet of polythene, but this should be slit or perforated to allow surplus water to escape.

Shelves slung from rafters or attached to side members can provide extra space and help to bring plants nearer to the light. Wire or plastic baskets can also be suspended above head level.

Soils and Composts

Collecting together the materials for John Innes compost. When making up compost, it is essential that all the ingredients are thoroughly mixed, so that plants receive a balanced amount of food

The soils or other growing media used for greenhouse plants are known as seed or potting composts. Standard composts will serve a wide variety of plants.

The most satisfactory soil composts are those known as the John Innes Composts.

The John Innes Seed Compost (J.I.S. for short) is prepared with 2 parts by bulk medium loam, 1 part granulated peat, 1 part coarse sand. To each bushel of this mixture add 1½ oz. superphosphate of lime and ¾ oz. ground limestone or chalk.

The John Innes Potting Compost is prepared by mixing 7 parts by bulk medium loam, 3 parts granulated peat, 2 parts coarse sand.

For the J.I.P. No. 1 Compost add to each bushel of this mixture ¾ oz. of ground limestone or chalk and 4 oz. of John Innes Base Fertiliser (2 parts by weight superphosphate of lime, 2 parts hoof and horn meal, 1 part sulphate of potash). For J.I.P. No. 2 use 8 oz. of J.I. Base Fertiliser and 1½ oz. of chalk or limestone per bushel of compost. For J.I.P. No. 3 use 12 oz. of J.I. Base Fertiliser and 2¼ oz. of chalk or limestone per bushel of compost. For J.I.P. No. 4 use 16 oz. of J.I. Base Fertiliser and 3 oz. of chalk or limestone per bushel.

The loam should be sterilised, since unsterilised soil may carry diseases. John Innes Seed and Potting Composts can be obtained ready mixed and so can several soil-less composts based on peat.

Pots and Containers

Flower pots are obtainable in a wide range of sizes. When potting up plants, one should be careful not to choose too large a pot in relation to the size of the plant

Greenhouse plants are grown in pots of various sizes and kinds and seedlings are usually raised in shallow boxes or trays or in special seed pans.

Pots and pans used always to be made of baked clay, but this is now being superseded by plastic which is lighter, easier to clean, and retains moisture and heat better. Seedboxes are usually made of wood and seed trays of plastic.

Pots are made in different sizes measured by the diameter across the top, which may be anything from 2 in. to 16 in. or thereabouts. For ordinary purposes, pots respectively 3, 4, 5, 6 and 8 in. across are the most useful. New clay pots are usually very dry and should be soaked in water before use, other-

wise they will absorb water from the compost. All pots must be kept scrupulously clean and provided with at least one good hole in the base for drainage.

Wooden boxes must not be treated with creosote as the fumes from this substance are harmful to plants. Boxes can be used as they are or treated with a harmless preservative such as copper naphthenate. Tubs are often painted.

All boxes and trays must also have adequate holes or slits to allow surplus water to escape. Provided that suitably porous seed and potting composts are used, no extra drainage material will be required. Tubs are usually on short legs or castors. This allows water to drain away easily.

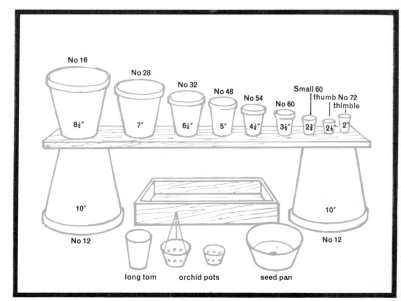

Potting

Feeding

Potting up young plants in plastic pots. The compost is firmed lightly with the fingers, and is then watered thoroughly to settle it more securely around the roots

Liquid feeding is especially useful for pot plants because the concentration of feed given can be so accurately controlled. Water dry soil before applying the liquid feed

As a rule plants are moved on only one, or at the most two, sizes of pot at a time. Thus a plant in a 3-in. pot is re-potted into a 4- or 5-in. pot, then into a 6- or 7-in. pot and so on. A little plant in a large pot is seldom happy and it is very difficult to give it the correct amount of water.

Potting becomes necessary when the roots of developing plants have occupied all the soil in their pots and the plants are in danger of becoming starved. It can be done at practically any time of the year except winter.

To re-pot a plant turn it over, holding the pot in one hand and placing two fingers of the other hand over the mouth of the pot, one on each side of the plant. Rap

the rim on something firm such as the edge of a potting bench, and the ball of soil should then slide out intact. Without disturbing the soil round the roots, place the plant on a little soil in the larger pot, trickle soil all round it and give the bottom of the pot a sharp rap on the bench to settle the soil in. With peat-based composts, nothing more is needed, but with soil composts a little firming all round with the fingers may be desirable. For very large pots a stick is occasionally used to ram the soil in round the edge.

Immediately after potting, water the compost well to settle it still more securely around the roots.

The John Innes and various proprietary peat-based seed and potting composts all contain sufficient plant food to carry plants on for a considerable period, but there will come a time when supplies begin to run out and extra feeding is required. To judge the right moment requires some experience, but condition of growth is a guide. Feeding is most likely to be necessary between May and August and is hardly ever required in autumn and winter.

Either dry or liquid feeds can be purchased for greenhouse plants, and the dry feeds are divided into those which should be dissolved in water and those to be applied as they are. In all cases manufacturers' instructions regarding

strength and method of application must be followed and should never be exceeded. It is better to give feeds that are too dilute than too concentrated.

A liquid feed containing minor as well as major foods can be made by suspending a bag of well-rotted manure in a tub of water and diluting the resulting liquor to pale straw colour. An alternative is seaweed extract used according to label instructions.

As a rule it is sufficient to apply liquid feeds about once every 7 to 10 days and dry feeds about once a fortnight. Dry feeds must be watered in and no more should be applied while any remains undissolved on the surface.

Sowing in Pots and Boxes

Primula obconica is a rewarding plant for the cool greenhouse. It can be raised from seed sown in March at a temperature of 15° C. (60° F.) and will then flower from December to March

Pots, pans and boxes in which seeds are germinated must be well provided with holes or slits through which surplus water can drain away. Cover these outlets with pieces of broken pot (crocks), small gravel or coarse peat so that they cannot be blocked by fine soil and then fill up with seed compost. Press the compost in gently with the fingers and smooth it off level with a straight-edged piece of wood. Firm composts based on loam, such as John Innes Seed Compost, with a smooth wooden block, but do not firm peat composts. When ready for sowing, the surface of the compost should be about $\frac{1}{2}$ in. below the rim of the receptacle.

Broadcast the seed thinly over the surface of the compost and cover by sifting soil, peat or sand over it. Very small seeds need not be covered at all, but both types should be protected by a pane of glass laid over the container (but not touching the soil) with a sheet of paper on top. The paper must be removed directly the seedlings appear and the glass a day or so later.

Water the seeds thoroughly using a watering-can fitted with a fine rose. For very small seeds, water by holding the pan for a few moments almost to its rim in a tub of water.

Germination and Watering

The sheets of glass used for covering seedboxes should be tilted slightly, to admit some air, once the seedlings appear and all the condensation wiped off daily

Most seeds of greenhouse plants will germinate in a temperature of 15 to 18° C. (60 to 65° F.) though seeds of warm house plants will germinate better at around 20° C. (68° F.). Some seeds germinate rapidly and seedlings may appear in 7 to 8 days, others are slow or irregular in germination, sometimes taking six months and occasionally a year or more. With the larger seeds it is usually possible to uncover one or two if germination is delayed to confirm that they have not rotted away.

Though many seeds germinate best in the dark, which is one reason for covering seed pans with paper, this is not true of all seeds as certain kinds will only germinate when they receive at least some light. There is a great dearth of accurate information on this matter, especially for the less common plants and so, when difficulty is experienced, it is wise to try some seeds in the dark and some in the light. Any shading must be removed immediately the first seedlings appear and glass coverings should be tilted slightly to admit more air, and entirely removed a few days later. Most seedlings quickly become drawn, i.e. long, thin and pale, if permitted to grow with insufficient light.

Seeds must have moisture and air for germination so the soil must be kept constantly moist but not sodden. Water is better given by semi-immersion than by overhead sprinkling.

watering seeds

Pricing Out

Seedlings are transplanted, or pricked out, once the seed leaves are well developed. Here, a box of seedlings is being watered overhead from a watering-can fitted with a rose

The first leaf or pair of leaves produced by seedlings are known as the seed leaves or cotyledons. In many plants they are quite different in appearance from the subsequent leaves, being un-broken in outline.

The seedlings unless sown very thinly will need to be transplanted to other trays or pans when still very small. This is known as pricking out and is best done either as soon as the seed leaves are well developed or when the first true leaves appear. As a rule the same soil or peat mixture for germination is used for pricking out, but for some strong growing plants a slightly richer compost is preferred, such as John Innes No. 1. The seedlings should be well watered the day before they are to be pricked out so that the soil around them is nicely moist. They are lifted very carefully with a sharp-ened stick or household fork, are equally carefully separated from one another and then replanted at least 1½ in. apart in holes made with a pointed stick or dibber. These holes must be large enough to accommodate all the roots and the soil should be pressed firmly around the roots with dibber or fingers. When pricking out into peat compost, which is light and easily worked, many gardeners prefer to use their fingers for the whole operation.

After pricking out, seedlings must be well watered in from a can fitted with a fine rose.

Care of Seedlings

Mignonette is one of the most pleasantly fragrant of annuals. Seed is sown in spring and the seedlings either planted out in late May or grown on as pot plants in the greenhouse

After being pricked out seedlings usually need to be kept in a still, moist, fairly warm atmosphere for a few days to get established. If a propagating frame is available inside the greenhouse they can be placed in this, alternatively they can be put in the warmest part of the house and shaded from strong sunshine. The seedlings may flag a little at first but as soon as they are seen to be growing again normal treatment should be re-sumed. Certain plants, particularly those grown primarily for their foliage, enjoy some shade much of the time, but most flowering plants like light, especially in the early stages of their growth, and become drawn and weakly if de-prived of it. One of the advantages of having shelves under the ridge in the greenhouse or above the staging is that seed trays and pans can be stood on these, so bringing the seedlings nearer the light.

Seedlings grow rapidly and need more water as they gain in size. It is usually best to use a can fitted with a moderately coarse rose which will supply plenty of water without washing the soil out. No feeding is needed.

As soon as the little plants have filled their new trays or pans they should be potted on singly into small (2½- or 3-in.) pots and a pot-ting compost. Care should be taken not to break roots or damage leaves. After potting the plants should be watered and kept in still, warm conditions for a few days.

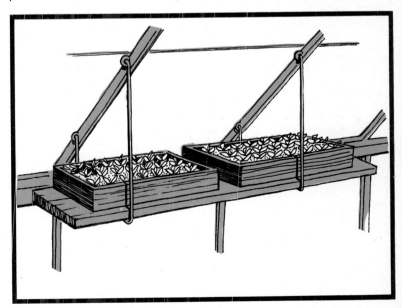

Hardening Off

If a frame is available, it will be extremely useful for hardening off plants that have been raised in a greenhouse. When the risk of frost is past they can be planted out of doors

Some plants raised or started under glass are planted out of doors later on. Care must be taken to see that the plant is properly prepared for the change in conditions, a process known as 'hardening off'.

A frame is of great assistance in hardening off, since it is possible to remove completely the protecting glass, or light, and give a degree of ventilation impossible inside a greenhouse.

First move the plant to the coolest part of the greenhouse and keep it as near the glass as practicable, giving it as much ventilation as possible without harming other plants in the greenhouse. Then remove it to a frame, continuing to increase ventilation whenever the

weather is favourable. On mild days remove the light altogether by day and only replace it for the night.

It is possible, however, to harden off without using a frame. Keep the plant a little longer in the greenhouse and then put it out of doors in the most sheltered place available. Cover it at night with suitably supported brown paper or hessian and, if frost threatens, cover it by day as well.

A period of from three to four weeks is usually required to harden off a plant properly.

Resting and Starting

These Poinsettias are resting under the greenhouse staging during the spring. At this time of the year watering should be reduced to the barest minimum

Few plants continue to grow all through the year and some have quite long resting periods, by no means always in winter. Plants that are resting need little or no water and some actually benefit from the fullest exposure to the sun. These may be placed on a shelf near the glass in the sunniest part of the greenhouse to enjoy a good baking.

Other plants may be stored away while resting, either in their pots or, if they have fleshy roots, they may be shaken out and stored quite dry. Correct treatment during the resting period can sometimes determine the freedom with which a plant will subsequently flower.

After their resting period plants must be restarted into growth, and this, too, must be done correctly.

Plants that have been shaken out of their soil are often started in damp peat in shallow trays and potted as soon as they have leaves and roots. Plants rested in their pots may simply be watered again or, if they are overcrowded, may be re-potted and then watered.

In either case water must be given rather sparingly at first and gradually increased as growth re-starts, the correct temperature for the plant being maintained throughout.

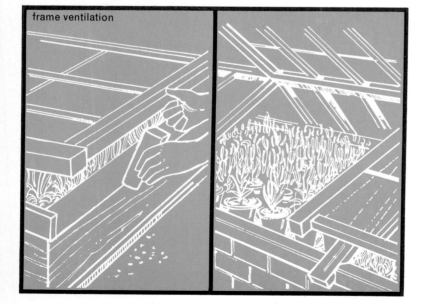

frame ventilation

Fumigation

Fumigation is an effective method of controlling pests in the greenhouse. Care must be taken when using the smoke generators and it will be necessary to keep out of the greenhouse for a few hours

In the greenhouse, pests and some diseases can most readily be controlled by fumigation. Special smoke generators can be purchased containing suitable chemicals. These, when ignited, will rapidly fill the greenhouse with smoke carrying the insecticides or fungicides with it and depositing them in a fine film on every part of the plants. Greenflies, caterpillars, whiteflies and most other troublesome insects can be controlled by this means, though for whitefly it may be necessary to repeat the fumigation at least twice at intervals of a fortnight.

To control red spider mites, which can increase rapidly under hot, dry conditions, fumigate the house with azobenzene smoke generators or use azobenzene in the form of an aerosol spray. Red spider mites are minute, rusty-coloured creatures living mainly on the underside of leaves to which they usually give a mottled, grey appearance.

A fungicide named tecnazene or TCNB can also be obtained in smoke generators and is useful for the control of botrytis or grey mould and other diseases.

Use smoke generators according to the manufacturers' instructions, first calculating in cubic feet the capacity of the greenhouse by multiplying the length, in feet, by the breadth and the height, measured mid-way between the eaves and ridge.

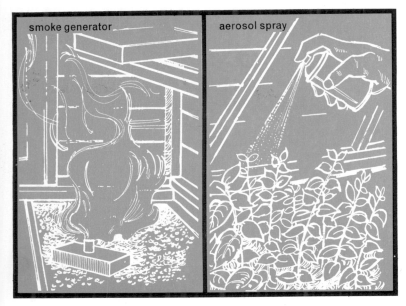

smoke generator   aerosol spray

Greenhouse Hygiene

To maintain a good display of healthy plants it is important that some attention is given each year to greenhouse hygiene, which is the most effective way of controlling many plant troubles

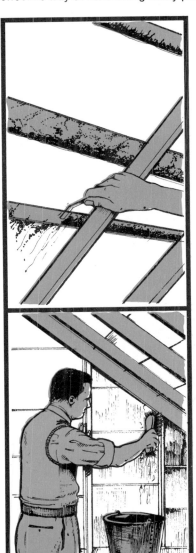

Some pests may establish themselves in the woodwork of the greenhouse and so it is a good thing if this can be thoroughly scrubbed at least once a year using warm water, a little detergent and just a dash of any good disinfectant. At the same time glass can be washed inside and out to remove grime and green scum.

Soil or peat. composts in pots and seed trays should not be used a second time since they may have become infected. One of the advantages of ring culture is that the used soil is so readily removed and the gravel aggregate can be flushed out with water.

Where crops such as carnations are grown in beds of soil these should either be renewed annually with fresh soil that has not been used previously for a similar crop, or the old soil should be partially sterilised, either chemically or by heat. The latter is best applied as steam, e.g. by suspending bags of soil over boiling water in a closed vessel, the aim being to keep the soil at 93 to 96° C. (200 to 205° F.) for 30 minutes. Formalin (40% formaldehyde) is commonly used for chemical sterilisation, 1 pint in 6 gallons of water will treat 3 bushels of soil. This treated soil should be thrown up into a heap and covered for 48 hours to trap fumes, after which it should be spread out and left until it has lost all smell of formalin. Do not use formalin in the house if it contains any plants. Proprietary sterilising chemicals are also available.

Propagating Plants

Special Methods

This summer bedding scheme uses a range of half-hardy plants which have been raised and grown on in a greenhouse for planting out when they are at their best

If a great many plants are to be raised from seed, cuttings or by other means, there is considerable advantage in having a greenhouse specially for this purpose or at least setting apart some section of the greenhouse for it. Young plants need to be moved frequently as they progress from seed pans to pricking out trays and then to pots, or from cutting beds to pots of increasing size. At some stages they need still, moist, warm air and at others they are better on shelves near the glass. All these varied conditions can be more easily supplied in a special house than in one which is mainly used for mature plants that have settled requirements.

The ideal propagating house will be in a particularly light position and will have a heating apparatus to meet all demands. It will be both an advantage and an economy to have one or more propagators or propagating frames installed within it as then the special conditions required by seeds and cuttings can be provided accurately and with the minimum use of fuel.

The propagating house should also be well provided with staging and shelves so that a large number of small plants can be accommodated and be tended easily. One of the commonest pitfalls of home propagation is to discover that one has inadequate room to grow on the large number of plants that can be produced from a few packets of seed.

It may be a great help to install electric lighting in the propagating house as much work is likely to be done in late winter and early spring when days are still short.

Either in or near the propagating house there must be room to carry out the necessary work. Seed trays will have to be filled with compost and sown with seeds; seedlings will need to be pricked out and later potted singly; cuttings will have to be prepared and so on. For all these jobs a solid wooden bench is ideal and it is unlikely that valuable greenhouse space will be spared for it, though some gardeners do manage with a portable bench that can be set up inside the greenhouse when required.

As a rule it is more convenient to make provision for all this ancillary work in a garden shed placed reasonably near to the greenhouse. Here potting ingredients, trays and pots can be stored, and tools kept conveniently to hand. The potting bench should stand in the window where it will receive maximum light and since much propagation is done early in the year when days are short, it will almost certainly be wise to make provision for artificial lighting and heating as well.

Propagation adds a new dimension to gardening and provides an insight into characteristics of some plants which cannot be obtained simply by cultivating mature specimens. For this reason alone it is worth carrying out some home propagation quite apart from the economy and satisfaction of producing one's own plants.

begonia leaf cuttings

saintpaulia leaf cuttings

In addition to the methods of increasing plants by seeds, cuttings and division, there are other means suitable for greenhouse plants.

Some kinds, notably the large-leaved begonias and also saintpaulias, can be increased from leaves. With begonias, mature leaves are laid flat on the surface of a mixture of moist sand and peat. Slits are made at intervals through the main veins and these wounded veins are then held close to the compost with wire pegs like hairpins. With saintpaulias, mature leaves are detached complete with leaf stalks, and are pushed into a mixture of peat and sand until most of the leaf stalk is covered. These leaf cuttings must be kept in a warm, moist atmosphere, preferably in a propagating frame. Little plants will, in time, form from each vein incision on the begonia leaves and from the leaf stalks of the saintpaulias.

Air layering can be applied to some semi-woody plants such as rubber plants, dracaenas, and crotons. If these plants get too tall and leggy an incision is made in the bark right round the stem 2 or 3 inches below the leaves; this wound is lightly dusted with hormone rooting powder and is wrapped around with damp sphagnum moss. The moss is bound in place with fillis or raffia and is covered with thin plastic film, tightly bound top and bottom. In time roots are formed from the wound into the moss and then the whole top of the plant is severed and re-potted.

Propagating Frames

A propagating case in a greenhouse containing soft-wood cuttings of various plants including begonia, abutilon, plumbago and coleus. A sandy compost is used as the rooting medium

This is the name given to frames used mainly for raising seedlings and for rooting cuttings. Such frames are often quite small and will stand inside a greenhouse, so giving double protection and providing the very still air that seeds and cuttings enjoy. It is, of course, much cheaper to maintain the necessary temperature inside such a frame than to heat up the whole of a greenhouse to the required level.

Propagating frames are best heated from below because seeds germinate and cuttings root most rapidly when the soil is a few degrees warmer than the air. Electric soil-warming cable is excellent for this purpose. Provided the frame can be tightly closed it is not as a rule necessary to shade it except for a few seeds that germinate better in the dark. Cuttings and seedlings grow better with good light provided this does not mean that they dry out rapidly, and this they will not do in a 'close' frame, that is, one with little or no change of atmosphere.

Seeds can be sown and cuttings inserted directly in a bed of good soil, such as John Innes or peat-based seed compost spread inside the propagating frame, or they can be sown and inserted in pots, in which case it is best to plunge the pots up to their rims in moist peat half filling the frame.

Mist Propagation

Laying the electric heating cables for a mist propagating unit. These propagators are an asset to any gardener, for they make the rooting of cuttings a relatively easy task

Mist is a device to keep cuttings fresh without confining them within a frame, box or bag, or shading them from sunshine. With free circulation of air the cuttings are less likely to succumb to disease, and full exposure to sunlight increases their rate of growth.

The moisture may be provided by frequent fine sprays of water. These may be controlled by some form of time switch or by an electronic 'leaf' which is sensitive to moisture. Various forms of apparatus can be purchased and must be installed according to the manufacturer's instructions.

Mist propagators may be placed in a greenhouse or frame. Some form of soil warming is desirable. An electrical soil-warming cable may be laid 4 or 5 in. beneath the surface of the bed or the propagator may be installed over hot water pipes or other heating apparatus. A very porous compost is required, either entirely sharp sand or a mixture of sand and peat with sand predominating. This may be in a bed or in pots, pans or boxes.

If the mist is controlled by a timing device this should be set to keep the leaves constantly damp and the soil moist but not flooded.

Mist propagators can also be used to germinate seeds.

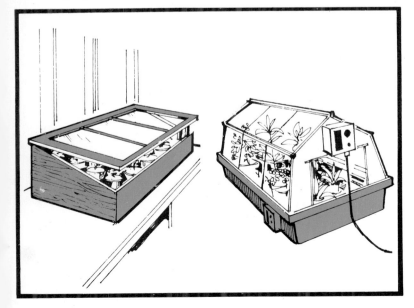

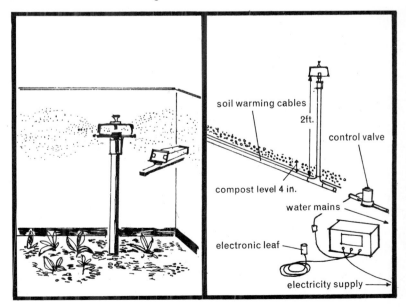

Growing in Frames

In a frame a controlled climate can be created to suit the needs of particular plants, just as it can in a greenhouse, and usually at considerably less cost. An added advantage is that when the protective lights (or other covering) are removed, plants are fully exposed to outdoor conditions in a way that is usually impossible with greenhouses. This can be of great assistance in the process of acclimatisation, called 'hardening off', which should precede the removal of plants from an artificial to a natural climate. The principal drawback of frames is their lack of headroom, which makes it impossible to grow tall plants in them or for the gardener to tend the plants with the same degree of protection for himself.

Perhaps the greatest value of frames is as an adjunct to the greenhouse. Used in this way they will serve both as an overflow for surplus plants and as a staging post for those plants that, having been reared in a greenhouse, are eventually destined for beds out of doors. In summer, with the protective lights removed, frames can provide a safe standing ground for many pot plants that are happier in the open. In winter, frames can be filled with small plants that require protection, though if this means full protection from frost then some system of heating must be provided. Considerable heating economies can be effected by covering frames with sacking or mats on cold nights. There are many winter-flowering plants which though quite hardy are often spoiled by wind and rain. In a frame they can be suitably protected without being unduly forced.

Frames are also excellent places in which to rear seedlings and root cuttings. Another use for frames is to ripen the bulbs of early-flowering plants such as tulips and sparaxis after they have finished flowering. By keeping the lights in place the rain will be kept from the bulbs. Air can be given by wedging up the lights rather than removing them or pushing them open.

When choosing and siting a greenhouse it is a good idea to choose and site the frame or frames that are to go with it, since then the whole layout can be made to look neat and efficient. It is often possible to have frames against the walls of the greenhouse where they will derive some protection from it. If the frames as well as the greenhouse are to be heated, considerable economies in installation can be made in this kind of way, perhaps by bringing heating cables or warm-water pipes from the greenhouse to the frame, or at least making certain that both can be supplied from the same source of heat. Any water supply can similarly be shared. It is desirable to have a hard path around frames and some means of stacking frame lights clear of the ground when not in use on the frames.

Types of Frame

Dutch lights are excellent for plants which require the maximum amount of light, since they are glazed with one large sheet of glass. A block of wood is used to prop up the frame light while ventilating

Frames are of many different types and sizes, but all have protective 'lights' that can be removed altogether or opened completely to allow plants inside the frame to be tended easily and to expose them to the outside atmosphere if required. Because of the comparatively small volume of air in a frame it is much cheaper to heat than a greenhouse with comparable standing space for plants, but the lack of headroom means that a frame is not suitable for tall plants.

The traditional type of frame with wooden sides and sliding lights is still one of the most popular and useful. Those used in nurseries and market gardens usually have lights measuring 6 x 4 ft., glazed with numerous panes of glass. Smaller lights, usually 4 x 3 ft., are better for gardens as they are more easily handled. Dutch lights measure 62 x 25 in. and are glazed with one large sheet of glass. They are excellent for winter crops and others requiring maximum light.

Frames may also have brick or concrete walls or be made of metal, plastic or glass fibre. Some have hinged instead of sliding lights. Some frames can be moved on metal rails and these are specially suitable for plants such as alpines which may be grown permanently in a frame, but which need only occasional protection.

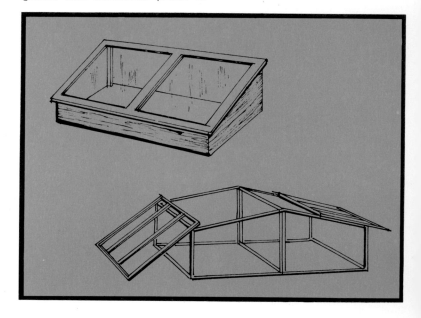

Heating, Hardening Off

When the weather is frosty it is a good idea to give some protection to frames at night by covering the lights with hessian or a similar material. This covering can be removed by day

A cold frame is one that is not heated in any way. It is most useful as an adjunct to a greenhouse, providing a place in which seedlings and cuttings raised in warmth can gradually be accustomed to the outside atmosphere. This is done by slowly increasing the ventilation until, when the weather is favourable, the lights can be removed altogether, first by day only, then later at night as well. This is known as 'hardening off'.

There are various ways of heating frames including the use of small oil heaters and hot-water pipes, but one of the most convenient methods is with special electric warming cables. These may either be buried in sand 4 to 6 in. beneath the soil's surface or they may be clipped around the sides of the frame. Soil warming is excellent for early seedlings and for rooting cuttings, air warming for plants that need frost protection in winter, and the temperature of both can be controlled by a thermostat if desired. Electric equipment in a frame must be entirely waterproof and should only be installed by a competent electrician.

Some protection can also be given by covering frames with hessian or something of the kind when the weather is frosty. This is particularly useful in spring when most frosts occur at night or early in the morning and the covering can be removed by day.

Hotbeds

A hotbed is made by placing a frame on a heap of fresh manure over which has been spread a 6-in. depth of soil and peat. This centuries-old idea can be used to advantage with many plants

When fresh manure decays it produces heat and a frame placed on top will trap the rising warmth and become a miniature hot house in which seedlings can be reared, cuttings rooted and warmth-loving plants given an early start.

Fresh strawy horse manure is the best material with which to make a hotbed. Failing this, well-wetted straw can be used treated with one of the advertised preparations for converting straw into mushroom compost. Another possibility is a mixture of autumn leaves, lawn mowings and weeds (especially nettle tops which rot well). Whatever is used should be built into a conical heap and left for about a week when it must be turned, well mixed and any dry parts watered. It will soon start to ferment vigorously and the temperature may rise considerably. The heap should then be turned again. A few days later it should be built into a flat-topped heap at least 18 in. longer and wider than the dimensions of the frame that is going to stand on it, and 2 ft. deep after having been well trodden down. A 6-in. depth of good soil or peat is spread on top and the frame and frame light placed in position. When the temperature well down in the heap has dropped to about 25° C. (77° F.) seeds can be sown, cuttings inserted or plants introduced. The warmth of the heap will continue to drop, and should remain effective for about 8 weeks.

soil warming unit

Plants for Unheated Greenhouses

Annuals

By making a succession of sowings, it is possible to have schizanthus in flower throughout the spring, summer and autumn. This lovely free-flowering annual is easy to grow

Only in the very mildest areas can an unheated greenhouse be expected to exclude frost throughout the winter. At this season, therefore, such a house is only suitable for plants that will withstand some degree of freezing. From about April to October it is very different, for then frosts are usually of short duration, sun heat can raise the temperature of the greenhouse to quite high levels by day even when it is cold outside, and stored heat will usually carry the house through the nights with little risk of the temperature dropping below freezing point. For these reasons during this period an unheated greenhouse can be used to grow quite a wide range of tender plants and also to raise seedlings, root cuttings and propagate plants in other ways.

If a conservatory is placed against a dwelling house, with perhaps french windows or a door leading directly into one of the rooms, it may derive quite a lot of warmth from the house, though even so it is unlikely to be fully protected against frost in winter unless it has some heating of its own. In winter such a conservatory can be used for the display of many hardy plants (including bulbs) in flower, also for nearly hardy plants such as cinerarias and winter-flowering primulas and for hardy or nearly hardy foliage plants such as clipped bay trees, fatsias, ivies, *Dracaena australis*, and the hardy palm, *Chamaerops humilis*. In summer there are few greenhouse plants that cannot be accommodated temporarily in it.

There is, of course, a half-way step from the completely unheated to the heated greenhouse, and that is the house with strictly temporary heating to be used only in emergencies. This is probably the way most beginners approach the problem, making do with portable oil heaters or something of the kind simply to exclude the worst frosts or to enable a start to be made with seed sowing a little earlier than would be wise in a completely unheated house. It is a very sensible compromise provided its limitations are realised, and it is one that, as experience and enthusiasm grow, is likely to lead eventually to a more generous level of heating.

Whether completely unheated or not, greenhouses which are to be run 'cold' most of the time must be sited with special care. They should be placed to catch all the sunshine that is going, but if they can also be sheltered from north and east by a building or hedge so much the better. The microclimates created in such places can be several degrees warmer than in a fully exposed position a few yards away.

Care during watering can also save the loss of a few degrees as water when evaporating takes heat from its surroundings. Therefore capillary benches should be allowed to dry out in the autumn and the plants grown with a minimum of water, care being taken not to spill water even on the path. Water during the morning to give any heat loss a chance to be made good before temperatures drop in the early evening.

Any hardy annual can be grown in an unheated greenhouse and some kinds, such as amaranthus, dimorphotheca, mignonette and schizanthus, make excellent pot plants. Seed of all these can be safely sown in late March or early April to give flowers in summer.

Even half-hardy annuals can be grown in an unheated greenhouse if sowing is delayed until April, or if seedlings are raised in a heated propagator or are purchased in April or May and potted. Among the best kinds for pot culture are antirrhinum, arctotis, *Begonia semperflorens*, Chabaud carnations, annual dianthus, diascia, felicia, heliotrope (strictly a perennial but easily grown as an annual), lobelia (especially the trailing varieties), molucella, nemesia, petunia (especially the large flowered and double varieties), salpiglossis, Ten Week stocks, ursinia, verbena and zinnia. *Cobaea scandens* and ipomoea varieties Flying Saucers or Heavenly Blue can be grown in the same way as climbers and will rapidly run up canes or spread along wires.

All these annuals are sun lovers and require no shading. They should be germinated and pricked out in J.I.S. or peat seed compost and then potted singly in J.I.P. No. 1 or peat potting compost. All should be watered fairly freely throughout and may be fed once a fortnight with weak liquid manure from the time they form their flower buds. Remove faded flowers.

Salpiglossis

mignonette

Biennials

The biennial stocks, such as the East Lothian and Brompton types, are more likely to survive the winter and will flower more freely when they are raised in an unheated house

wallflower

Some biennials make excellent pot plants for an unheated greenhouse or conservatory. Wallflowers can be had in bloom several weeks earlier than if grown out of doors. East Lothian and Brompton stocks are far more likely to survive and flower freely than they would in any but the mildest places in the open. The dwarfer forms of the Canterbury Bell make first-rate pot plants and its relative the tall Chimney Bellflower, *Campanula pyramidalis*, will produce striking 5-ft. spikes of bloom provided it does not get frozen too severely. Sweet Williams are completely hardy and can make a brilliant display.

Seed of all these can, if wished, be germinated outdoors in May though it is usually safer to sow in a frame. Seedlings can also be grown on for a while outdoors or planted out in a frame, but should be potted individually in J.I.P. No. 2 or peat potting compost before they get too large. Thereafter they can stand out of doors or in a frame until October, after which they should be rehoused and water should be applied much more sparingly. The plants are discarded after flowering. Some of the winter-flowering primulas, and particularly *Primula malacoides* and *P. kewensis*, can be grown in a similar manner except that seed should be germinated in pots and the seedlings grown on in pots throughout. They need only frame protection in summer but should go into the greenhouse by late September.

Herbaceous Plants

Some of the herbaceous plants, such as the astilbe shown above, make excellent pot plants for an unheated greenhouse but an annual re-potting is usually essential

A number of herbaceous plants grow well in pots and even in an unheated greenhouse can be in bloom several weeks ahead of their normal flowering time. Plants can either be purchased or lifted from the open ground and transferred to pots. This is usually done in October or November, though it can also be done in spring, in which case it is unwise to bring the plants into the greenhouse before the following autumn. Throughout the summer the plants can stand outdoors.

Since most herbaceous plants grow rapidly annual re-potting is usually essential. As the plants get too large for comfort they can be split up into smaller pieces. Water sparingly in winter, fairly frequently in spring and summer and feed with weak liquid manure about once a fortnight from June to August inclusive. Watering can be reduced by plunging pots to their rims in soil, sand or peat when they are put out of the greenhouse after flowering.

Among the most useful kinds are primroses, polyanthus and doronicum for spring, dicentra and astilbe for early summer. Francoa, though not completely hardy outdoors, usually survives in an unheated greenhouse and so does the Mother of Thousands, *Saxifraga tomentosa*, an attractive trailing plant. Violas and pansies can be grown in quite small pots but are often difficult to over-winter. Both are readily raised from seed.

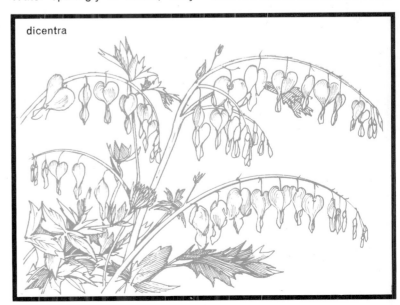

dicentra

Bulbs in Pots

For spring flowering, this novel pot was planted with tulip bulbs in early autumn. The pot requires careful planting as each bulb must be placed with its 'nose' by a hole

Many different types of bulbs can be grown successfully in an unheated greenhouse. For spring flowering only hardy kinds should be chosen, such as narcissus, tulip, hyacinth, crocus and the early bulbous-rooted irises, since they will have to be potted in early autumn and will make their growth in winter. For summer flowering some more tender kinds can be grown, such as tigridias, tritonias and zephyranthes. These need not be potted until March or April, when even an unheated house should provide frost protection.

In most cases the bulbs (or corms) can be planted almost shoulder to shoulder, but a little more space should be left between the very small irises, tigridias, tritonias and zephyranthes. For all kinds either J.I.P. No. 2 or peat-based compost is suitable.

All should be watered rather sparingly at first, then with increasing freedom as growth proceeds until the leaves begin to turn yellow and wither away, which they will in May and June for spring-flowering bulbs and in early autumn for most summer-flowering bulbs. This is the signal to reduce watering until the soil is quite dry, when the bulbs can be removed from the soil and stored until re-potting.

It is an advantage if narcissus, tulips and hyacinths can be plunged under 2 inches of sand or peat in a shady place outdoors for 8 to 10 weeks before they are brought into the greenhouse.

Camellias

There are many lovely varieties of *Camellia reticulata*. All are vigorous plants and ideal for training on wires or trellis. Those with double flowers can be grown to greater perfection indoors

All kinds of camellia make excellent pot or tub plants for unheated greenhouses and the very vigorous varieties of *Camellia reticulata* can be trained on the back wall of a lean-to greenhouse or conservatory. Varieties with large double flowers and those with double flowers of very formal shape can be grown to greater perfection in a greenhouse or conservatory than is usually possible out of doors where these flowers are often damaged by frost, wind or heavy rain. For the same reason this is an excellent way to grow the beautiful varieties of *C. sasanqua* which flower in autumn and winter.

It is best to start with young plants in pots, which can, if wished, be purchased in flower. If any are to be planted permanently in the greenhouse a bed of lime-free loam mixed with plenty of peat should be prepared for them. Pot plants are grown in a mixture of 4 parts by bulk lime-free loam, 2 parts peat and 1 part coarse sand with 4 oz. John Innes base fertiliser added to every bushel.

Stand pot or tub grown plants outdoors from May to October in a sheltered place. Ventilate permanently planted camellias very freely in summer and shade from direct sunshine. Water freely in spring and summer, moderately in autumn and winter. Feed every 10 to 14 days from May to August with weak liquid manure. If plants grow too large stems can be thinned or shortened in late May.

anemone-centred camellia

Hydrangeas

These popular pot plants are best renewed annually from cuttings. No chalk or limestone should be added to the compost if blue flowers are required and a 'blueing' compound may be used

These make excellent pot plants, for which they are best renewed from cuttings annually, though old plants can be grown in large pots or tubs in a border of soil within the greenhouse.

Prepare cuttings in March or April from firm, non-flowering stems. Insert the cuttings in sand and peat in a greenhouse or frame with a temperature of 10 to 15° C. (50 to 60° F.). When well rooted pot singly in 3-in. pots in J.I.P. No. 1 or peat-based potting compost. If blue flowers are required, make sure there is no chalk or limestone in the compost, and use a special hydrangea 'blueing' compound according to instructions.

Water freely and grow on in a greenhouse, with shade from strong sunshine. No artificial heat is required from May to October and plants can be put in a frame from June to September.

Pot on into 5-in. pots and J.I.P. No. 2 or peat potting compost when the smaller pots are full of roots and remove the tip of each plant about a fortnight later to encourage branching. Return them to the greenhouse in October and at the same time pot on the largest plants to 6- or 7-in. pots in similar compost.

Water rather sparingly from November until January and maintain a minimum temperature of 7° C. (45° F.). Then raise the temperature to 10 to 13° C. (50 to 55° F.) and water more freely for early flowers.

Other Shrubs

The unheated greenhouse is useful for providing winter protection for some of the early-flowering and slightly tender shrubs. *Rhododendron edgworthii*, shown above, is just such a plant

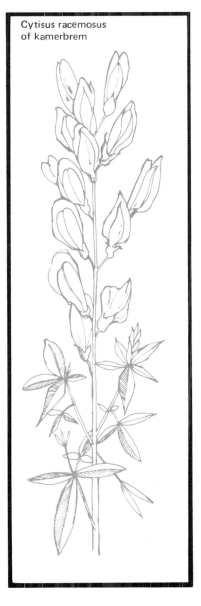

Cytisus racemosus of kamerbrem

Many other shrubs grow well in pots in an unheated greenhouse. Some, such as *Cytisus canariensis*, the shrub with scented yellow flowers in spring commonly known as 'genista', are a little tender but are usually safe in an unheated greenhouse provided they are not overwatered in winter. So are *Deutzia gracilis*, with sprays of small white flowers in spring and *Prunus triloba flore pleno*, a pretty relation of the almond with double pink flowers in spring. The Bridal Wreath, *Spiraea thunbergii*, is frequently grown as a white spring-flowering pot plant, and *Choisya ternata*, the Mexican Orange Blossom, is also very suitable.

Rhododendrons and azaleas make compact root balls and even quite big specimens can be grown in large pots or small tubs. Some rhododendrons are a little tender or flower very early, e.g., Christmas Cheer, *R. moupinense, R. ciliatum, R. praecox*, and like protection.

All shrubs should be potted in November, usually in J.I.P. No. 2, though for rhododendrons and azaleas no chalk or lime should be included. They are watered moderately in winter, freely in spring and summer and may stand outdoors from May to October. Feed fortnightly from June to August with weak liquid manure and re-pot annually in November. Genista, spiraea, deutzia, prunus and choisya can be pruned after flowering. Rhododendrons and azaleas should only have the faded flowers removed.

The Alpine House

Alpine House Management

An alpine house is a greenhouse devoted solely or mainly to plants which might otherwise be grown in a rock garden. Many of these will be genuine mountain plants but not necessarily all of them. Some will come from rocky places at low altitudes, others may simply be small plants which look right in the company of true rock plants. There are two major reasons for growing such plants in an alpine house: one, that it enables many of them to be grown to greater perfection than is possible in the open garden; the other that as many flower very early in the year it is easier to enjoy their beauty in the comfort of a greenhouse than it is out of doors. Since many of these plants come from very cold places it might be supposed that greenhouse protection is the last thing they would require. In fact, in their native habitats they are often covered deep in snow for the greater part of the year, emerging when the snow melts for a few weeks of hectic life and then returning to hibernation again. In lowland gardens they miss their snow covering, never become properly dormant, start to grow much too early and then have their flowers and possibly their leaves damaged by frost, wind and heavy rain. All these hazards can be overcome in a well managed alpine house.

A frame or series of frames is almost a necessity as an overflow for an alpine house, a place in which to keep plants while they are dormant or making little contribution to beauty. Frames have the advantage over greenhouses that the protective glass can be completely removed if desired, which can be very useful in summer to keep the temperature down. Even with full ventilation a greenhouse is usually a good many degrees warmer than the outside air on sunny days. An alpine house must be well provided with ventilators, all along the ridge if possible, and at the sides as well, so that when required a current of air can flow right through it. Staging is almost essential to bring the plants closer to eye level where they can be appreciated more fully and cared for most easily. It is an advantage if this staging has a solid, not a slatted, top on which a layer of pea gravel can be spread. This will absorb moisture and on sunny days will help to maintain the cool moist atmosphere which most rock plants enjoy.

Though most alpine houses are unheated this is not really ideal. Artificial warmth may not be required very often but there are occasions when it is desirable to exclude frost, certainly very severe and prolonged frost, and others when the air gets too moist and a little drying out is advantageous. The heating is unlikely to be required for more than that, so can be on a much more modest scale than in most greenhouses and will be correspondingly economical to run.

An unheated greenhouse may be used exclusively for the cultivation of spring-flowering alpines or rock plants and it is then known as an alpine house

All alpines enjoy a good circulation of air, so ventilation of the alpine house must be as free as circumstances permit. From April to October ventilators will be wide open most of the time and frame lights will only be required to keep off excessive rain, particularly from bulbs and tubers that are at rest. Even in winter it will be possible to keep the top ventilators open much of the time, only closing them when severe cold threatens to lower the temperature well below freezing point. In autumn especially, when the air is often excessively wet, it may be necessary to use a little artificial heat while keeping the top ventilators open to maintain a steady circulation of air and to dry it out a little.

This is particularly necessary for plants with leaves densely covered in hairs or down which can rot away from excessive moisture.

If frames are available it may be possible to use the alpine house itself mainly for display, moving many plants into it just before they are about to come into flower, or when their foliage is at its best. In a frame, pans can be plunged to their rims in sand, pea gravel or peat and this will help to keep them moist and so reduce the frequency of watering.

Although most plants will appreciate all the light possible from October to April, from May to September most will benefit from light shading, either with muslin or green shading compound.

alpine house with internal shading

muslin

Small Bulbs

The delicate flowers of many of the early-flowering bulbs can be grown to perfection in an alpine house where they are protected from wind and rain. *Iris reticulata* Harmony is a delightful choice

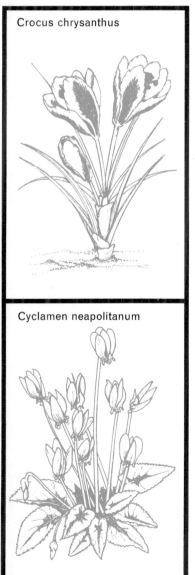

Crocus chrysanthus

Cyclamen neapolitanum

It is very early flowering bulbs that best repay cultivation in an alpine house since here their fragile blooms are protected from wind and rain. This applies to such irises as *Iris histrioides*, blue, *I. reticulata*, violet-purple and *I. danfordiae*, yellow; also to many crocuses, especially the numerous varieties of *Crocus chrysanthus* in orange, yellow, blue, purple and white. The large-flowered snowdrops and the early-flowering snowflake, *Leucojum vernum*, can be grown in pots, and so can the varieties of *Anemone blanda*, which may be blue, pink or carmine. Others worth their space are small species tulips such as *Tulipa violacea*, *T. orphanidea* and *T. batalinii*, the small fritillaries and *Tecophilaea cyanocrocus*.

The small-flowered cyclamen species, such as *Cyclamen orbiculatum*, which flowers in winter and *C. neapolitanum*, which flowers in autumn, make good alpine house or frame plants, and if given sufficient room in their pans they will increase themselves by self-sown seeds.

All these like a mixture of 2 parts peat, 1 part loam and 1 part sand. All should be removed to a frame after flowering or can be plunged to their rims in any sheltered place. There they will die down completely. The bulbs can be shaken out and re-potted in August, but the cyclamen are best left undisturbed, being transferred to wider pans as necessary. Seedlings can be prized out gently and re-potted separately.

Campanula and Allies

Although not easy to grow out of doors, *Edraianthus pumilio* makes an excellent pot plant for the alpine house where it can be protected from winter dampness

Many of the small species of campanula make good plants for the alpine house. These include *Campanula allionii* with quite large, purple bell-shaped flowers in June; *C. elatines*, a creeping plant with downy leaves and starry, blue-purple flowers in July; *C. waldsteiniana* only 3 in. high with starry violet-blue flowers in summer. *C. warleyensis*, a dainty little garden hybrid with small double flowers on thread-like stems in summer, and *C. zoysii* with pale blue flowers, tubular but crimped at the mouth, produced in June.

Related to these are the various species of edraianthus and phyteuma. The former have bell-shaped purple flowers which in *Edraianthus pumilio* and *E. serpyllifolius* are produced in May and June on slender stems.

Phyteumas are known as horned rampions and have unusual flowers rather like clusters of long necked onions. One of the most striking is *Phyteuma comosum*, which makes a little hummock of prickly leaves with lilac and purple flowers in June.

Most of these will grow in a mixture of 2 parts peat, 1 part loam and 1 part sharp sand. Water them fairly freely in spring and summer, sparingly in winter. All, except *Campanula warleyensis* which must be divided in spring, can be increased by seed. Campanula seeds need light for germination.

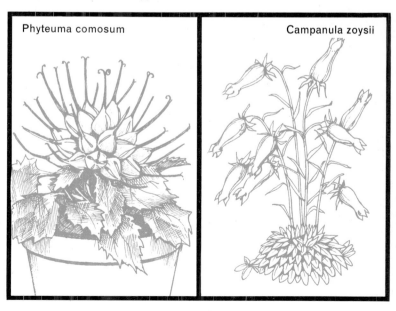

Phyteuma comosum

Campanula zoysii

Cassiope and Relatives

Andromeda polifolia produces its clusters of bell-like flowers in May. This charming dwarf shrub grows to about 12 in. and should be placed out of doors in summer if possible

The cassiopes are small evergreen shrubs related to the heathers but considerably more difficult to grow. *Cassiope lycopodioides* and its varieties and hybrids are the most satisfactory and beautiful, capable of completely covering a pan with a close hummock of small evergreen leaves and bearing white urn-shaped flowers in April.

Nearly related to these and forming similar mats or tussocks covered in small evergreen leaves are the phyllodoces. *Phyllodoce empetriformis* has red and purple flowers and *P. nipponica* white flowers and both these excellent kinds flower in April and May.

Then there is *Andromeda polifolia*, another of the heather tribe, a little evergreen bush with clusters of pink urn-shaped flowers in May. It tends to be a little straggly in habit but there are improved forms which are much more compact and are to be preferred for pot or pan cultivation.

All these little shrubs should be grown in a mixture of 4 parts peat and 1 part each of lime-free loam and coarse sand. They should be watered fairly freely in spring and summer, sparingly in autumn and winter. In summer they are happiest out of doors in a cool sheltered place protected from direct sunshine and frequently syringed to keep their leaves moist. All can be increased by seed, or by cuttings in July and August rooted in sand and peat.

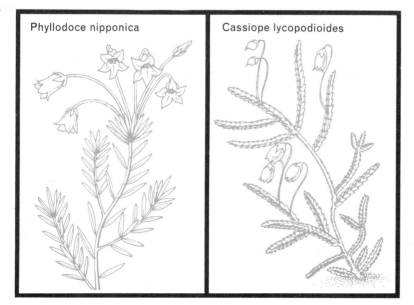

Phyllodoce nipponica

Cassiope lycopodioides

Gentians

The large trumpets of *Gentiana sino-ornata* are produced in September. All the gentians should be grown in a lime-free compost and most resent any root disturbance

Gentiana sino-ornata

Gentiana septemfida

Gentiana acaulis

There are gentians to flower in spring, summer and autumn, and all the prostrate or tufted kinds make excellent pot plants. A favourite is *Gentiana acaulis*, with large, narrowly trumpet-shaped, deep blue flowers on tufts of evergreen leaves in April or May. *G. sino-ornata* and *G. macauleyi* produce flowers of similar size and colour in September but have trailing stems which die down in winter. *G. septemfida* is a sprawling plant bearing clusters of deep blue flowers in late summer. *G. verna* has quite small flowers in April and May but the blue colour is particularly intense. There are many other species and hybrids. Most gentians dislike lime, though there is a considerable difference between species and both *G. acaulis* and *G. septemfida* may sometimes be found thriving in quite chalky soil. But for the alpine house it is best to grow them all in lime-free composts and to use lime-free water. A mixture of 2 parts peat and 1 part each of lime-free loam and sand will suit most, but for the autumn-flowering kinds the proportion of peat can be doubled.

All need to be watered freely in spring and summer and kept moist in autumn and winter. Species can be increased by seed, but hybrids and garden varieties must be increased by careful division in March, or immediately after flowering for the spring-blooming kinds. Since most kinds resent root disturbance division should only be done when essential.

Lewisias

Waxy, delicately shaped flowers in May and June are the rewards to any gardener who introduces the lewisias to his alpine house. *Lewisia howellii* is illustrated above

Lewisia cotyledon

In addition to the wild lewisias, such as *Lewisia howellii* with sprays of salmon flowers in May and *L. tweedyi* with large apricot flowers in June, there are a number of garden hybrids which seem easier to grow. These show considerable variation in colour and flower size but most flower freely and make excellent pot plants for an alpine house. They all need specially well-drained pots and like a mixture of equal parts lime-free loam, peat and coarse sand. Most should be watered sparingly in autumn and winter, fairly freely in spring and summer, but *Lewisia rediviva* dies down completely in July and from then until growth starts in December should be kept quite dry. In summer all appreciate light shading. All can be increased by seed though seedlings of the hybrids may vary in habit and colour. Some can also be divided in spring, but others make a single rosette of leaves on top of a carrot-like root which cannot be divided. Sometimes leaf cuttings can be induced to root in summer.

Another rosette forming plant which makes a good pot specimen is *Morisia monantha*. The handsome rosettes of dark green evergreen leaves are studded in May with bright yellow flowers. This is an easy plant to grow in a mixture of equal parts loam, peat and sand. It should be watered fairly freely in spring and summer, very sparingly in autumn and winter and can be increased by root cuttings in June.

Hardy Orchids

Pleiones are hardy orchids and will do equally well in a cold frame or a warm greenhouse. They make good window-sill plants provided they receive sufficient sunheat

Cypripedium calceolus

Several hardy orchids can be grown successfully in the alpine house. Among the most beautiful of these are the pleiones with pink or white flowers rather like small cattleyas in shape and freely produced in spring. They can be grown in well-drained pans in a mixture of 3 parts lime-free loam, 2 parts peat and 1 part sharp sand with a sprinkling of bonemeal. Pleiones are grown from bulb-like structures (pseudobulbs) which should be buried to half their depth in this compost, and 3 or 4 in. apart. Water sparingly at first then freely as growth progresses, but keep almost dry and in a frost-proof place in autumn and winter when they are at rest. Increase is by division of the pseudobulbs when re-potting after flowering.

Bletilla striata, sometimes known as *Bletia hyacinthina*, has small magenta flowers similar to those of pleione in form, but produced in loose 9-in. spikes in July and August. It should be grown in a mixture of 2 parts peat and 1 part each lime-free loam and sand, needs to be well watered in spring and summer, and shaded from direct sunshine. Like pleione it should be kept nearly dry and frost free in autumn and winter.

Other orchids that may be tried are *Cypripedium calceolus*, the chocolate and yellow Lady's Slipper Orchid, and *C. reginae*, the rose and white Moccasin Flower, both flowering in early summer. Soil and treatment are as for bletilla, but the plants are slightly hardier.

Oxalis and Others

Produced on short stems set amidst dainty leaves, the large pink flowers of *Oxalis adenophylla* brighten the months of May and June. Oxalis appreciates some shade while in bloom

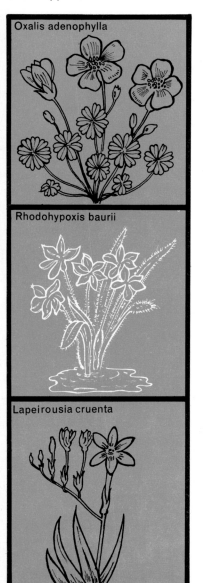

Oxalis adenophylla

Rhodohypoxis baurii

Lapeirousia cruenta

Oxalis adenophylla and *O. enneaphylla* are similar tuberous-rooted plants with deeply-divided grey-green leaves and large flowers, lilac-pink and white respectively, on short stems in May and June. Both will grow well in a mixture of 2 parts peat, 1 part each loam and sand. They should be watered freely from April to August, but as the leaves yellow and die down water must be reduced and the soil kept just moist, no more, in autumn and winter. Though they are sun lovers they appreciate a little shade while in bloom.

Similar treatment suits *Rhodohypoxis baurii* except that the loam must be lime free and no water at all is required from October to March. This delightful little plant has bulbous roots, grassy leaves and carmine flowers like fire-flies on 2-in. stems from May to September.

Lapeirousia cruenta must also be kept quite dry in late autumn and winter. It produces its 9-in. sprays of small, starry, orange and crimson flowers in August and September and will grow in a mixture of equal parts loam, peat and sharp sand.

It is grown from corms which should be potted in March, five to seven in each 5-in. pan. Water sparingly at first, freely when growth appears, but discontinue watering when the leaves die down. It is wise to keep the pans in a frost-proof greenhouse or frame in winter as the little corms are none too hardy.

Primulas

Primula pubescens Mrs J. H. Wilson breaks into colourful heads of flowers in May. Increase this attractive plant by dividing the roots in July, or by sowing seed when ripe

The primulas most suitable for cultivation in pots or pans are the European species related to the auricula. These include *Primula auricula* itself, a plant with leathery leaves more or less covered in white meal for which reason it is sometimes called Dusty Miller. The primrose-like flowers are borne in clusters on 6-in. stems in April or May and in many colours.

Primula pubescens is similar but smaller and neater, usually violet, lilac, crimson or white. *P. viscosa* is closely allied to this and also has a range of colours. *P. allionii* produces its rose-pink flowers in clusters on very short stems. It has a pure white variety. *P. glutinosa* has violet-blue flowers on 3-in. stems and *P. marginata*, with lavender flowers, is twice that height and has serrated silver-edged leaves. There are several varieties differing in depth of colour. Others in the same group are *P. clusiana* and *P. villosa*, both with carmine, white-eyed flowers.

All these flower in spring and can with advantage be outside in a fairly cool, partially shady place from June to October. All will grow in a mixture of equal parts loam, peat and coarse sand with plenty of broken crocks or small pebbles for drainage in the bottom of each pot or pan. They should be watered freely while in growth and never allowed to get really dry. They can be grown from seed or be increased by division as soon as they have finished flowering.

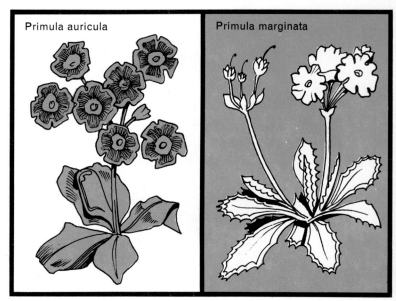

Primula auricula

Primula marginata

Saxifrages

Saxifraga grisebachii wisleyensis, one of the aptly named Silver Saxifrages, is an outstanding and highly decorative plant for the alpine house

All the early-flowering Cushion Saxifrages make beautiful specimens for the alpine house and as they spread they can be moved from pots to pans of ever greater width to display their full beauty. This applies to white-flowered *Saxifraga burseriana* in all its varieties, and to the scores of garden raised hybrids in white and various shades of yellow and pink. The Silver Saxifrages, such as *Saxifraga aizoon*, *S. cochlearis*, *S. cotyledon*, *S. longifolia*, and hybrid varieties like Tumbling Waters, are also excellent and flower in May and June. Then there is *S. grisebachii* with hummocked rosettes of silvered leaves from which in March arise crozier-like flower stems set with crimson bracts.

All these and many other kinds will thrive in the same soil mixture as that recommended for primulas but with a little powdered chalk added for the Silver Saxifrages. All like some shade in summer. The pans can be moved to a cooler place as the weather gets hot.

All should be watered freely in spring and summer, but the drainage must be good. In winter they should be kept rather dry.

The garden varieties are increased by careful division after flowering. Rosette-forming types can also be increased by detaching rosettes in June and inserting them as cuttings in sand and peat. Species are increased by seed, which is the only way of propagating *S. longifolia*.

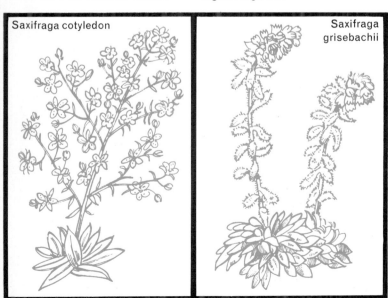

Saxifraga cotyledon

Saxifraga grisebachii

Shortia and Others

Fringed petal edges to trumpet-shaped flowers make *Schizocodon soldanelloides* a must for alpine-house enthusiasts. These unusual flowers appear in March or April

Shortia uniflora

Soldanella alpina

Schizocodon soldanelloides

The shortias are woodland plants, happier in a shady frame or plunge bed in summer than in an alpine house, but benefiting by being brought into the alpine house for a few weeks while flowering. They make low clumps of rounded shining evergreen leaves and have broadly bell-shaped white or pale pink flowers with fringed petals on 6-in. stems in April. *Shortia galacifolia* and *S. uniflora* are the two kinds grown. They need a mixture of 4 parts peat to 1 each of lime-free loam and coarse sand, and should be watered freely with lime-free water from March to September. Syringe daily with water in summer and only re-pot every second or third year, after flowering.

Soldanellas also have bell-shaped flowers with fringed petals, but they are smaller and the rounded leaves die down in winter. *Soldanella alpina* and *S. montana* both have lavender-blue flowers in April. Grow them in a compost of 2 parts peat, 1 part loam and 1 part coarse sand and treat as shortias. Slugs attack them readily and can be controlled with slug killer. *Schizocodon soldanelloides* looks like a pink and white soldanella, is related to shortia and requires exactly the same treatment.

Ramonda and haberlea make flat rosettes of leathery leaves from which spring in May and June short stems carrying clusters of lavender-blue or white flowers. They can be grown in the compost recommended for soldanella.

Plants for Heated Greenhouses

As soon as some form of heating is introduced the greenhouse owner's control over climate is increased and with it the range of plants which can be grown. Nevertheless, it is too simple a view to regard plants as divided into two groups, those that are hardy and will withstand frost, and those that are tender and are injured or killed by frost. Many tropical plants will die long before temperatures anywhere near freezing point are reached and the so-called hardy plants also differ greatly in the amount of cold they will stand. Even plants closely related and very similar in appearance may differ in the temperature ranges they will survive and only experience can prove just what those temperatures are. When in doubt it is wise to err on the side of keeping plants a little too warm than letting them become too cold.

In the following pages temperatures are referred to in four classifications, those of the cold greenhouse, cool greenhouse, intermediate greenhouse and warm greenhouse. These terms are explained on page 216, and though it is not necessary to adhere rigidly to any of these regimes they do give an accurate indication of the temperature ranges which particular plants prefer. There is no truth in the idea that warm-house plants are any more difficult to grow than those requiring lower temperatures.

Under glass plants often react more violently to direct sunshine than they would in the open. For this reason many plants regarded as sun lovers will not object to, and may actually appreciate, light shading from direct sunshine from about May to September. This can be convenient because although it is possible to shade plants individually it is much easier to spray the glass on the sunny side with a shading compound or to pin muslin under the rafters and leave it there for several months.

The provision of a correct degree of humidity is much more difficult. Most plants thrive in the kind of atmosphere gardeners usually describe as buoyant, which really means that it is pleasant to human beings as well as to plants, feeling congenial to the skin, neither searingly hot nor depressingly damp. But there are many tropical plants that like to grow in air saturated with moisture and which soon become yellow leaved and unhappy if the air gets too dry. At the other extreme are fleshy leaved and woolly leaved plants that are accustomed to dry air and soon fall victims to decay if grown for long in humid conditions. There is really no way of making plants with extreme requirements of this character happy within the same small greenhouse. Wisdom lies in choosing as companions plants that enjoy similar conditions or, if a wide selection is desired, either providing separate greenhouses for different groups or dividing one greenhouse into several compartments with well constructed partitions to prevent circulation of air from one to the other.

Abutilon, Hibiscus

Abutilons are very attractive plants for the cool greenhouse. Their peak flowering period is during the summer but this can be extended by careful management

These are both fine, shrubby plants, the greenhouse abutilons with hanging, bell-shaped flowers which may be white, yellow, orange or crimson according to variety and *Hibiscus rosa-sinensis* with large, trumpet-shaped flowers which may be scarlet, rose, pink, yellow or buff and are double in some varieties.

Both are best purchased as rooted plants, but they can be easily increased by cuttings of firm young shoots in a propagator in summer or early autumn.

Grow in J.I.P. No. 2 or peat potting compost in the smallest pots that will accommodate the roots comfortably. Quite good specimens can be grown in 6- or 7-in. pots, but old plants may require small tubs. Alternatively, they can be planted permanently in soil beds in the greenhouse.

Water freely in spring and summer, rather sparingly in winter. Shorten overlong or straggly stems each spring. Maintain a minimum winter temperature of 7° C. (45° F.) for abutilons and of 10° C. (50° F.) for hibiscus but no artificial heat should be required from May to September inclusive. Do not shade in summer.

Both abutilons and *Hibiscus rosa-sinensis* have a very long flowering season which is at its peak in the summer but some flowers can be had almost throughout the year if adequate temperatures can be maintained.

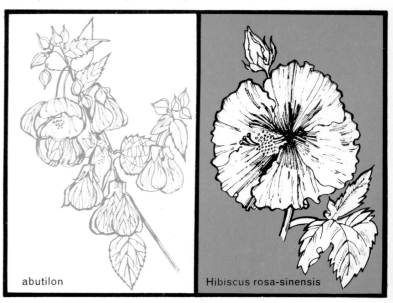

abutilon

Hibiscus rosa-sinensis

Acacia, Mimosa

Flowering in the spring, *Acacia armata* makes an excellent pot plant. It requires little more than frost protection and in summer can stand outdoors in a sunny place

The shrubby plants with fluffy yellow flowers which are commonly called mimosa are in fact acacias and the only true mimosa commonly grown in greenhouses in this country is *Mimosa pudica*, known as the Sensitive Plant because of its strange habit of folding its leaves when touched.

Some acacias make excellent pot plants and will flower in spring in greenhouses with little more than frost protection. The common 'mimosa' of the florists, *Acacia dealbata,* is beautiful but rather too large. *A. armata* and *A. drummondii* make better pot plants.

Grow them in J.I.P. No. 2 or peat-based potting compost and re-pot when necessary, using the smallest pots that will contain the roots comfortably. Good specimens can be grown in 6- to 8-in. pots. Shorten straggly shoots immediately after flowering and water fairly freely in spring and summer, rather sparingly in autumn and winter when a minimum temperature of 7° C. (45° F.) should be maintained. In summer plants may be stood out of doors in a sunny place.

Grow *Mimosa pudica* from seed sown in spring in a temperature of 15° C. (60° F.). Pot seedlings in J.I.P. No. 1 or peat potting compost in 3-in. pots and move on to 5-in. pots when necessary. Water fairly freely and keep in a light, airy greenhouse. It is best to renew from seed annually.

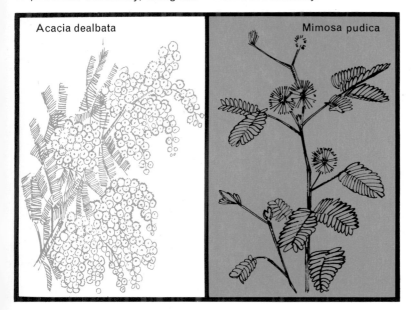

Acacia dealbata

Mimosa pudica

Acalypha and Others

Spectacular variegated foliage is a feature of *Breynia nivosa roseo-picta*. This shrub reaches a height of 3 to 4 ft. and is a marvellous addition to the range of greenhouse foliage plants

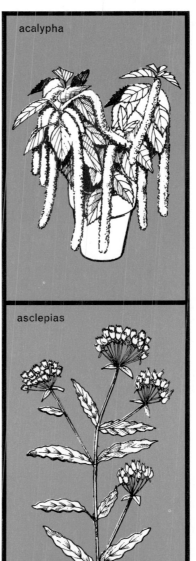

acalypha

asclepias

The two species of acalypha usually grown require similar treatment but are very different in appearance. *Acalypha hispida* has small magenta flowers produced in summer in long slender tassels, for which reason it is known as Red-hot Cat-tail or Chenille Plant. *A. wilkesiana* has inconspicuous flowers but handsome coppery-green leaves which may be edged with pink, red or yellow in some forms. It is known as Copper Leaf. Both are shrubby plants to be grown in a warm greenhouse in J.I.P. No. 2 or peat-based compost. They need normal watering but a really moist atmosphere in summer with shade. Increase is by summer cuttings.

Asclepias currassavica, known as Blood Flower, is a handsome flowering plant with strong, erect stems terminated by branched clusters of small flowers, purplish-red in bud, red, orange and yellow when open. It flowers for much of the summer and has an all-yellow variety with an even longer flowering season. Asclepias can be grown in J.I.P. No. 2 or a soil border in a cool or intermediate house but should be watered sparingly from November to March. Increase is by seed, division in spring or summer cuttings.

Breynia nivosa, also known as *Phyllanthus nivosus*, is a small shrub. Its variety *roseo-picta* has leaves splashed with pink, red and white. It needs the same treatment as *Asclepias currassavica* and is increased by summer cuttings.

Achimenes and Others

Achimenes are charming plants for hanging baskets. They also make splendid pot plants if the tips of the shoots are pinched out occasionally and some support is provided

Achimenes, columneas and aeschynanthus are related plants with showy flowers all summer and are excellent for hanging baskets. Achimenes are weak stemmed but can be made into bushy, erect plants if the tips of shoots are pinched out occasionally to encourage branching and a few twiggy branchlets are provided for support. Colours are pink, red, purple-blue and white. Columneas and aeschynanthus are trailing and have orange-red flowers.

Achimenes die down in autumn and their little cylindrical roots can be stored dry in a frost-proof place and then restarted in spring in a temperature of 15° C. (60° F.). Columneas and aeschynanthus grow all year and need a minimum winter temperature of 13° C. (55° F.).

Grow all these plants in J.I.P. No. 1 or peat-based compost. Plant five or six tubers of achimenes in each 5-in. pot or place them 2 or 3 in. apart in a hanging basket and cover with 1 in. of compost. One good columnea or aeschynanthus plant is sufficient for a 6-in. pot or hanging basket, but young plants should be started in 3-in. pots and moved on.

Water freely in spring and summer. Allow achimenes to dry off completely in autumn but water the others moderately in autumn and sparingly in winter. Increase achimenes by seed or tubers; columneas and aeschynanthus by cuttings in spring in a well-warmed propagator.

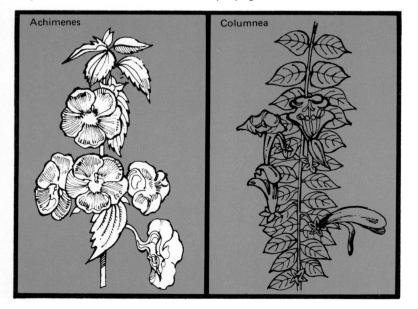

Anthurium, Arum Lily

The highly coloured spathes of *Anthurium andreanum* will look beautiful over a long period. These striking plants demand a humid atmosphere from February through to October

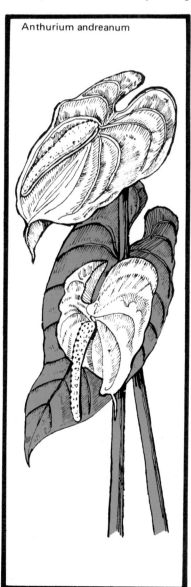

Anthurium andreanum

Both these plants carry their true flowers in a spike-like yellow spadix round or behind which is a large spathe, shaped like a shield, pink, scarlet, crimson or white in anthurium, rolled into a funnel and white or yellow in Arum Lily (richardia or zantedeschia). Both flower in spring or early summer.

Grow in J.I.P. No. 1 or peat-based potting compost in the smallest pots that will contain the roots comfortably and pot on as necessary. Quite good plants can be produced in 6-in. pots, but old Arum Lilies may require 7- or 8-in. pots.

Water anthuriums freely in spring and summer and damp down frequently to maintain a moist atmosphere. Shade from direct sunshine. Water and damp down less in autumn and winter and maintain a minimum temperature of 13° C. (55° F.). Re-pot in March and keep the crown of the plant well up above the compost.

Pot Arum Lilies in July or August, water sparingly at first but more freely as growth develops and really freely in spring. Reduce the water supply after flowering and keep the plants nearly dry for a few weeks before re-potting. Maintain a minimum temperature of 7° C. (45° F.) in winter, or 3 to 6° C. (5 to 10° F.) higher if early flowers are required.

Asparagus and Others

An occasional pot plant of *Grevillea robusta* makes a good foil for flowering plants. Individual specimens will soon grow too big but replacements can easily be raised from seed

The kinds of asparagus grown in greenhouses are foliage plants and are often referred to as asparagus ferns, though they are in no way true ferns. The two commonly cultivated are *Asparagus plumosus*, with feathery foliage, and *A. sprengeri*, with narrow leaves and long trailing stems. This is a favourite plant for hanging baskets and *A. plumosus* for foliage to be used with cut flowers.

The grevillea grown in greenhouses, *G. robusta*, is also cultivated for its rather fern-like leaves, but unlike the asparagus, it is a shrubby plant which in time becomes too large for convenience and so is usually renewed every few years from seed. Asparagus can be increased from seed or by dividing the old plants in spring.

Sow seed of both asparagus and grevillea in spring in J.I.S. or peat seed compost in a temperature of 15° C. (60° F.). When the seedlings are about 2 in. high pot them directly into 3-in. pots in J.I.P. No. 1. or peat-based potting compost and move on to larger pots and J.I.P. No. 2 or peat potting compost as necessary. Good plants can be grown in 5-in. pots. Shade from direct sunshine from May to October. Water freely in spring and summer, moderately in autumn and winter, and use artificial heat only to maintain a minimum temperature of 7° C. (45° F.). Train the stems of *Asparagus plumosus* up wires.

Azaleas

The lovely varieties of the evergreen Indian azalea can be raised in a greenhouse and then removed to the dwelling house when they start to come into flower

The azaleas grown in greenhouses, and very popular for indoor decoration when in flower, are all bushy evergreen shrubs. Their colour range is from white and palest pink to crimson with some salmon and orange-red varieties. The varieties fall into three groups: very early azaleas which can be forced from October to flower at Christmas or early in January; mid-season varieties which can be forced from December to flower from late January to early March, and late varieties which can be forced from January to flower in March or April.

The best way to start is to buy flowering plants and grow them on in a cool greenhouse. Pick off the faded flowers and stand the plants out of doors in a sheltered, partially shaded place. Keep them well watered throughout and from May to September syringe daily with water. Feed every 10 to 14 days from May to August with weak liquid fertiliser. Return the plants to the greenhouse in October before there is a serious frost. For early flowers use early varieties and maintain a minimum temperature of 10 to 13° C. (50 to 55° F.). For later flowers use mid-season varieties and keep in a cool house until December when the temperatures may be raised as above, or use late varieties and grow in cool house conditions throughout. Repot after flowering, using 3 parts peat, 1 part lime-free loam and 1 part sand.

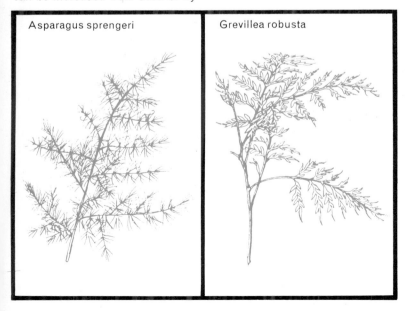

Asparagus sprengeri   Grevillea robusta

Tuberous-rooted Begonias

The begonia family is a very important one in the greenhouse. Tuberous-rooted begonias make up one group and this variety, Sam Phillips, is an excellent example

The double-flowered varieties of tuberous-rooted begonia make excellent pot plants and the small flowered 'pendula' varieties are equally attractive in baskets. Both can be grown from seed or tubers. The colour range is white, yellow to orange, and pink to crimson.

Sow seeds from January to March in J.I.S. or peat seed compost in a temperature of 15 to 18° C. (60 to 65° F.). Do not cover with soil, only with glass and paper. Prick out as soon as possible into similar compost and later pot singly in 3-in. pots in J.I.P. No. 1 or peat-based compost, moving on as necessary to 5- or 6-in. pots (or baskets) and J.I.P. No. 2.

Alternatively, start tubers in February to March by half burying them in moist peat in a temperature of 16° C. (61° F.). When they have two or three leaves pot as for seedlings.

Grow throughout in a temperature of 15 to 20° C. (60 to 68° F.), shading from sunshine from May to October. Water freely while in growth and feed every 7 to 10 days with weak liquid fertiliser from the time the first flower buds appear. Maintain a cool moist atmosphere throughout and ventilate freely in hot weather. Tie the flower stems individually to short canes. Remove the small female flowers beside the larger male ones. In October gradually reduce the water supply, let growth die down and then cut it off and store tubers dry at not less than 4° C. (40° F.).

planting tubers

Winter Begonias

Winter begonias need a minimum winter temperature of 13°C. (55°F.) but they respond with a wonderful display of flowers during that season. This is the variety Exquisite

The winter-flowering begonias are very beautiful plants but not as easy to grow as the summer-flowering kinds. All can be grown from cuttings of young shoots in spring, rooted in a propagator with a temperature of 18° C. (65° F.).

Pot rooted cuttings in 3-in. pots in J.I.P. No. 1 or peat-based potting compost, re-pot in 4- or 5-in. pots when necessary, and move the largest plants into 6-in. pots for flowering. Water freely and grow on in a minimum temperature of 15° C. (60° F.). Maintain a fairly moist atmosphere and shade from direct sunshine from May to September. In autumn and winter maintain a minimum temperature of 13° C. (55° F.) rising to 18° C. (65° F.) with sun heat. Place several split canes round each plant with encircling ties as support.

After flowering, water sparingly for a few weeks to rest the plants, then cut back the stems, and give more water to restart growth. Take cuttings when the young shoots are sufficiently long.

One of the most popular, Gloire de Lorraine, has fibrous roots, but some other kinds with larger flowers, such as Optima, have semi-tuberous roots. These need specially careful watering in winter since the tubers may decay in too wet a soil. They should not be attempted unless steady winter temperatures of around 15° C. (60° F.) can be maintained.

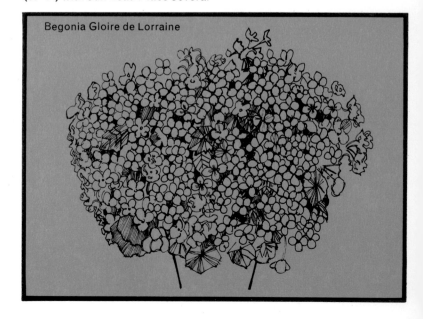

Begonia Gloire de Lorraine

Begonia rex

The large heart-shaped attractively marked leaves of *Begonia rex* make it a handsome foliage plant. Easy to grow, it well deserves a place in any greenhouse

The many varieties of *Begonia rex* are grown for their large heart-shaped leaves which may be green or purple variegated with silver. They are herbaceous plants with thick creeping rhizomes and can be increased by division in spring which is also the best time for planting or re-potting. An alternative method of propagation is to cut off mature leaves in July, make incisions through the leaf veins and then lay them on damp soil or peat and sand in a close moist atmosphere. Plantlets will form from the cut veins and when large enough can be detached and potted. *Begonia rex* can also be grown from seed treated as for tuberous-rooted begonias.

Begonia rex can be grown in a cool greenhouse but is happier in an intermediate house. It should be potted in J.I.P. No. 2 or a peat-based potting compost, or can be planted directly in a bed of fairly rich soil containing some peat. It enjoys shade and can be grown underneath the greenhouse staging. Plants should be watered freely from May to September, fed fortnightly with weak liquid fertiliser, and the atmosphere should be moist. In spring and autumn they should be watered moderately, and rather sparingly from December to February.

Begonia masoniana, sometimes known as Iron Cross because of the shape of the black markings on each green leaf, is grown in the same way.

Begonia masoniana

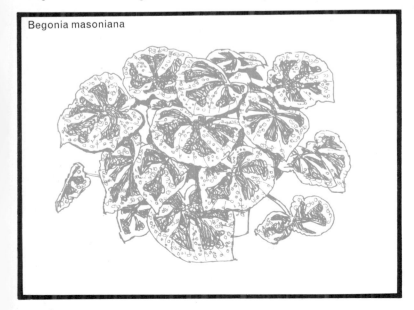

Other Begonias

Begonia Lucerna is a vigorous hybrid capable of growing into a massive ornamental plant. All these begonia species and their hybrids are easy to propagate, particularly by means of cuttings

Begonia haageana

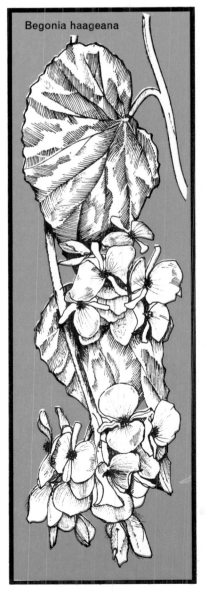

The begonia family is a large one full of good material for the greenhouse. In addition to the types separately described there are numerous species that are easily grown and very decorative. Most also have a long flowering season. *Begonia coccinea* is 5 to 6 ft. high with pendant sprays of scarlet flowers from May to October. *B. evansiana* is shorter and has small pink flowers all summer. *B. fuchsioides* makes long slender stems which can be trained against a wall. Its sprays of small pink flowers are produced from autumn until late spring. *B. haageana* has large leaves green above and purple beneath and pink flowers in summer. Lucerna and President Carnot are good hybrids in a similar style. *B. sutherlandii* is a foot high and has orange flowers all summer. There are many more.

All these can be grown in pots in J.I.P. No. 2 or peat potting compost in an intermediate greenhouse, or the summer-flowering kinds (particularly *B. evansiana* and *B. sutherlandii* which are nearly hardy) in a cool house. The summer-flowering kinds should have normal watering; the winter-flowering kinds should be rested and kept a little dry for a few weeks after flowering. All should be shaded and given a moist atmosphere in summer.

All species can be raised from seed as described on page 246. Some can be increased by division in spring and most by cuttings of non-flowering shoots in summer.

Beloperone, Jacobinia

Beloperone guttata is called the Shrimp Plant because of its sheath-like pink bracts. It will flower all year if a minimum temperature of 10°C. (50°F.) can be maintained

Beloperone guttata is known as the Shrimp Plant because of the sheath-like pink bracts which cover the nodding flower spikes. There is a greenish-yellow variety and also a dwarf variety only about 12 in. high against a normal 18 to 24 in. All flower almost throughout the year if a minimum temperature of 10° C. (50° F.) can be maintained. They will grow well in J.I.P. No. 1 or equivalent compost, and will survive in a cool greenhouse (though may not then flower all winter for which an intermediate house is necessary). Water normally. Increase by cuttings.

Jacobinias are of two distinct types, one with close heads of flowers at the tops of the stems, the other with tubular flowers scat-tered singly all over the plant. *Jacobinia carnea* (or *Justicia carnea*) with pink flowers in August and September is the most popular of the first type. It will grow to 6 ft. but can be kept at 3 ft. if it is fairly hard pruned after flowering. *J. pauci-flora* (or *Libonia floribunda*), with scarlet and orange flowers from autumn until summer, is the most popular of the second type.

Both plants can be grown in J.I.P. No. 2 in an intermediate house. *J. pauciflora* can be put out-doors or in a frame from June to September. Water both normally except that *J. carnea* can be kept a little dry for a few weeks after prun-ing. In the greenhouse in summer they need light shading. Increase by cuttings of firm young growth.

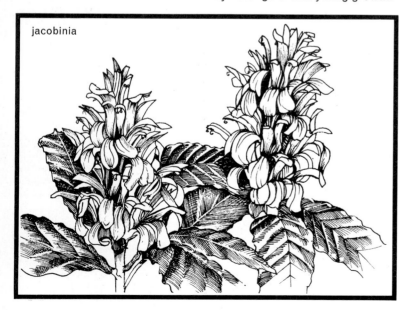

jacobinia

Billbergia and Relatives

The bromeliads are a family of curious rosette plants. Many are remarkable for the colour and variegations of their leaves as well as for their flowers, as shown above in *Billbergia nutans*

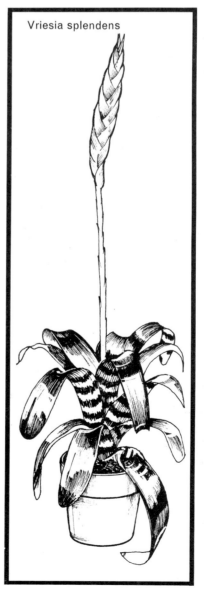

Vriesia splendens

Billbergia nutans belongs to the bromeliads. It makes clumps of rather stiff narrow saw-edged leaves and from June to August has slender 12- to 18-in. arching flower stems with drooping tubu-lar green and blue flowers sur-rounded by pink bracts. It is quite easy to grow in a cool or inter-mediate greenhouse in J.I.P. No. 1, requires light shading from June to October and very little water in winter. Water normally during the rest of the year and feed occa-sionally in summer.

Many other popular bromeliads, such as aechmea, nidularium and vriesia, have strap-shaped leaves forming stiff rosettes with a hollow, often called a 'vase', in the middle. These leaves may be mottled or grey-green or be handsomely variegated and in some, e.g. *Neoregelia carolinae*, are scarlet around the vase. Others are hand-some in flower – *Aechmea fasciata* with heads of blue flowers and pink bracts, and *Vriesia splendens*, with spikes of scarlet bracts. Cryp-tanthus carries its curious bronzy leaves in rosettes without a vase.

All these like an intermediate or warm house, well shaded and humid in summer. Most should be watered normally except that the central vase, if present, should always be full of water. Keep cryptanthus rather dry in winter. All can be grown in equal parts of sand, peat and osmunda fibre in the smallest pots that will contain them. Increase is by offsets re-moved in spring.

Boronia and Others

Bouvardia is a beautiful evergreen shrub with lovely waxy flowers. These are produced during the autumn and winter and are available in white, pink and red

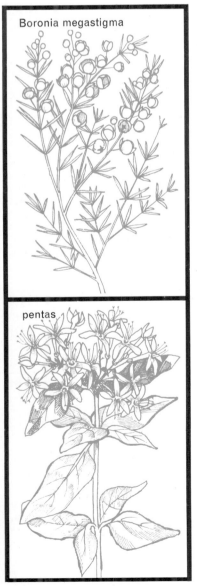

Boronia megastigma

pentas

Boronias are small evergreen shrubs, the most popular of which, *Boronia megastigma*, has very narrow leaves like those of a heath and maroon and yellow flowers from February to May. Others grown are *B. elatior*, carmine and *B. heterophylla*, purple. They can be grown in a cool greenhouse without shading and can be stood out of doors in a sunny place from June to September. They should be grown in J.I.P. No. 1 with some extra peat and must be watered carefully as they resent very wet soil, particularly in winter. Increase is by cuttings in summer in a propagator or under mist.

Bouvardias are also evergreen shrubs. The brightly coloured tubular flowers are freely produced in terminal clusters on 2- or 3-ft. stems from October to February and may be single or double, pink, scarlet or white. Plants should be grown in J.I.P. No. 2 and kept in an intermediate house, lightly shaded in summer or stood outdoors in a sheltered place from June to September. They are watered normally but after flowering they should be cut back and watered sparingly for three or four weeks. *Bouvardia longiflora*, which has white scented flowers, can be grown fairly successfully in a cool house.

Pentas lanceolata resembles bouvardia in appearance and requires similar treatment. It has rosy purple, pink or white flowers in autumn and winter.

All can be increased by spring cuttings in a propagator.

Browallia and Others

Celosias are half-hardy annuals which can be grown as pot plants or raised in the greenhouse for bedding out in summer. There are two types, one of which, *Celosia plumosa*, is illustrated

Browallia speciosa is an attractive annual that will flower in a cool or intermediate greenhouse from July to December if two sowings are made. The first should be in February or March, the second in May or June. Raise the seedlings in J.I.S. compost and transfer them singly to 4-in. pots in J.I.P. No. 1. Water fairly freely throughout and do not shade. Good varieties are Major, blue, Silver Stars, white and Sapphire, blue. All are about 1 ft.

Celosias are also annuals. Two quite distinct types are grown, *C. plumosa*, the Prince of Wales' Feather, with plumy sprays of yellow, orange, red or cerise flowers, and *C. cristata*, the Cockscomb, with flowers in similar colours crowded into flat, twisted heads like a cock's comb. Both are summer flowering and make excellent pot plants for a cool greenhouse. Seed should be sown from February to April and seedlings treated as for browallia. Plants can be stood outdoors in a sunny sheltered place in summer.

Celsia arcturus looks like a small verbascum or mullein, to which it is related. It is a half-hardy herbaceous plant readily raised from seed which can be sown in March to give plants to flower in September–October or in June–July to flower from April to July or later. Seedlings should be raised in the same way as browallia and if to be over-wintered should be kept in a cool greenhouse. It is often discarded after flowering.

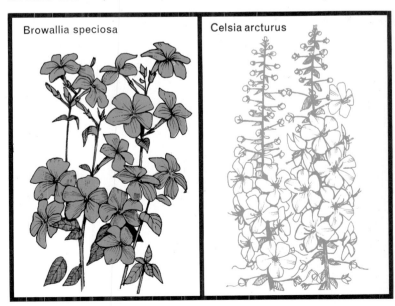

Browallia speciosa

Celsia arcturus

Brunfelsia, Gardenia

Brunfelsia calycina, a native of Peru, is a rewarding plant to grow provided a minimum winter temperature of 10°C. (50°F.) can be maintained. The fragrant flowers are produced for most of the year

Brunfelsias are low-growing evergreen shrubs with showy flowers produced most of the year. They can be grown in a cool house, but are happier and flower more continuously in an intermediate house. They can be grown in large pots in J.I.P. No. 2 or peat-based compost or be planted directly in a bed of good loamy soil. They should be shaded in summer and kept in a moist atmosphere. Water freely from April to October and feed occasionally from May to July with weak liquid fertiliser. Water rather sparingly from November to March but do not allow plants to become really dry. Prune lightly each spring. Increase by cuttings of firm young shoots in June and July in a propagator. *Brunfelsia calycina*,

with violet-blue flowers, is the most popular species.

Gardenia jasminoides, the Cape Jasmine, is an evergreen shrub requiring similar treatment and also capable of flowering on and off throughout the year, especially in intermediate or warm greenhouses. It should be grown in J.I.P. No. 2 with normal watering. Shade lightly in summer if under glass, but plants can be stood out of doors from June to September in a sunny sheltered place. Increase by cuttings of young shoots in March and April in a propagator. Most of the varieties cultivated have double flowers. All are very sweetly scented. *G. j. veitchiana* is specially recommended for winter flowering.

gardenia

Caladium, Codiaeum

Caladiums are among the most beautiful of greenhouse foliage plants. They have very attractive large shield-shaped leaves marked with green, white, pink and rose

Both these plants are grown solely for their highly decorative foliage. The leaves of caladiums are large and shield-shaped, green, white, pink or rose, variously veined, mottled and edged with one colour on another. Codiaeums, more familiar to many gardeners by their former name, croton, are bushier in habit and have evergreen, lance-shaped or oval leaves beautifully mottled in green, yellow, orange, crimson and bronze.

Caladiums have tuberous roots which should be potted in March in either peat-based potting compost or J.I.P. No. 1 with an additional 25 per cent. of peat. Water sparingly at first, freely as growth starts, and grow in a temperature of 18 to 24° C. (65 to 75° F.) through-

out, maintaining a moist atmosphere. Shade from strong sunshine but grow in good light as this helps to develop the full colour of the leaves. In autumn the water supply should be greatly reduced and in winter the plants should be kept in a minimum 13° C. (55° F.).

Pot codiaeums in spring in J.I.P. No. 2 or peat-based potting compost and grow on under the same conditions as caladiums. Do not dry off in autumn but water moderately from then until spring and maintain a temperature of about 15° C. (60° F.) or a minimum of 13° C. (55° F.).

Increase caladiums by division at potting time; codiaeums by cuttings of firm young shoots in a warm propagator in summer.

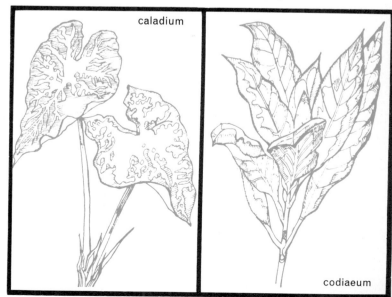

caladium

codiaeum

Calceolarias

The gaily coloured, pouched flowers of calceolarias are often spotted with contrasting hues. The varieties differ in height and all make excellent pot plants

The greenhouse calceolarias all have large pouched flowers in a variety of colours including yellow, orange, red and crimson, often with one colour brilliantly spotted or splashed on another. There are both tall and dwarf varieties, the former 15 to 18 in. high, the latter 9 to 12 in. and all make first-class pot plants to flower in a cool greenhouse in May and June. They are grown as biennials to be renewed from seed annually.

Sow seed in J.I.S. or peat-based seed compost in an unheated greenhouse or frame in May or June. Prick out the seedlings into boxes of similar compost and when they have formed a few leaves each pot them singly in 3-in. pots in J.I.P. No. 1 or peat-based potting compost. They should be shaded from direct sunshine, watered fairly freely and given ample ventilation. Indeed, since they are nearly hardy plants, at this stage and until late September they are really better in a frame than in a greenhouse.

They should be potted on into 4-in. pots and, if necessary, once again into 5-in. pots, in J.I.P. No. 2 or peat potting compost, and after September should be kept in a light greenhouse with a minimum temperature of 7° C. (45° F.). Water rather sparingly in winter but give more water in spring. The taller plants will need careful staking.

Callistemon, Clerodendrum

Clerodendrum thomsoniae is a striking evergreen climber with clusters of flowers during the summer and autumn. It looks attractive when trained over a crinoline frame

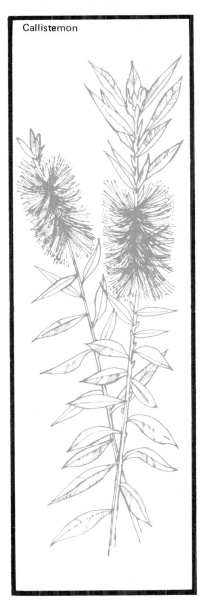

Callistemon

Callistemons are evergreen Australian shrubs with dense spikes of pink, red or yellow flowers. They make excellent pot plants grown in J.I.P. No. 2 compost in a sunny greenhouse with no more than frost protection in winter. From May to October the plants can stand out of doors; in mild places they can be planted permanently out of doors. Good kinds are: *Callistemon coccineus*, red and yellow, *C. lanceolatus* and *C. speciosus*, scarlet or crimson and *C. salignus*, pale yellow.

Two very different kinds of clerodendrum are grown in greenhouses, *Clerodendrum fallax*, a shrubby plant with handsome heads of scarlet flowers in summer, and *C. thomsoniae*, an evergreen climber with clusters of red and white flowers in summer and autumn. Both can be grown in pots, or *C. thomsoniae* can be planted in a bed and trained up a greenhouse wall or over a crinoline frame in a minimum 10° C. (50° F.).

Grow in John Innes No. 1 or peat potting compost. Pot in spring in the smallest pots that will contain the roots and re-pot as necessary. Water freely in spring and summer, sparingly in autumn and winter and prune after flowering. Cuttings may be prepared then and rooted in a propagator at 18 to 21° C. (65 to 70° F.). *Clerodendrum fallax* can also be raised from seed sown in spring in 18 to 21° C. (65 to 70° F.).

Campanula, Exacum

Exacum affine, a delightful greenhouse annual, can be seen in flower throughout the summer, autumn and winter depending on the time of sowing. The flowers are very fragrant

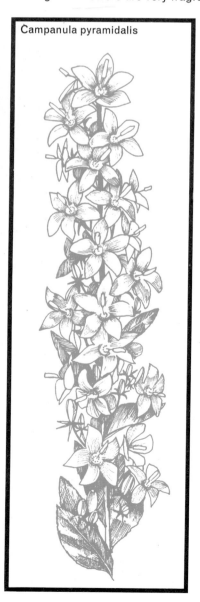

Campanula pyramidalis

Two very different campanulas are commonly grown in greenhouses. One is *Campanula isophylla*, a trailing perennial with star-shaped lavender or white flowers in August and September. It is an excellent plant for hanging baskets and is easily grown in J.I.P. No. 1 or peat-based potting compost, in sun or shade. It should be watered normally and can be increased by division in spring.

Campanula pyramidalis is known as the Chimney Bellflower because of its narrow 4- to 5-ft. spikes of blue or white flowers in June and July. It is grown as a biennial from seed sown in March or April in a cool or unheated greenhouse. Seedlings are raised in J.I.S. compost, potted singly into J.I.P. No. 1 and later moved on to larger pots and J.I.P. No. 2. Pots up to a 10 in. diameter may be required eventually. Plants can stand outdoors from June to September. Watering is normal throughout.

Exacum affine is a bushy annual 9 to 18 in. high with lilac-blue and yellow, scented flowers freely produced from August to December according to date of sowing. Two sowings are usually made, one in March, the second in June, in J.I.S. compost and a temperature of 15° C. (60° F.). Seedlings are potted singly in J.I.P. No. 1 and may later be transferred to 4-in. pots and J.I.P. No. 2. They should be watered fairly freely, should be grown in a cold or cool house with good light and a fairly damp atmosphere.

Canna, Hedychium

Hedychium spicatum acuminatum is a member of the Ginger family. It reaches a height of 3 ft. and is grown in the same way as the other species described below

The canna or Indian Shot is a tropical plant with broadly lance-shaped, green or purple leaves and showy spikes of summer flowers, red, yellow, orange or pink, often blotched with one colour on another. It has fleshy roots which can be stored dry in winter and can be grown on with very little artificial heat. Roots should be potted in February, March or April in J.I.P. No. 2 or peat-based potting compost and started into growth at 15 to 18° C. (60 to 65° F.). Thereafter they should be watered freely, fed every 10 to 14 days from June onwards with weak liquid fertiliser and given plenty of light and sunshine. In October water can be gradually withheld and when growth has died down the roots, in their soil, can be stored dry in any frost-proof place. Plants can be grown from seed but this should be soaked for 24 hours then nicked and germinated at 20° C. (68° F.).

Hedychium gardnerianum has similar, but always green, foliage and short broad spikes of pale yellow, scented flowers in summer. It, too, looks tropical but can be grown in a cool greenhouse if it is kept nearly dry all winter. In an intermediate house it can be given more water and will keep on growing, and this treatment also suits orange-red *H. coccineum* and white *H. coronarium*. Otherwise they are grown like cannas, except that they are best planted in a bed of good soil. *H. gardnerianum* is from 4 to 6 ft. the others 3 to 4 ft.

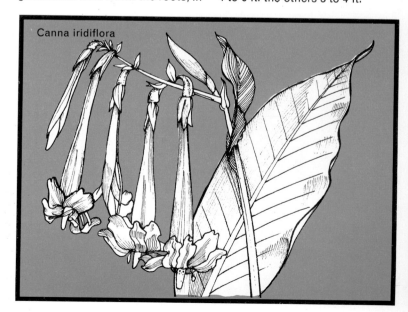

Canna iridiflora

Capsicums

Capsicums are grown both for their decorative value and their culinary uses. They are easily raised from seed and can be grown in a cool greenhouse or a sheltered place outdoors

capsicum

In addition to the culinary varieties of capsicum grown for their edible fruits there are a number of ornamental varieties differing in the shape and colour of their fruits. These sweet peppers or chillies can make highly decorative pot plants and are also useful for floral arrangements. They make bushy plants usually with the fruit carried above the foliage, and these fruits may be oval, conical or pencil shaped, erect or pendulous, straight, curved or twisted, green, yellow or red.

All are grown as annuals from seed sown from January to March in a temperature of 18° C. (65° F.). Raise the seedlings in J.I.S. compost, prick them out in J.I.P. No. 1 and pot singly in J.I.P. No. 2. Grow on in a sunny greenhouse, temperature 13 to 18° C. (55 to 65° F.), watering freely. Plants can be hardened off in a frame in May for planting out of doors in early June in good soil and a warm sunny place. Or they may be grown on in pots, 4 to 5 in. diameter for the popular dwarf 8- to 12-in. varieties, or up to 7 in. diameter for the tall 2- to 3-ft. varieties. They can either be kept in a sunny, well ventilated greenhouse or in a frame and must be well watered and fed every 10 to 14 days with weak liquid fertiliser from the time the first fruits are set. Plants in flower should be syringed daily with water to assist setting of the fruits. Tall varieties must be staked and tied. The ripe fruits retain their colour for a considerable time.

Cinerarias

Cinerarias are easily grown from seed and they are excellent subjects for the cool greenhouse. Flowering during the winter and spring they bring welcome colour at this time

anemone-centred cinerarias

multiflora cinerarias

Cinerarias are herbaceous perennials but are almost invariably grown from seed as biennials, being discarded after flowering. Only double-flowered varieties which set no seed are grown from cuttings and nowadays these are rarely seen.

The daisy-like flowers in a range of rich colours including shades of blue, violet, purple, crimson and scarlet, often with a white zone around the central disc, are produced in fine heads from November to May according to the time of sowing and the temperature available. There are Stellata varieties with small flowers, Multiflora varieties with flowers of medium size and large-flowered Grandiflora varieties. There are also dwarf varieties 12 to 15 in. high compared with the normal 18 to 24 in.

Seed should be sown in April, May and June for the longest flowering season. Sow in J.I.S. or peat-based compost in a temperature of 13 to 15° C. (55 to 60° F.). Prick out seedlings into similar compost and later pot singly in 3-in. pots in J.I.P. No. 1 or peat-based potting compost. Grow on in a light, unheated greenhouse or frame with shade from direct sunshine only. From late September onwards keep plants in a cool unshaded house. Water fairly freely in summer, sparingly in winter and ventilate as much as possible whilst maintaining a minimum temperature of 8° C. (46° F.). In a stuffy, warm, damp atmosphere cinerarias are liable to rot at soil level.

Perpetual Carnations

There are many kinds of perpetual-flowering carnations and new ones are introduced every year. Peppermint Sim, shown above, originated in America

Zuni is another variety of the perpetual-flowering carnation. These plants are grown for their importance as cut flowers rather than for any decorative value in the greenhouse

Provided that a minimum winter temperature of 7° C. (45° F.) can be maintained, perpetual-flowering carnations will bloom all year. They enjoy cool, airy conditions and dislike damp, which encourages stem diseases, and excessive heat, which can produce serious attacks by thrips and red spider.

Perpetual carnations can be grown from seed but the quality and colour of the flowers is very variable and the more usual way is to start with young plants of named varieties and renew these at least every second year by cuttings. These are prepared from November to March from non-flowering side growths that appear midway up the flowering stems. These sideshoots are broken out when

about 3 in. long and are rooted in sand in a glass-covered box or frame with just a little bottom heat. When well rooted they are potted singly in 3-in. pots in J.I.P. No. 1 compost and are moved on as necessary, first to 5- or 6-in. pots and later to 7- or 8-in. pots. Young plants are best purchased in spring and potted into J.I.P. No. 2.

Plants should be watered moderately throughout, just sufficient being given to keep the soil moist.

Break out the top two joints of each plant when it has made eight pairs of leaves and repeat the process on the sideshoots that result from this first stopping when they have produced six pairs of leaves. Do not stop after the first week of June if winter flowers are required.

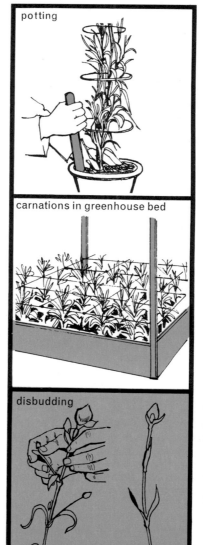

potting

carnations in greenhouse bed

disbudding

Each plant must be staked, preferably with special wire carnation supports which are readily adjustable as the plants grow. Two-year-old plants may be 4 or 5 ft. high. Keep the plants in a light, well ventilated house without any artificial heat from May to October. Alternatively, from June to September the pots may be plunged to their rims in peat or sand in a sunny, sheltered place outdoors. No shading is required at any time. Framed plants should be returned to the greenhouse before there is frost, and during autumn and winter all should be kept at a temperature of 10 to 15°C. (50 to 60° F.) which can fall occasionally to 7° C. (45° F.).

When the plants form flower buds carefully remove the small side buds and retain only the topmost bud on each stem. This disbudding is not necessary with some rather small-flowered kinds known as Spray carnations.

The greenhouse should be fumigated occasionally, especially from May to August, to destroy thrips and red spider mites. It is unwise to attempt to keep plants after their second year as they usually become weak.

There are a great many varieties in a wide colour range, but perpetual carnations lack fragrance. This is found in the Malmaison carnations which are grown in a similar manner but only flower in spring and summer. As a rule they are increased by layering in July and are only stopped once.

taking and rooting cuttings

Citrus, Avocado

The Calamondin Orange, *Citrus mitis*, will add interest to any cool greenhouse. To encourage the formation of flowers and fruits it is important that plants receive maximum sunshine in summer

avocado pear

Citrus is the name for all the oranges, lemons and grapefruits, any of which can be grown as greenhouse plants. But the best, as it is the neatest in habit and usually the most prolific, is the Calamondin Orange, *Citrus mitis*. Like other kinds this has shiny evergreen leaves and white fragrant flowers in spring and early summer. The fruits are small and resemble those of a tangerine.

All citrus varieties should be grown in a cool house and may be placed outdoors in a sunny sheltered place from June to September. They can be grown in large pots or tubs in J.I.P. No. 2 compost. Water freely in spring and summer, moderately in autumn, sparingly in winter. No shading is required and sunshine is essential to ripen the growth and ensure flowering and fruiting. Overgrown or badly shaped plants can be pruned lightly after flowering when it can be seen where the fruits have set. Increase is by summer cuttings of firm young growth in a propagator, or from pips.

Persea americana is the Avocado Pear, a large evergreen tree with handsome foliage which is only suitable for pot culture as a young plant. It is raised from seeds which can be obtained from purchased avocado pears. These germinate readily in J.I.S. or peat-based seed compost in a temperature of 15 to 18° C. (60 to 65° F.) and can be grown on in J.I.P. No. 2 in a cool or intermediate house or a sunny window until they get too large.

Clianthus, Erythrina

Clianthus looks very attractive when sprawled over a support or another plant. The striking flowers have given rise to the descriptive common names of Lobster Claw or Parrot's Bill

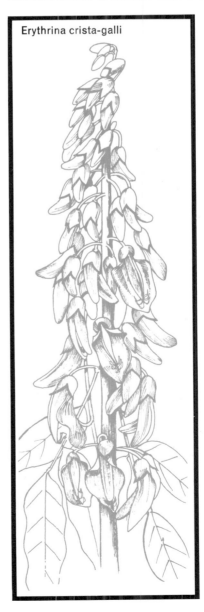

Erythrina crista-galli

Two very different species of clianthus can be grown in the greenhouse. *Clianthus puniceus*, the Lobster Claw or Parrot's Bill, is a vigorous shrub, usually evergreen under glass, with long slender stems which are best tied out on a trellis or wires. The scarlet or pure white flowers are shaped like a lobster's claw and appear in May and June. The Glory Pea, *C. dampieri*, is a more sprawling plant with greyish leaves and scarlet flowers, each with a prominent black blotch. It is difficult to grow on its own roots and is often grafted on to *Colutea arborescens*.

Both species can be grown in a cool greenhouse in J.I.P. No. 1. *C. puniceus* is really best planted in a bed of good loamy soil, but it can be grown in large pots or tubs. It can be raised from seed sown in spring or from summer cuttings of firm young shoots in a propagator. Both kinds need much sunshine and should be watered freely from April to October, sparingly from November to March.

Erythrina crista-galli, the Coral Tree, requires similar conditions and treatment and its crimson flowers, borne in late summer in long spikes, also resemble lobster claws. It is a shrub with fleshy roots but it can be cut hard back each March and will then make arching growths 4 to 6 ft. in length. Keep almost completely dry in winter and at all times give all the light and sunshine possible. It can be fed fortnightly with weak liquid fertiliser from May to August.

Coleus

Coleus, with their handsomely coloured leaves, are splendid plants for the amateur's greenhouse but grow best in a minimum winter temperature of about 13°C. (55°F.)

One of the most useful foliage plants for the greenhouse is the coleus with its nettle-shaped leaves in various colours, often with one colour splashed or zoned on another. As a rule mixed colours only are offered in seed though it is possible to produce varieties that will come reasonably true to colour. More usually these specially selected colours are reproduced by cuttings.

Seed is sown in March or April in J.I.S. or a peat-based seed compost in a temperature of 18° C. (65° F.). Seedlings are transferred to 3-in. pots in J.I.P. No. 1 or a peat-based compost and are later moved on into 5-in. pots in similar compost. The tip of each plant is pinched out when it has made four pairs of leaves. Alternatively, plants can be restricted to a single stem until they are 12 to 18 in. high and then pinched to form little standards. Either way, sideshoots are again pinched at four leaves.

Cuttings of young sideshoots root readily in late summer in a close frame or propagator.

Grow throughout in a cool or intermediate house, the latter being preferable if plants are to be over-wintered as they are readily attacked by grey mould at temperatures below 13° C. (55° F.). Water freely from April to September, sparingly for the rest of the year and shade lightly from June to September. They can be fed with weak liquid fertiliser from June to August.

Correa, Chorizema

The small pea-like flowers of *Chorizema cordatum* show a brilliant combination of colours. This Australian shrub will reach a height of 5 ft. but it resents any root disturbance

Correa alba

Correa reflexa

The correas are attractive little Australian or Tasmanian evergreen shrubs with pendant tubular flowers freely produced for many months from late winter onwards. In Australia they are known as Native Fuchsia. They are sufficiently hardy to be grown outdoors in the mildest parts of Britain, but are more reliable and also earlier flowering in a cool greenhouse. They can either be grown in fairly large pots in J.I.P. No. 2 compost, with a little extra sand as they appreciate good drainage, or be planted in a border of loam with which plenty of peat and sand has been mixed. Water moderately in spring and summer, less in autumn and winter. Light shading is beneficial. If they get too large they can be lightly pruned in late spring. Increase is by summer cuttings of firm young growth. The kinds most likely to be available are *Correa alba*, creamy white; *C. backhousiana*, cream tinged with green; *C. pulchella*, pink and red, and *C. reflexa* bronze red and yellow.

The chorizemas, or Flame Peas, also from Australia, are evergreen shrubs and require similar conditions to correas with even greater emphasis on sharp drainage and careful winter watering. They have small, brightly coloured pea-like flowers very freely produced in spring and summer. They can be raised from summer cuttings of firm young shoots, which should be potted singly as soon as rooted and then grown on without root breakage which can cause death.

Crossandra, Aphelandra

Silver Queen is a lovely variety of *Aphelandra squarrosa louisae*. Aphelandras grow best in a greenhouse but can be taken into the dwelling house for short periods

Aphelandra squarrosa louisae has already been mentioned as an evergreen house plant. In the diminished lighting of a room, however, it seldom flowers well and is valued chiefly as a foliage plant. In an intermediate or warm greenhouse, with only light shading in summer from direct sunshine and plenty of moisture in the air from May to September, it will produce plenty of its very handsome flower spikes in summer. Each spike is composed of close packed yellow flowers that look almost as if they are carved out of wood. Aphelandra should be grown in J.I.P. No. 2 or peat-based compost. Plants should be watered freely in spring and summer but sparingly in autumn and winter. They can be fed with weak liquid fertiliser every fortnight in summer. After flowering, stems can be shortened to keep plants compact and bushy. Increase is by cuttings of young growth in a propagator.

Crossandras are related to aphelandras and require similar conditions but if anything slightly more warmth, which makes them happier in the warm rather than the intermediate greenhouse. They, too, produce their showy flowers in short, close packed, terminal spikes. *Crossandra infundibuliformis* (*undulifolia*), with orange flowers in spring, is the kind most usually seen. It can be raised from seed sown in a temperature of 18 to 21° C. (65 to 70° F.), or from cuttings as for aphelandra.

Crossandra infundibuliformis

Cuphea, Manettia

Cuphea ignea comes from Mexico and is of interest for the delicate, slightly charred-looking flowers, which appear over a long season and have given rise to the common name of Cigar Flower

Manettia inflata

Cuphea ignea is known as the Cigar Flower because its little scarlet tubular flowers are black and white at the tip as if charred. They are produced continuously from spring to autumn. It is a bushy perennial about 1 ft. high, sufficiently hardy to grow outdoors from June to September. For the rest of the year it requires cool house treatment. It is easily raised from seed sown in a temperature of 15° C. (60° F.) in March or from spring cuttings of young shoots in a propagator. It should be watered normally and can be grown in 4-in. pots in J.I.P. No. 1 or peat-based compost. *C. microphylla*, with yellow and red flowers, is also grown.

Manettias are slender climbers also with small tubular flowers produced for much of the year. *Manettia bicolor* and *M. inflata* are most commonly seen, both with red and yellow flowers, but more yellow in the former and red in the latter. They need more warmth than the cupheas and should be grown throughout in an intermediate or warm house with plenty of humidity and shade from direct sunshine from May to October. They will thrive in J.I.P. No. 1 or peat-based compost, or can be planted in a border of good loam with some peat and sand. Canes should be provided for the slender stems to twine around. Water normally, feed with weak liquid fertiliser every 14 days from May to August and prune as needed in February. Increase is by cuttings in May or June in a propagator.

Cyclamen

One of the outstanding greenhouse plants, cyclamen need careful treatment throughout their culture. Given the correct conditions, however, they will present a beautiful display

seedling plants

plant potted singly

cyclamen

The lovely butterfly-like flowers of the cyclamen are produced from autumn to spring, and particularly attractive are the varieties with heart-shaped leaves heavily marbled with silver.

Sow seed in August in J.I.S. or peat-based seed compost in an unheated greenhouse or frame. Germination may be irregular so carefully lift out the seedlings as they reach the two-leaf stage and prick them out in similar compost. Keep them in a greenhouse all winter, minimum temperature 7° C. (45° F.), watering rather sparingly, and in March or April pot singly in 3-in. pots in J.I.P. No. 1 or a peat potting compost. At this stage maintain a minimum temperature of 10° C. (50° F.) rising to 15 to 18° C. (60 to 65° F.) with sun heat, and water fairly freely. In June, pot on into 5-in pots in J.I.P. No. 2 or peat potting compost and grow on, ventilating freely and shading from strong, direct sunlight only. The plants may be kept in a frame from June to September. Return them to the greenhouse in late September and maintain a temperature of 13° C. (55° F.) if early flowers are required.

In spring after flowering gradually reduce water until the leaves die down, then keep almost dry in a frame. In July re-pot, keeping the corms almost on top of the soil. Water more freely and return them to the greenhouse in September. Cyclamen may be kept thriving for many years.

Cyperus, Cycas

The feathery foliage of *Cycas revoluta* makes it a very decorative plant for use in large greenhouses where a suitable range of temperature can be maintained

Cyperus alternifolius

Cyperus alternifolius is known as the Umbrella Grass because of its bare stems each bearing at the tip a circle of narrow green leaves arranged like the ribs of an umbrella. It is usually about 18 in. high and is a distinctive foliage plant for cool greenhouses. There is a variety with white variegated leaves. Both can be grown in J.I.P. No. 1 compost in pots which should either be well watered in spring and summer or may be stood nearly to their rims in a pool. In summer the Umbrella Grass is quite happy out of doors. *C. papyrus*, the Egyptian Paper Reed or Papyrus is more tender and larger. It can easily reach 8 ft. and the green leaves are more numerous, much narrower and drooping. Treatment is similar to that for *C. alternifolius* except that an intermediate or warm house is required. Increase is by division in spring.

All species of cycas require a lot of room and the temperature of an intermediate or warm house. Apart from that they are not difficult to grow in J.I.P. No. 2 with normal watering and shade, plus a very humid atmosphere from May to September. Plants sometimes form suckers which can be carefully detached with roots in spring and potted. Alternatively, plants can be increased by seeds sown in spring in a temperature of 26 to 30° C. (80 to 85° F.). The kinds most often seen are *Cycas circinalis*, with leaves up to 10 ft. long and *C. revoluta*, the Sago Palm, with leaves 2 to 3 ft. long.

Datura

Datura sanguinea is a large shrub growing from 4 to 8 ft. high and producing its spectacular flowers, each of which may be up to 8 in. long, in summer

Three species of datura, all shrubby with large white trumpet-shaped hanging flowers, are known to gardeners by the same popular name, Angel's Trumpet. They are *Datura arborea*, *D. cornigera* and *D. suaveolens*, and the last named has the additional attraction of fragrance. Both *D. cornigera* and *D. suaveolens* have double-flowered varieties and the double *D. cornigera* is sometimes sold as *D. knightii*, an erroneous name. Yet another kind with narrower more tubular flowers, yellow deepening to orange or red at the mouth, is *D. sanguinea*. It is hardier than the others and can be grown out of doors in some very sheltered places. All are quite happy outside from June to September

and make handsome specimens for sunny sheltered patios and terraces. In winter keep them in a cool or intermediate house.

All can be grown in J.I.P. No. 2 compost in large pots or tubs. They should be watered freely in spring and summer and may be fed fortnightly in summer with weak liquid fertiliser. Plants can be pruned quite severely in autumn, so that they take up less room in the greenhouse, and will make well branched heads the following year. Increase is by cuttings of firm young shoots in spring in a propagator. Young plants may be restricted to a single stem until they are from 1 to 4 ft. high and then can be pinched to make them branch, so forming standards.

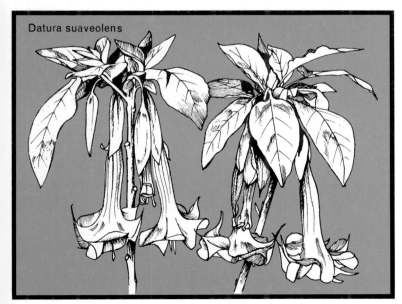

Datura suaveolens

Didiscus and Others

The delicate clusters of flowers of *Didiscus caeruleus* are produced in summer and have earned it the common name of Blue Lace Flower. Didiscus (also called trachymene) is a half-hardy annual

Trachelium caeruleum

Lobelia tenuior

Didiscus caeruleus, the Blue Lace Flower, has small lavender-blue flowers in flat clusters on slender 18-in. stems in summer and is easily grown in a cool house. Seed should be sown in spring in a temperature of about 15° C. (60° F.) in J.I.S. or peat seed compost, seedlings pricked out into the same compost and later potted singly into 4-in. pots in J.I.P. No. 1 or peat-based potting compost. They should be watered freely throughout, fed occasionally in summer and lightly shaded.

Trachelium caeruleum, the Blue Throatwort, also produces its small violet-blue or white flowers in clusters all summer on stems 18 to 36 in. high. Though a herbaceous perennial it is usually treated as an annual or biennial, being raised from seed sown in spring, or for longer, earlier flowering, in mid-summer. Spring-sown seedlings are grown in exactly the same way as didiscus except that 5-in. pots are likely to be required. Summer-sown seedlings are overwintered in a cold or cool house and may need to be potted on into 6- or 7-in. pots in spring.

The trailing varieties of the common lobelia and also *Lobelia tenuior* are usually grown as pot plants or in hanging baskets. Though perennial they are mostly grown as half-hardy annuals, seed being sown in early spring in a temperature of 15 to 18° C. (60 to 65° F.) and then grown on in the same way as didiscus, but without shade. In summer plants can be outdoors.

Epacris, Eucalyptus

Epacris are Australian plants which will flower in winter under cool greenhouse conditions. There are two species commonly grown, this one being *Epacris longiflora*

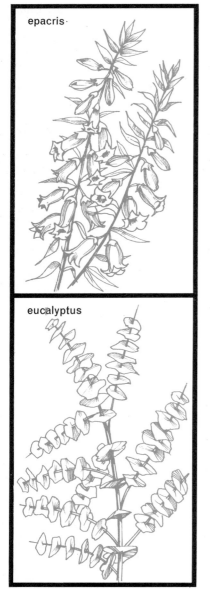

epacris

eucalyptus

Epacris are small evergreen shrubs flowering in winter. They are known as Australian Heath and have a superficial resemblance to some of the South African winter-flowering heaths. They are, however, unrelated and have longer, more tubular flowers than most heaths. The colour range is from white to carmine. Plants are best grown in a peat-based compost in a cool greenhouse and can be accommodated in a frame in summer. No shading is required. They must be watered carefully throughout, the compost kept moist, not sodden. Plants should be pruned fairly severely each spring after flowering to keep them bushy. Increase is by seed sown on peat in a cool greenhouse or by cuttings of firm young shoots in a propagator.

Eucalyptus are the Australian evergreen Gum Trees. Most are on the borderline of hardiness, grow readily and rapidly from seed and stand hard pruning well. They can be grown as cool (or even cold) greenhouse pot plants, at least for a few years, after which they can be replaced with new seedlings. Seed germinates readily in spring in a temperature of 13 to 15° C. (55 to 60° F.). Seedlings should be potted singly in J.I.P. No. 1 or peat-based compost and be moved on as necessary into J.I.P. No. 2. They should be watered normally, fed with weak liquid fertiliser fortnightly in summer and grown without shade, and can be cut back each spring. In summer plants can stand out of doors.

Euphorbias

Showy, red bracts make the Poinsettia, *Euphorbia pulcherrima*, a very popular pot plant at Christmas time. Poinsettias are easy plants to cultivate in a heated greenhouse

This is a big family of plants, some succulents grown solely for their strange foliage and some hardy perennials. The three most important flowering kinds for the greenhouse are *Euphorbia pulcherrima*, *E. fulgens* and *E. splendens*.

Euphorbia pulcherrima is the Poinsettia, which is popular at Christmas time because of the handsome scarlet or pink bracts which surround the insignificant flowers. It is not a difficult plant to grow but needs the temperatures of an intermediate greenhouse. It is usually grown from cuttings of young shoots 2 to 3 in. long taken in spring and rooted in a propagator. When well rooted these are potted singly in 4-in. pots in J.I.P. No. 2 or peat-based potting compost. The temperature is gradually lowered and in summer the plants are grown in a lightly shaded house with a fairly humid atmosphere. Water freely and feed every 7 to 10 days with weak liquid fertiliser. Water moderately in autumn and winter and maintain a minimum temperature of 13° C. (55° F.). Plants in flower can be brought indoors for a few weeks but should then be returned to the greenhouse. After flowering, watering is reduced until for two or three weeks in early spring the soil is almost dry. Then stems are cut back to about a third, watering is resumed and the temperature is raised to at least 18° C. (65° F.) to start new growth and provide further cuttings.

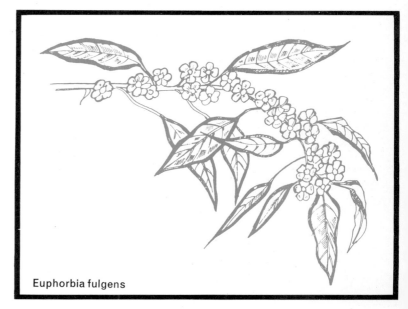

Euphorbia fulgens

The flowers of *Euphorbia fulgens* are, in fact, coloured bracts. This is also the case throughout the Euphorbia family, the true flowers being very insignificant

Gerberas are native to South Africa, hence their common name of Transvaal Daisy. These attractive daisy-like flowers are often used for flower arrangements and bouquets

Euphorbia splendens

Francoa ramosa

gerbera

Euphorbia fulgens is a shrub with slender stems wreathed in winter with clusters of small orange-scarlet flowers. These stems are usually supported in such a way that they arch gracefully and display their flowers well. It is a plant requiring treatment very similar to that of *Euphorbia pulcherrima*, the Poinsettia, but it prefers a slightly higher temperature in winter and is happier in a warm rather than an intermediate house. The long flower stems are often cut for use in floral arrangements, and this does the plants no harm since it encourages branching from low down and, as with the Poinsettia, produces early new growth to be used as cuttings. However, since the plants are smaller and less leafy there is not the need to restart from cuttings each year.

Euphorbia splendens has orange-red flowers larger than those of *E. fulgens* and produced in summer. It is a stiffly branched shrub armed with spines and known as the 'Crown of Thorns'. It makes a good pot plant in J.I.P. No. 1 compost in a cool or intermediate greenhouse without shade at any time. Water freely in spring and summer, sparingly in autumn and winter. *E. splendens* grows well in a sunny window provided the temperature never drops below 7° C. (45° F.).

Francoas are known as Bridal Wreath because of their slender 2- to 3-ft. sprays of flowers in summer. *Francoa ramosa*, which is pure white, is the species most commonly seen, but *F. appendiculata*, in which the flowers are flushed with red, is also grown. Both are herbaceous perennials, hardy out of doors in very sheltered places and easily grown as pot plants in a cold or cool greenhouse or a well-lighted window. Grow in J.I.P. No. 2 or peat-based potting compost. Water normally and shade lightly in summer, at which season plants can be placed out of doors or in a frame if wished. Increase is by division in spring, the best season for re-potting.

Gerbera jamesonii is a beautiful South African plant known as the Transvaal or Barberton Daisy. The large daisy-like flowers produced from late spring throughout the summer have very narrow petals which may be pink, red, terra-cotta, orange or yellow. There are both single and double varieties. All are suitable for cultivation in a cool, well-lighted greenhouse. They need sharp drainage, careful watering and free ventilation except in cold weather. They are grown from seed sown in early spring or from cuttings in spring. Grow on in J.I.P. No. 1 compost with extra sand or grit, maintain a minimum winter temperature of 7° C. (45° F.) and do not shade at any time. Water sparingly in autumn and winter, fairly freely in spring and summer.

Fuchsias

Globba, Ixora

Greenhouse fuchsias are accommodating plants for they can be grown as bushes, standards or in hanging baskets. These graceful flowers belong to the variety Coralle

Ixoras are evergreen shrubs of great beauty. They are natives of tropical areas and require warm greenhouse conditions for successful cultivation in this country

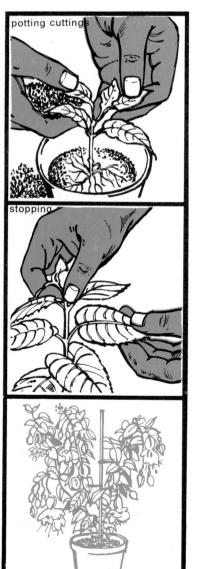

potting cuttings

stopping

staking

Fuchsias flower more or less continuously from May to October. There are a great many varieties; some have single flowers, some double, some are erect, some spreading or trailing, and all are easily grown from cuttings.

Cuttings of firm young shoots will root readily in a propagator at practically any time from spring to autumn but March–April and August–September are particularly convenient times. Pot cuttings as soon as they are well rooted into J.I.P. No. 1 or peat-based potting compost in 3-in. pots. Pot on into 5-in. pots and J.I.P. No. 2 or peat potting compost when the smaller pots are full of roots, and, if necessary, pot again into 6- or 7-in. pots.

Water freely in spring and summer and very sparingly in winter if the greenhouse is inadequately heated, but moderately if a minimum temperature of 10°C. (50°F.) can be maintained. No artificial heat is required from April to October. Shade from strong direct sunshine and ventilate freely. Most varieties can be placed out of doors from May to September.

Plants can be grown on one stem as standards, or if grown as bushes or for hanging baskets they should have the tip pinched out when 2 to 4 pairs of leaves have been made, and the sideshoots should be treated similarly. All sideshoots on the standards should be removed until the required height of the stem is reached, then treat as a bush

These are handsome tropical plants for well warmed greenhouses. Globbas are herbaceous in growth and belong to the ginger family. The flowers are curiously formed, carried in terminal sprays, red and yellow in *Globba atrosanguinea* and *G. schomburgkii*, magenta and yellow in *G. winitii*. Like many tropical plants they have a long and rather unpredictable flowering season.

Ixoras are evergreen shrubs, 2 to 3 ft. high with shining leaves and clusters of brilliantly coloured flowers, narrowly tubular in form except at the mouth which flares open like a star. Most of the varieties cultivated are garden raised hybrids and the colour range is from yellow to orange-red. All produce their flowers in summer.

Both plants should be grown in a warm greenhouse, the ixoras either in a peat-based compost or in J.I.P. No. 1 with extra peat, the globbas in normal J.I.P. No. 1 or peat-based compost. They should be watered freely in spring and summer, moderately in autumn and winter and can be fed fortnightly in summer with weak liquid fertiliser. During the summer they should be shaded from direct sunshine and a humid atmosphere should be maintained.

Ixoras can be increased by cuttings of firm young shoots in spring or summer in a propagator at a temperature of 21°C. (70°F.); globbas by division in spring, the best season for re-potting.

ixora

Gloxinias

Hybrid gloxinias, with their velvet-textured petals, are impressive plants to grow in the greenhouse or the home. The flowers can range in colour from white to pink, red and purple

Gloxinias are extremely showy plants with velvet-textured leaves and fine trumpet-shaped flowers in a range of brilliant colours. They are in flower from about mid-summer until early autumn and have tuberous roots. They can be grown either from these tubers or from seed.

Sow seed from January to March in John Innes Seed Compost or a peat-based seed compost in a temperature of 15 to 18°C. (60 to 65°F.), covering only with a piece of glass and paper laid over the pan. Remove the paper directly the seeds germinate and the glass two or three days later. Prick out the seedlings in similar compost while still small and when they have a few leaves, pot in 3-in. pots in John Innes No. 1 Potting Compost. As the pots fill with roots move the seedlings on to 4-in. and then to 5- or 6-in. pots, at the last stage using J.I.P. Compost No. 2.

Grow throughout in a temperature of around 15 to 18°C. (60 to 65°F.) shading from direct sunshine from May onwards, and water the seedlings freely, maintaining a fairly moist atmosphere by damping down at least once a day in summer. In October, gradually reduce the watering and from November keep the plants quite dry. Tubers can be shaken clear of soil and stored at not less than 10° C. (50° F.). In February or March set the tubers shoulder to shoulder in seedboxes of peat, water moderately and start at 15° C. (60° F.).

Gloxinia

Winter Heaths

Erica canaliculata is a good heather for cultivation under glass. Ideally, winter heaths need a special compost made up of 3 parts sphagnum peat and 1 part lime-free sand or grit

The winter heaths and heathers are all South African varieties of erica. Several of the best kinds, such as *Erica hyemalis* with pink and white flowers, *E. gracilis* with rosy-purple flowers and *E. nivalis* with white flowers, are grown in great quantities for the Christmas pot-plant trade. Unfortunately, commercial growers often trim the roots to such an extent before sending the plants to market that they have little chance of surviving more than a few weeks. It is better to start with young plants that have not yet flowered.

Pot these in a mixture of three parts sphagnum peat and one part lime-free sand or grit. Water carefully but adequately, keeping the soil moist and never allowing it to dry right out. Grow in a well-ventilated sunny greenhouse with a minimum winter temperature of 7° C. (45° F.). From June to September the plants will be better in a frame with free ventilation and with the pots plunged to their rims in moist peat to keep the compost from drying out. Shade only from the strongest sunshine.

Winter heaths can be increased in autumn by cuttings of firm side-shoots inserted in peat and sand in a temperature of 15° C. (60° F.). When rooted, pot in 3-in. pots and do not pot on until they are well filled with roots.

Erica hyemalis

Heliotrope, Humea

The fragrant flowers of heliotrope are produced in summer, and it is a popular bedding plant. Heliotropes do not need much heat at any time but are damaged when temperatures approach freezing point

Humea elegans

The common purple heliotrope or Cherry Pie, so popular as a summer bedding plant, also makes an excellent pot plant; and *Heliotropium peruvianum*, the wild plant from which the garden varieties have been developed, is sufficiently vigorous to cover a pillar or part of a wall if suitably supported.

Heliotrope can be grown from seed sown in spring in J.I.S. or peat-based seed compost and later potted singly in 4- or 5-in. pots in J.I.P. No. 2 compost. They should be watered fairly freely in spring and summer, moderately in autumn, sparingly in winter. Since they are so easily raised from seed many gardeners prefer to discard them after flowering.

Humea elegans is a biennial with slender 5-ft. stems bearing loose pendant sprays of small reddish-brown flowers in late summer and early autumn. It is known as the Incense Plant because of the distinctive aroma of its foliage. Seed should be sown in late spring or early autumn in J.I.S. or peat-based seed compost and germinated in a temperature of 15° C. (60° F.). Seedlings are potted singly in J.I.P. No. 2 or equivalent. Plants are over-wintered in a cool or intermediate greenhouse and moved on again in spring into 7- or 8-in. pots. Each stem must be staked and the plants given plenty of light. Great care must be taken not to overwater in winter and careful but adequate watering is essential throughout.

Jacaranda, Lagerstroemia

Jacarandas are grown in greenhouses and conservatories primarily for the beauty of their fine foliage; this is especially evident in young plants, as shown above

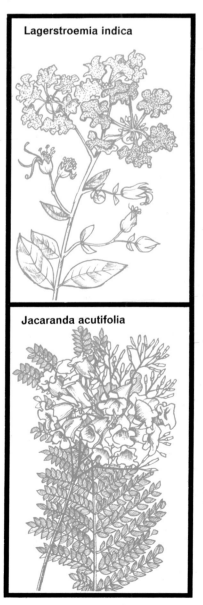

Lagerstroemia indica

Jacaranda acutifolia

In frost-free climates *Jacaranda acutifolia* (or *mimosifolia*, the name by which it used to be known) is one of the most admired of flowering trees. It can be grown just as readily in frost-proof greenhouses, the only difficulty being to find room to accommodate it. However, though young plants are unlikely to flower they are worth growing for their foliage. Plants can be raised from seed sown in J.I.S. or peat-based seed compost in a temperature of 15 to 18° C. (60 to 65° F.) in spring, seedlings being potted on as necessary in J.I.P. No. 1 or equivalent compost. Jacarandas should be watered normally and should be given as much sun and light as possible. They can be cut back in spring to delay the time at which they will get too large.

Lagerstroemia indica, the Crape Myrtle, is a deciduous shrub or small tree also much used for street planting in warmer climates. It can be grown readily in a frost-free greenhouse and, unlike the jacaranda, quite small specimens will produce the long terminal sprays of curiously crimped pink flowers. There are also white, mauve and heliotrope varieties. If desired it can be trained on the back wall of a lean-to greenhouse or conservatory. Treatment is as for the jacaranda except that plants are raised from cuttings of firm young shoots in spring or early summer in a propagator. Fairly hard pruning each spring not only keeps plants in bounds but encourages flower production.

Lantana, Verbena

Lantana camara is a colourful shrub which has a long flowering season and can be used for bedding out in summer. It must be pruned hard back each spring or it will become straggly

verbena

These plants are related and have a strong resemblance but the lantanas are, in general, more bushy than the verbenas. Both are readily grown in any sunny, frost-proof greenhouse.

The garden varieties of lantana are usually 2 or 3 ft. high and have pink, red, yellow, orange or white flowers produced continuously from spring to autumn. Seed can be sown in spring in J.I.S. or peat-based seed compost in a temperature of 15 to 18° C. (60 to 65° F.), seedlings being potted in J.I.P. No. 1 or equivalent compost and grown on in a cool or intermediate greenhouse without shading. They should be watered normally and can be pruned fairly severely each spring to keep them bushy and compact. Alternatively, cuttings of firm young shoots can be rooted in a propagator.

There are many different verbenas but the best to grow as pot plants are those marketed as half-hardy annuals for summer bedding. In fact, though readily raised from seed in exactly the same way as lantanas, they are not annuals but half-hardy perennials and they can just as easily be increased by cuttings. They are sprawling or bushy plants with showy flowers in a wide range of colours including pink, red, crimson, blue, mauve, and white. Culture is the same as for lantana and the flowering season almost as long. Many people will prefer not to attempt to over-winter them but to renew annually from seed.

Lippia and Others

Nerium, popularly known as oleander, makes a good greenhouse plant and under the right conditions it will reach a height of 6 ft. or more. The leaves, stems and flowers are poisonous

All these are shrubs which can be grown in a frost-proof greenhouse in large pots or tubs, or planted in beds of soil. Lippia is grown for its strongly lemon-scented leaves and is popularly known as lemon-scented verbena. Luculia has showy heads of sweetly scented pink flowers in late summer and autumn. Nerium is popularly known as oleander and has showy rose or white flowers. Its leaves, stems and flowers are poisonous.

Grow all three in J.I.P. No. 1 compost or in good loamy soil with a scattering of bonemeal and re-pot when necessary in March or April. Grow in full sunlight without shading throughout and water freely in spring and summer, very sparingly in winter, though luculia must be kept well watered through the period it is in flower, which may well be into November. Keep luculia in the smallest pots or tubs that will contain the roots or, if planted in a border, contain the roots with bricks or slates to promote free flowering.

Shorten the stems of luculia and nerium in December or January; cut back lippia almost to the base in February. Maintain a minimum winter temperature of 7° C. (45° F.) for luculia and nerium and of 2° C. (35° F.) for lippia. No artificial heat is required for any of these plants from April to October. Increase by summer cuttings.

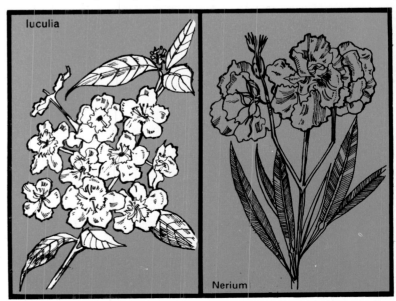

luculia

Nerium

Medinilla, Oxalis

The fine flowers of *Medinilla magnifica* make this one of the most eye-catching of plants. It comes from tropical areas and must be given warm conditions with a minimum winter temperature of 15°C. (60°F)

Oxalis purpurata bowiei

Medinilla magnifica really is a magnificent plant with large, shining evergreen leaves and fine hanging trusses of rosy-pink flowers topped by lighter pink bracts in late spring and early summer. It always excites admiration but it does need a warm greenhouse with a minimum winter temperature of 15° C. (60° F.). It can be grown in J.I.P. No. 2 compost with extra peat to provide a rather spongy mixture. Water freely in summer when a moist atmosphere must be maintained with a fair amount of shade. In winter only sufficient water should be given to keep the soil just moist, with increasing supplies as growth restarts in spring. Plants can be fed every fortnight from late spring throughout the summer. Increase is by cuttings of firm young growth in spring in a propagator at 20 to 24° C. (70 to 75° F.).

There are numerous species of oxalis suitable for greenhouse cultivation, all small tuberous-rooted plants with somewhat clover-like leaves and loose sprays of flowers produced mainly in spring. *Oxalis deppei*, rose, *O. purpurata*, purple and its larger variety *bowiei* are recommended. All can be grown in J.I.P. No. 1 or peat-based potting compost, about 5 little tubers in each 4- or 5-in. pot, in a cool greenhouse without shade. Pot in autumn, water sparingly in winter, freely as growth increases, then after flowering gradually reduce the water supply and keep quite dry in late summer until it is time to re-pot and start the tubers.

Mimulus, Reinwardtia

Reinwardtia trigyna is an evergreen shrub which produces its bright, showy flowers at a most useful period from autumn to spring, when colour can be rather scarce

Mimulus aurantiacus

The best mimulus for the greenhouse is *Mimulus aurantiacus*, sometimes still called by its old name of *Diplacus glutinosus*. It is a small, rather straggly evergreen shrub which produces a non-stop display of orange or coppery-red flowers from spring to autumn. It will grow 3 ft. high but can be kept shorter and more bushy by spring pruning. It should be grown in J.I.P. No. 2 or peat-based compost in a cold or cool greenhouse with all the light and sunshine possible. If necessary it can stand out of doors throughout the summer. Water fairly freely in spring and summer, very sparingly in autumn and winter.

The hybrid Monkey Flowers or mimulus usually sold as half-hardy annuals for summer bedding also make showy cold or cool greenhouse pot plants. They can be grown in J.I.P. No. 1 or peat-based potting compost, should be watered freely and shaded from direct sunshine. They are best discarded after flowering.

Reinwardtia trigyna is an evergreen shrub about 2 ft. high with showy yellow flowers produced from autumn until spring. Though it will grow in a cool house, flowering is more reliable and continuous in an intermediate house. Grow in J.I.P. No. 2 compost or plant in a bed of good loamy soil. Water normally and feed occasionally in summer with weak liquid fertiliser. Do not shade at any time. Prune fairly severely each spring as soon as flowering stops.

Myrtle, Leptospermum

Red Damask is a free-flowering variety of *Leptospermum scoparium*. Leptospermums are unusual plants for the greenhouse and, as most kinds are vigorous, they are better grown in borders of soil

The common myrtle, *Myrtus communis*, is a shrub with evergreen leaves, small, white sweetly scented flowers freely produced in summer, followed by blue-black fruits that are edible. It can be grown outdoors in sheltered places, but it is safer in a cool house and its compact variety makes an excellent pot plant. As an alternative to a tub which can be wheeled out in summer it can be planted in a bed of good loam, and if of the ordinary variety, its stems can be trained to trellis or wires. In pots or tubs plant in J.I.P. No. 2 compost, water normally and in the house give sufficient shade in summer to break direct sunshine. There are several other kinds such as *M. luma* with handsome cinna-mon and cream bark; *M. lechnreiana* which flowers (on very young plants) in May; and *M. ugni*, which has the most palatable fruits. All can be grown in the same way but preferably in beds of soil.

Leptospermum scoparium is a New Zealand evergreen shrub which can be grown in exactly the same way as the myrtles. The leaves are very narrow, the flowers small, white, pink or carmine, single or double and very freely produced in May and June. For pot cultivation the best variety is *nanum* which only grows about 1 ft. high against 6 ft. or more for most of the others.

Both myrtles and leptospermum can be increased by summer cuttings in a propagator.

Myrtus communis | Leptospermum scoparium

Nepenthes, Sarracenia

Few plants are more bizarre in their appearances than those which are insectivorous. *Sarracenia purpurea* is just such a fascinating plant, though it is unnecessary to provide it with insects

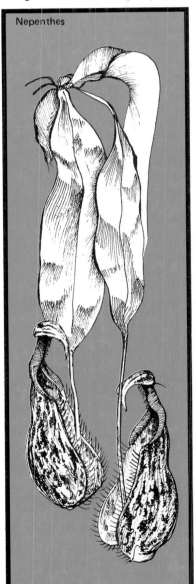

Nepenthes

Both nepenthes and sarracenias are known as Pitcher Plants because they catch and digest insects in pitcher-like structures. Those of nepenthes being rather like old-fashioned pipes hanging on slender stems and in some species highly ornamental; those of sarracenia are narrower and more vase like and grow up from the ground. In cultivation it is unnecessary to give them insects.

Nepenthes are usually grown in hanging baskets, often made of teak like those used for some orchids. The compost used is 2 parts peat and 1 part chopped sphagnum moss and plants are re-potted when necessary in March. They require warm house conditions with a very humid atmosphere at all times and shade from all direct sunshine throughout the year. Water freely from March to September and moderately from October to February. Increase is by cuttings of one-year-old shoots in peat and moss in a propagator at 26 to 30° C. (80 to 85° F.).

Sarracenias are much hardier and can be grown in a cool greenhouse, but they also need a damp atmosphere and shade and the same mixture of peat and chopped sphagnum moss. They can be grown in pots and are very suitable for Wardian cases or plant cabinets. Water freely from April to October, sparingly from November to March and syringe daily with water in summer. Increase is by division in March or April which is also the best time for re-potting.

Pelargoniums

Regal pelargoniums provide a brilliant show of colour in May, June and July. The many varieties cover a very wide colour range. This one is called Stardust

Pelargonium is the correct name for the greenhouse and summer bedding plants commonly called geraniums. There are numerous types, classified as Zonal-leaved, Ivy-leaved, Scented-leaved and Regal, and all can be grown in a greenhouse with a minimum temperature of 10°C. (50°F.).

All can be grown from cuttings of firm young shoots taken in spring or late summer. When well rooted, pot the cuttings singly in 3-in. pots in J.I.P. No. 1 or peat-based compost and grow on in a light greenhouse. Water moderately and maintain a fairly dry, airy atmosphere. Pot on into 5-in. pots and J.I.P. No. 2 or peat potting compost when the smaller pots are full of roots. The old plants should

be fed fortnightly in summer.

Place ivy-leaved pelargoniums at the edge of the staging or in hanging baskets so that they can trail naturally, or train them up trellis or canes. Pick off the flower buds of scented-leaved pelargoniums as the flowers are small and unattractive. Cut back regal pelargoniums after they have flowered in June or July and stand them out of doors, making cuttings from the new shoots when they appear.

Zonal-leaved and ivy-leaved pelargoniums will flower all summer and even in autumn if some flower buds are picked off to rest the plants, but those bedded out must be brought back into the greenhouse in late September.

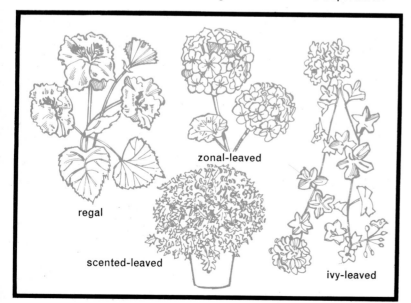

regal

zonal-leaved

scented-leaved

ivy-leaved

Petunia and Others

Petunias, which might well be considered the most popular of all bedding plants. The colour range includes many shades of red, purple, blue, salmon, pink, yellow and white

Petunias are grown from seed sown in spring in J.I.S. or peat-based seed compost in a temperature of 15 to 18°C. (60 to 65°F.). The seedlings are pricked out in the same compost and later potted singly in 4-in. pots in J.I.P. No. 1 or peat-based potting compost. No artificial heat should be necessary after April. Grow in a sunny greenhouse without any shade and water fairly freely throughout, but be careful not to splash the water over the flowers. Feed once a week from June onwards.

Impatiens holstii and *I. sultani* are similar plants popularly known as Busy Lizzie. They have gay pink, red, purple or white flowers which with sufficient warmth can be produced throughout the year.

They are perennials often grown from seed in the same way as petunias, but with shade from strong sunshine in summer. Plants can also be grown from cuttings of firm young shoots in spring or summer. In a cool or intermediate house or a sunny room plants can be over-wintered easily and kept for years. Water moderately in autumn and winter. The variety with variegated leaves must be increased by cuttings.

Vinca rosea, the Madagascar Periwinkle (*now Catharanthus roseus*), resembles the Busy Lizzie and like it can flower all the year. Treatment is the same as for impatiens but it needs an intermediate or warm greenhouse and prefers J.I.P. No. 2.

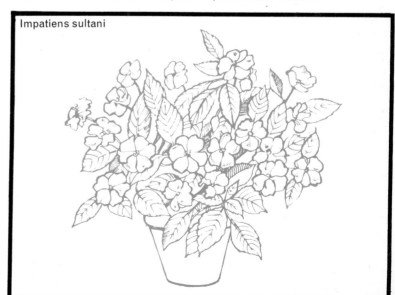

Impatiens sultani

Primulas

The yellow flowers of *Primula kewensis* make it quite distinct from other greenhouse primulas as this colour is missing among the other groups. It is pleasantly scented

Primula malacoides

Primula sinensis

Primula obconica

Of the four primulas which will flower in a greenhouse during the winter months, *Primula obconica*, *P malacoides*, *P. sinensis* and *P. kewensis*, the first two are the most rewarding. *Primula obconica* carries its quite large, blue, pink, salmon, crimson or white flowers in loose heads, and will keep on flowering most of the year. *P malacoides* has smaller flowers in larger, loose sprays, the colour range being pink and heliotrope to light crimson. *P. sinensis* has flatter heads of large pink, salmon, orange, crimson or blue flowers with fringed or waved petals. *P. kewensis* has sprays of scented yellow flowers and the leaves of some varieties are dusted with a mealy powder, or farina.

Sow seeds of *Primula obconica* and *P. sinensis* in March or April and *P. malacoides* and *P. kewensis* in May or June in J.I.S. or peat-based seed compost and germinate in a temperature of 15°C. (60°F.). *P. obconica* and *P. sinensis* germinate best in the light, so do not cover the seed pans with paper. Prick out the seedlings into J.I.P. No. 1 or a peat-based potting compost and, when they touch in the boxes, pot singly in 3-in. pots in similar compost. Pot on into 5-in. pots and J.I.P. No. 2 or peat-based potting compost.

Water fairly freely and grow in a cool, well-ventilated greenhouse or, from June to September, in a frame. From October on keep at a minimum of 7°C. (45°F.).

Protea and Relatives

Protea reflexa is one of the more unusual proteas. These South African plants have handsome flowers which can be used to make highly effective flower arrangements

The proteas are handsome shrubs with leathery leaves and extraordinary egg-shaped or conical flower heads, often 6 in. across, the tightly packed flowers encased in overlapping pink, red or yellow bracts. Allied to them and with flower heads of similar form are leucadendron and leucospermum.

All can be grown in cool or intermediate greenhouses or conservatories in large pots or tubs in peat-based potting compost or a mixture of 3 parts peat or leafmould, 2 parts sharp sand and 1 part lime-free loam. Alternatively, they may be planted in a bed of peat with which some lime-free loam and coarse sand has been mixed. A fairly open, free draining soil is essential. They also need plenty of sunlight and should not be shaded at any time of the year. If in pots or tubs they can be stood out of doors from June to September in a sunny, sheltered place. Water fairly freely from March to September, very sparingly from October to February.

Proteas and their relatives can be raised from seed sown in the autumn or late winter in the soil mixture recommended above and germinated in a temperature around 15°C. (60°F.) without any shading. Seeds germinate better if well soaked in warm water before sowing. Prick out singly into 3- or 4-in. pots in the same compost and pot on before roots penetrate through the drainage holes as proteas resent root breakage.

protea

Rehmannia and Others

Roses

Ruellia macrantha is a semi-shrubby plant which grows 2 to 3 ft. high and makes a decorative pot plant provided it is cut back hard each spring after flowering

Chicago Peace, an attractive sport of the famous rose, Peace, is a good variety for greenhouse cultivation in pots. The flowers are particularly large and slightly fragrant

Rehmannia angulata

ruellia

Torenia fournieri

Rehmannia angulata is a showy, easily grown plant. Its 2- to 3-ft. flower stems are freely produced in summer and carry almost throughout their length light purple bell-shaped flowers. Though a herbaceous perennial it is often grown as a biennial from seed sown in early or mid-summer in an unheated greenhouse or frame. Seedlings are grown on first in J.I.P. No. 1 and later, when they reach the 6-in. pots in which they will flower, in J.I.P. No. 2 compost. Water normally throughout and grow in a frost-proof house shaded in summer. Pinch out the tips of plants when about 9 in. high.

Ruellia macrantha is semi-shrubby, 2 to 3 ft. high with heads of rosy-purple trumpet-shaped flowers in winter and spring. It can be grown in a cool house but probably will not flower so early or reliably as it will in an intermediate house. It should be grown in J.I.P. No. 2 with normal watering and shade from direct sunshine. Prune hard each spring after flowering and increase by cuttings of firm young shoots in a propagator.

Torenia fournieri is a half-hardy annual, 1 ft. high, producing in summer and autumn trumpet-shaped violet-purple and blue flowers with a yellow throat. It should be raised from seed sown in spring in J.I.S. or peat-based compost. Pot singly in J.I.P. No. 1 or equivalent and grow on in a light, frost-proof greenhouse with normal watering. Give some support to the slender stems.

Any varieties of rose may be grown in greenhouses and this is the best way to enjoy some of the rather tender old kinds such as the climbers Niphetos, white, and Maréchal Niel, sulphur yellow. But these take up a good deal of room and are most suitable for training up the back walls of lean-to greenhouses or conservatories. They should be planted permanently in a bed of rich loamy soil and treated in much the same way as outdoor roses. No artificial heat is needed, or only enough to exclude frost.

Bush varieties are more suitable as pot plants and those with very shapely flowers are most popular. Young plants should be potted in 8- or 9-in. pots in autumn in J.I.P. No. 3 or equivalent compost. They can stand outdoors or in a frame until mid-winter when they should be pruned really hard and left for a further three or four weeks. They can then be brought into a light greenhouse, either unheated or slightly heated according to how early flowers are required. Subsequently they are watered freely and, when flower buds appear, fed every 10 days with weak liquid fertiliser. They should also be sprayed occasionally with a green-fly killer. After flowering they are moved out of doors and pots can be plunged to their rims. They must be well cared for all summer and in autumn should either be re-potted or generously topdressed with rich soil, some of the old top-soil being removed to make room.

pruning pot-grown roses

Saintpaulias

Saintpaulias are commonly known as African Violets. There are varieties with violet, purple, red, pink or white, single or double flowers, which, in the right conditions, are produced almost continuously

leaf cuttings

These are the plants commonly known as African Violets. They make almost flat rosettes of velvety dark green leaves and produce violet, purple, pink or white, single or double flowers almost continuously throughout the year.

Grow saintpaulias in J. I. P. No. 1 with 25 per cent. extra peat or in a peat-based potting compost. Good plants can be obtained in 3½-in. pots. They should be kept in a minimum temperature of about 13° C. (55° F.) away from direct sunshine and in as moist an atmosphere as possible. Saintpaulias do well in plant cabinets, Wardian cases and bottle gardens. Water freely in spring and summer and moderately in autumn and winter when it is particularly important to avoid splashing the leaves or allowing water to lodge in the crowns of plants.

Increase saintpaulias by sowing seed in spring or summer in John Innes or peat seed compost and germinate in a temperature of 18° C. (65° F.). Prick off seedlings into similar compost and when their leaves touch, pot them singly in 3- or 3½-in. pots. Alternatively, grow saintpaulias from well-developed leaves removed in summer complete with leaf stalk and inserted like cuttings, leaf stalk first, in peat and sand in a propagator with a temperature of 18° C. (65° F.).

Smithiantha, Gesneria

Smithianthas are very attractive greenhouse plants producing spikes of tubular yellow, pink, orange or scarlet flowers in summer, well complemented by velvety leaves

gesneria

These plants are closely related and their correct nomenclature is somewhat confused. All have tubers which are stored dry in winter in the soil in which they have been growing. Shake out these tubers in March and re-pot them singly in 5-in. pots in peat-based compost or a mixture of equal parts loam, leafmould and peat with 2 parts of sand. Only just cover the tubers, water rather sparingly at first, then freely and keep in a temperature of about 13° C. (55° F.) rising to 15 to 21° C. (60 to 70° F.) in summer. Shade from direct sunshine. After flowering gradually reduce the water and store pots on their sides quite dry from November to March in a frost-proof greenhouse.

They can also be grown from seed sown in January or June in a temperature of 15 to 18° C. (60 to 65° F.). Seedlings from a June sowing are kept growing all the first winter in an intermediate house and will start flowering the following spring. Seedlings from a January sowing will start to flower in late summer and are rested in winter like plants grown from tubers. The seedlings are raised in peat seed compost, pricked out into the same compost, and later potted individually like the tubers.

All these plants have velvety leaves and are 12 to 24 in. high. Smithianthas, sometimes called naegelia and popularly known as Temple Bells, are in many colours, e.g. yellow, orange, pink and red. *Gesneria cardinalis* is orange red.

Solanum, Ardisia

Solanum capsicastrum is often known as the Winter Cherry because of the brightly coloured berries which are produced during the late autumn and winter. Attractive bushes can be grown in 5- or 6-in. pots

Ardisia crispa

The Winter Cherry, *Solanum capsicastrum*, is a very popular winter house plant because of its abundant orange fruits the size of cherries. Purchase plants then, or grow them from seed sown in a warm greenhouse or a sunny window in February or March. Pot seedlings in John Innes No. 1 or peat potting compost and stand them out of doors in a sheltered, sunny place from June to September, pinching out the tips of shoots occasionally to make the plants bushy. Syringe daily with water while the plants are in flower in early summer, water freely from April to October, moderately at other times and feed from May to August. During the winter keep in as light a place as possible, in a minimum of 7° C. (45° F.).

Ardisia crispa, also sometimes known as *A. crenulata*, is grown for its scarlet berries and these remain decorative from autumn until spring. It is a neat evergreen shrub which makes an excellent pot plant for a cool or intermediate house. Grow in J.I.P. No. 2 or equivalent compost, water normally, shade lightly in summer and ventilate as freely as outside temperatures allow while plants are in flower to assist pollination. Syringe frequently in summer. Overgrown plants can be pruned in late winter before sap starts to rise strongly. Increase is by seeds sown in spring in a temperature of 18° C. (65° F.), or by cuttings of firm young shoots in a propagator.

Sparmannia, Prostanthera

The evergreen shrub, *Sparmannia africana*, has large leaves and is an ideal plant for the bigger greenhouse as it can reach a height of 10 ft. unless pruned periodically

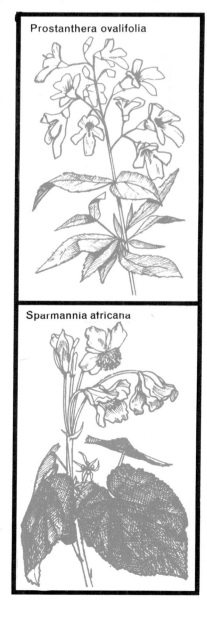

Prostanthera ovalifolia

Sparmannia atricana

Sparmannia africana is a big, bushy evergreen shrub with large, soft, green leaves and white flowers with purple stamens, produced almost throughout the year. It will grow to 10 ft. but can be kept down to 3 or 4 ft. by periodic pruning, but this inevitably interferes with the continuity of flowering. Cultivation is similar to that for pelargoniums, plants being grown in J.I.P. No. 2 or peat-based potting compost in a light, cool or intermediate house. They should be watered normally and can be stood outdoors in a sunny place in summer. Increase is by cuttings of firm young shoots in spring or summer. Late winter is the best time for any really hard pruning.

The prostantheras are also evergreen shrubs suitable for cultivation in a cool greenhouse, either trained against a wall or grown in pots and pruned each year after flowering to keep them from becoming straggly. Three of the most popular kinds, *Prostanthera ovalifolia*, *P. rotundifolia* and *P. violacea*, have small leaves, clusters of small lilac or purple flowers in spring and will reach a height of 6 to 8 ft. The leaves are aromatic, hence the common name of Mint Bush. All three are sufficiently hardy to be grown outside in some very sheltered places, and, under glass, only require frost protection. Water normally and do not shade. Pot-grown plants can stand outdoors in summer. Grow in J.I.P. No. 1 compost and increase by cuttings of firm young growths in summer.

Strelitzia and Others

Streptocarpus, Streptosolen

The exotic flowers of strelitzia appear in spring and early summer and it is easy to see how the common name, Bird of Paradise Flower, has arisen. Strelitzias thrive in a sunny position

Streptocarpus are excellent subjects for the cool greenhouse. Their funnel-shaped flowers are available in purple, blue, red and white and they are in bloom from spring through to autumn

musa

Musa is the name of the fruit producing banana, which for ornament is grown primarily for its very large leaves, though greenhouse plants will also produce crops. Most kinds are too large to make good pot plants and are best grown in tubs or planted in a border of good soil, but *Musa sanguinea* is 4 ft. and can be grown in a large pot. *M. basjoo* is the hardiest and can be grown in any frost-proof greenhouse. Culture is as for strelitzia but with rather more water in winter and a very moist atmosphere in summer.

Heliconias have broad banana-like leaves and stout stiffly erect flower spikes bearing brightly coloured boat-shaped bracts. In some varieties the flower stem is red and in some the leaves are marked or veined with red. Heliconias should be grown in a warm greenhouse as for bananas, but with little water in winter. Shade well in summer. All these plants belong to the banana family. *Strelitzia reginae* is known as the Bird of Paradise Flower because its orange and blue flowers look rather like the head of a crested bird. It has broad leaves, reaches a height of 3 ft. and flowers in spring and early summer. It should be grown in large pots in J.I.P. No. 2 or can be planted in a border of good soil with some peat and rotted manure. It needs a cool or intermediate house, should be watered freely in spring and summer, sparingly in autumn and winter. Re-pot in spring and divide old plants.

Streptocarpus have funnel-shaped blue, pink, red or white flowers on 9- to 12-in. stems from late spring to autumn. They are usually grown from seed though they can also be increased by leaf cuttings in summer in a propagator. Sow the seed in J.I.S. or peat-based seed compost in February or March and germinate in a temperature of 15° C. (60° F.). Prick out the seedlings in similar compost and later transfer singly to 3-in. pots in J.I.P. No. 1 or peat-based potting compost. Water fairly freely throughout and shade from direct sunshine. No artificial heat is required from May to September, but in autumn a minimum of 13° C. (55° F.) should be maintained, which can drop to 7° C. (45° F.) after flowering.

Streptosolen jamesonii is a sprawling evergreen shrub which can readily be grown as a climber to a height of 6 to 7 ft., or be trained over a wire balloon frame. Alternatively, if the tips of the shoots are pinched out occasionally it can be made into a more compact bush. It has clusters of bright orange flowers in summer and is a showy plant easily grown in any frost-proof greenhouse. Grow it in J.I.P. No. 2 compost, water normally and do not shade at any time. Shorten the previous year's stems fairly severely each February. Increase by cuttings of firm young shoots in spring or summer in a propagator.

Streptosolen jamesonii

Greenhouse Bulbs

Acidanthera, Watsonia

The handsome watsonias are not difficult plants to grow provided a frost-proof greenhouse or some other form of protection is available during the winter

Strictly speaking bulbs are modified buds built up of layers of overlapping fleshy scales, as can be seen very clearly when an onion is cut in half and the scales fall apart. In some bulbs, particularly lilies, the scales are so loosely arranged that they are quite obvious, in others, such as the hyacinth, they are so closely packed that outwardly the bulb appears solid.

As a rule when gardeners speak of bulbs they are extending the term to include corms, which really are solid right through, except for the membranous coat on the outside. Typical examples familiar to most people are the corms of gladiolus and crocus, and if these are cut in half their solid structure will become apparent.

This difference is really a technicality of interest only to scientists. Because of its affinity to a bud a bulb is often a complete plant in embryo. Packed tightly within it are leaves and flowers, and since the outer scales themselves are packed with food, moisture and warmth are all that are required to bring the plant to maturity. This can be seen most dramatically with hyacinths, which are often grown in special glasses designed to support them just above water into which their roots can descend. Placed in a sunny window and given no attention other than maintaining the level of water in the glass, the hyacinth will grow strongly and produce flowers of excellent quality.

By contrast, a corm is purely a storage organ, really a thickened stem with no leaves or flowers coiled within it ready to develop if given the correct conditions, though these are in the buds beneath the scales and care must be taken not to get them knocked off. The corm exists to give the plant a good start when conditions for growth are right, but it packs no guarantee within itself that the growth will culminate in flowers.

The moral of this is that good fat bulbs provide about the most foolproof method of starting to garden. It really is a very satisfying experience for a beginner to be given, say, a fine hippeastrum bulb and a few simple instructions and to be rewarded in a matter of weeks with a display of opulent flowers sufficiently good to win a prize in any show.

But to be sure of this happy result the bulbs must be good. Small bulbs will contain small flowers or no flowers at all, though if grown on well they may produce flowers another year. For instant success, however, one must buy good bulbs and these naturally enough cost more than small bulbs of the same variety.

This emphasis on size is nothing like so important with corms. Very small ones may only be suitable for growing on and building up stock for future years, but medium size corms can be just as satisfactory (occasionally even more satisfactory) than the largest, which may be more expensive. So when shopping for bulbs and corms spend your money where it will produce the best results.

Acidantheras look a little like gladioli, producing fragrant, white, maroon-blotched flowers on 2-ft. stems in August and September. They can be grown out of doors in well-drained soils and warm, sheltered places, though it is best to lift the corms in the autumn and store them in a frost-proof place until the spring. They al o make excellent pot plants for an unheated greenhouse.

Pot in spring four or five corms in each 4-in. pot in John Innes No. 1 or peat-based potting compost. Water moderately at first, then freely as growth starts, but reduce the water supply after flowering and keep the corms quite dry from November until February.

Watsonias are also allied to gladioli but the flowers are more tubular and the sword-like leaves are evergreen. In mild places, particularly near the sea, they can be grown out of doors but in most parts of the country they must be kept in a frost-proof greenhouse at least during the winter, or be covered with cloches or frames. Apart from this they are not difficult to grow. They have no resting season, so water moderately throughout the year, increasing the amount slightly as the flower spikes form.

There are a great many different kinds of watsonia, of which *W. ardernei*, white, *W. beatricis*, apricot to orange-red and *W. stanfordiae*, rose purple or scarlet, are typical.

acidanthera   watsonia

Agapanthus, Clivia

Babiana and Others

Clivia nobilis, with its large clusters of trumpet-shaped flowers in late winter and early spring, is an impressive plant for the home or greenhouse

Babianas are excellent subjects for the cool greenhouse and in some favoured districts they may be grown out of doors. The trumpet-shaped flowers are in a range of bright colours

The African lilies or agapanthus, which are not true lilies, are, like clivia, natives of South Africa. They both make fleshy roots and have rounded heads of flowers, blue or white in the African lily, orange-red or yellow in clivia.

The big African lily, *Agapanthus umbellatus,* is often grown in large pots or tubs so that it can be stood out of doors in summer when in flower and removed to a frost-proof greenhouse in winter. The small African lilies, *A. mooreanus* and Headbourne Hybrids, are hardier and can be grown out of doors in sunny sheltered places.

Clivias are also grown in large pots or tubs, but they flower in late winter and spring, too early to be put out of doors. Like *Agapan-*

thus umbellatus they require complete protection from frost in winter.

Grow these plants in good, loamy soil or in John Innes No. 2 Potting Compost, watering freely in spring and summer, and sparingly in autumn and winter. Do not shade the plants at any time of the year.

Increase them by dividing the roots in spring, or after flowering in the case of clivia.

babiana

sprekelia

tigridia

Babianas, ixias, sparaxis, sprekelias and tigridias can all be grown in a sunny, frost-proof greenhouse. Babianas have little sprays of blue, rose or carmine flowers on 6- to 12-in. stems in May and June. Ixias have sprays of starry red, crimson, orange, yellow or white flowers on wand-like 2-ft. stems in spring. Sparaxis, known as the Harlequin Flower because it often combines two contrasted colours, may be red, crimson, purple, yellow, orange or white, is 12 to 15 in. high and spring flowering. Sprekelia, or Jacobean Lily, has large scarlet, spidery-looking flowers in June on stout 1-ft. stems. Tigridias, Tiger Flowers, also 1 ft. high, have gleaming red, pink, orange or yellow flowers, often handsomely spotted with one colour on another. Each bloom only lasts for a day, but a succession of buds opens for weeks in summer.

Grow all these bulbs in J.I.P. No. 1, placing 5 to 7 bulbs in each 4- or 5-in. pot, except for sprekelia where one bulb to each pot is sufficient. Plant babianas, ixias and sparaxis in autumn and over-winter in a cool house. Plant sprekelias and tigridias in spring in a cold or cool house. Water all sparingly at first, freely while they are growing, but gradually reduce the water supply after flowering and then keep the bulbs dry until re-potting. Over-winter those for spring planting in a frost-proof cupboard or room.

All can also be raised from seed sown in a cool house in spring.

agapanthus

clivia

Eucharis and Others

Eucharis grandiflora is a very handsome plant for the warm greenhouse. It has broad shining leaves and numerous erect stems bearing large, intensely fragrant flowers

Amazon and spider lilies are related bulbous-rooted plants with white flowers. The Amazon Lily, *Eucharis grandiflora,* is the most tender and likes a well-warmed greenhouse with temperatures from 15 to 24°C. (60 to 75°F.). The nodding flowers, shaped rather like those of a narcissus, are very fragrant and carried in clusters on 18 to 24-in. stems. It may flower twice or even three times a year, chiefly in winter and spring.

The spider lilies get their name from the long, narrow, spidery segments around the small, funnel-shaped flowers. They belong to two genera, hymenocallis and pancratium and are sometimes listed as ismene. All varieties flower in summer and are nearly hardy.

Pot eucharis bulbs in spring, one bulb in each 6-in. pot, in John Innes No. 2 or peat-based potting compost. Water freely in spring and summer, rather sparingly for a few weeks in autumn, and then more freely again as the plants come into flower.

Spider lilies should be grown in similar soil and 5- or 6-in. pots, but reduce the water supply progressively in autumn and keep the bulbs quite dry from November to February when they are at rest. A minimum temperature of 4°C. (40°F.) is sufficient in winter and little or no artificial heat is required from April to October.

Eucomis and Others

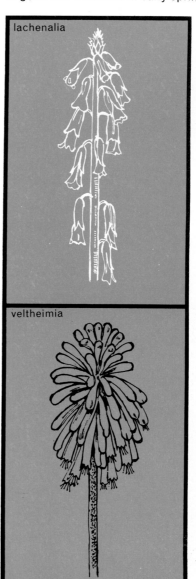

Veltheimias originate in South Africa and make excellent plants for a frost-proof greenhouse. *Veltheimia viridiflora* is the easiest species to grow and it flowers in early spring

Eucomis punctata is known as the Pineapple Flower. It has strap-shaped, brown-spotted leaves and 18-in. spikes of pale green flowers in July-August. *E. undulata* is similar, but has a tuft of leaves at the top of the flower spike.

Lachenalias are South African bulbs with 1-ft. high spikes of hanging, bell-shaped flowers, mostly orange or yellow though occasionally pale blue, in late winter and spring. They have acquired the popular name of Cape cowslip, though the resemblance to a true cowslip is slight.

Veltheimias are also South African bulbs flowering in winter and spring and the tubular pink or reddish flowers are clustered in little heads like red-hot pokers.

All these plants make excellent pot plants for frost-free greenhouses. Pot the bulbs of lachenalia and veltheimia in August or September, five or six bulbs in each 5-in. pot, in John Innes or peat-based potting compost and grow in a light, airy greenhouse with a minimum temperature of 7° C. (45° F.). Water rather sparingly at first, but more freely once the leaves appear. Gradually reduce the water supply after flowering and keep the plants quite dry in July before re-potting them in August. The pots can stand in a frame or a sunny place out of doors during the summer.

Pot eucomis bulbs in February or March, water freely in summer and keep dry from November to February.

Freesias

It is possible to have freesias in flower throughout the winter and spring by starting batches in succession. These charming plants are quite easy to grow

The little funnel-shaped flowers of freesias are carried in curved sprays on slender stems and are highly fragrant. Freesias can be grown either from seed or from corms, and by using both methods it is possible to have flowers from November until April.

Sow the seed thinly in 5-in. pots in February or March in a temperature of 15 to 18° C. (60 to 65° F.). Do not transplant the seedlings but grow on in an airy greenhouse until June and then stand them in a frame or out of doors in a cool, partly shaded place, bringing them back into the greenhouse in late September. Water the plants freely during this period, but after flowering reduce the water supply steadily and keep them quite dry during June and July when the corms can be shaken out and re-potted.

Corms are potted in August, five or six to a 5-in. pot, in John Innes or peat potting compost and are grown on in the same way as seedlings. Later batches of corms can be potted up until November. Dry the plants off after flowering and continue as before.

Specially prepared freesias can be purchased for growing out of doors. Plant in mid-April in a sheltered, sunny place, water in freely and support them with bushy twigs when the flower spikes appear in summer. As a rule these prepared corms will not flower outside a second year.

Gloriosa, Haemanthus

Gloriosas are lovely climbing plants for the warm greenhouse and they are not difficult to grow. The showy, flame-coloured flowers are abundantly produced throughout the summer

Gloriosa, sometimes called the glory lily or the climbing lily, has scarlet and yellow nodding flowers in summer and climbs to a height of 4 or 5 ft.

Pot the tubers from January to March, one in each 6-in. pot or three in an 8-in. pot, in J.I.P. No. 2 or peat-based potting compost. Water rather sparingly at first, then freely as the plants start to grow. Keep in a temperature of 15 to 21° C. (60 to 70° F.), shading only from strong, direct sunshine, and provide canes for the plants to climb on. After flowering, gradually reduced the water supply and store quite dry in winter in a temperature of 13° C. (55° F.). If little artificial heat is available do not start the tubers before March.

Haemanthus, also known as the blood lily, has wide fleshy leaves and globular heads of starry crimson, scarlet or white flowers in summer. Pot the bulbs in February or March in J.I.P. No. 1 or peat potting compost and grow in a sunny greenhouse without shading, watering moderately at first, freely as growth begins. Keep a minimum temperature of 7° C. (45° F.) but artificial heat is unlikely to be required from April to October as the plants are nearly hardy. Reduce the water supply after flowering and from November until restarting keep the plants dry in a frost-proof place. Do not re-pot every year as these plants flower most freely when rather pot-bound.

Gloriosa

haemanthus

Hippeastrum

The spectacular hippeastrums normally flower in the spring and summer and they are available in white, pink and red. However, specially prepared bulbs can be bought for Christmas flowering

hippeastrum

The large, funnel-shaped red, pink or white flowers of hippeastrums are carried on stout 2-ft. stems in spring and early summer and are extremely showy. Hippeastrums are also known as Barbados lilies and amaryllis, but since this last name belongs to a quite different plant, the Belladonna Lily, it can be confusing to use it. They are grown from bulbs which can be purchased in winter or spring.

Pot bulbs singly in John Innes No. 2 Potting Compost in successional batches from January to March to extend the flowering season. Place one bulb in each 5-, 6- or 7-in. pot, only half burying the bulb in the soil. Grow in a light greenhouse or a sunny window in a temperature of 15 to 18° C. (60 to 65° F.), water freely and feed occasionally with weak liquid manure or seaweed extract but do not shade at any time. In September, reduce the water supply progressively and from November until the bulbs are restarted keep them quite dry. Only re-pot them every third or fourth year as hippeastrums flower most freely when their roots are rather crowded. When the bulbs are not re-potted, scrape off an inch of top soil and replace this with fresh potting compost.

Specially prepared bulbs for Christmas flowering can be purchased in the autumn. Pot them as soon as available and grow in a temperature of 21° C. (70° F.).

Lilies

Lilium speciosum rubrum flowers in late summer and autumn. As they are stem rooting, the bulbs should be placed low down in the pots to allow room for a topdressing as the stems develop

Almost any lily can be grown in the greenhouse, but most popular for the purpose are *Lilium longiflorum*, with trumpet-shaped fragrant white flowers in spring and early summer; *L. formosanum*, rather similar in flower but a much taller plant and flowering in late summer; *L. auratum*, with very large, richly fragrant, bowl-shaped white flowers splashed with gold and spotted or banded with crimson in some varieties, also late summer flowering and *L. speciosum*, with nodding reflexed flowers, white flushed with pink or red, produced in late summer or autumn. There are several varieties.

All can be grown in unheated greenhouses but a little artificial warmth in late winter and spring will make *L. longiflorum* flower earlier.

Pot all these lilies in autumn or winter as soon as bulbs can be obtained. Use John Innes No. 1 or a peat-based potting compost without any lime or chalk. Keep them in a cool but frost-proof place and water sparingly until growth starts, then water freely, and grow on in a temperature of about 15° C. (60° F.), shading from direct sunshine. Tie the flower stems to canes pushed well into the soil and after flowering gradually reduce the water supply. When the leaves have died, keep the bulbs quite dry until they are re-potted in the autumn or early winter.

Lilium longiflorum

Lily of the Valley, Tuberose

The very fragrant flowers of the Tuberose can be produced at almost any time of the year by potting the bulbs successively and growing them in a warm greenhouse

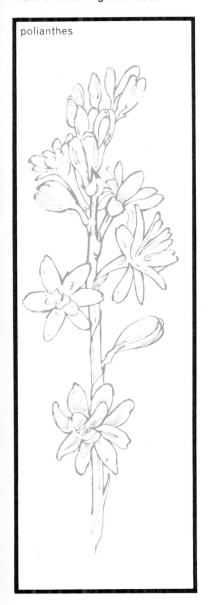

polianthes

Lily of the valley or convallaria is not really a bulb but a fleshy crown. Specially selected strong crowns can be purchased in autumn or early winter for forcing into early bloom. Plant these crowns almost side by side in pots or boxes filled with moist peat and keep them in a warm, dark, moist place, such as under the greenhouse staging, until new growth is 3 to 4 in. high, then lift them on to the greenhouse staging. Maintain a temperature of 10 to 15° C. (50 to 60° F.), and keep the peat constantly moist. Cut the flowers as they open and then either discard the plants or harden them off in a frame and plant out of doors in a partially shaded place. Do not force again for at least three years.

The Tuberose or polianthes is a Mexican plant with spikes of intensely fragrant white flowers which can be produced at almost any time of the year by potting the bulbs successively and growing them in a warm greenhouse at 15° C. (60° F.) or more. Pot one bulb in each 4-in. pot (or four bulbs in a 6-in. pot) in J.I.P. No. 1 or peat potting compost and treat as advised for lily of the valley. Bulbs can be placed in a warm, sunny place and gradually ripened off for flowering again, but it is usually more satisfactory to start afresh with new Tuberose bulbs and lily of the valley crowns each autumn or spring.

Nerine, Vallota

Some nerines can be grown outdoors in well-drained soil and a warm, sunny position. In the greenhouse, all kinds bring welcome colour in the autumn months

Vallota speciosa

Guernsey lily is the popular name of nerine, and Scarborough Lily of vallota. Both are excellent late-flowering pot plants grown from bulbs in a greenhouse. One kind of Guernsey lily, *Nerine bowdenii*, with heads of rose-pink flowers in September and October, is also sufficiently hardy to be grown out of doors in sunny, sheltered places. Other Guernsey lilies are available in various colours from pink and mauve-purple to scarlet. The Scarborough Lily has heads of trumpet-shaped scarlet flowers on stout 18-in. stems in August–September.

Pot bulbs singly in autumn in 4- or 5-in. pots and grow in a sunny greenhouse, minimum temperature 7° C. (45° F.). Water moderately at first, fairly freely while the plants are growing in late winter and spring, but keep Guernsey lilies just dry in a warm sunny place during June and July. The Scarborough Lily should never be quite dry, but should be watered rather sparingly in summer until the flower spikes appear, when it can be watered freely.

Do not re-pot annually as these plants flower most freely when the roots are crowded. Feed the plants in spring with weak liquid fertiliser or seaweed extract.

Greenhouse Climbers

Allamanda, Aristolochia

The trumpet-shaped flowers of allamanda are produced from April to September. This climber may be grown in a large container or in the greenhouse border

In this section are included in addition to the true climbers some shrubby plants which are most conveniently treated as climbers because their stems are long and flexible. However, they have no natural means of support and must be tied to wires, trellis work or something of the kind.

True climbers may attach themselves by means of tendrils, in which case the supports provided for them must be sufficiently thin for the tendrils to twist around them; or they may actually twine around anything convenient which they touch, which means that they can encompass quite large objects such as posts or pillars. A third group may cling with suckers or aerial roots, by which means they can ascend a wall with no other assistance.

If the climbers are relatively small plants they can be grown in pots into which three or four bamboo canes have been thrust to provide support. Many more are vigorous plants which are happiest when planted directly in a bed of soil and given plenty of space to fill, such as the back wall of a lean-to greenhouse or conservatory or the area beneath the rafters where wires have been strained to hold them up. Some climbers of intermediate vigour can be made into handsome shrub-like specimens by training them over a dome-shaped wire support. This was once very fashionable and might well be used more freely again, especially where such plants can be grown in tubs and used effectively out of doors in summer, perhaps for the decoration of a patio or terrace garden.

A little discretion needs to be exercised in introducing permanent climbers to small greenhouses. All may seem fine for the first year, but once the plants become established they may grow rapidly, monopolise space and cut off a great deal of light. Most of the passion flowers (passiflora) have this tendency, and the fine perennial morning glory, *Ipomoea learii*, and the deliciously scented *Jasminum polyanthum* are two other plants strictly for the large greenhouse or conservatory. There is one good way of growing these vigorous climbers which, though seldom seen, is entirely practical. This is to plant the climber inside the greenhouse but to allow it to grow wholly or mainly outside the house. To do this a hole must be left in the side wall or some other convenient part of the greenhouse or conservatory and all growth arising from the roots guided through the hole and trained up the outside. Treated in this way the stems of quite tender plants may survive many winters and, if they do get killed, more stems are likely to grow from the protected roots to take their place another year. This is a similar practice to the one often adopted for grape vines, though for them with the opposite purpose of allowing the roots to be outside and the stems inside.

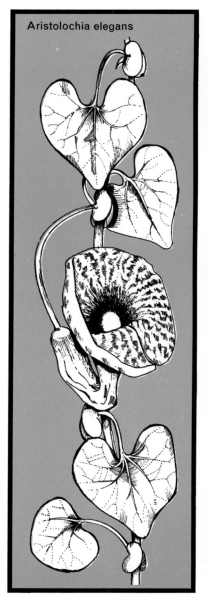

Aristolochia elegans

Allamanda cathartica is one of the most handsome climbers, a vigorous plant with shining yellow trumpet-shaped flowers produced from April to September. It can be grown in an intermediate or warm greenhouse in large pots or tubs filled with J.I.P. No. 2 compost or, better still, planted in a border of good loamy soil with some peat and a sprinkling of John Innes base fertiliser. Its long slender stems need to be tied to wires or other supports. It should be watered normally and shaded from strong sunshine. The previous year's growth can be shortened severely each February and in summer the tips of any shoots that extend too far can be pinched out. Propagation is by cuttings of firm young shoots in spring in a well warmed propagator.

Aristolochias are vigorous twiners with curiously shaped flowers like curved funnels. One hardy kind, *Aristolochia durior*, is known as the Duchman's Pipe, an allusion to the shape of its flower. But more attractive for the intermediate greenhouse is *A. elegans*, the Calico Flower, with large, wide-mouthed flowers, white mottled and netted with purplish-brown. It flowers in August and can be grown in large pots or be planted in a bed of soil as for allamanda. Water freely in spring and summer, sparingly in autumn and winter and shade in summer. Growth can be shortened, if overgrown, in February. Increase by early summer cuttings in a propagator.

Bougainvillea, Plumbago

Bougainvillea makes a splendid cool greenhouse climber and the glorious blossom provides a magnificent display for most of the summer. The colour range includes magenta, pink and orange

Both bougainvillea and plumbago are vigorous and showy climbing plants which grow freely out of doors around the Mediterranean, but will not survive frost. They can be grown successfully in greenhouses with a minimum winter temperature of 7°C. (45° F.) and need little or no artificial heat from May to September. Bougainvilleas have magenta, rose, pink or orange flowers and plumbago has pale blue flowers. Both are in flower for most of the summer.

Pot in March or April in 8- to 10-in. pots in J.I.P. No. 2 compost or plant in a bed of good soil to which some peat and bonemeal has been added. Water freely in spring and summer but rather sparingly in autumn and winter.

These plants should be grown in full sunlight with plenty of ventilation in summer. Feed the plants once a week from May to August with weak liquid manure and train the stems to wires attached beneath the rafters, or up the back wall of lean-to greenhouses. In March, shorten all sideshoots to a few inches and remove weak or overcrowded stems altogether. Then let the greenhouse temperature rise a little, water more freely and restart the plants into growth. They can be increased by cuttings of firm young growth in summer in a propagator.

Cassia and Others

Cassia corymbosa is a colourful shrub for a frost-proof greenhouse and the long branches also lend themselves to being trained against a sheltered sunny wall

Clematis indivisa

Coronilla glauca

Cassia corymbosa is a sprawling shrub, the long flexible stems of which can be trained against a wall, around a pillar or to wires strained beneath the rafters. It is evergreen and produces its clusters of yellow flowers very freely in late summer and autumn.

Most clematis grow best out of doors, but Clematis indivisa (C. paniculata) is rather tender and grows well in a cool greenhouse. It is evergreen and has white flowers in May and June. C. florida bicolor (or sieboldii) has white flowers with a central ring of narrow purple segments and is another kind that appreciates shelter, and some hybrids with large double flowers are seen to greatest perfection under glass.

Coronilla glauca is a bushy evergreen which can readily be trained against a wall. It can be grown outdoors in sheltered places but is safer in a greenhouse, and with a little warmth will produce, most of the year, small yellow pea flowers pleasantly scented by day.

All these plants can be grown in any frost-proof greenhouse, but will flower most reliably in a cool house. Grow in large pots or tubs in J.I.P. No. 2 compost or plant in a bed of good loamy soil. Water normally, and lightly shade clematis in summer. Prune early-flowering clematis after flowering, and coronilla in spring as necessary to fill available space. Increase all by summer cuttings in a propagator, cassia also by seed in a temperature of 15 to 18° C. (60 to 65° F.).

Cestrum, Fremontia

Fremontias are tender shrubs which must be given frost protection in winter. They flower freely in summer and need well-drained soil and a position in full sun

Cestrums are slender stemmed shrubs best treated as climbers in the greenhouse where they can be trained against walls or up pillars. They produce clusters of hanging, tubular flowers, orange-yellow in *Cestrum aurantiacum*, red in *C. elegans* (also known as *C. purpureum*) and *C. newellii*, yellow in *C. parqui*. All these flower in summer and can be grown in a cool greenhouse either in large pots in J.I.P. No. 2 compost or, preferably, planted in a bed of loam with some peat and sand and a sprinkling of John Innes base fertiliser. Water normally and shade lightly from strong direct sunshine in summer. Prune in February by shortening the previous year's growth. Increase by cuttings of firm young growth in summer in a propagator, temperature 18° C. (65° F.).

Fremontia californica and *F. mexicana* are very similar, evergreen shrubs with long pliable branches which can readily be trained against a wall or on a trellis. The leaves have a spicy odour, the flowers are yellow, saucer shaped and freely produced all summer. Fremontias can be grown in any sunny frost-proof greenhouse or conservatory in just the same way as cestrums, except that they require no shade but benefit from all the sunshine available. If overgrown prune lightly in the spring. Increase by seed sown in spring in a temperature of 15 to 18° C. (60 to 65° F.) and pot the seedlings singly in small pots in J.I.P. No. 1.

Cestrum newellii

Cobaea and Others

Thunbergia alata is better known to many as Black-eyed Susan. It succeeds best when treated as an annual and it makes a splendid plant for a hanging basket

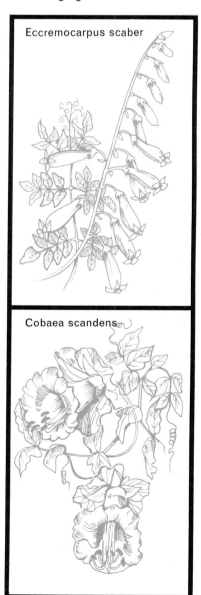

Eccremocarpus scaber

Cobaea scandens

Cobaea scandens is a fast growing perennial but so readily raised from seed that it is often grown as an annual. The purple or white flowers are cup shaped with a saucer-like green calyx behind each and the plant is known as the Cup-and-saucer Vine. It can be grown in any frost-proof greenhouse or even in an unheated house if the plants are purchased in spring and discarded in autumn. Seed should be sown in March in J.I.S. or peat-based seed compost in a temperature of 15 to 18° C. (60 to 65° F.), the seedlings being potted singly in J.I.P. No. 1 and later moved on into larger pots in J.I.P. No. 2 or planted in a bed of good soil. Water freely in spring and summer and, if plants are retained, rather sparingly in autumn and winter. Do not shade. Cut back the vines each February.

Eccremocarpus scaber is also a perennial sometimes treated as an annual. The tubular orange or orange-red flowers are produced from July to October and like the cobaea it climbs vigorously supporting itself by tendrils. Cultivation is similar but plants should be kept almost dry in winter.

Thunbergia alata is a slender twiner known as Black-eyed Susan because each orange, buff or white flower has a black centre. It is usually grown as an annual from seeds sown 3 or 4 in each 3-in. pot in J.I.S. or peat-based seed compost and germinated as for cobaea. Later re-pot the seedlings in 6-in. pots and J.I.P. No. 1.

Dipladenia and Others

Dipladenia is a delightful climber for the heated greenhouse, flowering throughout the summer. It should be shaded from hot sunshine and kept in a fairly moist atmosphere

Dipladenia, mandevilla and trachelospermum are related twiners, the first two climbing readily, the third needing some help. Dipladenias are evergreen and have quite large funnel-shaped flowers, white in *D. boliviensis* and pink in *D. splendens*. There are also garden varieties with deep rose or crimson flowers. *Mandevilla suaveolens*, Chilean Jasmine, is deciduous with white, fragrant flowers. *Trachelospermum jasminoides*, Chinese Jasmine, is also sweetly scented. Its white flowers are small but numerous, its leaves evergreen and leathery. *T. asiaticum* is similar. All are summer flowering.

Pot them in spring in J.I.P. No. 2 or peat-based compost in large pots or plant them in a bed of good

soil to which some peat and sand and a sprinkling of John Innes base fertiliser have been added. Grow the dipladenias in a warm or intermediate house, the mandevilla and trachelospermums in any frost-proof greenhouse. Water normally. In summer, shade and maintain a fairly moist atmosphere.

Cut back the previous year's growth of dipladenia and mandevilla nearly to the base in February and in summer pinch out the tips of any shoots that are growing too long. Trachelospermum only requires some thinning in February.

Increase all these plants by cuttings of young growth in summer, rooted in a propagator with a temperature of 18 to 21° C. (65 to 70° F.) for dipladenia, the most tender.

dipladenia

mandevilla

Fuchsia, Pelargonium

This display is formed from varieties of zonal pelargoniums which have been trained up the wall of a lean-to greenhouse. Among those used are Penny, Dryden, King of Denmark and The Speaker

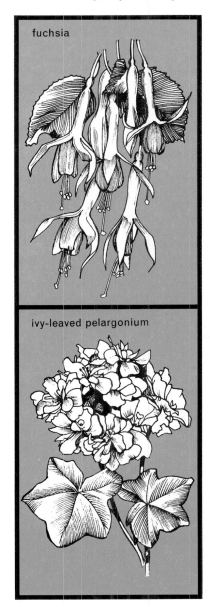

fuchsia

ivy-leaved pelargonium

Some varieties of fuchsia with long whippy stems can be trained as climbers either around a pillar or up a back wall of a lean-to greenhouse or conservatory. Vigorous species such as *F. arborescens*, *F. boliviana*, *F. cordifolia*, *F. corymbiflora* and *F. fulgens* can also be grown in the same way. All can be grown in large pots or tubs in J.I.P. No. 2 compost or, better still, planted in a bed of good loam with the addition of peat and sand and a sprinkling of John Innes base fertiliser. They need a cool house temperature and should be watered freely in spring and summer, moderately in autumn, sparingly in winter. They can be fed every 10 to 14 days in summer with weak liquid manure and should be shaded in summer from direct sunshine only. Tips of badly placed shoots can be pinched out at any time and, if necessary, plants can be pruned more severely in February.

Ivy-leaved pelargoniums are naturally trailing plants which can readily be trained up walls, trellis work etc. Some vigorous zonal-leaved varieties can also be trained in a similar way, though they will take longer (perhaps several years) to reach a height of 5 or 6 ft. and will require a good deal more summer pinching and training to get growth where it is required. Soil and culture are as for fuchsias, but no shading is required at any time.

Propagation of both fuchsias and pelargoniums is described elsewhere (pages 78 and 84).

Hoya, Stephanotis

Hoya bella is a trailing plant suitable for a hanging basket and flowering during the summer. It grows better in a higher temperature than is needed for *H. carnosa* and thrives in a warm greenhouse

stephanotis

Both these beautiful greenhouse climbers have waxen-textured flowers so that hoya is popularly known as the Wax Flower and stephanotis as the Clustered Wax Flower. In fact, though related, they are not much alike as the pink and white flowers of hoya are carried in little flat circular clusters, whereas the pure white tubular flowers of stephanotis hang in irregular clusters. Both flower in summer, *Hoya carnosa* rather late.

Pot *Hoya carnosa* in March in J.I.P. No. 1 or peat potting compost or plant in a bed of good loam with peat and a scattering of bone-meal added. Grow in a minimum temperature of 7°C. (45° F.) rising to 15° to 18° C. (60 to 65° F.) with sun heat. Water freely in spring and summer, rather sparingly in autumn and winter, but never allow the plants to become dry. Shade in summer from strong direct sunshine only. The stems should be trained to wires.

Hoya bella is a smaller, trailing plant suitable for hanging baskets. It should be treated in the same way as *Hoya carnosa*.

Stephanotis should be grown in a similar way but in a higher temperature, especially in winter when a minimum of 13° C. (55° F.) is desirable. Feed the plants once a week from May to August with weak liquid manure and spray them occasionally in summer with malathion to keep down mealy bugs and scale insects.

Ipomoea and Relatives

Ipomoeas, with their wide funnel-shaped flowers, are among the most popular of twining plants. They like a position where they will receive as much sun as possible

These are the plants that many gardeners know as convolvulus or morning glory. They are vigorous twiners with widely funnel-shaped flowers produced freely in summer, and all are sun lovers. Several of the most popular are grown as annuals, among them *Ipomoea purpurea* (sometimes called *Convolvulus major*) with purple, crimson or white flowers, and *I. tricolor* (or *rubro-caerulea*) with sky blue, blue and white or reddish-purple flowers. *I. learii* (or *Pharbitis learii*) has deep blue flowers becoming purple and is a perennial.

Related to these, though considerably different in appearance are *Quamoclit lobata* (or *Mina lobata*) with small curiously shaped tubular red and yellow flowers and *Quamoclit pennata* (or *Ipomoea quamoclit*) with scarlet trumpet-shaped flowers.

Though their names seem confused cultivation of all these plants is simple. All can be raised from seeds sown singly in small pots in spring in J.I.S. or peat seed compost in a temperature of 15 to 18° C. (60 to 65° F.). The annual kinds make good pot plants in J.I.P. No. 1 or peat potting composts and can be given canes or trellis to twine around. The perennial kinds are better planted in a bed of good soil and allowed to grow up a wall or on wires beneath the rafters. All will thrive in cool or intermediate houses. Water freely in spring and summer; perennial kinds sparingly in winter. Do not shade.

ipomoea

Jasmines

The charming flowers of the Primrose Jasmine, *Jasminum primulinum*, are to be seen from March to May. It likes a sunny position and the stems should be trained to a support

Jasminum polyanthum

There are several beautiful jasmines which are either partially or completely tender. *Jasminum primulinum* has large semi-double yellow flowers produced in spring. It is known as the Primrose Jasmine and is a sprawling shrub rather than a climber, though its long, slender stems can be easily trained to a wall or trellis. *J. polyanthum* produces its clusters of white richly scented flowers freely, mainly from February to May under glass. It is a vigorous twiner which will wrap itself around any convenient support. *J. angulare* has white fragrant flowers all summer; *J. sambac* is an evergreen twiner with fragrant white flowers almost throughout the year; *J. rex* has the largest flowers of all, white and up to 2 in. across and *J. grandiflorum* has masses of white sweetly scented flowers in summer.

All these jasmines are best planted in borders of good loamy soil, though they can be grown in large pots or tubs in J.I.P. No. 2 or equivalent compost. *J. primulinum*, *J. polyanthum* and *J. angulare* are happy in any frost-proof greenhouse and are excellent climbers for a cool conservatory. The other kinds are grown in intermediate or warm houses. All require normal watering and should be lightly shaded in summer. The warmhouse kinds should also have a moist atmosphere in summer. All can be pruned after flowering as necessary to keep them within bounds. All are readily increased by cuttings or layers.

Lapageria, Bomarea

Lapageria is a beautiful climber for a slightly heated greenhouse or a shaded, sheltered wall and it thrives in a lime-free loam. The waxy bell-like flowers appear in the summer

Lapageria rosea is a slender, evergreen twiner with large, hanging bell-shaped flowers in summer. The flowers may be rose or white and have an almost wax-like texture. The plant is known as the Chilean Bellflower. It is nearly hardy and can be grown in any completely frost-proof greenhouse either in large pots in J.I.P. No. 1 or peat-based potting compost, or planted in a bed of good lime-free loam and peat, with a sprinkling of John Innes base fertiliser. Water freely in spring and summer, moderately in autumn, sparingly in winter, and shade from May to September. Feed every 10 to 14 days from May to August with weak liquid fertiliser. The plant needs a trellis or wires for support. No pruning is normally needed. Increase by layering.

Bomareas are twiners related to the Peruvian Lily (alstroemeria) and with similar flowers. One of the best for cool greenhouse cultivation is *Bomarea caldasii* in which the orange-coloured flowers are produced in large clusters in winter and spring. Cultivation is very much the same as for lapageria, except that there is no need to avoid lime in the soil, summer shading is not essential and the resting period, when little water is required, is in autumn. Plants can be raised from seed sown in a temperature of 18° C. (65° F.) in spring, seedlings being grown singly in small pots. Alternatively, divide the roots in spring.

bomarea

Maurandia and Others

Maurandia erubescens, with its dainty leaves and trumpet flowers, makes a charming climber for a cool greenhouse. It should be grown in a fairly rich compost, such as J.I.P. No. 2

Maurandia are slender climbers supporting themselves by tendrils and producing trumpet-shaped flowers from spring to autumn. Two kinds are commonly grown, *Maurandia barclaiana*, rose and sometimes white and *M. erubescens*, pink and white.

Rhodochiton atrosanguineum (*R. volubile*) is a twiner with small lilac-pink and dark maroon flowers dangling from the stems like tiny peg dolls. It is known as Purple Bells and flowers in summer.

Senecio mikanioides (*S. scandens*) belongs to the same family as the groundsel and ragwort. It is a vigorous twiner with shining, evergreen, ivy-like leaves and clusters of golden-yellow daisy-like flowers in autumn. It is sometimes grown as a house plant for its foliage, but is unlikely to flower unless it gets a lot of light.

All these plants can be grown in a cool greenhouse either in large pots in J.I.P. No. 2 compost or planted in a bed of good loam with some peat and sand and a sprinkling of John Innes base fertiliser. Watering is normal except that the rhodochiton should be watered very sparingly in winter. All can be pruned in spring if necessary.

Rhodochiton is so readily raised from seed sown in spring in a temperature of 15 to 18° C. (60 to 65° F.) that it is sometimes treated as an annual. Maurandias can be increased by seed or by cuttings in a propagator, which is also the best method of increasing the senecio.

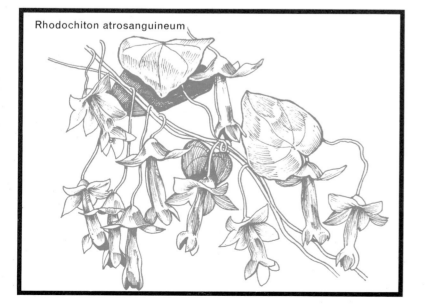

Rhodochiton atrosanguineum

Passiflora

All the passion flowers are remarkable and strangely beautiful. *Passiflora allardii* has fine flowers produced in summer, and there are many others to choose from

Passiflora caerulea

The passifloras are known as passion flowers because the circular flowers, often decorated with a ring of filaments and with central, cross-like organs, were thought to represent the Passion of Christ. All are vigorous climbers with tendrils, and flower in summer.

Passiflora caerulea, with blue and white or all white flowers, is one of the hardiest and can be grown out of doors in very sheltered places. *P. allardii* is similar, but has even finer flowers with some pink as well as deep purplish-blue and white. *P. antioquiensis* has large hanging flowers shaped like parasols, rose red in colour. *P. quadrangularis*, which produces the fruit known as grenadilla, also has large flowers, white, heavily veined and netted with purple and fringed by long hanging filaments. *P. edulis* has white and purple flowers then egg-shaped edible fruits.

All can be grown in large pots or tubs in J.I.P. No. 1 compost, but are easier to manage in a bed of good loam. Most are happy in either a cool or intermediate house, but *P. edulis* and *P. quadrangularis* prefer the latter. All should be watered freely in spring and summer, sparingly in autumn and winter, and need never be shaded. They can be cut back to within a foot or so of the base each spring or they can be permitted to retain main stems to which the side growths are shortened. Increase is by summer cuttings in a propagator or the species from seed in a temperature of 18° C. (65° F.).

Solanum and Others

Tibouchina is a very rewarding climber for the cool greenhouse and produces its striking flowers throughout the summer and well into the autumn. They are complemented by the velvet-textured leaves

Solanum jasminoides is a vigorous twiner with evergreen leaves and sprays of slate-blue and yellow (or white and yellow) flowers from July to November. It needs plenty of room though it can be pruned fairly severely each spring. *S. crispum* has purplish-blue and yellow flowers in late summer, but is a sprawling shrub or scrambler rather than a true climber, so its long flexible stems should be tied to suitable supports. *S. wendlandii* has larger flowers and is bushier.

Sollya heterophylla is a slender twiner bearing clusters of nodding sky-blue flowers in late summer and autumn. It is known as the Bluebell Creeper, more from the colour than the flower shape.

Tibouchina semidecandra is a vigorous sprawling shrub, its long lax stems being readily trained against a wall or to wires strained beneath the roof. It has velvety leaves and clusters of fine violet-purple flowers produced all the summer and most of the autumn.

All these climbers can be grown in a cool greenhouse either in pots in J.I.P. No. 2 or peat-based potting compost or in a bed of good loam, with plenty of peat and sand mixed in for the sollya. Do not shade at any time, or only lightly in summer for the tibouchina if its leaves show signs of scorching. Prune in February as necessary to fill available space, and pinch tips of tibouchina as necessary in summer. Increase by cuttings in spring or summer in a propagator.

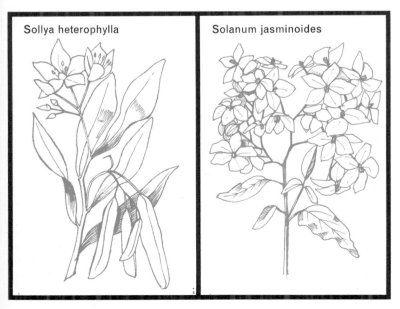

Sollya heterophylla

Solanum jasminoides

Trumpet Vines

Many related plants are known by the collective name of Trumpet Vine. *Campsis radicans*, shown above, is one of the most useful for providing fast cover

Bignonia capreolata

The botanical name of the trumpet vines is rather confused, but here are included climbers variously known as bignonia, campsis, doxantha, pandorea, podranea, pyrostegia and tecoma. All produce handsome clusters of funnel- or trumpet-shaped flowers in late summer and autumn, usually orange-red, orange, salmon red or pink. Some are twiners, a few, including *Campsis radicans*, support themselves by aerial roots like an ivy, and some are scramblers which need a little tying to take their long flexible stems where they are required. All need a good deal of room.

All trumpet vines can be grown in a cool greenhouse either in large pots or tubs of J.I.P. No. 2 compost or in a bed of good loamy soil. All are sun lovers and should not be shaded at any time because unless their growth is well ripened no flowers will be produced. They should be watered freely in spring and summer, moderately in autumn, sparingly in winter, and may be fed fortnightly from June to September with a high potash liquid fertiliser. All can be cut back severely in February and can be increased by cuttings in summer or by layering.

Recommended kinds are *Campsis grandiflora* with large, deep orange and red flowers; *C.* Madame Galen, salmon red; *Bignonia capreolata*, red and yellow and *Podranea ricasoliana*, pink.

Greenhouse Chrysanthemums

The flowering time of chrysanthemums is controlled partly by temperature and partly by night length. It is possible to manipulate both and so produce chrysanthemums throughout the year, and commercial producers of cut flowers and pot plants do exactly that. For the private gardener it is usually more convenient to allow the seasons to take their natural course and to grow the greenhouse chrysanthemums to flower from October to December or January.

There are a great many varieties which are classified according to the shape and size of their flowers and are also divided into Early Flowering, October Flowering and Late Flowering according to their natural flowering season. It is only the last two groups that need to be flowered in greenhouses, but all classes are usually over-wintered in frost-free greenhouses, are increased in cool greenhouses and grown on with frost protection at least until May.

The main flower type divisions are as follows: Single, up to five rows of petals and a button-like central disc; Incurved, petals curling inwards to form a ball-like flower; Intermediate, inner petals curling inwards and outer petals curling outwards; Reflexed, all petals curling outwards; Anemone-centred, like singles but with a low cushion of very short petals in place of a central disc; Thread-petalled or Rayonnante, petals rolled lengthwise like thin quills; Spoon-petalled, petals rolled for part of their length but open at the ends like little spoons; Charm, many small flowers on a bushy plant; Cascade, similar to Charm but with a looser habit.

All chrysanthemums are nearly hardy and do not need a great deal of warmth at any time. They must be protected from frost and also, in winter, from excessive moisture, which can do them just as much injury. From late May or early June until the end of September all chrysanthemums are better out of doors than under glass. In consequence the chrysanthemum routine fits in very well with that for tomatoes which can take their place in the greenhouse in summer, or they may be used with begonias, gloxinias or summer-flowering annuals which do not make much demand upon greenhouse space until about May.

Although greenhouse chrysanthemums are usually grown in pots, most varieties with normal culture grow too tall to make good decorative plants to use indoors. Their proper place is in the greenhouse or conservatory where there is plenty of room for display or to provide cut flowers. The dwarf pot plants that are available in florists' shops and at garden centres are produced partly by treatment with dwarfing chemicals, and partly by growing in controlled day lengths, so that plants can be brought into bloom before they have made much growth. However, there are a few naturally dwarf varieties such as Blanche du Poitou, Blanche Poitevene, Marie Morin, Yellow Morin, Dorothy Wilson and Dwarf Rose. These should be grown from April or May cuttings to flower from September to November.

Propagation

Anemone-flowered chrysanthemums, with their distinctive cushion of florets in the centre of the bloom, are ideal for flower arrangements. They are available in many different shades

All chrysanthemums can be raised from seed but usually this method is only used for the Charm and Cascade varieties as others give variable results. The seed is sown in February or March in a temperature of 15 to 18° C. (60 to 65° F.) in J.I.S. or peat-based seed compost. Seedlings are pricked out 1½ in. apart in J.I.P. No. 1 or peat-based potting compost and are then treated in the same way as plants raised from cuttings.

Cuttings are prepared between January and May from young shoots, 2 to 3 in. long, growing from the roots of old plants which have been cut hard back after flowering and kept moderately moist in a temperature of 7 to 10° C. (45 to 50° F.). Each cutting is cut off cleanly just below a joint, the lower leaves, if any, are removed and the base is dipped in hormone rooting powder. The cuttings are inserted in a mixture of equal parts coarse sand, loam and peat in pots or shallow boxes. They are rooted either in a propagator or on the open staging of the greenhouse, in which case they will need rather more watering and overhead spraying to prevent excessive flagging. An air temperature of 10° C. (50° F.) should be maintained and the soil should be warmed from below to 15° C. (60° F.).

When rooted, cuttings should be potted in 3- or 3½-in. pots in J.I.P. No. 1 or peat-based potting compost and grown on in a cool greenhouse. Shade for a few days then allow all the light available.

Growing On

The Cascade chrysanthemums are delightful pot plants which can be raised from seed. It should be noted, however, that the plants take up a considerable amount of space

As soon as the small pots are full of roots plants should be moved to 5-in. pots and J.I.P. No. 2 or peat-based compost. A few weeks later a further transfer will be necessary to 7- or 8-in. pots and J.I.P. No. 3 or peat-based compost. At this stage each plant should be provided with one strong 4-ft. cane for support.

Meanwhile the growing tip should be removed from each plant when it is 8 or 9 in. high and the tips of side growths similarly removed when they are 8 or 9 in. long. This encourages good branching from low down but it is not always wise to retain all the branches that result. The number retained will depend on the kind of flowers required. For very large exhibition blooms three stems to each plant may be ample. At the other extreme for a big display of small flowers a dozen or more stems may be required. However many stems are retained each should be looped individually to the central cane to prevent breakage. Very large plants may require several canes angled to lean outwards at the top to allow for the spread of the stems.

In late May (or as soon as danger of severe frost is over) plants should be placed out of doors in a sunny position. Stand the pots on a gravel or cinder base and tie the support canes to wires strained horizontally between posts driven in at the ends of each row of pots. Leave some room between rows.

Flowering

The late-flowering chrysanthemum Mavis Shoesmith. This is a good large-flowered incurved variety and is typical of the very popular exhibition type

Throughout their growing season chrysanthemums must be watered freely. From mid-June until the first petal colour is seen in the opening flower buds plants should be fed every 7 to 10 days with weak liquid fertiliser, for preference a special chrysanthemum fertiliser.

When flower buds start to appear it is necessary to decide whether large flowers (one to each stem) are required or sprays of smaller flowers. If the former, only the terminal bud on each stem should be retained, all others being removed at an early stage. If sprays are required the terminal bud is removed and all side buds kept.

Cascades are stood in summer on a raised plank running east/west, each plant with a cane sloping to the north to which the main stem is tied. This cane is gradually lowered, other canes being lashed to it for support, and side growths are pinched.

At the end of September all plants are returned to the greenhouse and grown with maximum light and as much ventilation as is consistent with maintenance of a temperature of 10 to 15° C. (50 to 60° F.). A little artificial heat may be necessary at times to dry the air and prevent decay of the opening flowers. After flowering, stems are cut down and pots kept with frost protection only until it is time to start growth again to provide a new lot of cuttings. Charm and Cascade chrysanthemums are usually discarded after flowering.

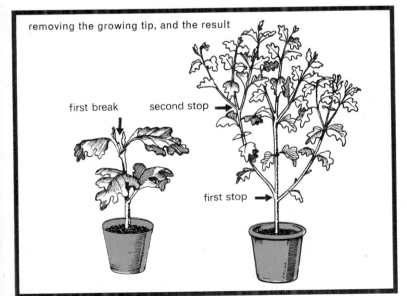

removing the growing tip, and the result

first break

second stop

first stop

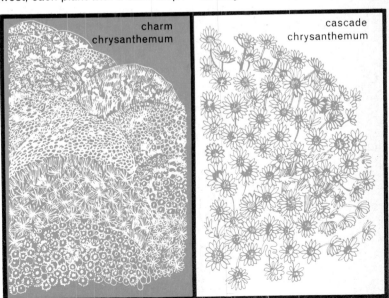

charm chrysanthemum

cascade chrysanthemum

Orchids

The orchid family is a very large one including thousands of distinct kinds growing naturally in many different parts of the world. Some are tropical plants and others, a number of which are native British wild plants, are completely hardy. In addition there are numerous hybrids and varieties.

Many orchids have thickened stems, known as pseudobulbs, which enable them to store food and moisture and rest for quite long periods. Some are epiphytic plants, getting most of their food from the air, but terrestrial orchids root and feed in the soil in the ordinary way. In nature many orchids grow in forests, the epiphytic kinds clinging to trees or damp rocks.

Because of these peculiar methods of growth orchids need composts very different from those used for most other greenhouse plants, and their management is also different. This does not mean that they are difficult to grow, in fact most orchid enthusiasts insist that they are among the easiest greenhouse plants to manage and they will withstand a great deal of ill-treatment. It does mean that a gardener who has been accustomed to handling other greenhouse plants must learn new ways when embarking on orchid cultivation. In particular, since many plants will be growing in spongy mixtures of sphagnum moss and osmunda fibre (perhaps even in completely synthetic materials such as expanded polystyrene if plants or composts are purchased from a commercial grower), normal methods of assessing soil moisture must be abandoned. In place of this the eye must be educated to observe by the look of leaves and composts when water is required. Fortunately, since the compost is so open and spongy it is almost impossible for it to become waterlogged and, since the atmosphere for orchids is usually humid, they do not dry out as rapidly as some other pot plants. Perhaps it is in identifying the resting season, which is a characteristic of many orchids with pseudobulbs, and in keeping them sufficiently dry during this important period in their annual cycle that the greatest difficulty arises. This is largely a matter of knowing the growth pattern of each species or hybrid and since there are many thousands of these it is impossible to deal with them in detail in a book of this character. There are numerous books devoted exclusively to the cultivation of orchids. There are also active orchid societies which publish useful literature on the subject and enable their members to exchange information. Commercial orchid firms are also always ready to assist customers and, because as a rule they grow nothing but orchids, they have an expertise which is unsurpassed.

Though it is possible to grow orchids in a mixed collection of greenhouse plants it is easier to provide the special conditions they require in greenhouses devoted exclusively to them. Houses specially suitable for orchids are produced by some greenhouse manufacturers.

Propagation

The belief that orchids are difficult to grow and expensive should not be a deterrent to the would-be grower, for there are many, such as these cymbidiums, which are fairly easy and inexpensive

Orchid seed is dust-like and produced in great quantity. In nature much seed never germinates and vast numbers of seedlings die young. In nurseries it is possible to germinate seeds in test tubes or flasks on agar (a special kind of jelly), impregnated with nutrient solution with all harmful germs excluded, so that a high percentage of the seed grows and the seedlings survive. This has made possible the immense increase in hybrid orchids, and unflowered seedlings with good parentage can often be purchased quite cheaply. But hybrids usually differ from their parents, sometimes for the better but often not, so purchasing unflowered seedlings is to some extent a gamble.

Divisions and cuttings reproduce exactly the plants from which they were taken. A system of taking minute cuttings from the growing tips of plants and growing them in slowly revolving flasks of nutrient solution has made it possible to increase selected plants far more rapidly. Small plants grown from these meristem cuttings are usually reasonably priced and can be grown on to flowering size in a few years.

Orchids are also still collected in the wild and imported and some firms specialise in selling such plants which can often prove very interesting.

Care of Plants

Potting and Dividing

The three main requirements of most greenhouse orchids, such as this miltonia, are an equable temperature, a moist atmosphere and no direct sunshine. It is useful to remember that orchids prefer rain water.

The genus *Dendrobium* is the largest one in the orchid family. This beautiful species, *D. thyrsiflorum*, is evergreen and the flowers appear in spring

Most greenhouse orchids need an equable temperature, a moist atmosphere and no direct sunshine. They can be grown in any adequately heated greenhouse, but one with solid walls rather than with glass to the ground is ideal, with slatted wooden blinds fitted outside to run on rollers 8 or 9 in. above the roof glass. Pots should stand on slatted staging about 6 in. above solid staging covered with small pebbles or grit that can be kept constantly moist.

Water the plants, if possible, with rain water. Established plants should be watered fairly freely while they are in growth, moderately for a few weeks after re-potting, and rather sparingly while at rest. Water paths and under staging at least once daily in spring and summer to maintain humidity, less frequently in winter, and syringe plants with water daily in warm weather. Alternatively, a mechanical humidifier can be fitted. Remove resting plants to the coolest part of the house. Shade from early April until the end of September, but if moveable blinds are fitted only use them in spring and early autumn during the middle period of the day when direct sunshine might harm the plants. If solid walls come above the staging level they will provide all the early and late shade necessary.

removing old compost

dividing plant

epiphytic orchid

Most orchids can be grown in a mixture of 3 parts by volume osmunda fibre and 1 part chopped sphagnum moss. These materials can be obtained from orchid specialists who often prepare and sell the required mixtures. For some strong-growing or terrestrial orchids the addition of 2 parts fibrous loam may give even better results, but the loam should be passed through a $\frac{1}{2}$-in. mesh sieve and only the soil left in the sieve used, the fine material being discarded.

Use a clay pot just large enough to contain the plant. Place enough pieces of broken pot (crocks) in the pot to fill it to one third, work some compost between the roots of the plant, place it in the pot and fill in the hollows with more compost.

When re-potting old plants remove most of the old compost and then divide the plant, keeping four or five pseudobulbs and a new growth to be potted on, and discard the rest.

As they grow, the epiphytic kinds will push roots out over the side of the pot or develop them in mid-air from stems or pseudobulbs. This is their natural habit and should not be interfered with.

Most orchids only need re-potting every second or third year but slipper orchids (paphiopedilum or cypripedium) may be re-potted every year. Spring is the best time, but not while plants are in flower.

Aerides and Others

Calanthe vestita is a terrestrial orchid from Burma and Malaya. The shining white flowers are carried on spikes up to 2 ft. long, which are produced during the winter

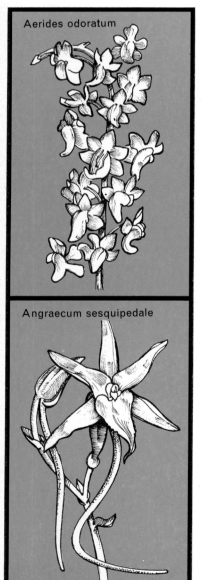

Aerides odoratum

Angraecum sesquipedale

The flowers of aerides are not big but they are numerous, carried in long arching spikes, and they last well. Colours are mainly pink, purple and white. There are many species from different parts of Asia and though all are epiphytes to be grown in sphagnum moss and osmunda or equivalent compost they differ in their temperature requirements. Most can be grown in an intermediate house, but a few need a warm house. All need shade in summer. Water well from May to October then sparingly.

Angraecum sesquipedale is a very distinctive orchid with fan-like clusters of leaves and hanging flower stems carrying large wax-white flowers each with a long slender spur like a tail. All angraecums can be grown in an intermediate greenhouse in any of the composts recommended for epiphytic orchids. Treatment is similar to that for aerides, but with slightly more water in winter as these orchids have no marked resting period.

In contrast *Calanthe vestita* goes completely to rest from about September to February, when it loses all its leaves and can be kept absolutely dry. It is then re-potted in a compost of loam with a little peat, chopped sphagnum and sand. At first it is watered sparingly, then as growth starts much more freely and it is grown in an intermediate house with light shade. The spikes of rose-pink and white flowers appear in winter during the resting period.

Cattleya, Miltonia

Cattleyas make especially good cut flowers and are much used by florists in corsages. Most flower in autumn and winter and the large blooms are brilliantly coloured

Cattleyas and miltonias are among the most gorgeously coloured of the orchids. Cattleyas have very large flowers, often in shades of magenta or mauve with or without white, and make fine cut flowers much in demand for corsages. There are a great many varieties including complex hybrids with other orchids, some of which have produced the most highly coloured flowers. They will grow well in intermediate house conditions and require only light shading. Most flower in autumn or winter and rest for a few weeks afterwards when water should be applied sparingly. For the rest of the year water freely but allow the compost to become almost dry before watering again.

Miltonias have flowers rather like huge pansies, often white, strongly blotched with rose or crimson. They flower in spring and early summer and good plants can be produced in 4- or 5-in. pots. They will grow well in cool house conditions, though the temperature should not drop below 13° C. (55° F.) at any time. They enjoy a fair amount of shade in spring and summer and a humid atmosphere, so should be watered throughout the year, though less frequently in winter than in summer. Annual re-potting is desirable.

Miltonia hybridises with odontoglossum to give odontonias. Like laeliocattleya, brassocattleya and brassolaeliocattleya (from cattleya with laelia and brassavola) they extend the colour range and form.

cattleya

miltonia

Cymbidium, Coelogyne

Dendrobium, Vanda

Coelogyne cristata is a very attractive orchid flowering in March and April on pendulous spikes. It needs a cool winter temperature and the roots should not be disturbed

Vanda caerulea is an orchid for the intermediate greenhouse. It should be re-potted very infrequently, but each spring as growth re-starts some of the compost should be replaced

Cymbidium and coelogyne are among the most popular of greenhouse orchids. The flowers, of many different colours, are carried on arching stems and last extremely well when cut. Plants are fairly large and have a tendency to flower every second year.

Cymbidiums are classed as cool house orchids and will survive even in greenhouses in which the temperature falls to 7° C. (45° F.) on occasions. They are epiphytic orchids but do well in composts containing some loam as recommended for terrestrial orchids (page 107). They grow throughout most of the year with a less marked resting season than many orchids so they should never be allowed to become dry.

Coelogyne cristata is a small, spreading orchid with white flowers hanging in short spikes in spring. It will thrive under exactly the same conditions as the cymbidiums with plenty of water in spring and summer. Only re-pot when absolutely necessary as large, old plants flower most freely. Plants can be kept going by replacing some of the old compost from time to time without actually removing them from their pots.

Most useful for the amateur's greenhouse are the hybrids of *Dendrobium nobile* which will thrive under intermediate house conditions. They have long, thin, cane-like pseudobulbs and clusters of white, yellow pink or purple flowers in winter and spring, often strikingly blotched with one colour on another. Hybrids of *D. phalaenopsis,* mainly in shades of rose and magenta, need warm house conditions. Water both groups freely in spring and summer but decreasingly during the autumn until the flower buds appear, when more water should be given. Maintain a humid atmosphere in summer and shade lightly. Every second or third year re-pot after flowering is completed.

Vanda caerulea is very distinctive, with wide sprays of pale blue flowers produced regularly each autumn. It requires intermediate house conditions. Water moderately at all times allowing the compost to become nearly dry before wetting it thoroughly again, and shade lightly in spring and summer. Direct sunshine will scorch plants but heavy shade pales the flowers. Re-pot very infrequently but replace some compost annually as growth re-starts in the spring.

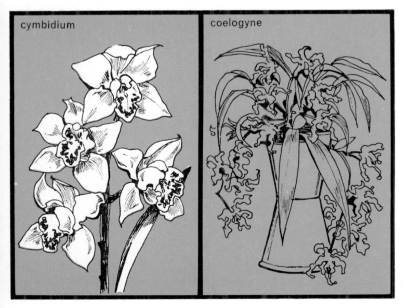

cymbidium

coelogyne

dendrobium

vanda

Odontoglossum and Others

The delicate flowers of *Odontoglossum crispum* are carried in slender sprays and are excellent as cut flowers. This orchid also makes a very attractive pot plant

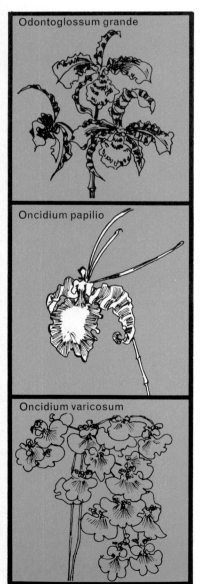

Odontoglossum grande

Oncidium papilio

Oncidium varicosum

There are a great many odontoglossums covering a wide range of colours and forms, but two types are of particular interest to gardeners. *Odontoglossum crispum* carries its white flowers in slender sprays and is first class both as a pot plant and as a cut flower. There are also a great many hybrids of the crispum type, but with flowers variously splashed with rose purple or maroon. All these need intermediate house temperatures. *Odontoglossum grande,* by contrast, will grow in a cool house and carries its large yellow and cinnamon-brown flowers in small spikes, usually of three. It is an easy orchid to grow, provided it is given a good rest with little water in winter. *O. crispum* and the hybrids have a less marked resting season, need very careful watering at all times, and are not the easiest of orchids to grow well.

Odontiodas are hybrids of *O. crispum* with cochlioda, which introduces red and rose shades.

Oncidiums usually have small yellow or yellow and brown flowers produced in large, branched sprays, but some have larger flowers produced successively, one or two at a time, for most of the year. One of these, *Oncidium papilio,* is known as the Butterfly Orchid because of the shape of its flowers. This and *O. rogersii* require warm house conditions, but the small *O. varicosum* can be grown in a cool house under similar conditions to cymbidiums. It flowers in autumn and winter.

Slipper and Moth Orchids

The slipper orchids, paphiopedilums, are terrestrial plants with highly distinctive pouched flowers. *Paphiopedilum insigne* is easy to grow in a cool greenhouse or even in a well-lighted room

Paphiopedilums are the slipper orchids still familiar to many people by the old name cypripedium. They are terrestrial orchids with highly distinctive pouched flowers usually carried singly on 1-ft. high stems. They are compact plants easily handled in small greenhouses. *Paphiopedilum insigne* and some kinds closely allied to it can be grown under cool greenhouse conditions, or even in well-lighted rooms, but the larger-flowered hybrids and those with mottled leaves require the greater warmth of the intermediate house. All like a compost containing some loam. They enjoy shade in spring and summer, ample humidity and, as they have no pseudobulbs and no marked resting period, must be watered all the year, but less frequently in winter than in summer.

Phalaenopsis (moth orchids) have white or pink flowers of highly distinctive shape carried in long spikes and produced at various times of the year. They are usually regarded as warm house orchids, but provided they are not over-watered in winter they can be grown under intermediate conditions. They like plenty of moisture in the air and a good deal of shade in spring and summer.

paphiopedilum

phalaenopsis

Small Orchids

The genus *Lycaste* has large, long-lasting, waxy flowers – characteristics which make it very popular. Flowering throughout the spring, it will grow in a cool greenhouse

Epidendrum vitellinum

Lycaste skinneri

Masdevallia ignea

Dendrochilums are very distinctive plants usually with small white or greenish-yellow flowers hanging in long slender chains. They are epiphytes and require a warm house.

Epidendrum vitellinum is a delightful orchid with vermilion flowers produced successively most of the summer. It can be grown in intermediate house conditions.

Lycaste skinneri, with white or pink flowers on short stems throughout the spring, will grow in cool house conditions with a little loam in the compost. It rests in winter, when it wants little water.

Masdevallia coccinea and *M. ignea* are small but brilliant orchids with purple, crimson or vermilion flowers in spring and early summer. They need cool house treatment and should be watered throughout the year.

Maxillaria is so called because it was thought that the flowers of some kinds resembled the jaws (or maxilla) of an insect. Those of *Maxillaria picta* are yellow and maroon, sweetly scented and produced in winter. It likes cool house conditions and should be watered sparingly in winter.

Sophronitis grandiflora and *Stanhopea tigrina* are both best grown in baskets suspended from the rafters of an intermediate temperate house. Water both throughout the year but sparingly in winter.

Zygopetalum mackayi, with curiously shaped flowers on erect stems in winter, likes an intermediate house and loamy compost.

Pests and Diseases

Florence Stirling, one of the many lovely hybrids of odontoglossum. As with all orchids, a careful watch must be kept for pests and diseases against which there are several effective controls

Orchids are attacked by most of the pests common to greenhouses. Red spider mites cause grey mottling of the leaves and thrips produce brown streaks on the flowers. Scale insects, like minute limpets, adhere to the leaves and exude a sticky fluid on which grows a black mould. Greenflies may cluster on the young shoots checking or distorting them, mealy bugs with their protective white waxy covering secrete themselves on the plants and slugs devour leaves or stems.

Many of these pests can be controlled by sponging the leaves occasionally with water containing a little white oil emulsion. Plants can be sprayed occasionally with malathion or derris or the house may be fumigated from time to time with smoke generators containing BHC. Slugs and snails can be destroyed by placing metaldehyde bait on the staging between the pots.

Diseases are less numerous and, on the whole, less controllable except by good cultivation and hygienic methods, including the removal of all dead or rotting leaves and stems. Occasionally viruses infect the plants causing ring-spotting, brown streaking or distortion. Infection is spread by greenflies and other insects, so if these are kept away trouble will be reduced to a minimum.

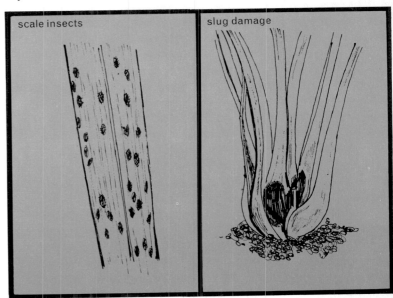

scale insects

slug damage

Greenhouse Ferns

Though a few ferns grow naturally in sunny places, most are shade lovers. They are, therefore, an excellent choice for a greenhouse that gets little or no direct sunshine. Some kinds make good indoor plants but many find the air of living rooms too dry for their liking, though if they are given periods of recuperation in a suitably damp place they may be kept in good condition indefinitely. One old-fashioned but still delightful way of reconciling the undoubted charms of ferns for indoor decoration with their love of moisture is to grow them in a conservatory or garden room with direct access from a living room. Here the ferns can be visible at all times and the fernery can be a pleasant place to sit in on hot days.

Another possibility is to grow ferns in rooms but inside special growth cabinets in which the moist conditions they like can be maintained without difficulty; or some small kinds can be grown in Wardian cases or bottle gardens.

Ferns are not flowering plants and their method of reproduction is markedly different from that of flowering plants. They produce dust-like spores in structures known as sori, which appear as brownish or blackish spots or patches on the backs of special leaves or fertile fronds. When these spores are sown under suitable conditions they develop into flat green plants, or prothalli, of a quite different character to the original fern. The prothalli carry male and female organs for fertilisation and production of a new generation of fern plants. Because of this method of sexual increase it is impossible to make the controlled crosses between ferns that are possible with many flowering plants. Instead, if an attempt at hydridisation is to be made between two different fern species, or even between varieties of the same species, spores of the two kinds must be sown together in the hope that when the prothalli develop, cross fertilisation (which is effected by mobile, water-borne male sex cells) will take place and some hybrids will eventually appear.

Some ferns produce little plantlets, like bulbils, on their fronds and if these fronds are pegged to the surface of moist peaty soil without being detached from their plants, the plantlets will develop and can be detached and potted singly. They will resemble their parents in every particular and provide a useful method of increasing some garden varieties with beautiful frond variegations. Division of the rhizomes or creeping stems produces similar results and is best carried out when re-potting in spring.

These frond variegations are not, as a rule, transmitted by spores though they do occur spontaneously, though rarely, by natural mutation or sporting. There are not so many of the frond variegations among the tender as among hardy ferns, probably because there has not been the same effort to search for them and preserve them.

Raising Ferns

Asplenium is an important genus of ferns which is known by the common name of spleenwort. This species, *Asplenium nidus*, prefers a warm greenhouse, though it will survive at lower temperatures

Ferns can be increased most readily by dividing large plants when replanting or re-potting. Take care that each piece contains a growing shoot or crown and roots. Where possible break up the large plants with the hands only, but if necessary use two hand forks thrust in back to back in the middle of the plant and lever them apart.

With plants such as *Asplenium bulbiferum* which make tiny plantlets on the fronds, peg these fronds to the surface of moist soil without removing them from the plant. When the plantlets begin to grow and form roots of their own, cut them out carefully with the soil attached and plant them in 3-in. pots.

To raise ferns from spores use moist peat seed compost in clean plastic pots. Make the surface quite level and moderately firm, dust the spores over it as evenly as possible and cover with a pane of glass. Keep the pot in a shady frame or greenhouse and when water is required give it by holding the pot almost to its rim in water for about a minute, then allow the surplus to drain away.

The prothalli will appear as green scale-like growths on the surface of the compost. Some weeks later tiny fronds will appear and when the little plants are large enough to be handled they can be carefully pricked out into pans or boxes of the same compost as used for potting ferns.

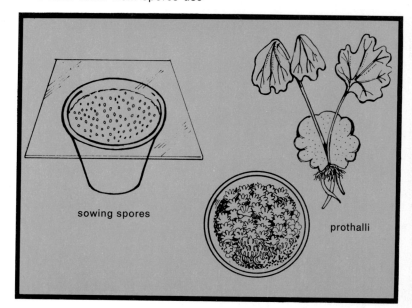

sowing spores

prothalli

Cultivation

Platycerium bifurcatum is aptly named the Stag's Horn Fern. It can be grown on a block of wood or cork and this can then be suspended so that the fern is growing on its side

Greenhouse ferns should be grown in a mixture of 2 parts by volume sphagnum peat or well-rotted beech or oak leafmould, 1 part medium loam and 1 part coarse sand or well-broken charcoal.

Re-pot when necessary in March but as a rule this need only be done every second or third year. Water the plants rather sparingly for the first few weeks after re-potting then more freely as the roots grow out into the new soil. Water established ferns fairly freely from April to September, and just sufficiently to keep the soil moist for the rest of the year.

Grow ferns in a north-facing greenhouse or in one that is shaded from direct sunshine, if necessary fixing slat blinds on the house so that the strong light is broken.

Ideal temperatures differ according to the kind of fern being grown but most of those commonly cultivated in pots will thrive in a winter minimum temperature of 7°C. (45° F.). It is unlikely that artificial heat will be needed from April to October inclusive when the problem is often to keep the greenhouse sufficiently cool. This will be helped by syringing with water the walls, paths and staging between the pots, but do not wet the fronds of the plants themselves.

Kinds of Ferns

Maidenhair ferns are amongst the most handsome of ferns. *Adiantum venustum* is a splendid greenhouse plant and, since it is almost hardy, it can be planted in sheltered places out of doors

Adiantum, the maidenhair fern, is one of the most popular and beautiful of all. There are numerous kinds, the most frequently grown being *A. cuneatum*. It enjoys warmth and in poorly heated houses may lose its leaves in winter, but new ones will appear in spring. *A. capillus-veneris* is much hardier and can be grown out of doors in some places, while *A. pedatum* is the hardiest of all and is often planted out of doors. It will lose its leaves in winter, but under glass it remains evergreen.

Of the aspleniums, known as spleenwort, by far the most popular is *A. bulbiferum*, so called because of the little plantlets which form like bulbils along the fronds and which readily grow into new plants. Great quantities of this fern are produced commercially as it is one of the best for room cultivation as well as for greenhouses. *Asplenium nidus* is very different in appearance and requirements, making a shuttlecock of long, undivided shining green fronds, and enjoying a fairly warm greenhouse though it will survive at lower temperatures.

Blechnum gibbum makes a plume of fronds on top of a short, thick stem, almost like a miniature tree fern. It is distinctive and easy and can be grown in rooms as well as greenhouses.

re-potting

Asplenium nidus

Blechnum gibbum

Kinds of Ferns

Woodwardia radicans is an ideal fern for the cool greenhouse or conservatory. It is important to keep it under cool conditions as in heat it is prone to attack from certain pests

Pteris arguta is one of the ribbon ferns and it should be grown in a warm greenhouse. It is an especially attractive fern with delicate, well-marked foliage

Cyrtomium falcatum

Davallia bullata

Cyrtomium falcatum is a popular commercial fern equally suitable for rooms or greenhouses. Known as the Holly Fern, because of the thick texture and dark green colour of the large segments of its fronds, it is very nearly hardy.

Davallia bullata is known as the Squirrel's-foot Fern, and *D. canariensis* as the Hare's-foot Fern, because of the shape of the brown, furry ground-hugging stems from which the finely divided fronds grow. They are among the loveliest of ferns, and there are numerous other beautiful davallias, many of which make good plants for hanging baskets.

Dicksonia antarctica is the Australian Tree Fern, which makes a great cartwheel of fronds on top of a stout, tall trunk. Young specimens can be grown in pots but as they get bigger they need to be planted in borders of soil. In sheltered seaside gardens in the south and west they can be grown out of doors in damp shady places.

Lygodium japonicum is one of the few climbing ferns and should be given bamboo canes or vertically strained wires around which it will wind itself. Its finely divided fronds are very attractive.

Woodwardia radicans can be grown out of doors in a sheltered position provided it is well protected in winter, and it is also an attractive plant for a hanging basket.

Nephrolepis exaltata is known as the Ladder Fern because of the ladder-like pattern of its fronds, which may be 3 ft. or more long. There are a great many varieties in some of which the fronds are so finely divided that they look like moss. All are easily grown in rooms or greenhouses.

Platycerium bifurcatum, known as the Stag's Horn Fern because of the antler-like appearance of its grey-green fronds, does not require soil and will grow well on a block of wood or cork to which it can be bound with a wad of sphagnum moss around its roots. The block can then be suspended so that the fern is growing on its side, which is its natural habit. Water the plants by immersing them for a few minutes, daily in spring and summer, much less frequently in autumn and winter. This fern can be grown in rooms.

Some of the greenhouse kinds of pteris are known as ribbon ferns because of the long, narrow, ribbon-like segments to the fronds. They are among the most popular of pot ferns because of the ease with which they can be grown in greenhouses or rooms. The principal kinds are *Pteris cretica* which has a variegated variety with a white stripe down the centre of each frond segment, and *P. serrulata* which has a lovely variety with crested fronds. *P. tremula* has more finely divided fronds and is equally easy to grow.

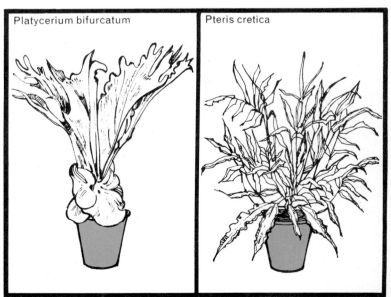

Platycerium bifurcatum

Pteris cretica

Filmies, Selaginellas

Keeping Ferns Healthy

Though selaginellas are not ferns, they are closely related and thrive under similar conditions. They are ideal plants for the front of a greenhouse staging and will also grow happily amongst ferns

A fernery, which can be established on a smaller scale than the one shown here, is the ideal way of maintaining the humid atmosphere which ferns enjoy and which discourages attacks from some pests

Filmy ferns have the most finely divided fronds of all, but require special conditions of quite dense shade and a very humid atmosphere. They are ideal for growing in Wardian cases, bottle gardens or plant cabinets in which the air is constantly saturated with moisture and the fronds are always damp.

There are numerous kinds, among the best being the Prince of Wales's Feather Fern, *Leptopteris superba*; the Killarney Fern, *Trichomanes radicans* and the Tunbridge Wells Fern, *Hymenophyllum tunbridgense*.

Selaginellas also grow well in similar damp, quite cool, shady conditions. They are not ferns, but they are allied to them; they are flowerless, produce spores and have minute leaves which give them a moss-like appearance. Most of them are quite small plants which can be grown among the ferns or along the front of the greenhouse staging.

There are numerous kinds such as *Selaginella caulescens*, one of the taller ones which often exceeds 1 ft.; *S. cuspidata*, low and tufted, the leaves margined with white; *S. emmeliana*, taller, green but with a white variegated variety; *S. kraussiana*, which soon creeps out of its pots to cover staging or floor and *S. uncinata*, of trailing habit and blue-green in colour.

Ferns hardly ever suffer from disease, though occasionally mould appears on those with very finely divided fronds, and rusts can develop. There is little that can be done about rust except to cut off and burn any affected fronds, but moulds can be checked by letting the air dry a little and dusting the fern with flowers of sulphur. Care must be taken not to mistake for rust disease the natural spore clusters which form on fertile fronds and which are a means of propagation.

Most troublesome pest is thrips, a tiny, fast moving insect which sucks the sap in the fronds causing pale discolouration (especially along the veins) and curling of the fronds. This insect thrives in hot, dry air, so one way of countering it is to maintain a proper degree of humidity. Another is to fumigate occasionally with BHC (lindane).

Another fairly common pest is greenfly, which sucks sap and causes fronds to curl and become distorted. Use a BHC fumigant.

Mealy bugs are protected by a coating of a white waxy substance. Fortunately this makes them conspicuous and they can be picked off and destroyed as seen. Though malathion and diazinon sprays will kill mealy bugs they also damage ferns, so cannot safely be used.

Another mealy bug may attack the roots. If seen when re-potting it should be carefully hand picked, the roots washed in soapy water and then replaced in fresh soil.

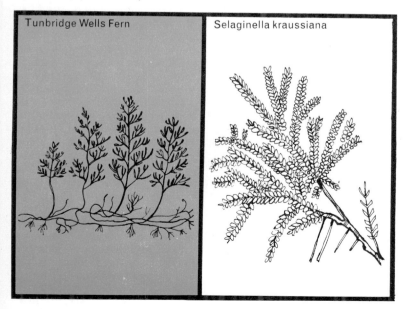

Tunbridge Wells Fern

Selaginella kraussiana

mealy bug

Greenhouse Calendar

January

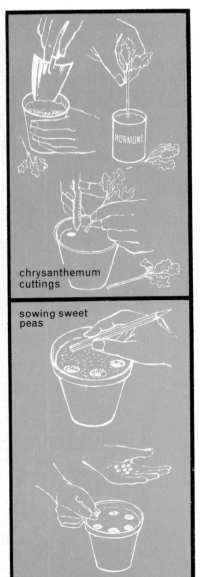

chrysanthemum cuttings

sowing sweet peas

Bulbs of the impressive hippeastrums should be started into growth in this month

Take cuttings of late-flowering chrysanthemums, and particularly those of large-flowered types required for exhibition. Root the cuttings in sandy soil in a greenhouse or a propagator in a temperature of 13 to 18°C. (55 to 65°F.).

Cuttings of perpetual-flowering carnations can also be taken and rooted in similar conditions. Prepare root cuttings of Oriental Poppies, anchusas, herbaceous phlox, verbascums, Californian Tree Poppies (or romneyas), ramondas, haberleas and morisias.

In a greenhouse with a temperature of 15 to 18°C. (60 to 65°F.), sow seed of antirrhinums, begonias, cannas, gloxinias, streptocarpus, Scarlet Salvias and verbenas. Sweet peas can be sown in a slightly lower temperature.

Place tubers of begonias and gloxinias and achimenes rhizomes in a temperature of 15 to 18°C. (60 to 65°F.) to start them into growth. Bring hippeastrum bulbs into a similar temperature to start growth.

Transfer pots and bowls of daffodils, hyacinths and tulips, as well as *Iris* Wedgwood, from their frame or plunge bed into a moderately heated greenhouse to bring them into early flower.

Bring early flowering rock plants and small bulbs in pots and pans into an alpine house or any unheated, well ventilated and well lighted structure to protect the opening flowers from wind, rain and frost.

February

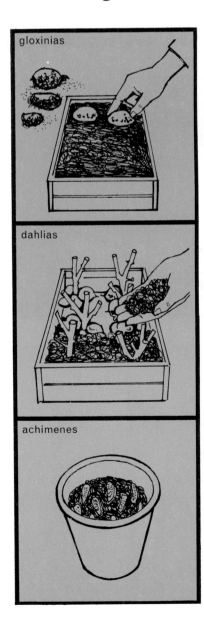

gloxinias

dahlias

achimenes

Cacti and succulents are always fascinating. Many can be raised from seed sown this month

Continue all the work recommended for January.

Start more dormant tubers of begonias, gloxinias and achimenes.

Place dormant dahlia tubers in large pots or boxes or pack them close together in a greenhouse border surrounded and just covered with soil. Maintain a temperature of 13 to 15°C. (55 to 60°F.) to start the tubers into growth so that cuttings may be taken when the new shoots are 2 to 3 in. in length.

Continue to take cuttings of chrysanthemums, particularly those required to provide cut flowers in autumn and winter or to make large decorative plants at that time of the year.

Prune *Luculia gratissima* and *Lippia citriodora*, the former by shortening the previous year's growth to a few inches, the latter by cutting back almost to the base. Most other greenhouse shrubs (not in flower) should only be pruned enough to keep them tidy.

Gradually reduce the water supply to poinsettias so that the plants can have a short rest before being pruned and restarted to provide cuttings for a fresh stock.

Sow freesias in a temperature of 15 to 18°C. (60 to 65°F.). If sown thinly in pots the seedlings can grow on undisturbed to flower in autumn and winter ahead of plants grown from summer-potted corms.

Sow seeds of cacti in a similar temperature and do not prick out early but wait until the little plants have formed good root systems.

The end of the month is a good time to sow seed of the bushy Charm chrysanthemums

In a greenhouse or propagating frame with a temperature of 15 to 18°C. (60 to 65°F.), sow seeds of many half-hardy annuals and bedding plants. These can include antirrhinums, begonias, cannas, impatiens, petunias, Scarlet Salvias, salpiglossis and verbenas. Towards the end of the month, sow dahlias and charm and cascade chrysanthemums.

Also sow various summer-flowering greenhouse plants, including celosias and Cockscombs, *Clerodendrum fallax,* greenhouse begonias, gloxinias and streptocarpus.

Prick out any seedlings from January sowings that are sufficiently large to be handled. Often seedlings transplant most suc-

cessfully when they have their first seed leaves and before they begin to grow the later leaves which are usually different in character. But with some very small seedlings, such as those of begonias and antirrhinums, this is just not practicable and it is better to wait until the seedlings have their first characteristic leaves.

Prune greenhouse plants that are to be trained as climbers in the house or are simply to be grown as well-shaped specimens. In the first category are bougainvilleas, the blue plumbago (Cape Leadwort) and ivy-leaved pelargoniums; and in the second, bouvardias, gardenias, fuchsias and zonal pelargoniums.

March

Re-pot greenhouse plants that have become pot-bound, are in need of a change of soil or need starting into growth. These will include ornamental varieties of asparagus, codiaeum (crotons), coleus, cacti and other succulents, ferns, fuchsias, palms, pelargoniums (geraniums), smilax and most house plants that are not actually in flower at the time.

Pot rooted cuttings of chrysanthemums and perpetual-flowering carnations and move earlier plants, that have already filled their first small pots with roots, into larger pots.

Continue to take cuttings of chrysanthemums and perpetual-flowering carnations. Early March is a good time to take cuttings of

Any plants, such as these codiaeums, which are pot-bound should now be re-potted

early-flowering chrysanthemums to be planted out of doors in May.

Take cuttings of dahlias as shoots reach a suitable length (2 to 3 in.). Pot earlier dahlia cuttings singly in 3-in. pots as soon as they are well rooted, and grow on in a light greenhouse in a temperature of 12 to 15°C. (55 to 60°F.).

Also take cuttings of fuchsias, heliotropes and pelargoniums and root in a propagating frame or box in the greenhouse. Pot on cuttings of any of these taken the previous summer or early autumn. Pinch out the growing tips as necessary to induce bushy plants.

Re-pot any orchids that are starting into growth. Large plants can be divided. Old pseudobulbs (back bulbs) are best discarded.

canna

bougainvillea

Christmas Cactus

Pelargonium

Greenhouse Calendar

March

Take cuttings of winter-flowering begonias, such as *Begonia* Gloire de Lorraine, also of poinsettias, and root in a propagating frame with bottom heat and a temperature of 18°C. (65°F.).

Also take cuttings of various greenhouse plants that are most conveniently reproduced in this way. These may include abutilons, bouvardias, coleus, daturas, gardenias, jacobinias, lantanas, and the double-flowered tropaeolums. All will root readily in a propagating frame and a temperature of 15°C. (60°F.).

Stop young perpetual-flowering carnation plants by breaking out the topmost joint of each plant when it has made about seven pairs of leaves. This will encourage side-shoots to develop and lead to the bushy plants which are so desired.

Divide large roots of canna, potting the divisions in the smallest pots that will contain them comfortably, and grow them on in a temperature of 15°C. (60°F.).

Pot smithianthas, one stolon in each 4- or 5-in. pot, and start into growth in a temperature of 18°C. (65°F.).

Pot September-sown schizanthus into 5- or 6-in. pots in John Innes No. 2 Potting Compost or a peat compost. Grow in a light position at a temperature of 10 to 15°C. (50 to 60°F.).

Re-pot anthuriums, also any house plants and ferns that need it.

Sow seed of browallia and exacum for late summer flowers.

Abutilon Fireball flowers in the spring. Take cuttings this month and root at 15°C. (60°F.)

April

Sow winter-flowering primulas of all kinds including *Primula malacoides*, *P. obconica* and *P. sinensis*. Germinate in a temperature of about 15°C. (60°F.).

Sow annuals, both hardy and half-hardy, for growing on as flowering pot plants in the greenhouse. Particularly suitable kinds are *Begonia semperflorens*, annual carnations, exacum, gazanias, nemesias, petunias, salpiglossis, *Limonium suworowii* (statice), ten-week stocks, verbenas and zinnias.

Continue to take cuttings of chrysanthemums and dahlias. Pot rooted cuttings singly and remove earlier potted cuttings of these plants to a frame to be hardened off. Chrysanthemums are hardier than dahlias and may therefore go into a frame a week or so earlier.

Pot on rooted cuttings of perpetual-flowering carnations, chrysanthemums, fuchsias, pelargoniums (geraniums) and other greenhouse plants into larger pots as they fill their small pots with roots.

Re-pot any old plants that appear overcrowded or pot-bound, i.e. with roots tightly wound round one another in the pot.

Re-pot cacti that have outgrown their pots, but annual re-potting is unlikely to be necessary.

Take cuttings of fuchsias and pelargoniums (geraniums) if stock is short or late flowering plants are required.

This is a good time for a major re-potting of all the plants which need it

Calceolarias may need staking and tying to support the weight of flowers

May

Perpetual-flowering carnations are planted into their final pots this month

Pot on begonias and gloxinias as they fill their pots with roots, and shade from strong sunshine.

Continue to take cuttings of winter-flowering begonias and poinsettias. Pot up singly any earlier cuttings that are well rooted and grow on in a temperature of 15 to 18°C. (60 to 65°F.).

Re-pot evergreen azaleas and camellias when they have finished flowering. A peat-based compost suits these plants well.

Gradually reduce the water supply to freesias and lachenalias that have been flowering during the winter or early spring so that they can rest for a while, but keep young freesias growing by watering them freely.

Pot on young cyclamen plants as they fill the smaller pots with roots.

Start late batches of achimenes and hippeastrums to give a succession of flowers.

Stake and tie greenhouse calceolarias carefully as they come into flower. The dwarf or nanus varieties do not require staking.

Fumigate the greenhouse with a suitable insecticide to keep down greenflies and other pests.

Continue to stop perpetual-flowering carnation cuttings.

Sow schizanthus to flower in summer and early autumn.

Start to harden off all plants that are to go outdoors in summer. Many plants, including greenhouse azaleas, can now be kept in frames, except in cold areas.

Shade greenhouses from strong sunshine unless plants are being grown that need as much sun heat as possible e.g. cacti and other succulents.

Give free ventilation by day but close ventilators early to trap sun heat, especially if there is a risk of frost.

Water pot plants freely and start to feed established plants with weak liquid manure.

Fumigate occasionally with nicotine smoke generators to kill greenflies, whiteflies etc.

Pot on spring-rooted cuttings of pelargoniums, fuchsias, winter-flowering begonias, poinsettias etc. as they fill the smaller pots with roots.

Pot late-flowering chrysanthemums into the pots in which they will grow on all the summer and flower in the autumn or winter. Place a bamboo cane in each pot and then stand the plants outdoors in a sheltered but sunny place on a firm ash or gravel base. Keep well watered.

Pinch out the tips of chrysanthemum plants grown for autumn or winter cut flowers or as decorative plants.

Insert cuttings of dwarf chrysanthemums to make small pot plants.

Also pot perpetual-flowering carnations into their final pots, usually 6 or 7 in. in diameter. Break out ends of side growths when each has made about 8 pairs of leaves.

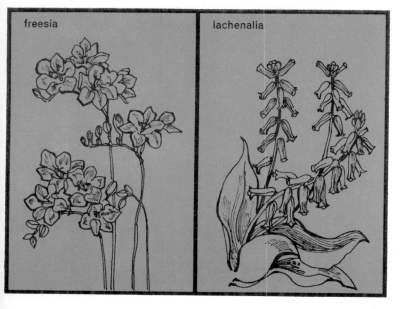

freesia

lachenalia

blinds

potting pelargonium

Greenhouse Calendar

May

The summer-flowering tuberous begonia Roy Hartley has large flowers of excellent quality

Gradually reduce the amount of water given to Arum Lilies, lachenalias, nerines and freesias that have flowered in winter and allow the plants to rest for a time. Place nerines in the sunniest part of the greenhouse so that they get a good baking.

Sow cinerarias in a greenhouse or frame. No artificial heat is necessary at this time of the year.

Prick out seedlings of winter-flowering primulas, such as *Primula malacoides, P. obconica* and *P. sinensis*. Grow on in a shaded greenhouse or frame and water fairly freely. Make further sowings for successive flowers.

Plant up summer-flowering begonias and gloxinias in the pots in which they will flower.

Grow on in a shaded greenhouse with only sufficient artificial heat to prevent the temperature falling below 10°C. (50°F.) at night.

Fill hanging baskets with geraniums, trailing lobelias and campanulas, pendulous begonias etc. and suspend them in the greenhouse for a few weeks to get established before hanging them outdoors.

Complete the hardening off of all plants that are to go out of doors in summer. Frame lights can be removed on all fine days.

Prune plants of *Euphorbia splendens* that are getting too tall and are not well branched.

Sow browallia to provide plants to flower in autumn and winter.

June

Cinerarias flower in winter and spring but the seed should be sown this month

Sow calceolarias and make further sowings of cinerarias and of winter-flowering primulas. This is a very good time to sow seed of *Primula malacoides.*

Prick out seedlings of cinerarias and winter-flowering primulas from earlier sowings, and pot the most forward seedlings singly in 3-in. pots.

Complete the potting of late-flowering chrysanthemums and perpetual-flowering carnations.

Stand out any remaining chrysanthemums on a gravel or ash base in a sheltered place out of doors. Perpetual-flowering carnations may be placed in a frame for the summer if the greenhouse is required for other purposes.

Many plants only require green-house protection when there is danger of frost, and can stand out of doors all summer.

See that greenhouses are well shaded on bright, sunny days, give ample ventilation to keep the temperature from rising too high, and damp down paths and stagings to maintain plenty of moisture in the atmosphere.

Pot on begonias and gloxinias as the smaller pots become comfortably filled with roots.

Stop all chrysanthemum plants that have not already been so treated by pinching out the top of each plant to make it branch. Some late-flowering varieties can be stopped twice; for such information consult one of the specialist chrysanthemum catalogues.

pricking out

hanging basket

standing out chrysanthemums

shading with whitewash

This regal pelargonium is Summertime. It is one of many varieties for greenhouse culture

Move young cyclamen plants into 5-in. pots as soon as they have filled the smaller pots with roots. Keep the plants growing all summer in a cool frame or a shady greenhouse and do not let them get dry at any time. Remove old cyclamen plants that have already flowered to a shady frame and give very little water until August.

Re-pot pot-grown auriculas. When doing this, examine them for root aphids (small grey lice on the roots), and if any are seen, wash the roots in a solution of an insecticide such as lindane, derris or malathion.

Many woody-stemmed plants, both outdoor and indoor, can be increased by cuttings taken between June and August and rooted in a propagating frame or box or in polythene bags in a greenhouse. Prepare cuttings from firm young shoots and insert a few each month as some may root more freely than others.

Towards the end of the month, when regal pelargoniums are no longer flowering freely, cut the plants back and place them in a frame or sunny place out of doors for a few weeks.

Fumigate occasionally with nicotine or other suitable smoke generators to keep down pests. Use azobenzene if red spider mite is troublesome.

While plants of *Solanum capsicum* are in flower syringe daily with water to encourage fruits to set.

re-potting cyclamen

July

spraying chrysanthemums

damping down

stopping carnation

Pot-grown chrysanthemums must now be kept well watered. Feed every 10 to 14 days

Water pot-grown chrysanthemums well and feed every 10 to 14 days. Spray with a good insecticide to keep them free of aphids and other pests.

Ventilate greenhouses freely in sunny weather. Many plants will require shading from direct sunlight and, except in the case of most succulents (including cacti) and carnations which prefer a dry atmosphere, water paths and syringe the walls and staging with water to maintain plenty of moisture in the air.

Stop young perpetual-flowering carnation plants for the last time by breaking out the end of each shoot.

Cuttings of many plants, including hardy trees and shrubs as well as those commonly grown in greenhouses, can be rooted in a close frame or under mist. Young growths that are becoming firm at the base make the best cuttings. Most will root more rapidly and certainly with bottom heat, i.e. the soil warmed from below so that it is at least as warm, possibly a little warmer, than the mean temperature of the air. The cut should be made through a node (where the leaf joins the stem), and the cut surface dipped into hormone rooting compound.

Fumigate the greenhouse occasionally to keep down pests. If whitefly appears several fumigations may be necessary to cope with the further batches of adult 'flies' that will emerge from the scales even after fumigation.

Greenhouse Calendar

July

Tennessee Waltz, a popular fuchsia for the cool greenhouse. Take cuttings from mid-July

Prick off winter-flowering primulas, cinerarias and calceolarias and pot singly those that have already been pricked off and have grown into sturdy little plants. Earlier batches already in pots should be moved on to larger sizes as soon as they fill the smaller pots with roots.

Make further sowings of calceolarias, cinerarias and *Primula malacoides* for successional flowering. At this season germination is just as good in a frame as in a greenhouse.

Pot on all young plants grown from cuttings, divisions etc. as they fill their smaller pots and from the middle of the month take cuttings of greenhouse fuchsias.

Keep nerines in the sunniest part of the greenhouse and do not water

them. Keep Arum Lilies rather dry for a few weeks before re-potting them in August. Stand regal pelargoniums outdoors in a sunny, sheltered place for a few weeks and water very sparingly.

Shade begonias and gloxinias well, water freely and feed them every 10 days or so with weak liquid manure. Stake and tie the flowering stems of begonias carefully to support the heavy blooms.

Take care not to allow the air to get too dry for those plants that thrive best in a moist atmosphere. This includes almost all foliage plants, ferns and orchids, as well as begonias and gloxinias. Keep paths and staging gravel wet, syringe between pots or install a humidifier.

August

Some flower buds may appear on late-flowering chrysanthemums during August and must be reduced to one per stem if large flowers are required.

Continue to ventilate greenhouses freely, to syringe frequently and to shade those plants that do not like intense heat or strong light. In small greenhouses it may be necessary at times to leave the doors open to keep the temperature down.

As the earliest batches of achimenes, tuberous-rooted begonias and gloxinias come to the end of their flowering period, gradually reduce the water supply and allow them to die down naturally.

Pot on winter-flowering primu-

This is a good time to begin planting up bowls of narcissus bulbs for winter flowering

las, cinerarias and calceolarias when they fill the smaller pots with roots, keeping them in a frame if possible as these plants do not like high temperatures.

Pot hyacinths, narcissi and other bulbs required for winter flowering. Bulbs for indoor flowering should also be planted now in bowls of bulb fibre. Keep them all in a cool, dark place for the time being or plunge pot-grown bulbs (but not bowl-grown ones) under 4 in. of sand or peat out of doors.

Pot veltheimias and keep in a sunny frame.

Sow winter-flowering stocks, also exacum and schizanthus to flower early next year.

greenhouse shading

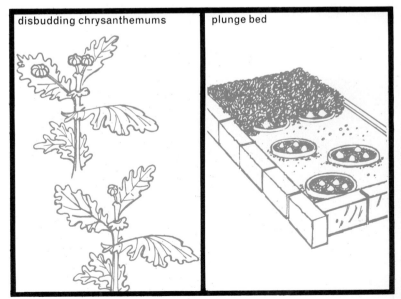

disbudding chrysanthemums

plunge bed

Lachenalia bulbs should be potted during August to flower in winter and early spring

starting an Arum Lily

potting freesia corms

Pot Arum Lilies or re-start those that have been resting during the summer by gradually increasing the quantity of water given to them.

Re-start nerines or purchase and pot bulbs in John Innes No. 1 Potting Compost, keeping the bulbs well up in the pots so that much of the bulb is exposed.

Re-pot freesia corms early in the month but keep them in a frame or a really cool greenhouse for the time being. Pot lachenalias or plant them in hanging baskets.

Sow cyclamen for flowering in the greenhouse the following year. Cyclamen seeds are often slow and irregular in germinating so prick out the seedlings as soon as they become sufficiently large, but do not discard the seed pans for several months. Re-pot in a shady frame old cyclamen corms that have been resting during the summer.

Cut back regal pelargoniums, start to water the plants more freely and when new shoots are 3 or 4 in. long take some cuttings.

Continue to fumigate the greenhouse occasionally. This is a month when whitefly, red spider mites and mealy bug can be troublesome. Azobenzene aerosols give good control of red spider mites, and mealy bugs may be sponged off with derris.

Take cuttings of zonal and ivy-leaved pelargoniums, also of fuchsias, gazanias, lampranthus (mesembryanthemums) and other plants of doubtful hardiness.

September

If greenhouses can be completely emptied they should be fumigated by burning sulphur in them, but the fumes are fatal to plants which must not be returned to the greenhouse until all traces of smoke have dispersed.

Make certain that the heating apparatus is functioning properly and carry out any necessary repairs before the winter. If the apparatus is thermostatically controlled check the operation and accuracy of the thermostat.

Cinerarias are liable to be attacked by leaf miner maggots which leave snaky white tunnels in the leaves. If these are seen, feel for the maggots in the leaves and kill them with the point of a penknife or spray them with an insect-

Cyclamen are among the most decorative of plants. Pot seedlings singly this month

icide such as BHC or trichlorphon.

Sow schizanthus for spring and early summer flowering, if not already done in August. Also sow any annuals required for use as pot plants in the greenhouse.

Pot singly any seedlings of cyclamen that appear from the August sowings but do not discard the seed pans or disturb the surface more than is essential as germination is often slow and irregular.

Continue to take cuttings of zonal and ivy-leaved pelargoniums, gazanias, lampranthus (mesembryanthemums), fuchsias.

Cuttings of coleus root readily in September and young plants are often easier to over-winter than old plants.

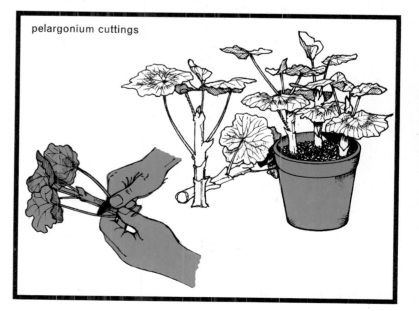

pelargonium cuttings

Greenhouse Calendar

September

The most popular lily for greenhouse cultivation is *Lilium longiflorum*. Pot the bulbs now

Many plants need all the light they can get in September and little shading is likely to be required. Syringing and damping down are also probably unnecessary except for a few moisture-loving plants.

Continue to pot bulbs for the greenhouse. This is a good time to pot *Lilium longiflorum* and other greenhouse lilies if the bulbs can be acquired so early. Pot a further batch of freesia corms for successive flowering.

Gradually reduce the amount of water given to begonias, gloxinias and hippeastrums so that they may ripen their growth. Old cyclamen corms re-potted in August will need increasing amounts of water as they start vigorously into growth. Nerines will also require more water as their flower stems grow.

Pot on winter-flowering primulas, calceolarias and cinerarias into the pots in which they will flower. Towards the end of the month bring them in from the frame where they have passed the summer back to a light, frost-proof greenhouse.

Also bring into the greenhouse any other tender plants that have been out of doors or in frames, including perpetual carnations, late-flowering chrysanthemums, Winter Cherries (solanums) and Indian azaleas. House plants which are returned indoors should have large leaves sponged of any dust.

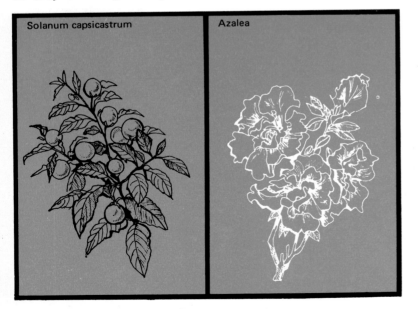

October

Primula obconica is available in a range of colours. It flowers in winter and for most of the year

If not already done in September, bring in late-flowering chrysanthemums and any other greenhouse plants that have been standing out of doors during the summer.

Gradually reduce the water supply to tuberous-rooted begonias, gloxinias, achimenes and ordinary hippeastrums so that by the end of the month they can be dried off completely for the winter.

Finish any potting on of young plants that was not completed in September, including winter-flowering primulas, cinerarias, calceolarias and cyclamen, but move the plants only if their pots are uncomfortably full of roots.

See that plants have as much light and as much room as possible and be careful when watering not to wet the leaves and crowns unnecessarily. Fertilisers should not be used at all during the autumn and winter months.

Continue to pot tulips, hyacinths and other bulbs for the greenhouse, including hippeastrums specially prepared for winter flowering. Bring in the earliest potted batches if they have formed plenty of roots and keep in full light in a temperature of 10 to 15° C. (50 to 60° F.).

Pot annuals sown in August and September, also winter-flowering stocks.

Disbud perpetual-flowering carnations, retaining only one flower bud per stem.

Pot a further batch of freesia corms to provide a succession of flowers.

November

Varieties of *Camellia japonica* make good pot plants for the cool greenhouse

Use sufficient artificial heat to maintain the necessary minimum temperatures for the plants being grown. Ventilate only by day when the weather is bright and there is sufficient sunshine to maintain a temperature of 13 to 15° C. (55 to 60° F.) and water carefully, only when it is really necessary.

Bring successive batches of bulbs in pots from frames or outdoor plunge beds into the greenhouse, but only when they have filled their pots fairly well with roots. At first the night temperatures should not be above 13° C. (55° F.) – less will do.

Pot astilbes, dicentras and other herbaceous plants to be gently forced in spring, also roses and shrubs such as Indian azaleas, camellias, hydrangeas, lilacs, genistas and deutzias.

Keep established Indian azaleas well watered and raise the temperature a little to around 15° C. (60° F.) if early flowers are wanted.

Continue to remove all diseased leaves and stems and to dust such plants with flowers of sulphur.

To support the lengthening flower stems of freesias, place a few sticks in the pots and loop raffia or fillis (soft string) around them.

Cut down indoor chrysanthemums as they finish flowering, keeping only enough plants of each variety for propagation purposes.

Reduce the water supply to smithianthas until quite dry and then store them like achimenes.

December

Poinsettias are a colourful sight this month. Red, pink or white varieties are available

Begin taking cuttings of perpetual-flowering carnations, choosing short sideshoots from about half way up the flowering stems.

Continue to cut back chrysanthemums as they finish flowering and to bring in successive batches of bulbs in pots to be forced gently in the greenhouse. Keep a close watch on temperatures, particularly now that nights are very cold. Many greenhouse plants suffer if temperatures fall below 7° C. (45° F.). If necessary, use auxiliary heating, such as an oil stove, if the main apparatus is inadequate.

Keep the air as dry as possible and water rather sparingly as plants suffer more from cold when overwet. Remove any diseased leaves and dust infected plants with flowers of sulphur or with thiram.

Give flowering plants such as winter begonias, cinerarias, lachenalias and primulas the lightest positions in the house and keep the glass as clean as possible at this time of the year.

Do not let poinsettias and saintpaulias get chilled while in flower.

Prune oleander by shortening to a few inches all growth made in the past year. Prune greenhouse roses, including any permanently planted climbing roses such as Maréchal Niel and Niphetos.

Examine tubers and bulbs in store including achimenes, begonias, cannas, gloxinias, hippeastrums and smithianthas and dust with flowers of sulphur if there is any sign of decay.

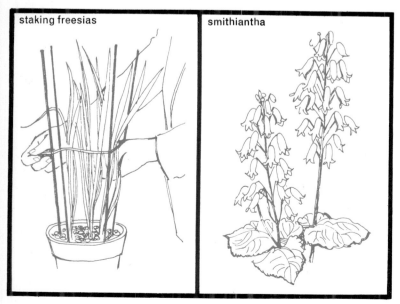

staking freesias

smithiantha

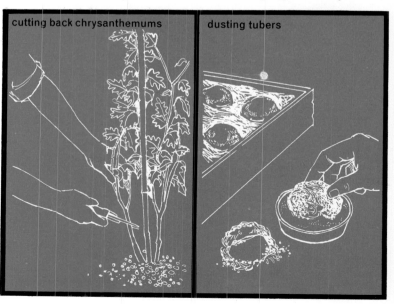

cutting back chrysanthemums

dusting tubers

INDEX

(*NOTE: Illustrated items are indicated by page numbers in italics*)

A

Abutilon *171, 242, 302*
Acacia *243*
    False *and* Rose (Robinia) *73*
Acaena *175*
Acalypha *243*
Acanthus *85*
Acer (Maple) *76, 215*
Achillea *93, 130*
Achimenes *244, 300, 303, 306, 308*
acid/alkaline test *27*
Acidanthera *274*
Aconite, Winter (Eranthis) *119*
Aconitum *88*
Acorus *195*
Acroclinium *185*
Adam's Needle (Yucca) *61*
Adiantum *297*
Aechmea *197, 248*
Aeonium *212*
Aerides *292*
Aeschynanthus *244*
Aethionema *130*
African Daisy *140*
African Lily (Agapanthus) *275*
African Violet (Saintpaulia) *228, 271, 309*
Agapanthus *275*
Agave *210*
Ageratum *144*
Aglaonema *195*
Agrostis *144*
Aichryson *212*
air layering *36, 228*
Akebia *64*
Alisma *159*
alkaline soil *27*
Allamanda *280*
Allium *115*
Almond *37, 70*
Aloe *210*
alpine house *236-41*
Alstroemeria *180*
Aluminium Plant (Pilea) *204*
Alyssum *132, 144*
Amaryllis *116*
Amaryllis (Hippeastrum) q.v.
Amazon Lily (Eucharis) *276*
Amelanchier *76*
American Currant (Ribes) *45*
Ampelopsis *63*
Ananas *204*
Anaphalis *92*
Anchusa *300*
Andromeda *238*
Androsace *130*
Anemones *85, 115, 116*
Angel's Trumpets (Datura) *259*
Angraecum *292*
annuals *30-33, 140-155*
    cold greenhouses *232*
annuals, half-hardy *179, 301, 302*
annuals, hardy *178, 302*

Antennaria *128*, 131
Anthemis *89, 91*
Antholyza *123*
Anthurium *194, 244, 302*
Antirrhinum *141, 300, 301*
Aphelandra *195, 257*
aphids: greenfly 7, *113*, 295, 299
    root aphids 305
Aponogeton *158*
Aporocactus *206, 208*
aquatic plants *158-9*
Aquilegia *88, 131*
Arabis *132*
Aralia *196*
Araucaria *196*
arbours *11*
Archangel, Variegated Yellow *175*
arches *10, 63*
Arctotis *140*
Ardisia *196, 272*
Arenaria *131*
Argyroderma *213*
Aristolochia *280*
Armeria *130*
Artemisia *92*
Artillery Plant (Pilea) *204*
Arum Lily *244, 304, 306, 307*
Aruncus *102*
Arundinaria (Bamboo) *39*
Asclepias *243*
Asparagus Fern *245*
Aspidistra *196*
Asplenium *200, 296, 297*
Asters *141*
Asters, perennial (Michaelmas Daisy)
    98, 173
Astilbe *102, 233, 309*
Astrophytum *208*
Aubrieta *125, 132*
Aucuba *81*
Aunt Eliza (Antholyza) *123*
Auricula *138, 240, 305*
Australian Heath (Epacris) *260*
Australian Tree Fern *298*
Autumn Crocus (Colchicum) *117*
Avena *144*
avenues *13*
Avocado Pear *204, 255*
Azalea *40, 194, 235, 245, 303, 308, 309*
    bonsai *215*
azobenzene *208, 227, 305, 307*

B

BHC insecticide/fumigant *295, 299, 307*
Babiana *275*
'balled' plants *25*
Balloon Flowers (Platycodon) *86*
Balsam *169*

Bamboo *39*
Banana (Musa) *273*
Banjo Fig *201*
Barbados Lily (Hippeastrum) *278*
Barberry *see* Berberis
Barberton Daisy (Gerbera) *261*
Barrel Cacti *209*
Bear's Breeches (Acanthus) *85*
bedding plants *168-71, 301*
beds, flower *12*
Beech *71, 80*
Begonia *168, 228, 246-7*
    (*see also* Greenhouse Calendar *300-309*)
Belladonna Lily (Amaryllis) *116*
Bellflower, Chilean (Lapageria) *285*
Bellflowers (Campanula) *86, 133*
Bellis *153*
Bells of Ireland (Molucella) *179*
Beloperone *197, 248*
Berberis *41, 78, 81*, 188
Bergamots *86*
Bergenia *85*
berries, shrubs with *188*
besom, lawn *19*
Betula (Silver Birch) *71*
biennials *152-5, 179, 233*
Bignonia *287*
Billbergia *248*
Birch, Silver *71*
Bird of Paradise Flower (Strelitzia) *273*
bird tables and baths *11*
birds: as pests 7
Black-Eyed Susan (Thunbergia) *66, 282*
black spot 7, *113*
Blackthorn *76*
Blazing Star (Liatris) *96*
Blechnum *297*
Bleeding Heart (Dicentra) *90*
Bletilla (Bletia) *239*
blood, dried *29*
Blood Flower (Asclepias) *243*
Blood Lily (Haemanthus) *277*
Blue Lace Flower (Didiscus) *259*
Blue Throatwort (Trachelium) *259*
Bluebell *123*
Bluebell Creeper (Sollya) *287*
Bocconia *85*
Bog Arum *159*
Bog Bean *158*
Bomarea *285*
bonemeal *29*
Bonsai *214-15*
Bordeaux mixture 113
borders, mixed *12*
Boronia *249*
botrytis *227*
bottle gardens *193, 296, 299*
Bougainvillea *281, 301*
Bouvardia *249, 301, 302*
Box *80, 168*
Brachycome *140*

Brambles (Rubus) 53
Brassaia 205
Brassica 27
Breynia 243
Briar, Sweet 111
bricks 9, 10
Bridal Wreath (Francoa) 233, 261
Briza 144
broadcasting, seed 32
Bromeliads 197, 248
Broom 42, 177
Browallia 249, 302, 304
Brunfelsia 250
Bryophyllum 213
budding 37
Buddleia 41
bulb planter 24, 114
bulbils 115
bulbs:
    for cut flowers 182, 183
    for garden display 114-25, 174
    in a greenhouse 234, 274-9, 300, 306, 308, 309
    in bowls 194, 300, 306
    in pots 234, 300, 306, 308, 309
    pests and diseases 125
    planting 24, 25, 119
    small 237
    storing 119
    structure 274
Busy Lizzie (Impatiens) 169, 194, 268
Butomus 159
Butterfly Orchid (Oncidium) 294

C

Cabbage, Skunk (Lysichitum) 159
Cacti 206-13, 300, 301, 302
    sowing 300
Caladium 250
Calanthe 292
Calathea 198
Calceolaria 251, 303, 306, 308
calcium carbonate 27
calcium hydroxide 27
calcium oxide 27
calendar, greenhouse 300-309
Calendula 33, 145
Calico Bush (Kalmia) 52
Calico Flower (Aristolochia) 280
Californian Tree Poppy (Romneya) 300
Calla 159
Callicarpa 188
Callistemon 251
Callistephus 141
Calluna 50
Calocephalus 171
calomel dust 21, 125
Caltha 159
Camassia 120
Camellia 42, 181, 234, 303, 309
Campanula 86, 133, 152, 155, 173, 237, 252
Campion 99
Campsis 287
Canary Creeper (Tropaeolum) 68
Candle Plant (Kleinia) 213
Candytuft 132, 144
canker 113
Canna 252, 300, 301, 302
Canterbury Bells 152, 155, 179, 233
Cape Cowslip (Lachenalia) 276
Cape Ivy (Senecio) 202

Cape Jasmine (Gardenia) 250
capillary bench 220
Capsicum 253
capsid bugs 7
captan 7, 113
Caralluma 212
carbon 29
carboys (Bottle gardens) 193
Carnations:
    border 36, 148, 185
    perpetual flowering 34, 254
    (see also Greenhouse Calendar 300-309)
Carrion Flower (Stapelia) 212
Caryopteris 43
cascades 157
Cassia 281
Cassiope 238
castor meal 29
Catalpa 73
Catananche 176
caterpillars 7, 113
Catharanthus 268
Catmints 87
Cattleya 292
Ceanothus 44, 69
Celastrus 64
Celosia 249, 301
Celsia 249
Cement and Concrete Association 10
Centaurea 89, 143, 171
Centranthus 173
Century Plant (Agave) 210
Cephalocereus 209
Cerastium 133
Ceratostigma 43
Cercis 73
Cereus 209
Cestrum 282
Chaenomeles (Japanese Quince) 57, 69, 181
chalk 27
chalk soils 172, 173
Chamaecereus 208
Chamaecyparis 72, 79
Chamomile lawns 14
Cheiranthus 155
chemicals see fertilisers; fungicides;
    insecticides; manures; weedkillers
Chenille Plant (Acalypha) 243
Cherry 71
Cherry Pie (Heliotrope) 264
children:
    flowers to grow for 172
    in the garden 8
Chilean Bellflower (Lapageria) 285
Chilean Jasmine (Mandevilla) 283
Chillies 253
Chimney Bellflower (Campanula) 252
Chimonanthus (Winter Sweet) 61
Chincherinchees 115
Chinese Jasmine (Trachelospermum) 283
Chionodoxa 117
chipping: seeds 33
chlordane 21
Chlorophytum 198
Choisya 50
Chorizema 256
Christmas Cactus 191, 209, 301
Christmas Rose (Helleborus) 87, 188
Christ's Thorn (Euphorbia) 211
Chrysanthemum (see also Greenhouse Calendar
    300-309) 178, 186-7, 301
    annual 143
    cuttings 34, 300
    disbudding 187, 306

greenhouse 288-9, 304, 305
    pot-grown 304, 305
Cigar Flower (Cuphea) 257
Cineraria 171, 253, 304, 306, 307, 308, 309
Cinquefoil, Shrubby (Potentilla) 56
Cissus 199
Cistus 43
Citrus 204, 255
Clarkia 142
clay soils 172
Cleistocactus 209
Clematis 64-5, 174, 281
Cleome 142
Clerodendrum 251, 301
Clianthus 255
climbers 62-69
    greenhouse 280-87
    roses 63, 105, 109, 112
Climbing Lily (Gloriosa) 277
Clivia 275
Clog Plant (Hypocyrta) 202
Clustered Wax Flower (Stephanotis) 284
Cobaea 66, 282
Cockscomb (Celosia) 301
Cocos 203
Codiaeum 195, 250, 301
Coelogyne 293
Coix 144
Colchicum 117
cold frames 231
Coleus 256, 301, 302, 307
coloured foliage 171
Columbine 88
Columnea 244
compost, garden 28
composts, potting see potting composts
concrete 9, 10, 157
Coneflowers (Rudbeckia) 88, 151
conifers 24, 70, 72
    deciduous 74, 75
    for bonsai 215
    hedges 79
Conophytum 213
conservatories 217
container-grown plants 6, 22, 25
    climbers 62
    roses 108
containers for plants 163, 165-7
Convallaria 182, 279
Convolvulus 146, 284
Coral Tree (Erythrina) 255
Cordyline 199
Coreopsis 91, 143
cormels 115
corms 115, 274
Cornflowers (Centaurea) 89, 143
Cornus 46
Coronilla 281
Correa 256
Cosmea (Cosmos) 142
Continus coggygria 59
Cotoneaster 44, 69, 81, 188
    for bonsai 215
Cotula 128
cotyledons 31, 213, 225
Cowslip, Cape (Lachenalia) 276
Crab Apples 72, 188
crane-fly 21
Cranesbill 134
Crape Myrtle (Lagestroemia) 264
Crassula 210
Crataegus 77, 188
creosote 63, 165, 222

Crinums *116*
Crocosmia *123*
Crocus *115, 117, 237*
Crocus, Autumn (Colchicum) *117*
Crossandra *257*
Croton (Codiaeum) *195, 250, 301*
Crown Imperial (Fritillaria) *120*
Crown of Thorns (Euphorbia) 211, *261*
Cryophytum 211
Cryptanthus 197
Cuban Lily (Scilla) *123*
cuckoo spit 113
cultivation *22-29*
   greenhouse *222-27, 300-309*
   perennials *82-4*
Cup-and-saucer Vine (Cobaea) *282*
Cuphea *257*
Cupressocyparis *79*
Cupressus 72
Currants (American or Flowering) *45*
Curtonus *123*
cut flowers: care of 178
cutting, flowers grown for *178-87*
cuttings: propagation by *34-5, 84, 305, 307*
Cycas *258*
Cyclamen *118*, 194, *258, 303, 305, 307*, 308
   species *237*
Cydonia *57*, 188
Cymbidium *290, 293*
Cyperus *258*
Cypress 72, *79*
Cypress, Swamp (Taxodium) 72, *75*
Cypripedium *239, 294*
Cyrtomium *298*
Cytisus *42, 177, 235*

D

Daboecia cantabrica 50
daddy-long-legs *21*
Daffodils *24, 114, 118-19, 182, 300*
Dahlias *115, 169, 186, 300,* 301, 302
Daisies, African *140*
Daisies, Gloriosa (Coneflowers, Rudbeckia) *151*
Daisies, Golden *91*
Daisies, Shasta or Moon *101*
Daisy (Bellis) *153*
Daisy, Barberton (Gerbera) *261*
Daisy, Livingstone (Mesembryanthemum) 146, 211
Daisy, Michaelmas (Aster) *98, 173*
Daisy, Transvaal (Gerbera) *261*
Daisy Bush (Olearia) *54*
Daisy Flowers *143*
damping down: greenhouses *221,* 304, *305*
Daphnes *45*
Datura *259, 302*
Davallia *298*
Dawn Redwood *75*
day, length of 191
Day Lily (Hemerocallis) *90*
Decaisnea 188
deciduous:
   hedges *80*
   shrubs 38
   trees 22
Delphinium 33, 34, *89*, 145
Dendrobium *291, 293*
Dendrochilum *295*
derris *295,* 305, *307*
design, garden *8-13,* 105, 160

Deutzia *46,* 235, 309
Dianthus 99, *134, 148, 155, 179*
diaznon 299
dibbers *24, 31*
Dicentra *90, 233, 309*
Dicksonia *298*
Didiscus *259*
die-back *113*
Dieffenbachia *200*
Diervilla (Weigela) *60*
digging *22-3*
Digitalis *153, 174*
dimethoate 7
Dimorphotheca *140*
dinocap 7, 113
Diplacus *266*
Dipladenia *283*
disbudding *110, 187, 306*
diseases *see* pests and diseases
dividing 36, 84
Dizygotheca *196*
Dog's Tooth Violet (Erythronium) *119*
Dogwoods *46*
Doronicum *91, 233*
Dorotheanthus 211
'dot' plants *168*
Doxantha *287*
Dracaena *199*
Dragon Plant (Dracaena) *199*
drainage:
   plant containers 165, 166
   rockery *126*
draw hoe 26
drills: sowing in *32*
Drumstick Primrose *138*
dry places: plants for *176*
Dusty Miller (Auricula) *138,* 240
Dutch hoe 26
Dutch lights *230*
Dutchman's Pipe (Aristolochia) 280
Duvallia 212
dwarfed trees (Bonsai) *214-15*

E

earthworms 21
Easter Cactus (Rhipsalidopsis) 209
Eccremocarpus *282*
Echeveria *213*
Echidnopsis 212
Echinacea 88
Echinocactus *209*
Echinocereus 208
Echinopsis *101,* 208
edging:
   for flower beds 168
   for lawns *18*
edging plants *144,* 168
Edraianthus *237*
eelworm *125*
Egyptian Paper Reed (Papyrus) 258
Elder *45*
Elaeagnus *47*
electricity 7, 8
   in the greenhouse 218
   pumps 156, 157
   soil-warming *229, 231*
Elettaria *205*
Epacris *260*
Epidendrum *295*
Epimedium *175*

Epiphyllum *207*
epiphytic plants *209, 290, 291,* 292
Eragrostis 144
Eranthis *119*
Erica 50, *263*
Erigeron *92*
Erinus *131*
Erodium *134, 176*
Eryngium *101*
Erythrina *255*
Erythronium *119*
Escallonia *47*
Eschscholzia *149*
estimating: quantities 9
Eucalyptus *181,* 260
Eucharis *276*
Eucomis *276*
Euonymus 48, 188
Euphorbia *102,* 211, *260-61,* 304
Evening Primrose (Oenothera) *100*
evergreens 26, 38, 70, *80-81*
'Everlasting' Flowers *92, 185*
Everlasting Pea (Lathyrus) *93*
Exacum *252, 302, 306*

F

F_1, F_2 hybrids 140
Fagus *71, 80*
fairy rings *21*
False Acacia (Robinia) *73*
False Castor Oil Plant (Fatsia) *196*
Fatsia *196*
feeding (*see also* fertilisers; potting compost)
   greenhouse plants 223
   house plants *192,* 194-205
   lawns *18*
Fenestraria *213*
Fern, Asparagus *245*
ferns 200, *296-9,* 301
Ferocactus *209*
fertilisers 15, 22, 29, 38
   lawns *18,* 21, *29*
Ficus *201*
Fig, Banjo *or* Fiddle-leaved 201
Filipendula *102*
Filmy Ferns *299*
Firethorn (Pyracantha) *57,* 69, 188
fish: garden pools 156, *157,* 158, 159
fish meal 29
Fittonia *201*
Flame Flower (Tropaeolum) *68*
Flame Pea (Chorizema) *256*
Flamingo Flower (Anthurium) 194
flower pots 222
flowers of sulphur 299, 309
foliage, coloured *171*
Forget-me-nots *153*
forking 22, *23*
formalin 227
formothion 7
Forsythia *39, 48*
fountains 156, *157,* 162
Foxglove *153, 174*
frames 7, *31, 35,* 226, *230-31*
frames, propagating *35, 229*
Francoa 233, *261*
Freesia (*see also* Greenhouse Calendar 300-309)
    277, 303, 307, 309
Fremontia *282*
Fritillaries *120*

frog flies (frog hoppers) 113
frost damage 26
fruits: shrubs 188
Fuchsia (see also Greenhouse Calendar 300-309) 49, 164, 170, 177, 262, 306
   climbers 283
fumigation see greenhouses
fungi: on lawns 21
fungicides:
   greenhouse 227
   lawns 21
   roses 113
Funkia 95
furniture: for patios 160, 161, 167

G

Gaillardia 94, 143
Galanthus 124
Galega 93
Galtonia 120
Gardenia 250, 301, 302
Garrya 47, 188
Gasteria 210
Gay Feather (Liatris) 96
Gazania 31, 302, 307
Genista 42, 235, 309
Gentian 135, 238
Geranium (see also Pelargonium) 170, 268, 301, 302, 307
   herbaceous 92
   rock gardens 134
Gerbera 261
germination 33, 224
Gesneria 271
Geum 91
Gibbaeum 213
Gingko 75
Gladiolus 114, 183
Globba 262
Globe Flowers (Trollius) 85
Globe Thistle (Echinops) 101
Gloriosa 277
Gloriosa Daisies (Coneflowers, Rudbeckia) 151
Glory Lily (Gloriosa) 277
Glory of the Snow (Chionodoxa) 117
Glory Pea (Clianthus) 255
Gloxinia (see also Greenhouse Calendar 300-309) 263, 300
Goat's Beard (Aruncus) 102
Goat's Rue (Galega) 93
Godetia 142
Golden Barrel Cactus 209
Golden Daisies 91
Golden Feather 171
Golden Rod (Solidago) 84, 93, 173
Goldfish Plant (Hypocyrta) 202
Goosefoot Plant (Syngonium) 200
grafting 37
Grape Hyacinth (Muscari) 117
Grape Vine 63
Grapefruit (Citrus) 255
grasses: for lawns 14
   ornamental 144
gravel: for paths 9
greenfly 7, 113, 295, 299
greenhouse plants:
   bulbs 274-9
   chrysanthemums 288-9
   climbers 280-87
   ferns 296-9
   orchids 290-95

greenhouses (see also Greenhouse Calendar 300-309)
   damping down 221, 304, 305
   fumigation 227, 303, 305, 307
   heating 190, 218
   hygiene and pests 227
   jobs to do 300-309
   management 216-227
   shading 217, 221, 303, 304, 306
   siting 11, 217, 232
   soils and composts 222
   staging and beds 221
   temperatures 216, 219, 242
   types 216-17
   ventilation 219
   watering 220, 224, 226, 232
greenhouses, heated 242
   plants for 242-73
greenhouses, unheated 232
   plants for 232-35
Grevillea 197, 245
grey leaved plants 92, 171
ground cover plants 175
'Growmore' fertiliser 15, 38
Guelder Rose (Viburnum) 60
Guernsey Lily (Nerine) 279
Gum tree (Eucalyptus) 260
Gymnocalycium 208
Gynura 202
Gypsophila 37, 94, 135

H

Haberlea 241, 300
Haemanthus 277
Halimium 136
Hamamelis (Witch Hazel) 61, 188
hanging baskets 164, 304
hardening off 31, 226, 231, 303, 304
hardy plants see herbaceous perennials; annuals, hardy and half-hardy
Hare's Foot Fern (Davallia) 298
Harlequin Flower (Sparaxis) 275
Harrisia 209
Haworthia 210
Hawthorn 77, 80
Hawthorn, Water (Aponogeton) 158, 159
Heathers 50
Heaths, Winter 263
heating:
   for greenhouses 190, 218
   frames 231
Hebes 49
Hedera 67, 202
hedges 78-81
   rose 111
Hedychium 252
'heel' cuttings 34
heeling in 23
Helenium 94
Helianthus 103, 151
Helianthemum 136
Helichrysum 185
Heliconia 273
Heliopsis 103
Heliotrope 169, 264, 301
Helipterum 185
Helleborus 87, 188
Hemerocallis 90
Hepatica 131

herbaceous perennials 82-103
   cultivation 82-4
   for cutting 180
herbaceous plants 9, 12, 22, 34, 36, 233
hermaphrodite form 64
Heron's Bill (Erodium) 134
Heuchera 87
Hibiscus 50, 194, 242
Hidcote 160
Himalayan Honeysuckle (Lycesteria) 53
Hippeastrum (Amaryllis) 116
Hippeastrum 278, 300, 303, 308
hoeing 26
Hollies, Sea 101
Holly 81
Holly Fern (Cyrtomium) 298
Hollyhocks 153
Honesty 185
Honeysuckle 66
Honeysuckle, Himalayan (Lycesteria) 53
Hoodia 212
hoof and horn meal 29
Hop (Humulus) 62, 68
hops, spent: fertiliser 29
Hordeum 144
hormone rooting powder 35, 36, 305
Hornbeam 80
Horned Rampion (Phyteuma) 237
Hosta 95, 180
hot, dry places: plants for 172, 176
hotbeds 231
Hottonia 158
House Leeks (Sempervivum) 139, 212
house plants 192-205
Howea 203
Hoya 197, 284
Humea 264
Humulus 62, 68
humus 22, 173
Hyacinth 121, 194, 300, 306
Hyacinth, Grape (Muscari) 117
hybrids 140
Hydrangea 51, 67, 235, 309
hydrated lime 27
Hymenocallis 276
Hymenophyllum 299
Hypericum 51, 136
Hypocyrta 202
Hypoestes 201

I

Iberis 132
Ice Plant (Cryophytum) 211
Ilex 81
Impatiens 169, 194, 268, 301
Incarvillea 96
Incense Plant (Humea) 264
increasing 30-37, 115
India-rubber Plant (Ficus) 201
Indian Bean Tree 73
Indian Shot (Canna) 252
insecticides 7
   bulbs 125
   greenhouse 208, 227, 295, 299, 305, 307
   lawns 21
   roses 113
   systemic 7
insectivorous plants 267
ioxynil 17, 20
Ipomoea 66, 146, 284

Iresines *171*
Iris *95*, *121*, 159, *183*, 188, *237*
iron: in the soil 22, 110, 172
Iron Cross (Begonia) *247*
iron sequestrol *110*, 172
Ismene *276*
Ivy *67*, *202*
Ivy, Cape (Senecio) 202
Ixia *184*, 275
Ixora *262*

J

Jacaranda *264*
Jacobean Lily (Sprekelia) *275*
Jacobinia *248*, 302
Japanese Quince (Chaenomeles) *57*, *69*, *181*
Japonica *57*, *69*, *181*
Jasmine *68*, *285*
Jasmine, Cape (Gardenia) *250*
Jasmine, Chilean (Mandevilla) *283*
Jasmine, Chinese (Trachelospermum) 283
Jekyll, Gertrude 160
Jerusalem Cross (Lychnis) *99*
Jerusalem Sage (Phlomis) *56*
Jersey Lily (Amaryllis) *116*
Job's Tears (Coix) *144*
John Innes composts 7, 30, 165, 166, *222*
Johnston, *Major* Lawrence 160
Judas Tree *73*
Juniper *74*, *215*
Justicia *248*

K

Kalanchoe 210, 213
Kalmia *52*
Kangaroo Vine (Cissus) *199*
Killarney Fern (Trichomanes) 299
Kingcups *159*
Kleinia *171*, 213
Kniphofia *83*, *90*
Kochia *171*

L

labour saving gardening 6
Laburnum *74*
Lachenalia *276*, *303*, *304*, *307*, 309
Ladder Fern (Nephrolepsis) 298
Lagerstromia *264*
Lagurus *144*
Lamium *175*
Lampranthus *211*, 307
Lantana *265*, 302
Lapageria *285*
Lapeirousia *240*
Larkspur *145*
Lathyrus *93*
Laurel *81*
Laurustinus (Viburnum) *60*, *81*
Lavatera *142*, *177*
Lavender *52*
Lavender Cottons (Santolina) *92*
lawn sand 20

lawns:
  aeration *20*
  care of *17-21*
  fertilisers *18*, 21, *29*
  grasses for *14*
  making and after-care *14-21*
  pests and diseases *21*
  preparing and sowing *15-16*, *32*
  turfing *16*, *17*
  verges *18*
  watering 17, *19*
  weeds *20*
layering *36*
  air *36*, 228
leaf curl *70*
leaf cuttings 228
leaf hoppers *113*
leaf miner 307
leatherjackets *21*
leaves:
  coloured and silver grey *171*
  sponging *192*
Lemaireocereus 209
Lemon (Citrus) 225
Lenten Rose (Helleborus) *87*
Leopard's Bane (Doronicum) *91*
Leptopteris 299
Leptospermum *177*, *267*
Leucadendron 269
Leucojum *124*
Leucophyta 171
Leucospermum 269
levelling: lawns *15*
Lewisia *239*
Leycesteria *53*
Liatris *96*
Libonia 248
lifting: herbaceous plants *84*
lights: in frames 230
Lilac *53*, 309
Lilium (Lily) *115*, *122*, *278*, *308*
Lily, Belladonna (Amaryllis) *116*
Lily, Blood (Haemanthus) *277*
Lily, Climbing (Gloriosa) *277*
Lily, Cuban (Scilla) *123*
Lily, Day (Hemerocallis) *90*
Lily, Glory (Gloriosa) *277*
Lily, Guernsey (Nerine) *279*
Lily, Jacobean (Sprekelia) *275*
Lily, Jersey (Amaryllis) *116*
Lily, Plantain (Hosta) *95*
Lily, Scarborough (Vallota) *279*
Lily, Spider (Hymenocallis) *276*
Lily of the Valley (Convallaria) *182*, *279*
lime and limestone *27*, 173
lime-hating plants 6
Limnathes *32*
Limonium *177*, 302
lindane *7*, 113, *125*, 299, 305
Linum *133*
Lippia *265*, 300
Liquidambar *73*
Lithops 213
Livingstone Daisy (Mesembryanthemum) 146, 211
loam 222
Lobelia *96*, *144*, 259
Lobivia 208
Lobster Claw (Clianthus) *255*
London Pride (Saxifraga) *137*
Lonicera *66*, *80*
Loosestrife *97*
Love-in-a-mist (Nigella) *147*

Luculia *265*, 300
Lunaria 185
Lupin *34*, *97*, 172
Lycaste *295*
Lychnis *99*
Lygodium 298
Lysichitum 159
Lysimachia *97*
Lythrum 97

M

MCPA 20
Macleaya *85*
Madagascar Periwinkle (Catharanthus) 268
magnesium 22
Magnolia *54*, 75
Mahonia *54*, *188*
Maidenhair Fern *297*
Maidenhair Tree 75
Maize *144*
malathion 113, 208, 295, 299, 305
Mallow *142*
Malope 142
Maltese Cross (Lychnis) *99*
Malus (Crab Apple) *72*, 188
Mammillaria 208
Mandevilla *283*
maneb 7
Manettia *257*
manganese 22
manure 22, 27, *28*, 231
Maple (Acer) *75*, *215*
Maranta 198
Marigold *145*
Marigold, Marsh (Caltha) *159*
marking out *9*
Marsh Marigold *159*
Masdevallia *295*
Maurandia *286*
Maxillaria 295
Meadow Rue (Thalictrum) *94*
Meadow Saffron (Colchicum) *117*
Meadow Sweet (Filipendula) *102*
meal: fertiliser *29*
mealy bugs *208*, *295*, *299*, 307
measuring: garden planning *8-9*
meat meal 29
mecoprop 20
Medinilla *266*
Medusa's Head (Euphorbia) *211*
Megasea (Bergenia) *85*
menazon 7
Menyanthes 153
Mesembryanthemum *146*, *211*, 307
metaldehyde 7, *295*
Metasequoia 75
methiocarb 7
Mexican Orange Blossom (Choisya) *50*
mice 7, 33
Michaelmas Daisy *98*, *173*
Mignonette *146*, 225, 232
mildew 7, *113*
Miltonia *291*, *292*
Mimosa *243*
Mimosifolia (Jacaranda) 264
Mimulus 159, *266*
Mina 284
Mint Bush (Prostanthera) *272*
mist propagation 229
Moccasin Flower 239

Mock Orange (Philadelphus) *55*
moles *21*
Molucella *179*
Monarda *86*
Monkey Flower (Mimulus) *266*
Monkshood *88*
Monstera *203*
Montbretia *123*
Moon Daisies *101*
Morisia 239, *300*
Morning Glory (Ipomoea) *66*, *146*, *284*
Moth Orchid (Phalaenopsis) *294*
Mother-in-law's Chair (Cactus) *209*
Mother-in-law's Tongue (Sansevieria) *205*
Mother of Thousands (Saxifraga) *205*, 233
mould: on ferns *299*
Mountain Ash 77, *188*
mowing *17*, 18
mulching 26, 27
Mullein (Verbascum) *103*
Musa *273*
Muscari *117*
Musk 159
Myosotis *153*
Myrobalan Plum 80
Myrtle (Myrtus) *177*, *267*

N

Naegelia *271*
Narcissus *117*, *118-19*, *182*, *306*
Nasturtium 68, *146*, *176*
Natal Vine *199*
Neanthe *203*
Nemesia *31*, *112*, *147*, 302
Neoregelia 197
Nepenthes *267*
Nepeta *87*
Nephrolepsis 298
Nephthytis *200*
Nerine *183*, *279*, 304, 306, 307, 308
Nerium *265*
Nicholson, *Sir* Harold 160
Nicotiana *147*
Nidularium 197, 248
Nigella *147*
Nitro-chalk 28
nitrogen 22, 29
Norfolk Island Pine *196*
Notocactus *208*
Nymphaea *158*

O

Oak tree 70
Obedient Plant (Physostegia) *100*
Odontioda 292, *294*
Odontoglossum *292*, *294*, 295
Oenothera *100*
offsets, cacti *207*
Old Man Cactus *209*
Oleander *265*, 309
Olearia *54*
Oliveranthus 213
Oncidium *294*
Onion, ornamental *115*
onion hoe *26*
Opuntia *209*
Orange (Citrus) *255*

orangeries 190, 191
Orchid *290-95*, 301
Orchid, Hardy *239*
Oriental Poppy (Papaver) *100*, 300
ornaments, garden *11*
Ornithogalum *115*
Osmanthus *54*
Oxalis *240*, *266*

P

pH value: soil *27*
Pachystachys 195
Paeonia (Peonies) *98*, *180*
Palm *199*, *203*, 301
Pancratium *276*
Pandanus *199*
Pandorea 287
Panicum 144
Pansy *154*, 233
Papaver *100*, *149*
Paphiopedilum *294*
Papyrus 258
Parrot's Bill (Clianthus) *255*
parterres *12*
Parthenocissus *63*
Pasque Flowers *131*
Passion Flower (Passiflora) *176*, *286*
paths *10*
patios *11*, *160-63*, 167
paving 9, *10*, *161*
    plants between *128*
Pea, Everlasting (Lathyris) *93*
Pea, Glory (Clianthus) 255
Pea, Sweet *32*, *149*, *300*
Peach *70*
peat 7, 22, 26, 27, 29
    for lawns *18*
Pelargonium (*see also* Greenhouse Calendar *300-309*) *170*, *194*, *268*, *283*, *301*, *303*, *305*, *307*
    cuttings *307*
Pennisetum 144
Penstemon *96*
Penta *249*
Peonies (Paeonia) *98*, *180*
Peperomia *204*
Peppers, Sweet (Capsicum) *253*
perennials *see* herbaceous perennials
pergolas 10, *11*, 63
Periwinkle, Madagascar (Catharanthus) 268
Pernettya *55*, 188
Perovskia *176*
Persea *255*
pests and diseases 7
    bulbs *125*
    cacti *208*
    ferns *299*
    greenhouse 227, *295*, *299*, 305, 307
    lawns *21*
    orchids *295*
    roses *113*
    virus 7
pests and diseases, control of *see* fungicides,
    insecticides, weedkillers
Petunia *148*, *268*, 301, 302
Phalaenopsis *294*
Philadelphus *55*
Philodendron *203*
Phlomis *56*
Phlox *99*, *137*, *148*, 300
phosphorus 22, 29

photoperiodic pattern 191
Phyllanthus 243
Phyllodoce *238*
Physalis 185
Physostegia *100*
Phyteuma *237*
Pieris *52*
Pilea *204*
Pileostegia *67*
Pine 70, *215*
Pine, Screw (Pandanus) *199*
Pineapple *204*
Pineapple Flower 276
Pinks 34, *99*, *134*, *148*
Pinks, Sea (Armeria) *130*
Piptanthus *176*
Pitcher Plants *267*
Pittosporum *181*, 205
planning, garden *8-13*, *105*, 160
plant cabinets and cases *193*
    plants for 296, *299*
Plantain Lily (Hosta) *95*
planting 22, *23-25*
    bulbs 24, 25
    perennials *82*
    roses *106-7*
    tools *24-5*
    trees and shrubs 24
Platycerium 297, *298*
Platycodon *86*
Plectranthus *202*
Pleiones *239*
Pleiospilos 213
Pleomele *199*
Plum, ornamental 76
Plumbago *281*, 301
Plume Poppy (Bocconia) *85*
plunge beds *306*
Podranea 287
Poinsettia 226, *260-61*, 300, 302, 303, *309*
Polianthes *279*
Polka Dot Plant 201
Polyanthus *138*, *154*, 233
Polygonatum *90*
Polygonum *64*, *100*, *133*
Pontederia 159
pools *8*, *156-59*, 162
Poplar 70
Poppy *149*
Poppy, Californian Tree 300
Poppy, Oriental *100*, 300
Poppy, Plume (Bocconia) *85*
Portulaca *146*
potash 22, 29
Potentilla *56*, *91*, *136*
pots, flower *222*
potting *223*
    cacti *207*
    orchids *291*
    re-potting *223*, 302
potting composts 7, 30, 165, 166, *222*
preservatives, wood *63*, 165, 222
pricking out *31*, *225*, 304
Prickly Pear *209*
Primrose *138*, *154*, 233
Primrose, Evening (Oenothera) *100*
Primula (*see also* Greenhouse Calendar 300-309)
    138, *224*, 233, *269*
    species for pots *240*
Prince of Wales Feather Fern 299
Privet *80*
propagating *30-37*, *228-9*
propagating case 229

propagating frames *35, 229*
Prostanthera *272*
Protea *269*
prothalli: ferns *296*
pruning:
   roses *107-9*
   shrubs *39*
Prunus 80, 188, 235
   almonds and peaches *70*
   cherries *71*
   laurel *81*
   plums and sloes *76*
pseudobulbs (Orchids) *290, 301*
Pteris *298*
Pulsatilla *131*
pumps, electrical 156, 157
Purple Bells (Rhodochiton) *286*
Purple Heart (Setcreasea) 198
Pyracantha 57, 69, 79, 188
Pyrethrum *101*, 171
Pyrostegia 287

Q

Quaking Grass *144*
Quamoclit 284
quantity surveying 9
Quick 77, 80
quick-lime 27
Quince, Common (Cydonia) 188
Quince, Japanese (Chaenomeles) 57, 69, *181*
quintozene 115

R

rakes and raking *15, 19*
Ramonda 241, 300
Ranunculus *116*
Rat-tailed Cactus *206, 208*
Rebutia *208*
Red-hot Cat Tail (Acalypha) *243*
Red-hot Poker (Kniphofia) *83*, 90
red spider mite 208, 227, 295, 305, 307
Redwood, Dawn 75
Reed Mace 159
refuse *27, 28*
Rehmannia *270*
Reinwardtia *266*
re-potting *223, 302*
resting periods *226*
Rhipsalidopsis *209*
Rhodochiton *286*
Rhododendron 27, *58*, 235
Rhodohypoxis *240*
Rhoeo *198*
Rhoicissus *199*
Rhus *59*
Ribbon Fern *298*
Ribes sanguineum 45
ridging *23*
Robinia *73*
Rochea *210*
rock gardens *126-9*
rock plants *130-39, 236*
Rock Rose (Cistus) *43*
Rock Rose (Helianthemum) *136*
Rodgersia *95, 180*
rolling: lawns *17*, 20
Romneya *300*

root aphids 305
rooting *35*
   hormone rooting powder *35, 36,* 305
Rosa rugosa scabrosa 33
Rose, Christmas (Helleborus) 87, *188*
Rose, Lenten (Helleborus) 87
Rose, Rock (Cistus) *43*
Rose, Rock (Helianthemum) *136*
Rose, Sun (Helianthemum) *136*
Rose Acacia (Robinia) *73*
Rose Campion (Lychnis) *99*
Rose hips *33*
Rose of Sharon (Hypericum) *51*
Rosemary *52,* 173
Roses *104-113*
   budding *37*
   climbing *63, 105, 109, 112*
   for cutting *184*
   in pots *270, 309*
   pests and diseases *113*
   planting *106-7*
   pruning *107-9*
   types *104-5*
Rowans 77, *188*
Rubber Plant (Ficus) *201*
Rubus *53*
Rudbeckia *88, 151*
Rue, Meadow (Thalictrum) *94*
Ruellia *270*
Rush, Flowering *159*
Russian Vine *64*
rust (disease) 113, 153, 299
Ruta *171*

S

Sackville-West, Victoria 160
Saffron, Meadow (Colchicum) *117*
Sage (Salvia) *150*
Sagittaria *159*
Sago Palm (Cyca) 258
Saint John's Wort *136*
Saintpaulia *228, 271*, 309
Salpiglossis *232*, 301, 302
Salvia *86, 150*, 300, 301
Sambucus *45*
Sanchezia *195*
Sansevieria *205*
Santolina *92*
Saponaria *133*
Sarracenia *267*
Savin (Juniper) 74
sawflies *113*
Saxifrage *137, 205, 233, 241*
Scabious (Scabiosa) *89, 147, 180*
scale insects *208,* 295
Scarborough Lily (Vallota) *279*
Schefflera *205*
Schizanthus *232,* 302, 303, 306, 307
Schizocodon *241*
Schizophragma *67*
Schlumbergera *209*
Scilla *112, 123*
Scindapsus *203*
scion *37*
Scirpus *159*
scree garden *128*
screening and climbing plants *62-9*
screens:
   for patios *10, 161*
   for plants *26*

Screw Pine (Pandanus) *199*
Sea Holly (Eryngium) *101*
Sea Pink (Armeria) *130*
seaside gardens 172, *177*
Sedum *102, 139, 213*
seed composts *30,* 222
seedlings: care of *225*
seeds:
   herbaceous plants *84*
   in a greenhouse *224-5*
   sowing *30-33, 178*
Selaginella *299*
Sempervivum *139, 212*
Senecio *56, 171, 202, 286*
Sensitive Plant (Mimosa) *243*
sequestrols 172
Setcreasea 198
shady places: plants for *174*
Shark's Head (Gibbaeum) *213*
Shasta Daisies *101*
sheds 11
Shortia *241*
Shrimp Plant (Beloperone) 197, *248*
Shrubby Cinquefoil (Potentilla) *56*
shrubs *38-61*
   cultivation *38*
   cuttings *34, 35*
   evergreen 22, *80-81*
   for bonsai *215*
   for cutting *180-81*
   hedges *81*
   in cold greenhouses *235*
   layering *36*
   planting *24, 25*
   pruning *39*
   spacing 9
   specimens *13*
   with berries and fruit *188*
Sidalcea *97*
Silenes *135*
Silver Birch *71*
silver foliage *92,* 171
singling *26*
sink garden *126, 129*
Siphonosmanthus delavayi 54
Sissinghurst Castle 160
Skimmia *55*
Skunk Cabbage (Lysichitum) 159
Slipper Orchid *294*
Sloe *76*
slugs 7, *208,* 295
Smilax 301
Smithiantha *271*, 302, *309*
smoke generators 227, 295, 303, 305
Smoke Tree (*Rhus cotinus*) *59*
snails 7, *208,* 295
Snow in Summer (Cerastium) *133*
Snowball Tree (Viburnum) *60*
Snowberry (Symphoricarpos) 188
Snowdrops (Galanthus) *124*
Snowflakes (Leucojum) *124*
Snowy Mespilus (Amelanchier) *76*
soil:
   cultivation *22-3*
   purchasing 9
   suitability 6
soil-warming *229, 231*
soils:
   acid/alkaline test *27*
   sterilisation 227
   variety of 172
Solanum 67, *272,* 287, 305, *308*
Soldanella *241*

Solidago *84*, *93*, *173*
Sollya *287*
Solomon's Seal (Polygonatum) *90*
Sonerila *201*
Sophronitis 295
Sorbus 77, *188*
sowing *30-33*
   broadcast *32*
   greenhouse *224*
spades *22*, *23*, *24*
Sparaxis 184, 275
Sparmannia *272*
Spartium junceum 42
Spathiphyllum *195*
specimen plants *13*
Spider Flower (Cleome) *142*
Spider Lily (Hymenocallis) *276*
Spider Plant (Aralia) *196*
Spiderwort (Tradescantia) *100*
Spindle Tree (Euonymous) *48*, 188
Spiraea 59, *81*, *102*, 235
Spleenwort (Asplenium) *296*, *297*
Sprekelia *275*
sprinkle bar *20*
sprinklers, lawn *19*
Spurge *102*
Squill *123*
Squirrel's Foot Fern *298*
Stachys lanata 175
Stag's Horn Fern *297*, *298*
Stag's Horn Sumach (Rhus) *59*
staking 24, 26, *83*
Stanhopea 295
Stapelia *212*
Star Cacti 208
Star of Bethlehem (Ornithogalum) *115*
Star of the Veldt (Dimorphotheca) *140*
Statice 185, *302*
statues *11*
Stephanotis *284*
sterilisation:
   of loam *222*
   of soil *227*
Stocks 25, *150*, 155, *233*, 302, 306
Stone mimics (succulents) *213*
stone walls *9*
Stonecrop (Sedum) *102*, *139*, *213*
'stools' (Chrysanthemum) *186*
Strawberry: layering *36*
Strelitzia *273*
Streptocarpus *273*, 300, 301
Streptosolen *273*
Succulents *206-13*, 300, 301
sulphate of ammonia *20*
sulphate of iron *20*, 21
Sumach, Stag's Horn (Rhus) *59*
Summer Cypress *171*
Summer Hyacinth (Galtonia) *120*
Sun Rose (Helianthemum) *136*
sundials *11*
Sunflower (Helianthus) *103*, *151*
surveying *8-9*
Swamp Cypress (Taxodium) 72, *75*
Swan River Daisy *140*
Sweet Briar (Rosa) 111
Sweet Gum (Liquidambar) *73*
Sweet Pea *32*, *149*, *300*
Sweet Sultan (Centaurea) *143*
Sweet William 155, *179*, *233*
Sycamore (Acer) *76*
Symphoricarpos *174*, 188
Syngonium *200*
Syrian Mallow (Hibiscus) *50*

Syringa (Lilac) *53*
Syringa (Philadelphus – Mock Orange *55*)
systemic insecticides *7*

T

Tagetes *145*
Tamarix (Tamarisk) *59*
Tavaresia *212*
Taxodium *75*
tecnazene 227
Tecoma 287
Temple Bell (Smithiantha) *271*
terraces *10*, *161*
Tetrastigma 199
Thalictrum *94*
thinning out *26*, *33*
thiram 113, 125, *309*
Thistle, Globe (Echinops) *101*
Thorn 77, 188
Thrift *130*
thrips 113, 295, 299
Thuja *79*, *173*
Thunbergia *66*, *282*
Thyme 14, *137*
Tibouchina *287*
Tigridia (Tiger Flower) *275*
Tobacco Plant *147*
tools:
   for cultivation *22-26*
   hedge *79*
   hoes *26*
   lawn care *15*, *17-20*
   planting *24-5*
Torch Lily (Kniphofia) *83*, *90*
Torenia *270*
trace elements 28, 29
Trachelium *259*
Trachelospermum 283
Trachycarpus *203*
Tradescantia *100*, *198*
transplanting 6, 22, 33
Transvaal Daisy (Gerbera) *261*
Trees: *70-77*
   for avenues *13*
   planting *24*, 70
   specimen *13*
Trees, dwarfed (Bonsai) *214-15*
trenching *23*
trichlorphon 307
Trichocereus 209
Trichomanes 299
trimmer:
   hedge *79*
   lawn *18*
Tritonia *123*
Trollius *85*
Tropaeolum 68, 146, *302*
troughs *163*, *165*
trowels *25*
Trumpet Vine *287*
Tuberose (Polianthes) *279*
tubers *115*, *309*
tubs *163*, *165*
Tulip Tree (Magnolia) *75*
Tulips 114, *124-5*, *182*, *234*, 300
Tunbridge Wells Fern *299*
Tunica *135*
turfing and turves 9, *16*, *17*
Typha *159*

U

Ulex *173*
Umbrella Grass (Cyperus) *258*
urea formaldehyde 29

V

Vallota *279*
Vanda *293*
vases *163*, 165
Veltheimia 276, 306
Venidium *140*
Verbascum *83*, *103*, 300
Verbena *151*, *265*, 300, 301, 302
verges, grass *18*
vernalisation *33*
Veronica *103*, *139*, 175
Veronica (shrubs) *see* Hebe
Viburnum *38*, *60*, 81, 188
Vinca *268*
Vine (Vitis) *63*
Vine, Kangaroo (Cissus) 199
Vine, Natal (Rhoicissus) 199
Vine, Russian *64*
Vine, Trumpet 287
Viola *112*, *139*, *154*, 233
Violet *36*, *139*, *187*
Violet, African (Saintpaulia) *228*, *271*, 309
Violet, Dog's Tooth *119*
Virginia Creeper *63*
virus diseases *7*
vistas and avenues *13*
Vitis *63*
Vriesia *197*, *248*

W

Waldsteinia *175*
Wallflower 152, *155*, *233*
walls 9, *127*, *161*
Wandering Jew (Tradescantia *and* Zebrina) *198*
Wardian cases *193*, 296, 299
water:
   plants *158-9*
   pools *156-9*, *162*
Water Hawthorn (Aponogeton) *158*, *159*
Water Lily *158*
Water Plantain 159
Water Violet *158*
watering 25, 26
   house plants and pot plants 7, *192*, *194-205*
   in greenhouses *220*, *224*, *226*, *232*, *300-309*
   lawns 17, *19*
Watsonia *274*
Wax Flower (Hoya) *284*
Wax Plant (Hoya) *197*
weedkillers, lawn 17, *20*
weeds:
   hoeing *26*
   lawn *20*, 17
Weigela *60*
white oil emulsion 295
White Sails (Spathiphyllum) *195*
Whitebeam *77*
whitefly 227, 305
Wig Tree (Rhus cotinus) *59*

window boxes 165, *166-7*
winds: protection against *26*
Winter Aconite (Eranthis) *119*
Winter Cherry (Solanum) *272, 308*
winter flowers *188*
Winter Sweet (Chimonanthus) *61*
Wisteria *69*
Witch Hazel (Hamamelis) *61*, 188
wood preservatives 63, 165, 222

Woodwardia *298*
worms 21

Y

Yarrow *93, 130*
Yew *79*
Yucca *61*

Z

Zea mays 144
Zebra Plant (Aphelandra) 195
Zebrina 198
Zinnia *151*, 302
Zygocactus *209*
Zygopetalum 295